Donny Whiliams
White on White

3.5

PSYCHOLOGY OF ADJUSTMENT AND HUMAN RELATIONSHIPS

PSYCHOLOGY OF ADJUSTMENT AND HUMAN RELATIONSHIPS

SECOND EDITION

James F. Calhoun
University of Georgia

Joan Ross Acocella

Random House
New York

Library of Congress Cataloging in Publication Data

Calhoun, James F.
Psychology of adjustment and human relationships.
Bibliography: p.
Includes index.
1. Adjustment (Psychology)   2. Behaviorism (Psychology)
3. Humanistic psychology.   I. Acocella, Joan Ross.
II. Title.   [DNLM: 1. Adaptation, Psychological.
2. Interpersonal relations. BF 335 C152p]
BF335.C34   1983   158   82-18078
ISBN 0-394-32906-6

Text Design: Karin Gerdes Kincheloe
Cover Design: Carol Grobe
Cover art: Mary Callery, *Perhaps.* 1950. Bronze. 70 × 55.7 × 30 cm.
Gift of Oliver B. James. University Art Collections. Arizona State University.
Production: Laura Lamorte

Manufactured in the United States of America.
Composed by Ruttle, Shaw & Wetherill, Philadelphia, Pa.
Printed and bound by R. R. Donnelly & Sons, Co. Crawfordsville, Indiana.

Permissions Acknowledgments

Robert E. Alberti and Michael L. Emmons, *Your Perfect Right: A Guide to Assertive Living,* Fourth Edition. Copyright © 1982 by Robert E. Alberti and Michael L. Emmons. Reprinted by permission of Impact Publishers, Inc., P.O. Box 1094, San Luis Obispo, CA 93406. Further reproduction prohibited.

A. Baum and G. E. Davis, "Reducing the Stress of High-Density Living: An Architectural Intervention," *Journal of Personality and Social Psychology,* 38 (1980), pp. 471–481. Copyright © 1980 by the American Psychological Association. Reprinted by permission.

Permissions Acknowledgments continued on page 452

TO THE INSTRUCTOR

Writing an adjustment text requires a certain daring, since, to a large extent, the authors decide what the subject matter is. In most other branches of psychology, the table of contents for a textbook is more or less fixed before the author comes along. In adjustment, on the other hand, the only requirement is that the book deal with the relationship between psychology and everyday life. This is a loose set of specifications, needless to say, and one that has produced widely different adjustment texts. Some are theoretically broad, others tied to one point of view. Some have concentrated on psychological information, resulting in something akin to introductory psychology texts. Others have concentrated on practical problem solving, resulting in something akin to "how-to" books.

In the first edition, we aimed for a combination of strengths—both psychological information *and* applications, both theoretical breadth *and* emphasis on those theories most relevant to normal adjustment. This method, we are happy to report, was very well received in the first edition, and therefore we have retained it in the second. The book's approach, then, is as follows:

General Procedure: To give approximately equal space to current psychological information and to practical problem solving, but to do this in such a way that the psychological information, once given, is almost immediately applied to the student's life.

Audience: First- and second-year students at two-year and four-year colleges. This book does not assume that the student has already taken courses in psychology, but it could be as useful to psychology majors who have had introductory courses as to non-majors encountering psychology for the first time. Most important, the book is geared not only to the late-adolescent freshman, but also to the many adults who are going back to college after having worked, married, and had children.

TO THE INSTRUCTOR

Goal: To teach students (1) what psychologists have learned about human behavior and (2) how to use this knowledge to evaluate and (if they so choose) change their own attitudes and behavior.

Theoretical Orientation: We present all the major theories of personality, and in dealing with various topics, we present whatever theories are most relevant. However, the goal of helping students to change their ways of thinking and behaving has led us to rely especially on two theoretical positions: (1) behavioral theory, for its valuable self-change techniques, and (2) humanistic-existential theory, for its insistence on the ability of individuals to choose, from day to day, how they will live their lives. In no way do we try to "sell" these theories to the student. However, our book, like most books concerned with self-change, has been influenced by these theories, and therefore they deserve mention here.

Subject: The individual's interaction with his or her self and with other people. That is what we mean by "adjustment"—the individual's way of influencing, and being influenced by, these two factors. Accordingly, these two factors are the topics of the two units of our book. In addition, there is a final chapter dealing with the physical environment—how it affects us and how we can affect it.

Method: As we have already stated, this book has as its two goals providing psychological information and helping students apply that information to their own lives. In keeping with these two goals, our chapters alternate between "information" and "application." (A glance at the table of contents will make this clear.)

General Information

Four of our chapters provide theoretical background on the general topics of the book.

- *Chapter 1*, "Adjustment: A Way of Handling Problems," outlines major personality theories.
- *Chapter 2*, "The Self: What It Is and How to Analyze It," describes various theories of the self.
- *Chapter 8*, "The Social Self: How We Interact," explains the major theories of social psychology.
- *Chapter 14*, "The Environment: How It Affects Us and How We Can Affect It," describes the theories of environmental psychology.

Specific Information

Five of our chapters describe what psychologists have been able to discover about the more specific topics covered in the book.

- *Chapter 3*, "The Self-Concept: What It Is and How It Develops"—This includes Rogers's theory of the self-concept, Festinger's theory of cognitive consistency, and a discussion of the self-concept as a self-fulfilling prophecy.
- *Chapter 5*, "Self-Control: What It Is and How It Develops"—The major mechanisms of learning (respondent conditioning, operant conditioning, reinforcement, etc.) are explained here.
- *Chapter 9*, "Social Perception: What It Is and How It Operates"—Attitude formation, attraction, and stereotyping are discussed in detail.
- *Chapter 11*, "Social Influence: What It Is and How It Operates"—This describes the processes of modeling, conformity, and persuasion, including persuasion in advertising.

TO THE INSTRUCTOR

• *Chapter 14*, "The Environment: How It Affects Us and How We Can Affect It"—This explains how the built environment (rooms, seating arrangements, buildings, neighborhoods, cities) influences human behavior and how people perceive their environments.

Practical Application

In eight chapters we take the student, step by step, through techniques for solving adjustment problems.

• *Chapter 2*, "The Self: What It Is and How to Analyze It"—This describes the procedure for analyzing an adjustment problem in order to discover ways of changing.

• *Chapter 4*, "The Self-Concept: How to Change It"—This introduces the student to cognitive restructuring through self-talk.

• *Chapter 6*, "Self-Control: How to Change It"—This emphasizes stimulus control and self-reinforcement.

• *Chapter 7*, "Three Self-Control Problems: Weight, Study Habits, and Anxiety"—This suggests specific techniques for dealing with these three problems. Included are the SQ3R study method, armchair desensitization, and the use of exercise for alleviating stress.

• *Chapter 10*, "Social Perception: How to Change It"—This shows how we can improve close relationships by revising unrealistic expectations.

• *Chapter 12*, "Social Influence: How to Change It"—This describes the reciprocal nature of relationships and how they can be improved by such means as listening to others more carefully, giving clear messages, and criticizing constructively.

• *Chapter 13*, "Three Social Problems: Making Contact, Becoming Assertive, and Fostering Intimacy"—This offers step-by-step procedures for overcoming shyness and nonassertive behavior, and it describes how intimacy can be fostered through informal interaction and self-disclosure.

• *Chapter 14*, "The Environment: How It Affects Us and How We Can Affect It"—This shows students how to analyze and change their behavioral responses to their environments.

Certain of these items are rare in the field of adjustment texts:

1. Thorough discussion of how to improve our perceptions of the people close to us (Chapter 10).

2. Discussion of how personal adjustment is affected by the environment (Chapter 14).

To our knowledge, the first edition of this book was the first adjustment text to discuss these matters in detail. Today they are still very special features of this book.

Extra Features

The information given in the chapters is supplemented by

• *Boxes*. These are brief inserts within the chapters, covering a wide range of topics that will be of special interest to the students—for example, problem-solving training for married couples, the use of sophisticated techniques of persuasion in presidential politics, and the recent research of Mahoney and others on self-control training for athletes.

• *Human Issues Essays*. These are short and (we hope) entertaining essays, sandwiched between the chapters. Each of them deals with a very important but very ordinary aspect of life—sex roles, love, sex, marriage, child rearing, midlife, work—providing current information and theories on these topics. Their purpose is to provoke the student to think seriously about those "life events" that for many of us simply happen, without our thinking much about what they mean.

Instructors may also find these essays helpful as starting points for discussion of the applications procedures outlined in the main text. For example, the essay on sex roles could provide a context for discussion of self-concept; the essay on marriage, for discussion of social influence. There is also a Human Issues essay on abnormal psychology, explaining how psychologists define abnormal behavior and what the major diagnostic categories (anxiety disorders, affective disorders, schizophrenic disorders) mean. This discussion has been carefully revised in keeping with the new DSM-III.

• *Appendix: "Getting Help."* This appendix explains the different kinds of psychotherapy that are available and gives the student some practical advice on how to go about getting psychological guidance.

Pedagogical Aids

To help the student learn what the book has to say, we have used a number of pedagogical aids.

• *Chapter Outlines.* The major headings of each chapter are presented in outline form at the opening of the chapter to give the student a clear preview.
• *Chapter Summaries.* A summary at the end of each chapter recapitulates the central points. This allows students to review what they have read.
• *Activities.* At the end of each chapter is a list of suggested activities—small "experiments" that students can conduct in their own daily lives (e.g., analyzing a television commercial). The activities reinforce the material in the chapters and help

the students see that the principles of psychology really do apply to ordinary life.

• *Projects.* Also at the end of each chapter is a suggestion for a project, larger in scale than the activities. In some cases, the project is an exercise in "consciousness-raising," to show the students how the principles outlined in the chapter do in fact apply to their own lives. In other chapters, the project proposes a step-by-step scenario for self-change. These projects can be used as homework assignments.
• *Glossary.* At the end of the book there is a glossary defining all the technical terms used in the book. Thus, students can easily look up terms whose meanings they have forgotten.
• *Definitions.* In the text of the chapter, new terms are italicized, and their definitions are not just implied; they are explicitly stated, so that the student knows exactly what the term means.
• *Examples.* As psychologists know, people tend to learn by observing others. Accordingly, we have provided plenty of "others" for the students to observe, in vignettes and in dialogues. When we explain a psychological principle or theory, we give an example of how it works in ordinary life. When we outline a self-change technique, we follow someone, step by step, through the procedure. (See, for instance, the "sample script" on pages 116–119: this teaches the student, by example, how to use self-talk to improve the self-concept.)

Finally, a book's most important pedagogical aid is its writing style. One of our major efforts in this book has been to make the chapters, line by line, as interesting and as clear as possible. We speak directly to the students, explaining psychological principles in a down-to-earth and commonsensical manner and inviting them, again and again, to look at their own lives in light of these theories. The text should be easy to read, but in no way does it talk down to the students—an approach that most students sniff out quickly and find insulting.

A note on pronouns: the regular use of "he" and "him" to describe human beings in general leaves out the female half of human beings in general. This problem cannot always be solved by using plurals, and the constant use of "he or she" is cumbersome. Therefore, our text alternates between male and female pronouns. This usage—or rather, the "she" part of it—may surprise some readers the first few times they encounter it, but we consider it the fairest and most realistic solution to the problem.

Most of the above, the broad outlines of the book, remain unchanged from the first to the second edition. What has been changed are specifics. Above all, the research presented in the chapters has been thoroughly updated in light of recent work. Furthermore, new material has been woven into all the chapters. It is impossible to list all of this material, but here is a sample of points on which the text has been enriched:

• Personality theory, including separate sections on the contributions of Erikson, Fromm, Maslow, Rogers, Frankl, Mischel, and the cognitive behaviorists (Chapter 1).
• The relationship between expectations and achievements (Chapter 3).
• Perfectionism (Chapter 4).
• The relationship between psychological well-being and the sense of control (Chapter 5).
• Controlling stress with exercise (Chapter 6).
• Self control in sports (Chapter 7).
• Sex-role stereotyping and attribution theory (Chapter 9).
• New research on the relationship be-

tween physical attractiveness and persuasiveness (Chapter 11).
• The effectiveness of growth groups (Chapter 13).
• The perception of loneliness (Chapter 13).
• Crowding and social behavior in college residences (Chapter 14).
• Stimulus overload and environmental awareness (Chapter 14).
• New Human Issues essay on work.

Changes have also been made in the pedagogical aids. The activities, instead of being distributed, like the boxes, through the text of the chapter, are now listed separately at the end. Both the activities and the projects have been substantially revised, on the basis of feedback from instructors as to which were most "do-able" and which less so. The majority of the projects are entirely new with this edition. They now include a number of self-assessment scales, which, aside from the fact that students seem to enjoy doing them, help students see that psychological principles do apply to their own lives and aid them in pinpointing areas where they might want to change.

That, in sum, is what the second edition of this book has to offer. Finally, as aids to teaching and learning, we have provided:

The Student Handbook: Readings, Cases, and Study Guide. For each chapter in the text, this handbook repeats the outline and offers additional learning aids: review questions with answers, and a selected reading (e.g., a case study or a description of some interesting research project) followed by questions.

The Instructor's Manual. This guide offers, for each chapter in the text, the following teaching aids: chapter outline; suggestions for demonstrations, classroom discussions,

TO THE INSTRUCTOR

student-involvement projects, and audio-visual aids; objective and essay questions for use in quizzes and examinations; questions and answers on the readings offered in the *Student Handbook*.

This book has benefited from much kind and expert assistance. The second edition still reflects, to a large extent, the help offered on the first edition by Random House editors Virginia Hoitsma and Paul Shensa in planning, by Paula Franklin in editing, and by Elaine Rosenberg in production. This time around, Virginia Hoitsma has once again been our primary, and extremely helpful, advisor. Our heartfelt thanks also to Judith Rothman, Senior Editor, Leslie Carr, Assistant Editor, and Deborah Connor Coker, Project Editor, for their valuable contributions at different stages. We have also received many fine suggestions from our reviewers:

Cheryl B. Bradley, Central Virginia Community College

Desmond S. Cartwright, University of Colorado

Fred S. Fehr, Arizona State University

Louis Fusilli, Monroe Community College

Darwin J. Goodey, Central Washington University

Bernard S. Gorman, Nassau Community College

Carol Grams, Orange Coast College

Gerald Rubin, Central Virginia Community College

Connie Schick, Bloomsburg State College

Ken Thompson, Central Missouri State University

As for our personal debts, James Calhoun wishes to thank his wife, Judy, for her support and encouragement. Joan Acocella thanks her husband, Nick, and her son, Bartholomew, who saw her patiently through this project.

JAMES F. CALHOUN
Athens, Georgia

JOAN ROSS ACOCELLA
New York City

TO THE STUDENT

Psychology is the study of human thoughts and behavior: what people think and do, and why. This particular psychology textbook is concerned with adjustment, the most practical side of psychology. The book has two goals: (1) to pass along to you some of what psychologists have discovered about ordinary, everyday behavior and (2) to show you how you can use these principles to solve ordinary problems in your own life—problems in seeing yourself realistically, problems in getting yourself to study, problems in meeting other people, problems in getting along with the people you care about, and many other types of problems as well.

Along with the main text of our chapters, we have included a number of aids—devices to help you learn the material and make practical use of it. If you take advantage of them, you will get more out of the book. They are:

Organization. The book is divided into two units: the self and others. Dealing with

these two things—and also with the environment, the subject of the final chapter—is what we mean by "adjustment." In each of the two main units, there are "information" chapters, which give psychological information, and "change" chapters, which tell you how you can change areas of your life if you want to. If you turn now to the table of contents and read the chapter titles, you will see what we mean by "information" chapters and "change" chapters.

Chapter Outlines. The first item in every chapter is an outline of that chapter. This will give you a broad idea of what the chapter is about before you start to read it. It is also useful for testing yourself before an exam. Just go down the list and see if you can recapitulate the main points covered under each heading and define any technical terms included in the heading.

Definitions. When we use a technical term for the first time, we italicize it and give a

TO THE STUDENT

clear, straightforward definition. It will help you to pay close attention to these definitions, since the terms are likely to come up again and again.

Glossary. At the end of the book there is a glossary, listing the technical terms in the book along with their definitions. So if you come across a term and have forgotten what it means, use the glossary to refresh your memory.

Activities. At the end of each chapter, there is a list of "activities," suggestions for things you can do (like analyzing a television commercial) to test the psychological principles we describe and to make use of them for your own benefit. The activities should be fun, and they should also help you learn the material. What we use, we learn.

Boxes. Scattered here and there in the chapters are the "boxes." These are short, boxed-in essays about interesting sidelights on the main points of the chapter.

Summaries. At the end of the text of each chapter comes the summary, which simply repeats the main points of the chapter in the form of numbered paragraphs. If you read the summary immediately after reading the chapter, it will help you to remember the material for the future. The summaries should also be helpful in reviewing the material for examinations.

Projects. The final item in every chapter is a "project," which is simply a longer activity. Like the activities, the projects are there to show you how to *use* psychological principles in your own life. And by using them, you will learn them.

Those, then, are our learning aids; together with the text of the chapters, they constitute the main body of this book. In addition, there are two special features:

Human Issues. Sandwiched between the chapters are eight "Human Issues" essays. They are there to give you information and psychological theories about some of the most ordinary but important aspects of living: sex roles, love, sex, marriage, child rearing, work, middle age, and old age. There is also a "Human Issues" essay on abnormal psychology: how psychologists define serious psychological disturbance and what forms it can take.

Appendix: "Getting Help." At the back of the book is one final essay, on how to get professional help if you have a psychological problem that you can't seem to solve for yourself. This essay describes the kinds of psychotherapy that are available and offers suggestions for finding a good therapist.

We wish you pleasure with this book—the kind of pleasure that comes from understanding. To many of us, personal problems seem totally personal, not something we share with the rest of the human race. Psychology teaches us that the very opposite is true: although each of us is unique, our problems are in fact quite similar to those of other human beings. It also teaches us that these problems follow certain rules, which means that we can understand them and go to work on them. To take hold of a problem in this way is an exhilarating experience, not only because it might result in our actually *solving* the problem, but also because it reminds us that our lives really do belong to us. Mysterious as life sometimes seems, it is not beyond our understanding. Nor is it beyond our control. Within limits, we can choose the kind of human beings we will be and the kind of lives we will live. If this book helps you find out what choices you have and to act on this knowledge, it will have done its job.

CONTENTS

CONTENTS

CONTENTS

PSYCHOLOGY OF ADJUSTMENT AND HUMAN RELATIONSHIPS

<u>OUTLINE</u>

MODERN LIFE: A NEW CHALLENGE
Increased Knowledge
Higher Expectations
Increased Freedom

ADJUSTMENT
What Is Adjustment?
Controlling Your Adjustment

WHAT IS GOOD ADJUSTMENT?
Factors in Evaluating Adjustment
The Situation
Values

PSYCHOLOGICAL THEORIES OF ADJUSTMENT
Psychodynamic Theory
Sigmund Freud: id, ego, and superego
Modern psychodynamic theory
Behavioral Theory
Walter Mischel: The interaction of person and situation
Cognitive behaviorism
Humanistic Theory
Abraham Maslow: The hierarchy of needs
Carl Rogers: The self theory
Existential Theory
Viktor Frankl: The will-to-meaning
The Psychological Theory of This Book

1

ADJUSTMENT: A WAY OF HANDLING PROBLEMS

It is Sunday afternoon. Some people have gone back to bed. Others have gone to the park or the movies or the library. Others are trying to deal with problems. Let us read the minds of some people in the last group.

Sam is wondering why he sat around with his friends in the cafeteria last night making jokes about the shy, odd little freshman who lives down the hall—and who was sitting two tables away in the cafeteria. What a petty thing to do! So why had he done it? Well, it was certainly easy to go along with the group. And you *could* make some very funny jokes about this guy. And what could Sam have done about the situation anyway? What if he had said to the group, "Look, let's not add to the guy's troubles"? He probably would have received a round of cold stares. And pretty soon he himself would be an oddball with no friends. But all the same, he feels ashamed.

Laura sits in her kitchen listening to her friend Cathy talk about her troubles. Cathy's troubles never get any better—or any more interesting. But Cathy never tires of talking about them, and Laura never has the courage to cut these sessions short. Wouldn't it be cruel to tell Cathy she doesn't have time to listen? How could she hurt Cathy's feelings like that? On the other hand, she has heard this bit about Cathy's husband so many times, and she wants desperately to finish the book she is reading.

Ralph looks at himself in the mirror and wonders whether he will ever manage to lose weight. Kay looks at the stack of books on her desk and wonders how she will ever pass the exam tomorrow. In fact, she wonders how she will ever be able to study at all, what with the noise in the house. Sara sits wondering whether the man she went out with last night liked her. Then she wonders why she is wondering whether someone likes her instead of vice versa.

These private struggles are nothing new.

On the contrary, they are illustrations of some of the most common problems in living. Such problems may be divided into two large categories. First is the problem of dealing with *ourselves:* controlling our work habits, eating habits, and other habits, enduring loneliness, living with our mistakes, learning to respect ourselves. Second is the problem of dealing with *others:* being kind to those who need kindness, resisting the temptation to go along with the group, finding a way to form intimate relationships, dealing with the inconveniences of living with other people.

These are not problems that can ever be solved once and for all; they are woven into life. So we handle them in the only way we can: by making changes and compromises from day to day. This process is called *adjustment.* And adjustment is the subject of our book.

Let us look briefly at what we will cover. The two units of our book will cover the two main categories of daily problems: self (Unit I) and others (Unit II). These two large categories are broken down into a number of separate topics, the subjects of our individual chapters.

Self-concept (Chapters 3, 4): How do you perceive yourself? Do you like what you see? Is your self-concept hurting you or helping you?

Self-control (Chapters 5–7): How well do you control your behavior? Are you eating more, studying less, and feeling more anxiety than you need to?

Social perception (Chapters 9, 10): How realistically do you see other people? And how are your perceptions of them affecting your relationships with them?

Social influence (Chapters 11–13): How *are* those relationships? Could you make them more pleasant and fulfilling?

In addition, we will present overviews of the self (Chapter 2) and of social relations (Chapter 8). Finally, in recognition of the great influence that our physical surroundings have on our behavior, we will include a final chapter on adjusting to the environment.

That, in brief, is what we will cover in the following chapters. As for the present chapter, we will use the rest of it to provide an overview of the topic of adjustment. First we will see how life in a modern society creates special challenges for personal adjustment. Second, we will take a closer look at the process of adjustment—how it actually works. Third, we will examine several theories of what constitutes good adjustment and explain what part these theories will play in the remainder of the book.

MODERN LIFE: A NEW CHALLENGE

Problems in living are not a modern invention. Yet the problems we face today are in many ways different from those of our ancestors. In the past century the quality of human existence has probably changed more than it did in the preceding ten centuries. To illustrate this fact, Alvin Toffler, in his book *Future Shock*, asks us to visualize human history as a series of lifetimes:

If the last 50,000 years of man's existence were divided into lifetimes of approximately sixty-two years each, there have been about 800 such lifetimes. Of these 800, fully 650 were spent in caves.

Only during the last seventy lifetimes has it been possible to communicate effectively from one lifetime to another—as writing made it possible to do. Only during the last six lifetimes did masses of men ever see a printed word. Only during the last four has it been possible to measure time with any precision. Only in the last two has anyone anywhere used an electric motor. And the overwhelming majority of all the material goods we use in daily life today have been developed within the present, the 800th, lifetime. (p. 14)

This does not mean that everything in human existence has been transformed. As a matter of fact, the joys that we find in life are probably the same ones that our great-grandparents and their great-grandparents found. Love, art, children, friends, a beautiful day, a good dinner, a success for which you worked hard—these are still the basic rewards of life.

What has really changed are the *problems* of living. For our ancestors, problems were often physical: staying alive, keeping warm, putting food on the table. For us, physical problems are not so pressing. As citizens of industrialized nations, we are generally well housed and well fed. What we have instead are existential problems: problems in choosing how we will lead our lives.

Where did these problems come from? In large part, they arose from three great changes in modern life: increased knowledge, increased expectations, and increased freedom. These three changes are precious gifts. But they also pose a very great challenge for living.

Increased Knowledge

In the eighteenth and nineteenth centuries it took weeks or even months for Americans to find out who their presidential candidates were. News traveled slowly. Today, with television, we can watch our political conventions at the very moment they are occurring. The Vietnam War, the astronauts' moon walk, the Watergate hearings, the return of the hostages from Iran—these momentous

events are beamed directly into our living rooms. Televised news is supplemented by magazines and newspapers. Any single edition of a metropolitan newspaper will offer you more information than you can absorb in a week.

What we do not find out through the communications media, we can find out through travel. In a matter of hours jets can transport us halfway across the world and deposit us in societies utterly unlike our own. In short, improved communications and transportation have made it possible for us to see and hear more different things than our ancestors ever dreamed existed.

Not only facts but also opinions come at us from all sides. Television, radio, books, newspapers, college lectures—from all these sources come different ideas as to what is right and wrong, normal and abnormal, good and evil. A student who comes to college believing that child molesters are evil may be told in her psychology course that child molesters are emotionally disturbed people who deserve compassion and psychological help. A housewife who has never dreamed of being anything but a housewife may be informed by a feminist magazine that her condition lies somewhere between slavery and prostitution. Whatever values we embrace, they must survive constant exposure to opposing values.

What do we do with all this information, and what does it do to us? On the one hand, knowledge is certainly preferable to ignorance. It feeds our curiosity, increases our tolerance, invites us to think in more complex ways, and allows us to base our beliefs on a foundation more solid than the folk wisdom on which earlier generations depended. On the other hand, it can be argued that the tidal wave of information has literally overwhelmed the modern consciousness, undermining beliefs, values, and tra-

ADJUSTMENT: A WAY OF HANDLING PROBLEMS

In contemporary industrial societies, transportation and communication networks provide almost immediate access to new information. (top left: © Frank Siteman/Taurus Photos; top right: © Leonard Speier 1982; bottom right: © Hervé Gloaguen/Viva/Woodfin Camp & Assoc.; bottom left: © Mark Godfrey/Magnum)

ditions. (This is certainly the opinion of those parents who want to censor textbooks.) Both views are to some degree correct. Our experience of the world is undoubtedly richer and more varied than that of a Nebraska farmer in 1850, but it is also much less stable. We are haunted by questions: Who am I? Where am I going? What should I believe? And for every question, ten different sources will give us ten different answers.

ACTIVITY 1.1

Although the amount of information available to us has increased at a phenomenal rate in the past few decades, we still tend to select the kind of information to which we are exposed. And what we generally select is information consistent with our own views.

Consider political information, for example. Some of us seek out conservative sources of information, while others of us listen only to liberal viewpoints. To understand where your political views come from, make a list of the sources from which you get information on politics, for example, books, magazines, newspapers, television and radio news broadcasts, and people. Rate each source according to the extent to which it challenges or supports your own views. You may find that most of what you read, see, and hear tends to confirm the political opinions you already hold.

Note that this selection process is a form of adjustment: by ignoring sources of information that we disagree with, we protect ourselves from the confusion of having our own opinions challenged. To see how this works, spend twenty minutes a day for a week reading or listening to sources of political information that you disagree with. (If you are a conservative, try reading *The Nation*; if you are a liberal, read *National Review*. Both will probably be in your school library.) At the end of the week, write a one-page summary of the experience. Did the opposition seem to make sense, too? Were you more bothered by it when it made sense or when it seemed unquestionably wrong?

Higher Expectations

Prior to the nineteenth century, it was the rare person who truly expected more from life than what his parents had received. If Mother was a peasant woman who got out of bed at sunrise every morning of her life to feed the pigs, then her daughters could almost surely expect the same future. If Mother's life was somewhat more comfortable, then her daughters could expect that much comfort. But there was little hope of "bettering" yourself. And for the most part, the same held true for sons as for daughters.

This iron law is no longer in force. Because of several factors—in particular, democracy, industrialization, free education, and the loosening of social-class structures—people in industrialized nations have been encouraged to generate high expectations for themselves. The waitress's daughter plans to become a physicist. The toll-collector's son hopes to become a surgeon. People divorced two or three times believe that *next* time it will work. We believe that we can have almost anything we want— love, power, wealth, happiness—if only we try hard enough.

Well, what about these high expectations? What have they done for us? To begin with, they have done a great deal of good. After all, it was high expectations that brought many of our grandparents and great-grandparents to the United States. They themselves worked on the docks and in the sweatshops, but with the expectation that their children would be free from hunger and that their grandchildren might even go

A Kentucky coal miner and his son. American children have a better chance than most of choosing their futures, but some have more choices than others. (© Earl Palmer/Monkmeyer Press Photo)

Immigrants arrive at Ellis Island in New York harbor at the turn of the century. The immigrants came in search of a better life. (The Bettmann Archive)

to college. For many, that hope was fulfilled. And we, the grandchildren—well-fed and educated—have to be grateful for it, and grateful, too, that we can hope to fulfill our own goals.

Nevertheless, it is also possible that we have learned to expect too much. While our grandparents had relatively simple ambitions, ours are often much grander. Intimate marriages *and* sexual freedom; close-knit families *and* personal autonomy; high-powered jobs *and* leisure time—all these things are valued as highly desirable. We want them all. But in most cases one will exclude the other, leaving us frustrated and with a sense of personal failure.

Furthermore, high expectations can lead to a sort of mindless and aimless searching that prevents us from putting down roots,

developing loyalties, and truly enjoying what there is to be enjoyed. We expect our jobs to be interesting, our marriages to be emotionally gratifying, and our environments to be comfortable. Well and fine. But in the process of pursuing this vision of happiness, we Americans change our jobs, our spouses, and our residences more frequently than any other people. This continuous shifting about suggests not fulfillment, but its opposite: a sense of restless dissatisfaction, for which our grandiose ambitions are largely to blame.

In sum, our high expectations are a classic case of the mixed blessing. On the one hand, they are the force that drives us to fulfill our highest goals. On the other hand, they pose the problem that we may never learn to take pleasure in what life has to offer us.

ACTIVITY 1.2

We all have expectations regarding our future. Rarely, however, do we stop to ask ourselves how realistic these expectations are. It's a good idea to examine them every now and then so that we can direct our lives toward realistic goals.

One set of expectations concerns work. Write down what kind of job you would like to be holding ten years from now. This may be vague, such as "working with people," or it may be as specific as "owning a sporting goods store." Then list the things you're doing now that you think will help you reach your goal: taking a certain course, working part-time, practicing a musical instrument, training in a sport.

Now look over what you've written and see how well your career goal and your present activities fit together. If you want to go into your father's construction business and are now studying accounting, your expectations are probably realistic—as much as they can be several years in advance. If, on the other hand, you want to be a neurosurgeon but are flunking biology, you may need to reexamine your expectations.

Increased Freedom

Freedom is another thing we have more of than did our ancestors. In other times and other countries people have died fighting for half the rights we take for granted. Freedom of speech, freedom of the press, freedom of assembly, freedom to worship as we choose (or not to worship at all)—most of these privileges were unheard of in even the greatest civilizations of the past.

And political freedoms are only half the story. In the home, children are more independent of their parents than ever before. In colleges, it is now the students who decide what they will study; what were once strict requirements are now electives. Indeed, it can actually be said that within limits, young people in industrial societies now *choose* what they will become. Their values, their votes, their jobs, their friends, their spouses, the number of their children—these matters are up to them.

Such freedom is truly exhilarating. It means we can set our own goals and go after

them; we can create our own lives. But at the same time our freedom is often somewhat bewildering. Many of us are not at all sure what to do with it.

For example, we have just said that in many ways young people can now choose what they will do and be as adults. But how do you decide what you will do and be? Human beings, unlike other animals, have very few instincts to tell them how to behave. In deciding what to do, they have had to depend on two sources of guidance: their well-developed brains and their culture—that is, the values and customs of their society. Let us take a look at this second source of guidance, our culture. How firmly can our culture guide us now? As we have seen, different facts and opinions come at us from all sides. Values differ from group to group and from generation to generation. In the past, the values of the culture were handed down from parent to child. Today, because the culture has changed so rapidly, parents' values may be simply irrelevant to the world their children have to deal with (Mead, 1970).

ADJUSTMENT: A WAY OF HANDLING PROBLEMS

In short, we can't depend on our culture to show us *the* way. It is bound to offer many different ways. So we must fall back on our brains, which, as we have said, are extremely capable. But intelligence alone will not get us through the business of living. When your husband asks you to quit school and go back to work because the family needs the extra money, you need more than brains to make your decision. You need values.

Another problem related to freedom is that of responsibility. Because we are allowed to make our own choices, we are responsible for the choices we make. A married woman, for example, can now choose (as her grandmother probably could not) whether to have a career or children or both. Whichever choice she makes, she cannot justifiably blame the consequences on society, human biology, men, or any other external force. The choice is hers. And therefore she is responsible for the consequences.

This responsibility can be a heavy burden.

Indeed, it is no coincidence that the idea of the "anguish of freedom" was developed in our century. Molding your own destiny can be a very exciting experience, but it can also be very anxiety provoking. According to the philosophers, the age of anxiety is definitely upon us. One sign of this is the immense quantity of tranquilizers Americans consume every year. Valium, only one of the more popular tranquilizers, is taken regularly by about thirteen out of every one hundred Americans (Carpenter, 1980). And this is to say nothing of those who relieve their tension with other tranquilizers or with alcohol or marijuana. We are a very nervous people.

With less freedom, we might have more peace of mind. Nevertheless, freedom, like knowledge and expectations, is not something most of us would want less of. We treasure our freedom. It is a rare gift. Yet it still leaves us the problems of deciding, alone, what to do with our lives and of living with our decisions.

Having a drink after work. Many people rely on alcohol or other drugs in the evening to relieve tension built up during the day. (© Barbara Alper 1982)

BOX 1.1
THE CULTS: FLIGHT FROM FREEDOM

An interesting development of the 1970s and 1980s has been the upsurge of evangelical religious sects in the United States. "Born-again" Christians, once a small minority, largely poor and rural, can now be found in all socioeconomic and geographical groups. In the 1980 presidential election, all three major candidates claimed to have been born again. Even more curious is the success of newer and more eccentric cults such as the Krishna Consciousness movement, the Church of Scientology, the Divine Light Mission, and the Unification Church of Reverend Sun Myung Moon. It is hard to say how many members these different sects have, because official figures are often inflated, but a recent estimate is that 3 million Americans now belong to religious cults of one kind or another (Conway and Siegelman, 1978). This is quite a substantial following.

What has made the cults so popular? There are many possible answers. One is that these groups provide a refuge from the anxieties of modern life by reducing what Western industrial societies have so greatly increased: expectations, freedom, and exposure to information.

In cults such as the Unification Church, freedom is severely limited. "I am your brain," Reverend Moon has said to his followers (quoted by Rice, 1976, p. 39), and the extent to which this is true can be seen in the way the Unification Church's residential centers are operated. Rules dominate every sphere of activity. Members are told when, where, and how they will work, eat, sleep, pray and behave in general. And there is little opportunity for deviation because almost all activities are conducted in groups. These groups, it should be noted, are segregated by sex. Along with drugs and liquor, sexual activity is forbidden, except to married couples, and even for the married it is controlled. (Newlyweds, for example, are not permitted to consummate their marriages for at least forty days.)

Marriage, too, is strictly regulated. In order to marry, one must first have put in seven years of service in the cult. Then the match may be proposed to Reverend Moon, who may or may not approve.

Information, likewise, is carefully selected. Moon's followers are offered a single system of beliefs, consisting largely of simple, black-and-white truths, and these are reinforced daily in lectures and prayer sessions lasting for hours. Questioning, even reasoning, is strongly discouraged.

As for individual expectations, they are prescribed by the organization. Unification Church members may be assigned to cook meals, wash cars, lead prayer meetings, or whatever. The most common jobs, however, are fund-raising and recruiting new members. Whatever the assignment, it is aimed at the development of the group rather than of the individual.

What do members receive in return? What draws them there and keeps them there? According to ex-members, the cults offer certain powerful rewards—above all, the pleasure of commitment and the sense of belonging. It is possible, however, that the greatest bonus the members receive for giving up their freedom is the relief of giving up their freedom. "Freedom is great," said one ex-cult member, "but it takes a lot of work" (quoted by Singer, 1979, p. 76). It also creates anxiety, a point that has been forcefully made by Erich Fromm (1941) and by existential writers. Free choice, after all, forces us to deal with many complicated problems: how to find friends, whom to date, how to handle sex, whether to try drugs, what to study, what kind of work to do, how to find a job, how to weigh your own needs against the needs of others. The cults offer ready-made solutions to such problems, and for that benefit many people are apparently content to trade in their freedom.

ADJUSTMENT

As we have just explained, difficulties—pain, disappointments, doubts, fears—have always been a part of life. And modern life has added its own new set of difficulties. It is therefore quite normal to have problems, even serious problems. It does not make you "crazy." It simply makes you human.

But let us get down to business. Normal as our problems may be, we still have to deal with them. How do we do it? Through the mechanism that is the subject of this book: *adjustment.*

What Is Adjustment?

Adjustment may be defined as your continuous interaction with your self, with other people, and with your world. These three factors are constantly acting on you and influencing you. And the relationship is reciprocal, for you are constantly acting on them as well.

Your self—that is, the sum total of what you already are: your body, your behavior, and your thoughts and feelings—is something that you are dealing with in every split second. Let us look back at the examples we gave at the beginning of this chapter. As Sam sat there mulling over his conformity to the group, he was interacting with his self. His self was influencing him, mainly by making him feel guilty. And he was influencing himself, partly by providing excuses for his behavior and partly by telling himself that, excuses or no excuses, what he did was shameful.

As for other people, it is obvious that they have a strong influence on us, as we do on them. Laura, by listening without complaint to Cathy's endless accounts of her troubles, influences her to go on talking. And Cathy, by reciting her woes at such great length, influences Laura not to do her reading.

Similarly, our world—the sights and smells and sounds that surround us as we go about our business—acts upon us, and we act upon it. If Kay can't study because of the noise in the house, then her environment is influencing her. Conversely, if she stuffs a towel under the door to block out the sound, she has turned the tables and influenced the environment.

Controlling Your Adjustment

At this point you may want to ask this question: If adjustment is something we engage in at every moment, something as natural and as automatic as breathing, then how can this process help us with our problems? The answer is that while adjustment may be natural, it is not necessarily automatic. It can be purposeful and deliberate.

Problems arise when the adjustment process starts going against us—when we are influenced by our selves or others or the environment to do things we wish we didn't do or to feel things we don't want to feel. But as we just saw, the tables can be turned. By finding out what is causing your problems, you can go to work on those causes and thus change the influence they have on you.

This does not mean that you can bend your self, your friends and family, and your world to fit all your requirements. Prices will still go up; friends will still disappoint you now and then; it may still rain on the day you planned to spend at the beach. On a larger scale, there are certain problems that may seem impossibly difficult to handle. For a person dealing with a serious drinking problem or other drug habit, it is often hard even to imagine life without the drug, to say nothing of actually living without it. Or, to take a somewhat more common problem, a person in the midst of a divorce may find that the sum total of adjustment demands—

comforting the children, dealing with the disapproval of parents and in-laws, learning to live without the other person, getting used to being alone, finding out how to date again, dealing with financial problems—is simply more than he or she can cope with.

Adjustment, in other words, involves genuine crises as well as more ordinary, day-to-day difficulties. When major crises occur, it is often a good idea to seek professional psychological help to get you through the adjustment process (see the Appendix for a discussion of different types of psychological help). For most of us, however, major adjustment crises are rare. The challenge of life is simply coping with a multitude of minor problems, things we *can* influence, such as getting along better with our parents, dealing with difficulties at work, studying more efficiently, and controlling anxieties. These "garden-variety" adjustment problems are the focus of our book.

But before we consider specific ways of altering our adjustment, we must ask ourselves what we are aiming for. What constitutes good adjustment?

WHAT IS GOOD ADJUSTMENT?

How can you tell whether a person is well-adjusted or poorly adjusted? During World War II thousands of Germans, to say nothing of other Europeans, knowingly cooperated with the German Gestapo in rounding up Jews and sending them off to concentration camps. These people later claimed that they were simply obeying orders. Were they maladjusted? Were they "sick"? Can we say that a whole nation of people is maladjusted?

Factors in Evaluating Adjustment

We are not suggesting that it is impossible to make sound judgments as to whether behavior is healthy or unhealthy, right or wrong. You have to make such judgments every day of your life. It must be kept in mind, however, that every time you judge human behavior (your own or someone else's), your conclusion will depend not only on the behavior in question but also on two other factors: the situation and your values.

The Situation

Many people would agree that prostitutes engage in abnormal behavior. No well-adjusted person, they say, would sell to strangers what is supposed to be a token of love. However, it appears that during the Vietnam War, one way in which a Vietnamese mother could help her daughter was to set her up as a prostitute. In this way the girl could at least earn a living rather than starve to death. And perhaps, if some soldier took a special interest in her, she could find a husband as well. To many mothers and their daughters, this was apparently a realistic, if not ideal, way of coping with the circumstances.

In other words, the way a person adjusts and our judgment as to whether it is a healthy adjustment depend very much on what the person is adjusting to. Some people can make a reasonable adjustment to one environment but not to another. In an environment that calls for spontaneous behavior (for example, a group therapy session), a person who is very restrained emotionally may seem maladjusted—repressed, overcontrolled, and so forth. Consider, on the other hand, a person in a situation demanding emotional restraint—for example, a psychiatrist talking to a client, a juror listening to a trial, the President of the United States addressing Congress. If any one of these people decided to "let it all hang out," he or she would probably be considered emotionally unbalanced or at least unfit for his or her job.

BOX 1.2
CHANGE, STRESS, AND ILLNESS

We all live through "life changes" that require adjustment. Two researchers, Thomas Holmes and Richard Rahe (1967), have developed a list of such events, rating them according to how difficult they are to adjust to. The ratings are expressed in "life change units," or LCU's. The higher the LCU rating, the more difficult the adjustment. The most taxing changes are the following:

Event	LCU's
Death of spouse	100
Divorce	73
Marital separation	65
Jail term	63
Death of close family member	63
Personal injury or illness	53
Marriage	50
Fired at work	47
Marital reconciliation	45
Retirement	45
Change in health of family member	44
Pregnancy	40
Sex difficulties	39
Gain of new family member	39
Business readjustment	39
Change in financial state	38
Death of close friend	37
Change to different line of work	36
Change in number of arguments with spouse	35
Mortgage or loan for major purchase (home, etc.)	31
Foreclosure of mortgage or loan	30
Change in responsibilities at work	29
Son or daughter leaving home	29
Trouble with in-laws	29
Outstanding personal achievement	28
Wife begins or stops work	26
Begin or end school	26
Change in living conditions	25
Revision of personal habits	24
Trouble with boss	23
Change in work hours or conditions	20
Change in residence	20
Change in schools	20
Change in recreation	19
Change in church activities	19
Change in social activities	18
Mortgage or loan for lesser purchase (car, TV, etc.)	17
Change in sleeping habits	16
Change in number of family get-togethers	15
Change in eating habits	15
Vacation	13
Christmas	12
Minor violations of the law	11

The interesting thing about this scale is that it lumps together positive and negative events. Marriage, for example, gets more points than being fired from your job, and an outstanding personal achievement is rated just one notch below trouble with in-laws. The point is that change *itself* is stressful, whether it is for the better or for the worse. Other researchers (for

Values

Our judgments as to whether people are well adjusted depends not only on the situation, but also on our values, our ideas about how people *should* behave. Let's assume that you believe people should act rationally—that they should not be superstitious or believe in miracles. Then you may agree with the modern psychiatrists who argue that Joan of

One of the most stressful adjustments in life is accepting the death of someone we care for. (© Jill Freedman/Magnum)

who had between 150 and 300 LCU's (Colligan, 1975).

Let us consider a hypothetical example. A woman with two children divorces her husband (73 LCU's) and moves to another city (change of residence: 20 LCU's), where she buys a house (mortgage of over $80,000: 31 LCU's). This leaves her broke (change in financial state: 38 LCU's). Nevertheless, she decides to go back to school (26 LCU's) and takes a part-time job in order to help pay for it (business readjustment: 39 LCU's). Her younger sister, who is having trouble at home, moves in with her (gain of a new family member: 39 LCU's) to help care for the children. Within a few months her life has become more settled, and she has even started dating someone (change in social activities: 18 LCU's), when she receives the news that her father has had a heart attack (change in health of a family member: 44 LCU's). We will leave her now in the midst of her problems and add up her LCU's for the past half year: 367. According to Holmes and Holmes (1970), she is now at a high risk for health problems.

To see how much change you have absorbed recently, go down the list and add up your own LCU's for the past year. If your score is less than 150, you are apparently meeting normal adjustment demands. A score of 150 to 199 suggests a mild degree of stress. A score of 200 to 299 indicates heavy stress. A score of 300 or more indicates extraordinary stress and a high risk of illness.

Rating scale adapted from: Holmes, T. H., and Rahe, R. H. "The Social Readjustment Rating Scale," Journal of Psychosomatic Research, 11 (1967), p. 215.

example, Sarason, Johnson, and Siegel, 1978) have disputed this claim, but more research is necessary before the issue can be decided.

Holmes and Holmes (1970) argue that too much change, positive or negative, can be damaging to your health. In a group of people who were rated for LCU's accumulated within the preceding year, 86 percent of those who had collected more than 300 LCU's had also suffered some major health problem. By contrast, health problems were found in only 48 percent of those

Arc was insane, since she claimed to have heard voices from heaven. If, however, you believe that people who have supernatural experiences are somehow special, then you may agree with the Roman Catholic Church

that Joan of Arc was not a madwoman but a saint.

Every judgment we make about whether we or someone else has "problems" reflects our values. Indeed, psychiatrist Thomas

Szasz (1967) claims that psychiatrists are nothing more than the moral policemen of our society, weeding out and sending off to hospitals those people whose behavior offends the values of our society. Once again, this is not to say you shouldn't make value judgments. It is wise to remember, however, that when you call someone (or yourself) "weird" or "sick," you are actually saying that this person's behavior contradicts your values.

PSYCHOLOGICAL THEORIES OF ADJUSTMENT

Psychology is the scientific study of human behavior and mental processes. This enormous topic is divided into a number of specialties, one of which is the *psychology of adjustment*. But in addition to being a subfield in itself, adjustment also draws from most of the other subfields of psychology. From *developmental psychology*, the study of how human beings change as they grow and develop, we get our information on how adjustment problems, along with techniques for adjusting, change over the life cycle. From *experimental psychology*, the study of general psychological principles via experimentation, we get our basic understanding of how human beings learn, how they think, and how their mental processes interact with their bodily processes. From *personality psychology*, the study of how human beings differ in their behavior, and from *clinical psychology*, which deals with the treatment of emotional and behavioral problems, we derive our understanding of various coping styles, the destructive along with the constructive. And from *social psychology*, the study of interpersonal behavior, we obtain knowledge about how people meet what is probably the greatest adjustment challenge: dealing with other people. Adjustment, then, cuts across most of the territories of psychology, taking what it needs from each.

To return to the problem of deciding what constitutes good adjustment, a number of psychological professionals have constructed theories that attempt to answer that question, among others. Several of these theories have become quite famous. Whether or not we realize it, they have influenced the way we look at life. And they have definitely influenced the ideas you will find in this book. Therefore, it is worthwhile for us to take a look at them.

Psychodynamic Theory

Psychodynamic theory explains human behavior as the product of forces operating *within* the mind, often without the awareness of the individual. Different theorists emphasize different forces, but almost all psychodynamic writers give primary attention to three mental processes: (1) *conflict* between mutually opposing motives, (2) *anxiety* over unacceptable motives, and (3) *defense* against such unacceptable motives (Bootzin and Acocella, 1980). We will first discuss the theories of Sigmund Freud, the founder of this school of thought. Then we will consider the ideas of more recent psychodynamic theorists.

Sigmund Freud: Id, Ego, and Superego

Sigmund Freud (1856–1939) based his theory of the personality on two very original ideas.* The first was that human behavior is ruled primarily not by reason but by ir-

---

*These ideas may not sound new to us now, but that is only because Freud has so heavily influenced modern thought. To most of his contemporaries, at least in the early part of his career, his theories seemed quite outlandish.

rational instincts—aggressive instincts, and above all, sexual instincts. The second idea was that only a tiny portion of our thoughts and actions emerges from conscious mental processes; the major influence on our behavior is the *unconscious,* a dark pool of memories and desires that either have never emerged into consciousness or have been repressed, that is, pushed out of consciousness, because they arouse fear or shame in us.

Working with these two basic ideas, Freud (1920) divided the human personality into three "branches," which he called the *id,* the *ego,* and the *superego.* The *id,* which operates in the unconscious, consists of those sexual and aggressive instincts that form the basis of human behavior. The id pushes for satisfaction of these instincts without regard for the limitations imposed by reality, reason, or morality. The *ego* is the thinking, perceiving, problem-solving part of the personality—in short, the reality-oriented part of the personality. Its primary role is to find ways to satisfy the id, but within the limits of reality, reason, and morality. The *superego* is the personality's moral code, similar to what we call the conscience, but a bit more stern. Its main function is to oppose the amoral strivings of the id.†

According to Freud, maladjustment, or *neurosis,* occurs when a person's upbringing has resulted in the development of a weak ego—an ego that cannot mediate between the id's demands for instinct-gratification and the superego's demands for morally acceptable conduct. When this happens, the individual falls victim to anxiety, fearing that his instincts will take over and that his superego will punish him for violating moral standards.

By contrast, a well-adjusted personality is one in which childhood development has allowed the id, the ego, and the superego to develop in some harmony. In this case, the ego can find ways to satisfy id instincts without violating the limits imposed by the superego and by reality. The id's irrational instincts still form the basis of emotion and behavior, but they are routed by the ego into realistic and morally acceptable channels—ideally, working and loving. Thus, a man with powerful sexual drives will not try to bed down every woman in sight, nor will he be overwhelmed by guilt over his sexual desires. Rather, the ego will find a compromise between the id (sexual desires) and the superego (prohibition and guilt). For example, the man could have a normal and loving sexual relationship with one woman and channel his excess sexual energy into some socially approved outlet, perhaps painting beautiful women. In sum, well-adjusted people are still, at the deepest level, impelled by the id, and therefore they still suffer id–superego conflicts. But with the help of a strong ego they are able to resolve these conflicts in constructive ways rather than wallowing in either self-indulgence or guilt.

Modern Psychodynamic Theory

Freud had a number of brilliant followers—particularly, Alfred Adler, Karen Horney, Harry Stack Sullivan, Erich Fromm, and Erik Erikson—all of whom eventually departed from Freud in one way or another. Each had his or her own new ideas. Together, however, they share two basic objections to Freudian theory.

---

†In using the terms *id, ego,* and *superego,* it is important to keep in mind that Freud did not mean them to be understood as actual entities or as sections of the brain, but simply as metaphors for the three main functions of the mind. To prevent misunderstanding on this score, many psychodynamic writers now speak of "ego functions" rather than "ego," "superego functions" rather than "superego," and so forth. For the sake of convenience, however, we will retain Freud's original terminology.

First, modern psychodynamic writers place much more emphasis on the ego than Freud did. As we have just seen, Freud regarded the id as the basic motivator of human behavior. The ego might censor or redirect the id's impulses, but it could not substitute any impulses of its own. Hence, crucial though its functions might be, the ego could not actually *explain* the personality. This was the privilege of the id. In opposition to this view, later psychodynamic theorists have argued that the functions of the ego—perception, memory, thinking, planning, problem-solving—are as important as id instincts, if not more important, in explaining human behavior. Several theorists (for example, Hartmann, 1958) have gone a step further, claiming that the ego does in fact have "impulses" of its own—that perception and the ability to walk, for example, stem from the ego alone, and not just as the ego's means of gratifying the id. With this shift of emphasis from the id to the ego, later psychodynamic theorists have come to view human beings as less irrational and more purposeful, less driven and more "driving," than did Freud.

A second important departure is that later Freudian theorists have given much more attention than Freud did to the *social* aspect of adjustment, the way in which the individual interacts with other human beings. To Freud, the major determinant of the adult personality was the way in which the id's biological instincts were satisfied at different stages of early childhood (whether the child was fed punctually or haphazardly, whether toilet training was handled gently or harshly, and so forth). To post-Freudians, the gratification of biological instincts is only one component of the individual's social development, and it is social development in general, the quality of the child's relationships with parents and peers, that the post-Freudians tend to see as the major force in the creation of the adult personality. Indeed, many of them go so far as to *define* adjustment in social terms: good adjustment equals the ability, and maladjustment the inability, to form intimate, loving relationships with others.

To illustrate these two important concerns of recent psychodynamic theory, we will look briefly at the ideas of Erich Fromm and Erik Erikson.

Erich Fromm: Personality and Society. Erich Fromm (1902–1980) in many ways exemplifies the post-Freudians' quarrel with Freud over the importance of the id. Fromm felt that Freud, by interpreting all human behavior as the masked expression of biological drives, had done a serious injustice to human nature. To Fromm, human goodness—the ability to love, the drive for truth and justice—was as real as human selfishness, and he saw no reason to explain it (as Freud did) as an outgrowth of selfishness.

Fromm's writings also exemplify the social emphasis of post-Freudian thought. In Fromm's view (1947), the adult personality is molded not so much by the individual's history of biological gratification as by the character of the society. Authoritarian societies will encourage the development of passive, dependent personalities; capitalist societies will tend to foster robot-like personalities, incapable of viewing themselves or others as anything but saleable commodities; just and idealistic societies will nourish what Fromm called "productive" personalities, capable of love and bent on fulfilling their potential. The "productive" personality is Fromm's ideal of good adjustment.

In Fromm's view, not only does the society create individual personality; through our personalities, we mold our society. To Fromm, this was a crucial point, since he felt that our society needed some remolding. His great fear was that Western industrial nations were fostering the sort of robot-like behavior described above. Many of his most popular books (for example, *The Art of Loving*, 1956) were appeals for the reorientation of our society away from market values and toward the values of truth and freedom.

Erik Erikson: Development in a Social Context. Erik Erikson (b. 1902), probably the most respected psychodynamic theorist alive today, is best known for his expansion of Freud's theory of child development. Freud believed that from birth to about the age of six, children pass through a series of fixed stages. What defines each stage is the major anatomical focus of pleasure and pain and, consequently, of psychological conflict. (Remember that Freud regarded all conflict as rooted in biological drives.) For infants, pain and pleasure are centered in the mouth; hence Freud called the first year the *oral stage*. In the second year, when toilet training begins, the crucial anatomical zone is the anus, and so this period is called the *anal stage*. From three to six years, the focus shifts to the genitals; this, then, is the *phallic stage*. In Freud's view, the quality of the adult personality depended on how much conflict the individual had suffered at each of these stages, up to age six. Inadequate care in the oral stage might produce a passive personality; overly harsh discipline in the anal stage might produce a stingy or "compulsive" personality; and so on.

Erikson's important contribution was to revise and extend Freud's developmental chart so that it stressed the ego over the id and social interaction over biological gratification. Erikson's developmental stages (1963), summarized in Figure 1.1, are differentiated not by anatomical zones but by "crises" involving the individual's relationships with others. In the first year, for example, the harmony or disharmony of the parent-child relationship results in either a trusting or a distrustful attitude toward others. In the second year, when toilet training and the ability to walk and talk offer the child increased independence, the parent-child interaction fosters either a sense of autonomy or feelings of self-doubt. Each of the remaining stages likewise involves a "crisis" that can be resolved constructively or destructively.

Several important differences between Freud's and Erikson's theories should be noted. First, in Erikson's system, ego functions (such as the ability to meet challenges and overcome difficulties) are more crucial than id strivings (physical gratification). Second, in Erikson's theory, the developmental crises and their outcomes are generally stated in social terms; they have to do with the individual's relations with other people. (Freud called his stages *psychosexual stages*; Erikson uses the term *psychosocial stages*.) Here again, as with Fromm, we see adjustment conceptualized as the capacity to form warm and trusting relationships. Another interesting point is that while Freud saw the personality as essentially formed by age six, Erikson's developmental scheme extends through adolescence and all the way through the adult years. Erikson considered adolescence an especially troubled and critical period, and it is partly due to his writings that this age group is given so much attention in our society. Finally, it is worth noting that Erikson's scheme, though based on Freud's, is far more optimistic. By stressing the creative, problem-solving ego and by asserting that we go on forming our characters even into old age, Erikson offers a heartening vision of the human personality—unrealistically heartening, in the opinion of strict Freudians.

ADJUSTMENT: A WAY OF HANDLING PROBLEMS

Erikson's psychosocial stages	Age	Successful resolution of crisis leads to
Basic Trust vs. Mistrust Consistent maternal care vs. negligence, irregular satisfaction of needs	First year	Trust, optimism, warmth
Autonomy vs. Shame, Doubt Assertiveness and physical self-control vs. dependence on parents and inability to be assertive	Second year	Sense of autonomy, pride of accomplishment
Initiative vs. Guilt Exploratory behavior and self-initiated activities vs. fearfulness and self-doubt	Third to fifth years	Development of conscience, self-worth, goal definition
Industry vs. Inferiority Cooperation and competition vs. fear of failing and feelings of inadequacy	Sixth year to puberty	Competence, mastery of skills, self-confidence
Identity vs. Role Confusion Integration of identity vs. role diffusion, lack of positive identity	Adolescence	Sense of continuity with one's past, present, and future; healthy sense of identity
Intimacy vs. Isolation Emotional vulnerability and ability to care deeply for another person vs. shallow interpersonal relationships and fear of commitment	Early adulthood	Ability to form stable commitments and close relationships
Generativity vs. Stagnation Need to be needed and desire to contribute vs. self-absorption and early invalidism	Middle adulthood	Productivity, creative concern for the world and future generations
Integrity vs. Despair Reflection and evaluation vs. regret for past life and strong fear of death	Old age	Acceptance of mortality and of the human life cycle, sense of peace

Figure 1.1   Erikson's stages of psychosocial development. At each stage of development, according to Erikson, the individual undergoes a new crisis, which, if she resolves it successfully, will lead to a new form of psychological strength. (Source: Erikson, 1963.)

Behavioral Theory

Behavioral psychology developed, in part, as a reaction against psychodynamic theory. The founders of behaviorism argued that it was irresponsible and unscientific to talk about psychology solely in terms of subjective events, that is, events that supposedly occurred in the mind but could not be observed or measured (emotions, memories, operations of id, ego, and superego). To correct this situation, they proposed that psychology be studied in terms of specific, measurable behaviors—things you could see, hear, and count (Watson, 1913)—and specific, measurable causes of these behaviors.

According to classical behaviorism, people engage in certain behaviors because they have learned, through previous experiences, to associate these behaviors with rewards. Likewise, people stop engaging in certain behaviors because these behaviors either have not been rewarded or have been punished. For example, depression could be explained as the discarding of cheerful and active behavior because some event (say, the death of one's spouse or the loss of one's job) has eliminated the rewards for this type of behavior. Thus, all behaviors, no matter how wholesome or destructive, are learned behaviors. Well-adjusted people are people who have learned behaviors that help them deal successfully with life's demands. And maladjusted people are people who have learned behaviors that prevent them from dealing successfully with life's demands.

In recent years, this theory has broadened considerably. Many behavioral psychologists now feel that behavior cannot be explained solely in terms of external rewards and punishments. Thoughts and emotions—in other words, internal events—must also be taken into account in any comprehensive theory of learning. A good example, as these theorists (for example, Bandura, 1971) have pointed out, is *observational learning,* or learning by watching others. When a teenaged boy begins to dress and walk like John Travolta, we cannot say that he does this because he has received any external reward for it. Rather, he behaves this way, it would seem, because he somehow expects that by acting like Travolta (or the character Travolta is playing) he will receive the rewards that Travolta receives. But this expectation is an internal event, not an external one. According to most modern behaviorists, not just observational learning but many kinds of learning are influenced by purely mental processes. We reward and punish ourselves with our thoughts and emotions (pride for accomplishments, guilt for misdeeds) as much as we are rewarded and punished by the outside world.

Walter Mischel: The Interaction of Person and Situation

A good illustration of the behaviorists' recent interest in internal events is Walter Mischel's (1973) theory that human behavior is the product of the interplay of the characteristics of the person with the characteristics of the situation. Strict behaviorists try to explain human actions in terms of the situation alone, the external events bearing down on the individual as he or she acts. According to Mischel, however, behavior issues from the interaction of external and internal events. On the one hand, there are *situational variables,* such as who is talking to you, where you are standing, how hot or cold it is, and so forth. These external factors will definitely affect your behavior, but not without the added influence of your *person variables,* internal factors such as your abilities, habits of mind, expectations, values, and plans. This theory, by turning once again to the unobservable processes of the mind, sacrifices the admirable precision of classical behaviorism. But at the same time it releases the individual from the extremely passive role assigned to him by classical behaviorism. To Mischel, the individual not only reacts to the environment but also evaluates it, interprets it, and acts on it.

Cognitive Behaviorism. The behaviorists' recent concern with mental processes has given rise to a whole new area of research, known as *cognitive behaviorism.* (The term is derived from *cognition*, which means mental processing—how we "know," perceive, learn, and think about things.) The central claim of cognitive behaviorism is that behavior is a response not so much to external events as to the mental processing of those events—the way we interpret them (Mahoney, 1974; Meichenbaum, 1977). Consider, for example, a person who has just been turned down for a job. There are a number of things she might say to herself—for example:

1. "I didn't like the look of that place anyway—a bunch of stuffed shirts."
2. "I guess someone else fit their job description better. I'll have to look somewhere else."
3. "That just proves it—I'm a failure."

Each of these interpretations will produce a different emotional response and consequently a different behavioral response. Thus, it is not actually the lost job opportunity but what the person makes of it that is the crucial influence on behavior. According to the cognitive behaviorists, good adjustment is the ability to interpret events in a realistic and (within reason) positive manner, so that the resulting behavior will be self-fulfilling rather than self-defeating.

Like Mischel's interactionist view, cognitive behaviorism lacks the precision of classical behaviorism, because thoughts cannot be counted and measured as exactly as external events. Again like Mischel's approach, however, cognitive behaviorism seems to offer a more complete explanation of human actions, by taking into account the inner life. It also raises the possibility that we can change self-defeating behaviors by changing our ways of interpreting events (a technique that we will return to in later chapters).

Humanistic Theory

Humanistic psychologists disagree entirely with the behaviorists' rather pragmatic approach to human existence. The humanists argue that ideal adjustment involves a great deal more than simply coping, or even coping successfully, with the circumstances of your life. Rather, it means developing all your potentials to the fullest. To illustrate this idealistic approach to adjustment, we will look at the theories of two influential humanists, Abraham Maslow and Carl Rogers.

Abraham Maslow: The Hierarchy of Needs

Abraham Maslow's (1908–1970) most lasting contribution to psychology is his theory of the *hierarchy of needs*. Maslow (1954) felt that the kinds of adjustment challenges addressed by psychodynamic and behavioral theories—satisfying biological needs, finding friends, learning to respect oneself—were actually only the preparation for the ultimate challenge, *self-actualization*, defined as the fulfillment of one's own completely unique potential. As you can see in Figure 1.2, Maslow ranked human needs in the following order: physiological needs, safety needs, belongingness and love needs, esteem needs, and the need for self-actualization. Each type of need must be reasonably satisfied before the next can be tackled. People must feel physically safe before they can establish intimate relationships; they must have some experience of intimacy before they can seek the esteem of others, and so on. But optimum adjustment occurs when the person has satisfied the first four categories of needs sufficiently to move on to self-actualization: the full, free expression of his or her own talents and capabilities. Maslow (1970) conducted research on the

ADJUSTMENT: A WAY OF HANDLING PROBLEMS

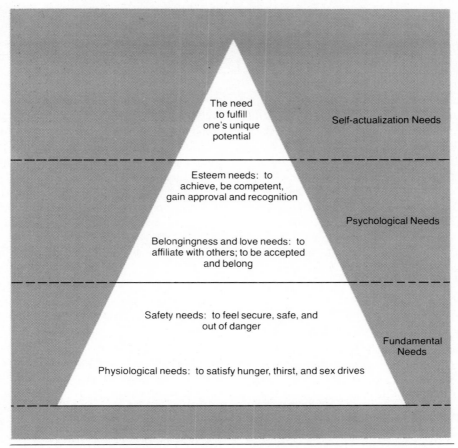

Figure 1.2   Maslow's hierarchy of needs. According to Maslow, fundamental needs (physiological needs and the need for safety) must be satisfied before we can move on to the satisfaction of psychological needs (the need for love and a sense of belonging, the need for esteem). These in turn must be taken care of before we can begin to satisfy the need for self-actualization. (Source: Maslow, 1954.)

characteristics of self-actualized people. Some of his findings are summarized in Box 1.3.

Carl Rogers: The Self Theory

Carl Rogers (b. 1902), like Maslow, defines adjustment in terms of self-actualization. His special contribution has been his *self theory*, which tries to explain why some people achieve self-actualization and others

do not. According to Rogers (1951), the key to self-actualization is the self-concept.* The self-concept is largely a product of our experiences in childhood, especially with our parents. All children naturally desire af-

---

* What we are here calling the "self-concept" Rogers actually called the "self." (Hence the name of his theory.) But since this book defines the "self" more broadly than Rogers does, we are limiting his term in order to prevent confusion. Rogers' theory will be discussed more fully in Chapter 3.

BOX 1.3
THE SELF-ACTUALIZED PERSON

In his effort to define the self-actualized person, Maslow singled out forty-eight people, living and dead, whom he felt had made extraordinary use of their potential. Included in the roster were such eminent figures as Baruch Spinoza, Thomas Jefferson, Abraham Lincoln, Albert Einstein, Albert Schweitzer, and Eleanor Roosevelt. After studying their lives, he concluded that they shared many other traits besides a knack for using their talents. In his book *Motivation and Personality* (1970), he listed fifteen characteristics that he found to be typical of self-actualized people. Six of these merit special attention:

Acceptance of self and others: Self-actualized people accept themselves and others as they are, rather than always wishing they were otherwise. They place a high value on the individuality and uniqueness of themselves and others.

Accurate perception of reality: Self-actualized people see things as they are, without shying away from painful or unpleasant information.

Intimacy with others: Self-actualized people tend to have a few, close friendships in which they reveal themselves fully. They are not intimate with many people, however, for they value their privacy and autonomy.

Personal autonomy: Self-actualized people are highly self-sufficient and have the strength to stand alone when necessary. They will stick by their own judgment even when others disagree. This inner strength helps them survive external losses and stress.

Problem-centered: Self-actualized people have a sense of mission in life. They make decisions on the basis of life goals, even if this means temporary sacrifice and frustration.

Spontaneity: Self-actualized people are spontaneous and simple. They respond to life in a natural, effortless way and are not bound by convention.

The nine other characteristics that Maslow found to be common in self-actualized people are a need for privacy, an appreciation of the new, a mystical sense of unity with nature and humankind, a feeling of brotherhood with all people, an ability to see other people as individuals (without being influenced by race, religion, and so on), clear ideas of right and wrong, a philosophical sense of humor, creativeness, and the ability to resist cultural influences that run counter to personal standards.

---

fection and approval. However, many parents make their approval conditional on certain kinds of behavior. They will love the child only insofar as she is whatever they want her to be: athletic or intellectual, aggressive or gentle, whatever. These conditions, if they are many and rigid, may cause the child to form an unrealistically limited self-concept. If her parents demand that she be gentle, for example, she will define herself as gentle no matter what she actually is. And consequently, to maintain a stable picture of herself, she will have to screen out of her awareness any experiences that contradict her self-defined gentleness. If she likes war movies or relishes competitive games or feels like hitting back at the child who hit her, all this must be denied. The unfortunate result is that this person's energies are wasted on the defense of an unrealistic self-concept when they could have been used for the full expression of what is actually her extremely varied experience of herself and the world. To Rogers, the crucial prerequisite for self-actualization is a broad and flexible self-concept, one that will permit us to absorb fully all our experiences and to express our full selves.

Both Rogers and Maslow have been criticized for naive optimism in believing that the full expression of all facets of the personality is a good thing, or even a feasible thing. To their followers, however, the humanists' optimism is probably their most precious contribution to psychology. Whereas psychodynamic theorists tend to view human beings as inherently selfish, the humanists see human beings as essentially loving and good. And whereas both the psychodynamic and behavioral schools see human behavior as determined largely by forces outside the individual's control, the humanists see human beings as free makers of their own destinies. Another important difference is that while other schools of psychology stress general laws of thought and behavior, the humanists stress the complete uniqueness of each person's own experience. Such a view sometimes sounds more like philosophy or religion than like science. Nevertheless, it is a welcome balance to the sometimes dreary and mechanical vision of life offered by more scientific schools of psychology.

Existential Theory

Like the humanists, the existential theorists in the field of psychology hold a dynamic view of the personality. This means they are most concerned with the individual's ability to move beyond simply coping. The ideal is not just to cope but to grow, to become something according to one's own personal ideals.

Unlike the humanists, however, the existentialists place great emphasis on the *difficulties* of breaking through to this state of free "becoming." A foremost difficulty, in their view, is the conformity and materialism fostered by the modern industrial societies. Existentialists in general are severe critics of modern society (e.g., Laing, 1967). They feel that the industrialized world, by encouraging people to deny their true inner selves, has created a widespread state of *alienation*, defined as a feeling of meaninglessness in life. Accordingly, the existentialists' writings often deal with the challenge of rediscovering meaning in modern life.

Viktor Frankl: The Will-to-Meaning

Viktor Frankl (b. 1905), a foremost thinker of the existential school, claims that traditional psychology has produced a distorted picture of the human condition by leaving out any consideration of the spiritual life: our search for the meaning of existence. In Frankl's (1962) view, the prime motivating force of human life is not the will-to-pleasure or the will-to-power, as psychodynamic theorists claim, but rather the will-to-meaning. The only way we can pierce through to the meaning of our lives is by pursuing values, which we do by working toward goals, caring for other people, and coming to terms with suffering. Frankl argues that this spiritual quest is an absolute necessity for psychological health. For without some sense of meaning in our lives, we cannot make responsible choices, and the process of making conscious, responsible choices is the only source of our dignity as human beings.

As this summary suggests, the existentialists, like the humanists, view behavior as the result of free choice. They also agree with the humanists that each person's perceptions and capabilities are utterly unique and that good adjustment means the full realization of one's capabilities. Where they differ from the humanists is on the matter of how this is achieved. For the humanists, self-actualization is somewhat automatic; like flowers, human beings will reach their full bloom if given the chance. For the existentialists, the fulfillment of one's potential is a more strenuous process, requiring painful struggles with loneliness and fear.

Understandably, the existentialists have not been accused of starry-eyed optimism, as the humanists have. Like the humanists, however, they have been taken to task for being vague and unscientific, for offering philosophy instead of science. To this they would reply that if such things as meaning and values cannot be measured scientifically, they are nevertheless major concerns of human life, and we ignore them at our peril.

The Psychological Theory of This Book

We have looked now at several different psychological theories. Some seem pragmatic, others idealistic, still others in between. But what about the theory of this book? What guidelines will we follow?

We will rely to some extent on all these theories. In keeping with post-Freudian theory, we will give special attention to the individual's social self—his relations with other people. In keeping with humanistic theory, we will stress the importance of the self-concept. And we will use Freudian theory to help explain various psychological phenomena, such as the development of self-control and the management of anxiety through defense.

However, the two theories on which we will rely most heavily are the most pragmatic and the most idealistic theories that we have discussed above. First, the pragmatic one: behavioral theory. This is meant to be a *practical* book, one that will show you specific ways to solve specific personal problems. Such problems can, of course, be taken to a professional therapist, and in some cases they should be. But behavioral psychologists have shown that many of these problems can also be solved right at home, by looking around you and inside yourself for the causes and then adjusting these causes. This is a commonsensical approach to ordinary problems, exactly what is needed for a book that aims to be practical. Therefore behaviorism (in its broadest sense) is the approach that will be most in evidence in our chapters, especially those dealing with how to change behavior.

Second, the idealistic theory (actually, a combined theory): the humanistic and existential argument that the most important factor of human life is individual potential. Humanistic and existential psychology, as we have seen, differ in certain respects. They agree, however, on this one central belief:

ACTIVITY 1.3

Which of the psychological theories of adjustment presented in this chapter makes the most sense to you? Remember that our judgments of what constitutes good and bad adjustment depend on our values and on the situation that one is adjusting to. Write a paragraph explaining how the adjustment theory you favor dovetails with (1) your values and (2) your situation in life. Whose life situation would it *not* fit? Whose values?

human beings have power over their lives. If problems are preventing you from pursuing your ideals and developing your special talents, you can energetically attack those problems. If you don't like what you are, you can change.

This faith in human potential, especially the potential for change, is the guiding spirit of our book. Our methods are pragmatic, our goals idealistic. The message is *choose*—and once you have chosen, be practical.

A final note: No matter which theory we are relying on, we will try to ground our observations in scientific findings. Through-out the book you will see sentences ending with names and dates enclosed in parentheses, like this: (Watson, 1913). These names and dates indicate the source of the statement we are making. (The sources are listed in full in the Bibliography at the back of the book.) In some instances, those sources are theoretical writings. In most cases, though, they are articles describing actual research, experiments that lead us to the observations and suggestions we make.

So much for our methods, our theory, and our goals. Let us turn to specific problems. First, the self.

SUMMARY

1. Modern technology has changed our lives and, in doing so, has increased our knowledge, our expectations, and our freedom. We are flooded with information, often conflicting and bewildering. Our expectations for our lives are high, frequently exceeding what is realistic and thus inviting disappointment. Our tremendous freedom leaves us with the responsibility of having to decide the direction of our lives, with little to guide us in our choices.

2. Such problems are normal and are experienced by all of us. We deal with them through the process of *adjustment*—that is, through continuous interaction with our selves, with other people, and with our world. By making this interaction more purposeful, we can solve many of our problems.

3. Judgments as to what is good or bad adjustment depend on our values and on the situation in which the behavior takes place. Behavior that seems normal in one situation may not seem so in another. And what looks like good adjustment according to one set of values may look like maladjustment according to another.

4. Psychology is the scientific study of human behavior and mental processes. The psychology of adjustment is a subfield of psychology and draws on a number of other subfields, including developmental, clinical, personality, social, and experimental psychology.

5. Psychological thinkers have developed a number of theories as to what constitutes good and bad adjustment. Psychodynamic theory sees behavior as the product of forces operating inside the mind and stresses the role of conflict, anxiety, and defense. Freud, the founder of psychodynamic theory, saw behavior as influenced primarily by biological instincts (id) affecting us at an unconscious level. Later psychodynamic theorists such as Erikson and Fromm have given more attention to problem-solving abilities (ego), as well as to the individual's social context.

6. Behavioral psychology views human actions as the product of learning, often via

rewards and punishments. Classical behaviorists attempted to explain behavior solely in terms of external events, because internal psychological events could not be scientifically observed. Theorists such as Mischel and the cognitive behaviorists have pulled back somewhat from this position and begun studying internal processes such as our interpretation of events.

7. Humanistic psychologists such as Maslow and Rogers feel that psychodynamic and behavioral theorists have placed too much emphasis on simply coping with life. In their view, good adjustment means self-actualization, the full realization of one's unique potential. According to Rogers' self theory, a broad and flexible self-concept is indispensable for self-actualization.

8. Existential psychologists, like the humanists, equate good adjustment with the realization of one's potential, but they do so from a more philosophical and "tragic" point of view. Frankl, for example, sees the key to adjustment as the struggle for meaning, without which we cannot make the truly free and responsible choices that are the only source of our dignity as human beings.

9. This book will try to show you how to use psychological theories and techniques to change self-defeating behavior. We will rely primarily on the practical techniques developed by behaviorists and on the humanistic-existential belief in the human being's power to change and grow.

PROJECT

Earlier in this chapter we described the challenges that modern life poses for us. Our point was that increased information, higher expectations, and greater freedom have made our lives extremely complex. But because you deal with these challenges every day, you may be only partially aware of them. To raise your consciousness concerning the wide range of events that influence your life, try the following exercise:

1. Buy the newspaper every day for one week.
2. Each day, make a list of the headlines on the front page.
3. Rate each headlined article on the following 5-point scales:
   a. How much that circumstance will affect your life
      (0 = no effect; 5 = great effect)
   b. How much that circumstance disturbs you
      (0 = does not disturb me at all; 5 = greatly disturbs me)
   c. How much you *could* do to change that circumstance or its effect on you
      (0 = nothing; 5 = a great deal)
   d. How much you *will* do to change that circumstance
      (0 = nothing; 5 = a great deal)

You may find that there are many more events affecting your life than you were actually aware of. Given our high expectations for our lives and our presumed freedom to create our own lives, we should ideally be controlling the circumstances that affect us. But how much control can you actually exert over most of the events that impinge upon your life? Part of the frustration of living in a modern technological society is knowing how many forces affect us and realizing how few of them we can actually hope to influence while still coping with the demands of daily life. Our freedom, then, has some limits.

HUMAN ISSUE:
ABNORMAL PSYCHOLOGY

In Chapter 1 we found that psychologists have a hard time agreeing on what it means to be psychologically "normal," or well-adjusted. Not surprisingly, they have an equally hard time agreeing on what it means to be psychologically "abnormal," or maladjusted. Most of them concede that it is abnormal for people to claim that they are God or to be so afraid of dogs that they cannot leave the house. But they cannot find a single answer as to what causes abnormal behavior or what it is exactly that distinguishes abnormal behavior from normal behavior.

DEFINING ABNORMAL BEHAVIOR

A time-honored criterion for defining abnormal behavior is *norm-violation*. Every society has a comprehensive set of norms, or rules for behavior, covering almost every aspect of life. In our society, for example, norms dictate that we wear clothing in public, that we not claim to hear the voices of angels, that we flirt only with people of the opposite sex, and so forth. Other societies have the opposite rules, for norms are relative to time and place. In general, however, we regard them not as relative but as absolute—clear-cut definitions of "right" and "wrong." Therefore, the violation of important norms is taken very seriously, and people who repeatedly walk down the street naked, claim to hear angels, and flirt with people of the same sex are widely regarded as "abnormal." The problem with the criterion of norm-violation is, of course, that it tends to set up social conformity as the ideal standard of behavior—a policy that is potentially very threatening to individual freedom. Nevertheless, most accepted categories of abnormal behavior are based on the norm-violation criterion.

Another important criterion for abnormality is *statistical rarity*. According to this standard, any behavior that deviates too far from the statistical average is designated as abnormal. It is on this basis, for example, that people are diagnosed as mentally retarded. The average IQ score is approximately 100. Any score that falls too far below this average (the cut-off point is about 68) is considered abnormal. The weakness of the statistical-rarity criterion is that it makes no distinction between desirable and undesirable deviations. After all, people who score over 132 on IQ tests are as rare as those who score under 68. Should they too be labeled abnormal? Furthermore, like the criterion of norm-violation, the statistical-rarity rule seems to place too much value on the ordinary.

A third criterion for defining abnormality is *personal discomfort:* If the person says he is extremely unhappy, then his behavior is abnormal and in need of treatment. This is a more liberal standard than norm-violation or statistical rarity, because it allows the person in question to be the judge of his own normality. The personal-discomfort rule is now widely used for the "neurotic" disorders and also for homosexuality. (According to the current diagnostic code, homosexuality is abnormal only when the person is distressed over being homosexual.) Useful as it may be for certain kinds of behavior, however, the personal-discomfort criterion is of little help when applied to socially disruptive behaviors. If a person rapes or kills with no regret, is he then normal? Are only *unhappy* alcoholics abnormal?

THE CLASSIFICATION OF ABNORMAL BEHAVIOR

Despite the general lack of agreement about abnormal behavior, psychological professionals still need a set of terms to describe the problem behaviors they see. Such terms have been developed over the years and have been gathered together into a unified classification system called *The Diagnostic and Statistical Manual of Mental Disorders*, or *DSM* for short. This classification system has a number of shortcomings. The most serious one is that the terms, all neatly classified, invite people to fall back on the so-called medical model, the habit of viewing abnormal behavior as if it were a medical disease. Seeing a term such as "schizophrenia," with a number of "essential features" listed after it, you might easily conclude that schizophrenia is a disease (like pneumonia or hepatitis) that people develop, whereas the truth is that schizophrenia—along with most of the other terms in the classification system—is simply a word psychologists and psychiatrists are in the habit of using to describe a certain kind of unusual behavior whose causes are largely unknown.

The *DSM* has recently been revised in such a way that it does not suggest the medical model. The manual now simply describes abnormal behaviors, as precisely as possible, without implying causes if causes are unknown. But medical-model thinking is still extremely common, partly because it is just an easy way to think about abnormal behavior. (How many times have you heard the phrase "mentally ill"?) Furthermore, there is evidence that certain serious disorders, such as schizophrenia and severe depression, do have some medical basis—a finding that has added further confusion. The point is not that the medical model is wrong, but that we have no evidence that it is right for most forms of abnormal behavior. Therefore, though we may find a person's behavior extremely weird, we have no right to say that it is "sick."

We will briefly describe two large categories of abnormal behavior: the "neurotic" disorders and the psychoses.

The "Neurotic" Disorders

The new diagnostic manual, called *DSM-III*, has dropped the time-honored term *neurosis* because it implies a cause (unconscious psychological conflict) that has never been proven. However, the term is still used by mental-health professionals to describe a broad category of disorders that, while they may cause extreme emotional distress, do not rob the person of reality contact. The "neurotic" may be unable to leave the house or hold down a job, but she still knows what is going on around her and is therefore unlikely to be hospitalized.

The "neurotic" disorders include a wide variety of patterns, some rare, some common. We will examine the most common category, the *anxiety disorders*, characterized by unreasonable and disabling fears.

In one pattern, called *generalized anxiety disorder*, the person feels a constant sense of tension and dread, but without knowing what he is afraid of. This "free-floating anxiety" may periodically escalate into *panic attacks*, during which the fear mounts to an almost unbearable level, causing sweating, trembling, heart-pounding, and other physical symptoms—a truly terrible experience that may last for hours and leave the person feeling exhausted and helpless.

A somewhat different pattern, though also marked by anxiety, is *phobic disorder*, characterized by an overwhelming fear of something which, as the phobic person realizes, poses no real threat. The phobia may be for dogs, for enclosed places (*claustrophobia*), for heights (*acrophobia*), or for almost anything. The point is that the object has been identified and therefore can be avoided. Unfortunately, this often means never leaving the house, a secondary condition known as *agoraphobia*. Many phobics remain housebound for years. Phobic disorder and generalized anxiety disorder are both very common.

Somewhat rarer is *obsessive-compulsive disorder*, in which the person either repeatedly thinks a disturbing thought (an *obsession*) or feels forced to engage repeatedly in some unnecessary act (a *compulsion*) or both. Obsessional thoughts often have a rather lurid quality. For example, the person may repeatedly imagine himself strangling his wife or masturbating in public and typically feels guilt-stricken over such fantasies. Compulsions, on the other hand, tend to center around duty and caution. Two of the most common compulsions are hand-washing (the person may wash his hands fifty or sixty times a day) and checking rituals (the person feels he must constantly interrupt his activities to go and make sure that he has done something he was supposed to do, such as lock all the windows and doors before going to bed). Just as phobics generally realize there is no rational basis for their fears, so obsessive-compulsives recognize that there is no objective need to keep washing or checking or whatever. Nevertheless, they feel forced to do so, and may experience terrible anxiety if they are prevented from fulfilling the compulsion.

The Psychotic Disorders

While neurotics are in fairly good contact with reality, psychotics are not. In *psychosis* the person's thoughts and emotions are so disturbed that he sees a very distorted picture of reality. He may see devils at the window, or he may hear Jesus Christ talking to him. These false sensory perceptions are called *hallucinations.* He may also come to believe that he *is* Jesus Christ—or that Martians are poisoning his food or that he has killed all his children or whatever. Such false beliefs are called *delusions.* Hallucinations and delusions, combined with other disturbances of thought and emotion, make it very difficult for psychotics to function in society. Therefore, it is psychotics who are generally hospitalized.

There are two main categories of psychosis: schizophrenia and the affective disorders. *Schizophrenia* is not, as is commonly believed, a form of "split personality." (That is an altogether different disorder, extremely rare.) Rather, it is a severe thinking disturbance, in which the person cannot concentrate or follow a logical train of thought. In addition, the schizophrenic's speech, perceptions, emotions, and general behavior are often confused and inappropriate. There are several patterns of schizophrenic behavior. In *catatonic schizophrenia*, the most obvious abnormality has to do with movement: catatonics will often assume some posture and then refuse to move for days on end—a pattern that may be interrupted by spells of extreme agitation. In *paranoid schizophrenia*, the most striking symptom is delusions of persecution; the person believes that someone—communists, the CIA, the Angel of Death, whoever—is out to "get" him. In *disorganized schizo-*

phrenia, the person becomes childlike, making funny faces, jumping off chairs, lapsing into fits of giggling, and wetting his pants. (The disorganized schizophrenic is probably the closest thing to what people think of as "crazy.") Most schizophrenics, however, show very unspectacular behavior. They are simply withdrawn and apathetic, particularly if they are taking chlorpromazine, a drug that is almost routinely administered to schizophrenics. Indeed, it is because of chlorpromazine's ability to suppress disorganized behavior that many schizophrenics have now been released from mental hospitals.

As disruptive as schizophrenia are the affective disorders. In the vocabulary of psychology, "affect" means emotion, and the *affective disorders* are severe disturbances of the emotions. What happens is that the person's emotions run to the furthest extremes. In *mania*, the person goes through periods when he is constantly "high"—impulsive, boastful, full of energy, feverishly active, and bursting with confidence in himself. While this might seem a desirable state, it is not, for the manic person is also irritable and jumpy, makes rash decisions, and may suffer from delusions of grandeur, claiming that he is a millionaire, the world's greatest composer, or something equally noteworthy. The opposite of mania is depression. In psychotic *depression*, the person periodically lapses into a state of total despair, weeping, blaming herself for imaginary sins, totally without hope for herself or the world. (There is also what is called *non-psychotic depression*, in which the depression is milder and the person maintains normal contact with reality.)

Sometimes a person will alternate between spells of mania and spells of depression—a pattern widely known as "manic-depressive illness." (Its technical term in *DSM-III* is *bipolar affective disorder.*) "Manic-depressive" is a term that people tend to throw around. However, the pattern is actually quite rare, as is simple mania. Simple psychotic depression, unfortunately, is quite common and often ends in suicide.

UNIT
I

SELF

<u>OUTLINE</u>

WHAT IS THE SELF?
The Self as a Construct
Five Aspects of the Self
The Unity and Continuity of the Self
The Dynamic Quality of the Self

SELF-ANALYSIS
Description
Objects of description
Methods of description
Preliminary rules for description
Further suggestions for description
Functional Analysis
Finding correlations
Pitfalls in looking for correlations
Forming a hypothesis
Testing the hypothesis
The Rewards of Self-Analysis

2

THE SELF: WHAT IT IS AND HOW TO ANALYZE IT

I think I'm okay on a lot of scores. Actually, I have to remind myself that I'm okay on a lot of scores. What I do is look at other people and see the problems they have. After all, I get high grades, I have some close friends, and I have enough money to go to school without having to take part-time jobs the way other people do. But as I said, I have to remind myself of these things, because when I just think about my SELF, what I think about are my problems.

I can't seem to get it together with a woman, and I think this is because of my whole personality. When I look in the mirror, I say to myself: How could this parent-pleasing jerk, this bookworm, ever get it together with a woman? In other words, it seems to me entirely logical that no one would want me. But other studious types have girlfriends. I don't know.

I go to parties. Sometimes I even take a date—usually a date that one of my friends has gotten for me. But I just don't know how to behave at a party, how to relax and have a good time and just let things happen. I look around and everyone seems so "cool," so loose. They've

studied all week, and now it's Friday night, and they're just hanging easy. For me, it's the opposite. I can study. Studying for me is easy. Classes too, because the professor usually likes me, and I have a lot to say in class. But parties are work, impossibly hard work: trying to look natural when everything inside me is so incredibly tight. Sometimes, when I'm at a party, I go to the bathroom just so that I can sit quietly and relax for a minute.

When I think about all this, I seem to myself very messed up. I'd like to do something about it, but it's all so huge and confused and awful. I just can't get a handle on it.

How *do* we get a handle on ourselves? Or even on any one problem that we have? After all, when we have a serious problem, it's usually not a new one. Often we've been struggling with it for years, and in the process, the problem has become surrounded by a murky cloud of negative feelings—shame, confusion, helplessness—so that we can no longer see it clearly.

Even when we aren't faced with a serious problem, it is still extremely difficult to understand ourselves. The human organism and its functioning are bewilderingly complex. The body alone is a vastly intricate mechanism. As for our behavior, we are capable of an infinite variety of actions. Our psychological processes are as rich and complex as our physical and behavioral processes, but they are even harder to understand because they cannot be directly observed.

How, then, do we begin to understand ourselves? The present chapter will offer some suggestions. The method we propose is that of systematic analysis. By way of introducing this method, the first part of the chapter will be devoted to describing what the self is. The second part will outline the basic procedures for analyzing the self.

WHAT IS THE SELF?

In reading Chapter 1, you may have been surprised to find the self being talked about as a separate entity—for example, "interacting with your self" as opposed to "interacting with yourself." What do we mean by this term, the *self?*

The Self as a Construct

In Chapter 1 we described the self as the sum total of what a person already is—body, behavior, thoughts, and feelings. This description, however, implies that the self is a thing or a collection of things. It is not. *The self may be defined as a hypothetical construct referring to the complex set of physical, behavioral, and psychological processes characteristic of the individual.* Note that we call the self a hypothetical construct. What this means is that we cannot use our five senses to prove that it exists. Rather, it is something that we say exists because we need a unifying term to describe

other things that we *can* experience with our five senses.

A good example of a construct is the word "soul," as it has been applied to certain black entertainers. Aretha Franklin, for example, is said to have "soul." What this means is hard for people to explain. Some would say that it has to do with the way Aretha Franklin sings. Others would claim that the key is her looks or the way she moves or talks. Actually, it seems that "soul" is simply the name people give to what they believe is *behind* all these special qualities, the "essence" that serves to unify and explain them. In just the same way, "self" is the name that a person gives to what he believes is the unifying principle tying together the many aspects of his personality.

Five Aspects of the Self

That there are many aspects to the self is a commonplace of psychology. First, and most obvious, is the *physical self,* the body and all the biological activity going on inside it. Though many people identify their selves with their minds rather than with their bodies, there is no question that when the body is endangered or actually damaged—for example, when a person's leg has to be amputated—the sense of self becomes threatened.

Second is a broad area that we might call the *self-as-process:* the constant flow of our thoughts, emotions, and behaviors. When we perceive a problem, respond to it emotionally, make a plan as to how we can solve it, and then take action, all these events are part of the self-as-process. The self-as-process, then, is the headquarters of adjustment, and as such, it will be the main topic of this book.

Third is the *social self,* a concept dear to sociologists. The social self consists of the thoughts and behaviors we adopt in response

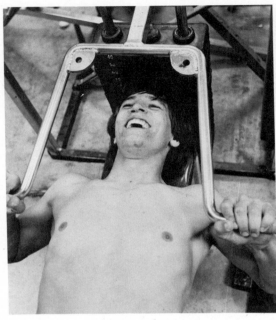

Working out in the gym. The current interest in sports and physical fitness has led many people to a rediscovery of the joys of the physical self. (© Ken Heyman)

What is this football player thinking about with such concentration? The minute-by-minute flow of our thoughts and feelings, along with our behavior, constitutes the self-as-process. (© Abigail Heyman/Magnum)

to other people and to the society in general. In society we enact certain roles—father, child, doctor, patient, employer, employee, and so on—and we identify with these roles very strongly. One study, for example, found that when people were asked "Who are you?" their first responses had to do with roles, such as "I am a student," "I am a Republican," or "I am the mother of three." Only after stating their roles did they go on to describe their traits, such as "I am industrious" or "I am outgoing" (Kuhn and McPartland, 1954). According to many sociologists (for example, Brim, 1960), our behavior is more a product of the role we are enacting at the moment than of any coherent inner "self." We tailor our behavior not only to roles but to individuals as well, adjusting our words and actions to make a certain kind of impression on whomever it is we are talking to. This is a matter that we will return to shortly. For the moment, it is simply important to keep in mind that one aspect of the self is designed for public consumption.

Fourth, there is the individual's own personal view of himself, the *self-concept*. Your self-concept is what comes to your mind when you think of "me." Each of us paints a mental portrait of himself, and though this portrait may be very unrealistic, it is still ours and has an immense influence on our thoughts and behavior.

Related to the self-concept is a fifth aspect of the self: the *self-ideal*, what you would like to be. The self-ideal is an extremely important determinant of your behavior. If your ideal is to be the first woman to become Pres-

For many people in college, the student role becomes the central component of the social self. (© Alex Webb/Magnum)

The self-ideal pushes people forward toward their goals. Behind the attentive gaze of these biology students may be the ideal of becoming a physician—or perhaps a professor like the one they are listening to. (© Erich Hartmann/Magnum)

Adolescence is a time of struggle to create a unified self-concept. This means trying on different roles, imitating different heroes. (Roswell Angier/Archive Pictures)

ident of the United States, you will act differently from a person whose ideal is to earn $25,000 a year and have a quiet family life. Furthermore, your self-ideal determines your self-concept; it is by measuring your actual achievements against your self-ideal that you form your self-concept.

The Unity and Continuity of the Self

So far, we have described five different aspects of the self. Is there any unity here? Can we talk about a single self? *The* self? The answer, we believe, is yes. Admittedly, there is a difference between the social self and the private self, or between the self-concept and the self-ideal. But remember that we defined the self as referring to a complex *set* of processes. The parts of the self are dependent on one another; they overlap and interconnect. If the physical self is damaged, the self-concept will suffer. If the self-concept is low, then the person's thoughts and behavior (self-as-process) will be troubled, and so on. In short, the units of the self fit together to form a whole. Like instruments in a band, each has its own part to play. But the final piece of music, the whole "you," is not any one unit or even all the units taken separately. It is all the instruments playing together, in harmony or in disharmony.

But what about continuity? As the individual moves from situation to situation, does the self remain the same? Not quite. As we mentioned earlier, social roles tend to mold behavior, regardless of individual characteristics. In the doctor's office you may be docile and passive, whereas on the job you may be a strong-willed "take-charge" person. With your parents you may be a mature, independent type, whereas with your spouse you may allow yourself to be more vulnerable and dependent.

Even regardless of roles, our behavior may be affected by characteristics of the people we are interacting with. One study, for example, found that many people can switch from voicing pro-war attitudes to voicing anti-war attitudes depending on whether the people they are talking to are pro- or anti-war (Newtson and Czerlinsky, 1974). Such adaptability is part of what is known as *impression-management* (Goffman, 1959), our habit of adjusting our words and behavior in such a way as to produce a desired impression on the people observing us—to make them like us, respect us, fear us, or whatever it is that we are aiming for. (See Box 2.1.)

ACTIVITY 2.1

Select a person whom you know extremely well and observe that person in at least three different situations: at home, at a party, at school, at work, or wherever. Note specific behaviors in each situation, including dress, way of moving, tone of voice, frequency of conversation, subjects discussed, and so on. Now write down your observations. First, state how the person differed from situation to situation. Second, describe in what ways the person remained the same (if she did remain the same) in these different situations. You will probably find that although behavior changes with the context, it still shows some continuity. (Your outgoing and free-spirited sister may be more subdued at work than at home, but even at the office she wears fuchsia-colored nail polish, jokes with the receptionist, and is on a first-name basis with her boss.) As you examine your own behavior, you will undoubtedly discover ways in which you too are consistent regardless of the situation. Your outward behavior may change from role to role because you are responding to different expectations. (Your grandmother expects you to be polite and tell her how you're doing in school; your sister does not.) But there is still a "core" personality operating in each situation.

It appears that not just behavior but even the self-concept may be affected by the situation in which we find ourselves. In a well-known experiment, fifty officer trainees in the navy were asked to write descriptions of themselves. A month later these fifty men were given "assignments." Half of them were told that they would be sent off in two-man work teams to solve rather intricate problems of fleet maneuvers. The other half were told that they would be working in two-man "leisure" teams; they too would be discussing fleet maneuvers, but their primary goal was to get along with their partners as well as possible. After the assignments had been made, the men were once again asked to describe themselves. Interestingly, the trainees suddenly became, in

BOX 2.1
IMPRESSION-MANAGEMENT: THE EXPERTS

Impression-management is probably a universal behavior. Anyone who has ever put on a suit for a job interview or cleaned the house when guests were coming has engaged in impression-management. Yet, as psychologist Mark Snyder points out, some of us engage in it more than others. Snyder (1974) has developed a scale to measure individual commitment to impression-management. Those who score high on the scale he calls "high self-monitors"; these people, he claims, tend to watch for signals as to how their behavior strikes other people and to adjust their behavior accordingly, so as to make the desired impression. Those who score low on the scale, the "low self-monitors," are more likely just to speak and do as they wish, with little thought of the impression they are making on others.

That people do differ in this respect has been shown in a number of interesting experiments. In one study, for example, a group of students was drawn into a discussion after having been given cues as to the most appropriate way to behave. Some of the students were given the idea that the discussion would be taped and played back to a larger group of students. Others believed that the discussion was private. One might predict that these differing expectations

would have little effect on the behavior of low self-monitors; they would do whatever they were going to do, regardless. High self-monitors, on the other hand, would presumably be influenced by the differing cues. Those who believed that their words were being taped might be less likely to conform to the group, since they would not want to show up on the tape as herd-followers. As for high self-monitors who believed that the discussion was private, they might be more likely to conform to group opinion, as this would make them more likeable to the others in the group. This, in fact, is what happened. Depending on whether they believed the discussion was private or taped, students who had shown up as high self-monitors on Snyder's scale tended to conform or disagree with group opinion. Those who scored as low self-monitors showed no such pattern; presumably, the social cues had little effect on their behavior (Snyder and Monson, 1975).

Clearly, the ability of high self-monitors to pick up social signals and tailor their behavior accordingly makes them naturals for certain professions, such as business and politics. But what about their moral and emotional lives? Doesn't high self-monitoring equal hypocrisy? Snyder avoids such judgments, claiming that

THE SELF: WHAT IT IS AND HOW TO ANALYZE IT

their own eyes, very well suited to the tasks ahead of them. Those assigned to work teams described themselves as more logical, organized, and efficient (in short, better workers) than they had a month before. And those assigned to the leisure teams now described themselves as more relaxed, tolerant, and friendly (in short, better "pals") than they had before (Gergen and Taylor, 1969).

To some psychologists and sociologists, such evidence suggests that there is no such thing as an underlying self that carries over from one situation to the next. Others insist that there is. As we have just seen, there exists good evidence for human changeability, yet our everyday experience suggests that people do have "core" personalities that endure over time. Think, for example, of a person whom you know well. You have seen

---

there is no reason to assume that high self-monitors use their impression-management skills for deception or manipulation. He does suggest, however, that what high self-monitors gain in likeability they may sacrifice in intimacy. It is generally accepted that a truly intimate relationship requires that the participants reveal their "true selves" to one another. But high self-monitors, accustomed to designing their words and actions to fit the situation, may not know *how* to reveal their true selves. Indeed, they may not even be able to locate a true self. The mask may have become the face.

A shortened version of Snyder's scale is given below. You may want to try it on yourself.

1. I find it hard to imitate the behavior of other people.   T   F
2. I guess I put on a show to impress or entertain people.   T   F
3. I would probably make a good actor.   T   F
4. I sometimes appear to others to be experiencing deeper emotions than I actually am.   T   F
5. In a group of people, I am rarely the center of attention.   T   F
6. In different situations and with different people, I often act like very different persons.   T   F
7. I can only argue for ideas I already believe.   T   F
8. In order to get along and be liked, I tend to be what people expect me to be rather than anything else.   T   F
9. I may deceive people by being friendly when I really dislike them.   T   F
10. I'm not always the person I appear to be.   T   F

For items 1, 5, and 7, take one point for each item that you marked false. For the remaining items, take one point for each item that you marked true. A total score of 3 or below suggests low self-monitoring; 4 to 6 places you in the middle; 7 to 10 suggests high self-monitoring.

A word of caution regarding self-report tests such as the one above: Such tests (and later chapters will include more of them) are fun to take and may give you useful information about yourself. However, the scores and the labels that go with them should be taken with a grain of salt. To begin with, many people are poor judges of their own character; others simply do not reveal themselves well on such tests (see the discussion of self-report tests on p. 46). Furthermore, there is always some question as to whether the trait the test is measuring actually exists. So do not feel that you must rush to the counseling center if you come up with a "bad" rating.

Source of scale: Snyder, M. "The Many Me's of the Self-Monitor," *Psychology Today*, March 1980, 33–92.

her act differently with her boyfriend, with her mother, with her professors, and with her friends. And yet she still acts somehow "in character." She is still a well-defined individual, not to be confused with anyone else. As psychologist Walter Mischel put it, "Each life has a coherence and continuity that are perceived both by the person and by those who know him" (1976, p. 493). Whether or not the existence of the self is scientifically provable, most people *believe* that they have a self. This belief makes the self an important issue for adjustment, and therefore we will make use of the concept.

The Dynamic Quality of the Self

Although the self may have unity and some continuity, it is not fixed. It is a set of *processes*, not a finished product. As the existentialists have pointed out, we are all in a state of "becoming," a state of growth and change. Our bodies mature and deteriorate. We learn new things and forget old things. Good experiences enhance our self-concept, and bad experiences deflate it. These changes, as we have stated, constitute our adjustment, our endless rubbing up against ourselves, others, and the environment. And we can direct our adjustment so that the changes it produces in us are changes of our own choosing.

The first step in this process of directing the future self is to analyze the present self. This brings us to the subject of self-analysis.

SELF-ANALYSIS

Analysis is the act of studying something by examining its essential features and their relation to one another. When we analyze a sentence, for example, we break it down into its parts—adjective and adverb, noun and verb—and we determine how those parts are related to each other: adjec-

tive modifies noun, adverb modifies verb. In the same way, when we analyze ourselves, we break the self down into specific feelings and specific behaviors. Then we try to discover how these elements of the self connect with one another: what causes what, what changes what.

The remainder of this chapter will be devoted to discussing how to analyze the self. You should keep in mind, however, that the method of analysis that we are introducing here will, in the course of this book, be applied not only to the self but also to social interactions and to our interactions with the environment. Indeed, this method is the foundation of all the "change" techniques offered in this book. (So study it carefully.) We will learn it first by applying it to the self.

Self-analysis, as we shall see, is an extremely methodical process. It involves two basic operations: *description* and *functional analysis*.

Description

The first step in solving a problem with the self is simply to describe the problem. This description has to be done rather carefully, however. Let's begin with an example of how *not* to describe a problem. Here is a student in an encounter group trying to explain what is troubling her:

> *I feel like I'm contradictory. . . and people keep hitting me with the* you're-not-what-you-seem *issue, and it's really wearing me down. . . it's like I feel I can only give part here to one person and part there to another, but then I become a bunch of parcels. If I could just get all my reactions together . . . (cited in Gergen, 1972, p.31).*

To the young woman who spoke these words, this is obviously a pressing problem. She feels that she lacks a coherent identity. But her problem, as it is described here, will not lend itself easily to self-analysis. It simply is not precise enough. We don't know whether she is describing an emotional state or a pattern of behavior. We don't know when the problem occurs or how severe it is. We don't really know what her goal is. Getting "all my reactions together": what exactly does this mean?

The fact is that when we talk about ourselves, especially about our problems, we habitually speak in vague terms such as these. However, a problem that is vaguely described is one that will be difficult to solve. We have to be able to see our opponent before we can tackle him.

Objects of Description

In describing a problem for the purpose of self-analysis, we should stick to one dimension of ourselves: the physical, behavioral, or psychological dimension. Trying to handle two or three dimensions at the same time is too difficult, at least for beginners.

A physical problem might be excess weight or high blood pressure; such problems are ideal for self-analysis because they are so easy to measure. Needless to say, however, not all of our problems are physical.

Behavioral problems are those that involve specific actions (or the lack of specific actions) on our part, such as smoking, stuttering, or failure to respond sexually. Behaviors are more difficult to analyze than simple physical attributes, because they are more complex. Like physical processes, however, they *are* observable, and therefore we can analyze them with some precision.

More challenging are problems in the psychological dimension. When we try to describe a mental characteristic, such as anxiety or compulsiveness, we are not even sure of what we are talking about. One person's definition of compulsiveness is, after all, as good as another person's, since compulsive-

Anxiety during exams may be a serious problem. But a more specific anxiety-produced behavior, such as nail-biting during exams (see the student in the first row), would be easier to analyze. (© Van Bucher/Photo Researchers, Inc.)

ness itself can never be isolated and observed. And since psychological processes cannot be observed, they are difficult to measure. This does not mean, however, that we should abandon all hope of analyzing our psychological problems. They are too important. And, in fact, they can be described and observed indirectly, as we shall see in the following section.

Methods of Description

Once we have limited our description to one dimension of the self, we have to choose a method of description. How do we go about stating exactly what the problem is, paring it down to the specifics?

The simplest and most accurate method of self-description is *physical measurement.* If you think you're fat, you can get on a scale and weigh yourself. Likewise, if you have chronic backaches, a doctor can measure your muscle tension. Would that all problems could be assessed so easily and so precisely!

A less precise but still valuable method of describing ourselves is *self-report.* In other words, we simply *say* how we feel or what we think of ourselves. One example of self-report is the descriptions that the naval officer-trainees wrote of themselves in the experiment described earlier (Gergen and Taylor, 1969). Another type of self-report is the psychotherapeutic interview: the client comes into the therapist's office, sits down, and tells the therapist what the problem is.

Therapists and psychological researchers depend heavily on the self-report method, but the problems with this method are obvious. In the first place, the person doing the reporting might distort the facts, deliberately or not, in order to appear more "normal." Lying, however, is not so serious a problem when we are producing information for ourselves. A more serious problem, though, is that many of us cannot describe ourselves accurately. Our judgments are subjective; they emerge from our own personal frame of reference. Can you always tell, for example, when you're tense and when you're relaxed? Researchers have found that some people have very little notion of what it means to be relaxed. Though they claim to be relaxed, measurements of their muscle tension clearly indicate that they are not. Likewise, many of us have difficulty saying to what extent we are hot-tempered or even-tempered, devious or sincere, optimistic or pessimistic.

Somewhat more precise as a means of description is the *performance measure.* Here what is described is what the person does rather than what he says about himself. For example, one group of therapists, in treating children who were afraid of dogs, measured each child's progress on the basis of how close he would come to a caged dog in a laboratory (Bandura, Grusec, and Menlove, 1967). In the same way, you can describe yourself on the basis of self-observation, that is, simply noting your own behavior objectively. This may involve nothing more complicated than looking in a full-length mirror to see whether your posture is slumped and withdrawn. Or you can speak into a tape recorder and then play it back to hear whether you really have an arrogant, intimidating tone in your voice, as people have said you do.

A more systematic method of behavioral self-observation is *self-monitoring,* that is, keeping regular and precise records of your behavior. Probably one of the first people to use self-monitoring was Benjamin Franklin. As a young man, Franklin decided he needed to strengthen himself in thirteen basic virtues, among them humility, sincerity, frugality, and industry. To measure his progress, he kept records in the following manner:

> I made a little book, in which I allotted a page for each of the virtues. I ruled each page with red ink, so as to have seven columns, one for each day of the week, marking each column with a letter for the day. I crossed these columns with thirteen red lines, marking the beginning of each line with the first letter of one of the virtues, on which line, and in its proper column, I might mark, by a little black spot, every fault I found upon examination to have been committed respecting that virtue upon that day. (1954, pp. 104–105)

Franklin's self-monitoring project, as you can see, was rather ambitious; thirteen virtues is a heavy load. However, simpler records can also be of use. A person who is trying to stop smoking can record when and in what circumstances she smokes. A person trying to lose weight can record his weight and his calorie intake on each day of the week. The result will be a much more specific description that is most useful in solving the problem.

An additional advantage of self-monitoring is that it will provide you with a *baseline*, a precise specification of your "prechange" behavior, to which you can compare your behavior once you begin trying to change. Imagine, for example, that you monitor your smoking for a week, without trying to cut down. You find that you smoke an average of twenty-four cigarettes a day. This, then, is your baseline. When you start trying to cut down, you can compare your daily cigarette consumption with this baseline figure to find out how well you're doing.

Self-monitoring is not a foolproof method of description. Like self-report, it is subject to distortion. And like physical measurement, it is usually limited to what is observable. For example, if you want to use self-monitoring to describe recurrent feelings of depression, you will get a more precise description by recording depressive behaviors (for example, staying in bed all day, crying, insomnia) than by recording depressive thoughts or feelings. If you record feelings, you are mixing the more subjective technique of self-report with the objective technique of self-observation.

Preliminary Rules for Description

In writing your self-description, you should follow three basic rules.

Rule 1: Simplicity. Self-analysis will be much easier if we restrict it to simple, well-defined units of behavior. For example, you should not choose a problem as large as "my constant anxiety." Instead, focus on one aspect of your anxiety, such as "insomnia on nights before exams" or "working myself into a sweat before going on a date." And don't worry that by choosing such simple behaviors, your analysis will be trivial or worthless. Every big problem is a collection of little problems. Once you have analyzed one simple problem, then you can tackle another, related problem, and then another and another. (They will become much easier as you go along.) The result will be a set of overlapping, interconnected analyses, adding up to a clear picture of whatever larger problem you may have.

Rule 2: Objectivity. Crucial to a usable self-description is *objectivity*—clear, accurate reporting, undistorted by one's personal feelings or opinions. In analyzing the self, it is not easy to be objective. There are very few things about which we have stronger feelings and opinions than ourselves. Furthermore, there are very few human motives so strong as the motive to avoid unpleasant truths about ourselves. Nevertheless, you can achieve a high degree of objectivity if you limit your description to observable behaviors. For example, if you have difficulty asserting yourself with other people, don't describe your problem by saying "I'm just a marshmallow." Instead, specify it in terms of actual behaviors: "When someone asks me to do something that I don't want to do, I usually say okay. But when I want something from someone else, I can't bring myself to ask." Your compliance with other people's unwelcome requests and your failure to make requests of your own are behaviors that someone else could observe. Hence your description is objective.

Rule 3: Specificity. Once you have pared down your description so that it is simple and objective, you need to fill it in with detail. In other words, you must be specific.

All the particulars of the problem should be included. Let's look back at our objective description of nonassertive behavior: you say okay to other people's requests, even when you don't want to, and then you hesitate to make requests of your own. This is objective, but it isn't specific. You have to fill in the details. Who makes these requests? Are the requests usually unreasonable? How do you feel when you say okay? What specific thoughts prevent you from saying no? (Yes, listen to your thoughts and put them into words on a piece of paper.) Are you angry afterwards? How do you know you're angry? What prevents you from making requests of your own? What do you say to yourself that discourages you from making the request? How do you feel afterwards? The more specific you are about the exact circumstances surrounding the problem, the easier it will be to pinpoint the causes of the problem.

Further Suggestions for Description

The following are a few additional suggestions for making your description as simple, objective, and specific as possible.

Limit Yourself to a Situational Description. It should be clear by now that the key to successful self-analysis is breaking down your complex behaviors into small, manageable units. One way to achieve this is to describe your problem only as it occurs in one particular situation. This is called a *situational description.* For example, our "marshmallow" person might describe his nonassertive behavior with his wife and only with his wife. Or a woman who overeats might limit her description to late-night snacks, describing in detail each midnight raid on the refrigerator. If you stick to a particular situation, problems with simplicity, objectivity, and specificity will tend to solve themselves.

Get Feedback. The details of your description should be clear enough so that another person, by reading your account, could easily picture the problem you are describing. Test yourself on this point. When you're satisfied with your description, show it to someone and ask him if he can get a mental "picture" of the problem as it occurs in a specific setting. If not, find out what's missing and then add the necessary details.

ACTIVITY 2.2

Objectivity in self-analysis is particularly important when we are dealing with something that we feel strongly about, such as our looks. Make a list of adjectives describing your physical appearance. Then, next to each adjective, write its opposite. (Next to "tall" write "short," and so on.) Go through your original list of adjectives again and see whether it is still accurate. Does an objective description of your various characteristics really fall somewhere *between* the first adjective and its opposite? You may find that this is often the case. If so, write a new and more objective list of adjectives to describe your physical appearance (for example, "slightly over medium height").

Whenever you write a description of yourself, keep in mind that the terms people apply to themselves are usually too absolute. Being objective means describing yourself not in black or white, but in precise shades of gray.

ACTIVITY 2.3

To help yourself in analyzing your thoughts and feelings, watch how these thoughts and feelings are carried over into behavior—behavior that could be monitored. Take a thought like "If I don't say the right thing, they won't like me." How does it affect what you do? Observe your own behavior when you are in the company of a person with whom you are not completely comfortable. Once you are out of the situation, write down how you acted on the above-stated idea. Were you reluctant to speak up? Did you pretend to agree when you really disagreed? Did you end up doing something that you dislike but that the other person wanted to do? By recognizing how your thoughts become translated into actions, you can become more aware of what you actually think and feel.

Use Self-Monitoring.   Probably the most useful means of making sure that your description is detailed and accurate is self-monitoring. Let's assume your problem is fear of speaking up in class. So you keep a record of every occasion when you are called on in class: how you felt before you started speaking, whether your voice quavered as you spoke, whether you trembled or perspired, what you said, what the teacher's response was, how the other people in the class reacted, how you felt afterwards, what you said to yourself when the ordeal was over. If you keep such a record for a week or so, you will have a series of mini-descriptions on which you can base your general description of your problem.*

How long should you keep records? This depends on the problem you are tackling. A behavior that occurs only on weekends may require several weeks of recording before you have enough information to condense into a clear and specific description. On the other hand, behaviors that occur very frequently may require only one day's observation. If a behavior varies widely across different situations, it may be necessary to observe it longer in order to create a consistent description. Similarly, a relatively complex behavior may require a longer period of observation than a simple one. (That is why working with a simple behavior or characteristic is recommended.)

Make a Graph. A final helpful technique in observing a behavior or characteristic that changes from day to day is to plot its fluctuations on a graph. A graph will not take the place of a description; it only provides material for the description. But the vivid zigzag of a line on a graph is sometimes more effective than anything else in calling your attention to the specific circumstances on which your behavior depends (see Box 2.2).

Functional Analysis

By producing a simple, objective, and specific description of our own behavior, we have completed the first step. We will now move on to the second step: functional analysis. *Functional analysis*, a technique drawn

---

* When a behavior occurs frequently throughout the day, it is often difficult to record every occurrence. In this case, you could *sample* the behavior by recording it only at fixed intervals or during fixed periods. Thus, rather than recording every time you smoke, you would record every other time, or you would record only the smoking that you do in the morning or in the afternoon or on weekends.

BOX 2.2
MAKING A GRAPH

To make a simple graph, draw a large "L" on a piece of graph paper. (If you don't have graph paper, use plain paper and fill in the interior of the "L" with a grid of evenly spaced horizontal and vertical lines, as on graph paper.) In graphing everyday behaviors, the vertical line should represent the rate of the behavior—for example, how many times you bite your nails, how many times you yell at your child—and the horizontal line should represent the time period. To make an entry on a graph, you find the appropriate time period on the horizontal line and then move your pencil up the vertical line rising from that number until this line meets the horizontal line corresponding to the frequency of the behavior (two yells, four nail-bitings) for that time period. Make a dot where the two lines cross. Then do the same thing for the next time period and the next. When you have recorded the rate of behavior for all the time periods on your horizontal line, you simply connect the successive dots with straight lines, and you have plotted your graph.

Let's imagine that Maria wants to describe her smoking habit. She decides that for three days she will record how many cigarettes she smokes, and what she is doing while she smokes them, each hour during the first five hours that she is awake. On Thursday, Friday, and Saturday she compiles the following records:

THURSDAY

Hour	Cigarettes	Activity
1	1	getting up
2	4	class
3	0	errands
4	5	studying
5	4	studying

FRIDAY

Hour	Cigarettes	Activity
1	0	getting up
2	4	class
3	1	coffee shop
4	4	studying
5	5	studying

SATURDAY

Hour	Cigarettes	Activity
1	0	getting up
2	1	washing hair
3	3	studying
4	4	studying
5	4	studying

These records translate into the following graphs:

from behavioral psychology (Skinner, 1953), is the examination of behaviors and the events and situations surrounding them in order to discover cause-and-effect relationships. In other words, what is causing the behavior?

Finding Correlations

The first step in functional analysis is to look for the clues. Your clues consist of correlations between the target behavior (your problem) and any other variable. (A *variable*

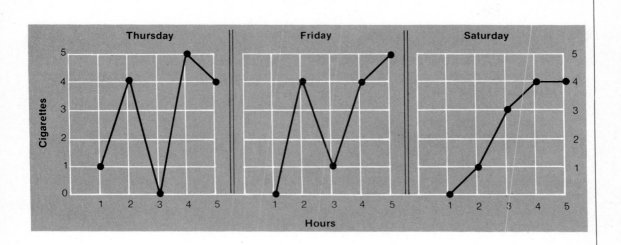

What do the graphs say? To begin with, Maria's smoking pattern on weekends seems to be different from her smoking pattern on the two weekdays. Her smoking "lines" on Thursday and Friday are quite similar. The line zooms up, drops back down, and then zooms back up again. What is she doing on those two mornings? As her records show, her morning activities on Thursdays and Fridays are basically the same. During the first hour (8:00–9:00) she gets up, dresses, and drives to campus, grabbing some breakfast along the way. During the second hour (9:00–10:00) she has her French class. During the third hour (10:00–11:00) she either sits with her friends in the coffee shop or does errands. During the fourth and fifth hours (11:00–1:00) she follows her new study regime:

2 hours a day in the library. So her heavy-smoking periods—hours 2, 4, and 5—are all related to schoolwork; she is either in class or studying in the smokers' lounge in the library. Looking at her records for Saturday, Maria realizes that they reveal the same connection. She spent the first two hours (10:00–12:00) on Saturday having breakfast, washing her hair, and talking on the telephone. Then she spent the afternoon writing a paper. So again her heavy-smoking hours were her "student" hours.

Maria now has at least one piece of solid information for a description of her smoking behavior. The times when she is most likely to pull out a cigarette are times when she is doing schoolwork, whether it's reading, writing, or participating in a class.

is a thing that can change.) When two variables are related in such a way that they change at the same time, either by increasing or decreasing, we call their relationship a *correlation*. The variables themselves are called *correlates*. If the correlates change in

the same direction (that is, they both increase or they both decrease), the correlation is said to be *positive*. If they change in opposite directions (that is, one increases as the other decreases), the correlation is said to be *negative*. Thus, if your cigarette consumption tends to increase when your anxiety increases and to decrease when your anxiety decreases, then there is a positive correlation between these two variables. But if you tend to eat less when you are having problems at work, then there is a negative correlation between your food consumption and the frequency of your work-related problems.

If your behavioral description is highly specific, it should contain hints of correlations. Take a look at Box 2.2. There appears to be a positive correlation between Maria's smoking and her academic activities. As the rate of academic behavior goes up, so does the rate of smoking. As a second example, let's look at a student's description of a problem familiar to many of us—cramming:

My teachers tell me I'm bright, but I do very badly (mostly Ds) on exams. My way of studying for midterm exams is as follows. About a week before the exam I start thinking about all the reading I haven't done for the course, but I'm still pretty confident that I can get it done in the last few days before the exam. That way, I figure, it will all be fresh in my mind. About three days before the exam I start getting scared. At that point I usually find someone to go out drinking with me. Two nights before the exam I sit in front of the television with a huge bag of potato chips—I'm completely miserable. The day before the exam I cut my classes, hole up in my room and read for about eight hours. I read Xerox copies that I've made of other people's lecture notes, and I read as much of the textbook as I can. I drink about twelve cups of coffee, and I'm scared stiff. I sleep maybe three or four hours that night. (I get my roommate to wake me up.) Then I have another cup of coffee, look at my study notes, and drive to campus. When I'm taking the exam, I try to concentrate, but I'm very tired, and my hands sweat, and I have this terrible feeling of dread. Afterwards I go back home and sleep for about twelve hours.

I know other people who do all right by cramming, so I'm not sure that cramming is the reason I get such terrible grades on exams. On the other hand, the only courses where I do well on midterms are my two language courses. In these courses you can't put off looking at the material, because you have to turn in worksheets three times a week. So by the time I get to the midterm, I've already done an awful lot of work, and there's not much to cram. I just review.

Here again the correlations seem fairly obvious. It is true that some students get by through cramming for exams, but in this student's case, cramming does seem to be correlated with poor performance, whereas studying a little bit at a time over an extended period seems to be correlated with good performance on exams. His experience, by the way, is consistent with research on learning. It has been found that people learn better (remember more information longer) through *distributed practice*—studying a little bit at a time on many different occasions—than through *massed practice*—studying for the same amount of time but packing it into only a few occasions (Underwood, 1961). Massed practice is what most of us call cramming.

In other cases, correlations are not so obvious. Where should you look? As we have seen, correlates are related in terms of time. So look for events that occur before, during, or after the target behavior. First, consider events that occur before the target behavior. If your problem is that lately you have been very depressed on Sunday mornings, ask yourself what you have been up to on Saturday nights. Perhaps you usually go out with your husband on Saturday night. If so, perhaps these evenings have recently been ending in arguments, resulting in an emotional hangover on Sunday morning.

Second, look at events that occur during the target behavior. Is Sunday morning the time you reserve to study for a course that you're afraid of failing? And does the depression seem to descend as you sit down with your book?

Third, examine events that occur after the target behavior. If you can't find any correlations by looking at Saturday night or Sunday, then what about Monday? Perhaps what is causing your depression is the dread of beginning another week at a boring job. Note that in this case it is not the event itself that is causing the target behavior. (A cause cannot come after its effect.) Rather, it is the anticipation of the event. After all, causes can be internal (that is, psychological) as well as external.

Pitfalls in Looking for Correlations

Correlations are not answers. They are hints at *possible* answers. In some cases they are also blind alleys. Sometimes two factors that seem to correlate actually have nothing to do with one another. For example, it is possible that the student who described the cramming problem is simply good at learning languages and not too competent in any other area of study.

A more common pitfall is what is called the *third-variable problem*. Here variable x and variable y correlate with one another, but neither one is caused by the other. Instead, both are caused by variable z. For example, you probably shiver more on days when you wear a heavy coat. Does this positive correlation indicate that wearing a heavy coat causes you to shiver or vice versa? No. Both variables are controlled by a third variable, cold weather. To take a trickier example, let's imagine that during periods when you can't seem to get along with your parents, you also have problems sleeping. It is possible that the fights with your parents are causing the insomnia. But it is also possible that both problems are caused by a hidden third variable, such as fears about schoolwork or worries that your girlfriend is losing interest. In other words, you can't assume that every correlation you spot amounts to a cause-and-effect relationship.

Another common source of confusion is the *circular relationship*. In this case each of two variables is both the cause and effect of the other. For a person who is both overweight and shy, for example, the excess weight may lead to shyness, but the shyness, by making him lonely and unhappy, may lead to further eating. Such vicious cycles are extremely common. Emotional problems lead to self-defeating behavior, which increases emotional problems, which aggravate self-defeating behavior, and so on.

A final problem with correlations is that even if circumstance x is causing behavior y, it is usually not the only cause. Human behavior is a thorny and complicated matter. Very rarely does a behavior have only one cause. Much more commonly, your overeating or your irritability with your parents is due to multiple causes—past and present, internal and external. Thus, as we sift through the correlates of our target behavior, we cannot expect to find the one and only cause. All we can hope is that we find an important cause.

Forming a Hypothesis

If you examine all the factors, internal and external, that could be related to your target behavior, it is likely that you will come up with many more correlations than you can handle. In sifting through these correlations for one that is most likely to reveal a causal relationship, simply use your common sense. If we look back to the "cramming for exams" description, for example, we find a number of correlations lurking in these two paragraphs. The writer's poor performance on midterms is correlated with (1) failure to study during the many weeks before the exam; (2) alcohol consumption three nights before the exam; (3) a television and potato chip binge two nights before the exam; (4) coffee consumption the night before the exam; and (5) sweaty hands during the exam, as well as a number of other factors. Which of these factors is most likely to be an important cause? That is, which of these factors, if changed, would be most likely to change the target behavior of doing poorly on the exams? (If he switched from potato chips to cupcakes or from coffee to tea, would this make a significant difference in his exam performance?) The answer that seems most logical is correlate number 1: the student's study habits. We cannot be sure that this is the cause, but of all the correlates, it seems the most *likely* to be a cause.

Once you have chosen the most suspicious-looking correlate, you have your proposed explanation of what is causing the target behavior. This is called your *hypothesis*, which you can now state as follows: variable x (your most suspicious-looking correlate) is an important cause of variable y (your target behavior). What you are saying here is that variable y is dependent on variable x. For this reason, variable y (the proposed effect) is called the *dependent variable*, and variable x (the proposed cause) is called the *independent variable:*

variable x (for example, study habits) = proposed cause = independent variable

variable y (for example, grades on exams) = proposed effect = dependent variable

Testing the Hypothesis

To find out whether your hypothesis is correct, you will have to engage in some *experimentation*. This means manipulating, or changing, the independent variable (study habits) and watching for corresponding changes in the dependent variable (grades on exams). In doing this, you should make a specific plan as to how you are going to change the independent variable. For example: "Instead of saving all that English and sociology reading for the night before the exam, I'll go to the library for two hours every day and study the material for those courses." And you must be equally specific about the kind of change you expect to see in the dependent variable: "I expect to get at least a C, maybe a B, on my next English and sociology exams." (Don't set your hopes too high at the beginning.)

Now you're ready to begin your experiment. Go ahead and make the changes you've proposed in the independent variable. Then watch to see if the expected change occurs in the dependent variable. (If the dependent variable is an everyday behavior, keep records.) If the desired effect occurs, your hypothesis may very well be correct.

It is also possible, however, that changes in the dependent variable are simply the result of chance or of your hopeful expectations. To make sure that you really have pinpointed a significant cause, maintain the change in the independent variable over a substantial period of time, for example, two exam periods. The more occasions on which you observe the desired effect, the more likely it is that you are dealing with a genuine cause-and-effect relationship.

Another way of checking your results is to apply the same method to a different but related dependent variable. Use that study technique not just for English and sociology, but also for your least favorite course. If manipulating the independent variable can bring about changes in the most stubborn dependent variable, you can assume that your hypothesis is correct. (For another method of testing a hypothesis, see Box 2.3.)

Of course, it is also possible that the de-

BOX 2.3
CHECKING YOUR RESULTS: THE REVERSAL DESIGN

Scientists try to be very thorough in testing whether a hypothesis that seems to work is really working—that is, whether changes in the dependent variable are in fact the result of changes in the independent variable. We have already discussed one method they use: manipulating the same independent variable to see if this will change a dependent variable different from the first one. (This is called the *multiple baseline design*.) Another method for checking whether an improvement is really due to your experimentation is called the *reversal design*. Here what you do is simply stop the experimentation (that is, stop manipulating the independent variable) and see if the improvement in the dependent variable disappears.

If you've stopped smoking or made peace with your parents through manipulating an independent variable, it would be foolish to meddle with these good results by switching to the reversal design. But imagine that your experiment was to see whether, by complaining, you could get your roommate to clean up the kitchen,

which is supposed to be her job. For three weeks you have complained whenever she left the kitchen a mess, and the result is that she now cleans it up 80 percent of the time, as opposed to 10 percent of the time before your complaining experiment. It is very likely that her sudden tidiness is the result of your complaints, but it *is* possible that your complaining had nothing to do with it. After all, your roommate may have (1) acquired a new boyfriend who likes only neat women, (2) switched her major to home economics, or (3) found a nest of cockroaches. To find out whether your complaints actually did the trick, you can use the reversal design. Simply don't complain for two weeks. If your roommate's clean-up rate returns to about 10 percent, then you are fully justified in concluding that your hypothesis was correct. With this particular roommate, griping does work. Now you can start complaining again every time she leaves the kitchen a mess. And you can try the complaining technique on whatever other annoying habits she has.

---

pendent variable will show no change at all, even after you have maintained the change in the independent variable for a fair trial period. This probably means that the two variables have no cause-and-effect relationship, or one so small as to be insignificant. Another possibility is that the dependent variable will show a change you didn't expect—a change that is unimportant or even undesirable. (For example, you stop yelling at your children, expecting that this will promote family harmony. Instead, the children simply stop listening to you.) In either

case, you should simply abandon your old hypothesis, re-examine your correlations, frame a new hypothesis, and go to work on it.

The Rewards of Self-Analysis

The immediate reward of self-analysis is of course the pleasure of solving a personal problem. But there are larger rewards as well. Repeated practice with self-analysis will help you perceive the *structure* of your experience: how this feeling sets off this behavior, how that experience gave rise to that feeling. This process should be somewhat like learning to fly an airplane. At first, when you look at the control panel, all you feel is confusion. But once you learn that this handle controls the wings, that lever controls the wheels, and so forth, the confusion disappears. Likewise, when you learn what causes what in your personal life, confusion will gradually give way to confidence.

SELF-ANALYSIS: AN OUTLINE

Self-analysis, in different variations, will be used throughout this book. Therefore it is important that you understand the procedure. As an aid, we offer the following outline of the steps described in this chapter.

A. Describing the problem:
1. Choose a problem as your target behavior, whether physical, behavioral, or psychological. (Note: For a first analysis, a physical or behavioral problem may be easiest to analyze.)
2. Decide on a method of description.
   a. Physical measurement.
   b. Self-report.
   c. Performance measure.
3. Apply the three basic rules of description.
   a. Simplicity: If you're worried about a big, general problem, focus on a simple unit of it.
   b. Objectivity: Stick to aspects of the problem that you can observe and measure.
   c. Specificity: Spell out the details of your problem.
4. Follow these additional suggestions for writing a description.
   a. Limit yourself to describing the problem only as it occurs in one specific situation.
   b. Show your description to someone else to see if he or she can get a clear picture of the problem; fill in missing details if necessary.
   c. Keep records through self-monitoring; use a mirror or tape recorder if needed.
   d. Plot your recorded behavior on a graph.
B. Functional analysis of the problem:
1. Look for correlations between your problem behavior and other variables.
   a. Try to identify positive or negative correlations.
   b. If correlations are difficult to find, examine events that occur before, during, or after the target behavior.
   c. Watch out for third variables and circular relationships.
2. Selecting the most likely correlation, develop a hypothesis, specifying the independent variable (the cause) that is affecting the dependent variable (the target behavior).
3. Test your hypothesis:
   a. Make a specific plan as to how you will change the independent variable.
   b. Set a target for improvement in the dependent variable.
   c. Change the independent variable.
   d. Examine changes in the dependent variable.
   e. If there is no change or only a very small change, repeat steps B2 and B3, using a different variable. Continue doing this until you see some lasting change in your problem behavior.

This understanding of why you do what you do and feel what you feel is often called *insight*. Insight not only replaces confusion with confidence. It also fosters personal growth. For once you understand what causes your feelings and behavior, you can usually find a way to change them. Hence it is no surprise that insight is a major goal of almost every form of psychotherapy.

Beyond the reward of insight, self-analysis can help us simply by creating a framework for information about ourselves. New information—for example, the discovery that your migraine headaches tend to come on days when you haven't had the courage to say no to an unreasonable request—can help you understand not only the problem in question (that is, your migraines) but related problems as well—for example, why you're still at a job you've been wanting to quit for more than a year. Furthermore, the frame of reference provided by self-analysis may encourage you to *gather* useful information. When you know what to look for, clues that were ignored before suddenly take on a new meaning and importance. Things begin to fit together into a coherent whole: a clear picture of what shapes your behavior into the forms it takes.

SUMMARY

1. The *self* may be defined as a hypothetical construct referring to the complex set of physical, behavioral, and psychological processes characteristic of the individual. There are many aspects of the self, including (1) the *physical self*, the body and its internal processes; (2) the *self-as-process*, the constant flow of the individual's thoughts, emotions, and behaviors; (3) the *social self*, the thoughts and behaviors we adopt in response to other people and to the society as a whole; (4) the *self-concept*, the individual's mental picture of himself; and (5) the *self-ideal*, the individual's image of what he would like to be.

2. The different aspects of the self are dependent on one another. Together, they show remarkable *unity*. And though we change from situation to situation, the self also seems to have some *continuity*. Finally, the self is *dynamic*—that is, in a state of constant change.

3. *Analysis* is the act of studying something by examining its essential features and their relation to one another. Analyzing the self involves two basic steps: *description* and *functional analysis*.

4. In describing ourselves, we may focus on a physical, behavioral, or psychological problem. Next we must choose a method of description. The various methods include *physical measurement, self-report, performance measures* and *self-monitoring*. The rules of *simplicity, objectivity,* and *specificity* should guide the self-description.

5. The second step of self-analysis, *functional analysis*, is the examination of behaviors in the context of the circumstances and situations surrounding them, in order to discover cause-and-effect relationships. The primary clues to search for in doing a functional analysis are *correlations* between the target behavior and other factors. Care should be taken in interpreting such correlations, since the search for cause-and-effect relationships

can be confused by a *third variable* or by a *circular relationship* between the variables.

6. A *hypothesis* is formed by proposing that a specific independent variable that correlates with the target behavior is a cause of that behavior. The final step of functional analysis is to test the hypothesis through *experimentation*. This means changing the *independent variable* and then watching the *dependent variable* (the target behavior) to see if it changes as well.

PROJECT

Many people are acutely aware of themselves, constantly mulling over their own thoughts and feelings, constantly wondering how they are coming across to those observing them. Others seem to take themselves quite casually, paying little attention either to their own mental processes or to other people's reactions to them. Three psychological researchers, Allan Fenigstein, Michael F. Scheier, and Arnold H. Buss (1975), have developed a scale that attempts to measure the degree to which people are conscious of themselves. The scale is reproduced below. To assess your own level of self-consciousness, rate each of the 23 statements as to how characteristic it is of you, from zero (extremely uncharacteristic) to 4 (extremely characteristic).

SELF-CONSCIOUSNESS SCALE

1. I'm always trying to figure myself out.	0	1	2	3	4
2. I'm concerned about my style of doing things.	0	1	2	3	4
3. *Generally I'm not very aware of myself.	0	1	2	3	4
4. It takes me time to overcome my shyness in new situations.	0	1	2	3	4
5. I reflect about myself a lot.	0	1	2	3	4
6. I'm concerned about the way I present myself.	0	1	2	3	4
7. I'm often the subject of my own fantasies.	0	1	2	3	4
8. I have trouble working when someone is watching me.	0	1	2	3	4
9. *I never scrutinize myself.	0	1	2	3	4
10. I get embarrassed very easily.	0	1	2	3	4
11. I'm self-conscious about the way I look.	0	1	2	3	4
12. *I don't find it hard to talk to strangers.	0	1	2	3	4
13. I'm generally attentive to my inner feelings.	0	1	2	3	4
14. I usually worry about making a good impression.	0	1	2	3	4
15. I'm constantly examining my motives.	0	1	2	3	4
16. I feel anxious when I speak in front of a group.	0	1	2	3	4
17. One of the last things I do before I leave my house is look in the mirror.	0	1	2	3	4
18. I sometimes have the feeling that I'm off somewhere watching myself.	0	1	2	3	4
19. I'm concerned about what other people think of me.	0	1	2	3	4

20. I'm alert to changes in my mood.	0	1	2	3	4
21. I'm usually aware of my appearance.	0	1	2	3	4
22. I'm aware of the way my mind works when I work through a problem.	0	1	2	3	4
23. Large groups make me nervous.	0	1	2	3	4

On starred (*) items—items 3, 9, and 12—reverse your rating before computing your total score. That is, if you have a 0, change it to a 4; if you have a 3, change it to a 1, and so on. If you have a 2, leave it as a 2. Now add up your score. The average total for college students is 58. If you score below 58, you are probably less aware of yourself than your fellow students. If you score above 58, you may well be more self-conscious than the average person.

How should you judge your score? Is it good or bad, for example, to be less self-conscious than other people? That depends on a number of factors.

For one thing, there are different kinds of self-consciousness. Although the above scale attempts to measure self-consciousness in general, Fenigstein and his colleagues point out that this general characteristic can be broken down into three more specific characteristics: (1) *private self-consciousness*, attention to one's own thoughts and feelings, (2) *public self-consciousness*, attention to the impression one is making on others, and (3) *social anxiety*, discomfort in the presence of others. (Public self-consciousness is similar to what we called self-monitoring in Box 2.1. Social anxiety is what most people mean when they use the term "self-conscious.") Each of these three characteristics is measured by different statements on the scale. Items 1, 3, 5, 7, 9, 13, 15, 18, 20, and 22 are indicators of private self-consciousness. Items 2, 6, 11, 14, 17, 19, and 21 measure public self-consciousness. Items 4, 8, 10, 12, 16, and 23 have to do with social anxiety. You might want to go back now and calculate subtotals for yourself on each of these mea-

sures. (Again, remember to reverse your rating on items 3, 9, and 12.) For the sake of comparison, the average scores for college students are 26 for private self-consciousness, 19 for public self-consciousness, and 13 for social anxiety.

With these subtotals, you are in a better position to judge whether your level of self-consciousness is serving you well or ill. But again, the judgment depends to some extent on what your goals are and how you want to live your life. An extremely high level of private self-consciousness could possibly be a handicap, for constant self-examination can cut into your spontaneity and productivity. On the other hand, if you want to make your living as a poet or as a psychotherapist, a higher-than-average level of private self-consciousness would probably be an asset. The value of public self-consciousness is likewise relative. Too much concern about the impression you are making on others can waste your time, divert you from your personal goals, and even make you seem hypocritical. However, if you want to be an actor, a trial lawyer, a salesperson, or a politician, you would do well to have a reasonably heavy dose of public self-consciousness. Social anxiety is probably the only aspect of self-consciousness that we can speak of in absolute terms: if you have a very high level of social anxiety, this is probably hurting you, no matter how you want to live. In Chapter 7 we will suggest ways of reducing social anxiety.

Scale adapted from: Fenigstein, A., Scheier, M. F., and Buss, A. H. "Public and Private Self-Consciousness: Assessment and Theory," *Journal of Consulting and Clinical Psychology*, 43 (1975), p. 524.

<u>OUTLINE</u>

DIMENSIONS OF THE SELF-CONCEPT
Knowledge
Expectations
Evaluation

THE NEGATIVE AND THE POSITIVE SELF-CONCEPT
The Negative Self-Concept
The Positive Self-Concept

THE DEVELOPMENT OF THE SELF-CONCEPT
Childhood Development: The Conceptual Anchor
Sources of Information for the Self-Concept
Parents
Peers
The society
Learning
Association
Consequences
Motivation
Problems in Learning
Insufficient or inconsistent feedback
Forbidden feelings: Rogers' self theory
Cognitive Consistency and Cognitive Dissonance
The self-concept as a prophecy

3

THE SELF-CONCEPT: WHAT IT IS AND HOW IT DEVELOPS

Poor study habits may help to explain why some intelligent students always do poorly on exams. But there is another possible explanation, having to do with the way people see themselves. This matter was explored by psychologist David Mettee (1971) in an experiment he did with several groups of high-school girls.

The girls were told that they were going to be given a five-part test to measure their "psychological sensitivity." After each part of the test, the girls would have a 2-minute rest period, during which the experimenter would score the part of the test they had just completed and tell them how they had done. The test was actually a fake; it didn't measure much of anything. The results were also rigged. Two groups, no matter what their answers, were told after each part of the test that they had earned very low scores, creating in their minds the belief that this was an area in which they would inevitably do poorly. Then, on the fifth part of the test, these girls received a

surprise: they achieved a very high score (again rigged). How did they deal with this unexpected success?

To answer this question, the experimenter asked the girls to re-take the fifth part of the test, the part on which they had just done so well, on the pretext that he had forgotten to hook up some part of his equipment during the first go-round.

One group of girls who went through this re-take believed that the next day they were going to be given a much more difficult test of "psychological sensitivity"—in other words, a test that they could expect to fail. A second group, on the other hand, were told that tomorrow they would be given an interview to measure their "psychological sensitivity"—an interview in which they might conceivably do well. What Mettee was interested in was the following question: Would these differing expectations as to future success or failure affect the girls' reactions to their surprise success on the fifth part of the test?

Apparently they did. The girls in the first group, who expected to fail in the future, gave much the same answers on the re-take as on the original. But the girls in the second group, faced with the possibility of future success (that is, in the interview), tended to change their answers on the re-take, thus undoing their unexpected success.

Why would anyone want to undo success? In order, perhaps, not to get one's hopes up. According to Mettee, the difference between the two groups in performance on the re-take might be explained as follows. The girls who believed they were definitely going to fail on a future test took their unexpected success as a fluke, something unrelated to their actual ability. Therefore it created no disturbance in their expectations for themselves. They were low in "psychological sensitivity" and that was that. But for the girls who believed that there was a chance of future success, the unexpected high score posed a threat. It might raise their hopes for themselves, only to have those hopes dashed again if they failed in the interview. Therefore, to protect themselves from disappointment, they changed their answers so as to fail rather than succeed.

This experiment suggests something that psychologists have long suspected—that our expectations for ourselves determine, to a large extent, how we will do in life. If we think of ourselves as successes, then we are likely to succeed. If we think we are failures, then we will actually *arrange* for ourselves to fail. In other words, the self-concept is a self-fulfilling prophecy.

* * *

Having learned the technique of self-analysis in Chapter 2, we can now begin to apply it to our own lives. An excellent place to start is with the self-concept, since this part of the self affects every aspect of our experience—our thoughts, our emotions, our perceptions, and our behavior. The self-concept has been an important topic in American psychology since the beginning of the century (James, 1910). Today it is the central focus of a whole school of psychological thought, the humanistic school (see Chapter 1). It is also a major concern of developmental, experimental, clinical, personality, and social psychologists and, increasingly, of the more cognitive-minded behaviorists. In our discussion, we will draw upon the findings of all these schools.

In Chapter 4, we will discuss ways of changing the self-concept. The present chapter will be devoted to describing and explaining the self-concept. What is the self-concept made up of? What do we mean by a positive self-concept and a negative self-concept? How does the self-concept develop? Why does it have the power to control behavior?

DIMENSIONS OF THE SELF-CONCEPT

As we saw in Chapter 2, the self-concept is your own personal view of yourself. This mental self-portrait has three dimensions: your knowledge of yourself, your expectations for yourself, and your evaluation of yourself.

Knowledge

The first dimension of the self-concept is what we *know* about ourselves. We carry around in our heads a list of labels that describe us: age, sex, nationality, ethnic background, profession, and so forth. Thus, a person's self-concept may be based on the following "fundamentals": twenty-five years old, male, United States citizen, Irish-American, shoe salesman, student.

These basic facts, it should be noted, place

ACTIVITY 3.1

As an exercise in understanding how people organize knowledge about themselves, make a list of ten labels that you feel identify you (for example, "student," "Italian-American," "opera fan," "pre-med major"). Put the most important label first and then list the others in order of decreasing importance. What do the selection and order tell you about your self-concept? (What if the order were reversed?) To what extent do you think your way of organizing information about yourself affects your behavior?

us in social groups—age group, ethnic group, occupational group, and so on. We also identify with other social groups that add to our list of self-labels: liberal Democrat, middle-of-the-road Republican, Roman Catholic, Protestant, upper middle class, lower middle class, member of commune, member of Future Engineers. Such labels can be switched at any time; the Future Engineer need only change into a pair of overalls and head for a commune. But as long as we identify with a group, that group gives us another bit of information that we work into our mental self-portrait.

Finally, in comparing ourselves to members of our groups, we label ourselves in terms of qualities. We categorize ourselves, relative to others, as spontaneous or restrained, generous or selfish, calm or hot-tempered, dependent or independent. Like most of our group-specific labels, the "qualities" we ascribe to ourselves are in no way permanent. We can either change our behavior or we can change the group to which we compare ourselves. Imagine that you label yourself "smart" because you graduated first in a high-school class of fifty students. However, if you enter a high-powered college and find yourself surrounded by students who graduated first in high-school classes of five hundred, you may suddenly feel that your label should be changed to "not-so-smart."

Thus, the important thing to remember

with regard to the knowledge dimension of the self-concept is that this information is rather unstable and subjective. Even information that seems totally fixed may be either highlighted or played down in our self-concept. Of the English diplomat Harold Nicholson, his son has written: "To him, sex was as incidental, and about as pleasurable, as a quick visit to a picture gallery between trains" (Nicholson, 1974, p. 148). Nicholson, like all human beings, was a sexual creature, but obviously his sexuality was not a major item in his self-concept. In the mental self-portrait of a successful call girl, on the other hand, sexuality might be the central item. In sum, our information about ourselves, no matter how objective, is organized subjectively.

Expectations

At the same time that we have a set of notions as to what we are, we have another set of notions as to what we *could* be (Rogers, 1959). In short, we have expectations for ourselves. These expectations constitute the ideal self, which we discussed in Chapter 2.*

---

* In Chapter 2 we described the ideal self as separate from the self-concept. However, as we shall see, the expectations that constitute the ideal self are also an essential component of the self-concept.

Our expectations for ourselves begin to take shape in childhood. These expectations are often based on the image of an admired adult. (Constantine Manos/Magnum)

ACTIVITY 3.2

According to Carl Rogers, if our real self (what we know to be true about ourselves) and our ideal self (what we feel should be) differ a great deal, we are likely to be unhappy with ourselves. The greater the difference, the greater the dissatisfaction. Being aware of this principle can help us deal with unhappiness.

Write down what grades you believe you are going to obtain in each of your courses this term. Next, write down what grade you think you *should* get in each course. Compare the two lists. You will probably find that the greater the difference, the greater your dissatisfaction with your current work in that course. You can deal with this problem in one of two ways: by revising your ideal or by revising your behavior. Look first at your ideal. Perhaps you are simply not proficient enough or not interested enough in languages to do A work in your German course. If so, you might want to revise your ideal downward to a B. On the other hand, you may feel that you really are capable of A work in German and that obtaining the ideal would be worth the effort. In that case, it is time to put forth the effort.

The ideal self differs considerably from individual to individual. One person may see his wonderful future self wearing a jacket with elbow patches and lecturing from a podium to a classroom full of students. Another person's future self may be installed in a mansion with an enormous white Lincoln Continental parked in front. Another person may see herself curing cancer or safeguarding the civil rights of the poor.

Whatever our expectations or goals, they generate the power that propels us into the future and guides our actions as we go. We may take on two jobs in order to buy that Lincoln Continental, or we may spend seven years in graduate school in order to ascend to that podium wearing those elbow patches. As we achieve our goals, we simply generate new ones. Thus, the "I-am" never stands alone in the self-concept. It is constantly being measured against the "I-could-be."

Evaluation

The third dimension of the self-concept is our evaluation of ourselves. We stand in judgment over ourselves every day, measuring what we are against (1) the "I-could-be," our expectations for ourselves, and (2) the "I-*should*-be," our standards for ourselves (Epstein, 1973). The resulting measurement is called our *self-esteem*—basically, how much we like ourselves. The greater the discrepancy between our picture of what we are and our picture of what we should or could be, the lower our self-esteem will be (Rogers, 1959). Thus, the person who is living up to her standards and expectations for herself—who likes who she is, what she is doing, where she is going, and the rate at which she is getting there—will have high self-esteem. On the other hand, the person who falls seriously short of his standards and expectations will have low self-esteem.

It matters little, in such a case, whether the standards are reasonable or the expectations realistic. If a student's standard for his academic performance is straight A's, then a B+ average (which for another student might be a source of high self-esteem) will create low self-esteem. College students have committed suicide over B's. Needless to say, our evaluation of ourselves is an extremely powerful component of the self-concept.

THE NEGATIVE AND THE POSITIVE SELF-CONCEPT

What is meant by a negative or positive self-concept? We will try to answer this question by describing a thoroughly negative and a thoroughly positive self-concept. Your own view of yourself probably falls somewhere between these two extremes. But by knowing the two extremes, you will be better able to judge which way your self-concept leans.

The Negative Self-Concept

As we just saw, the self-concept has three dimensions: knowledge, evaluation, and expectations. What does the person with a negative self-concept know of himself? Very little. There appear to be two characteristic types of negative self-concept. In one, the person's view of himself is markedly disorganized: he has no sense of a stable and integrated self. He does not really know who he is, what his strengths and weaknesses are, or what he values in life. This condition, which may be taken as a sign of maladjustment in adults, is a common and normal condition among adolescents, whose self-concept often becomes temporarily disorganized in making the transition from the role of child to the role of adult (Erikson, 1968).

The second type of negative self-concept is almost the exact opposite of the first. Here the self-concept is too stable and too organized—in other words, rigid. Possibly as the result of an excessively strict upbringing, the individual creates a self-image that allows for no deviation from the set of iron laws that in his mind constitute "respectability."

In both types of negative self-concept, new information about the self is bound to cause anxiety, a sense of threat to the self. (A fuller definition of anxiety will be given in Chapter 7.) For in neither case is the self-concept varied enough to absorb a variety of information about the self. Every day the human mind experiences a vast assortment of different impulses, memories, and perceptions, all of which reflect on the self. Thus, in order for us to understand and accept ourselves, our self-concept has to be equipped with a fairly wide spectrum of "personality pigeonholes" (for example, "my hot temper," "my generosity," "my adulterous fantasies," "my stubbornness") in which we can store a variety of different facts about ourselves. In other words, the self-concept, ideally, must be both organized *and* broad. The person with a disorganized self-concept or a narrow self-concept simply has no mental categories to which he can relate conflicting information about himself (Sullivan, 1953). Hence, he either shifts his self-concept continually, or he protects his ironclad self-concept by distorting or denying the new information.

As for self-evaluation, a negative self-concept by definition involves a negative judgment of the self. Whatever the person is, it is never good enough. Whatever she achieves seems paltry compared to what others achieve. (As Ralph Waldo Emerson once said, obviously in a moment of discouragement, "Any work looks wonderful to me except the one that I can do.") Furthermore, because she is repeatedly faced with new information about herself which she cannot properly assimilate, and which

could undermine her self-concept altogether, she is typically the victim of constant anxiety. This anxiety only serves to do further damage to her self-esteem, which in turn creates further anxiety—in other words, a classic vicious cycle.

What does the person with a negative self-concept expect of himself? Either too little or too much (Rotter, 1954). For example, a student with a negative self-concept may enroll and get passing grades in notoriously easy courses, or he may set some impossible goal (for example, a semester of straight A's) and, of course, fail to achieve it. In either case, he has set himself up for yet another blow to his self-esteem, either by attaining a goal that no one, including himself, considers an achievement, or by falling short of his goal. In both instances, there is probably a self-fulfilling prophecy at work. Believing that he cannot achieve anything of value, the individual arranges his expectations in such a way that he in fact does not achieve anything of value. This failure, in turn, damages his already feeble self-esteem, which in turn aggravates the rigidity or disorganization of his self-image. In sum, it is all of a piece, each part reinforcing the other to create a single, cruel mechanism of self-defeat.

The Positive Self-Concept

If you place a high value on the virtue of humility, then you might assume that a truly positive self-concept is a rather dangerous quantity. After all, if a person feels that everything about himself is perfect, won't he be unbearably conceited? And if he loves himself so much, wouldn't he be likely to take advantage of others in order to gratify his own wishes? The answer to these questions is that the basis of the positive self-concept is not so much admiration of the self as it is *acceptance* of the self. And this quality is more likely to lead to humility and generosity than to arrogance and selfishness.

What makes this self-acceptance possible is that the person with a positive self-concept has an extremely thorough knowledge of himself. Unlike the too rigid or too loose self-concepts that we have just discussed, the positive self-concept is both stable and diversified. It contains a large number of different "personality pigeonholes" in which the person can store information about himself—negative information as well as positive (Chodorkoff, 1954). Thus, the person with a positive self-concept can understand and accept a great many different facts about herself: "I am competent as a lawyer but not very competent as a housewife"; "I love my son but last night I dreamed that I watched him drown in the bathtub"; "I have no intention of committing adultery, but there are times when I wish I could." Because she can mentally absorb all this information, none of it poses a threat.

Because the positive self-concept is large enough to accommodate the entire range of the person's mental experience, her evaluation of herself is positive. She is able to accept herself for what she is. This does not mean that she never disappoints herself or that she fails to recognize her faults as faults. However, she feels no need to apologize for her existence. And by accepting herself, she accepts other people as well. As Erich Fromm (1947) pointed out, the love of oneself is a prerequisite for loving others.

As for expectations, the person with a positive self-concept sets goals that are appropriate and realistic. Like everyone else, he may fantasize periodically about being a rock star or winning the heavyweight championship of the world or discovering the cure for cancer in a single, brilliant experiment. But the objectives that he actually sets for himself are realistic. That is, there is substantial likelihood of his achieving them. At the same time, they are worthy enough so that achieving them will be just cause for self-praise.

However, even more important than realistic expectations of achievement is the individual's general expectation with regard to life: his idea of what life has to offer him and how he should approach the world. It is perhaps in this area more than any other that a positive self-concept constitutes an invaluable asset. Let us look back for a moment at our central point regarding the positive self-concept. Because it is large enough and diversified enough to assimilate the whole of the individual's experience, new information poses no threat, arouses no anxiety. What this means is that the individual can encounter life head-on. Unlike the person whose negative self-concept is walled up in a fortress of defenses, the person with a positive self-concept can come forth and shake hands with life. Life to him is a process of discovery. He expects it to interest him, surprise him, and reward him. As a result, he acts with courage and spontaneity and treats other people with warmth and respect. And because he approaches life in this way, life will in fact interest, surprise, and reward him. Thus, the positive self-concept, like the negative, is part of a circular relationship. But it is not a vicious cycle; it is a benign cycle.

THE DEVELOPMENT OF THE SELF-CONCEPT

The self-concept, needless to say, is an extremely important aspect of the self. Indeed, it is capable of making your existence happy or miserable. Where does this powerful belief come from, and how does it grow? What answers we have to these questions come primarily from the developmental psychologists' observations of children, along with the research of learning theorists and the observations of humanistic therapists.

Childhood Development: The Conceptual Anchor

At birth you had no self-concept—no knowledge of yourself, no expectations for yourself, and no evaluation of yourself. Indeed, you had no awareness of yourself as separate from your environment (Caplan, 1973). You did not know whether the thing you were holding on to was your foot or your toy, and you didn't care. If you saw your hand move, you didn't know it was yours. To be sure, you experienced physical sensations— warmth, cold, pleasure, pain. But you had no idea that these sensations resulted from the interaction of two independent factors: you and your environment. And, of course, you had good reason to be ignorant of your independent status, since you were utterly dependent on others for the fulfillment of your needs.

This state of fusion with the environment did not last long, however. Slowly, day by day, you began to differentiate between the "me" and the "not me." You discovered that it was *your* thumb that you were sucking. You realized that those were *your* toes down there and that you could make them move when you wanted to. As your sense of self consolidated, you began to form an idea of the relationship between the "me" and the

Because parents provide food, cuddling, and tender care, they acquire great value in the child's eyes. This value then broadens to include other human beings. (© Sylvia Johnson 1980/Woodfin Camp & Assoc.)

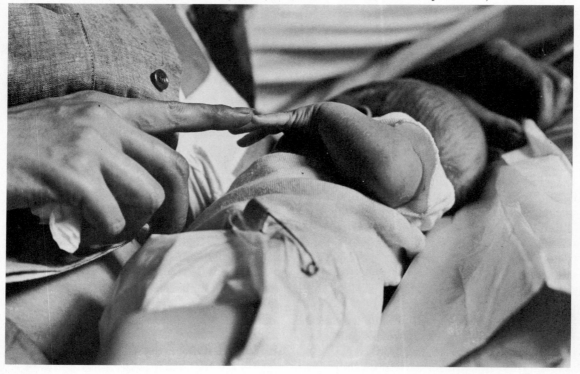

"not me." Most important, you learned that the "not me" world included people—creatures who, unlike the lamp or the crib-post, did things for you and responded to the things you did. Thus, very early in your life, you learned to place great importance on human beings (in this case, your parents), since they could fulfill—or fail to fulfill—your most urgent needs: warmth, food, physical contact (in the form of cuddling), and eventually, social interaction.

On this foundation—the discovery of your physical self as separate from the environment, and the discovery of the importance of other people—you began to construct your self-concept. At first this probably involved only a few vague notions, the condensation of repeated experiences with physical pleasure or pain. Vague though they were, however, these early notions formed the *conceptual anchor* (Asch, 1946) for your view of yourself, the kernel from which your self-concept would grow. If you were treated with warmth and affection, your conceptual anchor probably consisted of positive feelings toward yourself. If you experienced neglect or rejection, then the foundation for your future self-rejection was laid (Coopersmith, 1967).

The greatest spurt of progress in the development of your self-concept took place when you began to use language (Weir, 1962) at about the age of one. By understanding what your parents and others said to you and about you, you gained more information about yourself. Furthermore, as you learned to think in terms of words, you began to see relationships among things and consequently to make generalizations. One of the things you began to generalize about was yourself: "I am little"; "I am good"; "I can dress myself"; and so forth.

At this point your picture of yourself was still an extremely rough sketch. But just as a sketch determines the basic form of a painting, so the young child's vague self-concept determines the nature of the future self-concept. What happens is this: the child will tend to take most seriously, and to incorporate into his self-concept, information that is *consistent* with the beliefs he has already established about himself (Anderson, 1965). For example, a child who considers himself unlovable will take to heart a rejection by a nursery school teacher, since her judgment of him matches what he already believes about himself. On the other hand, a child who thinks of himself as lovable will tend to ignore a rejecting teacher, since the information she is giving him ("You are bad; I don't like you") does not fit into his mental picture of himself ("I am good; people like me").

For a child who already has a negative self-image, any criticism or rejection simply confirms his sense of worthlessness. (Burk Uzzle/Magnum)

BOX 3.1
DEFENSE MECHANISMS

Even if a person has developed a reasonably healthy self-concept, there will always be aspects of her psychological experience (e.g., ugly dreams, unacceptable sexual desires) that violate the standards she has set for herself. How do we manage to prevent these intruders from blackening our picture of ourselves? In formulating his theory of the personality, Sigmund Freud (1936) concluded that human beings unconsciously resort to various distortions of reality in order to protect themselves from the anxiety that comes from recognizing one's baser instincts. These distortions he called *ego defense mechanisms*. Let us look at a few of these stratagems by which we defend ourselves from unwelcome information about ourselves.

REPRESSION

Repression is the most common of all the defense mechanisms, and it is the basis on which the others operate. In *repression* a person experiencing an unacceptable impulse unknowingly forces that impulse out of his awareness and into the unconscious mind (see Chapter 1). For example, a child who feels intense jealousy of his baby sister and wishes she would be run over by a car may simply banish this intolerable thought from his consciousness. This does not mean that the hostility actually disappears. It may surface in his dreams, and it may affect his behavior in subtle ways. But his self-esteem remains unaffected, at least superficially.

PROJECTION

In *projection* the individual, experiencing an impulse that is threatening to his self-esteem, unconsciously transfers the unwanted impulse to another person and then poses as the innocent victim. For example, a man terrified by what he imagines are his own homosexual inclinations may complain that homosexuals are always making disgusting passes at him and that he has trouble fending them off.

DISPLACEMENT

Displacement, like projection, involves a transfer of emotion. In displacement, however, what is switched is the object, rather than the originator, of the emotion. Let us take as an example a woman whose self-concept does not allow her to feel hostility toward her child. She has read a lot of books on how to raise emotionally healthy children and considers herself the ideal "loving mother." It would be very threatening for her to deviate from this self-image, since it constitutes the basis of her self-esteem. Thus, at the end of a day on which her son has tortured the cat and flushed all his underwear down the toilet, she still remains calm and affectionate with the child. So far, she has been able to repress her hostility. But when her husband comes home from work, she finds some pretext to lash out at him and thereby release her bottled-up anger.

Fortunately for the child in the first example, a budding negative self-concept can be altered by new experiences of competence or esteem, if these experiences are repeated on a regular basis. (Hence the immense importance of teachers in early childhood development. They are with the child every day and therefore can do considerable repair work on a damaged self-concept.) However, as the child grows, his self-

REACTION FORMATION

Reaction formation involves repressing a feeling inconsistent with one's self-esteem and then professing the exact opposite of that feeling. For example, a woman who is troubled by her own sexual desires may rail against the rise in "immorality" and join her local League of Decency in order to stamp out pornography. Again, as with the other defense mechanisms, the person engaging in reaction formation is not conscious of his self-deception.

INTELLECTUALIZATION

In *intellectualization*, a rather subtle defense mechanism, the person hides unacceptable feelings behind a smokescreen of fancy intellectual analysis and thereby avoids the pain of confronting these feelings head-on. For example, a person may spin out impressive-sounding generalizations about how difficult it is for two generations to understand one another, how parents and children invariably disappoint one another, and how we are all alone as we face the existential void, whereas what she really means is: "My mother never loved me, and I hate her for it."

RATIONALIZATION

Rationalization is the substitution of "respectable" motives for "unrespectable," instinctual motives in explaining one's behavior. For example, a man may ransack his children's trick-or-treat bags after the children have gone to sleep and then explain to his wife that he is protecting the children from tooth decay, whereas the real reason is that he simply wanted to eat the candy. Rationalization is an extremely common defense mechanism.

SUBLIMATION

Of all the defense mechanisms, only sublimation is truly constructive. In our discussion of Freudian theory in Chapter 1, we brought up as an example a man with powerful sexual drives who channeled that excess energy into creative expression—portrait painting—while maintaining one intimate relationship with a woman. This is sublimation, the rechanneling of impulses away from forbidden outlets and toward more creative outlets that are consistent with one's self-esteem. Freud (1930) argued that civilization itself was the result of centuries of collective sublimation.

How do defense mechanisms affect the self-concept? Are these common self-deceptions damaging to the self? Yes and no. On the one hand, the defense mechanisms are, to some degree, useful adaptive techniques. We all resort to them and, according to Freud (1936), we have to resort to them in order to adjust to the demands made on us by reality and by our own consciences. On the other hand, defense mechanisms can also prevent us from looking at ourselves realistically. If the individual's image of himself must continuously be protected from his true feelings, then this is a good indication that his self-concept is rigid and unrealistic and that he is making it more so by blocking out large chunks of his experience.

concept solidifies and becomes more resistant to serious change. The self-concept of course continues developing throughout life, but it tends to develop along the lines established in early childhood.

Sources of Information for the Self-Concept

Who tells us what we are? Where do we get the information, expectations, and judgments that make up our self-concept? To some degree, we learn simply from ourselves. Our bodies teach us that we are separate from the world. They also teach us our relation to the world. Unable to reach a cupboard, the child learns that he is a small creature. When he can dress himself, he learns that he is a capable person. However, if we depended only on ourselves, we would probably never form anything resembling a self-concept. The major source of information for the self-concept is our interaction with other people.

The first modern thinker to state this fact was the sociologist Charles Horton Cooley (1922), who introduced the notion of the "looking-glass self." According to Cooley, we use other people as mirrors to show us who we are. We imagine how we appear to others and how they judge us, and this inferred appearance and judgment become our picture of ourselves. Cooley's idea was later expanded by another sociologist, George Herbert Mead (1934). Mead proposed that the self develops in two stages: first, we internalize (incorporate into ourselves) other people's attitudes toward us; second, we internalize the standards of the society.

In other words, the self-concept is a social creation, the product of our relationships with others. Let us examine some of these "others" and the ways in which they place their stamp on the self-concept.

Parents

Our parents are the earliest social contacts we have, and the most powerful. The infant depends on her parents for her food, shelter, and comfort—indeed, for her survival. Consequently, the parents take on an immense importance in the child's eyes. And because of their godlike importance, what the parents communicate to the child has better staying power than any other information she receives throughout her life.

Our parents provide us with a constant flow of information about ourselves. Furthermore, they are instrumental in establishing our expectations; a child whose parents believe that he will be lucky to get through high school is unlikely to go on to college. Finally, and most important, our parents teach us how to evaluate ourselves. They provide us with the standards—the "I-should-be"—against which we measure ourselves. (Lying means we are bad; a favorable report card means we are good.) Even more crucial than the parents' explicit standards is their general attitude toward the child. However the parents treat the child, the child assumes that this is how he *deserves* to be treated. His sense of his own value as a person comes from the value they place on him (Coopersmith, 1967). And this parent-derived self-judgment endures. Researchers have found that even in adult life, people still tend to evaluate themselves as they feel their parents evaluate them (Jourard and Remy, 1955).

Peers

A child's peer group is second only to his parents in influencing the self-concept. For a while it is enough to have the love of one's parents, but eventually the child needs the approval of the other children on his block or in his classroom. And if this approval is not forthcoming—if the child is teased, scorned, or left out—the self-concept will suffer.

Beyond the matter of approval or disapproval, the role the child carves out in his peer group is likely to have a profound impact on his view of himself. Here we have a classic circular relationship. There is no question that the child's self-concept determines to some degree whether he becomes the group leader, the group mischief-maker, the group clown, or the group goody-goody. But by enacting his role, he reinforces his

THE SELF-CONCEPT: WHAT IT IS AND HOW IT DEVELOPS

vision of himself as leader, mischief-maker, clown, or goody-goody. And this role, along with the self-judgments that it entails, tends to endure into his adult social relationships.

The Society

Young children place little value on the accidents of their birth: the fact that they are black or white, WASP or Italian-American, the son of the local banker or the daughter of the local drunk. But their society does place value on such facts. And this value is eventually communicated to the child and incorporated into the self-concept.

An interesting example of this process comes from a study of the Ashanti tribe of West Africa. The Ashanti believe that a child's personality is determined in large part by the day of the week on which he is born. The Ashanti also tend to name their children according to the day of birth. For example, boys who are born on Monday are usually named Kwadwo and are expected to be quiet, peace-loving types. On the other hand, boys born on Wednesday are typically named Kwaku and are expected to become rough, aggressive trouble-makers. Interestingly, the local police files on crimes of violence overflow with accounts of misdeeds perpetrated by Kwakus, whereas Kwadwos have an unusually low delinquency rate (Jahoda, 1954). Obviously, Monday's child and Wednesday's child absorbed into their self-concept the expectations of others and fulfilled these expectations.

It seems clear that for many years the same mechanism operated in the case of black children in the United States, much to their disadvantage. Studies from the 1950s and early 1960s (Kardiner and Ovesey, 1951; Maliver, 1965) indicate that black was anything but beautiful to the black children of this era. They felt inferior, and it is almost certain that their expectations and achievements were stunted as a result. More recent

The society already has an opinion about these American Indian children, whether they know it yet or not. And prejudice can deeply affect the self-concept. (Dennis Stock/Magnum)

The black-is-beautiful movement of the sixties helped many parents to instill in their children a feeling of pride in their ethnic status. (Leonard Freed/Magnum)

ACTIVITY 3.3

Although the self-concept changes as we grow older, elements that became part of it early in our lives tend to persist. Frequently we take these aspects of ourselves as "givens" simply because they have been with us for so long. But it is useful to look at such givens and test their validity, especially if we want to change how we see ourselves.

One aspect of the self-concept that tends to be established early is our idea of how athletic we are. Describe yourself now in terms of athletics: what sports, if any, you're good at; whether you enjoy participating in sports; how often you do participate; how

BOX 3.2
HOW TO ENCOURAGE HIGH SELF-ESTEEM IN CHILDREN

There is no guaranteed formula for teaching a child to like himself. But one study by psychologist Stanley Coopersmith (1967) of children with high and low self-esteem has indicated that certain child-rearing practices may have a lot to do with determining a child's self-esteem.

ACCEPTANCE
The parents of Coopersmith's high self-esteem subjects tended to offer their children a warm and loving acceptance, which the children apparently incorporated into their self-concepts. Although the parents disciplined the children firmly (see next item), this discipline was enforced by the parents, and interpreted by the children, as a function of the parents' concern for the child.

RESTRICTIONS AND DISCIPLINE
An interesting finding of Coopersmith's study was that the high self-esteem children were

punished just as often as the low self-esteem children. The difference was in the nature and timing of the punishment. Low self-esteem children were given very few guidelines for their behavior. The parents were permissive—or, one might rather say, neglectful—until at last they lost patience. At this point they punished the child through harsh and humiliating treatment and by withdrawing love. By contrast, the parents of high self-esteem subjects were notable for the strict demands they made on the child and for the firmness with which they enforced them. Thus they provided the child with a clear moral structure that he could use in judging and controlling his own behavior. If restrictions were violated, the child was punished. But the disapproval was aimed specifically at the behavior, not at the child as a person. As a result, though the high self-esteem children complained about how strict their parents were, they still tended to see the demands and punishments imposed by their parents as justified.

you rate on such general skills as running, throwing, and so on. Next, ask your parents or someone who knew you as a child to describe your childhood athletic ability. Then compare the two descriptions. You may find a good deal of continuity. (Your parents felt that you lacked coordination, and you still think you're a poor athlete.) This type of comparison will alert you to the way in which old aspects of your self-concept, learned years ago, can influence you now. (Maybe you were poor at sports because your eyesight was bad; even though you eventually got glasses, you still stay off the tennis court.) To change your self-concept, you first need to be aware of the old assumptions, and then to challenge them.

DEMOCRATIC PRACTICES

Within the firm limits they imposed, the parents of high self-esteem children were willing to listen respectfully to the children's arguments, to reason with them, and to explain the purpose of the restrictions. Furthermore, they preferred to gain compliance by offering rewards rather than by threatening to punish (though, as we have seen, they did not hesitate to punish when necessary). The parents of low self-esteem subjects, on the other hand, wasted no time reasoning with their children. (Indeed, there was little to reason about since there were so few rules.) When they wanted obedience, they simply used force.

In sum, the formula that Coopersmith came up with is: approval, clearly defined and strictly enforced limits, and a democratic respect for the child's individuality within those limits. This formula may not work for all children, but it worked for those studied by Coopersmith— white, middle-class boys aged ten to twelve.

(**Michael Hayman/Photo Researchers, Inc.**)

studies (Rosenberg and Simmons, 1971; Hraba and Grant, 1970) suggest that black children are no longer invariably burdened with low self-esteem. This change, however, is due not to the children but to the society. Like our parents and our peers, our society tells us how to define ourselves. And we listen.

Learning

Our self-concept is the product of learning. This learning goes on every day, usually without our being aware of it. *Learning* may be defined as a relatively permanent psychological change that occurs in us as a consequence of experience (Hilgard and Bower, 1966). Through the experience of falling in the bathtub and getting his nose full of water, a child may learn to fear water. The same principle operates in the learning of the self-concept. A short child, through the experience of being called "shrimp" and other unflattering names by his classmates, learns that shortness is not a valued trait (in boys, at least) and therefore questions his own value. In the learning of the self-concept, there are three important factors that must be considered: association, consequences, and motivation.

Association

John Locke, the seventeenth-century English philosopher, was the first to point out that we tend to think via *associations*—that is, learned connections between different things. If a person has experienced x and y together in the past, then the thought or experience of x on later occasions will call up the thought of y. And as behaviorists have pointed out, either object can take on, in our minds, the qualities of the other. For example, we may find, as adults, that silverbacked hairbrushes seem particularly attractive to us because a long-dead grandmother

whom we loved as a child used to brush her hair with one. This process of thinking and valuing via associations is basic to the formation of the self-concept. For example, by associating hairy chests with masculinity or large breasts with femininity (see Box 3.3), we may learn to like or dislike our own bodies, depending on whether or not they meet the cultural standard.

However, the most important association we can ever make, in terms of the future self-concept, takes place long before we are ever aware of such cultural stereotypes. As we have seen, one of the most crucial steps in the development of the self-concept is the infant's learning to value his parents as very special features of his environment. This does not happen because anyone has told him to honor thy father and thy mother. Rather, it probably occurs because the child comes to associate his parents with the physical gratifications they give him, especially food and physical contact (cuddling). His instinctively positive response to these gratifications of his bodily needs broadens to include his parents. And eventually the value the child places on his parents broadens to include people in general. Hence, learning through association is a basic cause of our condition as *social* creatures. And as we have seen, social interaction is largely responsible for teaching us our self-concept.

Consequences

For most of us, virtue is seldom its own reward. We take the actions that we take because, in the past, these actions have been rewarded. And we avoid the actions that we avoid because, in the past, these actions have been punished. This again is learning by association; we associate the action with its consequence—with what it *gets* us. Learning via consequences is largely responsible for creating our standards for ourselves and, consequently, our self-evaluations.

BOX 3.3
SELF-CONCEPT AND BODY IMAGE: BEING FLAT-CHESTED IN A BOSOMY WORLD

Body image—the individual's mental picture and evaluation of his own body—is an integral part of the self-concept. After all, it is a physical body in which the self gets around in the world. More important, it is as a body that we present ourselves to other people. And most of us would like the presentation to be attractive.

The body image is generally formed by comparing one's own physical endowment with cultural standards of beauty. Such standards vary widely from society to society. For example, the Bushmen of Africa feel that the most glorious physical attribute a woman can possess is a set of enormous buttocks—a feature that many American women spend hours in reducing salons trying to eliminate. Other African tribes feel that a woman's breasts are there simply to feed babies, whereas Americans for years have considered breasts the ultimate sexual drawing card.

The problem with such cultural ideals of physical beauty is that very few of us achieve them. And for those who fall drastically short of the ideal, self-esteem can suffer badly. Particularly for the adolescent, furtive locker-room comparisons of one's own penis or bustline with those of the other kids can be extremely discouraging.

The following is a story that many women will find familiar. It is an account, by essayist Nora Ephron, of what it was like to be a flat-chested adolescent when all her friends were developing bustlines:

I started with a 28 AA bra. I don't think they made them any smaller in those days.

My first brassiere came from Robinson's Department Store in Beverly Hills. I went there alone, shaking, positive they would look me over and smile and tell me to come back next year. An actual fitter took me into the dressing room and stood over me while I took off my blouse and tried the first one on. The little puffs stood out on my chest. "Lean over," said the fitter. (To this day, I am not sure what fitters in bra departments do except to tell you to lean over.) I leaned over, with the fleeting hope that my breasts would miraculously fall out of my body and into the puffs. Nothing.

"Don't worry about it," said my friend Libby some months later, when things had not improved. "You'll get them after you're married."

"What are you talking about?" I said.

"When you get married," Libby explained, "your husband will touch your breasts and rub them and kiss them and they'll grow."

That was the killer. Necking I could deal with. Intercourse I could deal with. But it had never crossed my mind that a man was going to touch my breasts, that breasts had something to do with all that, petting, my God, they never mentioned petting in my little sex manual about the fertilization of the ovum. I became dizzy. For I knew instantly—as naive as I had been only a moment before—that only part of what she was saying was true: the touching, rubbing, kissing part, not the growing part. And I knew that no one would ever want to marry me. I had no breasts. I would never have breasts.

Ephron, N. Crazy Salad: Some Things About Women. New York: Bantam, 1976, pp. 3-4.

Too much babying and attention in response to a child's temper tantrum can result in more temper tantrums. (Ken Heyman)

Imagine a child who comes home with an excellent report card. His parents kiss him, tell him what a smart boy he is, take him out for an ice-cream cone, call up Grandma to read her the whole report card, and so forth. As a result of being so richly rewarded, the child learns the value placed on academic achievement. Consequently, in the future he himself is likely to praise himself for academic success and blame himself for academic failure. Likewise, a child who is consistently scolded or spanked (that is, punished) for making small mistakes—such as spilling his milk or putting his shirt on inside out—may grow up to be a perfectionist about his own behavior, since he has incorporated into his self-concept the rule "I should never make mistakes." In sum, our self-ideal and, as a result, our self-esteem are to a large degree the outcome of learning

through consequences. The standards against which we evaluate ourselves are the rewards and punishments of yesteryear. (Associations and consequences will be discussed in greater detail in Chapter 5.)

Motivation

The more value we attach to a reward, the more likely we are to engage in whatever action will produce that reward. Learning, in other words, involves *motivation*—the state of arousal we experience when working toward a goal. In early childhood, when we are highly motivated to win our parents' approval, we learn to do the things they approve of—clean up our rooms, say "please" and "thank you," refrain from throwing food at our sisters and brothers. In adolescence, on the other hand, we are more motivated to win our peers' approval. Therefore we learn to do the things that *they* approve of (and that our parents may not approve of), such as speaking in the local teen-age jargon, wearing what the gang wears, and acting extremely unruffled and confident ("cool"). In short, what we learn depends to a large degree on what is motivating us.

Psychologists (among them, Coopersmith, 1967; Epstein, 1973) have suggested that certain types of motivation are particularly powerful in the learning of the self-concept. One is simple curiosity. Children spend many hours a day seeking out information about themselves and their world. They explore everything within reach. They pull the dog's tail to see what will happen. They throw temper tantrums to see if this will get them attention from their parents. And the information they receive as a result of such experiments has a profound effect. If the temper tantrum does in fact attract attention ("Johnny, what's the matter? What happened to Mommy's boy?"), then this tactic is likely to be repeated.

Two other motives that are thought to be

extremely important in the learning of the self-concept are the desire to achieve (Moss and Kagan, 1961) and the desire for self-esteem. Thus, rewards and punishments related to these motives—such as praise for drawing a beautiful picture or criticism for being messy—will be carefully incorporated into the self-concept.

Problems in Learning

Problems in learning mean problems in the self-concept. We have already suggested a number of things that can go wrong in the learning process. Let us look more closely at these factors.

Insufficient or Inconsistent Feedback

We already know that our environment, and especially the people who inhabit it, give us feedback about ourselves, and this feedback is eventually organized into a self-concept. Perhaps the most serious problem that can occur in this area is insufficient feedback. Children who have no parents, for example, will have difficulty gaining information about themselves and discovering how they fit into the scheme of things. More common, however, is the problem of parents who withdraw from their children, leaving them without any information about themselves other than the fact that Mother and Father are not interested in them. Such neglect has been shown to be a major cause of negative self-concept (Coopersmith, 1967). Nor are parents the only ones who can be stingy with feedback. It has been argued that one of the reasons women have lower expectations for themselves than men is that teachers give much more attention and feedback to boys than to girls (Serbin and O'Leary, 1975). Consequently, boys are more motivated to achieve, and they are better instructed in how to do so.

The quantity of feedback thus appears to be an important factor in the growth of the self-concept. However, the quality of the feedback is also crucial. For one thing, feedback should be consistent. A child who is subject to inconsistent discipline will have great difficulty assembling a set of standards against which to evaluate himself. Apparently, many parents tend to ignore their children's misbehavior until the proverbial "last straw," at which point they react with fury (Coopersmith, 1967). The problem here is that the last straw—the act for which the child is finally punished—may have been a trivial misdeed or even an accident, such as spilled milk or a wet bed, whereas much more serious mischief, such as stealing, cheating, or cruelty to other children, may have been ignored along the way. Furthermore, the misdeed that constitutes the last straw will probably vary every time. The result is that the child never learns to discriminate between proper and improper behavior. He simply behaves as he wishes, knowing that at some point his parents will explode but not knowing how to act in order to prevent the explosion.

Forbidden Feelings: Rogers' Self Theory

Another type of harmful feedback is that which requires the child to deny his own feelings—a problem that has been explored by the humanistic theorist Carl Rogers. We have already glanced at Rogers' *self theory* in Chapter 1. Let us now examine it more closely. Rogers (1951) regards the human personality as the interaction of two elements: (1) the *organism*, the individual's actual experience, and (2) the *self*, the individual's image of himself—that is, the self-concept. According to Rogers, the key to emotional health is the development of a self that is congruent with the organism. In other words, the person's self-concept should be as broad as his experience, so that new adventures and new thoughts and feelings can be fully savored and evaluated, rather than screened out on the grounds of "That's not me" or "That's unworthy of me."

Rogers (1959) feels that most of us do more screening out than is good for us, because we are taught to in early childhood. All children, he claims, automatically seek "positive regard" (approval), especially from their parents. But many parents are willing to bestow positive regard only on the condition that the child deny certain portions of his experience. For example, the child should not only refrain from hitting his baby brother; he should feel no *desire* to hit and no pleasure from hitting. The child should not only refrain from masturbating; he should not *want* to masturbate. To obtain the parents' positive regard, the child accepts these "conditions of worth" and incorporates them into his self. The organism's sexual and aggressive feelings are thus banished from the self, and the self becomes narrower than the organism. Of course, the forbidden feelings don't go away; they are still there. But now, instead of being recognized and perhaps used in some self-enhancing way, they function merely as threats to the unrealistically narrow self. The result is anxiety and stunted personal growth. Rogers believes that this process is responsible for many serious psychological disturbances. He also claims that at a less intense level it operates in most people's lives, interfering with their self-actualization.

Cognitive Consistency and Cognitive Dissonance

In 1957 the psychologist Leon Festinger put forth his theory of cognitive consistency and cognitive dissonance. Festinger's claim was that one of the most powerful motives in human life was the drive for *cognitive consistency*, the experience of having our beliefs fit comfortably with one another and of hav-

ing reality fit comfortably with our beliefs. When two cognitions (that is, beliefs or perceptions—see Chapter 1) conflict with one another, the individual experiences the opposite of cognitive consistency, a state of mental discomfort called *cognitive dissonance*. And he will attempt to resolve the dissonance by twisting one cognition to conform with the other (Festinger, 1957). Thus, according to Festinger, the individual will automatically resort to distortion in order to resist a challenge to what he already believes (see Box 3.4).

According to many psychologists, this principle is one of the central keys to the development of the self-concept. As we have noted earlier, a child's conceptual anchor, even if it is negative, will operate as the standard by which he sorts out feedback concerning himself. Likewise, adults tend to perceive reality in ways that conform with their self-concept. In one experiment, subjects were first tested for self-esteem, and then they were given a very difficult perceptual test. After the perceptual test the subjects were asked to explain their level of success or failure. As might be expected, the subjects who had scored high on the self-esteem test tended to attribute their success to internal factors—their own ability—and to explain their failures as the result of external factors, such as chance or temporary visual confusion. The low self-esteem subjects, on the other hand, tended to explain their failures as failures of ability and their successes as the result of chance (Fitch, 1970). In other words, the low self-esteem subjects, rather than give themselves credit for their success, chose an explanation consistent with their derogatory view of themselves.

This tendency may be related to sex differences. One study (Deaux, White, and Farris, 1975) found that, in general, men prefer games of skill, presumably because they believe they *have* skill. Women, on the other

BOX 3.4
REDUCING DISSONANCE

If you are one of those people who still refuse to use seatbelts in a car, what would you say to the evidence that not wearing a seatbelt increases the likelihood of serious injury if you are in an accident? To achieve cognitive consistency, as Leon Festinger describes it, you might respond in one of two ways. You might argue that the data are worthless. After all, how many miles have you driven without having been in an accident, much less a serious one? Or you might argue that you'd rather take the risk of being injured in an (unlikely) accident than go through the hassle of buckling yourself into a constraining seatbelt every time you get into a car. The point is, you would resist information that was inconsistent with your current behavior—information, in other words, that made you feel cognitive dissonance.

Festinger (1957) and his colleagues have conducted a number of studies in which people have been forced to experience cognitive dissonance. In one study (Festinger and Carlsmith, 1959) college students were put through an extremely boring hour-long experiment, one by one. When the experiment hour was over, each subject was asked, for the sake of research, to tell the next subject, who was waiting in an adjoining room, that the experiment was lots of fun. In other words, they were asked to lie. Half the subjects were paid $1 for their help; the other half were paid $20. They were then asked to rate the experiment in terms of how interesting it was. On the average, the subjects who were paid only $1 gave the experiment a rating about 4 times higher than the subjects who were paid $20.

This is a curious finding, but in terms of cognitive consistency, it is quite predictable. The subjects who had been paid $20 were able to justify to themselves the fact that they had told a lie: after all, they were well paid for it. But those who were paid only $1 had no such justification. Consequently, they were left with the problem of reconciling their boredom during the experiment with the fact that they had told another student that the experiment was very interesting. There were only two ways for them to resolve their dissonance: change the lie or change their opinion of the experiment. The first would be embarrassing. Furthermore, it was impossible; the other subject was already gone. So they chose the second route and decided that it was a rather interesting experiment after all.

---

hand, were shown to prefer games of chance, presumably because they have more faith in this completely arbitrary factor than in their own abilities. This pattern may be changing, however. The recent upsurge of female interest in sports, which are almost invariably based on skill, suggests that women are beginning to trust their abilities—and that they are weary of stereotyped images of femininity (Rohrbaugh, 1979).

Going back to the tendency of low self-esteem people to refuse credit for success, how can this be squared with what we said earlier: that one of the most basic human motives is the drive for self-esteem? It appears that like everyone else, people with negative self-concepts crave the acceptance and approval of others, but when they get it, they distrust it because it contradicts their expectations (Jacobs, Berscheid, and Walster, 1971). In other words, it creates cognitive dissonance. Faced with this dilemma, they cling to what they are sure of—that they are not worth very much—and discard the positive feedback as insincere or mistaken. This self-defeating line of reasoning is nicely illustrated in a statement by one of Carl Rogers' clients:

> When people tell me they think I'm intelligent, I just don't believe it. I just—I guess I don't want to believe it. . . . It should give me confidence, but it doesn't. I think they just really don't know (cited in Rogers, 1951, pp. 504–505).

As the saying goes, nothing succeeds like success. And nothing generates self-contempt like self-contempt.

The Self-Concept as a Prophecy

Karen Horney, one of the major proponents of modern Freudian theory, described the negative self-concept as the "perfect double crime" (cited in Moustakas, 1974, p. 34). Parents or peers may have initiated the process, but the victim of the "crime" eventually becomes an accomplice. As we have just seen, people reinforce their self-concepts, whether negative or positive, by adjusting their perceptions so that they are consistent with the self-concept. Likewise, it appears that people adjust their behavior to accord with their self-concepts. As we suggested in our descriptions of the positive and negative self-concept, people with high self-esteem set up successes for themselves, and—strange as it may seem—people with low self-esteem appear to engineer their own failures. We have already seen a demonstration of this sad fact—Mettee's experiments with the high-school girls, discussed at the opening of this chapter. The principle has been confirmed by other researchers as well.

In one experiment, researchers assembled a number of subjects who had scored in the bottom third of a self-esteem test. These subjects were then divided into two groups: those who indicated that they were sure their negative view of themselves was accurate, and those who showed some uncertainty about their negative self-concept. Then all the subjects were given the task of matching a number of geometric shapes on a board. In each of the two groups, half the subjects were told that the task was purely a matter of luck; the other half were told that their success would depend entirely on skill. (The latter was true; the task involved skill alone.) Then, halfway through the test, the researchers mentioned to the subjects

---

ACTIVITY 3.4

Through an unrealistic self-concept, we may program ourselves into problems. For instance, if we regard ourselves as lazy, we probably accomplish less than we would if we thought of ourselves as energetic.

Do you think you're lazy? If so, pick a day and list what you do that day under the headings of "Energetic Behavior" and "Lazy Behavior." You may find that you actually got a lot of things done or that your "lazy" activities were really times of needed relaxation. (If you don't think you're lazy, then choose some other weakness and its opposite.) If your weakness is not as serious as you thought it was, it may be time to revise that aspect of your self-concept.

that they were doing well. Normally, such positive feedback, in addition to the experience of "getting the hang" of the task, would have the effect of increasing the subject's success rate. The researchers hypothesized, however, that one set of subjects would resist this boost: the subjects who were certain of their negative self-concept and who

BOX 3.5
SELF-ESTEEM AND HONESTY

Low self-esteem may lead not only to failure but also to dishonesty—a possibility that was suggested in an experiment conducted by Eliot Aronson and David Mettee (1968). In the first stage of the experiment, a number of college women took a personality test, after which they were told the "results." As usual, the results were rigged. No matter how they had actually scored on the test, one group of women was given positive feedback; they were informed that their personalities were mature, deep, interesting, and the like. A second group was given negative feedback—that they were relatively immature, shallow, uninteresting, and so forth. A third group was given no feedback.

Immediately afterward, the subjects moved on to a second test, involving a game of blackjack. The experimenter told them that the purpose of the game was to measure their ESP in relation to their personality profiles. Actually, it was a test of whether they would cheat if given the chance. On 4 hands out of 35, each subject, when she was supposed to be "hit" with one card, received two by "mistake" from the machine that was dealing the cards. Of the two, the top card—the one the subject was supposed to have received—put her over 21, which would cause her to lose the hand. The question was whether the subject would give back the extra card, thereby losing the hand, or substitute it for the rightful card and thus win the hand. It should be added that the subjects were in booths designed so as to make it seem almost impossible to be caught cheating. Furthermore,

they were betting, so that if they decided to play it straight and return the extra card, they would lose money as well as the satisfaction of winning the hand.

The experimenters' hypothesis was that those subjects who had been given negative feedback regarding their personalities would be more likely to cheat than those who had been given positive feedback. Their hypothesis was borne out. In the list of subjects who cheated at least once, there were more than twice as many negative-feedback subjects as positive-feedback subjects. The subjects who had received no feedback on their personalities fell almost exactly in between.

This is a very interesting experiment, for it raises the possibility that the consequences of low self-esteem—or at least of a temporary blow to self-esteem—may be quite far-reaching. Other studies (for example, Maracek and Mettee, 1972, discussed on pp. 82–84) have shown that people with low self-esteem will avoid making full use of their abilities, presumably because they don't think very highly of their abilities. But what this study suggests is that such people will also compensate, through dishonesty, for what they feel they cannot achieve through their abilities. This in turn suggests that low self-esteem may be an important cause of criminal behavior. Parents may want to bolster their children's self-esteem not only to increase the children's chances of success as adults, but also to keep them out of jail.

had been told the task involved skill rather than luck. The hypothesis proved true. A respectable level of improvement was shown by those who were uncertain as to their negative self-concept (regardless of whether they believed the task involved luck or skill) and by those who were certain of their negative self-concept but believed the task involved only luck. The only ones who showed virtually no improvement were the subjects who felt certain about their negative self-concept and believed that their skill alone was being tested (Maracek and Mettee, 1972). For them, success would have created cognitive dissonance by violating their firm belief that they lacked ability. And so they managed not to succeed.

This principle appears to operate not only in task-oriented situations but also in interpersonal relations. As the Chinese philosopher Mencius said many centuries ago, "A man must first despise himself, and then others will despise him." People who like themselves tend to be liked by others, whereas those whose self-esteem is low have little chance of winning the esteem of others (Horowitz, 1962; Coleman, 1961). Apparently, we cue people as to how they should respond to us. They will value us as we value ourselves.

What all of this points to is a fact that we have suggested repeatedly throughout this chapter—probably the most important fact about the self-concept: *the self-concept is not so much an objective picture of ourselves as it is a prophecy that we make about ourselves—a prophecy that we ourselves then fulfill.* In the words of Sidney Jourard, a foremost humanistic theorist:

> When a person forms a self-concept, thereby defining himself, he is not so much describing his nature as he is making a pledge that he will continue to be the kind of person he believes he now is and has been. One's self-concept is not so much descriptive of experience and action as it is prescriptive. The self-concept is a commitment. (1974, p. 153)

Positive self-concept leads to positive experience leads to positive self-concept leads to positive experience, and so on, endlessly. The same is true if you substitute "negative" for "positive" in that sentence. Our self-concept and our experience interlock to form a closed circle, vicious or benign. However we judge ourselves, other people are prone to judge us in the same way. What we expect from life, life tends to give us. What we believe about ourselves, we are likely to become.

And therefore, if we are concerned about what we will become, we should take a close look at our self-concept. This is the business of Chapter 4.

SUMMARY

1. Your *self-concept* is your mental portrait of yourself. It is composed of *knowledge* about yourself, *expectations* for yourself, and *evaluations* of yourself. Your knowledge about yourself is the information that you have about yourself: your age, sex, appearance, and so on. Your expectations for yourself are your ideas about what you could be. Your evaluation of yourself is your measurement of what you are against what you feel you could and should be. This evaluation determines your level of *self-esteem*.

2. In its extreme form, a *negative self-concept* is characterized by inaccurate knowledge of the self, unrealistic expec-

tations, and low self-esteem. A *positive self-concept* is characterized by a broad and diversified knowledge of the self, realistic expectations, and high self-esteem.

3. Although we are born without a self-concept, it begins to develop almost from birth. We begin by differentiating between sensations and feelings that come from ourselves and those that come from the environment. Early experiences of pleasure or pain, affection or rejection, form the *conceptual anchor* for the future self-concept. As we begin to use language and encounter more and more experiences, the self-concept takes shape and solidifies, resisting major change.

4. The information, expectations, and judgments that make up the self-concept come primarily from interactions with others. Our *parents*, as our earliest and most powerful "others," provide the basic framework for the self-concept. Our *peers* are second only to our parents in influencing the self-concept. Finally, the *society* in which we live contributes to the development of the self-concept.

5. Crucial to the formation of the self-concept is *learning*—the relatively permanent psychological change that occurs in us as a consequence of experience. Three aspects of learning that are important in forming the self-concept are *association*, *consequences*, and *motivation*.

6. Because the self-concept is the product of learning, problems in learning can damage the developing self-concept. Two such problems are inadequate feedback and inconsistent feedback. A third form of harmful feedback is that which requires the child to screen out substantial portions of his experience. According to Rogers' *self theory*, this creates a *self* (self-concept) that is narrower than the *organism* (experience) and thus blocks personal growth.

7. Festinger has proposed that the motivation to maintain *cognitive consistency* is a powerful factor in the formation and maintenance of the self-concept. Once we have formed a basic image of ourselves, we will reject or distort perceptions that are inconsistent with that image, and respond to perceptions that are consistent. As a result, the image becomes increasingly more entrenched. Further, we tend to behave in ways that are consistent with our image of ourselves. Thus, the self-concept is a self-fulfilling prophecy.

PROJECT

On the basis of work done by William Stephenson (1953), Carl Rogers and his associates used a test called the Q-sort for assessing a person's self-concept. What the Q-sort does is measure the difference between the person's real self (how he actually sees himself) and his ideal self (how he would like to be). Rogers, you will recall, regards the self-concept as crucial to psychological well-being. In his view, the success of psychotherapy could be measured by the differences between a person's Q-sort results before and after therapy. If a Q-sort done at the end of therapy showed substantially less difference between the real self and ideal self than a Q-sort done before therapy, then the person's self-concept had become more positive, and the therapy could thus be considered a success.

The following is a test similar to the Q-sort. It uses 50 items from a study by Butler and Haigh (1954). To determine the degree of difference between your real and your ideal self, follow the procedure outlined below.

1. The first objective will be to determine how you see yourself now. To do this:

a. Read through the 50 statements listed below, mentally noting those items most characteristic of the way you see yourself now and those items most *un*characteristic of the way you see yourself now.

b. Using a pencil (so you can erase if you change your mind) and writing in the column under "real self," put a "1" next to the *five* items most characteristic of the way you see yourself now.

c. In the same column, put a "5" next to the *five* items most *un*characteristic of the way you see yourself now.

d. In the same column, put a 2 next to *twelve* items that are moderately characteristic of the way you see yourself now.

e. In the same column, put a 4 next to *twelve* items that are moderately *un*characteristic of the way you see yourself now.

f. This should leave you with sixteen items that are not particularly characteristic or uncharacteristic of the way you see yourself now. Next to these items, put a 3 in the "real self" column.

g. Go back over your ratings of all fifty items and make sure you are satisfied with them. If you are not, change them. Once you have done this, you will have a rough picture of how you see yourself now.

2. The second objective will be to determine how you would *like* to see yourself. To do this:

a. Take a piece of paper and cover the "real self" column so that you cannot see your ratings in that column.

b. Repeat steps a–g, above, but this time rate the statements according to how characteristic or uncharacteristic they are of your *ideal self*—the person you would like to be. Place your ratings in the "ideal self" column.

3. The third objective will be to determine the degree of difference between your real self and your ideal self. To do this:

a. Figure out the *difference* between your two numerical ratings for each statement. For example, if for a given statement you wrote a "5" in the "real self" column and a "1" in the "ideal self" column, the difference between the two ratings for that statement is 4.

b. Add up the differences for all fifty statements. The larger the total, the greater the difference between your real self and your ideal self, and the greater, in all probability, your dissatisfaction with yourself. (Obviously, if your real and ideal selves were identical, there would be no differences between the ratings in the two columns and thus the total differences would be zero.)

c. Keep in mind those statements for which the difference between your "real self" and "ideal self" ratings was as great as 4. These are probably areas in which you are very unhappy with yourself. You might want to work on them in later chapters, when we come to the subject of how to change thoughts and behavior.

Real Self	Ideal Self	
_____	_____	1. I am likable.
_____	_____	2. I put on a false front.
_____	_____	3. I often feel humiliated.
_____	_____	4. I am relaxed and nothing really bothers me.

THE SELF-CONCEPT: WHAT IT IS AND HOW IT DEVELOPS

——— ———	———	5. I am a hard worker.
——— ———	———	6. I am intelligent.
——— ———	———	7. I have a feeling of hopelessness.
——— ———	———	8. It is difficult to control my aggression.
——— ———	———	9. I am self-reliant.
——— ———	———	10. I understand myself.
——— ———	———	11. I am a good mixer.
——— ———	———	12. I tend to be on my guard with people who are somewhat more friendly than I had expected.
——— ———	———	13. I usually feel driven.
——— ———	———	14. I am satisfied with myself.
——— ———	———	15. My decisions are not my own.
——— ———	———	16. I am assertive.
——— ———	———	17. I am a hostile person.
——— ———	———	18. I have initiative.
——— ———	———	19. I am ambitious.
——— ———	———	20. I feel apathetic.
——— ———	———	21. I don't trust my emotions.
——— ———	———	22. I am tolerant.
——— ———	———	23. I am a rational person.
——— ———	———	24. I am poised.
——— ———	———	25. I have the feeling that I am just not facing things.
——— ———	———	26. I try not to think about my problems.
——— ———	———	27. I am contented.
——— ———	———	28. I am no one. Nothing seems to be me.
——— ———	———	29. I despise myself.
——— ———	———	30. I am sexually attractive.
——— ———	———	31. I just don't respect myself.
——— ———	———	32. I am liked by most people who know me.
——— ———	———	33. I am afraid of a full-fledged disagreement with a person.
——— ———	———	34. I am confused.
——— ———	———	35. I am a failure.
——— ———	———	36. My hardest battles are with myself.
——— ———	———	37. I can usually live comfortably with the people around me.
——— ———	———	38. I have a horror of failing in anything I want to accomplish.
——— ———	———	39. I usually like people.
——— ———	———	40. Self-control is no problem to me.
——— ———	———	41. I really am disturbed.
——— ———	———	42. I feel insecure within myself.
——— ———	———	43. I have to protect myself with excuses, with rationalizing.
——— ———	———	44. I am a responsible person.
——— ———	———	45. I am unreliable.
——— ———	———	46. I have a warm emotional relationship with others.
——— ———	———	47. I am worthless.
——— ———	———	48. I am responsible for my troubles.
——— ———	———	49. I make strong demands on myself.
——— ———	———	50. I have few values and standards of my own.

Source: Butler, J. M., and Haigh, G. V. "Changes in the Relation between Self-Concepts and Ideal Concepts Consequent upon Client-Centered Counselling," in C. R. Rogers and R. F. Dymond, eds., Psychotherapy and Personality Change. *Chicago: University of Chicago Press, 1954, p. 62.*

HUMAN ISSUE:
SEX-ROLE DEVELOPMENT

Picture this scenario: She showers and dresses while he prepares breakfast and packs the children's lunches for school. Then he throws on his robe and drives her to the station so she can catch the 7:30 train to the city. He spends the day doing household chores, while she helps plan a sales campaign. When she arrives home in the evening, he has dinner waiting. Afterward, he does the dishes, cleans up, and puts the children to bed while she relaxes with the newspaper.

Several years ago, this little drama would have been almost unheard of. Now, although still not common, such departures from the usual do occur. What makes them unusual, of course, is that they reverse the sex roles we associate with males and females. Most of us have grown up thinking that a woman stays home and takes care of the children (presuming she *is* married and *has* children—both considered to be part of the usual pattern), while the man works outside the home to support the family.

Now, women's liberation and similar movements are questioning stereotyped sex roles. Their challenges have brought new urgency to an old issue: which differences between men and women are innate—that is, biologically determined—and which ones are learned from society? Could we say, for example, that a female is "born" to tend the home and hearth, while a male "inherits" the drive to venture out into the world?

THE BIOLOGICAL CONTRIBUTION

The major physical differences between males and females are the product of internal secretions called hormones. Human males have a particular mix of hormones, heavily weighted toward hormones called androgens. Human females have a different mix, with a lesser dose of androgens. These hormonal differences create the anatomical differences between males and females—that is, that girls are born with vagina and uterus, boys with penis and testicles. They are also responsible for the secondary sexual characteristics that emerge in puberty, such as a deeper voice and facial hair in the male, breast development and menstruation in the female.

Is it possible that hormones affect not just the body but also the mind, creating biologically determined male and female behaviors? Some experiments do point to this conclusion. One study found that girls who, because of glandular disorders, were exposed before birth to abnormally high levels of androgens tended to become "tomboys" and began dating later than other girls (Money and Ehrhardt, 1972). Another study found that children whose mothers had taken synthetic androgens during pregnancy to prevent miscarriage scored significantly higher on tests of physical aggression than their brothers and sisters who had not been exposed to the extra dose of androgens (Reinisch, 1977).

Perhaps, then, biology does play some role in behavioral differences between the sexes. If so, this would be easy to explain in evolutionary terms. For many thousands of years our prehistoric ancestors lived in societies in which the men went out to do the hunting, while the women remained near the campsite caring for the children and gathering vegetable foods. According to the theory of natural selection, this role division would tend to encourage biologically based behavioral differences. Any inborn traits that predisposed men toward independence and aggression, and women toward nurturing, stay-at-home behavior, would tend to become more pronounced in the species, while the opposite characteristics (male passivity, female aggressiveness) would be suppressed (Gagnon, 1977).

Such a theory sounds logical, but opposing it is a wealth of evidence that "male" and "female" behaviors are the product not of biology but of social conditioning.

THE SOCIAL CONDITION

If sex-linked behavior were biologically determined, we would expect males and females to enact pretty much the same roles in all societies. But they do not. Anthropologist Margaret Mead, in her investigation of three cultures in New Guinea (1930), found widely differing attitudes regarding "appropriate" behavior for males and females. In one society, both men and women were equally gentle and nurturing. In another, both sexes were equally aggressive. In a third, the women were enterprising and efficient, while the men were vain and gossipy—a reversal of Western stereotypes. Mead's conclusion, supported by other anthropological studies as well, was that every society works out its own conceptions of "male" and "female" behavior and then enforces those standards through socialization.

Feminist writers agree and have stated their case with bitter forcefulness. Betty Friedan's book *The Feminine Mystique* (1964), for a while the bible of the

Women's Liberation movement, argued that Western culture has brainwashed girls into believing that the only socially acceptable and psychologically fulfilling role they could play was that of housewife-mother. Another major feminist writer, Kate Millet (1970), has claimed that our male-dominated society uses every possible resource, from the social sciences to literature to religion, to protect male power. Thus, women remain subservient, serving men's needs while suppressing their own.

Between these two opposing viewpoints—biological determinism and social conditioning—there is now a third, "interactionist" position, which holds that behavioral differences between the sexes are the result of an interplay between biology and society. According to this view, hormonal differences may establish a direction, but it is socialization that pushes us in that direction.

LEARNING SEX ROLES

The big question is whether sex-role socialization has a biological basis. As for the existence of sex-role socialization, there is no question. It is all around us—a program that begins on the day of birth. In the beginning, the parents are the major sex-role instructors. They dress a baby boy in blue, give him a football when he's old enough to throw it, and encourage him to think about what he'd like to be when he grows up. They dress a baby girl in pink ruffles, press a doll into her tiny hands, and encourage her to be attractive so that she can get married.

Schools pick up where parents leave off or, rather, reinforce what parents are still teaching at home. Boys are expected to do well in math and science, girls in reading and music. Overall, there is more pressure on boys to excel in school (and to continue schooling longer), since they will "need" education more in their future lives. Textbooks reinforce the stereotypes of competent male and passive female.

Books are just one of the media that continue the sex-role teaching begun by the parents. Television, through both programs and advertising, presents the average American woman as a vacantly pretty housewife whose greatest happiness is a well-waxed kitchen floor. Though the average TV husband is no bargain either, most of the adventurous characters, whether doctors or detectives, are males.

In recent years, largely because of women's liberation, this scenario has been modified somewhat. There has been a major effort to remove sexism from textbooks. Television networks now use female news commentators and sometimes even feature women rather than men (or, more often, women in addition to men) as the bold young doctors, police officers, and reporters of the typical television series. Most important, the increasing number of women in responsible and prestigious positions provide young girls with models for achievement. But such changes are still relatively slight compared to the continuing manifestations of male dominance in the society.

LIVING WITH THE STEREOTYPE

Becoming a Man

In many ways, the development of the male can be seen as a reaction against being female. From birth, the male child, like the female, is weak and dependent and cries easily. But he is trained to reject these "feminine" traits and become strong, independent, and restrained. Though a boy's closest early contacts are with his mother, he must resist being "tied to her apron strings."

This negative approach to male sex-role development has several unfortunate consequences for men. One is that it pressures them into "macho" behavior—acting the tough guy, aggressive and competitive, who shows no weaknesses or emotions. Such an unrealistic self-concept, requiring an almost superhuman suppression of self-doubt and feeling, can result in ulcers, heart attacks, and breakdowns.

A second unhappy consequence is that the American male frequently grows up with a negative attitude toward females or anything thought to be feminine. The prevailing image in this case is the James Bond type, who sees women basically as sexual commodities. A man burdened with this attitude has a lot of trouble establishing a warm, loving relationship with a woman.

Becoming a Woman

At first glance, it might seem that in our society females have a better chance for healthy emotional development. A little girl is not punished for being dependent, nor is she discouraged from expressing emotions. The presence of her mother provides her with a model whose behavior she can imitate. But all is not entirely smooth for the girl child. Prohibitions hem her in and discourage her from being independent. She is steered away from activities that teach competition and achievement.

The consequence for many American women has been a sense of limited perspective, of few possibilities for the future. Women learn a negative self-concept and thus, lacking confidence in themselves, often achieve far less than they might. The cost of imposing second-class citizenship on women is great both for individuals, whose growth as human beings is stunted, and for society at large, which loses the talent and creativity women could supply.

Becoming Androgynous

In recent years, more and more people have come to see traditional sex roles as prisons, and have urged that we accept behaviors that do not conform to the stereotypes. This does not necessarily mean the kind of role reversal we described at the beginning of this essay. Urging women to jump into the rat race that many men are finding dehumanizing is not likely to produce a better society.

One answer is *androgyny* (a term that combines the Greek words for "man" and "woman"). What this means is that each of us recognizes, and expresses, the "masculine" and "feminine" traits in ourselves. As one writer put it: "Men must learn to sing, to decorate, to garden, to play, to cry, to open up huge areas of self once blocked off, while women must escape from the isolation of housework, from their low self-esteem, from their denial of self" (Heilbrun, 1974, p. 132).

Sandra Bem has suggested (1975) that people who see themselves as androgynous, and act out both masculine and feminine sides of their natures, are more flexible—adjusting to a wider variety of situations and relationships—than people who conform to traditional sex-role stereotyping. Androgyny, as some research is beginning to show (Tunnell, 1981; Wiggins and Holzmuller, 1978), may well provide the key to happier and more productive lives for both men and women.

<u>OUTLINE</u>

ANALYZING THE SELF-CONCEPT
Description
Isolating the problem
Situational description
Functional Analysis
External variables
Internal variables
Negative self-talk and irrational beliefs

HOW YOU WERE FOUND GUILTY:
A REVIEW IN THE COURT OF APPEALS
Distortions and Denials
Faulty Categorizing
Old Standards
Perfectionism
Conventionality
What the other guy thinks

CHANGING THE SELF-CONCEPT
Setting the Goal
Getting New Information
Cognitive Restructuring: New Self-Talk
Listening to self-talk
Talking back
Acting on your back-talk
The results

THE SELF-CONCEPT UNDER REVISION:
A SAMPLE SCRIPT

4

THE SELF-CONCEPT: HOW TO CHANGE IT

Let's look back for a minute at the person whose words we quoted at the opening of Chapter 2. He has more to say:

When I'm in class, I'm a real person. The other students in the class look up to me—even envy me, probably—and that makes me feel good. I've usually done the reading. I have questions. I have answers. I'm there. I'm in a world that I can understand and where I'm competent. I count for something in that world.

At parties I'm not even a person. I'm worth about as much as the paper cup they put the beer in. Less, even. I just can't do that kind of relaxed (and sort of sexy) give-and-take between men and women—the talking, the dancing, the kidding around, the knowing when to press your leg up against hers and how to take it away without wondering whether she's wondering why you took it away. I can't be "loose." I watch other people doing these things, and I just stand there on the sidelines, drinking a beer, sweating like mad, and wishing I had never left my room. The truth is, I'm a social incompetent. It's not my world. I don't belong there.

I said before that I still go to parties. But actually, I don't go much anymore. (I did last year, and I was miserable every time.) On Saturday nights I'm usually back at my apartment alone, with my books. When I'm through studying, I read novels. My friends have sort of labeled me as the "intellectual." (That's why I don't go out. So they think.) And I suppose that's what I'm going to become—the "intellectual" and only that—since it's only in relation to my schoolwork that I really feel comfortable.

So there I am, with my books to keep me warm, and everybody thinking that's all I want out of life. And there I'll be, every Saturday night of my life. Just me and my books.

This student's name is Larry. Let's look for a moment not at his overt behavior, but at his self-concept. In Larry's self-concept, two labels stand out: "bookworm" and "social incompetent." As we saw in Chapter 3, the self-concept is self-perpetuating; it provides its own nourishment. Thus, Larry the Bookworm expects to enjoy his schoolwork and do well in it, and he does, which in turn reinforces that label and that expectation. Likewise, Larry the Social Incompetent expects to be nervous and miserable at parties, and, not surprisingly, he is. Such experiences have by now reinforced the "social incompetent" label to the point where he is giving up socializing altogether; the whole thing just seems hopeless. So in both cases we have the classic circular relationship: expectation determines outcome determines next expectation determines next outcome and so on.

Such circles can, however, be broken. This does not mean that the whole self-concept must be revised. Rather, we must identify the specific self-labels that are causing problems for us and attack the expectations arising from those labels. This can be done through the technique we learned in Chapter 2: self-analysis.

ANALYZING THE SELF-CONCEPT

Analyzing the self-concept is a rather subtle matter, since problem-causing self-labels, unlike problem behaviors, are internal. They exist only in our minds. However, they are also intimately related to external situations and behaviors. Thus, if we stick closely to these observable matters, and if we take care to proceed methodically, the troubled areas of the self-concept can be analyzed successfully. The analysis involves two steps: description and functional analysis.

Description

Before you begin describing whatever it is that bothers you about your self-concept, turn back to Chapter 2 and review the basic procedure for description. Most crucial of all is the necessity of writing down your description. This will help focus your thinking and "keep you honest"—that is, prevent you from meandering off into hazy generalizations. As you write, keep in mind the three basic rules for description: simplicity, objectivity, and specificity.

Isolating the Problem

It is not easy to be simple, objective, and specific when talking about problems in the way we view ourselves. Indeed, sometimes even locating the problem is hard. We don't usually think of our self-labels as separate units. Rather, in our minds these labels get "gummed up" together, forming a vague and shapeless mass. Hence, we have to be strict in our thinking in order to isolate the self-label that is causing us problems.

Let's look, for example, at Larry's description of himself at the beginning of Chapter 2. He looks in the mirror and, in his gloom, sums up his "whole personality" as that of a "parent-pleasing jerk," a "bookworm." This, then, is his self-concept at that moment. But where is the problem label here? Is it the "parent-pleasing"? Probably not. There is nothing wrong with pleasing your parents, as long as this doesn't interfere with your own self-fulfillment. The reason Larry mentions his "parent-pleasing" with such scorn is simply that his parents are the *only* ones he is pleasing at the moment. He wouldn't mind pleasing his parents if at the same time he were pleasing himself and perhaps someone else as well. So "parent-pleasing" is not the issue.

Well, what about "bookworm"? Is this the basic problem label? Certainly not. Larry is obviously a "natural" as a student, and what self-respect he still has is based on his academic success. The only reason the "bookworm" label is included in his self-criticism at this moment is that he sees his "book-worm" identity as *all* that he has. And he wants more; specifically, he wants to "get it together with a woman." Hence, his studiousness begins to look to him like a loser's substitute for the "real" thing. But if he had the "real" thing, his studies could be a real thing too. In other words, his studiousness is not the problem. If other facets of his self-concept were changed, he could be happy thinking of himself as a bookworm.

But he could not be happy thinking of himself as a jerk. This, of course, is the problem label. It is a big, vague label, but in the course of his discussion of himself, Larry has clarified what he means by it. He means that he is a social incompetent, or, more specifically, that he is a social incompetent with the opposite sex. The cause and the evidence for this self-label is that when he goes to a party he can't relax and meet women—or, if he is with a woman, he can't

enjoy himself with her because he can't be "loose."

In describing your own problems with your self-concept, you have to follow the procedure we have just been through with Larry. Trim away the irrelevancies until you have isolated the basic negative self-label. Write it down and then pare it down to its simplest, most objective, and most specific form. What do you really mean by saying to yourself, for example, that you are "no good" or that you "can't cope"? Clarify the self-label. For example, "What I mean by no good is that I use men: I get what I want out of them and then I leave them for somebody else," or "What I mean by saying that I can't cope is that whenever the pressure gets heavy at work, I immediately develop a throbbing headache and have to go home."

Situational Description

Once you have pinned down your self-label in specific terms, make it even more specific by describing a situation in which this self-label goes to work. Larry, for example, described his behavior at parties: standing on the sidelines, watching other people do the things he wishes he could do, feeling "incredibly tight" inside, sweating, sneaking off to the bathroom just to sit down and relax. In the same way, you should write a real-life "story" to back up your self-label. Describe the circumstances, what you do, how you feel, and what you say to yourself before and after whatever you do. Then show your story to a person who is close to you and ask for feedback. Is the account specific enough? Can your friend get the feel of the situation? If not, get out your pencil again and make the story more specific.

Once you have completed the description, you can start looking for causes. What is behind this negative self-label?

"Being loose." (© Stephen Shames 1981/Woodfin Camp & Assoc.)

ACTIVITY 4.1

Write down eight different social situations in which you frequently find yourself—for example, participating in a class, eating dinner with your family (or roommates), playing cards with your friends, talking on the phone to your parents, anything that you do with some regularity. Then pick your most serious general criticism of yourself (lazy, selfish, pushy, insensitive, self-conscious) and write down how well this criticism applies to you in each of the eight situations you have listed. You will probably find that it applies to only a few situations. Remember that while we tend to criticize ourselves in general terms, we live our lives in specific situations. Therefore, if you are going to criticize yourself, the most accurate way is to stick to situational problems—"rude to my parents (but not to my boyfriend)," "aggressively overcompetitive in sports (but not so much in the classroom)," and so forth.

BOX 4.1
LOSING YOUR SELF IN PRISON

One bright Sunday morning a police car, with sirens screaming, swept through the town of Palo Alto, California, stopping at different houses to arrest students. The suspects were charged with felonies, spread-eagled against the car, searched, handcuffed, and taken to the police station. From the station they were transferred to the "Stanford County Prison." There they were stripped, deloused, given uniforms with identification numbers printed on front and back, and locked up in windowless cells under the watchful eye of uniformed guards armed with billy clubs.

Actually, this "prison" was the basement of the Stanford University psychology building, done up in imitation of a prison. And both the "prisoners" and the "guards" were simply ordinary college students who had volunteered for a two-week study of prison life.

Social psychologist Philip Zimbardo and his colleagues (Zimbardo et al., 1972; Haney and Zimbardo, 1977) wanted to find out what the effect of a prison environment would be on the behavior and self-image of ordinary people. We know that in real prisons, guards are often tyrannical and abusive, and that prisoners, for their part, are often passive and self-demeaning. But such people may have been leaning in this direction before they ever entered a prison. To what extent is it the prison itself—the physical circumstances of the place and the roles that people enact there—that produces these unwelcome psychological effects? This is the question the experimenters were trying to answer. To do so, they recruited students through a newspaper ad, selected only those who seemed most stable emotionally, divided them at random into two groups, "prisoners" and "guards," and launched their experiment.

With some exceptions (for example, physical violence was forbidden), the daily routine of the "Stanford County Prison" was designed to sim-

Functional Analysis

As we learned in Chapter 2, functional analysis begins with the search for correlations, "connections" whereby changes in the variable you are examining seem related to changes in an independent variable. The self-concept may be affected by two kinds of variables: external variables and internal variables.

External Variables

Let us first consider external variables, the physical stimuli that impinge on us from our environments. These unquestionably af-

fect the self-concept. Hospitals, with their long, grim corridors and medicinal smells, help make incoming patients feel that they are genuinely sick. Prisons, with their high walls, barren cells, and stall-less bathrooms, help to make prisoners feel powerless and degraded (see Box 4.1). Even more ordinary physical circumstances can affect the self-concept. Imagine yourself as a new student on registration day at a large college or attempting to cash a check in a strange bank at lunch hour on a Friday or trying to renew your driver's license on a crowded day at the motor vehicle bureau. The institutional surroundings, the long lines, the windows separating you from the people whose help you

---

ulate important features of actual prison life. The guards were instructed to keep "law and order" and were given a number of rules to enforce. The prisoners had little to do, and for what they wanted to do—smoke a cigarette, go to the bathroom, write a letter—they had to get permission from the guards.

These normal, well-adjusted college students stepped into their new roles with amazing speed. Within a few days many of the prisoners began to lose hold on their former self-concepts. One of them described the experience:

I began to feel that I was losing my identity. The person I call [his own name],... the person who volunteered to go into this prison . . . was distant from me, was remote until finally, I wasn't that. I was #416—I was really my number. (Zimbardo et al., 1972, p. 12)

Their behavior reflected their loss of self-respect; they became passive, servile, and sneaky. A number of the guards showed a corresponding change in self-concept, becoming self-righteous, petty, and abusive. To quote one of them:

I was surprised at myself.... I made them call each other names and clean the toilets out with their bare hands. I practically considered the prisoners cattle, and I kept thinking I have to watch out for them in case they try something. (Zimbardo et al., 1972, p. 9)

The experiment was supposed to last for two weeks, but after six days it was called to a halt. Five of the prisoners had had to be sent home, with symptoms ranging from severe depression to psychosomatic skin rash. This left too few prisoners to continue; it also suggested that it might be dangerous to continue. Furthermore, the experiment had already made its point: In a very brief time, prison circumstances can radically affect the self-concept even of normal, well-balanced people who know that they are only participating in an experiment and will be released shortly. What then must be the effect of such circumstances on the self-concepts of people for whom the prison is for real?

need—all these physical factors will contribute to making you feel small and helpless. The self-concept, then, is to some degree the mirror of simple, measurable external factors.

Internal Variables

But let us reconsider for a moment the example we just looked at. Is is really *just* the physical circumstances at the registrar's office or the motor vehicle bureau that make you feel like a small, apologetic person? Think back to Gergen and Taylor's experiment with the naval recruits, described in Chapter 2. Was it really a voice of a superior officer issuing assignments that made the recruits' self-concepts shift in the direction of efficiency or affability?

The early behaviorists would have answered yes to all these questions. Because science could measure only the external variables, only the external variables could be taken into account as possible causes (Watson, 1924). However, as we found out in Chapter 1, behavioral psychology has, in the past thirty years, expanded into a broader perspective. Current behaviorists generally acknowledge the importance of cognitive (thought) processes (Bandura, 1977; Goldfried and Davison, 1976; Mahoney, 1974; Meichenbaum, 1977; Thoresen and Mahoney, 1974; O'Leary and Wilson, 1975). And they attempt to study these processes. In keeping with this theoretical shift, many psychologists now argue that the self-concept is determined not so much by external events as it is by our own private interpretation of these events: "It is not the environmental consequences *per se* which are of primary importance, but what [the person] says to himself about those consequences" (Meichenbaum and Cameron, 1974, p. 103). Or, as Shakespeare put it, "There is nothing either good or bad but thinking makes it so."

According to this view, it is not the long lines and the window-protected officials at the motor vehicle bureau that deflate your self-concept. It is the interpretation that you place on these external variables: "I don't count for much here."

The world affects us from the outside, but our interpretations of the world are the product of what we are on the inside. As a result of our learning history, we all carry within us a set of "person variables" (Mischel, 1973)—that is, highly individual styles of *thinking* about what happens to us (Chapter 1). And as we think, so will we feel (Beck, 1976; Ellis, 1973). Albert Ellis and Robert Harper (1978), major publicists of this theory, have conceptualized the process as a series labeled A-B-C: A (activating event) is cycled through B (the individual's belief system) and emerges as C (the emotional consequence). In other words, events don't lead directly to feelings about ourselves. Rather, events are filtered through our personal beliefs, and our feelings about ourselves come out at the other end. Thus, the shift in self-concept shown by Gergen and Taylor's naval recruits would not be the direct result of their new assignments; it would be the result of their feeding this information through their belief systems, which told them, "My personality should be suited to my job."

Negative Self-Talk and Irrational Beliefs

Unfortunately, many of our beliefs are quite irrational, which means that the A-B-C process can lead to mistaken and painful emotional conclusions. Let us look, for example, at a conversation between Albert Ellis and one of his clients. This client's problem was that he drank too much, felt guilty toward his wife for drinking too much, and then drank some more in order to forget his guilt.

Therapist: A (or what we call an Activating Event or Activating Experience), in this case, represents the fact that you've done badly and that your wife castigates you for your mistakes. And C (an Emotional Consequence) stands for the fact that you feel like a fool and keep drinking yourself into a stupor. You look at A, what seems her justifiable blame, and you look at C, what seems your own justifiable feeling of shame; and you say to yourself, "Well, A naturally leads to C. She rightly sees my behaving badly and blames me for this crummy behavior."

Mr. S.: Well, *doesn't* A lead to C in this case? Shouldn't I admit my mistakes and blame myself for them? How else will I ever change?

Therapist: No, A does not automatically lead to C, as you think it does. Rather, between A and C comes B—your Belief System about A. And B stems from your general philosophy of life . . . the philosophy that you *should* blame yourself (down or damn yourself as a total human) for doing the wrong thing, for making serious mistakes. Therefore, when your wife verbally rips you up at A, you *interpret* her criticism (at B) as accurate and you *agree* with her hypothesis that not only does your *behavior* stink but that *you* turn into a thorough stinker for behaving in that stinking way. You *then*, as a direct result of your Belief System (at B), bring about the Emotional Consequences you get (at C): including considering yourself hopeless (and) taking to drink (Ellis and Harper, 1978, pp. 119–120).

Ellis's tone is rather bossy, but he has a point. It would have been much more reasonable for Mr. S. to acknowledge that he had made serious mistakes and then simply to correct the mistakes as well as he could.

This would have eliminated both the unnecessary guilt and the drinking. But his beliefs got in the way.

In the same way, according to Ellis, many of us defeat ourselves via widely accepted but irrational beliefs. You may find this idea hard to accept. No one likes to think that his head is programed, particularly with mistaken notions that distort his perceptions. But if you listen carefully to what goes on in your mind, you will find that you do in fact carry on a mental conversation with yourself—what psychologists call *self-talk*—and that this conversation reflects a number of beliefs, many of them quite unreasonable. (Check yourself against the list in Box 4.2. How many times have you become very upset on the basis of one of these beliefs?)

Given, then, that we talk to ourselves, interpreting—often incorrectly—what we see around us. What does all this have to do with the task of finding variables that correlate with our negative self-labels? Simply this: the statements we make to ourselves should be considered prime suspects.

Imagine a woman who thinks she is unattractive. A married couple whom she knows (and who apparently do not think she is so unattractive) invite her to dinner so that she can meet a man they think she would like. As she drives to their house on that evening, the self-talk passes silently through her brain: "He won't like me. I'm ugly. And I can't stand to try to be charming, to try to make him like me, and then have him never call. Why should I try when I know it's not going to work? I can't take the rejection. I'll just stick with Marion in the kitchen." So she spends most of the evening in the kitchen with Marion, and the man, discouraged by her avoidance of him, never even has a chance to decide whether or not he likes her. He never calls, of course. (Why should he?) And because he doesn't call, her

---

BOX 4.2
IRRATIONAL BELIEFS: THE CLASSICS

According to Ellis (1958), most emotional disturbances, both "normal" and neurotic, are caused by irrational beliefs. The following are some of the most troublesome:

1. The idea that it is a dire necessity for an adult to be loved or approved by everyone for everything he does. . . .
2. The idea that certain acts are wrong, or wicked, or villainous, and that people who perform such acts should be severely punished. . . .
3. The idea that it is terrible, horrible, and catastrophic when things are not the way one would like them to be. . . .
4. The idea that much human unhappiness is externally caused and is forced on one by outside people and events. . . .
5. The idea that it is easier to avoid than to face life difficulties and self-responsibilities. . . .
6. The idea that one needs something other or stronger or greater than oneself on which to rely. . . .
7. The idea that one should be thoroughly competent, adequate, intelligent, and achieving in all possible respects. . . .
8. The idea that because something once strongly affected one's life, it should indefinitely affect it. . . .
9. The idea that it is vitally important to our existence what other people do, and that we should make great efforts to change them in the direction we would like them to be. . . .
10. The idea that one has virtually no control over one's emotions and that one cannot help feeling certain things.

Ellis, A. "Rational Psychotherapy," Journal of General Psychology, *59 (1958), 35–49.*

---

image of herself as unattractive is reinforced.

Here, and in most other cases of negative self-labeling, the independent variable that needs manipulating in order to change the self-concept is the person's self-talk, based on irrational beliefs—for example, that it's better not to try than to try and fail or that rejection is a catastrophe that cannot be endured. It is this self-talk that is maintaining the negative self-label. (The negative self-talk leads to self-defeating perceptions and behavior, which reinforce the negative self-talk, and so on—another circular relationship.) How we can change our negative self-labels by changing our self-talk is a subject we will deal with later in this chapter. First,

we have to prove to ourselves that the job is worth doing, that we're not just fooling ourselves into thinking we're better than we are. To convince ourselves of this truth, we need to look for possible flaws in the reasoning that led to our current style of self-talk. How did you decide that you were unloveable, stupid, spineless, lazy, or whatever your secret sin is? Let's see.

HOW YOU WERE FOUND GUILTY: A REVIEW IN THE COURT OF APPEALS

Imagine a courtroom. A criminal trial is going on. This is a rather unusual trial, however. All the jurors have already decided that the defendant is guilty. They knew it before the trial started. While the defense attorney tries to present the evidence of his client's innocence, the jurors tell jokes and read magazines. The defense attorney introduces exhibits x, y, and z, and the judge gets up and throws them in the wastebasket. Witnesses for the prosecution come in and testify: "I know he's the one, because he has shifty eyes," "I know he did it, because the president of the Chamber of Commerce told me he did," "I know he's guilty, because it's just the kind of thing he would do." The defense attorney is not allowed to cross-examine the witnesses. At last all the "evidence" is in. In his final instructions to the jury, the judge says, "Listen, if you have any trouble making your decision, just ask yourself: How does this person's behavior stack up against, say, Jesus Christ's?" The jurors confer for eight seconds and then they hand in their verdict: "Guilty."

How would you like to be the defendant in this trial? The truth is, you probably have been. We would be outraged if our society convicted people of crimes in this way. And yet most of us have convicted ourselves of crimes (stupidity, worthlessness, social incompetence, and so on) on the basis of procedures no more outrageous than those we have just described.

Fortunately, you have a second chance. You can appeal the conviction. So now you are a judge in the court of appeals, and your job is to review the transcript and decide whether your self was given a fair trial. Or, to put it in psychological terms, your job is to reexamine how you created your negative self-label and decide whether it was fairly arrived at. Was it based on realistic standards or on utterly impossible ideals? Did you weigh the information about yourself carefully, or did you bend it out of shape in order to make it fit with preconceived notions of your inadequacy?

Distortions and Denials

By definition, information that you have distorted or denied is no longer available to you in its original form. It has either been banished from your sight or mangled beyond recognition. But you can still reconsider decisions you have made about yourself in the past and ask yourself how accurate they were.

Imagine that as a college freshman, living away from home for the first time in your life, you panicked, became desperately homesick, returned home after one semester, and transferred to the local state college so that you could stay at home and commute to school. As a result of this experience, you created the self-label "chicken-hearted overdependent person" and installed it in the forefront of your self-concept. Now, three years later, it's still there. So reexamine the experience. What have you screened out? What evidence have you tossed in the wastebasket?

Well, as it happens, the time when you left to go to college was also a time when your younger sister was involved in some very self-destructive experiences with drugs, and you were quite upset over this. Needless to say, you had good reason to want to be home. Another interesting fact: you managed, in spite of your extreme misery during that first semester, to end up with a B average. Certainly this doesn't support your belief that you were a total failure that semester or that you can't achieve anything when you're on your own. Furthermore, perhaps you *were* an overdependent person three years ago, but are you still?

In other words, you must cross-examine yourself. Remember the powerful drive for cognitive consistency (Chapter 3). Our attention is selective; we tend to see only those things that fit our already-established beliefs. What doesn't fit, we ignore, screen out, or misinterpret. How many times have you mentally rejected a compliment ("He's just being nice," "She doesn't know what she's talking about") when you should have accepted it and felt good about yourself? How many times have you decided that you acted like a fool in a group of people, when no one present gave you any indication that he/she thought you were acting like a fool? How many times have you rationalized (that is, explained away) your achievements, so that they no longer looked like achievements? ("Oh, I only did well on that exam because the professor is an easy grader.") How many times have you jumped to unwarranted negative conclusions about yourself?

Picture the following scene. Two individuals, both of whom possess the *same* speaking skills, are asked on separate occasions to present a public speech. The two individuals differ in the degree to which they fear speaking in public: one has high speech-anxiety, while the other has low speech-anxiety. During each speaker's presentation some members of the audience walk out of the room. This elicits quite different self-statements or appraisals from the high and low speech-anxiety individuals. The high speech-anxiety individual is likely to say to himself: "I must be boring. How much longer do I have to speak? I knew I never could give a speech," and so forth. These self-statements produce anxiety and result in the very speech-anxiety behavior that the person fears (i.e., they become self-fulfilling prophecies). On the other hand, the low speech-anxiety individual is more likely to view the audience's departure as a sign of their rudeness or to attribute their leaving to external causes. He might say something like: "They must have a class to catch. Too bad they have to leave; they will miss a good talk" (Meichenbaum, 1975, p. 358).

It is possible, of course, that the second

For many people, speaking in front of an audience is an anxiety-provoking experience. Self-talk can either relieve or increase the anxiety. (Sepp Seitz/Magnum)

speaker was giving himself a break. (Who knows? Maybe his speech *was* boring.) But when was the last time you gave yourself a break in interpreting ambiguous feedback? Keep in mind the fact, proven in numerous psychological studies (for example, Shrauger and Terbovic, 1976), that people with low self-esteem tend consistently to underrate their performances. If you have a strong negative self-label, then you fall into this low self-esteem category. So rerate your performances, past and present, with an eye toward raising your score. Don't worry about giving yourself too many extra points. They probably couldn't equal the number of points you've lost through denying and distorting the evidence that should have been in your favor.

Faulty Categorizing

"I know he's guilty, because it's just the kind of thing he would do," said one of the witnesses for the prosecution. How many kinds of things do you imagine yourself capable of doing? As we learned in Chapter 3, an important feature of the positive self-concept is a broad image of the self. The positive self-concept contains a wide variety of mental categories, so that the person can organize, assimilate, and—most important—accept many different kinds of information about herself. If the categories of the self-concept are too few, then they become too general ("I am neurotic," "I am not too bright"), and this encourages negative self-labeling.

To see how this process works, let's look back at Larry's self-concept. At the center of his image of himself are two enormously broad categories: social incompetence and academic excellence. The second category may be fairly accurate. The first category, on the other hand, looks very suspicious. After all, hasn't Larry admitted (in the excerpt in Chapter 2) that he has friends—close friends? Making and keeping friends are not academic activities; they are social activities, and tremendously important ones. Thus Larry is not a total social incompetent. In fact, his social behavior is maladjusted in only one respect (admittedly an important one): he is afraid of meeting and interacting with women in social situations. Thus, his discomfort at parties should be filed under a more specific self-concept category, entitled "Social Fear of Women." As long as he sticks with the huge, vague, inaccurate category "Social Incompetence," he will get nowhere, because this category not only deprives him of credit for his areas of social competence but also fails to specify any actual emotions or behaviors on which he could go to work in order to solve his problem. The result is that his negative label is self-perpetuating.

As you review the history of your negative self-label, check to see if you have made this same mistake. If, for example, you consider yourself timid, ask yourself whether you're timid in every respect—with friends, with instructors, with the opposite sex, with your parents. (Are you physically timid as well? Are you afraid to pet a big dog, dive off a diving board, ski down a hill?) You will probably find that your self-label needs to be chopped up. If so, then go ahead and chop. Your self-concept will be better off for it. To be timid is one thing. To be timid in front of your father and your instructors (that is, authority figures) is another thing altogether, much less shameful and much more subject to change.

If you divide your general self-labels into a number of specific self-labels, you will come to accept the fact that human behavior, including yours, does not come in black or white, but rather in shades of gray. Furthermore, it contains many contradictions. Walt Whitman had an answer to this problem:

Do I contradict myself?
Very well then I contradict myself.
(I am large, I contain multitudes.)

You contain multitudes, too, and once you have created in your mind a corresponding multitude of self-categories, you will be able to perceive yourself more accurately. If you spend a whole semester playing bridge with your friends and end up with a D average, you can file this information properly. For example, it might go under "I have a terrible weakness for bridge," "I sometimes avoid challenges out of fear of failure," and "I am capable of making stupid decisions"—none of which is totally self-condemning and all of which invite efforts at improvement. You will *not* file your D average under "I am worthless," a self-category that (besides being untrue) is vague, discouraging, unworkable, and therefore self-perpetuating.

Old Standards

To go back to the question the judge put to the jury: How *does* your behavior measure up against Jesus Christ's? And while we're at it, how does your physical grace compare with Muhammad Ali's? How does your intelligence look next to Einstein's? How does your batting average stack up against George Brett's? Probably not too well. (For other people to compare yourself to, see Box 4.3.) If you are bothered by this—or by the fact that your society or your friends might not approve of everything you do—then it's time to reexamine the standards you have used in evaluating yourself.

Perfectionism

A negative self-label, by definition, is a statement to yourself that you've failed to live up to your standards. What about the standards by which you've condemned yourself? Are they realistic? Are they appropriate for you as an individual? Was there ever any chance of your measuring up to them?

Imagine that your standard for yourself is that you should always be "cool." This means that you should invariably have the right thing to say (preferably witty), that you should never be embarrassed or tongue-tied, that you should never stumble over your feet, that you should never spill your coffee all over your blouse (especially on a date), that you should know "when to press your leg up against hers and how to take it away without wondering whether she's wondering why you took it away," that you should never have to sneeze into your hand for lack

Will he drop that Coke in his lap? If so, he loses his "cool." (Bob Comas/Rapho/Photo Researchers, Inc.)

of a Kleenex, and that—God forbid—no one should ever have to tell you that your fly is unzipped. Well, what does this have to do with human existence? Nothing whatsoever. It is an impossible ideal. Furthermore, there is some question as to whether it is even an attractive ideal. After all, a person who is always so completely in control of himself and of the situation would seem to lack the emotional vulnerability necessary for human intimacy.

Yet many people label themselves "jerks" (to use Larry's term) because they fail to live up to their standard of Mr. or Ms. Cool. Other people label themselves as inadequate because they fail to meet their standards of perfect intelligence, perfect generosity, perfect honesty, a perfect figure, or a perfect something else. In short, the result of a per-

BOX 4.3
HOW TO MAKE YOURSELF MISERABLE

Comic writer Dan Greenburg (1966) has put together what he calls a "vital training manual," *How to Make Yourself Miserable,* designed to help its readers attain "the elusive and much sought-after goal of Total Personal Misery." In the section on evaluating your accomplishments in life, he offers the following exercise:

Compare yourself with these four ordinary people who were chosen at random.

Twenty-six-year-old patent office clerk, A. Einstein, formulated theory of relativity.

Swedish singer, Jenny Lind, was so popular that men paid $653.00 per seat to see her.

Youthful piano player, W. A. Mozart, had already composed his first symphony and three sets of sonatas by the age of eight.

Civil servant, Abdullah al-Salim of Kuwait, receives a salary of $7,280,000 per week. Every two hours and forty minutes he earns the equivalent of the average American's lifetime income.

Source: Greenburg, D., with Jacobs, M. How to Make Yourself Miserable. *New York: Random House, 1966, p. 51.*

fectionistic standard is self-contempt. (Another common result is contempt for others. After all, you're not the only one who can't live up to such a standard.)

People who hold perfectionistic standards often realize that this causes them unhappiness, but they are willing to pay the price for what they feel is improved performance. If they weren't perfectionists, they reason, they would slip down to second-rate. Research suggests that they are mistaken. Recent studies of insurance agents (Burns, 1980a,b), advanced gymnasts and racquetball players (Mahoney and Avener, 1977; Meyers et al., 1979), and law school students (Beck and Burns, 1979) have all indicated that those who punish themselves mentally for less-than-perfect performance tend to do *worse*, not better, than those who forgive themselves for mistakes and bad days.

As we learned in Chapter 2, all of us secretly contemplate an ideal self. But the ideal self should function as a helpful guide for our behavior and as a pleasurable fantasy into which we can escape periodically. It should *not* function as a tyrant, constantly cracking the whip over us, constantly "putting us down." So take a close look at the standard that generated your negative self-label. Was it reasonable? Did it allow for errors? Did you expect never to lose your temper with your children? Was it essential to get an A on every exam? Did you imagine that, unlike most other people, you would never have too much to drink and find yourself in a compromising position with someone you didn't even particularly like?

If your self-ideal, upon cross-examination, turns out to be tyrannical and inflexible, then it's time to adjust both your standards and the negative self-label that they generated. Set realistic goals. Take your ideal self with a grain of salt. Learn to forgive yourself for failing. Rejoin the human race. If you still feel that trying and failing is a disgrace,

you might consider the words of Fritz Perls, the founder of Gestalt psychotherapy:

> I love all the imperfect meetings of target and arrow that miss the bull's eye to the right and to the left, above and below. I love all the attempts that fail in a thousand ways. There is but one bull's-eye and a thousand good wills. . . . Perfectionism is a curse, and a strain. . . . Don't be afraid of mistakes. Mistakes are not sins. Mistakes are ways of doing something different, perhaps creatively new. (Perls, 1972)

Conventionality

Perfectionism is one way of worshiping false gods; conventionality is another:

> Many people regard cultural values as absolutes and have never paused to consider their relativity. They are entirely molded by the culture and assimilate all its contradictions. Conventionality is seen as extremely important rather than superficial, and folkways and mores are considered anything but perfunctory. Thus, millions of people are capable of justifying bloody warfare but not masturbation. (Lazarus, 1971, p. 171)

Our society has an important influence on the self-concept. We internalize social norms and then judge ourselves accordingly. Thus, a man might label himself "effeminate" because he tends to cry during sad movies. Likewise, a married woman who loves her husband might secretly label herself a "whore" because ten years ago she had a single brief adulterous episode. In both cases the standard generating the negative self-label is a social standard.

Before we turn over to society the right to tell us whether we're good or bad, worthy or worthless, we have to ask ourselves whether our society is infallible. For hundreds of years a substantial segment of our society considered black people good for picking cotton and not much more. For many more hundreds of years it was an accepted belief in Western societies that if a woman worried her "pretty little head" too much about intellectual matters, she was unattractive, not too normal, and possibly dangerous; her little head was no longer pretty. Needless to say, if George Washington Carver or Madame Curie had allowed such social values to interfere with their self-concepts, our world would be poorer for it.

This is not to say that social standards are always incorrect—only that they are not always correct. They are relative to time and place. They have changed and will change again. They are not carved in stone. Hence, we must decide for ourselves which social standards we will adhere to and which ones we will ignore. Should a man of sixty-five who enjoys sex label himself a "dirty old man" because our society presumes that sex is for the young? Should a married woman label herself "selfish" or "odd" if she and her husband decide not to have children? Should a man label himself "worthless" because he cannot find a job?

In rethinking the origins of your negative self-label, ask yourself what social standards, unquestioningly accepted as eternal truths, might be lurking behind it. Examine these standards rigorously. (Why *shouldn't* a man cry during a sad movie?) If they don't survive the questioning, then your negative self-label needs revision.

What the Other Guy Thinks

Said the witness: "I know he did it, because the president of the Chamber of Commerce told me he did." We may consider this absurd. Equally absurd is our habit of allowing our self-esteem to stand or fall on the basis of other people's judgments of us. All of us desire approval, particularly from people we

For many teenaged boys, sports are as much a contest for approval as they are a source of pleasure. (© Jim Anderson/Woodfin Camp & Assoc.)

love and respect. But too much reliance on the approval of others can do great damage to the self-concept. In the first place, you can never really know what other people think of you. Furthermore, their opinions change. Therefore, if you rely on their approval in order to start liking yourself, you are doomed to wait eternally, for their approval will never be absolute or final. Second, other people, even the ones you most respect, are not always right in their judgments of you. And why, after all, should their opinion of you count for more than yours? Third, to quote Abraham Lincoln's old chestnut, "You cannot please all the people all the time." If you try to do so, you will end up with a severely fragmented self: one piece molded to the standards of person x, another piece designed to please person y, another piece fashioned to win the approval of person z. In other words, you will have given your self away (Moustakas, 1974).

Of course, there is nothing wrong with seeking and enjoying the approval of others, just as there is nothing wrong with respecting cultural values or setting high standards for yourself. The question again is: How much? According to many psychologists (for example, Ellis, 1958), the constant craving for approval—and the self-condemnation that results when that craving is not satisfied—is a major cause of emotional maladjustment. This type of problem may be particularly common in large technological societies such as our own. Sociologist David Riesman (1950) argues that because of the constant shifting of social values in such societies (see Chapter 1), the individual is unable to construct a firm set of internal expectations as to how he should behave. Hence, he becomes "other-directed," constantly looking to those around him to tell him what he should be and do.

How "other-directed" have you been? Say to yourself the words of your negative self-label: "I am a loser because I am still a virgin at age twenty"; "I am a failure because I don't make enough money"; "I am insensi-

tive because I get bored listening to my roommate's constant problems." Do you hear in the background some familiar voice? Who informed you that all self-respecting people have lost their virginity by age twenty? Your sister? Who told you you *should* make more money? Your father-in-law? Who gave you the idea that you *should* always listen to your friends' problems with interest and sympathy? Your friends? By placing too much faith in the opinions of others, you condemn yourself to sweat and strain eternally under the "tyranny of the should" (Horney, 1950)—the constant feeling that you are not quite measuring up, that your behavior never quite fills the bill. And this feeling of course translates into negative self-labels.

So examine the "shoulds" on which your negative self-label is based. Are they yours, or are they someone else's? If they are someone else's, why are you still punishing yourself emotionally for not obeying them? What would happen if you discarded these "shoulds"? Would your mother be disappointed in you? Would your friends laugh at you? If so, would this be a catastrophe? Just as learning to make mistakes helps heal the self-concept, so does learning to endure the disapproval of others. If you consult your-

ACTIVITY 4.2

As an exercise in pinpointing the source of negative self-labels, do the following. On a given day, write down every self-critical thought that crosses your mind. At the end of the day, review the list and for each self-critical thought, write a brief answer to the following three questions. First, what is the standard (perfectionism, conventionality, other people's judgments, etc.) on which this self-criticism is based? Second, from whom do you think you picked up this standard? Third, do you really subscribe to the standard wholeheartedly? You may find that many of your self-criticisms are simply knee-jerk reactions, based on standards you don't really believe in when you think about them carefully.

self, first and foremost, as to what you should be—or, better yet, want to be—some people will admire you, some people will like you, some people will get angry at you, and, now and then, somebody might even go so far as to hate you. Teach yourself to live with this. For if you don't consult yourself, you may find eventually that you no longer have any self to consult. Instead, you will have only a collection of other people's "shoulds," each of them trailing an accusatory label.

CHANGING THE SELF-CONCEPT

As we said in Chapter 3, the self-concept is not an objective, factual report on the self. Rather, it is a subjective vision. It is a prophecy of what we will be and an unconscious commitment to fulfill that prophecy. Well, the prophecy can be changed. We have just reviewed the forces that influenced and changed it in the past. If the self-concept that has emerged from this process contains negative labels—prophecies of inadequacy

---

BOX 4.4
PERFECTING NEGATIVE SELF-TALK

In *How to Make Yourself Miserable* Dan Greenburg (1966) gives instructions on perfecting your negative self-talk in a number of specific situations. Here are his suggestions for making yourself miserable in two ordinary situations:

Basic Worries About Giving and Receiving Gifts

When buying a gift for somebody, worry about the following:

(1) They already have one.
(2) Not only do they already have one, but they hate it.
(3) The gift they're getting me will be much more expensive and mine will look cheap next to theirs.
(4) They're not getting me anything at all.
(5) They'll get me something I already have, or something I hate, and when I go to the store to return it I'll run into them at the exchange counter.

Basic Worries About Waiting

What to think about while waiting for the results of a job interview:

(1) I asked for too much money.
(2) I asked for too little money.
(3) I appeared too eager.
(4) I didn't appear eager enough.
(5) I don't deserve such a good job.

What to think about while waiting for someone who's late for an appointment:

(1) I'm waiting in the wrong place.
(2) An emergency came up at the last minute, they can't make it, and they don't know how to reach me.
(3) They probably aren't coming. They probably never intended to come.
(4) Everybody who passes by knows how long I've been waiting and is laughing at me.
(5) I was a little late myself and they've already been here and gone.

Source: Greenburg, D., with Jacobs, M. How to Make Yourself Miserable. *New York, Random House, 1966, pp. 20–21.*

and failure—we can subject the self-concept to new and healthier influences. How this is done will be the subject of the rest of this chapter.

Setting the Goal

The first step is to set a goal. Look again at your description of your negative self-label. Then write down a brief description of how you would like to behave instead. Make sure that this goal is free of perfectionism, excessive conventionality, and overconcern about other people's approval. And as with the other descriptions you have written, try to make it simple, objective, and specific. Larry's goal description, for example, might read something like this:

I want to get up the courage to go to parties again. And when I'm there I want to be able to relax and talk to people and have a good time—not hang around in a dark corner feeling self-conscious. Most of all, I want to be able to go up to a woman and talk to her without practically having a heart attack. I want to sit and have a conversation with her without worrying constantly about whether she likes me. If she doesn't like me—or if I don't like her (how about that!)—then I find somebody else. But if she does like me and if I like her, then I would like to ask her out, and then go out with her, and then ask her out again, and so on. (Maybe other women too.) And then I wouldn't have to spend all my Saturday nights at home pretending that I think the extra-credit reading in political science is far more interesting than women.

Getting New Information

The next step in changing your negative self-label is to look for new information about yourself in this area. Most of us avoid seeking out information about aspects of ourselves that we dislike. We're afraid of what we will find. But if you are going to change your self-concept, you need proof, in the form of information, that the change is justified. So go out and look for it.

Work up the courage to ask other people for feedback on your looks, your intelligence, your conversational abilities, or whatever it is that you feel is your weak point. Look in the mirror. Listen to yourself as you talk. Watch how others respond to you. And as you look and listen, force yourself to endure cognitive dissonance. In fact, you should pay the closest attention to any information that makes you uncomfortable because it seems to you inconsistent and confusing. This is a good sign that the information you're getting is violating the preconceived notions that make up your self-concept. When this happens, resist the drive toward cognitive consistency. Don't screen out or distort the information. Look at it squarely. In doing so, you will be playing the part of the good scientist, who considers *all* the evidence, not just the evidence that supports his hypothesis. This is how scientists find the truth, and it is how you will find it.

Imagine, for example, that Larry's roommate, Sal, has a girlfriend named Nancy. One day at school Larry runs into Nancy. She tells him that the staff of the college paper, for which she writes, is having a party on Friday night, and she suggests that he drop in. He suddenly feels somewhat embarrassed and confused, and he picks up the signal. Ordinarily, he would simply have concluded that she felt sorry for him or that she was willing to endure having him at the party in the hope of getting him to write for the paper. But now he forces himself to hold in his mind, without distorting it or even interpreting it, the fact that Nancy has asked him to come to the party. He returns to his apartment and walks over to the mirror: "My ears stick out a bit, but no one has ever said anything about it. And I *do* have a nice smile. Maybe, maybe . . ." That night Larry is reading in the kitchen when Sal walks in. Suddenly Larry, very embarrassed, asks Sal a question:

Larry: Sal, if you were a girl and I came up to you at a party and sort of made conversation, do you think you'd like me?

Sal: If I were one kind of girl I might love you, and if I were another kind of girl I might not. There are lots of kinds of girls. But what do you care? I thought you only wanted your professors to like you.

Larry: You seriously think that some girls might think I'm attractive?

Sal: Sure. Why not?

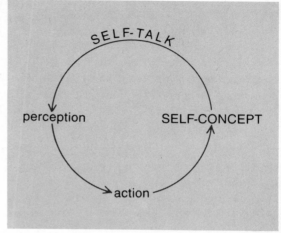

Figure 4.1 The circular relationship of self-concept, perception, and action. The relationship is mediated by self-talk.

Cognitive Restructuring: New Self-Talk

The gathering of new information about the part of yourself that you dislike will prepare you for the final step in changing your self-concept—that is, *cognitive restructuring,* or changing your self-talk. Earlier in this chapter we said that our self-concept and our perceptions and actions exist in a circular relationship, mediated by our self-talk (see Figure 4.1). We talk to ourselves in a way that is consistent with our self-concept ("I'm too much of a jerk for that girl over there to be interested in me"). The self-talk then molds our perceptions ("That's why she won't look my way"). The perception, in turn, molds our actions ("So I'll just stay here in the corner"). And the action, in turn, reinforces the self-concept ("What a jerk! Here I come to a party and all I do is stand alone in a corner").

But, as we said earlier, the circle can be broken. The best place to do this is at the moment when the self-concept is sending out its message to the organs of perception—

that is, at the moment when self-talk begins. This is not to say that we will interrupt the self-talk and cut it off. On the contrary, we will listen to it very carefully (Meichenbaum, 1977). And then we will talk back to it on the basis of reason and reality.

Don't forget: our self-talk is not gospel. Rather, it is a collection of sentences that we have internalized in the course of our past experiences. By saying new sentences to ourselves, we simply initiate a new experience. As our new sentences are internalized, they will replace the old ones. And as a result, more positive and realistic self-labels will come to replace our negative and self-defeating labels. Let's examine the procedure.

Listening to Self-Talk

Catch yourself at a moment when you're feeling bad about yourself. Instead of just sitting there and suffering passively, listen to your self-talk. What are you saying to yourself to make yourself feel so miserable?

ACTIVITY 4.3

As an exercise in learning to hear your own self-talk, do the following. Force yourself to perform some action that would normally cause you anxiety, such as speaking up in class or asking someone for a loan. After doing so, write down what you said to yourself before, during, and after the discomforting action. Then, being as objective as possible, examine the statements to see how realistic they were.

Mentally enunciate the words in clear, plain English.

Talking Back

Now cross-examine yourself on the statement that you've just enunciated in your mind. What is the evidence to support your self-statement? Could the evidence be interpreted in any other way? (Are you absolutely sure that she invited you to the party because she felt sorry for you?) Stick to raw reality and use it to combat preconceived ideas. Stick to reason and use it to combat unreason.

Acting on Your Back-Talk

If your old self-talk breaks down under cross-examination, then force yourself to perceive and to act on the basis of the arguments that broke it down. ("Since there's no good evidence that she's feeling sorry for me—she never seemed to feel sorry for me before—then maybe she really wants me to come to the party. Okay, I'll go. Maybe I'll meet someone.") Your altered perceptions and actions cannot help but be more positive and rewarding than those generated by your old negative self-talk. And these rewards will encourage you to go on giving yourself positive back-talk. Thus, the old vicious

cycle will be replaced by a benign one: rational self-talk leading to realistic perception leading to self-fulfilling action leading to positive self-concept leading to rational self-talk—and so on, around the circle again.

This will not happen overnight. Years of negative self-talk cannot be erased in a few hours of reasonable back-talk. But eventually the old negative sentences will have to give way in the face of new, more positive experiences resulting from your back-talk. This method has proved effective in increasing creative thinking (Meichenbaum and Cameron, 1974); relieving fears of exams, of public speaking, and of other people (Cooley and Spiegler, 1980; Kanter and Goldfried, 1979; Meichenbaum et al., 1971; Linehan, Goldfried, and Goldfried, 1979); and in combating a variety of ordinary emotional problems such as drinking and marital strain (Ellis and Harper, 1978). It can also be effective with your self-concept. After all, the various problems that we just listed invariably involve negative self-labels.

The Results

One result of using cognitive restructuring on yourself is that you will simply feel better. And that is all to the good. However, there is something even more important involved—the matter of freedom. The endless progression of negative self-statements, distorted perceptions, and self-defeating actions forms a chain that can bind you hand and foot. Once you break this chain, you become free to assess your life more objectively and to make more reasonable decisions. Instead of constantly "backing into" life, pulled into the future while your mind is still oriented toward the self-definitions of the past, you can turn your face forward and see where you are going. Then you can enjoy the reward of freedom: the ability to

---

BOX 4.5
SELF-CONCEPT AND TENNIS

As a result of growing interest in recent years, over 30 million Americans now face one another across the nets as they slug it out on the nation's tennis courts. According to Nathan Cobb, Alvin Kahn, and Stanley Cath (1977), most of these people do not play as well as they could, because their self-image gets in the way. As these three psychologists see it, people carry their self-image onto the court and often spend more time trying to score points in a struggle with their views of themselves than in the contest with their opponents. For these people, tennis is not so much a game, played for exercise and fun, as it is a battle to prove their own self-worth.

To a tennis player who needs to justify herself on the court, her performance becomes a measure of her emotional state. Off-court insecurities and negative self-labels surface in a game. The insecure player is threatened by every successful volley by her opponent, destroyed by every mistake of her own. She condemns herself for her failure to return an easy forehand and curses her lousy backhand. To worsen matters, each failure carries over to the next volley, causing her to think more about the last play than what she is currently doing. This distracting interference makes her play even more poorly. The whole episode often turns into a nightmare of mistakes and self-condemnation, with the crushed player finally leaving the court in a state of total self-negation.

Cobb, Kahn, and Cath make several suggestions to the tennis player (or competitor of any sort) in dealing with these self-concept problems. They recommend that you not play at all on days when you feel unsettled and your self-image isn't very positive. When you do play, stop and ask yourself if your last mistake was such a big deal. Was missing that overhead such a disaster? Recognize that mistakes don't mean the end of the world, or even of your tennis career. Forget the previous point. Let each new volley be a whole new beginning. Start over fresh each time. Don't brood about the last point, successful or unsuccessful. If you find yourself getting upset, take a break. Stop and relax before continuing. Aim your aggression toward your opponent, not yourself. He's the one you're trying to beat, not you. Don't spend a lot of time analyzing your thoughts or motives. Instead of focusing on what is going on in your head, figure out how to beat your opponent.

While these suggestions won't cure a negative self-concept or eliminate a sense of insecurity about yourself, they will help you function better in sports. Thus, a good source of exercise and pleasure won't turn into an occasion for further demolition of a shaky self-concept.

generate your own personal goals and move toward them, rather than struggling endlessly with what you were told was naughty or nice in another time and another place.

THE SELF-CONCEPT UNDER REVISION: A SAMPLE SCRIPT

It is eleven o'clock on Friday night. The party has been going on for two hours, but Larry is still at home reading. He can't concentrate, however. All he can think of is the party. A furious battle is going on in his mind between his old self-talk and his new self-talk.

OLD TALK: *You'll end up in the corner again. Nancy may come over and talk to you for a few minutes, because she feels sorry for you, but then she'll slip away. And then you'll be alone. Your face will get all sweaty, and people will see it. They'll know how nervous you are—what a jerk you are, what a loser.*

NEW TALK: *Who cares what Nancy feels or what Nancy does? Nancy is* Sal's *girlfriend. You want to meet a girl and tonight there's a party where girls are sitting around, and you've been invited. Go, you dummy. There's just a chance that this time it will be different. And if it isn't, what have you lost? You can't concentrate on that book anyway.*

This kind of talk and back-talk goes on for another half hour. Finally, the back-talk wins. Larry decides to go. He gets up, puts on his jacket, and leaves. He is scared stiff; he is thinking he should have worn a different shirt; he is sure the party is over by now. But he keeps walking toward the address that Nancy gave him. He arrives at the party, gets himself a beer, says hello to Nancy and Sal, and then, as usual, gravitates toward a dark corner of the room. Alone, he watches the others. Except for Nancy and Sal, there

is not a single familiar face in the room. Then one strange face suddenly starts to look familiar. It is a woman who was in his sociology course last semester. She is sitting alone on a couch. Larry watches her from his corner. The old talk and the new talk resume their battle.

OLD TALK: *Forget it. She's too good looking. Her date's probably in the bathroom and will be back any second. Even if she's not with a date, she's looking for somebody better-looking and more relaxed than you.*

NEW TALK: *Is she carrying a sign saying what kind of man she's waiting to meet? No. You have absolutely no proof that she wouldn't like you. Give her date exactly one minute to get back from the bathroom. If no date appears, you're going up to her. The time is now.*

The minutes passes. She is still alone, gazing across the room. Nervous and sweating already, Larry forces himself to go over and sit down next to her.

He: Hi. I remember you from the Social Problems class.

She: I remember you, too. You're Mr. Fallon. I saw you come in.

He: I'll tell you what. You don't have to call me Mr. Fallon. My first name is Larry.

She: I have a cousin Larry. (*She giggles.*)

OLD TALK: *What a dumb remark. She doesn't know what to say. She's trying to get rid of me.*

NEW TALK: *But she's smiling. And she remembered me. She even noticed me when I came in.*

He: Well, what's your cousin Larry like?

She: He's awful.

THE SELF-CONCEPT: HOW TO CHANGE IT

OLD TALK: *She hates me. God, get me out of here. Why did I ever do this? Tonight she's going to have a good laugh with her friends telling them how she got stuck on a couch with a jerk named Larry Fallon.*

NEW TALK: *But she's still smiling. And if she really thinks I'm as awful as Cousin Larry, then in a minute she'll say she has to go get a drink, and then she'll disappear into the crowd. And if she does, so what? I'll find somebody else. Or I'll go home and try again in three years.*

He: I'll bet you've grossly misjudged your cousin Larry. I'll bet he's a really sensitive person with a beautiful mind. I'll bet he even has a closetful of really great clothes that he never wears when you're around because you don't appreciate him.

She: (*laughing*) My name is Fran. Do you have a cousin Fran?

He: No, but I have an Aunt Fran. She has warts all over her face and wears a red wig. (*She laughs.*)

OLD TALK: *Now she probably thinks I'm really weird.*

NEW TALK: *What difference does it make? She laughed, didn't she? Ask her if she wants another beer.*

OLD TALK: *If I ask her if she wants another beer, she'll have to decide whether she wants to be stuck with me while she drinks the whole beer. Why put her to the test? She'll probably say she's just seen a friend she has to talk to, and so long, good to see you again. And then I'll go back to my corner.*

NEW TALK: *If she leaves, I don't have to go back to my corner. Nothing awful will have happened. Besides that, I want another beer.*

He: I'm thirsty. Do you want another beer?

She: No thanks. I've had enough.

He: Okay. I'll be back in a minute. (*He walks across the room to the beer keg.*)

OLD TALK: *What a dumb move. I was right—she doesn't want to sit with me through another beer. I insulted her with the stupid joke about Aunt Fran. She's gone by now. She's across the room, talking to someone else. About me, I'll bet. Don't turn around and see her gone. Just walk away. Go into the bathroom and rest. If you walk away, then you've rejected her. But if you turn around and she's gone, then she's rejected you.*

NEW TALK: *She laughed at the Aunt Fran bit. Maybe she's just not thirsty. Maybe she's sitting there looking at my back. And if I walk away, what will she think? And why walk away, when what I really want to do is go back and talk to her? Take the chance. Turn around. There's at least a fifty-fifty chance she's still there. TURN AROUND!* (*He turns around. She is still there. He heads back toward her, trying to look very casual. He sits down next to her again.*)

She: You know, I've been thinking about your Aunt Fran. I've taken a lot of psychology courses, and the psychologists say that you can develop physical problems from having emotional problems. I'll bet your Aunt Fran got those warts because her nephew Larry was so hostile toward her. And then she got so upset over the warts that her hair fell out and she had to get a red wig. Such a shame. Particularly when you consider how beautiful she was before . . .

He: (*laughs*) I don't have an Aunt Fran. Do you really have a cousin Larry?

She: Yes, and he really *is* awful. But his last name isn't Fallon.

OLD TALK: *She's telling me she likes me. After three minutes of conversation she's telling me she* likes *me. She must be a loser. She must be desperate. Look, she has acne scars. She's desperate.*

NEW TALK: *You have acne scars too, dummy. And she doesn't look desperate. She looks completely relaxed. And she's good-looking even with acne scars.*

OLD TALK: *But if she likes me, what do I do? Do I have to take her home? What am I going to do with a girl who likes me? If I lay a hand on her, she'll probably scream. What have I gotten myself into?*

NEW TALK: *You've gotten yourself into a three-minute conversation with a girl. You haven't promised to marry her. So just talk to her. Worry later about taking her home.*

OLD TALK: *Maybe she's going home with somebody else.*

NEW TALK: *Maybe she isn't.*

Larry and Fran talk, mostly about their courses, for about an hour. By then it is one o'clock in the morning.

She: I have to go. I was up till two this morning. If I don't get some sleep pretty soon, I'm going to have to check into the hospital.

He: Okay. Good night. Good to see you again. (*She starts collecting her purse, sweater, and so on.*)

OLD TALK: *You've bored her to tears. She's sorry she came to the party. She's going to go back to her apartment and tell her roommate what a loser she got stuck with at the party. She was too polite just to get up and find somebody else. So she sat for an hour with a loser.*

NEW TALK: *She didn't act bored. Stop worrying about what she says to her roommate. What do you care about her roommate? Tell her you'll walk her home.*

OLD TALK: *I can't. I just can't. I'd have to decide whether to put my arm around her while we're walking. I'd have to decide*

what to do at the door. I just can't deal with that tonight. I can't deal with her alone out there in the dark. I have to stay in this room, where there are people, where it's safe.

NEW TALK: *Okay. Compromise. Ask her for her phone number.*

She: (*hesitating*) Well, goodnight. (*She keeps fooling around with her purse.*)

He: Listen, why don't you give me your phone number? If you're not in the hospital, maybe we could have coffee some day next week.

She: (*smiling*) That would be nice. (*She writes her phone number on a paper napkin and gives it to him.*)

He: I'll give you a call during the week. Be nice to your cousin Larry in the meantime.

She: (*laughs*) Goodnight.

He: Goodnight. (*She leaves and Larry sits there finishing his beer.*)

OLD TALK: *I should have walked her home. I'm a jerk. Any other guy in this room, if he had been in my position, would have walked her home. I blew it. I completely blew it. I chickened out.*

NEW TALK: *Okay, you chickened out of walking her home. But you managed to get her phone number. How much do you expect to change in one night? And what does it matter what any other guy in this room would have done? You did a lot. You talked to her; you got her phone number; she even acted as though she wanted to have coffee with you. And you got through a whole party without going into the bathroom to rest. Congratulations.*

Larry goes back to his apartment, undresses, and gets into bed.

OLD TALK: *For a whole hour we talked about school. She's a bookworm, too. She's a jerk just like me.*

NEW TALK: *Just because she likes school, does that make her a jerk?*

OLD TALK: *I'm into schoolwork, and I'm a jerk.*

NEW TALK: *You* think *you're a jerk. But it's not because you're a good student. You like* being *a good student. You think you're a jerk because you can't meet girls. And now you met a girl.*

OLD TALK: *What if she doesn't remember who I am when I call? I shouldn't call. She won't know who I am.*

NEW TALK: *How is she going to forget who you are in two days' time? The worst thing that can possibly happen is that she will turn you down flat. And she didn't look as though she meant to do that. In fact, she looked as though she wanted you to walk her home. All that fumbling with her purse and taking so long to leave. She* liked *you.*

After four days, Larry, now very scared and furiously engaging in positive self-talk, calls her up and asks her out for coffee. To his very great surprise, she accepts.

OLD TALK: *But if I take her out for coffee and she* still *likes me, what do I do with her then?*

NEW TALK: *You'll figure out something.*

OUTLINE: CHANGING THE SELF-CONCEPT

A. Analyzing the problem:
1. Isolate the basic problem label.
2. Describe your problem in situational terms.
3. Search for correlations, watching out especially for negative self-talk.
4. Review the background of your problem to check for such causes as:
   a. Distortions and denials.
   b. Faulty categorizing.
   c. Perfectionism.
   d. Conventionality.
   e. Other people's judgments.

B. Changing the self-concept:
1. Set a goal.
2. Gather new information about this aspect of yourself.
3. Engage in cognitive restructuring:
   a. Listen to your old self-talk.
   b. Talk back to this old self-talk, cross-examining it to get at the reality.
   c. Act on your back-talk, substituting new behavior to accompany your new, more rational self-talk.

SUMMARY

1. Although analyzing the self-concept is a rather subtle matter, it can be done if we stick closely to external situations and behavior and if we proceed methodically. Our method of analysis involves the same procedure described in Chapter 2: *description* and *functional analysis.*

2. In the description, we detail the negative self-label and the situations that give rise to it. In the functional analysis, we look for correlations between the negative self-label and various internal and exter-

nal variables. Particularly important is the internal variable of negative *self-talk*, along with any irrational beliefs on which this self-talk is based.

3. In order to understand how the negative self-label arose, we need to reexamine our interpretations of past experience. Keeping in mind the theory of cognitive consistency, we should look for *distortions* and *denials* of information inconsistent with the negative self-label. Furthermore, we should look for *faulty categorizing* of information, and recategorize that information.

4. A critical examination of our old standards is also appropriate, since many of us generate unrealistic or inappropriate expectations for ourselves. We tend to demand perfection in ourselves, which leads us to criticize ourselves constantly for not achieving it. By following social values too slavishly, we allow *conventionality* to rule our lives. We may also rely too much on what other people think about us.

5. In changing a negative self-label, we can begin by setting for ourselves a realistic goal. Next, we gather new information about ourselves by talking to others, asking for feedback, and forcing ourselves to tolerate feedback that is inconsistent with the negative self-label.

6. After gathering new information, the final step in changing a negative self-label is *cognitive restructuring*—that is, changing our self-talk. This is accomplished by listening to negative self-statements, cross-examining ourselves on these statements, and then talking back to ourselves in a more realistic and positive way. Finally, as the negative ideas are broken down by our cross-examination, we should act on our back-talk. This will lead to more rewarding experiences, which will reinforce the new positive self-talk.

PROJECT

Perfectionism, as we learned in this chapter, not only creates emotional distress. It may also interfere with your performance, making you even less perfect than you would be if you let up on yourself. How perfectionistic are you? Psychologist David Burns (1980b) has developed a perfectionism scale, presented below. To test yourself, rate each of the ten statements on how much it applies to you. Use the following code:

+2 = agree strongly
+1 = agree somewhat
 0 = feel neutral

−1 = disagree somewhat
−2 = disagree strongly

_____ 1. If I don't set the highest standards for myself, I am likely to end up a second-rate person.

_____ 2. People will probably think less of me if I make a mistake.

_____ 3. If I cannot do something really well, there is little point in doing it at all.

_____ 4. I should be upset if I make a mistake.

_____ 5. If I try hard enough, I should be able to excel at anything I attempt.

THE SELF-CONCEPT: HOW TO CHANGE IT

———— 6. It is shameful for me to display weaknesses or foolish behavior.

———— 7. I shouldn't have to repeat the same mistake many times.

———— 8. An average performance is bound to be unsatisfying to me.

———— 9. Failing at something important means I'm less of a person.

———— 10. If I scold myself for failing to live up to my expectations, it will help me to do better in the future.

To compute your score, add up all the numbers. (If you are not sure how to add plus with minus numbers, do the following. First, add up all the minus numbers. Then, add up all the plus numbers. Subtract the smaller total from the larger total, keeping the plus or minus sign of the larger total.) Burns claims that about half the population is likely to score between +2 and +16.

If your score is relatively high—for example, +8 or more—you might want to work on your perfectionism. Burns suggests two exercises. First, write down the specific benefits you derive from perfectionism.

Then, write down the disadvantages. You will probably find that the disadvantages outweigh the advantages.

Second, Burns recommends that perfectionists make out a "pleasure-perfection balance sheet." Make four columns on a piece of paper. In the first column, list four or five activities that you are going to engage in on a given day. In the second column, predict, by means of a percentage, how satisfying you think each activity will be (0% = completely unsatisfying; 100% = completely satisfying). At the end of that day, record in the third column how satisfying each activity actually turned out to be. And in the fourth column, estimate how effectively you performed each activity. (Use percentages in the last two columns also.) You may find that perfection and satisfaction are not as closely related as you think. That is, you may get as much, if not more pleasure out of activities at which you are far from perfect than from those that you perform with great competence. Here is a sample "pleasure–perfection balance sheet" (adapted from Burns, 1980b):

Activity	Predict how satisfying it will be	Record how satisfying it actually was	Estimate how effectively you performed
Paint kitchen chairs	30%	95% (It was fun!)	20% (It took a long time and I made an awful mess.)
Write paper for English course	70%	40% (It was a boring topic.)	85% (I'm a pretty good writer.)
Give driving lesson to my son	50%	90% (We had a good time.)	50% (I lost patience twice.)
Write letter to old friend	80%	50% (There wasn't much to say.)	90% (It was as good as it could be.)

Source of scale: Burns, D. D. "The Perfectionist's Script for Self-Defeat," *Psychology Today,* Nov. 1980, p. 44.

<u>OUTLINE</u>

WHAT IS SELF-CONTROL?
Self-Control and External Control
Self-Control and Freedom
Perceived Locus of Control

THE DEVELOPMENT OF SELF-CONTROL: PROCESSES
Respondent Conditioning
Operant Conditioning
Reinforcement
Extinction
Generalization and Discrimination
Shaping
Modeling
Avoidance Learning
Intermittent Reinforcement

THE DEVELOPMENT OF SELF-CONTROL: RESULTS
Bodily Control
Control Over Impulsive Behaviors
Reactions to the Self
Problems in Self-Control

5

SELF-CONTROL: WHAT IT IS AND HOW IT DEVELOPS

A major problem in even the best-run nursing homes is apathy on the part of residents. Silent, staring into space, many of them act as though they were all but dead. Two researchers, Ellen Langer and Judith Rodin (1976), reasoned that a basic cause of this apathy might be that nursing-home residents have so little responsibility. They don't control their world; it is controlled for them. To test this hypothesis, the researchers decided to make a few small changes on one floor of a well-run nursing home in Connecticut. The residents of the floor were called to a meeting in the lounge, where the administrator of the home gave them a little talk emphasizing their control over their lives. He suggested to them that they might want to have the furniture in their rooms rearranged. He listed the choices that they should be making about how to spend their time. He urged them, if they had any complaints, to voice them, and he asked them for suggestions as to some kind of formal mechanism for registering complaints. He told them that next week's movie was being shown on Thursday and Friday, and that they should decide which night they wanted to go. Finally, he passed around a box of houseplants as gifts to the residents, telling them to take whichever one they liked and adding that the plant was theirs to care for.

On another floor of the same home, the administrator made a similar speech. Here, however, the emphasis was not on what the residents could do for themselves, but on what the staff would be happy to do for them. Again the movie was announced, but in this case the residents were told that they would be informed as to which night they were scheduled to see it. Again the plants were distributed, but this time the nurse handed each resident a plant, rather then let them choose, and the administrator said that the nurses would water and look after the plants.

Needless to say, the opportunities for control given to the first group were almost pathetically small. Nevertheless, they seem to have made a substantial difference. Three weeks after the meetings, the two groups were asked to rate themselves, and were independently rated by the nurses, on their level of happiness and activity. The ratings for the "responsibility" group were significantly higher than the ratings for the "no responsibility" group. The "responsibility" residents were reading more, talking more, visiting more, attending the movies more often, putting more mileage on their wheelchairs. A follow-up study conducted 18 months later found that these improvements were still in evidence (Rodin and Langer, 1977).

What this experiment suggests is something that should be fairly obvious: the more control we have over our lives, the happier and more productive we are. Self-control—how much we have and how to exercise it—is something we learn in the course of development. That learning is seldom ideal, however. In many cases, what we learn is to let the environment and our old habits control us, rather than vice versa. This problem, and its possible solutions, will be the subject of Chapters 5, 6, and 7. In this chapter (Chapter 5) we will examine the development and characteristics of self-control. In Chapters 6 and 7 we will discuss how we can turn the tables on our development—that is, improve our present style of self-control by using the very same mechanisms that produced it.

WHAT IS SELF-CONTROL?

Self-control is a person's influence over, and regulation of, his physical, behavioral, and psychological processes—in other words, the set of processes that constitute his self.

(This is the general meaning of the term. Behavioral psychologists have also given "self-control" a stricter definition, which we shall look at in Chapter 6.) In Chapter 4 we saw an excellent example of self-control: Larry's self-talk program, through which he manipulated his psychological processes and, in turn, his behavior.

Before we examine the origins of self-control, we need to consider why self-control is necessary. Why do we have to control ourselves constantly? Why not simply "stay loose" and just somehow "be"? There are two reasons why not: one social and one personal.

First, we do not live alone, but in groups, in societies. And the other people in the group have to be protected against whatever our "just being" might involve at the moment. After all, as Freud pointed out, human beings are motivated by strong sexual and aggressive drives. Furthermore, we have needs to satisfy: needs for food, drink, warmth, and so on. Hence, it is seldom that we are just "being"; usually we are doing. And what we do has to be controlled so that it does not disrupt the social order or infringe on the comfort and safety of others. This is true not only of our own society, but of all known societies.

Second, every human being absorbs from his culture certain standards of competence, beauty, success, virtue, and other desirables. In order to meet these standards, self-control is needed. This is particularly the case in our own achievement-oriented society. Our society encourages us constantly to set higher and higher goals for ourselves. And to achieve these goals, we have to learn, again and again, to control our impulses and choose long-term goals over immediate gratifications. If you want to go to graduate school in two years, you can't go bowling the night before a final exam, much as you might want to. If you want to rear a family, you may have to stay home with a sick baby

Many young people postpone the rewards of income and independence and spend several years in college, with the hope that this will ultimately bring them greater rewards. (Guy Gillette/Photo Researchers, Inc.)

on the night when you had tickets to go to a concert. In sum, personal goals, as well as social stability, require that we exercise control over ourselves.

Self-Control and External Control

Self-control is often considered the opposite of external control. In self-control, the individual sets her own standards for performance, and she rewards or punishes herself for meeting or not meeting these standards. In *external control*, on the other hand, someone else sets the standards and doles out (or withholds) rewards.

> If a rat, after having received his food pellet, were to place it aside, jog twenty laps around his cage, and then consume his reward, we could talk of self-control. (Thoresen and Mahoney, 1974, p. 25).

But if an experimenter were to train the rat to run twenty times around the cage before he could receive his food pellet, then we would be talking about external control.

The reason the distinction between self-control and external control is important is that most of us, unlike the rat, have considerable opportunity to choose between the two. Imagine, for example, that you enjoy speeding while you drive along the highway to school. You have two choices. First, you can exercise self-control. This might mean checking the speedometer every three minutes or having it hooked up to a buzzer that would make a loud sound as soon as you exceeded the speed limit. Every three days that you drive without speeding, you reward yourself by going to the movies. (If you speed, no movie.) Thus, you are controlling both your behavior and your rewards.

The other alternative is external control. Here you would simply go ahead and speed, thereby putting your rewards and punishments in the hands of others: the police (who may give you costly speeding tickets), the courts (who may eventually take your license away), the local car pool (on which you will have to depend once you lose your license).

As this example illustrates, the more self-control you exert, the less subject you are to external control. And this, of course, is the reason why self-control is considered a valuable skill. As long as you have to depend on external control, your life is largely in the hands of others. By exerting self-control, on the other hand, you become, to a degree, the master both of yourself and of the rewards you receive from the environment.

Self-Control and Freedom

If we consistently exercise self-control, making choices for ourselves rather than letting others make them for us, are we then truly free? Can we ever make the claim of the English poet William Henley: "I am the master of my fate, I am the captain of my soul?" Possibly. The existential psychologists, as we read in Chapter 1, argue that human beings are indeed free and therefore fully responsible for their actions. Most people in our society agree with this position. Indeed, the society's practice of punishing people for violating the law presupposes that such people made a free choice to violate the law.

While many psychologists, like the rest of the society, personally support the notion of the freedom of choice, as scientists they lean toward *determinism*, the idea that human behavior is largely caused by external forces. They have two interesting arguments in their favor. The first is that none of us is able to control all the environmental factors that influence him. One person may have been born blind; another person may have grown up in a depressing, crime-ridden ghetto; another person may have been reared by an alcoholic mother. Surely such people have limited freedom of choice. Even ordinary misfortunes—illness, the lack of enough money to go to school, the inability to get a job during an economic recession— severely restrict our choices. No matter which way we turn, we are still subject to a large degree of external control. It may be

argued (and it has been, many times) that while these external constraints affect the body, the "spirit"—that is, the part of us that generates our ideals and emotions— soars above them. However, the stories of those who have survived prisoner-of-war camps, Nazi concentration camps, and Russian penal colonies suggest that filth, cold, hunger, and cruelty can conquer the spirit as well as the body. Ideals crumble and the emotional life becomes dominated by groveling fear.

The second argument in favor of determinism is that even when we are controlling ourselves, our decision to do so and our way of doing it are controlled by external factors (Skinner, 1953). For example, a person who quits smoking does not do so because his judgment alone tells him he must. Rather, he does so because his doctor has told him that smoking is endangering his health, because cigarettes are expensive, because his wife nags him, and/or because many of his friends object to his smoking in their presence.

In view of these two arguments, should we conclude that, far from being completely free, we are completely controlled? No. By choosing between alternatives rather than letting the alternatives choose us, we still exercise a large measure of freedom. The

ACTIVITY 5.1

For hundreds of years, people have been debating the question of how much freedom human beings really have. Many of us find it easier to think about this issue in personal terms rather than in large abstractions.

List three free choices that you have made in your life—for example, to stop smoking, to break off a relationship, to attend the college you went to, maybe even to have your hair cut or grow a beard. Then list the anticipated rewards and punishments, *controlled by others*, that influenced these choices. Your list will probably show you that what you think of as free choices are not totally free.

fact that our choices are influenced by external factors does not mean that they aren't choices all the same (Kaplan, 1964). Whether we talk back to our self-talk or hook up a buzzer to our speedometer, we are acknowledging that our behavior is influenced, but at the same time we are making ourselves one of the influences. In doing so, we are, perhaps, not totally free, but neither are we simply the playthings of our environment.

Perceived Locus of Control

For centuries, and particularly in the past hundred years, the question that we have just examined—free will versus determinism—has been hotly debated. However, the question of how free we are may be less important than the question of how free we *think* we are (Kanfer and Karoly, 1972). A recent addition to the vocabulary of psychology is the term *perceived locus of control* (Rotter, 1966): our notion of who or what controls our lives. As we mentioned earlier, most people reject determinism on philosophical grounds. However, when individuals are asked whether they do in fact cause the things that happen to them, opinion is divided. Some people claim that whatever happens to them is largely the result of their actions and personality. Others believe that their success or failure is controlled from the outside: by "luck," by the society, or simply by other, more powerful people (Lefcourt, 1966). As we have seen in the last two chapters, our expectations have a powerful impact on our behavior. Thus, it should come as no surprise that people who believe they control what happens to them appear to have greater success in controlling what happens to them—in working up the motivation to act (Lefcourt, 1966; Rotter et al., 1972) and in resisting feelings of helplessness and depression (Seligman, 1975; Strickland, 1974).

It has also been suggested that people who believe in their control are better at resisting disease and death (Bettelheim, 1943; McMahon and Rhudick, 1964; Lefcourt, 1973). In this connection, it is worth noting the mortality rates among the nursing-home residents described at the opening of this chapter (Rodin and Langer, 1977). At the time of the experiment there was no indication that either of the two groups was in better or worse health than the other. Yet in the 18 months following the experiment, the death rate for the "responsibility" group (those who were given the talk on their choices and who selected their own plants) was exactly half that of the "no responsibility" group (those who were not reminded of their choices and whose plants were selected for them)—15 percent as opposed to 30 percent. The death rate for the entire home in the 18 months preceding the experiment was 25 percent.

It seems, then, that regardless of how much control we actually have, a *belief* in one's control makes a great difference. Psychotherapists consistently find that before a client can change, he must come to the point where he stops blaming his mother, his schoolmates, his toilet training, or whatever, and starts examining what *he* has done to contribute to his current problems. What he himself has done, he himself can undo. The same principle applies to behavioral control outside the consulting room. If you believe you can control your behavior, then you probably can.

THE DEVELOPMENT OF SELF-CONTROL: PROCESSES

Psychologists have come up with a number of different theories to explain how we develop the capacity for self-control. One of the most famous and comprehensive theories of self-control is Freud's account of the development of the superego. As we read in

In their early years, children learn to identify with the parent of the same sex. (left: © Ellen Pines Sheffield/Woodfin Camp & Assoc.; right: © Ken Karp)

Chapter 1, the superego was Freud's term for the individual's moral standards and self-ideals—similar to what we call the conscience. According to Freud, the superego develops in the child as the final outcome of a forbidden passion, the famous *Oedipus complex.* Freud (1933) believed that all children between the ages of three and six go through a period in which they long to do away with the parent of the same sex and take sexual possession of the parent of the opposite sex. This desire gives rise to a painful conflict, for at the time they still love the parent of the same sex. Furthermore, they are terribly afraid that that parent will discover their unsavory desires and take violent revenge. Eventually they resolve the conflict through a sort of compromise. They give up the incestuous desire (which is then repressed), and instead of coveting the place of the same-sex parent, they *identify* with that parent, adopting his or her sexual orientation, mannerisms, values, and (most important) moral standards, as dictated by the society. These standards become the super-

ego, which thereafter functions to prohibit the gratification of socially unacceptable yearnings. In its turn, the ego—which, as we learned in Chapter 1, is the more constructive, reality-oriented branch of the personality—represses these yearnings and rechannels them into more acceptable outlets.

A number of other schools of psychology have studied the development of self-control in the growing child. However, the only major challenge to the Freudian theory has come from the behaviorists, armed with the findings of experimental psychology on how people learn. Whether or not behavioral theory is accurate regarding the earliest origins of self-control, the learning mechanisms outlined in this theory have proven very successful in solving problems in already-established patterns of self-control. For this reason, we shall discuss them in some detail.

Respondent Conditioning

As we pointed out in Chapter 3, people learn by associations. The first scientific demon-

TABLE 5.1
RESPONDENT CONDITIONING:
LEARNING THROUGH ASSOCIATIONS

	NEUTRAL STIMULUS	PLEASANT OR PAINFUL STIMULUS	BEFORE CONDITIONING	CONDITIONING	AFTER CONDITIONING
Pavlov's experiment	Bell	Food	Bell elicits no response	Bell is paired with food, which elicits salivation	Bell alone, without food, elicits salivation
McDonald's advertising goal	Yellow arches	Hamburgers	Arches elicit no response	Arches are paired with sight of juicy hamburgers, which elicits salivation	Arches alone, without sight of hamburgers, elicit salivation
Child learning not to touch oven door	Oven door	Burning sensation	Oven door elicits no response	Touching oven door is paired with burning	Sight of oven door, without burning, elicits avoidance

stration of this fact was provided by the famous dog experiments of Ivan Pavlov, the Russian physiologist. Pavlov found that if he consistently sounded a bell about a half-second before giving his experimental dogs their food, the dogs would eventually salivate at the sound of the bell alone, with no food anywhere in sight. In other words, the dogs now associated the bell with the food, and consequently the bell called forth the same response (salivation) as the food. This type of learning is called *respondent conditioning*. Its principle may be stated as follows: a neutral stimulus (for example, the bell) is paired with a pleasant or painful stimulus (for example, the food) until the organism learns to respond to the neutral stimulus as it would to the pleasant or painful stimulus (see Table 5.1).

Let us look at an example from our own lives. If we repeatedly watch a television commercial in which two big yellow arches (neutral stimulus) are paired with pictures of juicy-looking hamburgers (pleasant stimulus), then those two yellow arches will eventually become associated with the pleasure of satisfying our hunger. Consequently, when we are driving along a road and see two big yellow arches, we may find our mouths watering and our stomachs growling—or so the McDonald's people hope. Likewise, Pepsi-Cola commercials present us with film clips of happy, carefree, healthy-looking people having all sorts of wholesome fun, while a voice sings to us about how, all across the nation, the "Pepsi generation" is "feelin' free, feelin' free, feelin' free." The idea, of course, is to get you to associate Pepsi-Cola with having a good time, so that you'll drink more Pepsi-Cola.

What does all this have to do with self-control? The major function of respondent

---

ACTIVITY 5.2

Respondent conditioning, as the text states, is a favorite technique of advertisers. Look at ten advertisements on television or in a magazine or newspaper. For each advertisement, ask yourself what neutral stimulus the advertiser is trying to get you to associate with what pleasant stimulus. Write down your answers. Which of these ads do you find most appealing? Does the degree of appeal have to do with how reinforcing you find that particular pleasant stimulus?

---

conditioning in the development of self-control is to lengthen, through chains of associations, our mental list of things that are pleasurable and painful. This broadens our range of emotional responses, which in turn dictate the ways in which we manipulate our behavior. Let us look at an example that we have already touched on in Chapter 3. A crucial step in infant development is the baby's learning, through respondent conditioning, to associate his parents (neutral stimulus) with the instinctively pleasurable stimuli of food, warmth, and cuddling. Thus, the parents take on an extremely high value. In turn, their approval and disapproval become emotionally rewarding and punishing in the child's eyes. Consequently, their approval or disapproval has the power to induce the child to postpone immediate gratification for the sake of large, long-term rewards—a process that is the essence of self-control.

Operant Conditioning

How *does* parental approval or disapproval mold behavior? In Chapter 3 we discussed the process of learning through consequences. The first person to study this process scientifically was the American psychologist Edward Lee Thorndike. In his most famous experiment, Thorndike placed a hungry cat in a box equipped in such a way that if the cat pulled a cord or pressed a lever, the door of the box opened. When the cat escaped through this door, it was given a piece of salmon to eat. Thorndike noted the time it took for the cat to escape each time it was put in the box. In the early episodes, the cat usually escaped only after a long period of fumbling about and clawing at the sides of the box. Gradually, however, the escape time became shorter and shorter. Eventually, when the cat was placed in the box, it almost immediately made the proper response, escaped, and received the food. Thorndike concluded that the reason the cat had learned the escape response so well was that this response had become associated with the food, which was the consequence of escaping. Hence, Thorndike formulated what he called the *law of effect*, which stated that responses that led to satisfying consequences were strengthened and therefore were likely to be repeated, while responses that led to unsatisfying consequences were weakened and therefore were unlikely to be repeated.

The learning process in which actions are strengthened or weakened by their consequences is called *operant conditioning*. It is important to note the differences between operant and respondent conditioning. In respondent conditioning, the pleasant or unpleasant stimulus precedes the response. In operant conditioning the pleasant or unpleasant stimulus follows the response.* Indeed, one learns to perform the response in order to experience the stimulus. Related to this first difference is a second difference, suggested by the names of the two types of conditioning. The result of respondent conditioning is simply a passive and automatic response: embarrassment, fear, desire, happiness, and the like. By contrast, the result of operant conditioning is deliberate action; the organism operates on the environment—in other words, *does* something—in order to achieve the desired result.

The ways in which operant conditioning induces self-control should be fairly obvious. Let's go back to the question we posed earlier: how does parental approval and disapproval mold behavior? If a child does crayon drawings on the living room wall and the consequence of this action is that his father yells at him and sends him to his room, the response of drawing on the living room wall is less likely to occur in the future, since it has been punished by the consequence of father's anger. Now let us imagine that the child goes to his room, takes out a piece of paper, and makes a handsome drawing for his father as an act of repentance. The likely consequence is that the father (who has calmed down by now) will say, "Good boy! *That's* what people draw on—paper. And what a nice picture! Fishes, ducks, very nice. . . . Why don't you come out of your room now." Thus, the response of drawing on paper rather than on walls is

"strengthened" by the reward of father's approval; it is more likely to occur in the future. As a result of these two episodes of operant conditioning, the child has learned a lesson in self-control: that when he has crayon in hand and wants to draw, he has to postpone his desire until he can find something appropriate to draw on.

Parents are not the only ones who supply the consequences that teach us self-control. The American psychologist B. F. Skinner (1953) has pointed out that our lives consist of a vast network of rewards and punishments that compel us to suppress, control, and channel our desires. Our employers, by offering the reward of money and the punishment of being fired, teach us to suppress until the weekend our desire to sleep till noon. Our schools, by offering us A's and F's and thus controlling our access to jobs and money, teach us that when we have a paper to write, we have to control our desire to loaf around with our friends. Traffic tickets, dinner parties, overdone steaks, sexual gratification, head colds, new clothes—all these things are rewards and punishments. And through the mechanism of operant conditioning, we learn to control and direct our behavior in order to obtain or avoid them. (For another application of operant conditioning, see Box 5.1.)

Reinforcement

In behavioral terminology, pleasant or unpleasant stimuli that strengthen a behavior are called *reinforcers*, and their effect is called *reinforcement*. The simplest type of reinforcer, called a *primary reinforcer*, is a pleasant or unpleasant one to which we respond instinctively, without learning (food, drink, heat, cold, pain). However, the vast majority of our reinforcers are not primary reinforcers, but *conditioned reinforcers*: stimuli to which we have attached positive

---

* Note, however, that in operant conditioning the pleasant or unpleasant stimulus does not influence the specific response that preceded it. That is over and done with. What this stimulus influences is the response we will make the next time we are in the same, or a similar, situation.

BOX 5.1
BIOFEEDBACK: A FORM OF CONDITIONING

In recent years, researchers have found that through the use of simple conditioning techniques, people can learn to control internal body processes that were formerly thought to be beyond voluntary control. People have learned to dilate their blood vessels, raise or lower their

(Ray Ellis/Photo Researchers, Inc.)

blood pressure, and even expand their bronchial tubes. They have done this through *biofeedback*, an operant conditioning technique in which responses are monitored by electronic beeps. For instance, men were trained to raise their blood pressure, increases being noted through electronic signals and rewarded by glimpses of nude pinup pictures. Eventually, a subject learns how to control the process in question well enough so that external feedback is not necessary.

Through biofeedback, people suffering from high blood pressure have been taught to lower their blood pressure, asthmatics have learned how to avoid attacks, and migraine patients have learned how to decrease headache pain. Biofeedback is also used to help people who have various neurological disorders control the effects of the disease. Epileptic patients, for instance, can reduce their seizures, and victims of Parkinson's disease can control tremors.

Research into the practical applications of biofeedback has only begun. Some scientists believe that one day in the future, anesthetics and painkillers will be unnecessary, because individuals will know how to block the impulses that now cause pain.

or negative value through association with primary reinforcers or with previously established conditioned reinforcers. For example, Grandmother becomes a conditioned positive reinforcer by being associated with the candy (primary reinforcers) that she gives us. And silver-backed hairbrushes become conditioned positive reinforcers by being associated with Grandmother (conditioned reinforcer).

Reinforcers act to strengthen behavior through two different types of consequences. The first is *positive reinforcement*, the presentation of a pleasant stimulus (for example, taking a child for an ice cream cone, or simply praising her, for exercising the self-control to clean up her room). The second type of reinforcing, or "strengthening," consequence is *negative reinforcement*, the removal of an unpleasant stimu-

ACTIVITY 5.3

Look back at Activity 5.2. Reread your list of the pleasant stimuli the advertisers were trying to get you to associate with their products. Make a list indicating which of these stimuli were primary reinforcers and which were conditioned reinforcers. Do you see any correlation between the appeal of the ad and whether the reinforcer was primary or conditioned?

lus (for example, releasing a child from captivity in his room).

As we have noted earlier, however, consequences can also weaken a behavior. Like "strengthening" consequences, "weakening" consequences are of two kinds, one involving presentation and one involving removal. The first is *punishment*, the presentation of an unpleasant stimulus (for example, yelling at a child or spanking her). The second kind is *extinction*, the removal of a stimulus that is reinforcing a conditioned response.

Extinction

The first three types of consequences, and their power in promoting self-control, should be fairly obvious. Extinction, however, requires a word of explanation. Most of our responses are maintained through reinforcement. If the reinforcement is eliminated, the response will eventually cease to occur. And that is exactly what happens in extinction.

Imagine, for example, that a person in your biology class consistently misses lectures and asks to borrow your notes. And you consistently lend them to her, even though you don't want to. By supplying the positive reinforcer (the notes), you have strengthened her note-borrowing response through operant conditioning. Finally, you get tired of being inconvenienced, and the next time she asks you to lend her your notes, you say, "I'm sorry, I can't. It just means too much trouble for me." Thus, you have removed the positive consequence that is maintaining her response. And as a result, her response of borrowing notes (or at least her response of borrowing notes from *you*) will eventually cease to occur. Psychologists advise using exactly the same tactic in discouraging a child's whining or temper tantrums. Such behaviors are maintained because they get the parents' attention. Once they are no longer reinforced by the reward of attention, they tend to disappear.

Generalization and Discrimination

The lessons we absorb through respondent and operant conditioning do not remain static, tied to the situation in which they were first learned. If they did, the crayon-wielding child in the earlier example might learn only that drawing on *living room* walls was forbidden, and thus he might simply move his operations to the dining room. Normally, however, our ability to make connections between things results in the rapid *generalization* of learning, whereby a conditioned response expands to include not only the original stimulus but similar stimuli as well. Thus, the child learns that not only the living room wall but all the walls in his house—indeed, all the walls in all houses—are inappropriate places to draw.

Needless to say, generalization saves us a lot of time in the operant learning of self-control.

Generalization is equally common in respondent conditioning. Perhaps the best example comes from a famous and rather inhumane experiment conducted by John B. Watson, the founder of behaviorism. Attempting to prove that emotions were the result of conditioning, Watson and one of his students set out to condition a fear of white rats in an eleven-month-old boy known as Albert B. Every time the child reached out for the white rat in Watson's laboratory, Watson struck an iron bar with a hammer, making a very loud noise that terrified the child. After just seven pairings of the noise with the white rat, Albert reacted with fright to the white rat. And interestingly enough, he reacted in the very same way (without further conditioning) to a rabbit, a dog, a fur coat, and a Santa Claus mask—in other words, anything that resembled the white rat. Thus, the fear of the white rat had generalized to all furry things (Watson and Rayner, 1920).

The effects of generalization can be offset somewhat by the opposite process, called *discrimination.* Discrimination means learning, through different conditioning experiences, to distinguish among similar stimuli and to tailor one's responses accordingly. The stimuli for which we learn specific responses through discrimination—and which eventually come to "trigger" that response—are called *discriminative stimuli.* To return to our example of the child with the crayons, the child learned, through the consequences provided by his father, to discriminate between two different kinds of surfaces: paper and walls. And paper, not walls, became a discriminative stimulus for drawing.

Likewise, through trying out the same response in different situations, we learn to

Girls training for the "Missy Junior Gloves Boxing Tournament." The mechanism of discrimination allows us to choose between appropriate and inappropriate outlets for aggression. (Abigail Heyman/Magnum)

discriminate between the situations in which that response is appropriate and situations in which it is inappropriate. We learn that sitting on the ground is fine if you're camping in the woods but not if you're at a garden party; that loud demonstrations of anger are permissible at home but not in the classroom or on the job; that it is fine to discuss your sexual adventures with a friend over coffee, but that it is not okay to discuss these matters with your great-aunt over Thanksgiving dinner.

These examples should suggest why discrimination is essential in the learning of self-control. It is discrimination that enables us to channel our needs and desires toward appropriate outlets. In this way we can satisfy ourselves, but without doing harm or giving offense. The child can go on making crayon drawings as long as he identifies what is appropriate to draw on. And you can laugh, cry, gossip, make love, quarrel, tell deep, dark secrets, and even throw dishes at the wall, as long as you pick the appropriate circumstances. Discrimination, then, cuts into spontaneity, but in the end it makes spontaneous behavior possible, by carving out a place for it within the bounds of personal and social values.

Shaping

In the kind of operant conditioning we have examined so far, the person must first produce the response, after which it is either reinforced or not reinforced. However, our more complex responses cannot be learned in this way, because there is so little probability of our producing them spontaneously. For example, if our educational system waited for students to compose well-written term papers spontaneously, it would end up waiting forever. Consequently this skill, along with our other more complex skills, is built up gradually, through a type of operant conditioning called shaping.

Shaping is the learning of a specific desired behavior through the reinforcement of responses that more and more closely approximate that behavior. In other words, the learner gradually refines and adds onto his skill, slowly shaping it into a complex response. For example, we are taught in school first to read and write, then to compose little book reports on index cards, then to write two-page "themes," and so on, until at last, after years of training, we are able to go home and produce a twenty-page term paper. At each successive stage we are rewarded for mastering the task, after which the task is made slightly more difficult.

Many of the complex operations we perform—speaking, getting dressed, brushing our teeth, reading, writing, cooking, driving a car, operating a computer or a cash register—are learned through shaping. The learning of any one of these skills requires considerable self-control. Once they are learned, they become the means by which we institute larger programs of self-control.

Modeling

Another extremely important method of learning a complex response is *modeling*, learning through imitating others. Before attempting to cook, we watch our parents cook. Before driving a car, we enviously watch our older sister drive. And when we finally perform these skills, we do what we have observed others doing. Actually, modeling often occurs in combination with shaping. In this case, we are reinforced for successive approximations of the modeled response.

When it occurs alone, however, modeling has a highly unique quality: it can mold responses without any direct reinforcement (Bandura, 1971). It seems that the mere power of social influence—the desire to be like other people, particularly people who seem powerful and attractive—is enough to make us imitate what we see. And since modeling has this unique capacity—the capacity to influence behavior without granting external rewards—it is particularly well suited to the teaching of self-control, which often, by its very nature, involves passing up immediate rewards. Laboratory experiments with children (Bandura and Mischel, 1965; Bandura and Kupers, 1964) have shown that modeling is extremely effective in transmitting two difficult skills that are utterly essential to effective self-control: delaying gratification and making self-rewards contingent upon satisfactory performance. Outside the laboratory, children watch their parents exercising these skills every day—allowing themselves to go for a Sunday swim only after they have finished the household chores, delaying buying a new car

BOX 5.2
WHO IS CONTROLLING YOUR BEHAVIOR?

It is not hard to see how operant conditioning affects certain areas of human behavior. If the consequence of your using a new bowling technique is a strike, you are likely to use that technique again in the future. If the consequence of your forgetting about the parking meter is a 25-dollar ticket, chances are you will keep the meter in mind next time. But what about more ordinary, everyday kinds of behavior, such as your way of eating or talking?

In the 1950s, when research on learning was still in its early stages, psychologist William Verplanck (1955) decided to try to find out whether a person's conversation could be controlled by reinforcement. He enlisted the students in his psychology course at Harvard as his experimenters. Each experimenter picked out a person and engaged him or her in conversation for thirty minutes. During the first ten minutes of the conversation, the experimenter recorded (1) how many statements the subject made and (2) how many of these statements were expressions of opinion—for example, sentences beginning "I think . . . " or "It seems to me . . . ." (By appearing to "doodle" during the conversation, the experimenters managed to do their recording without the subjects' being aware of it.) During this first ten minutes, the experimenter did not agree or disagree with any of the subject's opinions. Then, during the second ten-minute period, the experimenter deliberately reinforced the subject's opinion-stating by voicing or nodding agreement every time the subject expressed an opinion or by paraphrasing the subject's opinion back to him. Finally, in the third ten-minute period, the experimenter tried to extinguish the subject's opinion-stating by withdrawing reinforcement. Every time the subject stated an opinion, the experimenter either disagreed or simply failed to respond. The question was: Would the subjects' rate of opinion-stating increase during the reinforcement period and decrease during the extinction period?

The experimenters were allowed free choice of subjects, experimental circumstances, and topics of conversation. Many of them experimented on friends or roommates. One used a date; another used an uncle. The conversations took place in a number of different locations— a restaurant, a dormitory, a hospital ward, and so forth. And the topics of conversation ranged from Marxism to Liberace to vacation experiences.

Regardless of the circumstances, the subjects tended to respond to the conditioning. On the average, they expressed opinions almost twice as often during the reinforcement period as they had during the first (baseline) period. And during the extinction period, their average rate of opinion-stating dropped back down to approximately the baseline level.

What this suggests is that the things we say to other people are controlled not only by us but also by those people. Without being aware of it, we let them cue us and guide us. As Verplanck points out, this finding simply confirms common-sense observations. (For example, aren't you freer in voicing your likes and dislikes to someone who you know agrees with you?) But it also raises some further questions. If a person, simply by expressing or withholding agreement, can cause you to shift your manner of speaking, imagine the effect that people have on you by using more powerful reinforcers, such as love, companionship, food, or sex.

until they have paid for the washing machine, putting off eating sweets until after dinner. And through observing, the child imitates these self-control responses.

But what about the things that the parents *tell* the child? Do their words have the same power as their actions in influencing the child's behavior? Apparently not. Modeling, as we have just seen, is an extremely powerful learning mechanism, quite powerful enough to override any "Do as I say, not as I do" approach to child-rearing. When verbal instructions are consistent with modeled behavior, they make the modeling lesson that much more compelling. But when the parents' words point the child in the opposite direction from the parents' behavior, the child is likely to go the way of the parents' behavior (Bryan and Walbek, 1970; Mischel and Liebert, 1966). Monkey see, monkey do, no matter what monkey is told. It is for this reason that child-rearing manuals make such a point of "consistency" in disciplining children. For example, a mother who spanks her son for hitting his sister is modeling the exact opposite of what she is trying to teach—that is, not to hit. As a result, the child may feel somewhat confused and guilty about his tendency to hit, but he is likely to go on hitting all the same.

Avoidance Learning

As important as what we learn to do is what we learn to avoid doing. This is especially true in the case of self-control. For, after all, a good half of self-control is simply doing without the immediate gratification of our desires. As we grow, we gradually learn *not* to do all the many impetuous things that, as very young children, we did without hesitation: running into the street without looking, picking up food by the handful and stuffing it into our mouths, stealing, hitting, wetting our pants, and the like.

The process of learning to avoid these inappropriate behaviors is, not surprisingly, called *avoidance learning*. Avoidance learning is a two-stage process (Bolles, 1975). In the first stage, we are reprimanded or punished for the behavior; thus, we learn, through respondent conditioning, to associate anxiety with the desire to engage in the behavior. In the second stage, we learn, through operant conditioning, that if we suppress that desire, the uncomfortable feelings that accompany it will also disappear (Mowrer, 1948). The second stage is a good example of negative reinforcement: relief from a painful stimulus (in this case, anxiety) reinforces the behavior (in this case, suppressing the unacceptable desire) that resulted in the removal of the stimulus. In all, avoidance learning allows us to avoid an unpleasant situation *before* it occurs.

Unlike many other learned behaviors, avoidance behaviors are extremely difficult to unlearn. There are two good reasons for this. First, the avoidance behavior is repeatedly rewarded by negative reinforcement, through the process we just discussed. Second, avoidance by its very nature rules out the possibility of extinction. That is, since the thing that the person is avoiding is in fact avoided, the person never has the chance to test whether his fear of it is justified. If, for once, he retested the situation and found that nothing horrible happened as a result, then the fear would disappear, and the impulse-avoidance response would extinguish for lack of its reinforcement (relief from fear). But as long as the person avoids the fear-producing situation, extinction cannot take place. Consider, for example, a child who is afraid of the water. Every time he stays home while the other kids go to the swimming pool, (1) his avoidance of water is reinforced by the relief from fear, and (2) he loses the chance to discover that he had nothing to fear.

This rather curious process accounts, in part, for the permanence of the many impulse-avoidance behaviors that we learn as children. Another important reason for the durability of these avoidance behaviors is that they are so heavily reinforced by the society and are consistently modeled by our elders, those large and powerful people whom we are so strongly motivated to imitate.

Intermittent Reinforcement

So far we have spoken of conditioning as though every response were accompanied by reinforcement. This may happen in a laboratory—a rat may get a food pellet every time he presses a bar in his cage—but it seldom happens in life. Human behavior is generally maintained by *intermittent reinforcement*. That is, our behavior is reinforced only after a number of responses or at intervals in time. We are not rewarded for every favor we do. Nor, if we lose twenty pounds, are we complimented every day on our appearance. Human life simply does not work that way. We have to go on producing the response and be grateful for the reinforcement when it comes.

Interestingly enough, responses that have been built up through intermittent reinforcement are much more permanent than those that have been reinforced continuously (Robbins, 1971). A reinforcement that appears every time, without fail, tends eventually to lose its power to strengthen behavior. The person gets enough of the reinforcer and therefore ceases to respond to it. If you give a child a cookie every time she makes her bed, she may eventually reach the point where she has had enough cookies, and consequently she may stop making her bed. But if you notice her bed-making and give her the congratulatory cookie only every three days or so, she will continue to find the cookie reinforcing and therefore will continue making the bed.

A second reason for the great effectiveness of intermittent reinforcement is that the person learns to go on responding even when the behavior is not reinforced (Jenkins et al., 1950; Ferster and Skinner, 1957). If a response is rewarded every single time, it tends to extinguish quickly once the rewards stop coming. But if a person has learned a response through intermittent reinforcement, he will not be surprised or discouraged if no reward follows the response. In fact, human beings can go on for years engaging in some behavior (such as "cleaning their plates") that was learned in childhood through intermittent reinforcement but which has long since ceased to be reinforced.

THE DEVELOPMENT OF SELF-CONTROL: RESULTS

What do we learn through all the various processes outlined above? Basically, we learn three things: how to control our bodies, how to control impulsive behaviors, and how to react to ourselves.

Bodily Control

At birth we are completely at the mercy of external control. We have no self-control whatsoever. All we can do is what our inborn reflexes cause us to do automatically: suck, blink our eyes, urinate and defecate, fall asleep. Within the first year after birth, however, we probably learn more about self-control than we will ever learn the rest of our lives. For it is in this year that we learn the basic skills of controlling our bodies.

Gradually, week after week, we pass the milestones of physical self-control. We learn to focus our eyes and watch a moving object.

SELF-CONTROL: WHAT IT IS AND HOW IT DEVELOPS

We learn to turn over and eventually to sit up. We also master the tremendously important skill of hand-eye coordination: the ability to reach out and grab something that we see. And by the end of the first year we have begun to develop two monumental skills: speaking and walking.

In part, all these skills are the result of simple physical development. For example, we learn to speak once our muscles and nervous system have matured to the point where we can control the movements of mouth and tongue. However, when the body is ready to learn a new skill, reinforcement is required in order to develop it and "stamp it in." To some degree, the skill supplies its own reinforcement. For example, once we master hand-eye coordination, we have the satisfaction of being able to pick things up and inspect them. But considerable reinforcement is supplied by our parents, who model, shape, and reward our emerging physical skills. For example, when the child first says "Dada," the delighted father laughs, kisses her, and joyously repeats the great word, all the time pointing to himself. Needless to say, the child has good reason to restage and improve upon her performance. Speech comes later to children reared in institutions (Provence and Lipton, 1962; Dennis and Najarian, 1957). For this, too, there is good reason: no one in such settings can supply the kind of reinforcement that parents can supply.

These early self-control skills—walking, talking, hand-eye coordination—are easy to take for granted. After all, we have been doing these things for twenty or thirty years, haven't we? Yes, we have. But that does not detract from their importance. They constitute our earliest experiences of self-control, and the rewards they bring constitute our motivation to increase our self-control.

An excellent example is the achievement of toilet training. Unlike walking and talk-

This small child struggles to master a flight of stairs. Such achievements are a result of both physical maturation and self-control. (Charles Harbutt/Magnum)

ing, this is a skill that does not emerge naturally. Nor do most children have any great desire to develop it. For two or three years they have been urinating and defecating in a nice warm diaper, whenever the spirit moved them. Why should they learn to postpone these functions—to say nothing of postponing them in order to perform them on a hard, cold, unfriendly-looking toilet seat? But they do learn, because their parents want them to. And once they have mastered the skill, they gain the reward of being free from parental nagging, of going off to nursery school without fear of embarrassment, and of feeling competent and grownup. This experience establishes in the child's mind a model for future efforts at self-control: initial unwillingness, gradual mastery, and the rewards of self-determination and social approval.

Control Over Impulsive Behaviors

Toilet training is an excellent example of yet another area of self-control development: the controlling of impulsive behaviors. Impulsive behaviors are those in which we take immediate action for the sake of immediate gratification. Hence, the controlling of impulsive behaviors involves two abilities: the ability to wait before acting and the ability to forgo immediate gratification for the sake of some larger future reward.

Teaching the control of impulsive behavior, particularly of the sexual and aggressive variety, is probably the major effort of childhood socialization (Aronfreed, 1968). This is particularly true in our own society, where the importance of deferring gratification has for centuries been upheld by what is called the "Protestant Ethic" (Weber, 1958): the belief that work is virtuous and that pleasure is somehow morally questionable. During the past few decades there has been considerable resistance to the Protestant Ethic. Many people have argued, with reason, that the stigma on pleasure and the endless postponement of rewards lead to a pinched, repressed, self-righteous existence, devoid of joy and spontaneity. Indeed, a number of the communes established in the 1960s were attempts to escape the Protestant Ethic and the high-pressure capitalist society associated with it. Nevertheless, even on a commune, the goats must be fed and the lettuce must be picked, no matter how much one would rather be doing something else. And in the thick of our complex technological society (where most people choose to remain), the postponement of rewards is a skill we must exercise every day, from hour to hour.

An excellent example is the case of the person who goes back to school after several years of working or staying home with the children. If she just continued to work or to stay at home, she would have many short-term rewards: more leisure time, more money. But for the sake of larger rewards in the future—an interesting job, a higher salary, the pleasures that come from broader knowledge—she forgoes these immediate gratifications.

Likewise, children are taught, day after day, that the more distant or abstract rewards of achievement, safety, health, and parental and social approval should outweigh their immediate desires. What determines whether they will go along with this program? To a large degree, it is a matter of prior conditioning. If a child has been praised for planning, waiting, and working toward goals, and if past promises of deferred rewards have in fact been kept, then the child is more likely to postpone small immediate rewards for the sake of larger future rewards (Mischel, 1966, 1968, 1974). Furthermore, if he must work and achieve something in order to obtain the deferred reward, his confidence in his ability to do the required work will affect his decision (Mischel, 1974; Mischel and Mischel, 1976). In other words, the crucial factors are trust, goal-orientation, and self-confidence, all of which are determined by prior learning.

Reactions to the Self

In discussing the mechanisms of learning self-control, we spoke primarily of external reinforcement. However, one of the most powerful enforcers of self-control is the reinforcement that comes from within: the individual's reactions to himself. Guinea pigs in laboratory cages do not pat themselves on the back for producing the response that the experimenter wants, nor do

Excessive drinking may be learned in childhood, through modeling, as children watch their elders using liquor in order to "unwind." (© Leonard Speier 1982)

they feel ashamed when they get lost in a maze. Human beings, on the other hand, constantly evaluate their own performances (Bandura and Whalen, 1964). This self-reinforcement may take the form of actual concrete rewards, as when we treat ourselves to a big steak after taking a test for which we studied very hard. Much more common, however—and probably more potent—is the reinforcement we supply in the form of our simple feelings about ourselves: pride for good performance, shame for bad performance.

Experiments have shown that patterns of concrete self-reinforcement are quickly learned through modeling (Bandura and Whalen, 1964; Mischel and Liebert, 1966). As for the intangible reinforcers of self-praise and self-accusation, they are probably learned through a combination of modeling and respondent conditioning. The child who has been scolded by his mother for hitting the dog over the head with a block associates this aggressive act with the withdrawal of his mother's love. And eventually he incorporates, through learning, both his mother's standard (aggression is bad) and the punishment (withdrawal of love). Thus, when he behaves aggressively in the future, or is tempted to do so, he withdraws his own love from himself (Sears et al., 1957; Aronfreed, 1968). In other words, he feels guilt. As we all know, guilt is an extremely painful stimulus, one that we will go to great lengths to avoid or get rid of. Hence, the self-controlling behaviors that prevent or relieve guilt are firmly stamped in by negative reinforcement, the removal of this painful stimulus.

Problems in Self-Control

If our conditioning for self-control were perfect, then our bodily control, our impulse control, and our self-reactions would serve us so efficiently that we could lead consistently happy, guilt-free, and constructive lives, blessed with complete approval by ourselves and by our society. In real life, however, one's self-control invariably has certain holes in it, little pockets in which self-defeating habits and guilt fester together, producing no solution. We smoke too much or drink too much or eat too much or lose our tempers constantly or put off writing papers until the last minute. How do we develop these problems in self-control?

According to behavioral theory, faulty self-control is developed in the same way as good self-control—that is, through learning. Self-control problems crop up in areas where learning has been either insufficient or inappropriate. In the case of insufficient learning, imagine a young child who works hard in school but receives no feedback (reinforcement) from his parents—no approval, no encouragement. As a result, his studying response is likely to die out, so that by the time he reaches high school, he will be unable to exercise the self-control to study for an exam. As for inappropriate learning, a good example would be a man who grew up with parents who constantly resorted to alcohol in stressful situations. Imagine, in addition, that as a teenager he was part of a crowd for which heavy drinking was an essential ingredient of the group's fun. With such models and such reinforcement, the man comes to associate drinking with release from tension, social acceptability, and good times. Only later does he discover that he cannot relax until he has had several drinks—in other words, that he is on his way to alcoholism. The fact that alcoholism tends to run in families (MacKay, 1961; Wood and Duffy, 1966) lends some support to this learning hypothesis. Child abuse is another problem that runs in families and that may be learned in a similar way. After years of observational learning and reinforcement, such behaviors, repellent as they may seem, can become automatic.

The English novelist Colin Wilson visualizes automatic behavior as the work of an "inner robot":

I am writing this on an electric typewriter. When I learned to type, I had to do it painfully and with much nervous wear and tear. But at a certain stage a miracle occurred, and this complicated operation was "learned" by a useful robot whom I conceal in my subconscious mind. Now I only have to think about what I want to say; my robot secretary does the typing. He is really very useful. He also drives the car for me, speaks French (not very well), and occasionally gives lectures at American universities. [My robot] is most annoying when I am tired, because then he tends to take over most of my functions without even asking me. I have even caught him making love to my wife. (1967, p. 269)

We all have inner robots—behaviors so firmly stamped in by prior associations that they almost seem to enact themselves, without waiting for us to enact them. Some of these conditioned responses, like the typing and driving of Wilson's robot, are quite useful. Others, however, are not. In our earlier years, we may have associated smoking with looking sophisticated, depression with failure, cheating on tests with being "one of the crowd," and so forth. Once these unfortunate associations were established, the behavior provided its own reward and thus began generating itself automatically, leaving us with serious self-control problems.

It is dangerous, however, to rely too heavily on images of robots or of responses somehow enacting themselves. These are simply figures of speech. The fact remains that if you smoke, it is *you* who smoke; if you react to minor setbacks by collapsing into depression, it is *you* who engage in this self-defeating response. And since you are the one who produces these behaviors, you are the only one who can put an end to them. How this can be done is the subject of our next two chapters.

SUMMARY

1. *Self-control* is a person's influence over, and regulation of, his physical, behavioral, and psychological processes. The development of self-control is important in order to get along with others and to meet personal goals. Self-control is often considered to be the opposite of *external control*. In the former, the individual sets

his own standards, while in the latter, the standards are set for him.

2. The exercise of self-control will not free us completely from control by external forces. Indeed, according to many scientists, our behavior is largely ruled by external forces. This theory is called *determinism*. Whether or not determinism is valid, there is no doubt that we can achieve greater freedom by controlling the external forces that influence our behavior.

3. The *perceived locus of control* in our lives may be more important than the actual locus of control. The more control we feel we have, the more control we will exercise.

4. The processes of learning are central to the development of self-control. Through *respondent conditioning*, we learn associations with pleasurable and painful stimuli, thus training ourselves to delay gratification. Through *operant conditioning*, we learn to control ourselves in order to achieve satisfying consequences. Our behaviors may be strengthened by *positive reinforcement* (pleasant stimuli) or *negative reinforcement* (the removal of unpleasant stimuli). Behaviors may be "weakened" through *punishment* or *extinction*.

5. When what a person learns in one situation or about one response is carried over to other situations or responses, *generalization* has occurred. When a distinction is made between situations or responses, the process is called *discrimination*. Complex responses can be learned either through *shaping*, the learning of a response through reinforcement of successive approximations of that response, or through *modeling*, the learning of a response by observing others.

6. Important in the development of self-control are two additional learning processes. In *avoidance learning*, a person learns to avoid an unpleasant stimulus. *Intermittent reinforcement*—the reinforcement of behavior at intervals rather than after each response—results in learning that is relatively permanent and resistant to extinction.

7. In the development of self-control, an infant first learns to control her body. Later she learns to control her impulses and delay gratification. Finally, she learns how to react to herself, internalizing parental standards and evaluating her own behavior.

8. Problems can occur in the development of self-control. Most of these result from insufficient or inappropriate learning.

PROJECT

As we saw earlier in this chapter, reinforcement is central to operant conditioning and to the development of our self-control. Almost any activity or experience can be a reinforcement if we find it pleasurable and if we make it contingent upon some behavior. For example, if you like to watch television, you could use it as a reinforcement for studying by promising yourself that you can watch television once you have completed your studies.

We have produced on the pages that follow a list of activities and experiences which you might find pleasurable and which you could possibly use as reinforcers for some activity you would like to increase (e.g., studying, reading, writing, exercising, etc.). Go through the list and next to each activity rate how pleasurable you find it, using a scale such as the following:

1 = not at all pleasurable
2 = slightly pleasurable
3 = fairly pleasurable
4 = very pleasurable
5 = extremely pleasurable

Go by *your own* feelings in rating each activity, since everyone differs in which activities they find pleasurable. At the end of the list, you will find some blank spaces. Use these to add any activities not in the list that you find particularly pleasurable.

1. Eating:
   _____ a. Ice cream
   _____ b. Candy
   _____ c. Fruit
   _____ d. Pastry
   _____ e. Nuts
   _____ f. Cookies

2. Drinking:
   _____ a. Water
   _____ b. Milk
   _____ c. Soft drink
   _____ d. Tea
   _____ e. Coffee
   _____ f. Beer
   _____ g. Wine
   _____ h. Hard liquor

3. Looking at:
   _____ a. Beautiful women
   _____ b. Handsome men
   _____ c. Sunsets
   _____ d. Paintings
   _____ e. Interesting buildings
   _____ f. Beautiful scenery

4. Solving:
   _____ a. Crossword puzzles
   _____ b. Mathematical problems

5. Listening to music:
   _____ a. Classical
   _____ b. Western country
   _____ c. Jazz
   _____ d. Show tunes
   _____ e. Rhythm & blues
   _____ f. Rock & roll
   _____ g. Folk
   _____ h. Popular

6. Having:
   _____ a. Dogs
   _____ b. Cats
   _____ c. Horses
   _____ d. Birds

7. Watching:
   _____ a. TV
   _____ b. Movies

8. Singing:
   _____ a. Alone
   _____ b. With others

9. Dancing:
   _____ a. Ballroom
   _____ b. Discotheque
   _____ c. Ballet or interpretive
   _____ d. Square dancing
   _____ e. Folk dancing

10. Watching (sports):
   _____ a. Football
   _____ b. Baseball
   _____ c. Basketball
   _____ d. Track
   _____ e. Golf
   _____ f. Swimming
   _____ g. Running
   _____ h. Tennis
   _____ i. Pool
   _____ j. Other

11. Reading:
   _____ a. Adventure
   _____ b. Mystery
   _____ c. Famous people
   _____ d. Poetry
   _____ e. Travel
   _____ f. True confessions
   _____ g. Politics

_____ h. How to-do-it
_____ i. Humor
_____ j. Comic books
_____ k. Love stories
_____ l. Spiritual
_____ m. Magazines
_____ n. Sports
_____ o. Medicine
_____ p. Science
_____ q. Newspapers
12. Playing (sports):
_____ a. Football
_____ b. Baseball
_____ c. Basketball
_____ d. Track & field
_____ e. Golf
_____ f. Swimming
_____ g. Running
_____ h. Tennis
_____ i. Pool
_____ j. Boxing
_____ k. Judo or karate
_____ l. Fishing
_____ m. Skin diving
_____ n. Auto or cycle racing
_____ o. Hunting
_____ p. Skiing
13. Shopping for:
_____ a. Clothes
_____ b. Furniture
_____ c. Auto parts & supply
_____ d. Appliances
_____ e. Food
_____ f. New car
_____ g. New place to live
_____ h. Sports equipment
_____ 14. Figuring out how something works
_____ 15. Playing a musical instrument
_____ 16. Gardening
_____ 17. Playing cards
_____ 18. Hiking or walking
_____ 19. Completing a difficult job
_____ 20. Camping
_____ 21. Sleeping

_____ 22. Taking a bath
_____ 23. Taking a shower
24. Being right:
_____ a. In guessing what somebody is going to do
_____ b. In an argument
_____ c. About your work
_____ d. On a bet
25. Being praised about your:
_____ a. appearance
_____ b. work
_____ c. hobbies
_____ d. physical strength
_____ e. athletic ability
_____ f. mind
_____ g. personality
_____ h. moral strength
_____ i. understanding of others
_____ 26. Having people seek you out for company
_____ 27. Flirting
_____ 28. Having somebody flirt with you
_____ 29. Talking with people who like you
_____ 30. Making somebody happy
31. Being with:
_____ a. Babies
_____ b. Children
_____ c. Old men
_____ d. Old women
_____ 32. Having people ask your advice
_____ 33. Watching other people
_____ 34. Having somebody smile at you
_____ 35. Driving a car
_____ 36. Being with happy people
_____ 37. Being close to an attractive man
_____ 38. Being close to an attractive woman
_____ 39. Talking to the opposite sex
_____ 40. Talking to friends
_____ 41. Playing video games
_____ 42. Winning a bet
_____ 43. Being in Church or Temple

_____ 44. Saying prayers
_____ 45. Having somebody pray for you
_____ 46. Having peace and quiet

Write in and rate any other activities that you find pleasurable:

_____ 47. _____
_____ 48. _____
_____ 49. _____
_____ 50. _____
_____ 51. _____
_____ 52. _____
_____ 53. _____
_____ 54. _____
_____ 55. _____
_____ 56. _____
_____ 57. _____
_____ 58. _____
_____ 59. _____
_____ 60. _____

4 = about once a day
5 = more than once a day

Rating of Opportunity	Activity
_____	_____
_____	_____
_____	_____
_____	_____
_____	_____
_____	_____
_____	_____
_____	_____
_____	_____
_____	_____
_____	_____

Now that you have rated all of the items and added some of your own, you need to identify those which are _both_ pleasurable and accessible to you. Thus, in the spaces below, write in those activities from your list that you rated with a 4 (very pleasurable) or a 5 (extremely pleasurable). Then rate these activities as to how often you have the opportunity to participate in them, using this scale:

1 = no opportunity
2 = about once or twice a month
3 = about once or twice a week

With this last list, you may have a set of activities which you find very pleasurable and which you have the opportunity to engage in often. These may be useful reinforcers for those behaviors which you are trying to increase or maintain, such as exercising, dieting, or studying. Should you find that none of the highly pleasurable activities occur frequently enough to be useful, try looking down your list for other activities which, while less pleasurable, may occur with sufficient frequency to be useful reinforcers. Once you have a set of activities which you can use this way, you will be well on your way to developing better self-control.

<u>OUTLINE</u>

ANALYZING YOUR SELF-CONTROL
Description
Functional Analysis

IMPROVING SELF-CONTROL
Manipulating Antecedent Stimuli
Environmental planning
Redirecting attention
Relabeling and organizing
Meddling with Responses
Chaining
Incompatible behaviors
Shaping
Manipulating Consequences
Utilizing feedback
Providing self-reward
Using the Premack Principle
Administering punishment
Three Don'ts

6

SELF-CONTROL: HOW TO CHANGE IT

In Homer's epic poem *The Odyssey*, the hero, Odysseus, must sail his ship past the island of the Sirens. The Sirens are sinister creatures, half bird and half woman, whose beautiful songs lure men to their death. Hearing the Sirens' voices across the water, sailors on passing ships fall under their spell and steer toward the island, where they eventually waste away and die. To protect his crew, Odysseus orders them to plug their ears with beeswax. But he himself, always hungry for new experiences, cannot bear to pass up the chance to hear the Sirens' songs. So instead of plugging his ears, he has his men tie him to the mast of the ship and promise not to release him, no matter how much he begs.

The ship approaches the island, and the Sirens' songs float across the water. The crew, with their ears plugged, do not hear, but Odysseus immediately falls under the Sirens' power. He writhes against his ropes and shouts to his men to untie him so that he can turn the ship. But the crew, as ordered, ignore his pleas, and the ship sails on toward home.

We mentioned in Chapter 5 that certain behavioral psychologists have given a strict definition to the term "self-control." That definition is as follows: *A person exercises self-control when, for the sake of a long-term goal, he deliberately avoids engaging in some habitual or immediately gratifying behavior that is freely available to him and instead substitutes a behavior that is less habitual or offers less immediate gratification* (Thoresen and Mahoney, 1974). Furthermore, according to most behaviorists, the act of self-control is made possible by *manipulating the internal or external variables that influence the behavior in question* (Skinner, 1953). Thus, self-control, strictly defined, involves three basic factors: 1) deliberate choice; 2) choice between two conflicting behaviors, one offering immediate gratification and the other offering a long-term reward; and 3) manip-

Odysseus passing the island of the Sirens. Note that he is tied to the mast. (New York Public Library/Picture Collection)

ulation of stimuli in order to make the one behavior less probable and the other behavior more probable.

According to this definition, then, a person who successfully gave up smoking five years ago is not exercising self-control when she refrains from smoking. She no longer has to manipulate environmental stimuli (for example, asking her friends not to smoke in front of her, pasting a picture of a cancerous lung on her wall) or even make a deliberate choice in order not to smoke; nonsmoking is now a habitual behavior. Odysseus, on the other hand, offers a perfect example of self-control. He knows how immediately gratifying it will seem to turn his ship toward the island of the Sirens, but he prefers the conflicting behavior of sailing onward, in pursuit of the long-term goal of reaching home. Therefore, he manipulates the environmental variables controlling the response of changing the ship's course. In the case of his crew, he uses beeswax to block off the stimuli that would tempt them to steer the ship toward the island. In his own case, he uses physical restraint. A less romantic but equally valid example of self-control is provided by the student who gets himself to go to the library rather than the coffee shop between classes by avoiding his friends on his way across campus, by taking a special route that bypasses the coffee shop, and by rewarding himself with a cup of coffee after the required three hours of study.

According to many psychologists, what freedom we have as human beings derives from this ability to meddle with the factors that influence our behavior:

> The truly "free" individual is one who is in intimate contact with himself and his environment (both internal and external). He knows "where he's at" in terms of the factors influencing both his actions and his surroundings. Moreover, he has acquired technical skills which enable him to take an active role in his own growth and adjustment. He is no mechanical automaton, passively responding to environmental forces. He is a personal scientist, a skilled engineer capable of investigating and altering the determinants of his actions (Mahoney and Thoresen, 1974, p. 141).

The purpose of this chapter is to help you become a "personal scientist." Having investigated and manipulated the determinants of your self-concept (Chapter 4), you are already halfway there. Our job now is to extend your scientific experiments to problem behaviors—behaviors requiring self-control. We shall begin by discussing how to analyze a problem in self-control. Then we will examine various techniques for dealing with the problem.

ANALYZING YOUR SELF-CONTROL

Before we can solve a self-control problem, we have to specify what the problem is and form a hypothesis as to what is causing it. In other words, we have to conduct another self-analysis.

Description

The first step in describing a self-control problem is, of course, to decide what problem you are going to work on:

> *My problem is that I'm disorganized, completely disorganized. By the time the final week of a course rolls around, I can't find my textbook. I've lost half my lecture notes, and what notes I have are completely jumbled. When I look at other people's notes—nice, neat notes in outline form—I don't know how they do it. Mine are just messy scribbles that are no help at all in studying for the exam.*

This is a common problem, and one that can easily be worked on. But before it can be worked on, it has to be described in a simple, objective, and specific manner. Being "completely disorganized" is far too broad and vague a problem. It has to be simplified, perhaps pared down to "I take messy lecture notes and tend to lose them." Then these behaviors have to be objectified—that is, stated in terms of precise, observable facts. Exactly how often do you lose the notes? And as for their messiness, what do you mean by this? Finally, the circumstances in which the notes are taken have to be described in specific detail. In Chapter 5 we talked about reinforcers and their power to influence behavior. In the functional analysis of your description we will be looking for the reinforcers that are causing your problem behavior. Possible reinforcers include internal and external stimuli, antecedents (stimuli preceding the behavior) and consequences (stimuli following the behavior). So make sure that your description supplies the information you will need. What exactly is going on inside you and outside you before, during, and after your note-taking?

> *Okay. Okay. My problem behavior is that I take messy notes and tend to lose them afterwards.*

BOX 6.1
SELF-CONTROL GONE WILD

Writer Judith Viorst has fun describing a woman whose long-term goals have become so numerous and diverse that they've gotten out of hand. Viorst calls her poem "Self-Improvement Program."

I've finished six pillows in Needlepoint,
And I'm reading Jane Austen and Kant,
And I'm up to the pork with black beans in
    Advanced Chinese Cooking.
I don't have to struggle to find myself
For I already know what I want.
I want to be healthy and wise and extremely
    good-looking.

I'm learning new glazes in Pottery Class,
And I'm playing new chords in Guitar,
And in Yoga I'm starting to master the lotus
    position.
I don't have to ponder priorities
For I already know what they are:

To be good-looking, healthy, and wise.
And adored in addition.

I'm improving my serve with a tennis pro,
And I'm practicing verb forms in Greek,
And in Primal Scream Therapy all my frustra-
    tions are vented.
I don't have to ask what I'm searching for
Since I already know that I seek
To be good-looking, healthy, and wise.
And adored.
And contented.

I've bloomed in Organic Gardening,
And in Dance I have tightened my thighs,
And in Consciousness Raising there's no one
    around who can top me.
And I'm working all day and I'm working all
    night
To be good-looking, healthy, and wise.
And adored.
And contented.

Here's what I mean by messy notes. To begin with, I take very few notes—usually less than a page. And none of the things that I write down are numbered or outlined. As a result, I can't tell later what the big, important points were and what the sidelights were. Also, the notes are sort of scrawled all over the page, every which way, with doodles here and there. Furthermore, I never seem to put the date on the notes or number the pages. So when I try to pull them all together—the ones I can find, that is—to study for the exam, I can't tell which page comes after which, or even which lecture comes after which.

As for what goes on when I take the notes:

Well, I usually sit at the back of the lecture hall with my friends, and there's generally some talking. Also, I'm often late. And since I've been rushing, I'm usually sort of flustered. Then, after I sit down, I have to borrow some paper from somebody and maybe a pen too, so that by the time I start taking notes, the professor is already about five minutes into the lecture. Then I don't seem to be able to concentrate too well on what the professor is saying. Half the time I'm either talking to someone or admiring somebody's shoes or just sort of looking around the room, checking everyone out. What am I thinking? I'm thinking about this, that, and the other thing. When my mind zeros back in on what the professor is saying,

And brave.
And well-read.
And a marvelous hostess,
Fantastic in bed,
And bilingual,
Athletic,
Artistic . . .
Won't someone please stop me?

*Viorst, J. "Self-Improvement Program," How Did I
Get to Be Forty . . . and Other Atrocities. New York:
Simon & Schuster, 1976, pp. 31–32.*

(© James R. Smith)

*I'm sort of lost, because I wasn't paying
attention before.*

*After the lecture is over and I look down
at my awful notes, I think, "Oh hell, I'll
borrow Larry Fallon's notes." (He's a person that my roommate, Fran, is going out
with. He takes beautiful notes.) So I stuff
my messy notes into my purse. (I never
do get around to buying a binder with
those little colored dividers for each
course.) Then I go out and have coffee
with my friends.*

The next step in this description would be
self-monitoring. Our disorganized student—
whose name, incidentally, is Clara—would
have to pick one course in which she takes

particularly poor notes and keep records for
a few weeks on some measurable aspects of
her note-taking behavior. A sample record
sheet, Table 6.1, appears on p. 154.

Such a record serves three functions. First,
it makes the description even more specific.
Second, records often reveal inaccuracies in
our descriptions. For example, Clara may
find that considerably more than five minutes of the lecture have elapsed before she
begins taking notes. Third, as we saw in
Chapter 2, by monitoring your behavior before instituting any self-control program,
you provide yourself with a baseline, or pre-
treatment standard, against which you can

TABLE 6.1:
LECTURE NOTES

	WEEK 1			WEEK 2			WEEK 3		
	Mon	Wed	Fri	Mon	Wed	Fri	Mon	Wed	Fri
Number of minutes of lecture time elapsed before beginning of note-taking									
Number of minutes spent attending to something other than lecture									
Number of pages of notes taken									
Coherence of notes (rated on scale of 1 to 10)									
Able to find notes one week after lecture? (yes or no)									

compare your behavior once you start trying to improve it.

Functional Analysis

We will not go too far in the functional analysis of Clara's problem. You should do this on your own. Remember the procedure for functional analysis. The first step is to look for variables that seem to correlate with the behavior in question, since these variables may be the reinforcers of the behavior. So examine the *external* stimuli that *precede* the behaviors of taking disorganized notes and of losing notes: professor already five minutes into lecture before note-taking begins; seat in back of lecture hall; presence of talkative friends; lack of paper; lack of binder; notes stuffed into purse. And how about the *internal* stimuli that *precede* these behaviors, such as being "flustered" on arrival and being inattentive during the

lecture? Could any of these internal or external stimuli be "setting off" the problem behaviors? (Needless to say, yes.) Now, what about the stimuli, external and internal, that *follow* the behaviors in question: the cup of coffee with the friends from that class (external stimulus) and the thought that reliable old Larry Fallon will come through with the notes (internal stimulus)? Could either of these consequences be reinforcing the problem behaviors? Again, the answer probably is yes.

Thus, there seem to be a number of antecedents and consequences contributing to Clara's problem. The same is probably true of your self-control problem. So just choose the variable that seems most likely, formulate your hypothesis, and go to work on that variable. If some antecedent stimulus is triggering your unwanted behavior, then you have to avoid or replace that stimulus. If some consequence is reinforcing that behav-

ACTIVITY 6.1

Unwanted habits may be subject to a great variety of environmental cues. If you are a smoker—and even if you are not trying to stop smoking—keep a record for one day of the circumstances surrounding your smoking. Every time you light up, just jot down in a notebook where you are and what you are doing at that moment. You will probably find that you respond to a number of specific signals-for-smoking in the environment. (People with weight problems can do the same exercise with between-meal eating.)

ior, then you have to arrange new consequences. In other words, you, the "personal scientist," have to experiment with the causes of your behavior. The remainder of this chapter will be devoted to suggesting ways in which you can conduct your experiments.

IMPROVING SELF-CONTROL

First, set your behavioral goal and make it reasonable. Don't tackle more than one problem behavior at a time. And with the one behavior you are working on, do not attempt the impossible.

After you've written down your description, your hypothesis, and your goal, you can begin experimenting with your behavior. The techniques for doing so are grouped under three headings: manipulating antecedent stimuli, manipulating responses, and manipulating consequences. In practice, many behavioral therapists try to attack their clients' behavior on all three fronts, and you may find it useful to do the same.

Manipulating Antecedent Stimuli

Just as a traffic light signals whether to stop or go, there are discriminative stimuli that act as *cues* (also called *setting events*) for our behaviors. For many people, turning on

the television is a cue for snacking. For some families, sitting down at the dinner table is a cue for quarreling. Such stimulus-and-response sequences can be changed—and more useful stimulus-and-response sequences can be instituted. There are three basic ways to do this. You can change the antecedent stimuli in the environment. You can redirect your attention toward the behavior. Or you can change your cognitive approach to the antecedent stimuli through relabeling and reorganizing.

Environmental Planning

Environmental planning means arranging the stimuli in your external environment so that they will cue the behaviors you want and will not cue the behaviors you don't want. Depending on whether you are trying to decrease or increase a behavior, environmental planning involves avoiding stimuli; building in or removing delays; and decreasing or increasing associations.

Avoiding Stimuli. When a child watching a horror movie crawls under his seat so as not to see Godzilla devour the Thing, he is avoiding a stimulus that he knows will elicit an undesirable response (terror) in him. Likewise, you can arrange your environment so that you avoid those stimuli that cause unwanted responses. If you're trying to stop smoking, you can give away your last pack of cigarettes. If you're dieting, you can banish pretzels and potato chips from your house. If you're sailing past the island of the Sirens, you can plug your ears. This is the old principle of "Get thee behind me, Satan."

Often the environmental rearrangements needed are amazingly simple. One psychologist cites the case of a man who was disturbed over the fact that he was constantly nagging and criticizing his four-year-old son. Through self-monitoring the father discovered that one inevitable cue for nagging was the fact that whenever the boy tried to pour a little ketchup on his food, he ended up drowning his entire dinner in a big red puddle. In order to remove this anger-cue, the father simply made sure that at every dinnertime the boy (a great ketchup-lover) was given a small bowl of ketchup with a spoon so that he could neatly spread the desired amount of it on his food. This modest little strategy ended the dinnertime battle (Schmidt, 1976).

Building In and Removing Delays. In the Middle Ages, a knight going off on a long journey would sometimes try to ensure his wife's faithfulness by outfitting her with a chastity belt—essentially, a pair of iron underpants with lock and key. (The knight took the key.) It is doubtful that the chastity belts always prevented infidelity. What they did, however, was to make infidelity much more difficult. They created delays. Attention, determination, and effort were required to get past these delays. The chastity-belted wife could not simply "fall into" adultery; she had to go out and find a bribable locksmith first.

In the same way, you can decrease the likelihood of problem behaviors by arranging your environment so that delays are built in between the temptation and the actual enactment of the behavior (Lando, 1977). If you're trying to cut down on smoking, you can keep your cigarettes in an inconvenient place, like the back of a high kitchen cupboard. Likewise, dieters are advised to put small portions on their plates, so that if they want seconds, they have to get up and walk to the stove to serve themselves. Another good delay technique for people on diets is to keep in their kitchens only foods that require preparation. You can grab a cookie and put it in your mouth almost automatically, but a piece of frozen fish has to be cooked before you can eat it (Stuart and Davis, 1972; McReynolds and Paulsen, 1976).

In all these cases, the effort and the delay, even when very slight, will make the forbidden fruit seem less tempting. Even more important, however, is the fact that the delay brings the act to the individual's *attention.* Bad habits thrive on inattention. When we begin attending closely to a behavior, on the other hand, that behavior is likely to change, whether or not we want it to (McFall, 1970; Bornstein et al., 1978; Nelson, 1977). Delays, in other words, prevent impulsive and automatic behavior; they force us to make conscious choices. To put it in Freud's terms, delays prevent the id from going to work before the ego and superego have had time to think it over. And given this opportunity to attend and choose, the ego and superego often win. (For additional examples of built-in delays, see Box 6.2.)

If you are trying to increase rather than decrease a behavior, you need to use exactly the opposite tactic. Remove delays. Make the behavior as easy and as automatic as possible. If you hate to sit down and pay the bills, but simply must do it tonight, then lay out the bills, the checkbook, and the pen on your desk before you leave for work. If you dislike vacuuming but want to start doing an hour's housecleaning every Saturday morning, put the vacuum cleaner in the middle of the living room before you go to bed on Friday nights. By cutting out delays in this way, you bypass that "moment of decision" in which you're likely to convince yourself that you're too tired, too busy, or whatever.

Decreasing and Increasing Associations. So far we've dealt only with those stimuli that are *necessary* to our behaviors—cigarettes for smoking, snacks for snacking, a vacuum cleaner for housecleaning, and so forth. But as we have seen, our behaviors occur not only because such necessary equipment is available, but also because certain stimuli or situations cue the behavior. For example, finishing a meal, opening a book, taking a break from a task, and having an alcoholic drink or a cup of coffee are all common cues for smoking. Thus, if we want to decrease a behavior, one good way is to cut the associational ties between that behavior and its environmental cue (Lando, 1977).

This can be accomplished through *stimulus-narrowing*. Essentially, this is an enforced program of discrimination learning (see Chapter 5). Rather than let yourself engage in the behavior in a wide range of situations, you allow yourself to engage in it in only one specific situation. If you want to

---

BOX 6.2
A FEW EVERYDAY EXAMPLES OF BUILDING IN DELAYS

CHRISTMAS CLUBS

If you kept your Christmas savings in a bureau drawer, it would be very easy for you to lay your hands on the money when you felt like going out for a steak but were short of cash. In order to dig into your Christmas Club savings, however, you have to wait until banking hours, go to the bank, stand in line, and so forth. By that time you would almost certainly have lost interest in the steak. (Christmas Clubs also utilize the principle of removing delays. By automatically taking the money out of your checking account every month, the bank relieves you of the delay, effort, and choice involved in transferring the funds yourself.)

WAITING PERIODS FOR DIVORCE

Though almost 50 percent of all marriages in the United States now end in divorce, our legal system still has certain mechanisms aimed at protecting the institution of marriage. Most states require that a married couple filing for divorce wait anywhere from several weeks to a year before they are given a legal hearing in which the divorce may be granted. The purpose of the delay is to give the couple a chance to reflect and possibly change their minds.

DOUBLE DATES

Parents of young teen-agers often encourage double dating or dating in groups on the assumption (conscious or unconscious) that sexual activity is less likely to go on in the back seat if another couple is in the front seat. In order to find privacy, a couple on a double date have to put forth some effort and endure some delay, which parents hope will give their children time to remember what Mother said.

cut down on cigarette consumption, for example, you can restrict your smoking to a "smoking chair," preferably located in some uninviting place such as the bathroom or the basement (Frederiksen and Simon, 1978). One therapist used this technique with a man whose sulking was creating serious problems in his marriage:

> The client was instructed to sulk to his heart's content but to do so in a specified place. Whenever he felt like sulking, he was to go into the garage, sit on a special sulking stool, and sulk and mutter over the indignities of life for as long as he wished. When he was through with his sulking, he could leave the garage and join his wife (Goldiamond, 1965, p. 856).

Once the response is separated from its usual environmental cues, these cues eventually lose their power to call forth the response.

This same technique, in slightly altered form, can be used to increase a behavior. In this case, instead of limiting the number of stimuli that cue a certain behavior, you limit the number of behaviors that are cued by a certain stimulus. You reserve a certain environmental situation for one behavior alone: the behavior you want to increase. Eventually the situation and the behavior will become so firmly associated with one another that you can make the behavior occur simply by putting yourself in the situation (Coates and Thoresen, 1977). If you want to increase your studying, for example, you can reserve your desk exclusively for studying. This is exactly what Goldiamond instructed one of his clients to do:

> It was . . . decided that her desk was to control study behavior. If she wished to write a letter, she should do so, but in the dining room; if she wished to read comic books, she should do so, but in the kitchen; if she wished to

daydream, she should do so, but was to go to another room; at her desk she was to engage in her school work and her school work only. (1965, p. 854)

During the first week of this regimen, she spent only ten minutes at the desk. But by the end of the semester (in time for final exams), she was able to stay at her desk for three hours a day—all of which time was spent studying.

Another way of manipulating behavior through environmental cues is simply to increase the number of stimuli that will cue the behavior. In other words, you equip your environment with reminders. If you speed while driving, you can paste pictures of gruesome automobile accidents on the dashboard. If you bite your nails, you can tie the proverbial string around your finger. If you fritter away your money, you can put a rubber band around your wallet (thereby building in a delay as well) and attach to it a note specifying what you *won't* be able to do at the end of the month (for example, pay rent, buy the new shoes you need) if you spend all your money at the beginning of the month.

Redirecting Attention

We have already mentioned how helpful it is simply to pay close attention to your behavior. The people who truly master a skill are usually those who can concentrate best on what they're doing. For example, Ted Williams, one of the finest hitters in the history of baseball, was known for his ability, when he was at bat, to screen out everything else in the ballpark and concentrate only on the ball. As the ball left the pitcher's hands and came toward the plate, Williams reportedly would keep his eye on its lacings. (Needless to say, he had excellent vision.) And by watching how the lacings spun or twisted, he could tell whether the pitch was

One activity requiring immense concentration is tennis. This tennis player has his entire attention focused on the ball. (© Al Kaplan/DPI, Inc.)

group of smokers were given a talk on the health hazards of tobacco-use and then were asked to record, for a certain period of time, every cigarette they smoked. Almost immediately, their tobacco-intake decreased. An even greater decrease was shown when smokers were asked to record not only the cigarettes they smoked but also the amount of nicotine they were taking in with each cigarette. In other words, you have a better chance of beating a bad habit if you are forced to think about it—particularly if you are forced to think of what is bad about it.

To combat inattention in dealing with your own problem behavior, you can, as described above, engineer delays. You can also set up the situation so that there is nothing to distract you from concentrating on your behavior. If you bite your nails while reading, make a rule that in order to bite your nails you have to put the book down and focus your mind on your nail-biting. If you tend to smoke while watching television, make a rule that you must turn off the television until you have finished the cigarette. If you overeat, start eating alone, and without television or reading material, so that you can concentrate on your meal (Stuart and Davis, 1972). You might increase your concentration by performing these behaviors in front of a mirror. Whatever you do, pay attention to the behavior.

Chances are that this regimen will not go on for long without some behavior change. As we have seen, increased attention in itself brings about behavior change, whether or not any change is desired. Furthermore, reading, television, people, and other distractions are potent reinforcers, whereas our habitual behaviors are actually rather boring. Consequently, when faced with a choice between the behavior without distractions (smoking without TV) and the distractions without the behavior (TV without smoking), we are likely to choose the distractions.

a slider, a curve ball, or a fast ball and swing accordingly.

Very few of us will ever have the concentration of great athletes or great dancers. But we *can* teach ourselves to control our attention when we're dealing with a troublesome behavior (Komaki and Dore-Boyce, 1978; Bornstein et al., 1978). Such behaviors, as we mentioned earlier, are often fostered by lack of attention. Smokers will often light a cigarette without even thinking about it. Likewise, nail-biters usually do not attend to the pain and inconvenience of their nail-biting; the behavior has become as automatic as breathing.

But if people are forced to think about unwanted behaviors as they are performing them, the behavior tends to decrease. This was shown, for example, in an experiment on smoking (Abrams and Wilson, 1979). A

Relabeling and Organizing

When you redirect attention, you are manipulating internal antecedent stimuli: your own perceptions. Another way of manipulating internal antecedents to help you control your behavior is to revise your labeling of a task and your approach to it.

Relabeling. Experimenters (e.g., D'Zurilla and Goldfried, 1973) have found that people can control irrational fears if they can be taught to relabel them: "It's not really this dog I'm so afraid of—it's the dog who bit me when I was seven. And he's surely been dead for years. (May he roast in hell!) So what am I afraid of?"

This form of self-talk can also be used to help us engage in behaviors that we would otherwise avoid. All it really involves is finding more positive labels for tasks that we label negatively (Goldfried, 1977). If you hate going to the laundromat on Sunday, you can examine your current label for the task—"that awful job of lugging the dirty clothes down to that drafty old laundromat"—and change it to "taking the clothes to the laundromat and getting a chance to read for an hour and a half without listening to the kids yelling at each other." Or if you have trouble starting work on a paper, you change the label so that it is only *starting* the paper, rather than actually writing the paper, that is so difficult. (Actually, this is often the case.)

Such tinkering with your perceptions may sound a bit like a child's game. But your revised label is usually every bit as accurate as your original one. More important, it will help you get started on what you have to do.

Organizing. Another useful stratagem for accomplishing unloved tasks is to organize the job (Kanfer, 1977). Map out the method by which the job will be done, deciding what deserves the most attention, what order you should follow, and so forth. People use this technique every day when they make lists of things they have to do. Such simple little lists reduce the day's labors to manageable proportions just by spelling out what needs to be done and—if the person is a sophisticated list-maker—in what order.

By applying this same technique to a specific task, you can actually turn it into a sort of game. If you have to iron, you can set a goal (five shirts and eight napkins) and plan to alternate between shirts (difficult) and napkins (easy). If you have trouble getting yourself to study, you can devise a different technique for each course, depending on what is most important in the course (Goldiamond, 1965; Menges and Dobroski, 1977). For your language course, where memorizing is important, you give most attention to flash cards and verb charts. For political science, where the text is boring but the professor is brilliant, you put your efforts into taking thorough lecture notes and reviewing them afterwards. For zoology, where the text is good and the professor is bad, you concentrate on outlining the textbook, and so forth. In this way, what seems to be a huge and horrible labor can be reduced to a set of clear and realistic duties, with enough variety to keep you from getting bored.

Meddling With Responses

We have concentrated so far on altering the antecedents of our behavior. A second approach is to attack the behavior itself.

Chaining

Often, a troublesome habit is a "chained" behavior—that is, a behavior that is actually a sequence of mini-behaviors, each of which constitutes the cue for the next. For exam-

BOX 6.3
WHAT ABOUT WILL POWER?

When a friend stops smoking or finishes some long and difficult task, we often say that he or she has "will power." This concept of *will* or *will power* was developed by Western philosophers to account for the ability of human beings to forgo immediate gratifications for the sake of long-term goals. While the body might be subject to numerous temptations, the will was directed by the higher power of reason, which could win out over such temptations.

Modern psychologists, in general, do not like to use the concept of will power. To begin with, the concept *seems* to explain the human ability to place long-term goals over short-term pleasures, whereas in fact it doesn't explain it, but only gives it a name. Furthermore, the implied explanation is that this ability comes from some mysterious inner force that is not subject to external influence—either you have it or you don't. That, clearly, is not the case. It takes control to paint a fence, cook a hamburger, or get out of bed on Monday morning, and the ability to go on a successful diet or to stop smoking appears to be just an extension of these more modest achievements.

In place of will power, many psychologists prefer the term *self-control*. This term implies no mysterious inner force, nor does it attempt to explain what it is that causes people to make short-term sacrifices for long-term rewards. Instead, it simply describes a behavior: the individual's conscious management of those external and internal variables that influence his or her behavior. The term, in other words, is less ambitious, but more accurate. Furthermore, it gives power back to the person. If you control your behavior, why should the credit go to some inner "something" whose existence cannot even be proven? Why not to you?

ple, smoking may look like a rather elementary response, but it actually involves a long chain of responses. The smoker must first buy a pack of cigarettes and store them somewhere (purse, pocket, desk drawer). Then she must withdraw the pack from where it is kept and, if it is unopened, remove the wrapper. Then she may tap the cigarette. Or, if the cigarette is filter-tipped, she has to look at it to see which end to put in her mouth. Once it is in her mouth, she must locate a pack of matches, open it, tear out a match, close the cover, and strike the match. Then she must hold the lighted match so that it ignites the end of the cigarette. Then she must inhale, bringing the smoke into her lungs, and exhale, breathing it out again. This inhalation-exhalation process continues, along with the occasional tapping of the cigarette to remove ashes, until the cigarette is almost consumed, at which point the smoker extinguishes it.

Chained behaviors offer excellent opportunities for self-control, because there are so many points at which we can jump in and interfere with the completion of the chain. The simplest way of interfering is, of course, simply to interrupt the chain by removing one of its links. For example, the smoker could 1) not buy the pack, 2) not reach for the pack, 3) not carry any matches. The earlier the chain is interrupted, the better. Like a ball rolling down a hill, a chained behavior gains momentum as it moves along. It is

---

ACTIVITY 6.2

The very process of chaining may make the getting-out-of-the-house-in-the-morning routine take so long that we either end up being late or have to start waking up earlier than we should. Write down, in order, all the things you do before leaving in the morning, and how long each activity takes. If you think you're spending too much time on the process, you may want to rearrange the chain. You can shorten it by taking care of some steps the previous evening. Pack the children's lunches while you're making dinner. Set the table for breakfast as you clean up after dinner. Lay out your clothes before you go to bed. With these tasks already done, you will probably be able to sleep a few minutes longer and still get off on time in the morning.

---

hard to interrupt the smoking chain once the cigarette has been lit. Likewise, it is difficult not to eat a potato chip once you are aiming it toward your mouth. (The chain should have been interrupted early, by not buying the potato chips or not entering the kitchen.)

A second approach is to scramble the chain—that is, rearrange the order. Striking the match before removing the cigarette from the pack is likely to result in considerable confusion and possibly burned fingers as well. The result is that you will be less eager to smoke. Here again, the purpose is to disrupt the automatic quality of the behavior and make you aware of what you're doing.

A third approach to chained behaviors is to lengthen the chain by adding extra links. If you want to cut down on television-watching, for example, you can store the television in a closet (better yet, a closet in the basement) so that you have to go get it and plug it in before you can watch it. Or, if you want to lose weight, you can do your food shopping on a day-to-day basis, so that overeating requires getting some money together and going to the store (Ferster et al., 1962; Stuart and Davis, 1972). In practice, this technique is almost identical to build-

ing in delays, and its purposes are the same: first, to make the "reward" more difficult to obtain and therefore less attractive, and second, to allow you the time and the awareness necessary for resisting the temptation.

With chain-lengthening, as with delaying, you simply reverse the procedure when you want to increase a behavior. Cut out whatever intermediate steps you can. For example, if you're trying to get yourself to wash the dishes right after dinner, dump them into soapy water as you clear the table; this will eliminate soaking later on.

Incompatible Behaviors

An old trick for cutting down on smoking is to chew gum instead. In doing this, the smoker is resorting to the useful technique of replacing the problem behavior with an *incompatible behavior*—that is, a behavior that makes the problem behavior difficult or impossible to enact. To use the incompatible-behavior approach, you have to begin by finding a good substitute, one that is reinforcing at the same time that it interferes with your problem behavior. If you tend to do your between-meal nibbling at about 10:00 A.M., reserve this time for some especially valued activity, such as reading the

SELF-CONTROL: HOW TO CHANGE IT

Should they start looking for an incompatible behavior?
(Bill Owens/Magnum)

morning paper or telephoning a friend (Ferster et al., 1962; Stuart and Davis, 1972). If you tend to get drunk on Friday night, start spending your Friday evenings at the movies (preferably double features). If you tend to turn on the television as soon as you walk into the house, keep a novel or a magazine on top of the television so that you can easily substitute reading for TV-watching. In all these cases, what you're doing is cutting the conditioned associations between the problem behavior and its environmental cues. At the same time you're creating an association between those cues and a harmless substitute behavior.

If you can't find a substitute, you can at least institute a waiting period before engaging in the problem behavior—somewhat like counting to ten when you're angry. (This is yet another subdivision of the technique of building in delays.) For example, you can

make a rule forbidding yourself to turn on the television until you've been in the house for a half hour. Here you are still cutting the association between the behavior and its cue. At the same time it's possible that during that half hour you'll find some other activity to fill the void, so that you may forget about the television after all.

Shaping

As we saw in Chapter 5, shaping is the gradual creation of a target behavior by moving toward it in very small steps. Through shaping you can ease yourself into smoking fewer cigarettes, consuming fewer calories, writing longer letters, jogging longer distances, studying for longer periods of time, and so forth.

When shaping a behavior, there are a few important rules to remember. The first is that the increase or decrease must be extremely gradual. Let's imagine, for example, that you want to use shaping to cut down on the length of your telephone calls. The first thing to do is establish your baseline—that is, determine the average number of minutes you currently spend per day on the telephone. Just check the clock at the beginning and end of each call. After each call, add the number of minutes to that day's running total. At the end of a week, figure out your average. Let's say that you find, to your horror, that your daily average is 130 minutes. You say to yourself, "Two precious hours a day spent yakking into the phone! And all I get for it is a sweaty ear. No wonder I never get any studying done. I'm cutting back right now to ten minutes a day." Wrong. No matter how disgusted you are with yourself, you shouldn't try to cut back too fast. If you do, you will very probably break your rule, become even more disgusted with yourself, give up hope, and abandon the shaping project altogether. Instead, you should decrease your telephone time very slowly, possibly in steps of 5 to 10 minutes.

A second rule for shaping: at every step of the way you should make sure that you feel perfectly comfortable with that step before moving on to the next one. Once you have averaged 120 minutes phone time per day for two days, don't jump to the next step right away. Give yourself two or three more days at 120 minutes. The purpose of shaping is not to make a big effort; it is to change *without* making a big effort. You want to make the new rate of response as natural and as habitual as the old rate of response. And habits are not created overnight. So take your time.

A final point regarding shaping is that you should try to deal with your behavior in terms of a measurement that can be broken up into very small units. In other words, don't measure your behavior in terms of big, vague units such as number of books read or number of phone calls. Stick to a dimension with small, regular units like calories or minutes. Such measures make it easier for you to observe your progress, and observing your progress is invaluable feedback. Second, they allow for flexibility across situations; you can make either two long phone calls or ten short phone calls and still stay within your limit. Finally, small units of measure make it easier for you to move in small steps and to adjust your steps. If steps are too large, you can cut them in half (for example, reduce telephone time by 5 minutes rather than 10 minutes at each step). Or if your steps are too small, you can increase them without having to go so far as to double them.

Manipulating Consequences

Until now, we have put off discussing one very important item, the thing that keeps you working at whatever self-control technique you happen to choose. That item is, of course, the consequences of your behavior. As we saw in Chapter 5, consequences influence behavior whether or not we manipulate them—indeed, whether or not we are even aware of them. When we do make ourselves aware of them and when we do manipulate them, they are a powerful ally in improving self-control.

Utilizing Feedback

Perhaps the most important consequence you can provide for yourself in a self-control program is feedback—information as to how you are doing. Feedback can come from a number of sources: a mirror (if you're trying to lose weight), a tape recorder (if you're working on your speaking abilities), an audiovisual tape (if you're trying to improve an athletic skill). Dancers, singers, actors, and athletes use such devices constantly.

Probably the most valuable source of feedback, however, is self-monitoring (McFall, 1977). Earlier in this chapter we mentioned the necessity of keeping records on your problem behavior in order to find out exactly how big the problem is and what stimulus might be triggering or maintaining it. But record-keeping should not stop once you have written your description of your behavior. When you move into the experimentation phase, you must go on keeping your records.

There are two reasons for this. First, the record will tell you whether the self-control technique is working. If it isn't, you can throw out your hypothesis and formulate a new one, or simply switch to a different self-control technique. Second, once you begin to improve, the record will provide you with precious positive feedback. As you look at the record of your declining calorie-consumption, alongside the record of your declining weight, you'll feel good about yourself: proud, self-disciplined, skinny, beautiful, and so on. These positive self-reactions are probably the most potent reinforcing consequences that you can use to strengthen your revised behavior.

An interesting sidelight on self-monitoring (and perhaps a third reason for using it) is that it is *reactive*. That is, the mere act of keeping records on a behavior leads to change (usually improvement) in that behavior, even when there is no conscious desire or effort to change (McFall, 1977). Psychologists have found this to be true in self-monitoring of smoking (McFall, 1970; Abrams and Wilson, 1979), classroom-disrupting (Turkewitz et al., 1975), studying (Broden et al., 1971; Johnson and White, 1971), dieting (Mahoney, 1974; Romanczyk, 1974), electricity-consumption (Winnett et al., 1979), even attendance and performance

For hours every day, dancers use mirrors to give them feedback on the grace and control of their movements. (Laimute E. Druskis/EPA, Inc.)

at swimming classes (McKenzie and Rushall, 1974). This fact should come as no surprise. As we have seen earlier, paying attention to our behavior makes an immense difference. When we're forced to watch what we're doing, we shape up. And keeping records is the best means of watching what we're doing.

Providing Self-Reward

In self-monitoring we provide ourselves with automatic internal reinforcement: the sense of competence and achievement. Positive self-reactions need not be simply automatic, however. When you've resisted temptation, you can engage in deliberate self-praise. In other words, pat yourself on the back verbally. Say to yourself, out loud, "Congratulations!" or "See, you can do it." If you're with other people, then switch to *covert* (that is, mental) *reinforcement*. Praise yourself in your mind, or imagine yourself enjoying the ultimate rewards of your self-control program: looking wonderful in a swimsuit, receiving a letter saying that you've been accepted into medical school, or saying to someone, very casually, "Oh yes, I used to smoke too, but I gave it up."

Going one step further, we can provide ourselves with external reinforcement as well. Indeed, the combination of self-monitoring, self-evaluation (that is, a sense of competence and achievement), and tangible self-reinforcement appears to be the most effective means of manipulating the consequences of our behavior (Bandura, 1969, 1971; Kanfer, 1977).

The most direct form of self-reward is positive reinforcement, giving yourself something nice as a consequence of having controlled your behavior. Thus, for every five pounds that you lose through shaping, you could buy yourself a new pair of pants (*not* a banana split). Or you could treat yourself to a new record for having managed, through relabeling, to give your apartment a thorough cleaning.

Whatever your rewards, they should be readily accessible, and you should present them to yourself as soon as possible after you have fulfilled your self-control requirement (Goldiamond, 1976). Once a self-control program is well under way, intermittent rewards (the new pair of pants for every five pounds lost, rather than a reward for every day of dieting) are best. As we have seen in Chapter 5, intermittently rewarded behaviors have a better chance of becoming permanent. But at the beginning it is usually a good idea to give yourself smaller rewards more often, since the frequent payoffs will help to reinforce the new behavior. If you follow these rules, you may end up choosing very modest rewards—a cup of coffee, an evening walk, thirty minutes to read the newspaper. No matter how modest, the reward is likely to work if it is something you truly enjoy and if you allow yourself to have it only when you have stuck to your self-control program.

Rules and Contracts. If you're going to try to control your behavior by manipulating its consequences, you have to spell out the behavior and the consequences. In other words, you have to make a *rule* for yourself. For example, if the behavior you're trying to control is your habit of tossing your clothes onto the bed whenever you change your outfit, then you might make the following rule: "Whenever I take off my clothes, I'll hang them up. If I do so, I can have a cup of coffee after dinner. If I fail to do so, no after-dinner coffee."

The necessity for rule-making may seem rather obvious. It should be remembered, however, that one reason why New Year's resolutions are such notorious failures is that they state grand, vague dreams of self-improvement ("I will stop wasting time,"

"I will lose weight," "I will be a nicer person") rather than specific behaviors and specific rewards for those behaviors.

For behaviors more complicated than hanging up your clothes—behaviors such as losing weight or improving study habits—you may want to go one step beyond rule-making and write a *self-contract* (Homme et al., 1969; Kanfer, 1975). This is simply a set of interlocking rules. The contract should specify your behavioral goal, your behavioral requirements for achieving it (for example, decrease calorie-intake by 100 calories per week and increase exercising by 1 minute per week), and your predetermined reward program. To supply yourself with both pressure and support, it is often helpful to involve someone else in your contract, perhaps by allowing him or her to control your rewards. (See, for example, Box 6.4.) Posting the contract in an appropriate place (over your desk for study problems, on the refrigerator for eating problems) will also serve to remind you, to pressure you, and to make the whole project seem that much more serious.

Using the Premack Principle

When you're trying to select valued and accessible reinforcers as consequences for your behavior, you should keep in mind what is called the *Premack principle*, after David Premack, the psychologist who formulated it. The Premack principle states that a behavior you voluntarily perform with high frequency can be used to reinforce a behavior you perform with low frequency (Premack, 1965, 1971). We have already mentioned the use of behaviors, as well as tangible goods, as rewards: taking a walk, reading the newspaper, and so forth. If you examine your daily activities very closely (or, better yet, keep a record for a few days), you will probably find a number of hidden voluntary behaviors that occur so naturally

BOX 6.4
A SAMPLE SELF-CONTRACT

Here is a self-contract drawn up by psychologist Jerry Schmidt to get himself to finish writing his book on self-control. (Technically, he is trying to increase his book-writing behavior.) Note that the contract involves another person, Schmidt's wife. She not only controls some of the rewards but also has her own set of contracted duties, which support and encourage Schmidt's efforts.

SELF-CONTRACT Self: _____Jerry Schmidt_____ _____February 9, 1975_____

Other: _____Karen Schmidt_____ **Date**

Goal:

_____To increase my book writing time_____

AGREEMENT

Self:

I agree to write on my self-change book for a minimum of eight hours each week. Any given writing interval must be at least two hours in length.

Others:

Karen Schmidt (my wife) agrees to read and comment on all written pages that occur during two-hour intervals, within the same day they are written.

CONSEQUENCES

Arranged by Self: (If contract is kept)

If I stick to the above agreement, at the end of each week (ending Friday at 5:00 P.M.) I will reward myself with an expensive cigar.

(If the contract is broken)

If I do not keep the above agreement during a given week I will do the yardwork by myself on Saturday.

Arranged by Others: (If contract is kept)

Karen will (1) read and comment on written pages finished during two-hour intervals; (2) type final copy each week I write for eight total hours; and (3) help me with the yard work for one hour on Saturday during each week I keep the contract.

Signed: _Jerry Schmidt_ **Witness** _Karen Schmidt_ **Review Date** _February 28, 1975_

Schmidt, J.A. Help Yourself: A Guide to Self-Change. *Champaign, Ill.: Research Press Co.*, 1976, p. 61.

and with such high frequency that you take them for granted. If you live in a college residence, what about the behavior of eating with your friends? If you have a job, what about the behavior of chatting with your coworkers for a few minutes every morning before starting your work? If you walk back from campus to the place where you live, what about the behavior of always taking a certain route because you like to look in the shop windows and perhaps stop in the bookstores along the way?

Such behaviors may seem unglamorous, but if you engage in them with great regularity, you must enjoy them, since they're not the kind of behaviors you're forced to engage in. Hence, these behaviors (in addition to the more obvious reward behaviors of watching television, reading magazines, playing tennis, and so forth) qualify as excellent reinforcers. Using the Premack principle, you can make the behavior of eating dinner with your friends contingent on having put in two hours of study time that afternoon. Or you can make the behavior of walking home by your usual route contingent on having done your allotted amount of exercise that morning. You may be amazed to find—when, for the first time, you are deprived of them—how much value you place on those modest daily rewards.

Administering Punishment

Because so many of us were socialized by punishments rather than rewards, we tend to feel that a self-control program is "soft" if it doesn't include punishments. However, as many psychologists (Skinner, 1948, 1953; Bandura, 1969) have pointed out, punishment is generally less effective than other learning techniques. (This applies not only to adult self-control programs but also to child-rearing [Bandura, 1962].) In the first place, people build up a resistance to punishment, with the result that the punishment ceases to have any effect unless it is constantly made harsher and harsher. Second, punishment does not teach new behaviors; it only tells you what behaviors are wrong. Third, and perhaps most important, punishment, even when it is self-imposed, results in bad feelings. The person being punished feels unhappy about himself, and these negative feelings are likely to generalize to the self-control program, resulting in its abandonment.

Punishment, then, should be used sparingly, if at all. Perhaps you feel that you really must "get tough" with yourself. In this case, limit yourself to what is called *positive self-punishment*. This means depriving yourself of some freely available

---

ACTIVITY 6.3

Test the Premack principle on yourself. Make a list of some of the things you do every day on a regular basis (watch television, shower, visit with friends, talk on the telephone, go for walks, change clothes, listen to the radio, read the newspaper, and so on). Make one of these activities for today contingent on your reading the next chapter in this book. You will probably find that you waste little time getting the chapter read, since you won't want to prolong the inconvenience of being unable to perform a habitual—and pleasurable—activity.

reinforcer—for example, "tearing up a dollar bill for every 100 calories in excess of one's daily limit" (Thoresen and Mahoney, 1974, p. 22). Definitely avoid *negative self-punishment*—that is, subjecting yourself to some freely avoidable unpleasant stimulus (for example, forcing yourself to keep your hands in ice-cold water for three minutes on days when you break your studying rules). Actually, however, neither form of punishment is useful enough to outweigh its unpleasantness. If you stick to self-monitoring and self-rewards, you will probably find that the disappointment of a day's failure and the loss of a hoped-for reward are punishment enough.

Three Don'ts

Don't create unrealistic goals or unrealistic requirements. Like the maker of New Year's resolutions, the person embarking on a self-control program is likely to say to himself in a fit of disgust, "Okay. This is it. Now I'm really going to do it. By next Thursday I'm going to be . . ." something utterly impossible to achieve by next Thursday: fifteen pounds lighter, an honors student, or whatever. Make your goal realistic, and when you're creating your self-control program, make your rules realistic. What two psychologists have to say about dieting rules applies as well to any self-control program:

BOX 6.5
UNEXPECTED RESULTS

In the rare case a self-control experiment will backfire, producing behaviors never dreamed of by the conscientious "personal scientist." For example, one psychologist decided that he would cut down on smoking through stimulus-narrowing. To eliminate the environmental triggers for smoking, he allowed himself to smoke only in the bathroom, whether at work or at home. Soon he found that this strategy had resulted in some unexpected respondent conditioning: when, outside the bathroom, he saw or smelled someone else's cigarette, he suddenly felt a desire to urinate (Thoresen and Mahoney, 1974).

Another psychologist tried to cut down on his smoking by using a reversal of the Premack principle: he would make smoking (high-frequency response) contingent on the hated task of reading psychological research reports in pro-

fessional journals (low-frequency response). Only when he sat down to read one of these reports would he allow himself to light a cigarette. His hope was that his smoking would become as infrequent as his report-reading. At the beginning it seemed that his hope would be fulfilled. His cigarette consumption did start to decline. As the days passed, however, he came to the awful realization that he was reading more and more research reports. Never before had he been so well informed on the research in his field! After three weeks of this "therapy," he found, much to his dismay, that his cigarette consumption was the same as before his self-control experiment. The only change in his behavior was that he had become an avid reader of research reports and that he now truly enjoyed this once-loathed activity.

It is tempting to make a list of perfectionistic rules, especially if you aren't hungry at the moment. This should be avoided. Remember that if you were perfect you wouldn't be fat. Rigid rules . . . are bound to be broken eventually, and that leads to a sense of failure. Stick with rules you think you can follow. (Mahoney and Mahoney, 1976, p. 43)

It is better to try for too little than for too much. If you find that your rules are too easy or your goal too modest, then you can simply revise them (gradually!) and proceed as before. But if your rules are too strict and your goal too grand, you will fail to meet your targets, become discouraged, and give up.

Don't expect either immediate results or continual results. It is possible that at the beginning you will see no improvement. Mark this up to the staying power of an old habit and keep trying. It is even more possible that you will reach plateaus—periods in which, no matter how hard you try, nothing happens. (For example, you are following your diet faithfully, but your body seems to pay no attention. For a whole week it has stubbornly gone on weighing 147 pounds.) Again, you must regard this as natural and wait it out. This brings us to our final don't.

Don't give up. If you have spent weeks at a discouraging plateau, or if your whole self-control program has been a plateau from the start, then reexamine your hypothesis or change your self-control technique. If this doesn't work, there is still no reason to assume that you're doomed to spend your life at the mercy of your problem behavior. The fault may well lie with the program rather than with you. One good solution is to consult a professional, who will help you design a better program and give you support and encouragement in following it. (See the section entitled "Getting Help," pp. 000–000.) And remember: Any learned behavior can be unlearned. All you need is careful planning and hard work.

SUMMARY

1. The first step in solving a self-control problem is to specify what the problem is and form some hypothesis as to what is causing it. This means starting with a description of the problem you're going to work on. You then keep careful records of your behavior through self-monitoring. These data will allow you to examine the external and internal stimuli that precede and follow the behavior. You can then locate correlations and form a hypothesis as to what is causing the behavior.

2. After completing your self-analysis, you can begin working toward improving your self-control. One basic approach is to manipulate antecedent stimuli. You can do this through *environmental planning*, which involves arranging external *cues* so they will trigger only the behaviors you want. Environmental-planning methods include avoiding stimuli, building in or removing delays between stimuli and responses, and decreasing or increasing associations by such means as *stimulus-narrowing* (a form of discrimination learning).

3. Another way to manipulate antecedent stimuli is to redirect your attention away

INCREASING SELF-CONTROL: AN OUTLINE

Whether or not you currently have a problem in self-control, exercising influence over yourself is a skill worth having and improving. As a skill, self-control needs to be practiced just like tennis or the piano. The following outline summarizes the approach described in this chapter. Try using it to gain greater control over a relatively simple daily activity such as brushing your teeth or watching television. Remember to keep written records as you go along.

1. Describe the problem:
   a. Write a simple, objective, and specific description.
   b. Use self-monitoring to flesh out the description.
2. Examine, in the description, the internal and external antecedents and the internal and external consequences of the behavior. Choose those you wish to work on and attack them as follows:

3. Manipulate the antecedents:
   a. Environmental planning: avoiding stimuli, building in or removing delays, decreasing or increasing associations
   b. Redirecting attention toward the behavior
   c. Relabeling and reorganizing
4. Modify the response:
   a. Interrupting, scrambling, lengthening, or shortening a chain of behaviors
   b. Substituting incompatible behaviors
   c. Shaping
5. Manipulate the consequences:
   a. Utilizing feedback on your progress, through self-monitoring
   b. Rewarding yourself covertly and overtly
   c. Choosing rewards on the basis of the Premack principle

from cues for the problem behavior and focus it instead on the behavior itself. A third way is to relabel tasks or organize them so that you can control them more easily.

4. A second basic approach to modifying behavior is to attack the response itself. When a troublesome habit is part of a *chain* of behaviors, interrupting, rearranging, or lengthening the chain may improve self-control. In other cases, it may help to engage in *incompatible behaviors*—behaviors that make the problem behavior difficult or impossible to perform. Shaping is also useful in modifying troublesome behaviors, especially if it is done very gradually and in easily measurable steps.

5. The consequences of our behavior have a powerful effect on us, whether or not we manipulate them. One of the most important consequences you can utilize is feedback—information on how well you're doing. Self-reward can also help you improve your self-control, whether in the form of covert self-congratulation or overt positive reinforcement. Making rules or writing out a *self-contract* will facilitate this process.

6. The *Premack principle* states that behaviors you voluntarily perform with high frequency can be used to reinforce behaviors you perform with low frequency. Using this principle, you can make things you enjoy doing contingent upon your doing things you may not like to do.

7. Because of the problems associated with punishment, this type of consequence is not recommended in a self-control program. If you do use it, limit yourself to *positive self-punishment* and avoid *negative self-punishment.*

8. In setting up your self-control program, three pitfalls are to be avoided: creating unrealistic goals or requirements, expecting immediate or continual results, and giving up too quickly.

PROJECT

All of us have to exercise some self-control. We have to save our money, get to work on time, talk ourselves out of depression and anxiety, write term papers, and so forth. Some people are quite adept at such control behaviors; others, less so. The following questionnaire was developed by Michael Rosenbaum (1980) to assess people's self-control skills. Since this chapter and the next are aimed at helping you increase such skills, it might be helpful now to take a rough measure of your present skills.

Go through the 36 statements and indicate how characteristic each statement is of you by circling the appropriate number in the columns next to the statement.

	Very Characteristic of Me	Rather Characteristic of Me	Somewhat Characteristic of Me	Somewhat Uncharacteristic of Me	Rather Uncharacteristic of Me	Very Uncharacteristic of Me
1. When I do a boring job, I think about the less boring parts of the job and the reward that I will receive once I am finished.	+3	+2	+1	−1	−2	−3
2. When I have to do something that is anxiety arousing for me, I try to visualize how I will overcome my anxieties while doing it.	+3	+2	+1	−1	−2	−3
3. Often, by changing my way of thinking, I am able to change my feelings about almost everything.	+3	+2	+1	−1	−2	−3
4. I often find it difficult to overcome my feelings of nervousness and tension without any outside help.*	+3	+2	+1	−1	−2	−3
5. When I am feeling depressed I try to think about pleasant events.	+3	+2	+1	−1	−2	−3
6. I cannot avoid thinking about mistakes I have made in the past.*	+3	+2	+1	−1	−2	−3
7. When I am faced with a difficult problem, I try to approach its solution in a systematic way.	+3	+2	+1	−1	−2	−3

SELF-CONTROL: HOW TO CHANGE IT

	Very Characteristic of Me	Rather Characteristic of Me	Somewhat Characteristic of Me	Somewhat Uncharacteristic of Me	Rather Uncharacteristic of Me	Very Uncharacteristic of Me
8. I usually do my duties quicker when somebody is pressuring me.*	+3	+2	+1	−1	−2	−3
9. When I am faced with a difficult decision, I prefer to postpone making a decision even if all the facts are at my disposal.*	+3	+2	+1	−1	−2	−3
10. When I find that I have difficulties in concentrating on my reading, I look for ways to increase my concentration.	+3	+2	+1	−1	−2	−3
11. When I plan to work, I remove all the things that are not relevant to my work.	+3	+2	+1	−1	−2	−3
12. When I try to get rid of a bad habit, I first try to find out all the factors that maintain this habit.	+3	+2	+1	−1	−2	−3
13. When an unpleasant thought is bothering me, I try to think about something pleasant.	+3	+2	+1	−1	−2	−3
14. If I would smoke two packages of cigarettes a day, I probably would need outside help to stop smoking.*	+3	+2	+1	−1	−2	−3
15. When I am in a low mood, I try to act cheerful so my mood will change.	+3	+2	+1	−1	−2	−3
16. If I had the pills with me, I would take a tranquilizer whenever I felt tense and nervous.*	+3	+2	+1	−1	−2	−3
17. When I am depressed, I try to keep myself busy with things that I like.	+3	+2	+1	−1	−2	−3
18. I tend to postpone unpleasant duties even if I could perform them immediately.*	+3	+2	+1	−1	−2	−3
19. I need outside help to get rid of some of my bad habits.*	+3	+2	+1	−1	−2	−3
20. When I find it difficult to settle down and do a certain job, I look for ways to help me settle down.	+3	+2	+1	−1	−2	−3
21. Although it makes me feel bad, I cannot avoid thinking about all kinds of possible catastrophes in the future.*	+3	+2	+1	−1	−2	−3
22. First of all I prefer to finish a job that I have to do and then start doing the things I really like.	+3	+2	+1	−1	−2	−3

Continued on next page

SELF

	Very Characteristic of Me	Rather Characteristic of Me	Somewhat Characteristic of Me	Somewhat Uncharacteristic of Me	Rather Uncharacteristic of Me	Very Uncharacteristic of Me
23. When I feel pain in a certain part of my body, I try not to think about it.	+3	+2	+1	−1	−2	−3
24. My self-esteem increases once I am able to overcome a bad habit.	+3	+2	+1	−1	−2	−3
25. In order to overcome bad feelings that accompany failure, I often tell myself that it is not so catastrophic and that I can do something about it.	+3	+2	+1	−1	−2	−3
26. When I feel that I am too impulsive, I tell myself "stop and think before you do anything."	+3	+2	+1	−1	−2	−3
27. Even when I am terribly angry at somebody, I consider my actions very carefully.	+3	+2	+1	−1	−2	−3
28. Facing the need to make a decision, I usually find out all the possible alternatives instead of deciding quickly and spontaneously.	+3	+2	+1	−1	−2	−3
29. Usually I do first the things I really like to do even if there are more urgent things to do.*	+3	+2	+1	−1	−2	−3
30. When I realize that I cannot help but be late for an important meeting, I tell myself to keep calm.	+3	+2	+1	−1	−2	−3
31. When I feel pain in my body, I try to divert my thoughts from it.	+3	+2	+1	−1	−2	−3
32. I usually plan my work when faced with a number of things to do.	+3	+2	+1	−1	−2	−3
33. When I am short of money, I decide to record all my expenses in order to plan more carefully for the future.	+3	+2	+1	−1	−2	−3
34. If I find it difficult to concentrate on a certain job, I divide the job into smaller segments.	+3	+2	+1	−1	−2	−3
35. Quite often I cannot overcome unpleasant thoughts that bother me.*	+3	+2	+1	−1	−2	−3
36. Once I am hungry and unable to eat, I try to divert my thoughts away from my stomach or try to imagine that I am satisfied.	+3	+2	+1	−1	−2	−3

To obtain your total, first reverse your score for all items with an asterisk: items 4, 6, 8, 9, 14, 16, 18, 19, 21, 29, and 35. (That is, if you circled −2 for item 16, change it to +2.) Then add up all the numbers. If you have forgotten how to add plus and minus numbers, see page 121.

In administering this test to college students, Rosenbaum found that men had an average score of about 26; women averaged about 28. If your score is higher than that average, chances are that you are already using many of the self-control techniques that we have described in this chapter. In that case, make a list of six of the activities in which you exercise self-control. Beside each, indicate which technique you use. You can use this as a guide for applying these techniques in other areas in which you wish to develop more self-control.

If you have a lower than average score, you may want to work on your self-control techniques. Begin by writing down two areas in which you are successful in exercising self-control (for example, saving money, driving within the speed limit, turning in papers on time, getting to work or to class on time). Next, describe which techniques you use in exercising this control (for example, relabeling, congratulating yourself mentally, imagining punishments). As you try to increase your self-control in other areas, it is a good idea to use first the techniques with which you have already had some success, before learning new techniques.

Source of scale: Rosenbaum, M. "A Schedule for Assessing Self-Control Behaviors: Preliminary Findings," Behavior Therapy, 11 (1980), 113–114.

OUTLINE

WEIGHT PROBLEMS
Analyzing Your Eating Habits
What exactly do you eat?
External antecedents
Internal antecedents
Eating behavior: The frenetic fork
Changing Your Eating Behavior
Stimulus-narrowing and redirecting attention
Delaying and chaining
Coverants
Changing Your Exercise Pattern

STUDY PROBLEMS
Analyzing Your Study Behavior
How much time do you spend studying?
How is the time distributed?
When do you study?
Where do you study?
How well do you concentrate?
What is your attitude?
What is your method of study?
Managing Your Study Time
Environmental planning
Scheduling
Getting the full use of your study time: The SQ3R method

ANXIETY
Analyzing Your Anxiety
Managing Anxiety
Environmental planning
Relabeling and self-talk
Desensitization
Stress and Physical Exercise

7

THREE SELF-CONTROL PROBLEMS: WEIGHT, STUDY HABITS, AND ANXIETY

In Chapter 6 we concentrated on the techniques of self-control, bringing in specific self-control problems only by way of example. This may lead some students to ask: "Well, what about my problem? How do I know that a technique that helps John Doe vacuum his house is going to help me get a grip on myself when I'm taking an exam?" This is a good question, and in this chapter we shall try to give you at least part of the answer.

Actually, no matter what your problem, almost any one of the techniques described in Chapter 6 should be of help if it is systematically applied. But psychological research has shown that certain techniques are particularly useful for certain problems. In this chapter we will discuss the techniques most appropriate for three of the most common self-control problems: weight, poor study habits, and anxiety.

Each of these problems constitutes an enormous topic. So in order to cover all three of them in the space of one chapter, we shall have to make certain assump-

tions. First, we will take it for granted that by now you are familiar with the procedure for describing a behavior. To tackle any of these problems, you will need a written description—simple, objective, and specific—such as we discussed in Chapter 2.

Second, we will assume that you are familiar with the self-control techniques explained in the last chapter. Here is a brief review:

1. *Manipulating antecedent stimuli:* environmental planning (avoiding stimuli, building in delays, removing delays, stimulus-narrowing, increasing associations); redirecting attention; relabeling and organizing.
2. *Meddling with responses:* chaining, incompatible behaviors, shaping.
3. *Manipulating consequences:* utilizing feedback, providing self-reward, making rules and contracts, using the Premack principle.

If any of these terms sounds hazy to you,

back and review the discussion of that technique in Chapter 6.

Finally, we will assume that you have a self-control problem and want to solve it. As we mentioned earlier, the three problems we will tackle are weight, poor study habits, and anxiety. Almost everyone in our society could use some help in controlling tension and anxiety. And most students, whether they are on the dean's list or on academic probation, could stand some advice on how to study in such a way that they learn more material in less time. As for weight, there are some people for whom this is no problem. If you are one of the fortunate ones, you can either skip this section or read it as a model for dealing with some other self-control problem.

WEIGHT PROBLEMS

According to the United States Public Health Service, one out of every four Americans has a weight problem. Therefore, the chances are good that you either have or will have this problem. (If you want to check, see Box 7.1.) What causes it is certainly no mystery. Unless you have a special medical problem, such as an underactive thyroid, your excess poundage is the result of either eating too much or eating the wrong foods or exercising too little—or (most probably) all three. Before launching any weight-control program, you should get a checkup from a physician. This will tell you whether you have a medical problem that is causing you to be overweight. If so, you might require a special diet or exercise program. It is probable, however, that your only medical problem is that you *are* overweight. If so, it's time to look for what you're doing wrong.

Analyzing Your Eating Habits

The first step is to state the problem. How much do you weigh? How do you look to yourself? (Take pictures. They will provide you with a visual baseline—the "before" of your "before and after.") How does it feel, physically, to be carrying around those extra pounds? And how does it feel emotionally? Do you feel embarrassed about your body? Do you hate to buy clothes? Do you avoid going swimming? Since our society places great value on slimness, particularly in the young, it is difficult to be overweight without suffering some psychological side effects (Wooley et al., 1979).*

Now for the next step: What are you doing to maintain those extra pounds?

What Exactly Do You Eat?

Overweight people often feel that life has dealt with them unjustly: "I eat the same as everyone else, but I gain weight and everyone else stays skinny"; "I just eat regular meals—I don't stuff myself—and I still gain weight." The truth is that many overweight people do eat "regular meals." However, they may also eat a great deal in addition to those meals. Or they may be eating the wrong foods.

The type of food you eat is particularly crucial—more so, probably, than the amount. After all, quantity is really important only for certain kinds of foods—foods that the body can use only in limited amounts. At the same time, there are other foods (many vegetables, for example) that even the soundest diets allow in unlimited amounts.

So before you rail against your fate, keep a strict record, for at least a week, of every-

---

* It is possible that our society places too much value on slimness. If, according to the Mahoneys' formula (Box 7.1), you are ten or twenty pounds overweight and you feel that you look good, then there is no reason why you should start feeling that you look bad. You may in fact look terrific. (Sophia Loren would certainly fail the Mahoneys' test.) If you are very heavy, however, you might need to lose weight simply for health reasons.

BOX 7.1
WHAT IS YOUR IDEAL WEIGHT?

In calculating how much you should weigh, you might use the following system, offered by Mahoney and Mahoney (1976). And then you might add a few pounds, since the Mahoneys are rather tough.

Many people try to determine how much they should weigh by reading height-weight tables, but since these tables often indicate average weights rather than optimum weights, the figures tend to be too high. There is, however, a formula for estimating your healthiest weight.

Adult women of average build can compute their ideal weight by multiplying their height in inches by 3.5 and then subtracting 110 from the product. Thus, a woman who is five feet tall should weigh about 100 pounds (60 × 3.5 − 110 = 100). For men of average build the formula is height in inches times four, minus 130. A six-foot man should weigh about 158.

It is reasonable to make allowances for bone structure and muscularity; even if Woody Allen and Rosie Grier were the same height they should not weigh the same amount. But be careful that in making these allowances, you don't mistake fat for muscle. And remember that if you are 30 pounds overweight, it is unlikely that the difference is all in your bones. (p. 43)

Mahoney, M, J., and Mahoney, K. "Fight Fat with Behavior Control," Psychology Today, *9, no. 12 (1976), 43.*

---

thing you eat. Let's look at the first two days of one such record:

Monday, Oct. 1

8:30	2 pieces of buttered toast, 1 bowl cornflakes with milk (light sugar), 2 cups black coffee
10:30	4 peanut-butter cookies, cup black coffee
12:45	tuna-fish sandwich on whole-wheat toast, dill pickle, glass of milk (10 oz.)
2:15	cup of coffee, half piece of toast with peanut butter
4:30	2 peanut-butter cookies
6:00	1 serving corn, 2 servings fish, 1 small boiled potato, 2 cups coffee
9:30	1 Coke (16 oz.) and about 25 potato chips
10:30	1 cup chocolate ice cream

Tuesday, Oct. 2

8:30	1 bowl cornflakes with milk (light sugar), 2 cups black coffee
10:00	Coke and doughnut
12:15	(restaurant) BLT sandwich, small serving coleslaw, cup of coffee
3:00	4 peanut-butter cookies, 1 Coke (16 oz.)
6:00	2 servings rice casserole, small salad with dressing, 1 slice buttered bread, 1 cup coffee
9:00	1 Coke (16 oz.) and 6 vanilla wafers
10:00	1 glass milk, 2 pretzel sticks

(Mahoney and Mahoney, 1976, p. 42)

This person has every reason to protest that his meals are not extravagantly fattening. But his between-meal snacks, which his record reveals in all their glaring junkiness, are enough to maintain a solid layer of fat. If he counted his calories, he would find that he consumes almost as many calories between meals as he does at mealtime.

Nevertheless, no matter how many embarrassing facts turn up on your eating record, you still need more information. If you eat two doughnuts on the way to school every morning and consume a jumbo bag of corn chips before bed every night, these eating habits are certainly a cause of your weight problem. But what's causing the eating habits?

External Antecedents

You will notice that the record shown above includes the time of the food consumption. Time is an important antecedent stimulus for eating. Many people, it seems, "eat by the clock," whether or not they're actually hungry (Green, 1978; Loro et al., 1979). Eating by the clock is actually a good idea as long as the "eat" buzzer of your internal clock goes off only three times a day—for breakfast, lunch, and dinner. But if it goes off seven or eight times a day, as in the eating record shown above, then you have a problem. You are not only eating too much; you are probably also eating the wrong foods. People don't generally broil chicken or toss salads for between-meal snacks. Rather, they tend to eat cookies, pretzels, doughnuts—anything that can be gobbled up quickly. Such foods are notoriously high in calories and low in nutritional value. So keep a careful record of your eating times. The clock may be an antecedent stimulus that needs controlling.

Another important antecedent stimulus that should appear on your record is the place where you eat (Abrams and Allen, 1974; Green, 1978; Loro et al., 1979). Eating in restaurants or coffee shops may lead you to eat more, either because you want to get

A street-fair buffet, with external antecedents galore. People on diets do best to eat at home, where they can avoid such temptations. (© Leonard Speier 1982)

your money's worth or because such places offer goodies not available at home. However, even if you always eat at home, it's important to note where, since this information is essential for environmental control.

A third antecedent stimulus you should note is any distraction that is present during an eating occasion: television, radio, a book or a magazine, people to chat with. (Or do you chow down at the movies or the ballgame, and go to movies or ballgames often?) Distractions result in inattention, and inattention, as we have seen, is a major contributor to self-control problems.

Finally, the consumption of alcoholic drinks or any other drug before or during an eating episode should be noted. Alcohol—and, even more so, marijuana—can desensitize you to feelings of fullness, so that your brain never gets the "stop" signal from your stomach.

Internal Antecedents

For some people, internal stimuli, especially emotions, are every bit as powerful as external stimuli in controlling eating behavior (Green, 1978). Tension, depression, loneliness, and frustration—all these feelings (of which overweight people seem to have more than their fair share) can be cues for overeating. In such cases, eating may function as comfort and compensation. When all other reinforcers seem lost, there is still the faithful reinforcer of putting food in one's mouth (Ferster et al., 1962; Stunkard and Kaplan, 1977). Or eating may offer the dubious reward of confirming an already negative self-concept—a common problem with overweight people—and providing new opportunities for guilt and self-blame. To combat these unhelpful mental processes, make sure you take notes on the feelings that seem to propel you toward the refrigerator or the doughnut shop.

Eating Behavior: The Frenetic Fork

One final matter that should be included in your records is the actual mechanics of your eating. How fast do you eat? Do you take big bites? How well do you chew? Do you already have the next bite on your fork while you're chewing? Do you cut up a piece of meat into bite-sized pieces at the beginning of the meal so that you won't have to endure the delay of cutting it, piece by piece, as you eat? Do you clean your plate? These are all leading questions. Some research has shown that many people with weight problems are rapid and intense eaters (Ferster et al., 1962; Gaul et al., 1975; Stunkard and Kaplan, 1977). This habit may contribute to weight problems, since rapid eating throws off your body's feedback system. After you begin to eat, it generally takes at least fifteen minutes for the body to register feelings of fullness (Harris, 1969). If in those fifteen minutes you've already finished your second helping, the body's "stop" signal will be of no use. You will have already eaten too much.

Changing Your Eating Behavior

Now that you have these very specific records of your eating behavior and have included them in your description, what do you do with this information? The first and most obvious step is to get a calorie chart from your local bookstore and count your average daily calorie-intake. Then compare this total to what your calorie-intake should be (see Box 7.2). This procedure will probably tell you two things: that you have to avoid high-calorie foods and that you have to cut down on your food consumption in general. How to do this? Look at your description for variables that might be controlling your present eating habits. Then start manipulating those variables.

As for the appropriate methods, we have already stolen some of our own thunder in Chapter 6. A number of the best weight-control techniques were mentioned there by way of example. Don't forget these examples. Decorating your kitchen walls with pictures of fat people will increase associations for not eating. Banishing snack foods from your house will help you avoid the fatal stimuli. A weight-control contract pasted to your refrigerator will help keep you honest. Saving a favorite activity for a time when you ordinarily succumb to the call of the cupboard will provide you with an incompatible behavior and help you control the antecedent stimulus of the clock (Stuart and Davis, 1972). Covert self-praise and tangible rewards will provide the necessary reinforcing consequences (Saccone and Israel, 1978; Israel and Saccone, 1979). Other techniques particularly useful for weight control are as follows.

Organizations such as Smokenders, pictured here, and Weight Watchers offer a very powerful form of reinforcement: group support and approval. (© Lawrence Frank 1982)

In this bakery window, several trays full of eating cues are displayed. One woman is clearly responding to the cues. (Erich Lessing/Magnum)

Stimulus-Narrowing and Redirecting Attention

For people with weight problems, there are hundreds of cues for eating: seeing food, passing a delicatessen or bakery, watching food commercials on television, watching television at all, going to the movies, reading, finishing reading, walking to class, walking home from class, and so on, endlessly. A logical approach, then, is stimulus-narrowing—cutting the associations that connect these stimuli with food. You can decide that you are allowed to eat only at 8:00 A.M., noon, and 6:00 P.M., or only at the dinner table, with a complete place setting (Ferster et al., 1962; Stunkard and Kaplan, 1977; Katell et al., 1979). One dieter made a rule that she could snack only at her dressing table. This stratagem not only eliminated her normal snacking cues, it also forced her to look at herself in the mirror as she ate (Williams and Long, 1979).

Stimulus-narrowing regimens generally serve a second purpose as well. That is, they

BOX 7.2
HOW MANY CALORIES DO YOU NEED?

How many eclairs can you afford to consume without getting fat? This depends on your ideal weight (see Box 7.1) and on your level of exercise. Mahoney and Mahoney (1976) offer the following system for determining your calorie allowance.

Begin by rating yourself on the scale below:

13	very inactive
14	slightly inactive
15	moderately active
16	relatively active
17	frequently, strenuously active

If you are a sedentary office worker or a housewife you should probably rate yourself a 13. If your physical exercise consists of occasional games of golf or an afternoon walk, you're a 14. A score of 15 means that you frequently engage in moderate exertion—jogging, calisthenics, tennis. A 16 requires that you are almost always on the go, seldom sitting down or standing still for long. Don't give yourself a 17 unless you are a construction worker or engage in other strenuous activity frequently. Most adult Americans should rate themselves 13 or 14.

To calculate the number of calories you need to maintain your ideal weight, multiply your activity rating by your ideal weight. A 200-pound office worker, for example, needs 2,600 calories a day, a 200-pound athlete needs 3,400 calories.

To estimate how many calories you are getting now, multiply your current weight times your activity level. If your weight is constant at 140 pounds and you are inactive, you are consuming about 1,820 calories a day (13 times 140). Subtract the number of calories you need for your ideal weight from the number of calories you are consuming, and you will know the size of your energy imbalance. (p. 43)

Mahoney, M. J., and Mahoney, K. "Fight Fat with Behavior Control," Psychology Today, 9, no. 12 (1976), 43.

ACTIVITY 7.1

It is likely that television advertising contributes heavily to weight problems in America. Hour after hour, TV shows us thin, happy people promoting high-calorie foods, thus creating an association between these foods and the social rewards of being attractive and popular. Watch three hours of television, either in one sitting or in several smaller doses. Write down a brief description of every food or beverage commercial you see. Note what the product is, whether in your opinion it is high or low in calories, and what associations the ad is trying to get you to make.

remove distractions and thereby focus your attention on eating, so that you cannot simply feed your face automatically (Stuart and Davis, 1972; Loro et al., 1979). This stimulus-narrowing-plus-redirecting-attention is the goal of a weight-control program that Goldiamond designed for one client:

> He was instructed to eat to his heart's content and not to repress the desire. He was, however, to treat the food with the dignity it deserved. Rather than eating while he watched television or while he studied, he was to devote himself to eating when he ate. If he wished to eat a sandwich, he was to put it on a plate and sit down and devote himself exclusively to it. Thus, reinforcing consequences such as watching television or reading would be withdrawn when he engaged in the behaviors of preparing the food, eating, and cleaning up. Responding to the refrigerator in between meals resulted in withdrawal of such consequences, as did going to the refrigerator while watching television. Television, studying, and other stimuli would lose their control of initiating the chain of behaviors and conditions that terminated in eating. Within one week, the young man cut out all eating between meals. "You've taken all the fun out of it," he said to me. (Goldiamond, 1965, p. 856)

To take the fun out of your snacking, reserve for yourself a snacking place remote from all fun. You will soon find those snacks much less tempting.

Delaying and Chaining

In Chapter 6 we gave some examples of the use of delays and chaining in weight control: small portions (forcing yourself to get up for seconds), grocery shopping on a daily basis (forcing yourself to go to the grocery store in order to break your diet), buying only foods that require preparation (forcing yourself to work and wait for your food).

The eating chain, however, is a long one, much longer than the smoking chain. Consequently, there are many other areas where you can stretch it out. Serve yourself your meal on a salad plate rather than a dinner plate; this will increase the number of trips you have to make to the stove in order to eat what you normally eat. You can also use chaining, combined with shaping, to slow down your fork action (Katell et al., 1979; Loro et al., 1979). First try taking smaller bites. Then allow yourself to put food on your fork only after you have thoroughly chewed and then swallowed what is in your mouth. Then put your utensils on the plate while you chew and swallow each bite. Then interrupt your eating altogether for thirty seconds, then a minute, then two or three minutes. Then practice these same delays while you're holding food on your fork. Finally—the ultimate in eating control—make a rule that you must always leave at least one bite of food on your plate when you finish eating.

Coverants

In Chapter 6 we mentioned the usefulness of covert reinforcement, in the form of mental imagery and self-talk, as a reward for "good behavior." You can also use premeditated mental activity as the *antecedent* for self-control behavior. Several researchers (Homme, 1965; Manno and Marston, 1972; Kingsley and Wilson, 1977) have found this technique to be effective in weight control. When handled in this way, mental sentences and images are called *coverants* (a contraction of *covert operants*). Coverants are generally used in pairs: one negative and one positive.

Imagine, for example, that you have the misfortune to be on a diet at a lavish wedding dinner. You've made it safely through the first four courses, but now you're standing in front of the buffet salivating over an array of fattening desserts. You hasten to rehearse your coverants (which you have established and practiced beforehand). First, your negative coverant: you imagine your old fat self standing in front of a mirror in a swimsuit, with layers of fat bulging and rippling out of the top and bottom; you look at yourself in total discouragement; you call up your friend and tell her you can't go with her to the beach. After concentrating on this negative coverant for a moment or two, you switch to the positive coverant. You imagine your future thin self—long, lithe, smooth, tanned—running happily along the beach in a swimsuit; people look up from their magazines and gaze at beautiful you; an entire volleyball game comes to a halt as you pass by. With this long-term goal shining before your eyes, you turn away from the buffet and go back to your seat.

By now it should be clear why such a covert imagery is called operant; it operates on your mind in such a way that temptation loses its power.

Changing Your Exercise Pattern

Exercising is an essential part of any serious weight-control program. Diet or no diet, you're still taking in calories. And if you spend all day sitting in a chair, you're simply not burning up enough of these calories.

To increase your rate of exercise, eliminate the antecedents of inactivity (Meyers et al., 1980). Avoid elevators; use the stairs instead. If you drive to school, park your car twelve blocks away from campus rather than three blocks away. If you take the bus, get off four stops before your usual stop and walk the rest of the way.

You should also create antecedents for exercise. In the same way that the student in the last chapter reserved her desk exclusively for studying, you can reserve a special

mat or throw rug in your bedroom exclusively for your exercises. Another extremely useful antecedent for exercise is companionship (Stuart and Davis, 1972; Zitter and Fremouw, 1978). Join your local Y or set up a regular tennis or jogging date with a friend.

As for consequences, the most indispensable reward is, as usual, feedback (Castro and Rachlin, 1980). Your daily exercise, like your daily weight and calorie-intake, should be carefully recorded so that you can have the satisfaction of contemplating your progress. Use other reinforcers as well. Praise yourself for doing your ten sit-ups and reward yourself by watching the eleven o'clock news or spending a half-hour with a magazine.

Whatever your specific techniques for increasing exercise, make sure that the increase is gradual. This applies to dieting as well. If you starve yourself to the point of nausea or exercise until your body is one large charley horse, you may lose weight, but not permanently. Permanent weight loss can be achieved only through the creation of new *habits* (Cohen et al., 1980). And habits, by definition, are not built in a day. So give your muscles time to adapt to the new exercise routine, and give your stomach and taste buds time to adapt to the new eating routine. In this way, your goal will not be achieved by next weekend, but neither will it have been abandoned by the following weekend.

STUDY PROBLEMS

To many students, studying means underlining an expensive textbook with a see-through yellow marker while half-listening to someone's stereo down the hall. Or, if there is an exam the next day, studying means drugging yourself with coffee or a diet pill and spending the entire night trying to

Cramming means trying to do too much in too little time. (Spencer Carter/Woodfin Camp & Assoc.)

cram into your head all the material that should have been learned gradually over the previous eight weeks. Such study habits generally result in enough learning to keep you off academic probation. And because they are reinforced in this way, they are maintained (Fox, 1962). But they constitute the least efficient way of learning.

Learning is the input, processing, and storage of information, which can then be retrieved at some later time. Lackadaisical reading to the tune of a distant stereo results in little processing and, hence, little storage. (How many times have you discovered, after reading five pages of a book, that you have almost no idea of what they said?) And last-minute cramming involves so much input in so little time that the processing and storage functions of the brain become overworked and inefficient. As a result, the information is stuffed in every which way, and when it has to be retrieved, it is difficult to find and even more difficult to organize. In short, neither of these techniques *works*

very well. In both of them, too much time is spent doing too little learning.

What, then, is the solution? Before working on the solution, we have to specify the problem. How, exactly, do you study?

Analyzing Your Study Behavior

To get a close look at your study habits, you should monitor your studying for two weeks. And these should be ordinary weeks, not during final exams. Your record, and the description that you distill from it, should include the following information.

How Much Time Do You Spend Studying?

Calculate your daily average. This is your rock-bottom variable. Contrary to campus wisdom, the amount of time spent studying is not the most important determinant of learning. Studying five hours a day is no guarantee of academic success. But since studying fifteen minutes a day is an excellent guarantee of academic failure, you do need to know how many hours you actually put in with the books.

How Is the Time Distributed?

Let's say that your total study time for two weeks is a modest twenty-eight hours—an average of two hours a day. But your record also shows that eighteen of those twenty-eight hours were clumped into three days: the day before your chemistry midterm, a night for writing an English paper, and one desperate Sunday when you felt guilty about being so far behind in all your reading. As we saw earlier, this type of learning—big chunks of study after long stretches of no studying—is called *massed practice*; the best example is cramming. The opposite of massed practice is *distributed practice*, learning in small, regular, evenly spaced sessions, such as two hours a night. In general, massed practice is much less likely than distributed practice to produce good recall (Kientzle, 1946; Spence and Norris, 1950; Underwood and Schulz, 1961).

When Do You Study?

At what time of the day or night do you put in your study time? By noting this on your record, you will have some essential information for environmental control. (For example, you'll know when to leave the phone off the hook.) Furthermore, you may pinpoint some problems. If you find that your reading puts you to sleep, but your record tells you that you tend to start your reading around 10:30 P.M., then your reading is probably not the only reason you're falling asleep.

Where Do You Study?

Describe the place in which you usually study. (If you don't have one or two places in which you usually study, you should. We'll come to this later.) How is the lighting, the temperature, the ventilation? Is the chair uncomfortable—or too comfortable? Do you (God forbid) study in bed? Most important of all, what about distractions? Is there a phone on the desk? *Can* you hear the stereo down the hall or a television in the next room? Is there a discotheque next door? Are your friends liable to pile through the door at any minute?

How Well Do You Concentrate?

Related to the subject of distractions is the matter of your concentration. Perhaps the deadliest enemy of studying is inattention. Stalk this enemy. If you sit down to study your history text for two hours, clock your-

This student might do well to look for a better place to study. (© George W. Gardner)

self as to how many of those 120 minutes are actually spent on history. Subtract the time spent looking at your fingernails, reading the graffiti on the library desk, and wondering whether you should shave off your moustache. The results of this simple arithmetic may dismay you. If so, you have an important variable to work on.

What Is Your Attitude?

How do you feel about your studying as you sit down to it? This will probably vary from course to course. But make a note on your record, as you begin each study session, of how you feel about the task in front of you. Do you *want* to learn this material, or do you hate the mere thought of it? Do you think you *can* learn it, or are you just going through the motions? Does studying make

ACTIVITY 7.2

Many of us find studying difficult because we approach it as work—something that we *have* to do. But most of us have also "studied" something just for the fun of it—piano, dance, cooking, photography, baseball, yoga, whatever. Often we approach these "fun" studies more efficiently than we do our school studies. Choose a subject that you studied for pleasure and describe specifically how you went about learning it. Chances are that you automatically used many of the self-control techniques described in these chapters. Did you, for example, try to get away from distractions so that you could concentrate? Did you study it often (distributed practice)? Did you measure your progress (self-monitoring) and congratulate yourself on gains (self-reward)? Your approach to your hobbies may give you some tips on how to approach your studies.

you anxious? It hardly needs to be said that such attitudes and expectations will affect your level of concentration and, consequently, the efficiency of your studying.

What Is Your Method of Study?

Above all, you need to describe the way you actually go about your studying (Richards et al., 1976). Do you organize the task? Do you set a goal (for example, "read ten pages," "have those five irregular verbs memorized") for each study session? If you're reading a textbook, what else do you do at the same time? Do you underline, take notes, outline? If you're studying a foreign language, what do you do with the vocabulary words at the end of the lesson? Do you try to memorize them then and there, or do you put this off until the midterm? If you're reading a poem, novel, or short story, do you take any notes at all? Your answers to these questions are extremely important. We said before that your raw number of study-hours per day is probably not the major determinant of success in learning. Excluding intelligence, the major determinant is, in all likelihood, your method of study.

Managing Your Study Time

Laying aside for a moment the matter of study methods, let's examine ways in which you can manage your study time: increase it, space it properly, and distill it into "pure" study time by increasing concentration.

Environmental Planning

Your description should indicate to you the antecedents that cue you *not* to study when you had meant to study. Whatever they are, plan your environment so as to avoid them. If you have a free hour between classes and plan to spend it in the library, don't try to get to the library by walking past a record or clothing store that you know you'll be tempted to enter; take a different path. If you study at home, either take the phone off the hook or tell the person answering the phone that you are officially not at home. (Taking the phone off the hook is better, because it removes temptation altogether. Or, if you have a jack phone, unplug it.) If you study in a dormitory, hang a sign on your door letting your friends know that they should knock only if the place is burning down.

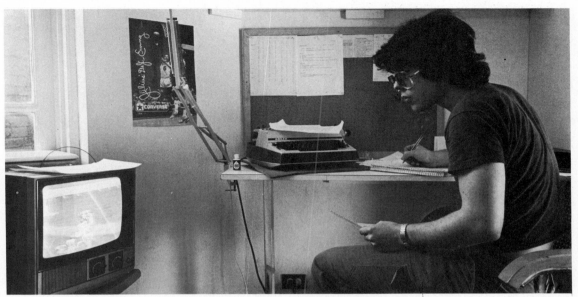

Time spent at the desk is not always time spent studying. When you clock your study time, make sure you include only the time you spend actually concentrating on the work. (© Joan Liftin 1980/Archive Pictures, Inc.)

Once you have managed to eliminate the antecedents for not studying, you can start controlling the antecedents for inattention. In a dormitory this may not be easy. There are few places on earth less congenial to concentrated studying than a college residence hall. Even if you manage to scare your friends away, you will probably still have to cope with a stereo in the distance, a bull session in the hallway, or a talkative roommate. Some dormitories have special study rooms where noise is forbidden. If you have one of these, move your operations down there. Or pick up your books and go to the library. In short, don't try to cope with distractions. Get away from them. People who study at home—especially people with children—might also hang a sign to discourage informal visits.

Wherever you decide to study, make sure you choose only one or, at the most, two places. And then bring your behavior under stimulus control by using these places *only*

for studying (Fox, 1962; Beneke and Harris, 1972; Harris and Johnson, 1980). In this way the environment will become a sure-fire cue for study behavior. Just as Goldiamond, in the case cited in Chapter 6, banished the student from her desk when she was doing anything besides studying, keep your study environment pure. Let us say that you have two study places: a special room in the library and the desk in your bedroom at home. If, after two hours in the library, you have finished your work and want to read a magazine, go to another room. At home, move your telephoning, letter-writing, bill-paying, Christmas-list-making, and so forth anywhere you like, as long as it is away from the desk.

Scheduling

Now that you have your study environment, unpolluted by any other associations, you have to deal with the problem of getting yourself to go there regularly. So we are back to the matter of distributed versus massed practice. These are very impressive-sounding terms, but they hide a very homely fact of life: people tend to procrastinate. A stitch in time may save nine, but it is the rare person who makes that stitch in time. Students, in other words, did not invent massed practice, but they still have to find a solution to the problem.

The most reasonable solution is a technique we have already discussed in Chapter 6: organizing the task. At the beginning of every week you need to make up a study schedule (Greiner and Karoly, 1976; Harris and Johnson, 1980), listing what has to be done each day of that week. From the schedules handed out by your professors, you know what work has to be finished each week. Your job is to break down those assignments into manageable daily tasks. Knowing that you have to read a 24-page chapter in your economics text this week, you divide that up into 8 pages a day for 3 days. Or if you have a short paper due on Friday, you schedule outlining for Monday, first-draft writing for Tuesday and Wednesday, and revision and typing for Thursday. (Don't schedule your weekends. You'll need them to make up for slips in self-control and to relax.) Make sure that your schedule is realistic, taking into account the other demands on your time: job, family, other courses, and the like.

Once you have done this breakdown for all your courses, you have a clear, precise schedule. Add to it a system of daily rewards—coffee, ice-cream cones, television time, goofing-off periods, browsing sessions in the bookstore or sporting goods store. (Keep in mind the Premack principle.) What you have then is a contract. Post this contract over your desk and check off your daily assignments as you complete them.

As for how you should get those daily assignments done, this again is a matter of scheduling. Each morning (or, better yet, the night before) you should make a timetable specifying when you are going to do your work. Consult your schedule as to what has to be done that day, estimate how much time it will take, add about 25 percent for study breaks, unexpected distractions, and what-have-you, and then write down when your study periods will be. For each study period, specify the goals. Do not use time (for example, one hour of economics reading) as a goal; as we have seen, "study time" can be frittered away on many things other than studying. Instead, your goals should be work completed—pages read, pages written, vocabulary words memorized, and so forth. For study periods exceeding an hour, specify reasonable study breaks. Thus, your schedule might look something like this:

Library	10:00-11:00	1) 8 pages of economics reading
		2) Memorize half the Italian vocabulary words
Library	4:00-6:15	1) Finish English reading (20 pages)
		2) Write outline for English paper
	5:00-5:15	*Study break in lounge*
Home	9:00-10:00	Do 4 physics problems

If you wish, you can arrange some trade-offs in your daily scheduling. For example, you could memorize all the Italian vocabulary words today and then read 16 pages of economics tomorrow. But avoid trade-offs involving more than two days; they can lead you right back into massed practice. And beware of trade-offs that postpone your least-loved tasks.

If all this scheduling sounds like something out of military school, consider what you will gain by it. Your attitude toward studying is almost certain to improve, since by organizing the task, you have stripped it of its awesome character. Even more important, such a schedule will allow you to keep pace with the assignments in all your courses. This should mean better learning, more active class participation, and higher grades. It also means that you are released from the vicious cycle of massed practice, where the Italian midterm means dropping everything else, then the English paper means dropping everything else, and so on.

Getting Full Use of Your Study Time: The SQ3R Method

Let us now return to the subject of your method of study. A number of psychologists (including Robinson, 1970; Fox, 1962) have pointed out that most students' textbook-reading methods are far too passive. Either they simply read the chapter and close the book, or they accompany the reading with the usual underlining. Either way, the student simply lies back and lets the material flow through his cognitive field. And much of it flows right out the other end.

What is needed, then, is a more active approach to reading. You need to meet the material halfway, "attack" it, make demands on it, and work along with it. Above all, you need to practice doing what you will be asked to do in classroom discussions and on exams—that is, recapitulate the material in your own words. These needs can be filled by using a study method designed by the psychologist F. P. Robinson (1970), the *SQ3R method*. The name is an abbreviation of the five tasks that the method requires you to perform: survey, question, read, recite, and review.

1. *Survey:* Before you start reading, look at the headings in the chapter and at the chapter summary, if there is one, to find out what the chapter's main points are. This will give you a framework within which you can organize the material as you read it. Before going on to the next step, make sure that you know what the chapter's goals are—what it is trying to teach.

2. *Question:* Now look back at the first heading, turn it into a question, and write down the question. Let's say, for example, that your chapter is entitled "The Founders of Modern Psychology" and the first heading is "Sigmund Freud." An obvious question would be "What ideas did Freud contribute to psychology?" By formulating this question, you increase your curiosity and turn your reading into a purposeful task—the task of answering that question.

3. *Read:* Read the section under that heading *to find an answer to your question.* In this way you must go digging in the material, actively searching for the essential points. The key to this type of reading is that it is selective. Your attention is focused on the most important material.

4. *Recite:* Having finished the section, look away from the book and recite to yourself from memory (out loud, if possible) the answer to your question. You should use your own words and give an example. Then turn to the sheet on which you wrote down your question, and jot down the answer in a few key words. Force yourself to keep these notes very brief. (If you can't answer the question, look at the material again until you can.) This reciting step is essential for "locking in" the material in your brain.

Repeat steps 2, 3, and 4 for each headed section in the chapter. Form your question, write it down, read to find an answer to it, recite the answer from memory, and jot down the key words. Do this until you have finished the chapter. The list of questions and key-word answers constitutes your reading notes.

5. *Review:* Immediately after you've finished the chapter, or that day's assignment in it, glance over your reading notes to review the major points and to get an overview of their relationship to each other. Make sure you know the meaning behind your key words. Then, for each question-and-answer section of your notes, cover up the key words, read the question, answer it, and then uncover your key words to make sure that your answer was correct. This review will help to prevent rapid forgetting, the forgetting of what you have just learned. And thereafter you should repeat the review of this material periodically (say, once a week) in order to prevent gradual forgetting—that is, forgetting over time.

The SQ3R method has been tested by students at a number of colleges and has proven quite successful in raising grade point averages (Beneke and Harris, 1972; Greiner and Karoly, 1976; Harris and Johnson, 1980). Nevertheless, keep in mind that the central purpose of this method is to help you remember and recapitulate *what the textbook said.* Don't forget that *you* should also say something back to the textbook. Think about what you're reading. Chew it over in

---

BOX 7.3
PRACTICAL HINTS FOR TAKING LECTURE NOTES

1. *Do the reading before the lecture.* Don't wait until Friday night to read the chapter that the lecturer has been discussing on Monday, Wednesday, and Friday. Such a reading lag makes it much more difficult for you to understand the classroom discussion and to take intelligent notes on it. Friday night (or Saturday morning) is when you should be starting the reading for *next* week's lectures.

2. *Before the lecture, review your notes from the last one or two class periods.* This will refresh your memory and help you see the direction in which the professor is heading.

3. *Take your notes in outline form.* Outline form is easy to read and forces you to organize the material into main points and subpoints— which is utterly essential.

4. *Mark items stressed in the lecture.* Teachers generally make no secret of what they consider the most important points of a lecture. Mark these points with asterisks or some other attention-getting symbol so that you will remember to study them carefully. You're likely to encounter them on the exam.

5. *Don't try to write down everything.* Listen first, then write down the essentials. Don't aim for complete sentences. And don't try to take down what the professor says word for word, except in the case of a definition or a short quotation. Remember: your notes should be an outline, not an essay.

6. *Be neat.* Write legibly, skip lines, follow a consistent system of indentation in your outline. And don't doodle on your notes. They are not playthings; they are tools for study.

7. *Review the notes after the lecture.* Reread your notes the same day or evening, reciting the major points. If they are disorganized, reorganize them. For maximum recall, use the SQ3R method as you review. With two or three pages of lecture notes, this should take about two or three minutes.

your mind. Relate it to what you already know from other courses and from your experience. If you disagree with what the text says, or if you have questions, or if you can think of interesting examples or comparisons, write these things down and bring them up in class. By doing creative thinking of this kind, you will learn a great deal more, you will take more pleasure in your reading, and—to return to the practical level—you will be well prepared for essay tests.

The instructions we have given for the SQ3R method are specifically tailored for conventional textbooks—textbooks with headings and summaries. The SQ3R method, however, can also help you in reading a book without headings, or even a poem or a novel. With such materials, just keep asking yourself questions ("What are the major themes in this novel?"; "What are the most striking images in this poem?"), looking for answers, jotting down key words, and reviewing.

ANXIETY

So far we have dealt with a physical problem, overweight, and a behavioral problem, poor study habits. We come now to an all-too-common emotional problem, anxiety. What exactly is anxiety? Psychologists have disagreed on this subject for decades. Some claim that "anxiety" is an unrealistic fear, a sense of threat in response to something that is not really threatening, whereas "fear" is by definition realistic—a fear of something that is truly fearful. Other psychological writers have used the terms "fear" and "anxiety" interchangeably, along with the terms "nervousness" and "tension." To avoid drawing overly fine distinctions in an area of psychology that is still very unclear, we shall stick to the term "anxiety" and use it to refer to *a feeling of fear (realistic or unrealistic), accompanied by a state of increased physiological arousal.*

How anxieties—particularly unrealistic anxieties—develop is another hotly debated question. Freud believed that when someone displayed an unrealistic anxiety, such as a fear of horses, it was simply a symbol of a much deeper fear—the fear that unconscious sexual or aggressive impulses would break through the ego's control mechanisms, seize their gratification, and bring terrible punishment down on the person as a result. This theory is still the basis of psychodynamic writings on anxiety.

The behaviorists, on the other hand, argue that unrealistic anxieties, along with realistic ones, are the result of respondent conditioning. In Chapter 5 we saw an example of this process: the famous experiment in which Watson and Rayner conditioned little Albert B. to fear white rats and other furry things by pairing the sight of the rat with a sudden loud noise. Such fears, once learned, are often maintained through avoidance behavior. Indeed, Albert B., who was never deconditioned by Watson and Rayner, may still be afraid of white rats today.

Whether anxiety is caused by unconscious impulses or by simple conditioned associations, what it involves—what it actually *feels* like—is fairly clear. A strong anxiety reaction has three components (Maher, 1966):

1. *Emotional:* The person has a conscious and intense feeling of fear.
2. *Cognitive:* The fear, as it escalates, eventually interferes with the person's ability to think clearly, solve problems, and handle environmental demands.
3. *Physiological:* The body's response to fear is to mobilize itself for action, whether or not any action is called for. This mobilization is largely the work of the *autonomic nervous system,* which

controls many of the body's muscles and glands. When the mind is seized by fear, the autonomic nervous system switches the body into a state of intense arousal. The heart pounds; pulse and breathing speed up; the pupils of the eye dilate; digestive and intestinal processes stop; blood vessels constrict; blood pressure rises; adrenal glands shoot adrenalin into the blood. Finally, blood is diverted into the skeletal muscles (the muscles responsible for voluntary movement), which become tensed and ready for action.

For the caveman who awoke to find some large, hairy creature in his cave, the physiological changes associated with fear were extremely useful; they all served to prepare him for action, whether by fighting or by running away. But for a person anxious about starting a new job, neither fighting nor running away is in order. Hence, the autonomic changes merely cause distress and embarrassment. Likewise, pent-up tension in the skeletal muscles results in aimless nervous movements (pacing, nail-biting, hair-twisting, and so on) and in chest pains and headaches.

While this description would suggest that anxiety is something we could all do without, the truth is that moderate levels of anxiety in appropriate situations are normal and healthy. (Our description was of an intense anxiety response.) If your common sense hasn't warned you against getting into a car with a drunk driver, then the fact that your heart is pounding as the car careens along the freeway may cause you to do something about the situation. In other words, some anxiety is appropriate, since there are some things that we *should* be afraid of. As Margaret Mead points out:

We have developed a society which depends on having the right amount of anxiety to make it work. Psychiatrists have been heard to say, "He

Although there are times when anxiety is quite appropriate, chronic anxiety can be a major adjustment problem. (Ken Heyman)

didn't have enough anxiety to get well," indicating that, while we agree that too much anxiety is inimical to mental health, we have come to rely on anxiety to push and prod us into seeing a doctor about a symptom which may indicate cancer, into checking up on that old life insurance policy which may have out-of-date clauses in it, into having a conference with Billy's teacher even though his report card looks all right. (1956, p. 13)

The problem arises when we experience too much anxiety—anxiety that is inappropriate to the circumstances. Such anxiety wastes our psychological and physical resources.

Furthermore, it makes us miserable. It deprives us of our sense of dignity, making us feel small and helpless. Fortunately, there is something we can do about it.

Analyzing Your Anxiety

Each person's anxiety pattern is unique. Some people appear to be generally more fearful than others. Psychologists have developed tests to identify highly anxious people. One such test, the Manifest Anxiety Scale (Taylor, 1953), rates the individual according to whether he answers "true" or "false" to items such as "I am usually calm," "I am a very nervous person," "At times I worry about things that I know don't really matter." However, more recent psychological research has demonstrated a point that should seem obvious: anxiety depends not only on "person variables" but also on the anxiety-provoking stimulus in question (Endler and Hunt, 1969; Breen et al., 1978; Kendall, 1978). Some people tremble at the mere thought of stepping out onto a fire escape but are completely relaxed when addressing an audience. Others can happily dangle on ropes from mountain ledges, while the act of knocking on a professor's office door makes them feel faint with fear.

Hence, the first step in controlling inappropriate anxiety is to pinpoint it. Saying, "I am a very tense person" won't do. You must determine the antecedents of your anxiety. What are the situations that make you so tense? Competing with others? Social "mixing"? Situations in which you have to prove to someone else your mental capability, such as taking an exam, writing a paper, or going through a job interview? Or is it something even more specific, such as making decisions or riding in elevators or even spending a weekend with your parents?

Once you've determined the general situation in which you become anxious, look for and record the specific antecedents of the anxiety response. If it is writing a paper that makes you anxious, what stimuli actually trigger your feelings? Is it the thought that tonight you have to sit down and outline the paper? Is it getting out the lined tablet and starting to write? And what are the thoughts that pass through your mind? Are you all right until you imagine the professor, red pencil in hand, reading the words that you're writing at this very moment?

Another internal antecedent you should consider is anxiety itself. Many of us, having been conditioned by past experiences to associate fear with failure and embarrassment, become terrified of our own fear. Thus, anxiety becomes a spiral. As we feel ourselves beginning to perspire under stress, we become more anxious and begin to tremble. This in turn causes further anxiety, which causes further behavioral signs, which cause further anxiety, and so on.

Finally, you should try to indicate in your description the consequences of your anxiety. What could be maintaining it? One thing to look at very carefully is avoidance behavior. As we pointed out in Chapter 5, avoidance nourishes anxiety. By relieving our anxiety through retreat, we deprive ourselves of the chance to subject that anxiety to reality-testing. That is, we never get the chance to say, "Well, that wasn't so bad after all"—an experience that would eventually result in the extinction of the anxiety. Furthermore, our relief upon retreating constitutes negative reinforcement, increasing the probability of our retreating again next time.

Another possible reinforcer of anxiety is a mistaken association between getting through a feared situation and having been anxious about it. Some students, after years of overanxious reactions to tests, come to associate anxiety with academic success. Through operant conditioning, passing the test begins to look like a reward for anxiety and consequently strengthens the anxiety response. (The same mechanism can maintain stage fright in actors and dancers.) Actually, the causal connection linking anxiety to efficient learning and good performance is completely false. Research has shown that although some degree of arousal is necessary for efficient learning, intense arousal actually interferes with learning (Ellis, 1972). And as for performance, anxiety, as we have seen, interferes with problem-solving abilities. At its peak, it can paralyze cognitive functions altogether.

Managing Anxiety

Once you have described the antecedents and consequences surrounding your inappropriate anxieties, you can begin experimenting with yourself. The most obvious method is to rearrange the antecedents—environmental and mental.

Environmental Planning

Some anxiety-provoking stimuli are, frankly, not worth the trouble of your learning how to handle them more calmly. In other words, some situations *deserve* to be avoided. If horror movies make you anxious, you don't go to a therapist to learn how to enjoy them. You simply don't go to them. By the same token, there is no reason why you should have to mediate quarrels between your parents if this role makes you tense, as it well might. Walk out and let them settle their difficulties themselves. In other cases you can avoid unnecessary anx-

BOX 7.4
SELF-CONTROL IN SPORTS

Very few people need self-control as much as star athletes. Hence, it is no surprise that some athletes are now experimenting with self-control training, particularly for handling anxiety. Studies have shown that anxiety can interfere seriously with athletes' concentration and thus damage their performance (Mahoney and Avener, 1977; Shelton and Mahoney, 1978; Morgan, 1978). To combat this problem, one group of researchers taught cross-country skiers to relax and then to imagine themselves competing in an important race. During this imaginary race, the subjects practiced stopping anxious thoughts (fears of inferiority, worries about the surroundings, etc.) and increasing self-statements that would aid their performance, such as "Kick hard!" Later they did the same cogni-

tive exercises while actually skiing. Compared to skiers who did not receive this treatment, the subjects found after three races that their disruptive thoughts had decreased significantly, while at the same time their concentration on their bodies and on the race had improved noticeably (Gravel et al., 1980).

In another study (Suinn, 1977), Olympic skiers were taught to make positive statements to themselves in order to counteract pain. While this was not a scientifically controlled experiment, one of the subjects won the first silver medal ever awarded to an American skier in Nordic skiing—which may mean something. Experimentation with self-control techniques in sports has only just begun, but we are likely to see a great deal more of it in the future.

ieties by simply planning ahead. This is one reason for using distributed practice in studying: you eliminate night-before-the-test terrors.

As we have mentioned, avoidance can be a dangerous tactic in dealing with anxiety, but only if you or someone else stands to lose through your avoidance. If being with your father makes you anxious, this is a problem you should probably deal with rather than avoid. Likewise, if you are afraid of dogs, you shouldn't use the tactic of avoidance. Dogs are everywhere; to avoid them, you would have to put drastic limitations on your activities. But if your brother's habit of bringing illegal drugs into your house makes you nervous, tell him not to do it. Don't subject yourself to unnecessary anxieties by being a "nice guy."

Relabeling and Self-Talk

What about anxiety-producing situations that cannot or should not be avoided? When you cannot eliminate the external cues for anxiety, you can still eliminate the internal cues—that is, your negative self-talk (Goldfried, 1977; Kanter and Goldfried, 1979). Look back at Ellis's list of irrational beliefs in Box 4.2, p. 102. At least two of them are sure-fire generators of anxiety: "the idea that it is a dire necessity for an adult to be loved or approved by everyone for everything he does," and "the idea that one should be thoroughly competent, adequate, intelligent, and achieving in all possible respects." On the basis of these ideas, we do what Ellis and Harper (1976) call "catastrophizing." That is, we take some misfortune (actual or anticipated), and instead of labeling it as a misfortune, we label it as a catastrophe—a calamity, a disaster, a thing from which we will never recover. And not surprisingly, we respond to this label by becoming anxious.

To reverse this cognitive process, we have to engage in the type of deliberate self-talk discussed in Chapter 4. This does not mean kidding ourselves with Pollyanna-type optimism. What you need is neither optimism nor pessimism, but simple realism. Train yourself to respond to anxiety as a signal, a signal for you to examine what you are saying to yourself. Listen to your self-statements: "This is terrible"; "I'll never make it"; "She'll never speak to me again." Then systematically combat these statements with more realistic ones: "This isn't too comfortable, but I've seen worse"; "A year from now, I'll look back on this and laugh"; "If she never speaks to me again, there are plenty of other people who will"; "If I fail the exam, I'll just have to take the course again. Anyway, I'll live" (Goldfried et al., 1974; Goldfried and Goldfried, 1975). In this way you interrupt the automatic behavior of labeling situations as bleakly as possible. And you institute the new behavior of labeling realistically. Reinforced by the lessening of anxiety, this new labeling method can become as automatic as the old alarmist method.

Desensitization

The purpose of the technique that we just described is to replace an old maladaptive response with a new, adaptive response. Another technique for achieving this same goal is desensitization, by now a classic treatment for anxiety. Developed by physiologist Joseph Wolpe, *desensitization* is based on the following principle: "If a response inhibiting anxiety can be made to occur in the presence of anxiety-evoking stimuli, it will weaken the bond between these stimuli and the anxiety" (1973, p. 17). As the "response inhibiting anxiety," Wolpe chose the state of deep muscle relaxation. As we have seen earlier, tension in the skeletal muscles is a physiological response that normally accompanies the psychological response of anxiety. How the two responses are related is not yet entirely clear, but one thing is certain: it is difficult for people to maintain their anxiety if their muscles are relaxed. And since Wolpe knew of a technique, developed in 1929 by the physiologist Edmund Jacobson (1964), for inducing deep muscle relaxation, he used this as the incompatible response to weaken the associations between anxiety and the stimuli that produced anxiety. Since its introduction, desensitization has proven extremely successful in a wide variety of specific anxieties (Kazdin and Wilcozon, 1976).

In desensitization the anxious person is first taught to relax her whole body. The procedure is described in Box 7.5, pp. 200–201. It is hardly mysterious or difficult. All that is required is the progressive tensing and relaxing of various parts of the body. Once the relaxation response is learned well, the anxious person subjects herself to her anxiety-provoking stimuli while in the state of relaxation. This pairing of muscle relaxation with the stimuli counteracts and eventually destroys the association between these stimuli and muscle tension. And as we have just seen, once the muscle tension is gone, the psychological state of anxiety tends to give way also.

The confronting of the anxiety-provoking stimuli may be done by imagining them; this method is called *armchair desensitization.* Or one may actually confront the stimuli in the flesh—a method called *in vivo* (that is, in real life) *desensitization.* In both cases, the person approaches the object of her fear very gradually. First she confronts a slightly fearful stimulus, then a more fearful one, and so on, until at last she is able to experience or imagine her worst fear while remaining relaxed. This graded series of anxiety-provoking cues is called a *fear hierarchy.*

Armchair Desensitization. To illustrate armchair desensitization, we will take the case of Chris, who had a problem familiar to many students: test anxiety. Chris' preliminary description of her problem is as follows:

For me exams are a total nightmare. (I do have nightmares about them.) When I even think of an exam that's coming up, my stomach sort of caves in. This is not because I'm a bad student. I do a lot of studying, and I think I learn a fair amount. But when I have to take the exam I become a puddle. I shake. I sweat. I have to go to the bathroom. At first, when the exam begins, I'm so panicked I can't concentrate. I look at the other students writing madly away, and I think, "Oh, my God, for them it's a breeze. In three minutes they're going to be miles ahead of me." Suddenly I know I'm going to fail. When I finally force myself to concentrate, I get all worked up trying to do each part of the exam perfectly, and as a result, I never have time to finish the test. Once I had a midterm exam in American Literature with four equally weighted essay questions. I got a 75—a perfect score on each of the first three questions and zero on the last question, which I never got to. So after practically killing myself studying for this exam, I came out with a D.

I feel completely defeated by the whole business, but aside from my husband, I can't bring myself to tell anyone about it. I'm too embarrassed. For a thirty-year-old woman to be so afraid of a test—it's crazy.

Chris finally ended up bringing her problem to the college counseling center, where she was given a booklet on progressive relaxation, containing the same instructions as in Box 7.5. She was told to go home and relax herself twice a day. At first, the psychologist said, each relaxation session would take about a half hour. Later, when Chris had learned the technique, it should take about fifteen or twenty minutes. Chris was also advised that if she didn't want to hold the booklet while she was trying to relax, she could put the instructions on a tape and play the tape to herself.

Chris mastered the relaxation technique within a week. She loved it; it felt like floating on waves. She even used it to get to sleep at night. But this still didn't solve her test problem.

Now the psychologist told her to construct a fear hierarchy having to do with test-taking—ten scenes, going from the mildly stressful to the most terrifying. Chris came up with the following scenes.

1. *My son tells me that he has a math test in school tomorrow.*

2. *A friend tells me that a professor whose course I want to take grades on the curve.*

3. *On the first day of the course, I look at the mimeographed schedule and see the date of the midterm, seven weeks away.*

4. *At the beginning of a lecture the professor says, "The midterm examination is next Friday. You will be responsible for . . . ."*

5. *In the last lecture before the midterm, the professor reminds the class not to spend too much time on any one question.*

6. *The night before the exam, I am sitting at my desk looking over my course notes.*

7. *I am driving to school to take the exam.*

8. *The professor says, "The bluebooks will be collected at exactly four o'clock."*

9. *The professor starts handing out the exams.*

10. *I get my own copy of the exam and start to read it.*

The psychologist approved Chris' hierarchy and told her to go home and begin her desensitization. In her first session, she was to relax herself and imagine scene 1 for five seconds. Then in the next few sessions she was to increase the time spent imagining scene 1 until she could get up to thirty seconds. When she had progressed to this point, she should switch her attention from the scene to the relaxed feeling in her muscles and concentrate only on that for thirty seconds. Then she should move on to scene 2. With scene 2 she should proceed exactly as she had with scene 1. She could then graduate to the next scene (repeating the same process) and the next, until she had reached the top of her fear hierarchy. If she experienced even the least bit of anxiety over any scene, she was to shut out the scene and focus only on relaxing for at least thirty seconds. Once she had relaxed again, she was to switch back to the *preceding* scene (the one before the scene that had aroused the anxiety) and get used to that scene again before trying to move forward once more.

Chris progressed smoothly up through scene 7, but she couldn't get past this point. Every time she tried to imagine the professor tolling that four o'clock bell of doom, her heartbeat would speed up, her body would tighten, and anxiety would flood her mind. She would try to go blank, but once this anxiety response had occurred a few times, she became very upset, imagining that the whole thing was hopeless. Finally, she called the psychologist, who said that this sometimes happened and that Chris should have called earlier, before allowing herself to become anxious again. The solution was to insert a few intermediate steps between steps 7 and 8. So Chris added the following scenes:

7A. *I go into the classroom and sit down at a desk.*

BOX 7.5
RELAXATION PROCEDURE

It may seem strange, but learning how to relax involves learning how to tense up—at least as a first step. You tense a muscle (like making a tight fist) and then release the tension by "letting go" of it (releasing your fist and letting the hand fall open). The release creates a momentum effect in the muscle, so that it becomes more relaxed than it was before you tensed it. Once you have completed this simple exercise with sixteen of the major muscle groups in your body, you will probably find that your body is relaxed.

The procedure for relaxing a muscle group is as follows:

1. Breathe in, hold the breath, and tense the muscle group for 5 to 10 seconds, concentrating on the tense feeling in the muscles.
2. Release the tension and breathe out.
3. Concentrate for 20 to 30 seconds on the relaxed feeling in the muscles. (Breathe normally.)

Do this two times in a row for each muscle group. Then, if it feels relaxed, go on to the next muscle group. We list the sixteen muscle groups below and how best to tense each of them. Remember to concentrate on the feeling in the muscles both when tensing them and when relaxing them. This is done so that you can differentiate between the two responses and learn to know when your muscles are relaxed.

Before beginning the relaxation procedure, there are a number of things you should know and do:

1. Allow yourself thirty minutes for the whole procedure. (It will take less time once you are skilled at it.)
2. Practice in a room where there are no distractions and where you will not be disturbed.
3. Wear loose-fitting, comfortable clothing. Take off glasses, earrings, watches, shoes.
4. Recline or lie down so that the chair, bed, or couch completely supports your whole body. Your muscles shouldn't have to support any part of you.
5. Put this book on your lap so you can follow the instructions as you go. (Once you learn them, practice them with your eyes closed.)
6. To learn the method quickly, practice twice a day in sessions spaced at least two hours apart. Practice is important. Do it regularly.
7. Remember to pay close attention to the feelings in your muscles, both when you tense tightly and when you relax before tensing again.

MUSCLE GROUPS
AND HOW TO TENSE THEM
The general progression is from the hands to the head to the feet. Do each group twice.

1. Right hand and forearm: make a tight fist with your right hand.
2. Right biceps: bend your arm at the elbow and tense as if you were lifting weights.

3. Left hand and forearm (same procedure as right).

4. Left biceps (same procedure as right).

5. Forehead and top of your head: frown hard, tensing muscles in forehead and top of head.

6. Nose and cheeks: squint, wrinkling nose and tensing muscles in nose and cheeks.

7. Mouth and jaw: clench your teeth, pull the corners of your mouth back toward your ears (forced smile).

8. Throat and neck: pull your head back and at the same time pull your chin down (make a double chin).

9. Chest and back: inhale, pull your shoulder blades together and down (as if you were standing at rigid attention).

10. Abdominal muscles: inhale and suck in abdomen.

11. Right upper leg: raise right foot about six inches, keeping leg stiff and straight.

12. Right calf: pull foot toward you, keeping leg stiff and straight.

13. Right foot: curl toes under and arch your foot.

14. Left upper leg (same procedure as right).

15. Left calf (same procedure as right).

16. Left foot (same procedure as right).

After you have finished, survey your muscles to determine if any still feel tense. If so, repeat the procedure with that muscle group. Once they are all relaxed, remain reclined, enjoying the feeling for a few minutes before becoming active again. The effect will wear off after about two hours.

7B. *I look at the clock; the exam starts in five minutes.*

7C. *The professor enters the room and opens his briefcase.*

Because she had let herself get so upset, Chris had to drop down to scene 4 in order to relax again. But she quickly worked her way back up to scene 7. Then, with the help of the intermediate steps, she progressed to scene 8 and eventually to scene 10.

In her first final exam that semester, Chris was somewhat nervous, but since the psychologist had told her this would happen, she did not let her nervousness make her more nervous. She simply applied herself to the task at hand, allotting to each section of the exam the appropriate amount of time before starting to write. She did well on that set of finals, and this success increased her confidence in the following semester's midterms. Chris still gets slightly keyed up when taking an exam—about as keyed up as everyone else.

Can You Desensitize Yourself? There is some question as to whether desensitization belongs in a self-help book. Traditionally, this therapy is administered by a psychologist; even Chris had advice from the counseling center. Yet recent research has shown that people can desensitize themselves to various sources of anxiety—including driving, public speaking, and authority figures— with little or no help from a therapist (Rosen et al., 1976; Spiegler et al., 1976; Goldfried and Goldfried, 1977; Harris and Johnson, 1980). They can do this simply by using tape-recorded instructions (Lang, 1969; Phillips et al., 1972). Hence, if you have a specific anxiety in a life that is otherwise reasonably happy, there is no reason why you shouldn't practice desensitization on yourself, using Chris as your model. Teach yourself to relax, following the instructions in

Box 7.5. Then create your hierarchy, using very gradual steps. After that, slowly ascend the hierarchy, making sure that you drop back one step at the first twinge of anxiety. And if you find that there is a step you cannot make, insert intermediate steps before that step, as Chris did.

In Vivo Desensitization. In armchair desensitization you imagine the thing you fear; with in vivo desensitization you go out and actually face it. This is not as terrible as it sounds, however, for once again, you approach the feared stimulus in very small steps.

The success of in vivo desensitization depends on conditioning yourself to associate some cue word, such as "calm" or "relax," with the state of deep muscle relaxation (Paul, 1966; Newman and Brand, 1980). This is done by saying the word to yourself each time you release the tension in a muscle group during the relaxation procedure described in Box 7.5. Eventually, through respondent conditioning, the mere thought of the word will result in substantial relaxation. And then you can use the word to relax yourself in non-armchair situations (Counts et al., 1978; Kirkland and Hollandsworth, 1980).

The next step is to create a hierarchy of behaviors that bring you closer and closer to the thing you fear. Thus, for example, if Larry Fallon from Chapter 4 were practicing in vivo desensitization, he might first practice deliberately sitting next to a strange woman in every class (and not doing anything about it), then addressing some very ordinary remark (such as "Do you have the time?") to a strange woman in every class, then making conversation, then going through these same steps at a party, then adding further steps. The final step would be to ask a woman for her phone number and then to call and ask her out. Before performing any one of these actions, he would relax himself as much as possible by saying to himself his cue word. And as with armchair desensitization, he would drop back one step at the first sign of anxiety.

A Caution. There is one potential problem with self-desensitization, whether armchair or in vivo. Fortunately, it is one that you can eliminate by understanding it beforehand. The problem is the possibility that when you hit a roadblock in the hierarchy, you will either push yourself forward, thereby imagining scenes without the appropriate state of relaxation or that you will give up,

---

ACTIVITY 7.3

Think of some fear that you have overcome in the past and write down how you managed to get over it. If, as a child, you were afraid of the water, did you learn to swim by going in water that was gradually deeper and deeper? If you used to be afraid to stand up to some person in your life who was pushing you around, did you use self-talk to overcome the fear? The point is that a technique you have *already* used successfully would be an obvious first choice in attempting to conquer other anxieties. So think of a method that has worked for you previously, write it down, apply it to a new problem, and describe the results.

saying to yourself, "Since this technique can't work for me, obviously I'm even crazier than I thought."

As with any form of self-control, you should expect plateaus in self-desensitization. You should also expect that progress will be very gradual, especially as you get nearer the top of the hierarchy. You won't become fearless in a week. Furthermore, you should be aware that self-desensitization without the help of a professional may simply not work for you. The research on self-desensitization indicates that it is successful for about half the people who try it (Clark, 1973; Rosen et al., 1976; Newman and Brand, 1980). If you are among the other half, don't conclude that you're a hopeless case or a lunatic. The reasons for failure are probably much less dramatic than that—for example, too few steps in the hierarchy, steps too far apart, failure to relax, failure to visualize the scenes. So instead of becoming panicked or depressed, simply consult a professional. (See "Getting Help," pp. 439–444.) He or she will either help you work out the snags in your desensitization or suggest a different technique.

Stress and Physical Exercise

So far, we have been discussing anxiety, a very uncomfortable condition that, fortunately, most of us do not experience on a constant basis. But many of us do live our lives in a state of excessive arousal; some call it "stress,"* others call it "tension." Although stress may not be as unsettling as anxiety, it still tends to make our lives less happy. It can also make them shorter. Illnesses such as ulcers, heart attacks, and hypertension (high blood pressure) have been directly related to stressful work situations (House, 1974). There are even studies (e.g., Locke, 1978) suggesting that cancer may be related to chronic stress.

In our society, stress is hard to avoid. As we saw in Chapter 1, the world we live in seems, by its very nature, to foster tension. But there are things that we can do to relieve stress, and exercise is apparently one of them.

Research on the relationship between exercise and psychological well-being is still in its early stages. There are many enthusiastic but poorly documented claims by physical fitness enthusiasts—that jogging brings peace, that tennis improves the personality—reports that tend to be curtly dismissed by more rigorous scientists. There is, however, a respectable group of studies indicating that physical fitness programs do enhance the self-concept (Hilyer and Mitchell, 1979; Martinek et al., 1978; McGowan et al., 1974). This, actually, should come as no surprise. As we noted in Chapter 2, changes in the physical self tend to bring about changes in the rest of the self, and that includes the self-concept. Furthermore, no matter what the actual changes in the body (or, more precisely, in the view of the body), the mere sense of mastery and control that most people derive from putting themselves through an exercise regimen may lend a new glow to the image of the self (Solomon and Bumpas, 1978).

More important for our immediate purposes is the evidence showing that exercise can have powerful effects on emotion—above all, that it can reduce stress and anxiety (Folkins and Amsterdam, 1977; Folkins and Sime, 1981). No one yet knows why this should be. Perhaps physical exertion releases chemicals in the brain that help to inhibit anxiety. Perhaps, like the muscle-relaxation technique described earlier, it counteracts psychological tension by counteracting physiological tension. Or maybe it

---

* Stress will be more precisely defined in Chapter 14.

simply takes people's minds off their problems. In any case, it does tend to alleviate anxiety and is also useful in dealing with many "psychosomatic" disorders that are often related to anxiety, such as insomnia (Walker et al., 1978) and heart disease (Martic, 1976).

We have already offered, in the section on weight problems, a number of suggestions for improving your exercise pattern. These techniques will work as well for stress as they will for weight control. And if sit-ups bore you, take up a sport such as tennis or jogging. At the same time that you are relieving stress, improving your health, and enhancing your self-concept, you may also meet someone nice, in case that was a source of anxiety.

SUMMARY

1. The chapter discussed self-control techniques appropriate for three common self-control problems: weight, poor study habits, and anxiety.

2. In dealing with weight problems, the first step is to analyze your eating habits. Ask yourself, and record, exactly what you eat, the external antecedents (such as the time and place of eating), and the internal antecedents (such as mood).

3. Among the most effective methods of changing eating behavior are stimulus-narrowing, redirecting attention, delaying, chaining, and using *coverants*. Exercise, an important aspect of weight control, can also be increased through self-control techniques.

4. Poor study habits are often reinforced because they allow the student to "get by" without failing. To improve your study habits, you must first describe them: how much time you spend actually studying, how you distribute your study time, when and where you study, how well you concentrate, what your attitude is, and what method you use in studying.

5. Among the ways in which you can improve the effectiveness of your study time are environmental planning, scheduling, and the use of a systematic method of study. A particularly helpful approach is the *SQ3R method*, in which you survey the material, form questions, read to find answers to the questions, recite the answers, and review your questions and answers.

6. *Anxiety* is a feeling of fear accompanied by a state of increased physiological arousal. According to behaviorists, it results from respondent conditioning. Intense anxiety involves emotional, cognitive, and physiological changes. Although moderate anxiety can be useful, extreme anxiety is often inappropriate to the situation and should be reduced.

7. To reduce anxiety, begin by pinpointing the situations in which you experience it. You should note antecedents and consequences, internal and external. Anxiety can be managed through environmental planning, relabeling, and self-talk. Another technique, *desensitization*, involves the substitution of a new adaptive response to counteract an old maladaptive response. After learning to relax his muscles, the anxious person is exposed, and gradually desensitized, to anxiety-provoking stimuli graded in a *fear hierarchy*. The stimuli can be imagined (*armchair desensitization*) or actually experienced (*in vivo desensitization*).

THREE SELF-CONTROL PROBLEMS: WEIGHT, STUDY HABITS, AND ANXIETY

PROJECT

One situation in which self-control techniques can be applied is a test. The testing situation has two specific characteristics. One is that it involves supplying information. In this respect it is the opposite of studying. Studying involves input—getting information inside you. Taking a test involves output—getting the stored information out in some intelligible form. The second characteristic of testing is that its purpose is evaluation. For this reason it is often a source of anxiety and, hence, can be a very unpleasant occasion.

Below is a checklist of nineteen self-control techniques to help you improve your information output and lessen your anxiety during tests. First read the list.

Things to do before going to the exam:

_____ 1. Get a good night's sleep the night before the exam.

_____ 2. Avoid discussing the test on the day it takes place.

_____ 3. Avoid any emotionally involving discussions or arguments on the day of the exam.

_____ 4. Try not to eat too much or get too much exercise before the exam.

_____ 5. Try to place yourself in a calm, comfortable, relaxing atmosphere before the test.

_____ 6. Allow yourself plenty of time before the test to eat lightly and get your supplies together.

_____ 7. Plan for and take extra pens and pencils (and erasers), extra paper to use for notes, a book or magazine, and a watch. (For longer tests, you might take a candy bar or a piece of fruit.)

Things to do before the exam begins:

_____ 8. Arrive at the test room early and pick out a seat that is comfortable and has good lighting.

_____ 9. Avoid sitting near doors, aisles, and other sources of distraction.

_____ 10. Put your watch where you can see it and lay out your test-taking materials.

_____ 11. While waiting for the test to begin, read a book or magazine and try to get your mind completely off the test situation.

_____ 12. Avoid talking to other students.

Things to do during the exam:

_____ 13. Read all instructions, ask for clarifications if necessary, and determine what you have to do and how much time you have in which to do it.

_____ 14. On one of your note sheets, write down your schedule (for example, how many questions to be answered by a certain time). Questions that count more should get more time.

_____ 15. If the test lasts more than an hour, schedule a five-minute break after each hour. During breaks, avoid conversation. Get up, stretch, have a snack.

_____ 16. As you move through the test, try to stay with your schedule.

_____ 17. On a test with many items, skip those that look extremely difficult. Come back to them when you have finished the other items.

_____ 18. Outline essay questions before answering them.

_____ 19. Use self-talk. Be positive. Tell yourself that you will do as well as anybody on the test.

Follow these suggestions when you take your next exam. After the exam, rate on a scale of 1 to 5 the usefulness of each suggestion. Those to which you give a 4 or 5 you should probably use when taking future exams.

UNIT
II

OTHERS

OUTLINE

OUR SOCIAL LIVES
The Need for Others
The Socially Created Self
Monkeys reared in isolation
Isolated and institutionalized children

STUDYING SOCIAL INTERACTION
The Complexity of Social Interaction
Theories of Social Psychology
Attribution theory
Role theory
Communication theory
Social exchange theory
Applying the Theories of Social Psychology to Adjustment

8

THE SOCIAL SELF: HOW WE INTERACT

Adjustment, as we have seen, is the continuous interaction that we carry on with ourselves, with other people, and with our world. In the six chapters of Unit I we concentrated on how we interact with ourselves. The main thrust of those chapters should by now be clear: we *can* influence ourselves in important ways; within limits, we can change who we are.

We now turn to the second factor with which we interact: other people—a major factor, needless to say. As Harry Stack Sullivan put it, "Persons are decidedly the hardest things we have to deal with" (1962, p. 246). They are also the most influential. People, more than anything else in the world, have the power to give us pain and pleasure. And no matter how many times we experience these feelings, their impact never diminishes. Warmth and anger, love and hatred—these feelings do not become ordinary. For the ninety-year-old as for the two-year-old, nothing carries such high

stakes as interpersonal relationships. It is no accident that poets often describe such relationships in religious terms. What we know of "heaven"—and of "hell"—we generally find out through our dealings with other people.

Thus, like the self, the relationship of self and other is a profound conception, with roots extending to the very depths of our experience. Yet from these invisible roots spring visible, concrete realities. A birthday card, a gentle or sarcastic tone of voice, a hand held out in greeting or raised in anger—these are the concrete particulars of our relationships with others. Furthermore, our relationships give rise to thoughts and emotions that we can enunciate in fairly plain English. Hence, if we wish to change our interactions with other people, we *do* have materials on which we can work in a scientific manner.

How? In Chapters 9 through 13 we shall discuss in detail the origins of our patterns

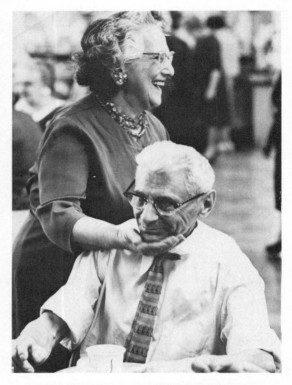

of perceiving and interacting with others and the ways in which these patterns can be changed. First, however, we must examine the dimensions of our social life and the current theories of social interaction. These two topics are the business of the present chapter.

People are the strongest influence on our emotional lives. What we feel, we generally feel in a social context. (*top far left*, © Ken Heyman; *top left*, Charles Harbutt/Magnum; *bottom left*, Bill Stanton/Magnum; *top right*, Burk Uzzle/Magnum; *bottom right*, Bill Stanton/Magnum)

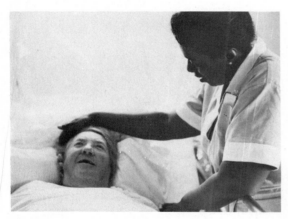

OUR SOCIAL LIVES

If someone asked you how your social life was going, you might reply that you were going out with someone interesting, that you'd been to a party on Friday night, and so on. In other words, we tend to apply the term "social" to recreational, pleasure-oriented interactions with others. Actually, however, the term applies to any interaction involving two or more people. A party is a social occasion, but so is having a fight with your mother or asking your neighbor to water your plants while you are away on vacation.

Human life is permeated with such interactions. Of course, other animals too have social interactions. Wolves hunt in packs. Gorillas and chimpanzees live in small groups, which buzz with social activity. Bees and ants form large communities and work together with admirable cooperation. But none of these animal groupings can compare with the social world created by the human animal—a vast network of groups and subgroups, personal and institutional, each with its own set of rules, duties, and satisfactions. Why this intense concentration on the social life? Why do human beings need other human beings so much, and what does this constant interaction do to us?

The Need for Others

Is the need for others an inborn trait—an instinct? Or is it simply a conditioned response, based on a learned association between our parents and the satisfaction of more primary needs, such as hunger and thirst? In an effort to answer this question, psychologist Harry Harlow (1958, 1959; Harlow and Harlow, 1962) devised what was to become a very famous experiment. Harlow took a number of infant monkeys away from their mothers at birth, so that none of them had the opportunity to "learn" a need for the social comforts of body contact and cuddling. Each of the monkeys was then reared in isolation, in a cage equipped with two artificial "mothers." One of the artificial mothers was made of wire mesh and equipped with a milk dispenser. This mother was strictly a food-giver. The second artificial mother was similar to the first in shape and size, but she had no milk dispenser. And instead of wire, she was made of soft terry cloth. This was the mother you could cuddle up to. Harlow's question was: with which of the two mothers would the monkeys spend the most time?

At the end of the 165-day experiment, he had a very clear answer. The monkeys by that time were spending an average of sixteen hours a day with the terry-cloth mother, as compared to one and a half hours a day with the wire mother. Hence, it was not an association with food that produced social attachment in these monkeys. Rather, it was a need for comforting physical contact—a need that the monkeys never learned from their own mothers but which emerged anyway (Harlow and Zimmerman, 1959).

If we can generalize from monkeys to human beings, Harlow's experiment strongly suggests that our need for contact with others is independent of our need for food and produces a stronger attachment. But the experiment still doesn't explain how this need emerges. Researchers have proposed various answers to this question. One theory holds that the parents act as a "releaser stimulus" eliciting the infant's instinctive social responses, such as clinging, cuddling, and smiling (Bowlby, 1958, 1969). Another major theory is the behavioral position (Gewirtz, 1972) that the parents become conditioned reinforcers by being associated with relief from hunger *and* relief from physical tension (through holding); their value then generalizes to other human beings, so that the child comes to value people in general.

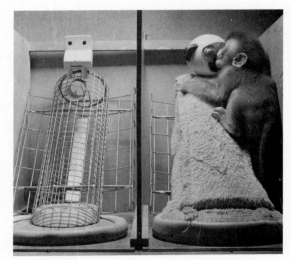

Harlow's rhesus monkeys chose to spend their time with the soft terry-cloth "mother" rather than the milk-giving wire "mother." (Courtesy, Harry F. Harlow, University of Wisconsin Primate Research Center)

Neither of these theories has been conclusively proved or disproved. Furthermore, what support they have generally comes from experiments with animals, and we can never be sure that what is true for a duck or a white rat is true for a human being. (Harlow's experiment raises the same question. However, the animal he chose, the infant rhesus monkey, is thought to be very similar to the human infant in its basic responses.)

So we have no final answer as to the original source of our need for others. But we do have some idea, both from scientific studies and from our own experience, *why* human beings seek out other human beings. To begin on the simplest level, human beings provide one another with stimulation—something on which to fasten their five senses, their minds, and their feelings (Casler, 1961). Deprived of stimulation, we not only become bored; eventually our thought processes can become seriously disturbed (Heron, 1957; Zubek, 1969). Second, we look

ACTIVITY 8.1

We are not always aware of just how much of our time is spent interacting with other people. For one day, keep a record of all your social interactions, noting how long each one lasts. Find the total and determine what percentage of your waking hours this represents. You may find that you are more involved with others than you thought you were.

to other human beings for the satisfaction of biological needs (Bowlby, 1969). Unlike infants, adults can find their own food, but to satisfy their needs for physical contact, including sexual contact, they need other people. Third, human beings look to one another for the gratification of a number of emotional needs: love, respect, appreciation, power, comfort (Rheingold and Eckerman, 1973).

The last factor, the need for comfort, appears to be a particularly powerful means of bringing people together. Several experiments have shown that people under stress—especially the stress of fear—are highly motivated to seek out others (Schachter, 1959; Zimbardo and Formica, 1963; Firestone et al., 1973). There are apparently two reasons for this. First, simply being with others and talking to them about a source of fear seems to help reduce the fear. Second, by comparing their own reactions to those of others, people are better able to organize and evaluate their feelings. The same two principles probably apply to grief as well, and may account for the amount of "socializing" that surrounds a death. Those who remember the assassination of President Kennedy will recall that it was a major feat to put through a telephone call that day, so jammed were the wires. An entire nation was on the phone, sharing its grief, unburdening it socially.

The Socially Created Self

People, then, need other people, and consequently they tend to spend a large portion of their waking hours in social interaction. What effect does all this social activity have on us? It teaches us the beliefs, values, and behaviors that are acceptable to the people around us and necessary for social interaction with them. From birth onward, through interacting with others, we learn to control our bodies, to speak, to think, to adopt the customs and rules of our community, to respond to other people, to care about them, and to adopt behaviors that dovetail with theirs. This process of learning-to-be-social is called *socialization*.

Without socialization, the human creature fails not only to become "social" but also to become what we think of as "human" in a psychological and behavioral sense (Clausen, 1968). "Human nature," wrote George Herbert Mead, "is something social through and through" (1934, p. 229). Take away the "social" and you take away most of the "human." All you are left with is raw biology.

Monkeys Reared in Isolation

The role of social interaction in the establishment of normal adult behavior was another focus of the rhesus monkey experiments conducted by Harlow and his colleagues (Harlow and Harlow, 1966; Harlow et al., 1971). In several studies these investigators removed infant monkeys from their mothers at birth, placed them in isolation chambers, kept them there for varying periods, and then returned them to group cages to see how they fared. They fared very poorly. Those that were isolated for over six months were fearful of the other monkeys, had trouble mating, and if they became mothers, ignored their infants to the point of endangering their lives. Those monkeys that spent their first twelve months alone did even worse. They crouched in corners, avoided all social contact, and to the extent that they showed any activity, acted in a bizarre manner. Now, animal behavior, as we know, is based in large measure on instinct, or inborn "coding." But social interaction is clearly required in order for the instincts to find their proper outlet, at least in the case of rhesus monkeys.

Isolated and Institutionalized Children

For obvious reasons, such experiments cannot be conducted on human infants. But life performs its own cruel experiments. Over the years, psychologists have had the opportunity to observe several children raised in total or almost total isolation from other human beings. One such child, for example, was Anna. Anna's mother, after trying and failing to get rid of her illegitimate daughter, finally closed her up in an attic room. Thereafter, the mother entered the room only to bring the child her food. Otherwise, Anna had no contact with human life. This went on for six years, until Anna was finally discovered by a social worker and removed to an institution. At that point the child bore no resemblance to the average six-year-old, or even to the average two-year-old. She wasn't toilet trained, couldn't talk, couldn't

even sit up, to say nothing of walking. Furthermore, she was totally unresponsive not only to human beings but to almost everything else as well. Her only skill was to feed herself. The experts who observed Anna's behavior—or lack of behavior—guessed that she was deaf and dumb, and possibly mentally retarded as well. But eventually, through patient training in a special school, she learned to walk, to play with blocks, to speak words and phrases (but not sentences), and even to interact with other children. Anna died at the age of eleven, and it is impossible to tell how much more progress she would have made. Yet, the progress she did make suggests that her handicap was not biological but social (Davis, 1948). Isolated from other human beings, she had been unable to develop any of the normal human responses for which she was biologically equipped. In short, "human nature" does not develop spontaneously; it is built up through interaction with others.

The same phenomenon has been observed in orphanages (Goldfarb, 1947; Goldenson, 1970). In one classic study, two researchers observed seventy-five institutionalized infants who were given everything *but* social attention. The babies had baths, regular diaper changes, airy rooms, and nourishing food. But the food was dispensed through propped bottles, and the babies spent their days in glass-walled cubicles. At eight months, these infants were already strikingly different from family-reared infants of the same age. They did not babble or smile. Indeed, they had almost no facial expression. When picked up, they didn't mold their bodies to the body of the person holding them. They showed little interest in toys or in people (Provence and Lipton, 1962). René Spitz (1945), a pioneer in the study of institutionalized infants, claimed that the high mortality rate in orphanages was due to the lack

BOX 8.1
GROWING UP ON
A KIBBUTZ

For the past sixty years, a kind of communal settlement called a kibbutz (plural: kibbutzim) has been in existence in Israel. Designed to encourage social equality, the typical kibbutz is a voluntary collective farm. In many kibbutzim, property is community-owned and child care is a collective responsibility. This type of kibbutz has been extensively studied by psychologists, who are particularly interested in how community child-rearing affects socialization and other aspects of early development.

In this kind of kibbutz, a child is placed in a brightly decorated nursery with other infants right after birth. During the first six weeks, his mother visits him as often as necessary to feed him. Gradually, however, the job of rearing the child is assumed by female caretakers, though the parents continue to visit the child, usually for an hour or two each day, using the time for affectionate play.

After a year, the child moves from the nursery to the toddlers' house, joining five of his peers. Caretakers look after the children, teaching them to feed and dress themselves. Most important of all, the children learn to interact with their peers, playing together and cooperating with one another.

At three or four, the child's education begins in a kindergarten consisting of eighteen children. The child remains with this group for several years, studying, working, and playing with them. They are together through grammar school, which lasts from ages seven to twelve. Though a child still has contact with her parents, the primary socializing agent is her peer group and the women who teach her.

Only when a child goes to high school away from the kibbutz is she separated from her peer group. She lives, works, and studies at the high school until the age of eighteen, learning a skill that will enable her to contribute to the kibbutz economy. When she graduates from high school, she returns to the kibbutz as an adult member.

Despite the fact that these children are separated from their parents and raised in a group context by multiple caretakers, studies indicate that they are intellectually equal to children reared in private homes (Rabin, 1965). In their emotional lives, however, they appear to be somewhat different from family-reared children. Bruno Bettelheim (1969), for example, has pointed out that in one-to-one relationships, kibbutz children seem to lack the intensity of feeling (both positive and negative) that is probably fostered in the family. Rather, because of their group-oriented socialization, they are most comfortable in group interactions and find emotional gratification primarily in the less intense and more generalized feeling of "togetherness" that is fostered in groups. Thus, while they are certainly as "normal" emotionally as family-raised children, their emotional lives have a different focus—a focus quite appropriate to group-oriented life on the kibbutz. Later studies have confirmed the emotional "normality" of kibbutz-raised children (Rutter, 1972). Much research remains to be done on these children, particularly as they pass through adulthood. Whatever this research reveals, it will cast an interesting light on the more usual, family-based socialization practices.

of tender handling—in other words, that some children actually die from social deprivation.

Social interaction, then, is vital for normal development, whether physical, intellectual, or emotional. Nevertheless, interaction itself by no means guarantees healthy development, just as isolated and institutionalized children are by no means the only human beings who are psychologically handicapped. The fact that disturbed interactions in childhood can create a disturbed adult is probably the best-known commonplace of psychology (Rutter, 1972). This idea, originated by Freud, became the central argument of the psychodynamic theorists coming after Freud, particularly Alfred Adler, Harry Stack Sullivan, Karen Horney, and Erich Fromm (Chapter 1). By now, the notion that maladjustment is the result of social problems—problems in relationships between people—has been accepted by every school of psychology. Indeed, some modern psychological theorists have gone one step further, claiming that maladjustment exists not in individuals but in social groups, particularly small, intimate groups such as the family (Satir, 1967; Minuchin, 1974). It is not the person who is disturbed; it is the interaction. Family therapy and marriage counseling are both based on this belief.

In sum, interaction—present or lacking, affirming or demeaning—can make *and* break the self. For better or worse, we are, as Mead stated, "social through and through."

Psychological disturbance in the individual may be merely a symptom of psychological disturbance in the family—for example, a conflict between parents and child. Many psychologists, therefore, treat the entire family rather than simply its most unhappy member. (Sepp Seitz/Magnum)

STUDYING SOCIAL INTERACTION

Because the social life is so central to the development of the self, it has generated a whole separate field of study, the field of *social psychology*. Whereas general psychology often studies the individual in isolation, the job of social psychology is to study interpersonal behavior. As we are about to see, this is no easy job.

The Complexity of Social Interaction

Imagine that you are eating alone in a crowded cafeteria. A man arrives, puts his tray down on your table, and sits down across from you. After a few minutes, he strikes up a conversation. What could be simpler? What could be more complex?

Consider just a few of the many external variables that will affect your response to him: his age, his clothes, his physical attractiveness. (If it were a woman instead of a man, this too would make a difference, of course.) Likewise, if he is what you consider handsome or what you consider ugly, if he has all his teeth or is missing a few, if he has on a three-piece suit or tennis shorts and a purple T-shirt, if he is ten years older than you or your own age—all these factors will influence your response to him before he even opens his mouth.

Once he does open his mouth, you have a great deal more to respond to: what he says to you and the tone in which he says it. Is he boring or interesting? Is he witty? Is he nosy? And what does he want from you? Is he just looking for a mealtime chat, or does he sound as though he is about to try to persuade you to join his religious sect?

Consider also his nonverbal behavior. Af-

This is the only free table in the restaurant. You sit down at it, and the man starts talking to you. What external variables does he present to you? How would you respond to them? (Alex Webb/Magnum)

ter all, his "body language" is surely communicating something to you. If he leans forward with an air of intimacy or if he sits back rigidly in his chair, this will elicit some reaction from you. You may also be affected by his table manners and his other mannerisms. Does he drum his fingers on the table? Does he slurp his coffee? Does he chain-smoke? Does he smile?

These, then, are some of the stimuli that will determine your response to him. Complicated as the picture seems, it has been grossly simplified. For we have implied that the cluster of stimuli presented by your dinner companion is stable. It is not. It changes from minute to minute. For every response that you make to him, the stimulus-picture (response) that he presents to you will alter. He will not run out and change his clothes,

ACTIVITY 8.2

It is difficult to be alert to the subtler characteristics of a person with whom we are interacting. We are too busy framing our own responses. But subtle signals can have a powerful effect on a transaction. Go to a place where you are likely to see people in conversation—for example, a coffee shop or a student lounge. Find two people (only two) who are interacting and observe them for five minutes. As you watch, write down any nonverbal behaviors—eye movements, head movements, hand gestures, crossing and recrossing of legs—that may be affecting their spoken interaction. You will probably find that your subjects are sending out many subtle messages, messages that might escape you if you were part of the conversation.

but he will say something new, and perhaps change his posture, tone of voice, or facial expression, *in reaction to your response to him*. And this change on his part will influence you to produce a new response—a "new" you (Patterson and Cobb, 1971). Each person's response, then, is the trigger for a new response from the other person. Thus, what we have in any human interaction is a chain, extending through time, of *reciprocal influences*—subtle changes that we bring about in one another.

Social exchanges, as you can see, are intricate phenomena. And our example involves only a simple *dyad*, an interaction between two people. As more people are added to the interaction, the complexity of course increases. Furthermore, our example concerns only one *transaction*—that is, a "piece" of interaction with a beginning and an end. (We can assume that the dinner conversation ended in one way or another.) Imagine how much more difficult it is to study a *relationship*—that is, a habitual pattern of transactions between two people, extending over time and involving its own unique set of emotional signals.

Finally, we must take into account one last factor: the social history of each of the participants in an interaction. Earlier, we gave a rather simple definition of social psychology: the study of interpersonal behavior. Psychologist Gordon Allport has provided a richer and more complicated definition, which bears looking at. Social psychology, Allport writes, is "an attempt to understand and explain how the feeling, thought, or behavior of individuals [is] influenced by the *actual, imagined, or implied* presence of others" (1968, p. 3, italics added). What Allport is saying is that the fellow across from us is not the only person influencing us in a social transaction. To every encounter we bring the influences of all the people with whom we have interacted in the past. If our beloved Uncle George used to slurp his coffee, then the coffee-slurping of our dinner companion may have pleasant rather than annoying associations. Similarly, we bring to every interaction an awareness of our membership in certain subgroups of the society as a whole. If you think of yourself as a member of the refined upper classes, then the other fellow's coffee-slurping is likely to seem unpleasant no matter what Uncle George used to do.

Theories of Social Psychology

Faced with all this complexity, social psychologists have, understandably, developed different theories as to which aspect of a social transaction is most central. Let us look at four of the most important theories.

Attribution Theory

As we have seen, one line of questioning that you might have pursued mentally as you talked to the stranger in the cafeteria is: What does he want from me? What is he up to? Why is he striking up this conversation with me? According to *attribution theory*, how you answer this question for yourself is the crucial determinant of your behavior in the transaction. *Attribution theory holds that the key to a transaction lies in the causes that each person assigns to the other person's behavior.* If you attribute the stranger's friendliness to the fact that he is just a nice, gregarious person who doesn't like to eat alone, then you are likely to respond to him in a friendly manner, encouraging his chitchat with chitchat of your own. But if you guess that he is leading up to something—that he *wants* something from you—then you may pull out a magazine and begin reading it very intently.

Why do we engage in this guesswork about what is causing the other person's behavior? According to Fritz Heider (1958), who originated attribution theory, the reason is that all human beings (not just psychologists) feel a strong need to make some sense out of human behavior. In order to organize their view of reality, people need to know *why* they and other people are doing what they are doing. More recently, Harold Kelley (1971), another major attribution theorist, has pointed out that we must assign causes to behavior in order to feel that we have some control over our interactions.

But how do we decide what causes to assign? According to Kelley (1967, 1973), there are a number of criteria that people use, almost unconsciously, in interpreting other people's behavior. One is *consistency:* How "typical" is this particular behavior of this particular person? The more typical it is, the more likely we are to attribute it to a personality "trait." The more atypical it is, the more likely we are to ascribe it to some very special external influence or to some unusual motive.

A second factor influencing attribution is *consensus:* Do other people agree with your interpretation? Imagine that a woman in one of your classes makes a particularly clever remark, and you conclude that she is witty and intelligent. But if people you trust tell you that this woman's brain is not her strong point, then you are likely to discard or at least reinvestigate your hypothesis.

A third important criterion is the perceived *likelihood* of the other person's behavior: Is this what people normally do in this situation? Let's say you're a man who is used to getting a great deal of attention from women. But a woman whose attention *you* have been trying to get persists in ignoring you completely. Rather than decide that she is brushing you off because you're unattractive, you may conclude that she is married, is afraid of men, or doesn't know a good thing when she sees it.

Finally, in making attributions, we take into account *external pressures*. You are having Thanksgiving dinner with your liberal roommate's conservative family. In the middle of dinner, one of her uncles declares that all welfare recipients should be put to work in salt mines. Your roommate goes on eating her turkey and says nothing. Instead of concluding that she has suddenly turned conservative, you would probably attribute her silence to a desire to keep the family peace on Thanksgiving. All four of these cri-

ACTIVITY 8.3

As psychologists like Heider and Kelley have suggested, we constantly assign internal causes to the behavior of others. Unfortunately, we often come up with the wrong causes, and as a result we may treat others unjustly. It's often possible to avoid errors by simply asking people why they did what they did.

Think of a recent occasion when a person did something that annoyed or upset you. Write down why you think the person did this. Then check your hypothesis—that is, ask the person why she did what she did. (You can often do this in an indirect way: "Boy, you really seemed preoccupied the last time I saw you.") Then compare her reply ("Oh, I was so upset by the grade on my last history quiz") with what you wrote down ("She thinks my conversation is boring"). You may well find that the other person had a perfectly plausible reason for what she did—a reason that had nothing to do with you. This may happen more often than you think, and it's a good idea to be alert to the problem.

teria, it should be noted, relate to Festinger's theory of cognitive consistency, discussed in Chapter 3. Our attributions are designed to confirm our mental ordering of the world.

However we interpret someone else's behavior, the question of whether we attribute it to internal or external forces is extremely important. An interesting finding, confirmed by a number of studies (Jones and Harris, 1967; Jones et al., 1968; Nisbett et al., 1971; Jones and Nisbett, 1973), is that we tend to assume that other people's behavior is due to internal causes, whereas we are likely to attribute our own behavior to external causes. (If I see a woman yelling at the bus driver, that's because she's an aggressive type. But if I yell at the bus driver, that's because he made a nasty remark to me or because my boss has been driving me crazy all day.) The reason this internal-versus-external question is important is that people are usually held more responsible for actions that are internally motivated. Since we can find more good, solid, external reasons for the things we do, we are more le-

nient with ourselves. (That causal relationship might also be reversed.) But whatever reasons we find—for our own behavior or the other person's—these attributions will affect our behavior in an interaction.

Role Theory

While attribution theory focuses on our ideas of why people behave as they do, *role theory* focuses on our ideas of what people are "supposed" to do. The term "role" is borrowed from drama. Consider, for example, the role of Hamlet in Shakespeare's play. This role has been played by thousands of different actors over the past three centuries. And each of these actors has created his own special Hamlet, while still remaining within the confines of the script. In the same way, according to role theory, human beings act out social roles (father, employer, student, doctor, and so on) that allow for a certain degree of individualism within the confines of a set of socially prescribed behaviors (Sarbin and Allen, 1968). Thus, a *social role* may

BOX 8.2
RELATIONS IN PUBLIC

A: Hi, how are you?
B: Fine, thanks, and you?

To you this may not seem a particularly interesting interchange. But according to sociologist Erving Goffman, such ritualized exchanges—greetings, congratulations, farewells, condolences—serve a very important function. In essence, they maintain our social lives, providing support for our established relationships and repairing any damage that may have been done to them.

In his book, *Relations in Public* (1971), Goffman analyzes what goes on in an ordinary greeting such as the one quoted above. In the first place, the greeting affirms the value that each participant places on the relationship. Note that in such a greeting it is required that you make some show of pleasure—usually a smile. The show of pleasure, along with the inquiries after the other person's well-being, is each person's way of saying to the other: (1) "I am happy to be with you" and (2) "The fact that we haven't seen one another for a while doesn't mean that I don't value you." The greeting may also include elements that reaffirm differences in status, as in military salutes, where the subordinate must salute first.

The same sorts of messages are communicated when two people are introduced to one another. In this situation, as Goffman points out, "a little dance is likely to occur; faces light up, smiles are exchanged, eyes are addressed, handshakes or hat-doffing may occur, and also inquiries after one another's health" (p. 78). The message sent out through this little ritual dance is "I am glad to have the chance to begin a relationship with you." Whether the message is sincere is another matter, but the dance can be modified to express reluctance.

According to Goffman, even the "Hi" that we toss out, without stopping, to a neighbor helps to maintain the relationship. It affirms the connection ("I value you") and at the same time defines its limits ("Our relationship is not close").

Goffman's studies are particularly valuable in that they focus on a neglected corner of social behavior. Love, marriage, parent-child relationships—these are things that we all worry about, and that sociologists and psychologists tend to study. But Goffman is one of the very few who has troubled to examine the little social rituals that we enact so mechanically—and, in his view, so meaningfully—every day.

---

be defined as the sum total of the expectations for behavior in a given position in a social structure. These expectations are more flexible than Hamlet's script, but they are still very much there and exercise immense influence over our behavior.

Each of us has a cluster of roles, and each role involves its own different set of expectations. If you (in your customer role) take a pen from your druggist's shelf, you are expected to pay for it. But if you (in your husband role) took a pen from your wife's desk and paid her for it, she would be very confused. Likewise, you may be expected to kiss your wife good-bye when you leave the house, but if you kissed your druggist good-bye when you left his store, *he* would be very confused.

OTHERS

According to role theory, the quality of our social interactions is determined by the appropriateness or inappropriateness of our behavior to the role we are enacting (Shaw and Costanzo, 1970). The people in an interaction are *role partners* (for example, husband and wife, druggist and customer). Each partner gives the other partner "cues" for role-appropriate behavior that will dovetail with his own. These cues—the druggist extending his hand for the money, the wife offering her cheek for the kiss—are called *role demands* (Biddle and Thomas, 1966). If the other partner ignores the cue and violates the role expectations, the interaction will be disturbed. The wife will be hurt and ask what is the matter; the druggist may call the police. As you can see, we put considerable pressure on our role partners to act according to their roles (Sarbin and Allen, 1968). And so does the society. People who steal from drugstores are not only disliked

Entering the work force means taking on a new role. This man's suit, his briefcase, even the style of his watchband are responses to role demands. (© Barbara Alper 1980)

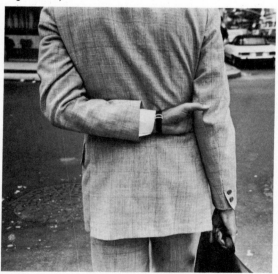

by druggists, they can be put in jail as well—so can judges who take bribes, parents who beat their children, and soldiers who refuse to obey orders. As these examples show, some role expectations are protected by law.

Thus, if we act appropriately in our different roles, our interactions will proceed smoothly and predictably. If we act inappropriately, our interactions will be confused and painful. Such role disturbances can take a number of different forms. One is simple *role failure*. Here the individual, out of unwillingness or inability to continue in the role, repeatedly disappoints the role partner's expectations—for example, the professor who continually misses classes or the student who continually fails to hand in papers.

Somewhat more complicated is the problem of *role dissensus*, in which role partners disagree on what is expected of one or both of them. For example, many modern marriages are disturbed by disagreements between husband and wife as to what their respective roles are. She expects the time and freedom to pursue a professional career. He expects her to stay at home, keep house, and care for the children. She expects him to share fully in these domestic responsibilities. He expects to relax and enjoy himself when he is at home. Such disagreements over marital roles have been found to have a very high correlation with sexual dissatisfaction, even in couples who describe their marriages as happy or even very happy (Frank et al., 1979).

A third form of disturbance is *role conflict*, in which the individual is faced with conflicting demands from his different roles. Imagine, for example, a not uncommon scenario: a man is working during the day and going to school at night and at the same time is married and has two children. The man thus has at least four important roles—worker, student, husband, and father—and they are bound to conflict with one another. On any given Saturday, for example, he may be faced with the mutually exclusive demands that he (1) go to the office and work overtime on a rush job (worker role), (2) write a paper that is due in his history class on Monday (student role), (3) attend a gymnastics meet in which his daughter is competing (father role), and (4) go shopping for a present for his wife, because tonight is their wedding anniversary (husband role).

For victims of role conflict, such situations tend to occur not just now and then, but with painful regularity. People often handle role conflict by deciding, consciously or unconsciously, which role would involve the worst consequences if it were ignored and then favoring that role over the others. Role conflict can also be relieved by asking role partners to ease up somewhat on their demands. For example, our harried worker/ student/father/husband might (1) tell his boss that he cannot come in on Saturdays except in extreme cases, (2) arrange with his professors for extensions on his papers, when necessary, (3) negotiate with his wife so that if he can't attend his daughter's gym-

nastics meet, at least she will be there, and (4) pick up a bouquet of flowers for his wife and tell her that she'll have her present in a few days. In other words, roles are not completely inflexible; they can be bent to accommodate other roles. (For a fourth type of role disturbance, see Activity 8.4.)

Role theory, particularly in light of its reference to "actors" and "scripts," sometimes seems to suggest that in our social lives we are "acting a part," not being "ourselves." However, as sociologists and psychologists have pointed out, roles, once we assume them, become fundamental components of the self. Indeed, people who have just retired from their jobs and parents whose children have just left home often have difficulty locating their "selves" once they have lost the central role of worker or parent. Likewise, the fact that we enact roles in our relationships with others does not mean that we are being artificial or unnatural. When a father tells his daughter to wear a sweater because it's cold outside, he is acting within the role of father—he wouldn't give this warning to his friends, for example—but he is acting with perfect sincerity and conviction.

ACTIVITY 8.4

Role clash, a disturbance in role relationships, occurs when we try to step out of one role and adopt a different one in relation to the same person. If your boss starts dating your sister, or if the new member of your therapy group turns out to be your English professor, then you are experiencing role clash (and so is he), which can be very awkward and uncomfortable. Try to recall an instance of role clash from your own life. Have you ever suddenly found yourself in a position of authority over a friend or vice versa? Have you ever tried to make the switch from boyfriend-and-girlfriend to "just friends"? Have you ever tried to do business with a friend? Whatever your encounter with role clash, describe it. What were the two roles that clashed? What were the role expectations for each of those roles? How did the two sets of expectations conflict with one another? What feelings did you experience?

Communication Theory

According to attribution theory and role theory, the course of a transaction is determined somewhere deep in the mental recesses of the participants, where each decides why the other person is doing what she is doing or whether what she is doing is what she is supposed to do. By contrast, *communication theory,* a third perspective of social psychology, focuses directly on what people *say* to one another. *Communication theory holds that people's statements to one another constitute the crucial factor in social interaction, because these statements serve to define the relationship for each of the participants.*

People need to know where they stand in a relationship—what the rules are, what they can expect. And these guidelines are set down by their communications to one another. By way of illustration, let us listen in on a telephone conversation.

He: Okay. I'll meet you at seven-thirty. The concert starts at eight.

She: I don't know if I want to go to the concert.

He: What do you mean? I told you two weeks ago I was getting these tickets.

She: That's just it. You're always *telling* me where we are going. You never ask me where I want to go. You just let me know when to be ready so that we can go where you want to go.

He: But how am I supposed to know, if you never say anything? I just sort of assumed you were enjoying the things *I* picked out. Why didn't you say something?

She: I don't know. I guess I should have. But I'm saying something now.

He: Okay. Let's not make a big deal out of this. The tickets didn't cost very much. I'll give them to somebody. . . . Wait a minute. Do you still want to see me tonight?

She: Yes.

He: Good. What do you want to do?

She: I want to go to the movies. . . . Listen, Jerry, I'm sorry I made you waste your money. This whole thing is half my fault. Next time I'll let you know beforehand.

He: Don't worry about it. I'll see you at seven-thirty.

Here two people are untangling a snare in their relationship by communicating to one another some very essential information about that relationship: (1) who will determine their recreational activities (from now on, both of them) and (2) whether or not they have enough affection for one another to override disagreements and bitter feelings (yes). In the same way, according to communication theorists, people's remarks to one another serve to define how each person judges the other, how much loyalty, affection, and forgiveness each expects to give and to receive, and, most important, what each person's rights and duties are.* According to one major communication theorist, every word we speak to one another is a comment on how we see the relationship: "Every message exchanged (including silence) defines the relationship implicitly

---

* Communication can be nonverbal (smiles, frowns, slumped posture, eye contact, avoidance of eye contact) as well as verbal. Imagine that you are trying to tell your father about some rather personal matter. He nods in a distracted way, avoids looking you in the eye, and keeps glancing back at the magazine he was reading. Without saying a word, he is communicating a very clear message: "I don't want to talk about this."

since it expresses the idea, 'this is the sort of relationship where this sort of message may be given' " (Jackson, 1959, p. 129). Such messages also allow us to "check up" on whether the other person agrees with our way of conceiving the relationship.

Predictably, communication theorists hold that disturbed relationships—particularly disturbed marriages, to which they have given careful attention—are the result of disturbed communications (Lederer and Jackson, 1968). The usual culprit is a pattern of unclear communications, where each person's desires, privileges, and obligations are left hanging in the air, never decisively pinned down. Imagine, for example, that your brother, who is rather shy, wishes you would include him in your social activities—introduce him to your friends and invite him along when you go out with them. However, he can't quite bring himself to communicate this desire. He waits for you to take the initiative, and eventually he begins to feel very hurt that you haven't. So he retaliates by criticizing your social activities, telling you that your friends are a bunch of morons and so forth. You, in the meantime, would have been happy to invite him along, but you thought he wasn't interested. And now that he is attacking your friends, you are even less likely to include him. Furthermore, you pay him back by telling him that you at least *have* some friends, whereas his only friends are the dog and the television set. Thus, as a result of faulty communication, a desire that could have been easily satisfied has gone unsatisfied, and you and your brother have each succeeded in adding a bit of unhappiness to the other's life.

Unclear communication seems to be particularly common and particularly frustrating in marriage. Psychologist C. H. Swensen offers a typical example:

A husband may decide to buy a new car but his wife [objects], claiming she doesn't like the make or the color of the car he proposes to buy, rather than admitting that she resents his claim of dominance over the car-buying area. So he forgoes buying the car, and criticizes her for spending money on a new dress. Neither can communicate directly with the other about what is going on in the relationship. Neither can explicitly take responsibility for defining or setting the limits to the relationship. (1973, p. 63)

It is because of situations such as this that psychologists and marriage counselors are so insistent on the necessity of honest feedback. Many of us find it difficult and embarrassing to "come clean" about our desires and expectations, but unless we do so, our intimate relationships will suffer. (In Chapter 12 we will give specific recommendations for communicating more honestly and directly in close relationships.)

Even more damaging than unclear communications are contradictory communications. Here each "relationship-message" is the opposite of the last, so that the victim of the contradictory messages can never figure out where he stands in relation to the other person. When the victim is a child, the consequences may be disastrous. For example, in what has been called *double-bind communication*, the parent rejects the child, and then, when the child responds by withdrawing, the parent accuses the child of being unloving. Thus, the child is caught in a double bind; whichever way he turns, he is wrong. According to Gregory Bateson and his colleagues (1956), who first described the double-bind pattern, the child's final refuge may be schizophrenia, one of the most severe forms of psychological disturbance.

In sum, communications chart the course of a relationship. When they are confused, the relationship suffers. When they are contradictory, the result may be a psychological catastrophe.

Social Exchange Theory

Whatever their attributions, role expectations, or communications, people do hope to get something out of their relationships. This, it might seem, would go without saying. Yet according to a fourth perspective of social psychology, *social exchange theory*, this fact is the central fact of social life. *Social exchange theory views relationships as determined primarily by their outcomes—that is, the profits that each participant derives.* J. W. Thibaut and H. H. Kelley,

two of the originators of this theory, have summarized it as follows: "Whatever the gratifications achieved in dyads, however lofty or fine the motives satisfied may be, the relationship may be viewed as a trading or bargaining one. . . . every individual voluntarily enters and stays in any relationship only as long as it is adequately satisfactory in terms of his rewards and costs" (1959, p. 37). Here "rewards" are whatever the person needs or likes, and "costs" are whatever the person does not need or like.

Rewards minus costs equals profit. This, according to social exchange theory, is the formula that we all carry in our minds as we pursue our relationships (Aronson, 1970). And as we pursue them, our main goal is to

Friends give us attention and affection and help us have a good time. We may take such rewards for granted, but according to social exchange theory, they are the mechanism that maintains the friendship. (© Jeff Jacobson/ Archive Pictures)

ensure that we *are* making a profit. No profit, no relationship.

Whatever the rewards or costs, the relationship will have a trade agreement, a sort of implicit "contract" specifying who gets what and who gives what (Homans, 1961). Like role expectations, such contracts are often talked about only when they are violated. When a father yells at his teen-age daughter, "As long as you're living in my house, you'll come home when I say," he is making explicit a cost-and-rewards agreement ("I give material support; you give obedience") that for years has been implicit.

As is obvious, social exchange theory is based on economics. It is also based on behavioral psychology. Rewards and costs, after all, are simply different words for positive and negative consequences. Furthermore, according to Thibaut and Kelley, it is through the principles of operant and respondent conditioning that we learn how to pursue rewards. We look for "cues" (conditioned discriminative stimuli) that in the past have been associated with rewards. And when we find the cues, we respond with behaviors (conditioned response) that have brought us rewards previously. If you need to ask your father for money, you may try to catch him in a good mood (conditioned discriminative stimulus), and then, in making your request, you will use whatever words and whatever tone of voice (conditioned response) have worked before.

By this time you may be asking yourself whether human relationships are truly so calculating. What about love? What about trust? Can every relationship actually be defined as a profit-making enterprise? If so, how does the bond between lovers or between husband and wife differ from a businessman's relationship to his stock portfolio?

A number of modern thinkers have also asked these questions. As we read in Chapter 1, Erich Fromm, in his book *The Art of Loving*, vehemently condemns what he sees as the infiltration of profit considerations into human relationships: "Modern man has transformed himself into a commodity" (1956, p. 105) and "consumes" other people like so many commodities. Arthur Miller makes essentially the same complaint in his play *Death of a Salesman*. When the hero, Willy Loman, outlives his usefulness to the company and is fired, he says to his employer,

> I put thirty-four years into this firm, Howard, and now I can't pay my insurance! You can't eat the orange and throw the peel away—a man is not a piece of fruit! (1955, p. 175)

What we have here is a conflict between idealism and materialism. It is probable, however, that our more intimate relationships contain some of each. For example, psychologists and sociologists specializing in the study of marriage have repeatedly pointed out that satisfying marriages are based on both tenderness *and* fairness. As two observers have put it, "Marriage requires two legs—love and justice" (Scanzoni and Scanzoni, 1976, p. 304). When the exchange of privileges and rewards seems unjust, negotiation ensues: "I work all day, just like you, so it's only fair that you do your share of the housework"; "We spent last year's vacation with your parents—*this* year we're going where I want to go." When negotiation fails, love may compensate for short-term injustice. But when negotiation breaks down time and again, love too may break down. In other words, whatever we think we *should* be doing in our intimate relationships, what we are doing is not just loving but also looking for a fair deal (see Activity 8.5). Hence, social-exchange theory, cynical as it sometimes seems, definitely applies.

BOX 8.3
GAMES PEOPLE PLAY

According to psychiatrist Eric Berne (1964), unhappy relationships are often based on "games"—that is, repetitive and stereotyped transactions in which one participant, while appearing to be in the right, actually takes advantage of the other(s). Berne divided human behavior into three modes: Adult (reasonable, mature), Parent (scolding, authoritarian), and Child (selfish, immature). The point of games is that they allow us to give vent to our Parent and Child impulses while still pretending to be Adults.

Here is Berne's description of the game he calls "Now I've Got You, You Son of a Bitch":

> White needed some plumbing fixtures installed, and he reviewed the costs very carefully with the plumber before giving him a go-ahead. The price was set, and it was agreed that there would be no extras. When the plumber submitted his bill, he included a few dollars extra for an unexpected valve that had to be installed—about four dollars on a four-hundred-dollar job. White became infuriated, called the plumber on the phone and demanded an explanation. The plumber would not back down. White wrote him a long letter criticizing his integrity and ethics and refused to pay the bill until the extra charge was withdrawn. The plumber finally gave in.
>
> It soon became obvious that both White and the plumber were playing games. In the course of their negotiations, they had recognized each other's potentials. The plumber made his provocative move when he submitted his bill. Since White had the plumber's word, the plumber was clearly in the wrong. White now felt justified in venting almost unlimited rage against him. Instead of merely negotiating in a dignified way that befit the

Adult standards he set for himself, perhaps with a little innocent annoyance, White took the opportunity to make extensive criticisms of the plumber's whole way of living. On the surface their argument was Adult to Adult, a legitimate business dispute over a stated sum of money. At the psychological level it was Parent to Adult: White was exploiting his trivial but socially defensible objection (position) to vent the pent-up furies of many years on his cozening opponent, just as his mother might have done in a similar situation. (pp. 85–86)

Other games described by Berne are "Let's You and Him Fight," "Ain't It Awful," "If It Weren't for You," "Schlemiel," "See What You Made Me Do," and "Why Don't You—Yes But." This catalogue covers everything from sexual teasing to tiresome complaining. In "Rapo," the game-player behaves seductively with another person and then is "shocked" and "disgusted" when the other person responds accordingly. In "Look How Hard I've Tried," the game-player makes a pretense of trying to deal with a problem (for example, a rocky marriage) and then quits—as he or she intended to do all along—claiming, however, to be innocent, since he/she *did* try.

Berne's descriptions are often funny, but the games themselves can be deadly. Indeed, Berne (1961) developed his own form of therapy, transactional analysis, in order to uncover destructive games in personal relationships. This is one of the numerous recent forms of psychotherapy that focuses less on the individual than on his or her interactions with others.

Berne, E. Games People Play: The Psychology of Human Relationships. *New York: Grove Press, 1964.*

ACTIVITY 8.5

Our relationships with others become troubled, according to social exchange theory, when what we put into the relationship exceeds what we get out of it. Approaching an interpersonal bond from the debit/credit point of view may seem cold, but it does provide a useful tool for assessing a relationship. Make a list of all the benefits you get out of your relationship with your closest friend, listing them in their order of importance to you. Next, write down the costs of the relationship, again in their order of importance. You will probably find that the credits outweigh the debits. If not, and if you do in fact consider this person a close friend, then there may be some benefits you are overlooking.

Applying the Theories of Social Psychology to Adjustment

In Unit I we suggested ways of describing, explaining, and changing aspects of the self. Now, in Unit II, the same description-explanation-changing method will be applied to aspects of our social life: our ways of perceiving other people and our ways of interacting with them. With each of these matters, as with the self, we will ask ourselves: What are the essential features of this matter? And how do the essential features relate to one another? What causes what?

Having just examined four different theories of social psychology, you may feel that we have given you four conflicting answers to these questions. After all, each of the theories claims that one element of social in-

teraction is the essential element, *the* independent variable on which all the other variables depend. However, since we are not social psychologists by profession, we need not take sides. We can benefit from all four theories. Taken together, they help us see the immense richness of social life, with so many variables intertwined in every transaction that takes place between two human beings. And taken separately, each theory points us toward important features of social interaction. The attributions we make, the roles we enact, the communications we use to define our relationships, and the costs and rewards we derive from our interactions—all these factors create the antecedents and consequences of our social behavior. Thus, we have no lack of materials to study.

SUMMARY

1. Our lives are permeated with social interactions. A need for comforting contact appears to be present from birth, as indicated by Harlow's studies of monkeys and by observations of human beings.
2. A major consequence of our interaction

with others is *socialization*, the process of learning to be social. Studies of isolated and institutionalized children indicate the utter necessity of socialization for normal social, emotional, and intellectual development.

3. *Social psychology* is the study of human interpersonal behavior. This is a very complex subject, as there are hundreds of factors affecting even the simplest transaction between two persons. Extended relationships are even more difficult to study.

4. Several theories have been advanced in an attempt to explain social interaction. Each one regards a different aspect of social interaction as most central.

5. *Attribution theory* holds that the key to a transaction lies in the causes that each person assigns to the other's behavior. Among the factors that affect our interpretation are (1) the consistency of the action with the person's past behavior, (2) the general consensus of others as to that person's personality, (3) the likelihood of the action in terms of what we know of human behavior, and (4) the possibility that the action has been influenced by external pressures.

6. *Role theory* holds that the quality of our social interactions is determined by our response to social roles—that is, sets of expectations for behavior in a given position in the social structure. According to role theory, disturbed relationships are due to role disturbances. In *role failure,* one partner, out of unwillingness or inability, simply ceases to fulfill role expectations. In *role dissensus,* role partners disagree on what role expectations they should be fulfilling. In *role conflict* a relationship comes under stress because one or more partners is having trouble reconciling the conflicting demands of his or her different roles.

7. *Communication theory* asserts that people's statements to one another are the crucial factor in social interaction, because these statements serve to define the relationship for each of the participants. According to communications theorists, the major cause of disturbed relationships (especially disturbed marriages) is unclear communication.

8. *Social exchange theory* views relationships as determined primarily by their outcomes—that is, the profits that each participant derives. This theory has been attacked for portraying human beings as unduly selfish and opportunistic, but studies of marriage suggest that marital success depends not just on love but also on the fair apportionment of rewards.

9. Following the same basic procedure that we used in conducting our self-analysis, we can analyze our social relationships, making use of all four theories to study the antecedents and consequences of our social behavior.

PROJECT

It will help you see how social interactions work if you analyze an interaction between yourself and one other person. To make the situation as simple as possible, limit it to a brief transaction with someone who does not already have a relationship with you—for example, a clerk in an uncrowded store, a secretary in an office at school, or the person who delivers your mail. Keep the transaction short—just one or two minutes long—so that afterward you can remember who said what and how each of you acted. (Wait until after the transaction to write down what took place.)

Below is an outline of the information you should try to collect. Use it both as a guide in observing the transaction and as an aid in writing your description of it. Remember to be objective and specific in everything you write down.

A. Behavior in the transaction (described like a script for a play)
  1. What was said:
     a. Record as accurately as possible what was said by whom; include laughter, coughing, and other such sounds.
  2. What was done:
     a. By the other person: Insert into the dialogue brief descriptions of what the other person did at each point in the transaction (hand, head, eye, and other body movements).
     b. By you: Insert into the dialogue brief descriptions of what you did at each point in the transaction.

B. Characteristics of the transaction
  1. When and where the transaction took place: describe the setting.
  2. Characteristics of the participants:
     a. Describe the other person (looks, sex, age, clothing, and so on).
     b. Describe yourself briefly.

  3. Roles of the participants:
     a. Describe the role the other person was playing, your expectations for behavior in that role, and whether the person fulfilled them.
     b. Describe the role you were playing and your expectations of it. (Note whether you think the other person's expectations of your role differ from your own.)

C. Outcomes of the transaction
  1. Attributions made:
     a. To what did you attribute the other person's behavior?
     b. To what did you attribute your own behavior? Can you think of other ways in which it might be interpreted?
  2. Consequences of the transaction:
     a. Describe what the other person got from the transaction, including positive and negative outcomes.
     b. Describe what you got from the transaction.

After you have completed this project, you may want to engage in a second and similar transaction with the same person to see how things change from one transaction to the next.

HUMAN ISSUE:
SEX

In 1977 the issue of homosexuality blew sky high as singer Anita Bryant led a crusade against gay rights legislation in Dade County, Florida. Though the legislation was defeated, this was less significant than the aftermath. Within days, homosexuals staged massive demonstrations across the country, inspiring many gays to come out of the "closet" and protest the attitudes that had kept them in the closet. The effects of this movement are widely felt today. Not just San Francisco and New York, but many cities across the country have gay neighborhoods where homosexual couples walk down the street hand in hand without drawing stares. The mayors of cities such as New York, Boston, San Francisco, and Washington, D.C., have openly sought political support from gay groups. National corporations, including AT&T and IBM, have publicly announced that they do not discriminate against homosexuals in hiring or promotion. Even Ann Landers is now counseling parents not to be ashamed of their homosexual children.

Clearly, attitudes toward homosexuality have changed. Actually, though, this is only one facet of a more widespread change, the so-called sexual revolution. The byword of this revolution is freedom of sexual expression—under whatever circumstances, with whatever partner, and via whatever activities one wishes. To some extent, that freedom has been won. More and more people engage in sexual activities before marriage, outside of marriage, and with members of the same sex. There is growing acceptance of forms of sex, such as oral-genital contact, that were previously forbidden. Our surroundings are pervaded by explicit sexuality. Advertising links sex to products as diverse as cigarettes and rental cars. Movies promise (and sometimes deliver) scenes of unbridled sexual gymnastics. Hundreds of books and magazines purvey in steamy prose the minutest details of sexual encounters.

SEX: WORK OR PLAY?

For a long time the predominant view in our culture was that the main function of sex was procreation; a man and a woman engaged in intercourse in order to produce children. This principle guided ideas about what was right and what was wrong in sexual activity. Since any sexual act that could not result in the birth of legitimate children was "bad," society severely condemned masturbation, homo-sexuality, and premarital and extramarital sex.

Over the past fifty years, the idea of sex as a means of reproduction has gradually been replaced by the concept of sex as play. By the early 1970s, so many Americans hoped to find what biologist Alex Comfort called *The Joy of Sex* that millions bought copies of his book (1972). The fact that standards of sexual behavior had changed did not suddenly become apparent in 1972, of course. Studies of human sexuality conducted more than twenty years earlier made it clear that many Americans engaged in a wide variety of sexual activity before and during marriage, and that very little of it had to do with reproduction (Kinsey et al., 1948, 1953).

With sex viewed as play, there has been more openness about varieties of sexual activity—masturbation, oral sex, group sex, and so on. This interest has been reflected in, and stimulated by, a spate of books describing techniques, most of which aim at meeting the needs of one's sexual partner in order to achieve orgasm.

The focus on sex as play has not been without problems. Some people have found that the heavy emphasis on what one writer termed "funsex" makes sexual activity as burdensome as work. Barraged by manuals, guides, and advice on how to be more competent, people become so concerned with performance that they can't enjoy what they're doing. Also, with the emphasis on simultaneous orgasm—which is not always possible or even desirable—those who don't achieve it may be oppressed by a sense of failure.

SEX BEFORE MARRIAGE

While society's basic view of sex has altered and our knowledge of human sexuality has increased, perhaps the most striking change of the sexual revolution has been in our views of sex before marriage. Not too many years ago, premarital sex was deplored, if discussed at all. Today it is widely recognized and accepted.

Why the Change?

The change in attitudes toward premarital sex can be traced to a number of factors. One of the most obvious is the increased availability of convenient birth control measures. Twenty-five years ago birth-control devices were limited to mechanical means, such as condoms and diaphragms, that were often unavailable to younger people. Today convenient birth-control pills, or the more permanent IUD, allow couples to enjoy sex without fear of pregnancy. Another factor is the availability of penicillin and similar antibiotics to control venereal disease. (It should be noted, however, that the incidence of sexually transmitted diseases has increased sharply in the past two decades.)

Other technological changes also helped to encourage premarital sex. The automobile gave couples both mobility and a degree of privacy. It became easier for them to meet, to go somewhere alone, and to have sex without fear of getting caught. Parental supervision was further reduced as greater numbers of young people went away to college. In the 1960s many campuses set up coeducational dorms where couples could live together if they wanted to.

An additional factor encouraging premarital sex has been the earlier onset of sexual maturity. The average age of a girl's first menstruation has steadily dropped from 17.7 in 1830, to 16.5 in the 1860s, to 14.2 in the 1920s, to 12.4 in the 1970s (Tanner, 1966; USDHEW, 1979). Many children no sooner stop wetting their beds than they reach puberty.

This earlier onset of puberty (which is happening to boys as well)—coupled with a tendency to postpone marriage until after college or graduate school—has resulted in a longer and longer period during which people are sexually mature but not yet married. The obvious solution, for many, is not to wait for marriage.

Differing Standards

Although ideas about premarital sex have changed, they are by no means uniform. Variations in attitudes have been revealed in several recent studies. Ira Reiss (1967, 1971), for example, found that permissiveness regarding premarital sex varied between males and females, blacks and whites, and Northerners and Southerners. (Males, blacks, and Northerners were generally more permissive.) He categorized the attitudes he found into four main groups: abstinence, the double standard, permissiveness with affection, and permissiveness without affection.

Most of those who believed in some sort of abstinence (some 42 percent of the college students Reiss interviewed in the 1960s) felt that sex before marriage was immoral because of religious sanctions. Others worried about infection or pregnancy.

The double standard, an old standby in American society, was favored by some

25 percent of Reiss's respondents. Firmly based on the notion of the inequality of men and women, the double standard allows men to be sexually active in order to work off energy and gain experience, but requires women to remain virgins until marriage. The problem of finding partners for the lusty males is solved mainly through the ancient profession of prostitution. When Reiss did his surveys, 60 percent of the men but only 20 percent of the women had engaged in premarital sex. The women may have subscribed to a variation of the double standard known as the transitional double standard; this allows a woman to have intercourse if she and her partner are in love and plan to marry.

Permissiveness-with-affection is an attitude that seems to be gaining ground. This standard favors premarital sexual activity as long as it is accompanied by love or strong affection. In a 1974 survey, over three-fourths of the men and almost two-thirds of the women questioned thought this type of sex was acceptable for both men and women (Hunt, 1974). This attitude may help account for the apparent increase in premarital sex revealed by another survey (Tavris, 1974, 1978). Of those surveyed, 80 percent of the women and 90 percent of the men had engaged in premarital intercourse.

Permissiveness without affection—what Reiss calls recreational sex—is also being viewed more tolerantly, especially by women. A survey from the late sixties (Luckey and Nass, 1969) found that only 6 percent of college women and 27 percent of college men approved of this sort of casual sex. But in a more recent poll (Hunt, 1974), 26 percent of women and 30 percent of men found it acceptable.

SEX OUTSIDE OF MARRIAGE

Just as our attitudes about sex before marriage have changed, so also have we become more tolerant toward sex outside of marriage. Legally, our society still supports fidelity in marriage by making adultery grounds for divorce. However, Kinsey and his colleagues (1948) and Hunt (1974) both found that approximately 50 percent of married males had engaged in extramarital sex. During the twenty-five-year period between these surveys, the proportion of women engaging in extramarital sex increased dramatically (Hunt, 1974; Tavris, 1974). A survey of *Cosmopolitan* readers—who, however, are probably more free-wheeling than the national average—found that 69 percent of the over-35 group had sampled extramarital sex (Wolfe, 1980).

There are various forms of extramarital sex, and apparently several motives behind it. Nonconsensual adultery—that which takes place without the knowledge of one's marriage partner—may range from a one-night-stand to a long-term, romantic affair. An essential element is secrecy. However, extramarital sex does not necessarily indicate a bad marriage or destroy a good one. According to Albert Ellis, if a wife or husband engages in extramarital sex for "positive" reasons—a desire for variety, a richer life experience, adventure—the marriage may actually benefit. "Disturbed" reasons, which may have the contrary effect, include hostility toward one's spouse and a desire to escape from marital problems (Ellis, 1969).

Consensual adultery, where a person's extramarital activity is known to his or her spouse, may take place more or less spontaneously once husband and wife have agreed not to expect sexual fidelity from each other. A different approach is "swinging," when a couple deliberately arranges to swap mates with one or more other couples. Swinging takes place within an organized framework and under definite rules. For instance, gossip is usually prohibited, and steps are taken to avoid emotional entanglements. Couples who swing—generally white-collar, educated, and "straight" in other respects—claim that this arrangement adds zest to marriage. But once again, the effect on the marriage seems to depend on the attitudes involved. According to one study (Gilmartin, 1977), swinging apparently can enliven a marriage if both husband and wife are truly comfortable with the arrangement; if not, it may create bitter conflict. Another study found the same to be true of "open" marriages (Knapp and Whitehurst, 1977). And in both cases, even if the arrangement works, this is only after the inevitable fears and jealousies have been worked through.

OUTLINE

THE DEVELOPMENT OF SOCIAL PERCEPTIONS
Infancy
Childhood
Adolescence

HOW DOES SOCIAL PERCEPTION OPERATE?
Unity
Consistency
Assumed Content
Implicit theory of personality
Structure: What Counts Most
Central traits
The primacy effect
Understanding and Control

ATTRACTION
Physical Attractiveness
Competence
Proximity
Similarity
Complementarity
Rewardingness

STEREOTYPING
Stereotypes: Accurate or Inaccurate?
The Damage Done by Stereotyping

9
SOCIAL PERCEPTION: WHAT IT IS AND HOW IT OPERATES

In 1954 psychologist Eugene Gollin performed an experiment with a group of students. He showed them some film clips in which a young woman displayed two different personality characteristics. In several of the scenes, the trait she revealed most clearly was generosity or kindness. She gave money to a beggar, helped a person who had fallen down, and the like. Other scenes focused on a different trait: promiscuity. In one scene, for example, she very casually and boldly offered herself sexually to a man.

After the film was over, the students were asked to write down their impressions of the woman. Faced with the two different characteristics shown in the film—generosity and promiscuity, not incompatible traits—one-fourth of the students simply reported that the woman was both generous and promiscuous. Another quarter of the students tried to integrate the two into a single, unified trait of generosity: the woman was a person who gave of herself—her time, her money, her body, and so forth. The remaining half of the students in the experiment did something that might appear surprising. They simply ignored one of the traits and reported the other, describing the woman either as promiscuous or as generous.

What Gollin was trying to study in his experiment was the process through which we form our *social perceptions*, our views of other people. And it is unlikely that he was surprised (or that any social psychologist would be surprised) by the fact that fully half the students in the experiment formed their social perception of the young woman by discounting half the evidence. For although social psychologists disagree on different theories, there is one principle on which they generally agree. That is, that *the formation of a social perception is a creative act.*

As we learned in Chapter 3, the self-concept, our view of ourselves, is often an extremely subjective product, full of distortions and fabrications. Likewise, the views that we have of others are far from being objective, scientific reports. In forming our social perceptions we are not scientists, who look only at the facts and all the facts. We are more like artists, who take from reality whatever facts fit the picture that we want to paint or that we have been taught to paint. The facts that don't fit, we throw out. (If the traits of generosity and promiscuity don't seem to fit well together, we discard one of them.) The facts that do seem to fit, we organize in such a way that they fit even better. Like the students who combined the woman's generosity and promiscuity into a single trait, we bend the evidence so that the pieces harmonize with one another, creating a single organic unity—a whole personality, structured and consistent.

This creative process of social perception is the subject of our present chapter. First we shall trace the development of social perception from infancy to adulthood. Second, we will discuss the specific mental processes governing adult social perceptions. Finally, we will examine two important facets of social perception: attraction and stereotyping.

THE DEVELOPMENT OF SOCIAL PERCEPTIONS

The mental patterns into which we fit other people—where do they come from? Where do we get our ideas of what a mother or a professor or a doctor should be like? Where do we get the notion that WASPS are repressed, fat people are jolly, whores have hearts of gold? And how do we learn to form a detailed and unified picture of another person in the first place?

The ability to form social impressions is developed during childhood, through the combination of two processes: (1) the biological maturation of the brain and (2) so-cialization, a process that we discussed in Chapter 8. As for the standards on which we base our impressions, these are formulated and reformulated throughout our lives. But here again the process of childhood socialization is particularly crucial, because it is childhood experiences that establish our most fundamental patterns of perceiving others. Let us therefore trace briefly the impact of childhood socialization on social perception.

Infancy

We cannot know for certain how the infant perceives others; by the time he is old enough to tell us what it was like, he has forgotten. Nevertheless, by observing infants at great length, psychologists have been able to make educated guesses regarding our earliest impressions of others.

First, the infant has an extremely limited awareness of others. As we saw in Chapter 3, a newborn baby has no clear idea either of others or of a self. This situation soon changes, however. Through repeated interaction with his parents (or whoever is in charge of his daily care), he gradually develops a stable picture of them. If they provide consistent, predictable, and affectionate care, the child will also come to develop trust in them (Erikson, 1963). And this trust, combined with the consistent reward of having his needs met, will give rise to *attachment*. In general, for example, an eight-month-old baby will smile at the sight of his parent's face. When approached or held by a stranger, on the other hand, he will usually howl in protest—a normal response called *stranger anxiety*. By the age of one year, most children will also show *separation anxiety*, crying furiously when separated from their primary-care parent.

The parent-child attachment on which these responses are based has an immense impact on future social perceptions, since it

In the first year of life, the child has only a hazy picture of others. Slowly, however, he develops his first strong attachment—to his parents. (Hella Hammid/Photo Researchers, Inc.)

is on the strength of this attachment that the child eventually absorbs his parents' standards for judging others. Through the first year, however, the child is aware of others only insofar as their behavior directly affects him, and he apparently judges others only on the dimension of good-familiar versus bad-strange.

Childhood

In the long span of learning that extends from age two up to adolescence, social impressions lose their infant crudity and take on a refinement approaching that of adult social perception. This progress is due primarily to two crucial developments. The first is the development of language. Based on an evolved mental capacity (Chomsky, 1972; Trotter, 1975) and learned through shaping and modeling, language allows the child to engage in more complex and meaningful social interactions and thus to

sharpen her social perceptions. Furthermore, language gives the child a vocabulary of social meanings. Many of the words that make up our language—words such as "don't," "please," "yes," "thank you," "love," "friend," "kind," "handsome," "bad"—do not stand for any concrete object or observable action. Rather, they are symbols of purely social meanings—symbols of the desires, emotions, and judgments that emerge from our dealings with others. By learning these symbols, the child is able to accumulate in her mind an increasing store of social meanings, which she can then use to form more complex and precise impressions of others (Mead, 1934; McNeill, 1970).

The second crucial factor in the refinement of the child's social perceptions is the rapid expansion of her social roles. No longer simply "baby" interacting with "Mommy" or "Daddy," the child gradually learns the important roles of brother or sister, student, and friend. Furthermore, by school age, sex roles are usually well learned (Thompson, 1975), while ethnic and socioeconomic roles are beginning to develop.

This expansion of roles influences social perceptions in three important ways. In the first place, every social role, as we learned in Chapter 8, carries a specific set of expectations. Children should love and obey; parents should love, nurture, and instruct. Students should study and raise their hands; teachers should teach and call on children. Boys should play with trucks and be aggressive; girls should play with dolls and be "nice." (This last role pair, needless to say, is now being widely challenged.) Note the word "should" in these sentences. Role expectations do not remain neutral—something you can do if you want to. Rather, they become *norms*, rules for behavior. And these norms, in turn, become the standards on which we base our social judgments. Since the child learns the expectations not only for her own roles, but also for those of her

OTHERS

By the time he goes to school, the child has usually learned a sex role. The combination of boots, toy rifle, and miniature motorcycle would indicate that this glowering little boy is fast learning the aggressive side of the male role. (Bill Owens/Magnum)

role partners (teacher, parent, and so on), she gradually learns a large set of behavioral norms. And on the basis of these norms she will eventually perceive a negligent parent as cold, a disobedient child as bratty, a teacher who can't keep order as incompetent, and so on. In short, through role-enactment the child comes to see role-fulfillment as a virtue and role-failure as a vice. She now has begun to judge.

Second, from each of her role partners the child adopts attitudes that color her social perceptions. Values, preferences, prejudices, stereotypes—all these are communicated to her in the classroom, on the playground, at the dinner table. The major source of attitudes is, of course, the parents (Jennings and Niemi, 1968; Epstein and Komorita, 1966).

They are the child's earliest, most constant, and most valued role partners, and they offer the most potent punishments and rewards. But as the years of childhood pass, school, church, television, and, above all, the peer group become important additional sources of social attitudes.

Finally, the give-and-take of repeated role enactment with numerous partners teaches the child to "take the role of the other" (Mead, 1934; Hoffman, 1979). The young child, like the infant, is "egocentric" (Piaget, 1951)—that is, she has no idea that anyone else has a point of view separate from her own. Through role-taking, however, she gradually learns that other people have their own special ways of looking at things. And she learns to empathize with them—to predict, understand, and identify with their feelings (Rubin and Schneider, 1973; Hoffman, 1977, 1979). For example, if her sister breaks a vase, she can say to herself, "Mommy will be angry," in recognition of her mother's feelings. (And she can identify with her sister's fear of the mother's anger.) Though not yet fully developed, this growing ability to put herself in someone else's shoes makes her perceptions of others clearer, more consistent, and better organized. As the child approaches adolescence, other people slowly begin to take shape in her mind as unified personalities.

Adolescence

The adolescent must take on several new and important roles: date, boyfriend or girlfriend, employee, and, eventually, adult. His student role also changes, involving heavier responsibilities. With this further expansion of roles, and with the increasing maturity of his thinking, the adolescent's social perceptions gradually become more and more refined.

To begin with, the adolescent is more attentive to the behavior of others; he simply

SOCIAL PERCEPTION: WHAT IT IS AND HOW IT OPERATES

picks up more social information. And his greater intellectual abilities permit him to organize a great deal of different, and even contradictory, information about one person into a unified whole, discriminating between the person's good and bad points. At the same time, the adolescent has more empathy than the child. He identifies easily with characters in books and movies, and in everyday life he is able to sympathize with others and guess fairly accurately at their motives. Furthermore, unlike the child, the adolescent can think in terms of abstract concepts (Piaget, 1952, 1967). Consequently he is able to judge people, and compare them with one another, on the basis of abstract notions of good and evil. In early adolescence, such conceptual thinking often leads to black-or-white judgments, but eventually it gives rise to more precise and discriminating moral perception.

HOW DOES SOCIAL PERCEPTION OPERATE?

We have just painted a picture of the increasing sophistication of social perception through infancy, childhood, and adolescence. Obviously, our conclusion should be that adults, having passed through these developmental stages, are experts at social perception. To some degree, this is true. As the theories of social psychology (Chapter 8) suggest, adults, in forming social impressions, manage to process many complicated and often ambiguous pieces of "information": attributions, role expectations and role performances, communications, costs and rewards. But as we pointed out earlier, the adult's way of handling all this information is to organize it into manageable structures. In the process, the information is distorted considerably.

It is a commonplace of psychology that we transform reality in the process of perceiving it. Reality itself—the whole range of stimuli available to us as we open our eyes and ears—is chaotic, confusing, and unstable, but our perception of it is not. We select only certain stimuli to notice, ignoring the others. And to those stimuli that we choose to perceive, we give structure, stability, and meaning (Rosch, 1978). The same rule applies to our perception of people. When we "size up" another person, we pay attention only to certain details of appearance and behavior, and we organize those details into a pattern of our own choosing.

What are the main characteristics of this pattern? We will examine four characteristics—unity, consistency, assumed content,

ACTIVITY 9.1

Being able to challenge misleading first impressions is a valuable skill. Select someone whom you do not know well but think you dislike—perhaps a fellow student in one of your classes or a member of an organization you belong to. Write down the reasons you dislike this person. Then engage the person in conversation after class or during a meeting. Look for aspects of his or her personality that contradict your initial impression. Next, review your list of "disliking" reasons and see if you should revise your impression. Doing this sort of exercise several times may make you less hasty in judging others.

and structure. Then we will consider why we give our social perceptions these characteristics.

Unity

Look at the following list of traits:

intelligent
skillful
industrious
warm
determined
practical
cautious

Can you form a picture of the person being described? Solomon Asch, a social psychologist famous for his studies of perception, read this list to a group of people and asked them the same question. The subjects had no difficulty whatsoever making the leap from a short list of adjectives to the image of a complete personality. One subject, for example, gave the following description: "A scientist performing experiments and persevering after many setbacks. He is driven by the desire to accomplish something that would be of benefit" (Asch, 1946, p. 263). From seven words, a whole person was created.

Outside the psychology laboratory, we don't get our information about other people in the form of adjectives. But like the subjects in Asch's experiment, we don't hesitate to take whatever snatches of information we have and use them to create a unified and complete personality.

Let's take an imaginary example. A seventyish woman speaks to you in the line at the supermarket. You complain that the checkout clerk is slow. She says, "Well, they don't make much—and look what they have to do all day." You notice her weary but pleasant smile, her slight foreign accent, her rather dowdy old coat. Then the encounter is over. However, you walk away from the supermarket thinking of her not as a collection of four or five stimuli (which is really all that was presented to you), but as a *person*. She is old, wise, kind, patient, stoical. Probably a widow without much money. She has suffered a lot, you are sure. Probably escaped from Europe during World War II, maybe lost some of her family in a concentration camp. You may not say all these things in your head, but you see her as a whole person, rounded and complete, with a personality and a life story all her own.

Consistency

As we saw in Chapter 3, the self-concept seems to obey what Festinger called the principle of cognitive consistency. In collecting information about ourselves, we pick up evidence that is consistent—and ignore or distort evidence that is inconsistent—with what we already believe about ourselves. This principle seems to apply to our social perception as well. Our mental pictures of other people, whether we have known them for ten minutes or ten years, are designed to be consistent. We make the traits fit together comfortably. If we pick up information that doesn't fit, we experience the uncomfortable state of cognitive dissonance. And to resolve that dissonance, we either screen out the new evidence or manipulate it until it *does* fit.

The drive for consistency is well documented in the Gollins study that we described at the beginning of this chapter. Although promiscuity and generosity are by no means mutually exclusive traits, three-quarters of the students apparently felt some dissonance between them. Consequently they did some doctoring of the evidence, either combining the two traits or simply ignoring one of them, in order to produce what to them was a more consistent description.

Likewise, if the kind, wise, dowdy old lady in the supermarket line had suddenly produced an exquisite, hundred-dollar-variety alligator handbag, you probably wouldn't have concluded that she was a rich woman who spent her days shopping and riding around in a chauffeured limousine. This would have been inconsistent with what you already "knew" about her. Rather, you would somehow have worked the handbag into your already-formed impression. Perhaps it was sent to her by her successful son, whose education she had worked hard to pay for. Perhaps it was given to her by her grateful staff when she retired as director of a nursery school. Perhaps she had had the handbag for thirty years. In other words, you would somehow make the new information fit with the impression that you had formed.

According to Asch, this habit of bending evidence to fit other evidence is one of the most basic facts of social perception:

> The moment we see that two or more characteristics belong to the same person, they enter into dynamic interaction. We cannot see one quality and another in the same person without their affecting each other. If one person is intelligent and cheerful, and another intelligent and morose, the quality of intelligence ceases to be the same in the two. (1952, p. 216)

The cheerful person's intelligence is lively and inquiring; he reads constantly and shares his ideas with his friends. The morose person's intelligence is somber and probing; he sits alone in his room meditating on the futility of life and the folly of human behavior.

What happens when we are unable to make the facts fit? We may screen out the inconsistent fact, as did half the students in the Gollins study. Or we may screen out the person. One group of researchers found that people like consistent personalities more than inconsistent personalities (Hendrick,

1972). Thus, if the wise old lady, instead of producing an expensive handbag, had donned a pair of butterfly-shaped sunglasses studded with colored rhinestones, you might just have given up and forgotten about her.

Assumed Content

Look back at the description that Asch's subject gave of the seven-adjective person and at the mental picture you formed of the woman in the supermarket. Aside from unity and consistency, they have a third characteristic in common. That is, many of the details they contain (a scientist, World War II refugee) are not directly suggested by the evidence; rather, they have been supplied by the perceiver. In our effort to create a unified and consistent picture of another person on the basis of scanty evidence, we simply fill in the gaps with details that seem to enhance and support our fundamental impression.

This added material is called the *assumed content* of a social impression. We look at our kindly, unkempt English professor and assume that his wife loves him and that he loses his keys regularly. We see that homely boy who works in the local gas station and we think how lonely he must be. Likewise, Asch's subjects were almost unanimous in concluding that the seven-adjective person, in addition to being what those seven adjectives said he was, was also persistent, honest, serious, and strong. At times we assign whole complexes of traits—a complete personality—on the basis of a single "clue" (Kelley, 1973). In one study, for example, subjects who were told that a person was intelligent expected him to be clever, reliable, deliberate, conscientious, active, and imaginative as well. When told that a person was inconsiderate, they expected that he would also be hypocritical, boastful, cold,

Take one person out of each of these pictures and fill in the assumed content. What kind of personalities do they have? What do they care about most in life? What were they doing most of this year? What will they be doing next year? What stereotypes are involved in your perceptions of these people? (See the discussion of stereotypes at the end of this chapter.) (*top left*, © Abigail Heyman/Archive Pictures; *bottom left*, Bill Stanton/Magnum; *top right*, Esaias Baitel/Rapho/Photo Researchers, Inc.; *bottom right*, Constantine Manos/Magnum)

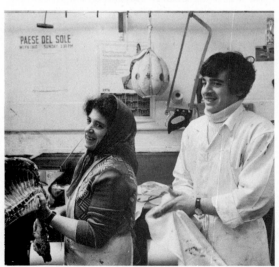

and irritable (Bruner et al., 1958). All on the basis of one adjective!

Implicit Theory of Personality

Where do these notions come from? What information bank supplies the assumed content? According to many psychologists, each of us has his own *implicit theory of personality* (Schneider, 1973), a set of beliefs about which traits go with which in the human personality. Shakespeare's Julius Caesar offers a nice example. Noticing the Roman senator Cassius, whom he distrusts, Caesar remarks to his friend Mark Antony:

> Let me have men about me that are fat,
> Sleek-headed men, and such as sleep o' night:
> Yon Cassius has a lean and hungry look;
> He thinks too much: such men are dangerous.

In Caesar's mind, being fat, being sleek-headed, sleeping easily, and being trustworthy are traits that go together, as do being lean, thinking too much, and being untrustworthy. Likewise, many of us assume that fat people are jolly, that extremely intelligent people have psychological problems, that a kindly, rumpled professor must be well loved, and that a homely gas-station attendant must be a social misfit.

In fact, the absent-minded professor may have a ghastly marriage, and the gas-station attendant may have a most exotic love life. The human personality is seldom as "logical" as our theories about it. (Indeed, implicit theories of personality are a major source of mistaken impressions.) Yet we cling to these theories because they fit our ideas of what is right and because they allow us to give to our impressions of others a sense of order, even if it is a false order. Furthermore, as we have just seen, it is our implicit theories of personality that supply the assumed content of social perceptions, rounding them out into satisfying wholes.

Structure: What Counts Most

In the process of assigning traits to others, we don't give all the traits equal value. Instead, like the artist, we structure our creation; we build it around a main theme. As Asch notes:

> Some [traits] become central, providing the main direction; others become peripheral and dependent. Until we have found the center—that part of the person which wants to live and act in a certain way, which wants not to break up or disappear—we feel we have not succeeded in reaching an understanding. (1946, p. 216)

But how do we locate the center, the hook on which we hang the other traits? In this area of research, the pioneer again was Asch, who isolated two factors—the "central trait" and the primacy effect—that influence our way of structuring social impressions.

Central Traits

Look at another list of seven adjectives:

intelligent
skillful
industrious
cold
determined
practical
cautious

Before reading any further, close your eyes and try to form a mental picture of this person. Now, if you turn back to page 244, you will see that this list is identical to the list we presented earlier, except for one item: "cold" has been substituted for "warm."

How important was this change? Did you imagine a person very different from the one you created on the basis of the earlier list? If you are anything like the subjects in Asch's 1946 experiment, the answer is yes. Half the group saw the first list, and as we have seen, concluded that the seven-adjective person was many good things in addition to his seven virtues. To the other half of the group, Asch showed the second list, with "cold" instead of "warm." And in spite of his remaining six virtues, the seven-adjective person lost his glow. One subject, for example, described him as "calculating and unsympathetic" and as "a rather snobbish person who feels that his success and intelligence set him apart from the run-of-the-mill individual" (p. 263). Whereas the general feeling of the first group was that the "warm" person would also be humane, generous, wise, humorous, happy, sociable, and popular, the second group generally agreed that these valued traits could not belong to the "cold" person.

But why? Objectively, there is no reason whatsoever why a cold person cannot be, for example, as wise or as humorous or as successful as a warm person. Yet this one change, this one adjective, colored the whole picture. Once a wonderful fellow, the seven-adjective person had become a person to avoid. Asch experimented further to see if other adjective pairs would have the same effect. For example, he used "polite" and "blunt" in place of "warm" and "cold" in the two lists, but the impressions formed by the two groups with these lists were much more similar than those of the groups with the "warm" and "cold" lists.

Asch concluded that there are certain personality characteristics, or *central traits*, that are more important to us than others. We place these traits at the center of our picture of another person and organize the rest of the picture around them. In the process of bending traits to make them consistent with one another, we tend to bend other traits to conform to the central trait rather than vice versa.

More recent experiments have confirmed the centrality of the warm-cold trait but

BOX 9.1
YOUR NAME CAN AFFECT YOUR LIFE

"What's in a name?" says Shakespeare's Juliet, ". . . a rose by any other name would smell as sweet." Juliet's point seems well taken, but according to psychological research, it is mistaken. To those who deal with you, your name apparently *does* mean something. It affects the way they perceive you, the expectations they have of you, and the way they treat you. An early study (Eagelson, 1946) found that people perceived Johns as kind and trustworthy, Tonys as sociable, and Agneses and Matildas as unattractive. Similar research (e.g., Buchanan and Bruning, 1971) found additional linkages: James and Michael were masculine; Wendy was feminine; James, Michael, and Wendy were active; Alfreda, Percival, and Isadore were passive.

Common names seem to do better than unusual ones. One study (Lawson, 1971) found that the owners of common names such as David, James, John, Joseph, Michael, Paul, Richard, Robert, and Thomas were seen as stronger and more active than those with less common names such as Bernard, Dale, Edmond, Ivan, Raymond, and Stanley. Even children have stereotypes about names, and these stereotypes seem to affect their interactions with their peers. Children with rather common names tend to be more popular than those with unusual names (McDavid and Harari, 1966).

Unfortunately, even teachers tend to be affected by the name game. Researchers found that teachers gave higher marks to children's essays when they were signed with "desirable" names such as Karen, Lisa, David, and Michael than when they were signed by "undesirable" names such as Elmer, Bertha, and Hubert. Indeed, teachers regarded children named Jonathan, James, John, Patrick, Craig, Thomas, Gregory, Richard, and Jeffrey as being better adjusted and likely to do better in school than children named Bernard, Curtis, Darrell, Donald, Gerald, Horace, Maurice, Jerome, Roderick, and Samuel (Hariri and McDavid, 1973; Garwood, 1976).

While these studies indicate the possible disadvantages of uncommon names, there is another side to the coin. Unusual names are easily remembered, as politicians (Abraham and Grover), entertainers (Aretha and Dustin), and sports figures (Vida and Reggie) could testify.

have failed to turn up any other trait that has as great an impact. Maybe this is predictable. After all, our idea of a person's warmth or coldness is basically our estimate of how willing that person would be to interact with us. And considering the immense value that we place on social interaction, it is no surprise that this quality of being open or closed to interaction should occupy a central position in our perception of another person.

However, if you examine the mental images that you have of your friends, you may find that in many cases you have organized the image around a central trait other than warmth or coldness. You may have, for example, a "sympathetic friend" whose other traits are organized in your mind around the trait of sympathy and whose behavior you tend to interpret in light of her sympathy. The same goes for your "fun-loving friend" and your "intellectual friend." In sum, we write a different story for each person we know, and each story has its own main theme.

The Primacy Effect

Your sister has a new boyfriend. The first time you meet him, he corners you and talks to you for an hour about football, a subject in which you have no interest at all. You come away with the impression that he is an inconsiderate bore. The next two times you see him, however, he says not a word about football. He participates in the general conversation and makes some witty and intelligent remarks. What is your impression of him now? Do you find him likable and interesting on the basis of the last two encounters? Do you average out the early minus and the later plus and come out with a neutral zero? Neither is likely. What is likely is that you still think of him as an inconsiderate bore. For psychological research suggests that first impressions, as our mothers and fathers told us, are quite lasting.

To test the impact of first impressions, Asch, in another experiment, presented one group of subjects with the following list of adjectives:

intelligent
industrious
impulsive
critical
stubborn
envious

Note that this list starts with two positive qualities and ends with two negative qualities, while the two qualities in the middle could be interpreted either positively or negatively. To a second group of subjects he presented exactly the same list but in reverse order. The two groups came up with very different perceptions of the person being described. The first group, having seen the positive qualities first, stressed these qualities; they saw a competent person who also happened to have some personality problems. The second group, who encountered the negative qualities first, saw someone with personality problems who also had a competence that was hampered by those problems. In general, the two middle traits—impulsive and critical—were sucked into the flow of the basic impression. The first group tended to see them in a positive light, the second group in a negative light.

What apparently happened was that the first two adjectives formed the pattern of the perception and the other adjectives were mentally cut and tailored to fit that pattern. Asch called this phenomenon the *primacy effect* and described it as follows:

> The first terms [that is, adjectives] set up a *direction* that exerts a continuous effect on the later terms. When one hears the first term, a broad, uncrystallized, but directed impression is born. The next characteristic is related to the established direction. The view formed quickly acquires a certain stability; later characteristics are fitted to the prevailing direction when conditions permit. (1952, pp. 212–213)

According to Asch, this principle (an extension of the theory of cognitive consistency) applies as well to life outside the psychology lab. First impressions—whether based on an adjective, a kind remark, or an hour-long lecture on football—do definitely count.[*]

When the primacy effect is positive, it is called a *halo effect*; when it is negative, it

---

[*] Under certain circumstances people may also be swayed by *recency effects*, in which the last impression, rather than the first, has the greatest impact. Political candidates, for example, often try to capture votes through a flood of television advertising in the last few days before the election.

is called a *devil effect*. Both are extremely resistant to contradictory evidence. Your sister's boyfriend is going to have to be on extremely good behavior in several more encounters before he can undo the "inconsiderate bore" image. Likewise, if your first paper for a course is particularly brilliant, leading the professor to conclude that you're an outstanding student, you will have to put in a number of bad performances before you can tarnish your halo, for once a first impression is established in a person's mind, he will bend all later evidence to make it consistent with that first impression. (For example, if you don't speak up in class, the professor may conclude that you are the shy type—not that you haven't done the reading.) Only when the later evidence repeatedly contradicts the first impression will the person give it up. But not willingly, since revising an impression means dismantling an entire, elaborate mental structure.

Understanding and Control

Let's sum up. In our social perceptions we (1) see a unified personality, no matter how fragmentary the evidence, (2) adapt pieces of evidence to one another to achieve consistency, (3) add further details, or assumed content, based on our implicit theories of personality, (4) structure all this material around a main theme, usually either a "central trait" or a trait based on the primacy effect.

This, needless to say, requires a great deal of cognitive work. Why do we do all this manipulating and arranging? Probably for the same reason that we make attributions regarding people's behavior: because we want to understand the other person. We aren't content to see him scientifically— that is, as a collection of stimuli. We want to know what he is "really like," what "makes him tick." Once we have organized

the stimuli into a coherent structure (distorting and adding on when we have to), we can attach a meaning to him. And this meaning, even if it is inaccurate, gives us the comforting feeling that we can predict his behavior and determine how we should behave toward him. In sum, what we gain from our social perceptions is a sense of understanding and a feeling of control in our interactions with others.

ATTRACTION

One of the most important outcomes of social perception is *attraction*. Do we like the other person or don't we? This is a decision we make every day, with little fanfare, but it is a crucial decision all the same. When we like people, we want to be with them. We call them up, we go out with them, meet their friends, borrow their books, sit for hours talking to them. And this interaction, as we have seen, has an immense impact on our lives and our personalities. It molds the self-concept. It forms our attitudes, inducing us to think and act as our acquaintances think and act. In turn, it influences our social perceptions; whom we will like this year influences whom we will like next year. Finally, social interaction can bring us enormous pleasure and enormous pain. Therefore, we have good reason to ask: Who are these people we hang around with? How did we choose them? What is it that makes us like another person?

Social psychologists have discovered that there seem to be certain definite qualities that attract us to others. These qualities will be discussed below. In reading about them, however, keep in mind that we are not describing hard-and-fast rules but simply statements of probability. For example, as we will see shortly, people tend to like people who are geographically close to them. This is the general rule. But as for the specific case—for example, whether you in particular will become friendly with your next-door neighbor—this will depend on many factors besides geographical closeness. To begin with, there are your "person variables," such as your age, sex, self-esteem, past learning, tastes, and values, and your neighbor's as well. Then there are the situational variables—whether she has ten cats and you are a cat-hater; whether there are other people on the block or in the building who are more appealing to you; whether there are expectations of neighborly socializing in the particular neighborhood. In sum, there are many different variables operating, and individual cases can easily break general rules.

With this caution in mind, let's look at the general rules. We will examine five important determinants of attraction: (1) physical attractiveness, (2) competence, (3) proximity, (4) similarity, and (5) rewardingness.

Physical Attractiveness

Most people are quick to deny that physical attractiveness has much to do with their liking of another person. After all, you can't tell a book by its cover. Beauty is only skin deep, and we are deeper than that. Psychological research indicates, however, that we aren't—or at least not to the degree we think we are.

In general, people tend to believe that what is beautiful is also good (Dion et al., 1972; Dion, 1980).* Apparently, this stereotype is active already in early childhood. Nursery-school children, when asked whom

they like best and who is best-behaved, picked for both categories those of their classmates whom adults judged to be the most attractive physically (Dion and Berscheid, 1972).

These attitudes may be picked up from adults, who clearly share the children's prejudice. In one interesting experiment, psychologist Karen Dion described to a large number of women a child's misbehavior, such as throwing rocks at a dog. Then she showed each woman a photograph of the supposed culprit. Half the subjects were shown attractive children; the other half were shown homely children. When asked to evaluate the seriousness of the child's act, the two groups came to very different conclusions. Those who had seen the pretty children found excuses for them. One subject, for example, concluded: "She appears to be a perfectly charming little girl, well-mannered, basically unselfish. . . . but like anyone else, a bad day can occur. Her cruelty . . . need not be taken seriously" (Dion, 1972, p. 45). The subjects who saw the homely children were much more stern in their judgments: this youngster was a serious offender. In the words of one subject, "the child . . . would be a problem to teachers. . . . She would be a brat at home. . . . All in all, she would be a real problem" (p. 45).

Adults' evaluations of other adults follow the same pattern. Physically attractive people are thought to be stronger, more sensitive, more modest, more sociable, more poised, more interesting, and more sexually responsive than less attractive people. We also tend to expect attractive people to be more successful in their jobs and marriages and to lead happier and more fulfilling lives than more ordinary-looking folk (Dion et al., 1972). Indeed, even being seen with someone who is attractive can put us in a more

* People also tend to agree about what is beautiful. Beauty may be in the eye of the beholder, but within a given society, most beholders tend to have the same general idea of what it means (Murstein, 1972).

favorable light (Sigall and Landy, 1973; Sheposh et al., 1977)—a factor that probably has much influence on many dating choices. However, people looking for long-term relationships are probably not well advised to seek out partners considerably more attractive than they. Recent research suggests that the closer a dating couple are in physical attractiveness—both of them gorgeous or both plain or both in between—the more likely it is that the relationship will last (White, 1980).

These data are rather discouraging. It seems unfair, even rather shameful, that we should like or dislike people because their genes, over which they have no control, sent them into this world beautiful or homely. One comforting thought is that the power of beauty may wear off once we get to know a person. Ellen Berscheid and Elaine Walster, two of the foremost researchers on the effects of physical attractiveness, claim that good looks have a much greater impact on first impressions than on later impressions (1969). But we have already seen the power of first impressions. Physically attractive people clearly have the edge.

Psychologists say that beautiful people are better liked. If you met this model at a party, would you like her better than you would a more ordinary-looking woman? (© Barbara Alper 1981)

ACTIVITY 9.2

To test the power of physical attractiveness, get out a high school yearbook and ask a friend to look at pictures of some of your old classmates. (Make sure that you cover up the names and any other words accompanying the pictures.) Out of about thirty photographs, ask your subject to pick out the ten people whom he or she thinks would be the most likeable. Repeat the same experiment with another subject. To what extent did the choices conform to the physical attractiveness of the people in the photographs? To what extent were your two subjects' choices the same? Did the two subjects actually pick the people who, in your opinion, were the most likeable? This may tell you something about the effect of physical attractiveness and about its special influence over first impressions.

BOX 9.2
YOU ARE WHAT YOU WEAR

Whether you care about clothes or think about them only when you're going to a job interview, what you wear does make a difference. In a series of studies, psychologist Leonard Bickman (1971) found that our clothes affect how other people react to us. One experiment involved two groups of people, one group well dressed (indicating high social status), the other group poorly dressed (indicating low social status). The people in both groups were instructed to leave a dime in a public phone booth, watch the booth until someone else entered it and started to make a call, and then ask that person whether he or she had found a dime there. Bickman found that subjects returned the dime to the well-dressed people in 78 percent of the cases, whereas the poorly dressed people got their dimes back only 38 percent of the time.

Another study involved petition-signing. One group of women wore dresses, high heels, and makeup; the others wore blue jeans, work shirts, and no makeup. They then canvassed passersby, asking them to sign a petition to outlaw detergents containing phosphates. Bickman found that many more people signed the petition when they were asked by women in dresses than when the women in jeans made the request. In other words, when political campaign managers ask volunteers to dress "straight" for door-to-door canvassing, they have a good reason.

Competence

Competent people—people who are good at what they do—also have an edge. We like them better than we do less competent people. There are limits to this rule, however. Have you ever worked with someone who seems to do everything perfectly—is always on time, always looks marvelous, always seems to know what the boss wants and how to get it done quickly? How much did you like her? Probably not *too* much. But what if you were back at work with Miss Perfect and she made some embarrassing blunder, such as throwing away an important document by mistake? Chances are that you would start to like her somewhat more. Her blunder would make her seem more human, more approachable.

This point—that we prefer competent people as long as they are not too perfect—has been confirmed by a clever experiment (Aronson et al., 1966). Subjects heard four tape recordings, supposedly of four people trying out for a quiz show. In all four tapes the person had to answer a series of very difficult questions. One of these people came across as a near-genius. In another tape the person performed equally brilliantly but admitted at the end that he had just spilled a cup of coffee all over his suit. In the third tape the person showed average competence in answering the questions. In the fourth tape the person was again average but also spilled his coffee. When asked which of the would-be contestants they liked best, the subjects preferred the second one, the near-genius who had spilled the coffee. And interestingly enough, the contestant they liked least was the average person who had spilled the coffee. In other words, while extremely superior people may be better liked for their blunders, ordinary mortals are not.

Proximity

What is the causal relationship between liking someone and seeing her often? Most people would guess that liking causes seeing. This is certainly true, but so is the reverse. *Proximity*, the other person's geographical closeness to you and hence her availability for interaction, is possibly the most important determinant of whether that person will be your friend. The closer she lives, the more you will see her. And the more you see her, the more you'll like her. Familiarity, in short, does *not* breed contempt.

The importance of proximity comes as a surprise to many people. We don't see ourselves as choosing our friends on the basis of who is merely available. But ask yourself how the friendships you have now first developed. Chances are that they developed simply through seeing the person regularly, either because you had the same classes in high school, or worked in the same drugstore, or lived in the same building. If you're married, ask yourself how available, geographically, your spouse was when you were first getting to know one another. For proximity is not only an important determinant of friendship; it is probably the most important limiting factor in our choice of whom we will marry (Catton and Smircich, 1964). "Cherished notions about romantic love notwithstanding it appears that when all is said and done, the 'one and only' may have a better than 50-50 chance of living within walking distance" (Kephart, 1972).

The classic study of the effect of proximity on attraction is that of Leon Festinger, Stanley Schachter, and Kurt Back (1950). These three researchers chose as their sam-

Neighbors are the best example of the proximity-leads-to-liking rule. Because they are just across the hedge, we tend to socialize with them, and the more we socialize with them, the more we like them. (© Michal Heron 1981/ Woodfin Camp & Assoc.)

ACTIVITY 9.3

Make a list of your five closest friends. (If you are married, include your spouse.) Then, for each one, explain in one or two sentences the circumstances in which your friendship developed. Were you in a class together? Did you work in the same office? Were you on the same bowling team? You will probably find that physical proximity has played a decisive role in your selection of friends.

ple a married-student housing project called Westgate West. The project consisted of seventeen two-story buildings, each with ten apartments. The apartments were assigned at random, so friends could not arrange to live close to one another. Hence, the researchers could assume that the friendships that existed in Westgate West had been formed there.

What were these friendships? Each resident was asked to name the three Westgate West residents with whom he or she socialized most often. The results were rather astounding. One might have predicted that the students would tend to choose their friends from the same building or from the buildings next door. As it turned out, however, not only did distances between buildings count; distances as small as 20 feet made an enormous difference. In the friend-listing, the people in the next apartment were twice as likely to be chosen as the people two apartments away, though the distance between their two front doors was only about 20 feet. Likewise, the people two apartments away were twice as likely to be chosen as the people three apartments away. In other words, three or four seconds of travel time managed to cut in half a person's chances of becoming a friend.

It should be added, however, that proximity is not a magical factor, guaranteeing attraction. Proximity is important only be- cause it results in interaction, which in turn results in attraction. Proximity without interaction stirs no warm feelings. In big-city apartment complexes, where it is often the custom *not* to socialize with fellow residents, next-door neighbors can go on for years exchanging nothing more than nods. Conversely, any factor besides proximity that increases the likelihood of interaction also increases the likelihood of attraction. In Westgate West, for example, the couples who lived next to the mailboxes and next to the foot of the stairwell (where the garbage cans were kept) turned out to be slightly more popular than the average. The reason is obvious. In terms of the likelihood of interaction, they were strategically located.

Similarity

Another major determinant of attraction is similarity. Among those who are geographically close to us, we tend to gravitate toward those who are most like us. This is something that you can probably confirm from your own experience. For example, you may have had the uncomfortable experience of finding that a close friend from your childhood or high-school years is no longer very attractive to you because different experiences in recent years (college, military service, marriage) have changed both of you. Once you were similar, and you were the

SOCIAL PERCEPTION: WHAT IT IS AND HOW IT OPERATES

best of friends. Now, having gone separate ways and developed different tastes and interests, you are no longer similar, and therefore it is no longer easy to be friends. This fact of life is a common source of discomfort at high-school and college reunions.

The birds-of-a-feather rule applies to a wide range of characteristics. According to research, we prefer people who are similar to us in intelligence, ability, race, socioeconomic status, and even size. Above all, we are drawn to people with attitudes similar to our own (Byrne, 1971). It has been shown, for example, that whites would rather associate with blacks who share their attitudes than with whites who hold opposing attitudes (Rokeach, 1968; Byrne and Wong, 1962; Moss and Andrasik, 1973).

In another study, psychologist Theodore Newcomb (1961) took over a large house at the University of Michigan and offered one semester of rent-free housing to male students who would give him a few hours of their time each week. All the men chosen were sophomores and juniors; none of them knew any of the others. Before the semester began, the men filled out questionnaires indicating their attitudes and values. Newcomb assigned roommates on the basis of these questionnaires. To some of the men he gave roommates similar to themselves; to others he gave dissimilar roommates. The semester began; the men moved in and met one another; and Newcomb waited to see

Friendships can grow out of shared interests, as in the case of these bicyclists. For centuries people have assumed that similarity leads to liking, and psychological research has confirmed that assumption. (© Leonard Speier 1982)

what would happen. What happened was that—roommate or no roommate—similarity of attitudes tended to determine attraction. The similar roommates liked each other and became friends; the dissimilar roommates disliked each other and sought more similar friends among other house residents. Thus, it would appear that computer dating services, which match men and women on the basis of attitudes, *are* on the

ACTIVITY 9.4

To what extent are your attitudes similar to those of your closest friends? Make a list of important attitudes held by a very close friend. Next make a list of your own attitudes. (Be as objective as you can.) Then make a list of attitudes held by someone you don't like. Compare your lists. Note the similarities and differences.

right track, silly as they seem to some people.

But why do we seek out our own kind? Why do we avoid the challenge of interacting with people of different outlooks? One likely explanation is simply that having someone agree with you is pleasant. It makes you feel that you are *right*—that the reality you see is really there and you are on top of it. Furthermore, disagreements over attitudes can be frustrating and exhausting. Now and then you may want to let your aunts and uncles know how wrong they are on the subject of busing, premarital sex, or whatever (and they may want to let you know how wrong you are), but no one would enjoy doing this every night. Constantly disagreeing with someone you are close to is painful.

Complementarity

There is one area in which the similarity-leads-to-liking rule may not apply as well as in others. That is the area of personality. In responding to other people's personalities, we may lay aside our interest in similarity and look instead for *complementarity*—that is, a personality that *meshes* with ours rather than being identical. Complementarity might be called the "Jack Sprat" rule. It does not necessarily mean that the two personalities involved are opposite, but rather that in certain important areas each person, by fulfilling his own needs, automatically fulfills the needs of the other person (Seyfried and Hendrick, 1973).

We are all familiar with complementarity stereotypes: the dominant wife and the meek husband, the hard-driving, ambitious executive and his stay-at-home, slipper-warming wife. As these examples indicate, much of the research on complementarity has focused on married couples. But friends may be complementary, too. The constant talker tends to find good listeners; the big-hearted, sympathetic person is often surrounded by friends with problems. Tom Sawyer chooses Huck Finn; Felix Unger chooses Oscar Madison.

Total complementarity of needs may, however, work against a relationship, particularly a marriage (Meyer and Pepper, 1977). For example, an extremely outgoing person may not do well with an extremely reclusive person. It seems that the best recipe for a close relationship is a combination of complementarity and similarity: complementarity in areas such as dominance-submissiveness and similarity in areas such as sociability and sense of humor.

Rewardingness

A final important determinant of attraction is *rewardingness*. As social exchange theory (Chapter 8) would suggest, we like people who reward us. In a sense, this is a subject we have already covered in our discussions of physical attractiveness, competence, proximity, similarity, and complementarity. Being associated with people who are good-looking and competent, having someone nearby to socialize with, having our opinions seconded and our personality needs met—all these things are rewards. And as we have seen, we prefer people who can supply them.

Another important reward, predictably, is the pleasure of being liked. We are drawn to people who show that they like us (Aronson, 1970). And, interestingly enough, it seems that we are particularly drawn to people who are critical of us at first and then decide that they like us (Aronson and Linder, 1965). Maybe we consider such people more discriminating, or perhaps we simply derive a special pleasure from winning over another person.

Finally, even ordinary, down-to-earth re-

The fact that rewardingness leads to liking may sound a bit cold and calculating when it is stated as a rule. But in real life, the process is quite natural. People who like us help us, and those who are kind to us of course arouse warmer feelings in us than do people who don't like us, don't help us, and aren't kind to us. (Charles Harbutt/Magnum)

wards can make another person more attractive to us. We like to think that we value our friends for what they are rather than for what they can do for us. But in actuality we tend to prefer people who do things for us—get us dates, lend us their cars, pay us compliments, listen to our troubles, invite us to their parties. Likewise, acquaintances who keep us on the phone too long, borrow our books and fail to return them, always need favors and are never there when we need a favor—in short, acquaintances who are high-cost and low-reward—tend not to become friends. Or if they are friends, they tend to be dropped. We also prefer people who are associated with rewards, even if they aren't directly responsible for them—for example,

people with whom we always seem to do enjoyable things. The more rewards we associate with a person, the more we like that person (Lott et al., 1969).

There are limits to the rewardingness rule, however. If a person likes you twice as much as you like her or if she constantly pays you compliments that you don't think you deserve or if she showers you with many more rewards than you can ever pay back, then you are likely to feel uncomfortable with her. Evidently, we all have a certain sense of what is appropriate, and we like to keep the balance sheet fairly even.

It should be noted that the rewardingness rule also works in reverse. That is, we try to supply rewards to the people we like by being responsive to their needs. We try to remember their birthdays, to do the favors they ask of us, to listen to them when they need to talk. And if we stop doing these things—that is, if we cease to supply rewards to the other person (or if he ceases to supply rewards to us)—there may be trouble in the relationship. In Chapter 12 we will examine interpersonal troubles more closely, and we will suggest various ways of increasing your rewardingness to other people by responding to their signals, by communicating with them more honestly and intimately, by offering more positive feedback, and by keeping your negative feedback constructive.

STEREOTYPING

Attraction, as we have just seen, is the result of several factors: availability, similarity, rewards, and so on. But there is a process that can short-circuit the connection between these factors and attraction. Imagine that your next-door neighbor is similar to you in attitudes, complementary to you in personality needs, competent in his work, and handsome as well, to say nothing of being geographically close and thus extremely available for interaction. But aside from taking note of his physical attractiveness and his proximity, you never give yourself the chance to find out all the good things about him. Why? Because you are black and he is white, or you are heterosexual and he is homosexual. Knowing that he belongs to a group different from yours, you assign to him a number of personality traits that you think "go with" that group membership. And this set of assigned traits blocks your access to any more accurate information. You have "placed" him; you don't need to know anything more.

This process—classifying people on the basis of their membership in a group and automatically assuming that they possess a cluster of traits that you associate with that group—is called *stereotyping*. It involves all the perceptual processes that we discussed earlier: the drive for unity and consistency, the filling in of assumed content, the structuring around a central trait. Here, however, the central trait is the person's membership in a specific group—the fact that he or she is a hippie or a police officer, a black or a white, a WASP or a Pole, a southerner or a northerner. And the implicit theory that in this case supplies the assumed content is not so much a theory of personality in general as it is a theory of group personalities: occupational types, racial types, ethnic types. This theory is the *stereotype*.

Stereotyping is a result of socialization. By taking roles, for example, we learn what boys and girls—and men and women—are "supposed" to be. And by adopting the attitudes of those around us, we learn what to expect from Italians, Irishmen, Catholics, Protestants, Jews, stockbrokers, sanitation workers, blacks, whites, Democrats, Republicans, and socialists. Thus, for most of us socialization is, in one sense, a training ground for stereotyping. As a result, most of

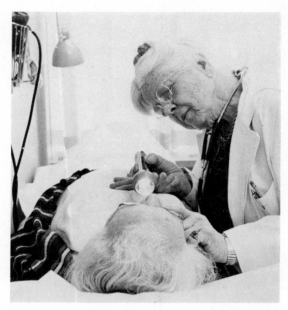

According to the stereotype, this woman should be sitting on the back porch knitting sweaters. Instead she is a doctor and probably has to work harder to prove her competence than someone who fits the "doctor" stereotype better—that is, a middle-aged male. (Raimondo Borea/EPA, Inc.)

us "naturally" engage in some stereotypical thinking. As the famous journalist Walter Lippmann noted:

> We do not see first, then define; we define first and then see. . . . We are told about the world before we see it. We imagine most things before we experience them. And those preconceptions . . . govern deeply the whole process of perception (1922, pp. 91, 90).

Hundreds of studies have proved this point to be true. To cite just one, a psychologist gave a group of subjects a list of personality characteristics and asked them to indicate which characteristic would be more typical of working-class people and which would apply to professional people. The subjects generally agreed that in contrast to working-class people, professional people had many sterling qualities: they were re-

Look at these two groups of men. What stereotypes of yours do they fit? Which group is more likely to vote Republican? drink too much? attend church regularly? write short stories in their spare time? (© Eric Kroll/Taurus; © Terry McKoy/Taurus)

sourceful, independent, complex, and fore-sighted, to say nothing of persistent, ambitious, and intelligent (Feldman, 1972). In other words, even the extremely broad and vague category of professional versus working-class carries with it a trait cluster, or stereotype—in this case, a positive stereotype.

You may think you're more open-minded than the subjects in this study. If so, ask yourself the following questions: Wouldn't you be more disturbed by the sight of a man crying than of a woman crying?* If you had a special medical problem and were referred to an expensive specialist, wouldn't you be surprised to walk into the doctor's office and

discover that he was physically handicapped? If you were told that a woman in your office was a lesbian, wouldn't you reinterpret some of her past behavior in light of this information?

Stereotypes: Accurate or Inaccurate?

According to most social psychologists, stereotypes are basically false. They exaggerate the differences between groups (for example, Irishmen are drunks; Jews don't drink), and they take no account of the millions of individual differences within groups. Furthermore, they often carry the totally unproven assumption that the group's behavior is biologically determined. Finally, many of the traits assigned through stereotyping are simply not there. For example, contrary to popular opinion, homosexuals do *not* have a distinct personality type. According to research (Gagnon, 1977), most homosexuals are indistinguishable from heterosexuals in per-

---

* In 1972 Edmund Muskie, the front-running Democrat in the presidential primaries, shed a few tears in public after his wife had been publicly slurred. Many newspaper editorials expressed serious concern over his emotional stability. Others implied that he was just a sissy. The voters seemed to agree. Muskie's lead slipped away, and he eventually lost the nomination to George McGovern.

sonality, as well as in manner and appearance. By the same token, women are *not* bad drivers; every year the percentage of women drivers responsible for automobile accidents is much smaller than the percentage of male drivers causing accidents.

However, many stereotypes do have some superficial truth. Women do, of course, cry more easily than men. Many blacks *are* musical, indeed much of America's musical talent has been drawn from the black population. Many homosexuals are, as is generally believed, promiscuous (Saghir and Robins,

1969; Bell and Weinberg, 1978; Gagnon and Simon, 1973); their sexual careers are often dotted with one-night stands. But what does this mean? Does it mean, as the stereotype usually implies, that female biology *makes* women more emotional or that blacks are "born with it" or that homosexuality and promiscuity "naturally" go together? On the contrary. The evidence indicates that these are learned behaviors.

Girls are taught at an early age that they are allowed to cry; indeed, in some situations, such as weddings and funerals,

BOX 9.3
NUMBER TWO TRIES HARDER

Studies have shown that people expect men to do better than women on most tasks. One unfortunate consequence of this sexual stereotyping is that when the evaluation of a performance requires judgment—rating a pianist's performance, for example—people will give it higher marks if they think it was done by a man (Goldberg, 1968; Muhr and Bogard, 1972). But what if the evidence *shows* that a man and a woman have done equally well on a task? Will this alter people's view of male and female abilities? It might. On the other hand, the woman's success might simply be explained in terms of something besides ability.

Using attribution theory, psychological researchers Shirley Feldman-Summers and Sara B. Kiesler (1974) postulated that there are four basic ways to account for an individual's performance on a task: the individual's ability, the difficulty of the task, the individual's motivation, and luck. Of these four factors, the first two are stable and predictable, while the second two are variable. The experimenters hypothe-

sized that since men were expected to perform better than women, any violation of this expectation would be explained in terms of variable factors, things one couldn't predict—in other words, motivation and luck. To test their hypothesis, they conducted two different experiments.

In the first experiment, each of the subjects was shown a set of problems in logic and mathematics, along with six answer sheets supposedly filled out by student "test-takers." On some answer sheets, the name of the "test-taker" was female; on others it was male. For each answer sheet, the subject was to rate the importance of four different factors—ability, motivation, luck, and task difficulty—in explaining the performance of the "test-taker." The main finding of this experiment was that no matter how well or poorly the "test-takers" did, the females' results were more frequently attributed to high motivation than the males' results.

In a second experiment, each subject was

SOCIAL PERCEPTION: WHAT IT IS AND HOW IT OPERATES

ACTIVITY 9.5

Advertisers frequently make use of stereotypes in linking certain types of people to their products. For example, a well-spoken, middle-aged man urges us to trust the such-and-such life insurance company; we are expected, via stereotyping, to assume that he must be reliable, serious, honest, and conscientious, and therefore to believe him. Likewise, when a roly-poly woman touts Ladrone's Frozen Pizza, it is hoped that we will respond favorably to the stereotype of a jolly, warm, giving Italian mama.

Watch two or three hours of television, noting how stereotypes are used in commercials. List the product, the type of person advertising it, and why you think the two are linked.

shown a written description of a successful physician. All the descriptions were identical except that for half the subjects, the physician being described was Dr. Marcia Greer, whereas for the other half it was Dr. Mark Greer. There were a few other experimental variations as well. For example, in some descriptions, it was noted that the physician took over his or her father's practice; in others, this detail was omitted. Again subjects were asked to rate the importance of ability, motivation, luck, and task difficulty in explaining the physician's success.

Here, as in the first experiment, the main finding was that women's success is more likely to be attributed to high motivation than men's success. But this experiment, unlike the first, showed significant differences in the attitudes of male and female *subjects*. The men generally viewed the female physician as less able than the male physician. If she took over her father's practice, then the men were more likely to see her success as due to luck or to her having had an easy task. If the father's practice wasn't mentioned, then they tended to attribute her success to high motivation. The female subjects saw it differently. To them, the male and female physicians were equal in ability, but the female

physician's success was due more to high motivation, whereas the male's was due more to his having had an easy task.

The experimenters speculate that the women's liberation movement may have been responsible in part for some of the attitudes revealed by the second experiment—for example, the female subjects' perception that men have an easier time of it. At the same time, the experiment also revealed a number of attitudes that women's liberation is bent on eradicating—above all, the notion that women have less ability than men. As for the belief that successful women have higher motivation than successful men, this belief is unlikely to benefit women, either in the job market or elsewhere, as long as it is coupled with the belief that they also have less ability than men. Women *already* have jobs that require hard work—nursing, secretarial work, and the like. What they want is an equal shot at jobs that call for great mental acuity and decision-making ability. A reputation for high motivation alone, without correspondingly high ability, is not going to win them such jobs. It may be that number two tries harder, but in the end, the rewards tend to go to number one.

women are actually expected to cry. Likewise, the entertainment industry is one of the very few respected and lucrative professions that has been open to blacks in the United States; it is no wonder that blacks have eagerly entered, and excelled in, this field or that music has become a central part of the "black experience." Finally, as for homosexual promiscuity, American society makes it rather difficult for homosexuals to establish long-lasting relationships. (Homosexual acts are still illegal in many states and homosexual couples are not generally welcomed by landlords.) Thus, it is not surprising that homosexuals tend to have short-term relationships.

In sum, the central falsehood of stereotypes lies in their determinism—the assumption that traits and behaviors that may or may not characterize a group are automatically, even biologically, connected to that group and that these traits consequently "define" the group, limiting its capabilities. (Women are emotional and therefore should stay home. Homosexuals are promiscuous and therefore wicked or unstable; either way, bad employment risks.) In reality, the traits are much more likely to be the result of stereotyping itself—the group definitions and group restrictions built into our socialization and our social attitudes.

The Damage Done by Stereotyping

Much is lost as a result of stereotyped thinking. The person doing the stereotyping sacrifices breadth and accuracy of perception. He limits his interests, his curiosity, his friendships, his understanding of humankind. Furthermore, he limits his personal growth. He cannot be gentle—that is too womanly. He cannot go to a neighborhood bar—that is too "working-class." God forbid he should take up interior decorating—people might think he was homosexual. In short, by boxing others in, he has boxed himself in as well.

Much more serious, however, is the damage done to the person stereotyped. He is locked into a limited definition of his personality and capabilities, a definition which may have nothing whatsoever to do with him but which he will probably internalize all the same. (Many working women accept lower pay on the assumption that men *should* earn more.) If the person rejects the stereotype and deviates from it, he is likely to be punished or at least discouraged. A woman entering a bar alone, a known homosexual running for public office—these people are taking their self-respect in their own hands. The path of least resistance, then, is to remain within your stereotype. By doing so, however, you accept unreasonable limitations on your potential. Essentially, you "buckle under" to the self-fulfilling prophecy.

There is one further problem. If the stereotype is a negative one, it carries with it an automatic negative evaluation, known by the familiar name of *prejudice.* Prejudice almost invariably damages the self-esteem of its victim. Several decades ago, before the "black is beautiful" campaign, black children thought white dolls were "nicer" than black ones (Clark and Clark, 1947). Likewise, a 1972 study found that women are more critical of a piece of writing when they think it was done by a woman than when they think it was done by a man (Muhr and Bogard, 1972). Thus, not only the restrictive definitions ("you are flighty, soft, and weak") but also the negative evaluation ("you are inferior") contained in the stereotype are internalized by the person being stereotyped, eroding confidence, courage, and self-respect.

Research from the past decade suggests that protest movements such as civil rights, women's liberation, and the Grey Panthers may at last have made some headway against stereotypes. In the early seventies there was ample evidence that people tended to associate undesirable traits with the elderly (Bennett and Eckman, 1973), with women (Broverman et al., 1970), and with blacks (Brigham, 1971). By contrast, a recent study of impression formation (McArthur and Friedman, 1980) failed to reveal any general tendency to rate these groups negatively. In fact, old people were rated more positively than young people, and women somewhat more positively than men. Such results may indicate an actual change in people's attitudes toward these groups. Alternatively, they might be the result simply of self-consciousness on the part of the subjects. As is so often the case, the subjects in this experiment were college students, who tend to be somewhat more exposed than the general public to liberal social and political views. Yet even if the subjects were bending over backward not to *look* prejudiced, this is perhaps the beginning of an actual resistance to prejudice—at least against women, blacks, and the elderly. (See also Box 9.3.)

Nevertheless, stereotypes still persist and are definitely a problem in social perception. So too are any cognitive processes that seriously distort our impressions of others in the name of unity or consistency. So too are impressions that focus on the surface—the person's looks, hair, clothes. In dealing with these problems, however, we must remember that we are not perfect: we can never perceive reality (in this case, the other person) pure and undistorted. Also, in order to perceive at all, the human mind generally requires a certain degree of imposed unity and consistency. In defense of superficial judgments, it may be said that the other person's surface is sometimes the only clear thing about him. But if we rely too much on surface, filling in the personality picture with our private notions about "people in general," then eventually we no longer see reality. We see only our own preconceptions. Such flawed perceptions can seriously damage our relationships and, consequently, our personal adjustment. This is the problem we will tackle in the next chapter.

SUMMARY

1. Our *social perceptions* are our views of other people. The formation of social perceptions begins in infancy, as the child first becomes aware of other human beings. This awareness is seen in the infant's early *attachment* to people and in the responses of *stranger anxiety* and *separation anxiety*. During childhood, the twin developments of speech and of expanded social roles introduce children to a greater number of social situations and help them to make finer discriminations. This development continues through adolescence, as young people learn to sympathize with others and to think in abstract terms.

2. The operation of social perception is characterized by four techniques that help us organize the many details of reality. First, in perceiving others, we attempt to create *unity* in our pictures of them. Second, we aim for *consistency*, incorporating new information that fits our initial perception and ignoring information that is inconsistent. Third, we may add information (*assumed content*) to make the perception complete. The assumed content is supplied by our own

implicit theories of personality. Fourth, we tend to *structure* our perceptions. We organize the total perception around a *central trait,* such as warmth. We are also subject to the *primacy effect;* in other words, we give great weight to first impressions.

3. One of the most important outcomes of social perception is *attraction,* or liking. A major determinant of attraction is *physical attractiveness.* Physically attractive people are viewed as generally better, happier, and more successful than unattractive people. Competent people also have an edge, although they are preferred only so long as they are perceived as not too perfect.

4. Four other factors affect attraction. *Proximity* makes a difference; the closer a person is to us geographically, the more we are attracted to him, since we have greater opportunity to interact with him. *Similarity* also makes a difference; we tend to gravitate toward those who are the most like us physically, emotionally, and attitudinally. On the other hand, *complementarity* draws us to those whose personalities are different from, but mesh with, our own personalities. Finally, *rewardingness* influences attraction; we tend to like those who like us and do things for us.

5. A process that short-circuits the operation of attraction is *stereotyping*—classifying people on the basis of their membership in a group and automatically assuming that any one member of the group has the traits that we associate with that group. Typically, stereotypes are inaccurate because they do not take into account individual differences, because they view behavior as biologically determined, and because they perpetuate false assumptions. They do a good deal of damage by locking us into limited definitions of our capabilities and thus blocking our growth.

PROJECT

Often one of the first questions we ask when we meet someone is "What do you do?" and we use this information to develop our impression of the person. Yet, as we have seen in this chapter, many professions are subject to stereotypes, which can lead to mistaken conclusions. You can see how this happens by subjecting your friends to a matching game.

1. Copy out the table shown below and ask two friends to match the twenty personal characteristics listed in the left-hand column with the four professions indicated at the top of the remaining columns. No char-acteristic should be used more than once, and the characteristics should be evenly apportioned. That is, each profession should end up with five characteristics. When the matches are completed, examine each five-characteristic group for unity and consistency. Do you detect an underlying stereotype?

2. Wait three days and then ask the same two friends to redo the matching exercise. This time, however, remove the professions from the top of the columns and replace them with the names given below. Give your subjects both the new table and the

following descriptions to go with the names. (Copy out the descriptions; don't show your subjects the book.)

a. Steve Jackson has been a police officer in Cincinnati for ten years. He and his wife have one child, a mentally retarded boy to whom they devote much of their time.
b. Ralph Lombardi, a marriage counselor, is divorced himself, dates a number of different women, and practices yoga for relaxation.
c. Jacqueline Krauss, an art teacher, makes some extra money each year by filling out people's tax returns.

d. Caroline Conrad, a successful lawyer, collects Japanese porcelain and donates time to the women's rights movement.

3. For each of your subjects, compare the results of the first and second matches. Note how even a little bit of additional information—none of it very inconsistent, in the above cases—can invalidate a stereotype. By keeping this in mind, you can help prevent yourself from drawing conclusions about people simply on the basis of profession—or any other group affiliation, for that matter.

	police officer	marriage counselor	art teacher	lawyer
empathetic				
aggressive				
athletic				
sincere				
disorganized				
cheerful				
obedient				
domineering				
sly				
reserved				
creative				
practical				
shallow				
intelligent				
stable				
self-confident				
short-tempered				
persistent				
rebellious				
articulate				

HUMAN ISSUE:
MIDLIFE AND AGING

Two hundred years ago, the average American could expect to live to the age of thirty-six. Today, we live much longer. Indeed, as prime minister of Israel, Golda Meir was working twenty-hour days in her mid-seventies. Given the wide range of the human record, it is risky to define "midlife" or "old age" in terms of rigid time periods. We do know, however, that forty is no longer young, and that seventy is quite a bit different from forty. For the sake of convenience, therefore, we may define midlife as the years from about forty to sixty-five, and old age as the period from about sixty-five on. Both stages involve adjustment to a number of physical, psychological, and social changes.

MIDLIFE: PRIME OR DECLINE?

For some people, the midlife years are the prime of life. According to Bernice Neugarten (1968), this is the time when people can feel a sense of satisfaction with their accomplishments. For other people, however, midlife is the beginning of the end. Life is more than half over. They have stopped growing up and have started growing old. They see that their options are limited. Suddenly they find themselves asking, "Is this all there is?"

Traps and Empty Nests

In many ways, midlife is a time of emotional stress. Erik Erikson (1964) has proposed that there are eight stages in the life cycle, each characterized by a choice between two approaches to life, one positive and one negative (see Chapter 1). In the middle years (the seventh stage), the individual chooses between generativity and self-absorption. Generativity is the capacity to develop a concern for others (for example, the future of one's society or of one's children). People who fail to develop this capacity may become increasingly absorbed in themselves.

Gail Sheehy, writing of "the predictable crises of adult life" (1977), differentiates between what she calls the midlife passage—the years from about thirty-five to forty-five—and middle age—the more or less safe harbor at the end of the trip. During the midlife passage, men and women struggle to reappraise their lives, sorting out illusion from reality in a search for authenticity. "The consensus of current research," says Sheehy, "is that the transition into middle life is as critical as adolescence and in some ways more harrowing" (p. 360).

Sheehy based some of her conclusions on the work of psychologist Daniel Levinson, who, with colleagues at Yale, studied a number of men ranging in age from the twenties into the forties (Levinson et al., 1978). These researchers saw the decade from thirty-five to forty-five as a painful one of questioning and re-evaluation, characterized by feelings of resentment, boredom, and a desire to escape. Another researcher, Fried, quotes a forty-year-old man saying:

> Sure, I feel trapped. Why shouldn't I? Twenty-five years ago a dopey eighteen-year-old college kid made up *his* mind that *I* was going to be a dentist. So now here I am, a dentist. I'm stuck. What I want to know is, who told that kid he could decide what I was going to have to do for the rest of my life? (1967, p. 59)

For women, midlife may be even more difficult. They have to deal with the physical and emotional stress of menopause. Furthermore, our society prizes a youthful appearance in women. Consequently, a woman's ego may be severely damaged when her mirror reveals the inevitable lines, gray streaks, and pouchy eyes. Children are another important factor. During the parents' middle years, children become adolescents and then leave the family. Adolescent turmoils may place considerable stress on middle-aged parents. And when the children do leave home, a woman who has devoted her life to her family may have a difficult time finding new sources of pleasure and self-esteem.

Social Changes

Extramarital sex seems to be fairly common in midlife (Tavris, 1974, 1978). In many cases husbands and wives seem to be searching not for new life partners but for assurance of their own worth and attractiveness. However, separation and divorce occur fairly frequently, too. (So does remarriage; people of this age have become used to living with another person, and are likely to continue doing so.)

For all its traumas, midlife offers some real advantages. With children grown up, parents have more time for social life. They may find new interests or develop old ones. Women who had quit work to stay home with their children may now rejoin the work force or go to college, and there is evidence that those women who do develop interests outside the home weather midlife most easily (Barnett and Baruch, 1981). Furthermore, having taken stock of themselves, the middle-aged often feel a freedom they never had before. A physiologist nearing sixty remarked:

I find that I'm telling the truth more often. I didn't realize I was lying. I just thought I had good, ladylike manners. The one thing in the world I always wanted was to have everybody like me. Now I don't give a damm. I want *some* people to like me, and I'll settle. (quoted in Sheehy, 1977, p. 507)

OLD AGE

The age of sixty-five, in the United States, is the time at which we become eligible for full Social Security benefits and discounts on transportation, movie tickets, and the like. But the clearest signal of old age is retirement. Today it is usually at seventy that an individual, regardless of skill or ability, is required to leave the work force. Some Americans welcome retirement as a time to enjoy leisure or even pursue a new career. For others, retirement and the other changes that accompany old age spell an ever-increasing sense of loss.

The Physical Signs

The most obvious changes that take place in old age are physical. The skin loses its elasticity, hangs more loosely, and becomes wrinkled. Teeth may be lost, making dentures necessary. As the bone structure weakens, height decreases, the chest and shoulders narrow, and the pelvis broadens. With weaker muscles, the body loses strength and reflexes slow down.

Internally, the body's systems are changing. The heart's capacity for work decreases, the circulatory system and lungs are less efficient, and there is often some loss in hearing and vision. People grow more susceptible to disease. They get sick more easily and take longer to recover. Broken bones and other injuries are slower to heal. Minor illnesses like colds can often lead to more severe illnesses like pneumonia.

A persistent myth in our culture is that intellectual functioning declines in old age. This is far from true. If an older person is isolated from others and given little to do but watch television all day, he or she may indeed become withdrawn and dull-witted. However, if a person remains active in an intellectually stimulating environment, mental activity is not significantly impaired. According to a recent estimate, only 8 percent of the aged are senile (Trippett, 1980).

Another myth about the aged is that they are incapable of sex—or ought to be, since our culture has a bias against sexual expression by the elderly. As one researcher put it, "What is virility at twenty-five is lechery at sixty-five" (Braceland, 1972). In reality, both men and women can have sexual intercourse well into their eighties (Masters and Johnson, 1970), and those who do seem to enjoy it. One man reported, "I asked my Grandma when you stop liking it, and she was eighty. She said, 'Child, you'll have to ask someone older than me'" (Tavris and Sadd, 1977). Unfortunately, many old people avoid sex because they feel it is somehow wrong, because they lack a partner, or because both sexes fear that the man will be impotent.

The Stresses of Aging

For many old people, the special stresses of aging can make their last years a period of tremendous depression and anxiety. One such stress is poverty. One out of every four Americans over sixty-five has an income below the poverty line (U.S. Bureau of Census, 1979). Another stress is loneliness. Old people who no longer work miss the contacts provided by employment. Their children are gone and may be living thousands of miles away. And at this age, death takes a heavy toll—of friends, of relatives, and of one's spouse. Because they live longer, women are more likely than men to experience these traumas.

One overriding difficulty for the aged comes from the attitude of society itself. It is a truism (but no less true) that American culture is youth-oriented. The other side of the coin is that we devalue the elderly. We invent euphemisms for them— "senior citizens," "golden-agers"—and tuck them away in hospitals and nursing homes. In a classic example of the self-fulfilling prophecy, people who are regarded as useless, self-involved, and befuddled often become just that.

Dealing with Age

Old people have come to form an ever-larger proportion of the American population. In 1900 only 4 percent of Americans were over sixty-five; by 1980 the total had increased to 12 percent. In a tradition approved by our pluralistic society, the aged have begun to organize themselves as a political pressure group. The Grey Panthers, formed in 1970, work on a wide range of issues, from seeking higher Social Security benefits to improving the image of the elderly in the media.

In Erikson's eight stages, the last involves a choice between despair and integrity. Old people who dwell on what they missed in life—the mistakes they made, the things they never had—may be swamped by despair. Those, on the other hand, who can look back on their lives with satisfaction are strengthened by a sense of personal integrity. One of the latter was this elderly man, interviewed after a long career as an architect: "I feel I've had a good life. I've had extraordinary enemies and extraordinary friends. And I'm still searching for delight" (quoted in Terkel, p. 265).

<u>OUTLINE</u>

PROBLEM PERCEPTIONS
Wishful Thinking
Outdated Images
The Case of Julie and Steve
Solutions
Throw him out
Make him change
Change the way you perceive him

ANALYZING SOCIAL PERCEPTIONS
Description
Situational description
Functional Analysis
External variables: The outer person
Internal variables

REEXAMINING EXPECTATIONS
The Primacy Effect
Distorting and Screening Out
Central traits
Inferred Qualities
Inappropriate Standards
Be like me
Make my dream come true
What the neighbors think
What you are supposed *to do*

CHANGING SOCIAL PERCEPTIONS
Gathering New Information
Incongruous, embarrassing, or threatening information
Feedback
Challenging Expectations Through Self-Talk
Listening to self-talk
Examining the expectation
Talking back
Acting on your back-talk
Are You Buckling Under?
Julie and Steve: A proposal

10

SOCIAL PERCEPTION: HOW TO CHANGE IT

We devoted our last chapter to describing the processes of social perception. What, in the end, is the outcome of these processes? A perception of a person whom we know fairly well has three dimensions—the same three dimensions that characterize the self-concept:

1. *Knowledge:* what we know (or think we know) of the other person—looks, behavior, past history, feelings, motives, and so forth.
2. *Expectations:* our idea of what the person could be and could do, combined with our idea of what he or she should be and should do.
3. *Evaluation:* our judgment of the person, based on how well the person (according to what we know of him or her) is fulfilling our expectations of him or her.

These three elements are intimately tied to one another. Each, in fact, is based on the other two. We *expect* our friend George to keep our deep, dark secret because we evaluate him as loyal and because we "know" that he has kept our secrets in the past. We *evaluate* him as loyal because we expect him to keep our secrets and because we "know" that he has kept our secrets before. And we *"know"* that he has kept our secrets because we expect him to do so and because we judge him to be loyal.

Thus, what we have, once again, is a circular relationship—specifically, a system of three interlocking circles, as illustrated in Figure 10.1. Because the circles interlock, each feeding material to the other, it is often difficult for reality to penetrate the system. George, after all, may have been telling your secrets to your worst enemy all along. You could easily have ignored any hints of this, since they would have been inconsistent with your evaluation and expectations of him. As was pointed out in Chapter 9, we find it quite easy to revise new evidence to fit an al-

OTHERS

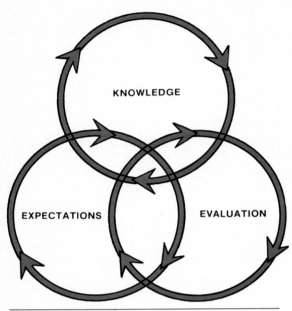

Figure 10.1

ready established social impression but quite difficult to revise the impression to fit new evidence.

What this means is that distortions in our perceptions of others tend to remain there. At times this creates no problem whatsoever. If your father, for example, thinks you are better-looking and smarter and kinder than you actually are, then you can simply count yourself lucky. We all need people who will see us more favorably than objectively—people who will give us the benefit of the doubt, who will automatically take our side, who will assume that the reason we didn't call was that we were too busy rather than too lazy. Love and loyalty depend on this kind of positive bias.

In other cases, however, distorted social perceptions can create serious conflicts in human relationships. This problem and how to deal with it will be the subject of the present chapter. To begin with, we will examine the ways in which inaccurate percep-

tions can damage our interactions with others. Then we will propose a method for undoing the damage.

PROBLEM PERCEPTIONS

We have already seen, in Chapter 9, how inaccurate perceptions can distort our responses to human beings in general, the people who walk in and out of our lives every day. We are too easily swayed by good looks. We accept or dismiss people on the basis of first impressions. We rely on stereotypes. We generalize and fantasize. As a result, our response to the man on the street or the woman down the hall is often far from appropriate.

A more serious problem is that we often do no better in perceiving those who are close to us: our parents, our sisters and brothers, our children, our spouses, our friends. In fact, we may do considerably worse.

Wishful Thinking

Our intimates mean a great deal to us. To some degree, our self-esteem, our happiness, and our sense of fulfillment depend on what they do and who they are. Consequently, we tend to mix a great deal of *wishful thinking* into our images of them (Bower, 1977). We want and need the person to be *x*, and therefore we see her as *x*. Yet at the same time, she is busy being *y*. And when we finally notice this disturbing fact, we feel cheated, as if she had broken a promise. The problem, of course, is that we made the promise for her. She had nothing to do with it.

The classic example of wishful thinking is the habit that parents have of nourishing fantasies about their children's future lives. The mother who regrets that she didn't go to medical school sees her bright little daughter as a future heart surgeon. When the bright little daughter grows up and an-

Our parents often think we are cuter, better-behaved, and more intelligent than a panel of unbiased observers would judge us to be. This is one type of unrealistic perception that we should simply accept and be grateful for. (Constantine Manos/Magnum)

the child is so dependent on his parents, he needs to see them as infinitely wise and capable. Therefore, in his eyes, they *are* infinitely wise and capable. In adolescence he makes the cruel discovery that they are only human, and he feels that they fooled him, cheated him, let him down. In short, we deceive ourselves about the other person, and then we blame the other person for deceiving us.

Outdated Images

A second difficulty is that our perceptions of those who are close to us are often out-of-date. Intimate relationships tend to be long lasting. As time passes, people change. Yet, as we have seen, once perceptions are established, they resist change (Wicklund and Brehm, 1976). So while the person being perceived grows and changes, the perception stays the same. The result is an *outdated image.*

Like the wishful image, the outdated image is a ripe source of conflict. The reformed alcoholic may be pained and angry to discover that no matter how sober he remains, his wife still thinks of him as having a "problem" and secretly turns down invitations to cocktail parties for fear that he will "slip." Likewise, adolescents constantly

nounces that she is going to art school, the mother feels betrayed.

Children, of course, make exactly the same mistake about their parents. Because

ACTIVITY 10.1

Choose two people to whom you are close. Write down the things about their physical appearance that you wish were different. You may well find that these "defects" affect your overall evaluation of them and even your behavior toward them. ("If Karen didn't have such heavy legs, I'd feel better about going to the beach with her." "I wouldn't mind introducing my sister to my friends if only she wouldn't wear such frumpy clothes.") You should ask yourself what these "defects" in appearance actually mean to you—what personal fears and ambitions underlie your concern about them. This may help you keep them in perspective.

BOX 10.1
A CASE OF PROBLEM PERCEPTIONS

In his novel *Something Happened* (1974), Joseph Heller portrays fear as the major component of people's perceptions of one another within a large company. Although this is an extreme example of distorted perception, it does illustrate the effects that social perception has on our behavior toward other people. It also shows the destructive side of those effects.

> In the office in which I work there are five people of whom I am afraid. Each of these five people is afraid of four people (excluding overlaps), for a total of twenty, and each of these twenty people is afraid of six people, making a total of one hundred and twenty people who are feared by at least one person. Each of these one hundred and twenty people is afraid of the other one hundred and nineteen, and all of these one hundred and forty-five people are afraid of the twelve men at the top who helped found and build the company and now own and direct it. (p. 15)

Sometimes the fear is mutual:

> In the normal course of a business day, I fear Green and Green fears me. I am afraid of Jack Green because my department is part of his department and Jack Green is my boss; Green is afraid of me because most of the work in my department is done for the Sales Department, and I am much closer to Andy Kagle and the other people in the Sales Department than he is. (p. 16)

And sometimes the fear is one-sided:

> In my department, there are six people who are afraid of me, and one small secretary who is afraid of all of us. I have one other person working for me who is not afraid of anyone, not even me, and I would fire him quickly, but I'm afraid of him. The thought occurs to me often that there must be mail clerks, office boys and girls, stock boys, messengers, and assistants of all kinds and ages who are

complain that their parents still see them as children—cuddly, cute, and helpless—whereas to them childhood is something they have left far behind.

Thus, two powerful forces, human hopes and human growth, tend to work against accurate perception in intimate relationships. This does not mean that our close relationships are doomed to frustration. Tolerance and affection make up for a great deal. Furthermore, as we saw earlier, some degree of distortion is quite harmless if it is positive. However, when one person holds an extremely inaccurate image of another, this is bound eventually to produce anger

and distrust. Indeed, it can threaten to destroy the relationship altogether. Let's look at a specific case.

The Case of Julie and Steve

Julie and Steve met while they were both seniors in college. Steve was a very fine student. He was also a rather carefree, disorganized, happy-go-lucky person. His wardrobe consisted of three T-shirts and a pair of baggy blue jeans. It was a rare day when his socks matched. Julie too was a reasonably good student, but unlike Steve, she had to work hard at it. He admired her efficiency

afraid of *everyone* in the company; and there is one typist in our department who is going crazy slowly and has all of *us* afraid of *her.* (p. 17)

The irony is that this one typist whom everyone perceives as going crazy is the happiest person in the office:

Her name is Martha. Our biggest fear is that she will go crazy on a weekday between nine and five. We hope she'll go crazy on a weekend, when we aren't with her. We should get her out of the company now, while there is still time. But we won't. Somebody should fire her; nobody will.

Oddly, she is much happier at her job than the rest of us. Her mind wanders from her work to more satisfying places, and she smiles and whispers contentedly to herself as she gazes out over her typewriter roller at the blank wall only a foot or two in front of her face, forgetting what or where she is and the page she is supposed to be copying. We walk away from her if we can, or turn our backs and try not to notice. We each hope somebody else will do or say something to make her stop smiling and chatting to herself each time she starts. When we cannot, in all decency, delay any longer doing it ourselves, we bring her back to our office and her work with gentle reminders that contain no implication of criticism or reproach. We feel she would be surprised and distraught if she knew what she was doing and that she was probably going mad. Other times she is unbearably nervous, unbearable to watch and be with. Everyone is very careful with her and very considerate. (pp. 17–18)

Heller, J. Something Happened. *New York: Knopf, 1974.*

and drive; she helped him keep his life in order. She admired his quick intelligence and his easygoing nature; he helped her relax. They dated regularly and married soon after graduation.

The following September Julie went to work as a secretary in a hospital in order to put Steve through law school. Julie's parents were not happy about this arrangement. But Julie said she wanted to "launch" Steve in his career; she would worry about her own career later. Steve, for his part, was willing to be launched. But he left the decision to Julie, and she decided.

In law school, Steve did very well, as usual, and after graduation, he was offered a job with a well-known law firm. Julie was delighted, and Steve was happy that she was so pleased. He hung his blue jeans in the closet, bought some suits and a briefcase, and went off to work at the law firm. Julie made sure his socks always matched.

But the law firm was very different from school. In return for his high salary, Steve found that he was expected to work about nine or ten hours a day. Furthermore, the atmosphere was hotly competitive. Everyone was jockeying for promotions. It seemed as though all the younger lawyers in the place were running a contest to see who could keep his office light burning the latest. Another thing that bothered Steve was that most of his clients were corporations. He had imagined himself working with human beings, on human problems. Instead, he was spending most of his time helping corporations save money on taxes. Tax law bored him.

But Steve didn't share too many of his complaints with Julie. She was so proud of him and of his job. Before, they had talked about her going to law school once they had enough money. But now she seemed more interested in his career than in starting one of her own. Furthermore, by now they had a baby. Julie seemed happy enough to stay at home with the baby as long as Steve was doing well. She was full of energy and full of ambition for him. Steve privately wished

he could put his briefcase in her hands and send her off to his job. He was sure she would do beautifully. For his part, he would have been happy to stay home with the baby.

As the months passed, Steve came to dislike his job more and more. But he also felt that it was partly because of this job that Julie valued him. The more he thought about this, the more anxiety he felt. He became jumpy and irritable, the complete opposite of his easygoing student self. He started sleeping badly and drinking too much.

Finally, he told Julie that he had to change jobs. And soon he found the job he wanted, with the Legal Aid Society. It paid about $7,000 a year less than his other job, but it had everything he wanted. The atmosphere was calm. He could wear his jeans to the

Distorted perceptions can cause great bitterness in marriage. Each partner keeps expecting the other to be something else besides what he or she is. And consequently each one is left confused and angry. (© Abigail Heyman/Archive Pictures)

office. He could leave work at five. He could relax and be himself again. Steve was happy.

Julie, however, was not happy. When Steve told her he wanted to leave the law firm, she had said everything that she knew she should say. Yes, he had a right to be happy. No, being a fancy tax lawyer was not the ultimate goal in life. Yes, they could, if they tried, live on less money. But she was angry. All that time typing admissions forms in the hospital—for this? So that Steve could *relax?* And where did that leave her? She felt she had nothing to be proud of, nothing to look forward to. All because Steve didn't want to overwork his brain. Suddenly he seemed to her lazy and selfish. He even began to *look* different to her. She hated his sloppy jeans, his slouched posture, his balding head, his big, silly grin. She lost interest in him sexually.

Steve, of course, was aware of her anger and was hurt and resentful in return. They didn't fight often. They simply kept their distance. Neither of them took any pleasure in the other one, but neither of them was willing to give up the marriage either.

Solutions

The problem with Julie and Steve is obviously one of inaccurate perception. Julie is trying to fit a round peg (Steve) into a square hole (her expectations of him). And most of us, at some time in our lives, do the same thing. When we say that our parents or children, our boyfriends or girlfriends, our husbands or wives or friends have disappointed us, what we are saying is that they have failed to conform to our perceptions of them.

What, then, do you do when you have a round peg and a square hole? There are three possible solutions. You can throw out the round peg and look for a square one. You can whittle away at the round peg until it fits a

square hole. Or you can whittle away at the square hole until a round peg can fit in it. Let us look at these solutions one at a time.

Throw Him Out

When a friend or a spouse fails to live up to your expectations of him or her, one choice is simply to end the relationship. This, of course, happens every day. People drop their friends and leave their spouses, sometimes for very good reasons.

For many married couples and many friends, however, the reasons are not quite good enough. The relationship is *not* a clear-cut hopeless case. The sense of attachment remains; it is simply a painful attachment. In such cases, the relationship deserves working on. (This is particularly true in a time when so many people complain that their relationships are shallow and brief.) And in the case of problems with our parents or our children, who can't be divorced or replaced, we need to make every effort at adjustment. But how, and what, do we adjust?

Make Him Change

A second solution is to ask the person to change, even force him to change, by threatening to end the relationship if he doesn't change (Bach and Wyden, 1969). In some instances, this is a fair tactic. For example, a spouse who beats the children or gets drunk every night should be asked to change—fast. In other instances, it is perfectly fair to ask the other person to change *with* you, in order to improve the relationship.

But before you demand any serious change in the other person, you have to ask yourself whether the demand is a fair one. Is he clearly violating your rights? Or is it that you would just like him to be a different kind of person?

The second question brings us to a rather subtle problem. Sometimes the other person unwittingly encourages our hopes that he will be "a different kind of person" (Frank and Kupfer, 1976). In a close relationship, the other person almost always senses the perception that you have of him. And if that perception makes you like him better, he will usually cooperate somewhat in maintaining it, even if it is inaccurate. To some degree, he will try to be, or seem to be, the thing that you want him to be. After all, he values your affection. But when this game infringes too greatly on his freedom, he will insist once again on being himself. And when you complain that he has violated your image of him, he will probably answer that your image of him is *your* problem; *he* is, and always has been, a unique individual, and is not about to be made over to your specifications.

In other words, inaccurate perceptions are usually not the fault of the perceiver alone. Nevertheless, the fact that the other person may have acted as an accomplice still does not mean that he is obligated, once the game is up, to conform to your inaccurate perception. For example, in the case just presented, Steve, wanting to please Julie, went along with her image of him. But she clearly has no right to *demand* that he be her idea of a fancy lawyer. In short, we have to consider, before we ask people to change, whether they truly owe it to us to change.

Change the Way You Perceive Him

If you don't want to throw away the round peg and don't have the right to pare it down to fit the square hole, then you have to go to work on the square hole. In other words, you have to change your perception of the other person so that it fits him better. But how? The rest of our chapter will be devoted to answering this question.

ANALYZING SOCIAL PERCEPTIONS

The first thing that must be said is that your social perceptions, like your self-concept and your pattern of self-control, *can* definitely be changed. Keep in mind that you have changed them many times in the past. For example, you certainly don't view your parents now the way you did when you were a child. As you matured, you changed your perception of them, probably without being aware of it. By the same token, you can, with full awareness and quite deliberately, change your present social perceptions if they are interfering with your adjustment. Remember: social perceptions are not sacred truths. Like the self-concept, they are pictures that we have pieced together—incomplete and often inaccurate. Therefore we have no reason to be sentimentally attached to them. If the picture doesn't resemble the person, go to work on it until it does.

First, however, you must analyze the perception to find out what the basic problem is and what is causing it. As before, analysis requires two steps: description and functional analysis.

Description

In order to conduct a useful analysis, we must, as we have seen, begin with a simple, objective, and specific description. Yet our view of another person, like our view of ourselves, is anything but simple, objective, and specific. On the contrary, it is complicated, subjective, and vague. Hence, the best procedure is the one we used in describing the self-concept—that is, isolating the basic negative label. If you had to lodge one complaint against the other person, what would it be? State this complaint and the emotion that goes with it: "My roommate is inconsiderate, and this makes me furious"; "My girlfriend isn't affectionate, and this makes me feel hurt."

Such a statement satisfies the requirement of simplicity. We are still left with the requirements of objectivity and specificity. In order to have some information to work on in your functional analysis, you have to fill out your statement with objective facts and specific details. What, objectively, does the other person do? And how, specifically, do you feel about it? To return to the problems of Steve and Julie, Julie's complaint has already been stated: Steve, in her eyes, is lazy and selfish, and her dominant emotion is clearly anger. She fills in the objective facts and specific details of her complaint as follows:

I look at him and I see all those brains and all that talent—wasted. He is really the smartest person I've ever known. He sees to the bottom of a problem before anyone else does. In school he always did better than anyone else with about half as much work. He was always at the top in everything.

Obviously, that kind of talent should be used. So I put him through law school, and sure enough, he got a beautiful job. And I saw him moving to the top again. Sure, the job was hard. But anything worth having takes work.

He doesn't see it that way, and that's why he chucked the job. He wants a job that will guarantee that he can read magazines on his lunch hour and be free at five o'clock so that he can come home and just hang around in those baggy old jeans. Mostly, he reads or watches TV or plays with the baby—anything that means no challenge, no pressure. They should have given brains to somebody else.

The problem is, it seems to me, that he just doesn't care very much about his family. All he cares about is himself. I'm hurt and angry. I feel as though he's not holding up his end of the bargain.

Now we have more information on Julie's negative labeling of Steve. Specifically, we can see that Steve's intelligence is extremely important to her and she felt she had a contract with him, based on that intelligence. These factors, as we will see shortly, should be important in the functional analysis.

Situational Description

At the bottom of Julie's complaint is one action: Steve's quitting his job. But many problems in our personal relationships have to do with repeated actions—a painful script that is played over and over again. At least once a week you manage somehow to have the same fight with your father at the dinner table. Or every other time you want to make love with your husband, the two of you go through the same discouraging round of teasing. In such cases, it is very useful to write a situational description, either included in or separate from your general description. We have already discussed situational descriptions in earlier chapters. In this case the situational description should be a paragraph or two depicting an actual situation in which the other person behaves according to your negative label of him and in which you respond with the negative emotion tied to that label. In other words, write out the script of that dinnertime fight or that no-I-don't-want-to-yes-I-do sexual routine.

Functional Analysis

Now that you have your description, you can proceed to the functional analysis. What is causing and maintaining the negative evaluation? As usual, there are two kinds of variables to consider: external and internal. We will start with the external variables, the most obvious.

External Variables: The Outer Person

Rather ordinary concrete facts about another person—what he is physically and what he says and does—can easily annoy us or make us uncomfortable (Williams, 1979). A person doesn't have to look like Count Dracula for his appearance to disturb us. One of Richard Nixon's major problems throughout his political career was that many voters thought his face, and particularly his smile, looked shifty. Likewise, a person does not have to kick a dog for us to respond negatively to his actions. He may do nothing worse than avoid eye contact with us while we're talking to him, and we will probably dislike him. Or if he is a friend, we will assume that he is angry with us or is hiding something from us. In other words, we definitely do care about the outer person. Indeed, we

A constant problem in Richard Nixon's political campaigns was that many people responded negatively to his face, and especially his smile, which sometimes seemed forced. This distrust was summed up in a political poster which showed a picture of Nixon with the caption, "Would you buy a used car from this man?"

evaluate the inner person on the basis of the outer person.

Therefore, in analyzing your problem perception, you should take note of external stimuli. Look at your description and pick out any facts that you wrote down about the person's body or clothes, his little habits, and his major actions. Julie, for example, is annoyed by Steve's quitting his prestigious job and his tendency just to "hang around," but she is also annoyed by his blue jeans, his slouch, and the fact that he is losing his hair. Though we may be embarrassed that such innocent little physical details can anger us, we must be aware of them if we hope to find the cause of our negative perception.

Internal Variables

The blue jeans and the slouched posture are, as we just saw, involved in Julie's negative evaluation of Steve. But are they really a primary cause? Interestingly, when Steve was in college, his posture was just as bad, and he wore jeans every day. That was when Julie met him. His appearance seemed to her charmingly casual. It was one of the things that attracted her to him. Why should this very same appearance seem oafish to her now?

Let us recall what we said in Chapter 4 about the influence of external and internal variables on the self-concept. External variables—a dreary room, a remark uttered in a certain tone of voice—can make people feel bad about themselves. But even behavioral psychologists, the psychologists who are most concerned with external, observable evidence, acknowledge that there is an important middle step between the external stimulus and its effect on the self-concept. That step is the person's interpretation of the external stimulus. And it is the interpretation, the internal stimulus, that directly affects the self-concept. As we saw,

Albert Ellis and Robert Harper proposed the A-B-C formula for this process: A (activating event) is fed into B (the person's belief system) and comes out as C (the emotional consequence).

This formula can be applied to social perception as well as self-perception. Our perception of another person is of course based on the external stimuli that the person emits in our direction, but not directly. It is based directly on the vibrations that those stimuli set off in our belief system. In the 1960s parents and school principals raged at male students who grew their hair long. Long hair on a male was considered effeminate, unclean, weird. Long-haired students were expelled from school and barred from graduation ceremonies. Their parents threatened to carry them bound and gagged to the barber. Ten years later, strangely enough, many parents and principals had long hair. Why? The belief system had changed. Long hair was no longer weird; it was fashionable. In short, if the external stimulus rubs the belief system right, the evaluation is positive; if the external stimulus rubs the belief system wrong, the evaluation is negative (Ross, 1977).

Expectations. Each of us has a special little belief system devoted to each of the people that we most care about (Rausch et al., 1974). A wife has a belief system organized around the image of her husband. A father has a belief system organized around the image of his daughter. These person-specific beliefs are our *expectations.* We mentioned expectations at the beginning of this chapter. They tell us what the other person could be and could do, and what he "should" be and "should" do. Against these coulds and shoulds we measure what we know about the other person. Is he doing what he could and should? If so, he makes us happy. If not, he makes us angry.

Expectations, then, are the key to understanding our negative evaluation of another person and the negative emotions that accompany it (Cohen, 1981). Let's return to Steve's blue jeans. In college, jeans were part of Julie's expectations of Steve. She expected him to be a bright student with a relaxed attitude toward life, and jeans fit quite comfortably into this little belief system. But once he graduated from law school she expected him to become something else: a well-tailored, hard-working, ambitious young professional. And so the jeans no longer fit into the picture. But once Steve changed jobs, the jeans reappeared daily. And they served to remind her at every turn that Steve was not going to fulfill her expectations of the "successful lawyer" husband. They were a symbol of her disappointed expectations.

Blue jeans, however, are no crime. And neither is working for the Legal Aid Society. Therefore, what Julie has to pinpoint, analyze, and change are her expectations. And if you wish to change a negative evaluation of someone you care about, you have to do the same thing.

Pinpointing Expectations. How can you pinpoint your expectations? First, look at your description. Whatever your main complaint is, your expectation should be something close to the opposite. This is clear in Julie's description. Steve, she claims, is lazy and selfish. Clearly, what he *should* be is a hard-working, well-dressed man who is concerned with pleasing her rather than pleasing himself.

However, this method—calculating the opposite of your complaint—will give you only a general idea of your expectations. You need to fill in the specifics by "interviewing" yourself at the exact moment when you experience a wave of negative feeling about the other person. Catch yourself in mid-spasm and ask yourself: What is he doing "wrong"? What should he be doing instead? Keep up this exercise for a week, always writing down the answer to your second question. At the end of this period, go through your notes. Eliminate the repetitions and move to the top of the list the items that were repeated most often. Then you will have a clear, specific list of your expectations, in order of frequency of disappointment.

REEXAMINING EXPECTATIONS

You have pinpointed your expectations. And having seen them in action, in your moments of anger, you know that these expectations are a major cause of conflict with the other person. So what do you do now? Can you simply throw out your expectations? Probably not. You have hung on to them in the face of plentiful evidence that the person is not going to fulfill them. It is not likely that at this point you can simply abandon them without a second look.

Thus, what you need is to take that second look. You need to reexamine your expectations and pick out the flaws in them. By doing so, you will find out what mistakes you have to correct in order to make your expectations more realistic. Furthermore—and this is important—you will prove to

yourself that your expectations *are* unrealistic. It is one thing to be told by a textbook that problems in relationships are often caused by unrealistic expectations and that these expectations should be corrected. It is another thing to face the evidence that *you* have actually created a distorted picture of another person: that you have done what the textbooks say people do. Only when you see the distortions—your own personal ones, not just Julie's—will you have good enough reasons, specific and personal reasons, to change.

So let us cross-examine your expectations.

The Primacy Effect

How much of what you expect from the other person is based on what the person was once, but is no longer? The primacy effect, as we have seen in Chapter 9, is the staying power of a first impression. It seems odd to imagine that first impressions might have anything to do with our perception of people we have known for years. Yet they do, in a more general sense.

As we noted at the beginning of this chapter, our impressions of our intimates tend to be out of date. We demand that they be now what they were five or ten years ago, or when we first knew them. Let us imagine that you are having problems with your marriage and that you take these problems to

---

ACTIVITY 10.2

Think about the last time you had a serious quarrel with someone close—your father or your spouse, for example. Write a brief description of the quarrel, including its subject, the grievances that each of you brought forth, and so on. Then think about and jot down the expectations involved in this situation: not only those you held of the other person, but also those you imagine he or she held of you. You will probably discover that a conflict in expectations was one of the underlying reasons for the clash.

your mother. She, you imagine, is the person you need right now. Whatever else she is, she has always been strong, firm, and decisive, and you are feeling very weak, shaky, and indecisive. But when you tell her your troubles, you find that she does not act as you expected. She cries, she flutters, she seems totally overwhelmed by the problem. You end up having to comfort *her* ("Don't worry—it'll be all right—it'll all be solved— don't worry"). But you go away feeling very angry. How could she be so weak, so flustered, so stupid? True, she has her own troubles. She was widowed two years ago and is now worried about having to retire early from her job because of arthritis. True, but she was always so strong, and this time you needed her strength. How could she have failed you like this?

People fail us by changing. But they have

BOX 10.2
THE PERCEPTION OF INSANITY

One place in which first impressions can have a powerful impact is the psychiatric ward. When a psychiatrist in a hospital diagnoses a new patient—that is, decides what kind of psychological problem the person has—he usually does so on the basis of a first impression, gathered in one interview with the patient. That first impression may be completely incorrect, but once it is converted into a diagnostic label, it becomes almost permanent. A very interesting study by David Rosenhan (1973) showed how this process works.

Rosenhan and seven volunteers went to eight different hospitals claiming that they had been hearing voices saying something like "hollow," "empty," or "thud." They all gave false names, and those who were in the mental health profession lied about their jobs. Otherwise, they answered truthfully all the psychiatrists' questions about their jobs, their marriages, and their lives in general. One was diagnosed as depressive. The other seven were diagnosed as schizophrenic. (For an explanation of these diagnostic labels, see the Human Issue essay entitled "Abnormal Psychology," pages 29–33.) And all of them were hospitalized.

From then on, each of the "pseudopatients"

acted completely normal. From the moment they were admitted to the hospital, all of them wanted very badly to get out, and the only way they could do so was to act as sane as possible. (They had all agreed not to give in and reveal that they were there as part of a study.) So they were model patients—friendly, well behaved, rational, cooperative. Yet no staff member in any one of the hospitals ever expressed any doubt that the pseudopatients were insane. They had been diagnosed as insane, and therefore they were insane.

Their hospital stays ranged from 7 to 52 days, with an average of 19 days. And when they were discharged, it was not because someone figured out that they were sane after all. The seven pseudopatients who had been diagnosed as schizophrenic were discharged with a diagnosis of "schizophrenia in remission"—that is, schizophrenia that for the time being had died down. Their "condition" had improved, and therefore they could go home, but only as insane people whose condition had improved. The first impression—that they were suffering from serious mental disturbance—was never questioned.

a right to change, just as we do. The failing, therefore, is not theirs. It is ours, if we cannot adjust our expectations to fit the present person rather than the past person.

Cross-examining for outdated expectations:

1. Review the list of your expectations for the other person.
2. Think back to earlier stages—perhaps the earliest stage—of your relationship with this person, and ask yourself what it was in the person that raised each of these expectations. Draw the connection between the qualities the person had and the expectations you formed. (For example, you should draw a mental connecting line between your expectation that your mother be a pillar of strength and the fact that she *was*, or seemed to be, a pillar of strength during your childhood and adolescence.)
3. Switch your focus from the past person to the present person, the person you saw last night or last week. Can those same connecting lines still be drawn? Does the person's present behavior indicate that she can still support the expectations that you based on her past behavior? If not, your expectations have to be brought up to date.

Distorting and Screening Out

How much information about the other person have you distorted or simply ignored because it didn't fit into your set of expectations? In the drive for cognitive consistency, we perceive very selectively the facts that are presented to us. On the basis of our implicit theories of personality (Chapter 9) and on the basis of wishful thinking, we choose the facts that "fit" and leave out the facts that don't fit. The result may be a very handsome set of expectations—well-rounded, consistent, admirable. But it may also be very inaccurate.

This is not to say that we are actually unaware of facts that don't fit our expectations of another person. (If we were unaware, we would never be disappointed.) A person may be very much aware—aware that her boss' solution to frustration is to have three martinis with lunch, that her son is not a good reader, that her husband is vain about his looks and primps in front of the mirror. The point is that this awareness does not alter her expectations (Hastie, 1980). The expectations are kept in an airtight compartment, uncontaminated by reality. What the other person does is one thing; what he could do and should do is another thing. Thus, the expectations remain the "rule" and the person's behavior is the exception to the rule—or rather, the breaking of the rule, the violation. The result, of course, is that the other person is condemned to the role of chronic offender. And you, the keeper of the rules, are condemned to constant anger or disappointment.

Central Traits

An excellent source of distortion-for-the-sake-of-consistency is the central trait. As we saw in Chapter 9, a central trait is a trait around which we organize our perception of another person. We settle on one quality, then make the person's other qualities conform in our minds to that central quality.

Look back, for example, to the case of Julie and Steve. It's clear from Julie's description that she has organized her perception of Steve around the central trait of intelligence. Steve is brainy—she makes this point repeatedly. But he is other things as well. For one thing, he appears to be a rather passive person. Yet, to Julie's thinking, passivity is inconsistent with intelligence. And since intelligence is, in her mind, his central trait, the "inconsistent" passivity is all the more unacceptable. So she screens it out; it has no place in her expectations for him. At the same time, however, Steve goes on being a rather passive person, with the result that Julie's expectations are constantly being violated.

The problem with central traits and with all other efforts at consistency in perception is that they oversimplify the other person's personality (Schneider et al., 1979). Think back to the self-concept. As we mentioned in Chapter 3, one of the most important qualities of a positive and realistic self-concept is diversity. When the self-concept is organized not into one or two qualities, but into a wide variety of "personality pigeon-holes," then the individual is able to understand and accept the wide variety of his feelings and actions. The same holds true of our concepts of others. When we try to understand them in terms of a limited but consistent set of expectations, they will be neither understandable nor acceptable. For other people's personalities, like our own, are wide, various, and often inconsistent.

Expectations, then, must be broadened—opened up to reality. Steve is both intelligent and passive. Johnny is bad at reading and good in math. Your husband is vain about his looks but modest about his achievements. These different qualities, even if they seem inconsistent, should be included in our expectations if we wish to understand and take pleasure in the other person.

Cross-examining for distorted expectations:

1. Review your list of expectations for the other person. Ask yourself how consistent they are. Do they all fit together nicely? If so, be suspicious.
2. Look back at your main complaint against the other person. How possible is it that this complaint is simply a negative reading ("lazy and selfish") of qualities that are quite natural to the other person (passivity, love of relaxation, lack of desire to "get ahead")? And how possible is it that you screened out these qualities because they were not consistent with your wishful expectations? If it *is* possible, then your expectations may need to be modified in light of the screened-out information.

Inferred Qualities

Just as we distort and screen out information about other people, so too do we add "information" of our own making. (See the discussion of assumed content in Chapter 9.) From the characteristics we actually see in a person, we *infer* other characteristics and tack them onto our set of expectations (Jones and Davis, 1965). Like distortions and screening out, inferences are based on our implicit theories of personality and on wishful thinking. We add what seems "logical" and what we would like to see.

Julie, for example, inferred from Steve's intelligence that he was also ambitious. To her this was logical: If you have brains like that, you use them to "get ahead"—to become "important" and "successful." And like most people, she found "evidence" when she looked for it. After all, didn't he take that job with the high-powered law firm? This might seem to Julie a reasonable attribution, but it is a false one. Steve took that first job not because he was ambitious, but because the job was offered to him and because Julie wanted him to take it. As usual, he did what seemed easiest—in this case, what others wanted him to do. But when the job proved too painful, he quit. And this left Julie with her expectations unfulfilled—expectations based on a mistaken inference, supported by mistaken attributions. This is what she means when she says, at the end of her description, that he is not holding up his end of the bargain.

Unfortunately, the bargain existed only in her mind.

Inferences can be very harmful. They create expectations that cannot be fulfilled and therefore almost guarantee disappointment. They should be carefully weeded out of your perception of the other person.

Cross-examining for inferences:

1. Look at your list of expectations. What are the personal qualities on which you base these expectations? Are you sure that the person really has these qualities?
2. Try to come up with facts to prove the existence of those qualities. Could these facts as easily be evidence for other qualities—qualities that you may not value greatly but that the person may have nevertheless?

Inappropriate Standards

A final factor that we should examine is the standards on which we have based our expectations. The standards we hold for the people close to us are usually much higher than those we hold for human beings in general. Furthermore, these standards often have nothing whatever to do with the individual to whom we apply them. They are dragged in from our earlier years, long before we ever knew this person. Nevertheless, they form part of our expectations and contribute to making these expectations unrealistic. Let us look at four common standards by which we measure people close to us: (1) ourselves, (2) our unrealized goals, (3) the opinions of people outside the situation, and (4) social conventions.

Be Like Me

One of the most inappropriate, yet one of the most commonly used standards for judging others is ourselves (Nisbett and Ross,

1980). An interesting recent study showed that women for whom femininity is an important feature of the self-concept are likely to perceive others in terms of their femininity or masculinity (Tunnell, 1981). For such a woman, obviously, the femininity of her daughter—also the masculinity of her son—is going to be an important issue. Another woman, whose self-esteem is based in large part on her success in business, will be more concerned over whether her children are doing well enough in school to land good jobs when they graduate. Woe to any tomboy daughter born to the first woman, and to any lackadaisical student born to the second!

If asked whether we ourselves constitute models for perfect behavior, most of us would probably answer no. Furthermore, many of us know what it is like to be on the other side—to be declared a disappointment because we chose to be different from someone (a parent, say) who cared about us. Yet we often repeat the same error in our own adulthood. We try to make people over into ourselves. We expect them to enjoy the movies we enjoy, to support the political candidate we support, to wear the clothes we find attractive, to see things *our* way. In doing so, we violate the other person's rights as an individual. Furthermore, we condemn ourselves to frustration, for the other person can never be turned into a duplicate of ourselves. And ironically, if we managed to intimidate her to the point where she did try to convert her personality into ours, we would probably lose respect for her.

Make My Dream Come True

A variation on the "be-like-me" standard is the "make-my-dream-come-true" standard. Here the measuring stick is not ourselves, but what we wish we were (Knudson et al., 1980). Unable or unwilling to pursue our goal, we seek to achieve it vicariously through the other person. The most common example is the parent who fantasizes a glorious professional career for his child and then feels cheated when the child does not fulfill the fantasy. But parents are not the only ones who engage in this self-defeating exercise. Spouses do it too. In the case of Julie and Steve, for example, it is clearly Julie who is the ambitious one in the family. Yet she expects Steve to fulfill her ambitions.

"Make-my-dream-come-true" is often the resort of the underdog—the parent who had to go to work before he could finish high school or college, the wife who feels (with some justification) that her husband has a better chance than she in the job market. Hence, their yearning for vicarious fulfillment is understandable. One's own ambitions, fulfilled or not, are one's own ambitions. The other person has *his* own ambitions. Trying to replace his ambitions with yours, like trying to replace his tastes and personality with yours, is a violation of

Parents often try to persuade their children to be like them. After all, to the parents their values, opinions, and lifestyle are the best, and why shouldn't their children have the best? (Robert A. Isaacs/Photo Researchers, Inc.)

his rights as a human being and an almost certain guarantee of conflict.

What the Neighbors Think

Most of us want other people to approve of the people we care for. We want our parents to like our girlfriend, our old high-school friend to like our new college friend, our college friend to like our brother. Yet this approval is not always offered. And when it isn't, this does not constitute permission for us to try to change the person being judged into a more "approvable" commodity.

Expecting those who are close to us to measure up to other people's standards is even more unjust than expecting them to fulfill our own private standards. It places the locus of approval outside the relationship. The person in question chose you and seeks your approval, but she should not have to worry about the approval of all the other people you associate with. To expect her to do so is an insult to her individuality. Furthermore, like other unrealistic standards, it breeds unnecessary bitterness in the relationship.

What You Are *Supposed* to Do

A final standard that can create unrealistic expectations is social convention: the standard social norms regarding what people are "supposed" to do. Roles, for example, are surrounded by norms. A man is "supposed" to be strong (not flighty or emotional), to take the initiative in sexual matters, and to solve problems in a rational manner. A woman is "supposed" to be gentle, emotional, and nurturing. But what if your husband is not fulfilling his socially decreed male role? What if he tends to be more gentle, warm, and sympathetic than you, while expecting you to take the initiative in sex and to be the rational problem-solver? One alternative is to take the side of society and condemn him for violating the social norm; since he is not man enough for society, he is not man enough for you. The other alternative is to ask yourself whether it is really necessary to your relationship that he be the "he-man" type. If this is not part of his nature, why should it be part of your expectations for him? If you're good at solving problems and if it's only the social norm that makes you feel uncomfortable making the first move in bed, then your expectations need revising to reflect the needs of your relationship rather than the conventions of your society.

Cross-examining for inappropriate standards:

1. Look at your list of expectations. Ask yourself what standards they're based on. Your personality and tastes? Your ambitions? The preferences of people outside the relationship? Social conventions?
2. Having located the standard, ask yourself what it has to do with the other person. Do you have the right to ask him to observe this standard?

CHANGING SOCIAL PERCEPTIONS

If you've found that your expectations don't stand up well under cross-examination, you need to change your perception of the person in question. You do this by experimenting with your expectations, the presumed cause of your negative perception. We propose a two-step method: (1) gather new information about the person and incorporate this information into your expectations, and (2) challenge expectations through self-talk.

Gathering New Information

As we saw earlier in this chapter, we tend to distort much of the information presented to us by the people close to us. We may simply ignore it, or we may alter it to fit our prevailing image of the person, or we may see it as an annoying exception to the "real" person—that is, the person of our expectations. In any case, the information is not permitted to influence our expectations. The first step in gathering new information about the other person is to pay serious attention to the information we're likely to distort. The second step is an active seeking out of information by asking for feedback on our perceptions.

Incongruous, Embarrassing, or Threatening Information

The best sign that we are receiving information that doesn't fit our perception of a person is a sense of mental discomfort. This may be simply a feeling of incongruity, or it may be more intense: a feeling of embarrassment or actual threat. Watch for these emotional signals and catch the information before you distort it.

Imagine, for example, that you are with your boyfriend. You expect him to be a secure and confident person, and you are always bothered when he shows signs of weakness. (This has caused problems between you in the past.) The two of you are talking to a group of people, and suddenly you hear your boyfriend giving a very exaggerated account of his achievements as a high school football player. The other people are impressed, but you are confused and embarrassed. Perhaps you're even a bit threatened. His need to impress these people, even to the point of dishonesty, doesn't fit your expectation. Before you distort this piece of information or classify it as an "exception" to your "rule" (expectation) and allow yourself to get angry, hold it fast in your mind. Has he ever done this before? Yes. Then your expectations are unrealistic. Your boyfriend

Father makes dinner while mother stays late at the office. Such role-adjustments, because they violate conventional patterns, may affect interpersonal perception. The husband, for example, may feel that the wife "should" be home making dinner. Such conventional "should's" must be carefully examined. (© Mark Antman/The Image Works)

has a weakness—a need to impress people, even to the point of tampering somewhat with the truth. And you should modify your expectations of him in view of that weakness, rather than screening it out.

By practicing this mental exercise every time your expectations are rubbed the wrong way, you will add considerably to your list of "personality pigeonholes" for the other person. The resulting perception will be less ideal than your original perception, but that's all to the good. Idealized perceptions have no place in intimate relationships (Luckey, 1960). They strait-jacket the other person, and in the end they lead to disappointment and rejection. Realistic perceptions, on the other hand, lead to intimacy, acceptance, and freedom.

Feedback

A second way of getting new information about the other person is ask him for it. That is, let him know how you perceive him and then ask him for feedback (Knudson et al., 1980).

We seldom consider telling the other person what we truly think of him. He simply has to guess at it, on the basis of our behavior. And if he doesn't like what he guesses ("You think I'm an idiot!" "You expect me to be more of an intellectual than I really am"), we can always claim that he misinterpreted our behavior. In this way mistaken perceptions can be maintained for decades.

To "come clean"—to tell the other person how you see him and how you interpret his behavior—might seem difficult or embarrassing. But unless you make some effort in this direction, you are really working in the dark. As one psychologist put it, "it is impossible to understand why a person behaves in a certain way in a certain situation unless you understand how he perceives that situation. . . . Behavior by itself explains nothing" (Swensen, 1973, p. 12).

To obtain feedback on your perception of the other person, talk to him in a calm and private moment. Tell him how you see him, including what your expectations are (you might show him your list) and how they are being disappointed. Then give him the opportunity to correct your perception. This is not to say that he necessarily has the absolute truth about himself. But by putting his perception of himself together with your perception of him, you may be able to construct a more accurate picture. And regardless of how accurate the picture is, he can definitely let you know which of your expectations he can, or wants to, satisfy and which disappointments you will have to live with. With this feedback, you can form a more realistic set of expectations.

Challenging Expectations Through Self-Talk

You now have new information. From cross-examining your expectations, you know how they should be corrected. From paying attention to discomforting information and from soliciting feedback, you know what should be added, modified, and omitted.

But information alone will not change your expectations. The expectations are old and have become automatic. They will not change in the light of your new information unless you deliberately and systematically use that information to combat them. This can be done through self-talk, the technique we learned in Chapter 4. (The self-talk procedure for changing social perceptions is similar to the self-talk procedure for changing the self-concept. Therefore, it might be useful at this point to review the earlier procedure, page 113.) To illustrate, we will put Julie through the exercise.

Listening to Self-Talk

Stop yourself at a moment when the person has done something you don't like and you're evaluating him negatively. Instead of simply feeling your anger or disappointment, articulate in your own mind the words to express your feeling. What *exactly* is he doing wrong?

Julie and Steve are at a party. Another lawyer asks Steve why he changed jobs. Steve says, "Oh, the pace was just too crazy. I'd like to do something in life besides work." Julie feels anger, and she enunciates it to herself: "Why couldn't he say he wanted to help the poor, or something respectable? Why does he have to admit that he's too lazy to work hard?"

Examining the Expectation

After enunciating your complaint, locate the expectation on which it is based. Ask yourself if it is a fair expectation, reflecting a realistic perception of the other person.

Julie locates the expectation. It is that Steve should want to hide his lack of strong career ambitions—that he should consider this shameful. She asks herself whether this is a fair expectation. It isn't. She may be ashamed of his lack of ambition, but she has no right to ask him to be.

Talking Back

If the expectation is not fair or realistic, talk back to it. Tell yourself in what way it is inappropriate. (Remember your cross-examination.) Then enunciate to yourself a more reasonable expectation, based on the new information you have gathered.

Julie talks to herself: "I can't expect him to be ashamed of wanting to take life easy. Just because he has brains, that doesn't mean he should be hell-bent on cashing in on them. No, this is not going to work. I have to expect that he's going to take his work in his stride and enjoy himself as much as possible. And I can't ask him to be ashamed of this. There's nothing shameful about it."

Acting on Your Back-Talk

Once you talk back to the old expectation, your negative evaluation and negative emotion—both of them based on that old expectation—will lose hold. Let them go. Act on the basis of your new expectation. In Julie's situation—after all, she is with a group of people—she can do little more than perhaps support his statement that the job was too hectic. But to Steve, these would probably be welcome words. And they would represent a small step toward an improved relationship.

Of course, a social perception that has been formed over a number of years can't be changed in one evening. In repairing negative social perceptions, as in repairing a negative self-concept, self-talk must be practiced repeatedly. But eventually the new knowledge and new evaluation of the other person will make the new expectations as automatic as the old. And then the circle of your perception, having been broken open and tinkered with, can once again close, in a new form. The vicious cycle of unrealistic expectations, incomplete knowledge, and negative evaluations will have become a benign cycle of realistic expectations, wider knowledge, and positive evaluations. And on the basis of this new perception, the relationship cannot help but become more honest and more accepting.

Are You Buckling Under?

We have one last question to address. If, to improve a relationship, you have to change your expectations, doesn't this amount to buckling under (and brainwashing yourself into liking it)? Aren't you getting the "raw end" of the deal?

It depends. And what it depends on is the justice of your complaint against the other person. As we pointed out earlier in this chapter, there are situations in which it is perfectly fair to ask the other person to change, or, more often, to ask him to change *along with you*. This kind of two-way adjustment will be the subject of Chapter 12.

But there are situations in which it is not fair to ask the other person to change, and those situations have been the subject of this chapter. When the demand is that the other person essentially alter his personality, simply because these alterations would be more to your liking, then the demand is unfair.

Here we encounter one of the central tenets of humanistic and existential psychology: interpersonal relationships, to remain healthy, must allow for individuality. Certain things we can negotiate; other things we must accept. And one thing we must accept and respect is the other person's "otherness": his uniqueness, his difference from us and from everyone else. This doesn't mean that we have to like everything about him. But it does mean that we should acknowledge, and fit into our expectations, the other person's *whole* self—including what we don't like along with what we do like. To acknowledge only a part of the other person and to look upon the other parts as clay for us to mold into a more attractive shape is to deny that person his individuality. He is what he is. He cannot be made over to give us a sense of fulfillment. He should be allowed to seek his own fulfillment, and we should seek ours.

Julie and Steve: A Proposal

The subject of self-fulfillment suggests a happy ending for the story of Julie and Steve. Self-talk may help Julie acknowledge Steve's whole self, and thus to improve the relationship. But Julie is still left with a bundle of unfulfilled ambitions and unexpended energies. This is a part of *her* self that she tried to satisfy through Steve. But Steve will not satisfy this part of her, and there is no good reason why he should. So perhaps it is time that she satisfy it herself—by dividing the housework with Steve, going to law school as she had once planned, buying her own briefcase, and becoming an ambitious lawyer.

SUMMARY

1. A social perception is an interlocking network of knowledge, expectations, and evaluations. Because each component reinforces the others, a social perception is a self-perpetuating system, highly resistant to change. Distortions in our views of others may endure for years, despite new information.

2. Two important causes of unrealistic social perceptions are *wishful thinking*, the habit of seeing others as we wish they were, and *outdated images*, images based on the person's earlier behavior, without consideration that he has since changed.

3. To change a social perception, we must begin by analyzing it. First we describe our view of the other person, focusing on a negative label. Filling out this label with a specific situational description is very helpful.

4. In the functional analysis of a social perception, we should examine both external and internal variables. An extremely important internal variable is our set of expectations regarding the other person. These expectations should be pinpointed.

5. Expectations that bring us into conflict with the other person should be reexamined in order to make them more realistic. We should see whether the primacy effect has biased our view, causing us to ignore changes in the other person.

We should also ask ourselves whether we are distorting or screening out information that does not "fit" with our expectations, particularly with a central trait that we have assigned to the other person.

6. Inferred qualities—qualities that we attribute to the person on the basis of other, related qualities—may encourage unrealistic expectations. Another common source of unrealistic expectations is *inappropriate standards*. Such standards may be based on ourselves, our unrealized goals, the opinions of others, or social norms.

7. If our expectations do not stand up well under cross-examination, we need to change our perception of the person in question. The first step is to increase our knowledge of the other person by resisting the temptation to screen out or distort information that seems to us incongruous, embarrassing, or threatening. We can also ask the other person for feedback concerning our perception of him.

8. This new information should be put to use in self-talk exercises—listening to what we tell ourselves about the other person, examining the expectation involved, talking back, and then acting on the basis of the revised expectation.

PROJECT

Examining your own perception of someone is probably the best way to learn the material that is discussed in this chapter. We have noted that one cause of inaccurate social perceptions is an outdated image—for example, a parent's image of an adolescent as a dependent child. Most of us have a brother, a sister, or a cousin with whom we have had a long relationship but whom we view negatively in some way. How accurate is the perception? Using such a person as the target, follow the procedure outlined in the chapter, presented below in fourteen steps. A suggestion: if you have several siblings or cousins to choose from, pick one whom you see relatively often, so that you can gather additional information, if necessary.

Describing Your Perception

Step 1: Begin with a general label. Put it into a single sentence, stating what the person does that you don't like and how you feel about it.

Step 2: Expand your statement with additional facts and details so that you develop a more complete picture.

Step 3: Tie this description to a situation or situations in which the person acts in accordance with your label. Write it all down.

Step 4: Add to your description concrete characteristics—what the person looks like, says, and does—that might be the source of your label. (If the person is not around, use a recent photograph to refresh your memory.)

Step 5: Using your description, look for discrepancies between what the person is or does and what you *think* he should be or do. List these discrepancies to pinpoint your expectations about him.

Examining Your Expectations

Step 6: To pin down outdated expectations, consider earlier stages of your relationship. What qualities did the person have that caused you to form your present expectations of him? Does he still have these qualities?

Step 7: To locate information that may have been distorted or screened out, ask yourself whether your expectations are based on what seems to you a central trait of this person. It may be that you have formed an overconsistent, and therefore unrealistically narrow, picture of the person on the basis of that trait.

Step 8: Review your expectations and see whether you can support them with specific examples of behavior. Those for which you cannot find evidence may well be inferred qualities; jot them down in a separate list.

Step 9: Now think about the standards you have used in arriving at your expectations. Are you asking the person to be like you, to fulfill your own unrealized goals, to win the approval of others, or to fit certain social conventions? Note in what ways you may be using these standards in making your judgments.

Changing Your Perception

Step 10: Decide whether your perception is accurate. If you feel it is, you have finished the exercise. If you feel it could be changed, go ahead with the remaining steps.

Step 11: Gather new information about the person. Look especially for behaviors that don't "fit," behaviors that are inconsistent with the perception you now have.

Step 12: Talk to the person. Tell him how you see him and ask him for feedback. Find out how realistic he thinks your view is. (If you feel that this would be harmful, ask others who know him and get their views.)

Step 13: Start paying attention to what you say to yourself about the person when you think of him or see him. Challenge your negative self-talk and provide yourself with alternative interpretations.

Step 14: Act on your new interpretation. Let the old expectations go as you enjoy the new relationship.

HUMAN ISSUE:
MARRIAGE

Almost everyone agrees that marriage in America has changed during the past few decades. The innocence of a fifties song like "Love and Marriage" (which "go together like a horse and carriage") seems quite obsolete in an era when bookstores offer us titles such as *The Case Against Marriage* and *Is Marriage Necessary?* Marriage is simply no longer the sacred institution it used to be. It is being picked apart and analyzed in terms of its usefulness to human beings. And often the conclusion has been negative. Many observers would agree with sociologist Mervin Cadwallader that marriage is a "wretched and disappointing institution" (1966, p. 66). Nevertheless, most young people expect to get married. And this is a realistic expectation, since, according to predictions, 95 percent of American men and 94 percent of American women will marry at some time in their lives (Glick and Norton, 1977, 1979). Marriage may be changing, but it is not going out of style.

WHY MARRY?

In the United States, romantic love is regarded as a necessary prerequisite to marriage. Without love, we are taught, marriage is hollow, even shameful. Love isn't everything, however. After all, most of us are likely to form several romantic attachments in our lives that do not end in marriage. Furthermore, when we do marry, love is not always the primary reason. In a survey of 4,000 married men and women, love was the most frequently given reason for marriage (56 percent of women, 39 percent of men), but the need for companionship (15 percent of women, 35 percent of men) and the desire to establish a home (26 percent of women, 26 percent of men) were close runners-up (Pietropinto and Simenauer, 1979).

Still, the motive, whether love or companionship, tends to be idealistic. Men and women today are less likely than earlier generations to look primarily for sexual satisfaction or economic support from a spouse. Instead, they want the true intimacy of a close, warm, and, above all, honest relationship. Within this relationship, most of them hope to continue to grow and develop as individual personalities (Rogers, 1972).

Whatever the feelings or goals of those who marry, studies reveal that additional factors also play a role in the actual selection of a mate. One is, simply, availability. The chances are good that we will marry someone who lives near us or someone with whom we work or go to school (Kephart, 1972). Another factor is similarity. As might be expected, marriage usually brings together people of the same race; census statistics show that 99.8 percent of whites marry whites, and 99 percent of blacks marry blacks. Social background, too, is apt to be similar (Belkin and Goodman, 1980).

ASSUMPTIONS AND ADJUSTMENTS

When two people marry, they enter into a contractual arrangement that binds them both legally and socially. In legal terms, the traditional assumptions have been that the wife will give up her maiden name and follow her husband wherever he goes; he in turn accepts the responsibility of supporting her and their children. In social terms, the traditional assumptions have been that the couple will live together permanently ("till death do us part") and carry out certain obligations toward each other ("love, comfort, honor, keep—in sickness and in health"). To carry out these contractual obligations, society has fostered the development of traditional sex roles, according to which husbands work outside the home as wage-earners and wives remain at home, taking care of the house and the children.

Although it is often the men who joke and complain about the "ball and chain" of marriage, they seem to benefit from it much more than women. Married men, compared to men who have never married, not only live longer but are far more likely to report themselves as "very happy" (Bradburn, 1969). Married women tell a different tale. They seem to be subject to more psychological disturbances than single women (Knupfer et al., 1966). And, according to sociologist Jessie Bernard (1973), they are far more likely than their husbands to report negative feelings about their marriages.

Bernard speculates that women's marital dissatisfaction is closely related to the limitations of the housewife role—a role that assigns them dull and repetitive chores and does not even reward them with pay, which, in our money-oriented society, seems to stamp their work as worthless. (See the Human Issues essay on sex roles, after Chapter 3.) Small wonder that one observer stated gloomily: "The institution we call marriage can't hold two full human beings—it was designed for one and a half" (Andrew Hacker, cited in "The American Family," 1970).

Feminists and others have been trying to make marriage big enough for two whole people. They have, for instance, encouraged married women to continue their careers or return to them. Many women have done so. Whether for self-fulfillment or just to make ends meet, approximately half of all married women now have jobs outside the home (U. S. Bureau of the Census, 1980). This step requires adjustment for both husband and wife. Many men have assumed a larger share of the domestic chores. But truly equal partnerships are extremely difficult to achieve, particularly if children are involved.

It is not only in the area of traditional work obligations that adjustments are being attempted. Obviously, when financial support is provided by both marriage partners, other legal assumptions may change as well. In recent years it has become more common for women to retain their maiden names when they marry, and a potential move is more apt to be a joint decision, based on mutual interests. If divorce occurs, it is no longer universally assumed that a husband owes alimony or that a wife gets custody of the children. At the social level, perhaps the most important single change has been in attitudes toward the permanence of marriage. More and more people believe that if a marriage does not result in happiness for both partners, it should be terminated.

TERMINATING MARRIAGE

With the pressures of changing expectations and sex roles, among other things, it is no surprise that divorces in the United States are on the upswing. Over twice as many were granted in 1980 as in 1965. Almost half of all marriages now end in divorce. Frequent as it may be, divorce is hardly ever painless. Both partners are likely to feel a sense of failure and a loss of self-esteem. Where there was hope, there is now uncertainty. Companionship gives way to loneliness. When friends take sides and familiar patterns of living are dissolved, the suffering can be intense. Severe depression, insomnia, excessive drinking, and health problems are all extremely common in people going through a divorce (Chiriboga and Cutler, 1979).

Two facts about divorce in the United States should be kept in mind. One is that the chances of a marital split are greater in some groups than in others. The rate is higher for blacks, for those under twenty-five, and for those with low incomes and fewer years of education. The other consideration is that divorced people tend to remarry. What this suggests is not that people are taking marriage lightly but that they are taking it very seriously—so seriously that they are willing to go through the pain of divorce and the trouble of finding a new partner in order to establish an emotionally satisfying marriage.

ALTERNATIVES

Because of changes in the functions of marriage, some couples have begun formally to modify the expectations that they have of each other. They may draw up an agreement to specify how they will handle housework and finances, how they will reach decisions about jobs and children, even whether they will take separate vacations. Another idea is the "growth contract," in which the traditional commitment of remaining married for marriage's sake is replaced by a concern with companionship, reciprocal affection, and individual fulfillment (O'Neill, 1972). Other people, instead of redesigning marriage, are trying out alternatives to marriage.

Living Together

As even etiquette books now recognize, a growing number of couples are living together without being married. The number of such households in the United States more than doubled between 1970 and 1980; for couples under the age of 25, the number increased by more than *eight* times during that period (U. S. Bureau of the Census, 1980). Many such arrangements seem to follow Margaret Mead's formula for "marriage in two steps" (1966). In Mead's scheme, a couple first enters into an easily dissolvable "individual marriage," with the understanding that they will have no children. If and when they decide to have children, and are emotionally and financially prepared to do so, they move on to a second and more formal "parental marriage," which is more difficult to dissolve and which is focused on the well-being of children. Likewise, many young couples simply live together until they decide to have children, at which point they marry.

Are they happier than traditional married folk? One researcher (Yllo, 1978) found that couples who live together have essentially the same problems and report the same rate of satisfaction as married couples. One important difference is that it is easier to dissolve the relationship—no lawyers, no hearings, just pack up and move out—but the pain of "splitting up" is as great as in a divorce.

Remaining Single

Because more and more people are considering marriage as an alternative rather than an obligation, the number of persons choosing to remain single is on the rise. In 1980, 20 percent of American households consisted of only one person—a 44 percent increase over the 1970 figure (U.S. Bureau of the Census, 1980).

The choice of remaining single is not without its problems, however. Our culture is still designed primarily for couples. There is a certain stigma attached to being single, an aura of irresponsibility. Unmarried men are sometimes thought eccentric (or homosexual). Unmarried women are still subject to the "old maid" label. Single people may be left out of social activities and are discriminated against legally. Single women often have trouble establishing credit, and single householders pay proportionately higher income taxes than do married householders.

Many who choose to be single insist that there is no reason to marry. They can avoid getting locked into an unhappy commitment, and are free to explore a variety of relationships with others. Others see the unmarried state only as a transitional phase on the way to eventual marriage or remarriage. Thus, marriage is still very much on people's minds, even when they are single.

OUTLINE

ATTITUDES
The Functions of Attitudes
The Origins of Attitudes: Three Sources
The Organs of Social Influence
Parents
Peers
Mass media

THE PROCESSES OF INFLUENCE
Modeling
Modeling and reinforcement
The characteristics of the model
Modeling and attitudes
Conformity
The group and its norms
The Asch study
The causes of conformity
The determinants of conformity
Persuasion
The determinants of persuasion
Propaganda

DIRECT INFLUENCE AND ADJUSTMENT
Reactance
An Active Approach to Influence

11

SOCIAL INFLUENCE: WHAT IT IS AND HOW IT OPERATES

If you sit in a dark room and look at a small pinpoint of light, the light will seem to move, even though it actually remains completely stable. This phenomenon, called the *autokinetic effect*, was used as the basis for a famous study of social behavior.

Social psychologist Muzafer Sherif (1935) exposed a number of subjects, one at a time, to the autokinetic effect. He seated each subject in a dark room and then turned a tiny light on and off several times. Each time, he asked the subject to judge how far the light had moved. This was a difficult task, since the subject, unable to see anything else in the dark room, had no point of comparison (such as the width of a chair) against which to measure distances. But eventually each of the subjects developed his or her own internal point of comparison: a *norm*, or mental standard, for determining what the "normal" movement would be. For one subject the light always tended to move four inches, or a

little bit more or less; for another subject the movement was always in the area of seven inches, and so on. Sherif concluded that when a human being finds himself in a situation ungoverned by norms, he simply creates his own.

But what if that human being is joined by others who have different norms? Does he stick to his guns? In the second stage of his experiment, Sherif repeated the same test, with the same subjects. But this time the subjects were questioned in groups of two or three, each of whom had established a different norm in the first stage of the experiment. On each trial, the subjects announced their answers one after the other. And interestingly, as the test proceeded, their responses became more and more similar. Each subject, listening to the others, adjusted his standard bit by bit until the separate standards converged into one standard. For example, in a group of two subjects where one subject had a standard of twelve inches and the other had a standard of four inches, both subjects gradually moved to a standard of eight inches.

Sherif's experiment is a classic demonstration of the most basic fact of social psychology: human beings are affected by other human beings. We may construct our own standards and act on them, but those standards and actions will have everything to do with the standards and actions of the people we know and have known. Thus, each person's self may be seen as one terminal wired to hundreds of other terminals and constantly buzzing with messages—messages being transmitted and messages being received. This transfer of messages, and its effect on us, is called *social influence*.

Social psychologists define the term "influence" more broadly than the general public does. Most people, when they speak of influence, mean direct influence, in which one person imitates another person or complies with the other person's wishes. (This, for example, is what your parents meant when they called your most amusing high school friend a "bad influence.") In the language of social psychology, on the other hand, *social influence occurs whenever we think or act in response to the prior action of another human being.* This definition covers a very broad spectrum of influence. It ranges from direct persuasion to the most ordinary "cued" behavior. When your high school friend says, "Let's go to that dirty movie at the Cinema I—Frank said it was really dynamite," and you say, "Well, er, okay," that is certainly influence. But when your friend says "So long" and you say "So long" back, that is influence too; your action is a response to his action. The first type of influence, in which we imitate or comply with others, may be called *direct influence*. The rest of the spectrum, in which other people's actions simply set conditions for

our actions, may be called *indirect influence*.

Both types of influence present their own challenges for adjustment. In this chapter we will deal with direct influence. We will begin by describing attitudes. Then we will discuss three processes by which attitudes are influenced: modeling, conformity, and persuasion. Finally, we will address the adjustment question: how can we preserve some measure of integrity and independence amid the crosswinds of different social influences?

ATTITUDES

When blacks come into the store—I work at the complaints counter in a men's clothing store—I can't say I treat them the same as whites. I figure they have gotten so many raw deals from stores: shoddy merchandise, high prices, snotty salespeople. So when a black man comes in and says his new sweater is unraveling or his new shirt self-destructed in the washing machine, I'm more likely to do something about it than I would be if the person were white.

What is being expressed here is an attitude. *An attitude is a cluster of ingrained beliefs and feelings about a certain object and a predisposition to act toward that object in a certain way.* Note that according to this definition an attitude contains three components: (1) a cognitive component (beliefs); (2) an emotional component (feelings); and (3) a behavioral component (actions). We can see these three components in the attitude expressed above. The speaker *believes* that blacks have been treated unjustly, *feels* sympathy toward them, and tends to *act* in such a way as to compensate them. Likewise, the attitude that is called "male chauvinism" involves a belief that it is right and natural for women to be dependent on men, a feeling of hostility toward women who compete with men, and a tendency to act on this belief and this feeling—for example, by promoting a male employee over a more qualified female employee and by holding doors and lighting cigarettes for women.

Let us look at two important aspects of attitudes: their functions and their origins.

The Functions of Attitudes

It can be safely said that for the individual, attitudes make social life possible. How? By serving three important functions (Katz, 1960). First, attitudes have an organizational function. The beliefs contained in our attitudes allow us to organize our social experience—to impose on it a certain order and to give it meaning. If your daughter comes home from school with a black eye, your attitudes about physical aggression, about females, and about children will allow you to categorize mentally the fact of this black eye and give it some meaning. Without this mental "fitting" and interpreting, you would have no basis on which to act.

Second, attitudes serve a utilitarian function: we use them to confirm other people's attitudes and thus gain social approval. At any party, you can observe attitudes being pumped for all their utilitarian value. Person 1 expresses an attitude, person 2 confirms it with an anecdote from his own experience, person 3 introduces a slight variation on the attitude, person 1 agrees. And all three bask in the warmth of their mutual approval.

Third, attitudes serve a protective function. They guard us from threats to our self-esteem. (This is similar to the function of the Freudian defense mechanism of projection.) For a person who has been through two unsuccessful marriages, a negative at-titude toward marriage in general can relieve feelings of failure. Likewise, for many people, negative attitudes toward other races provide a comforting sense of superiority.

The Origins of Attitudes: Three Sources

Where do our attitudes come from? We certainly weren't born liking or disliking big business, respecting or rejecting organized religion. Where did we get these ideas?

Social psychologists have located three main sources of attitudes. The first is personal experience. Attitudes can be the result of pleasant or painful experiences with the object of the attitude. If your vacation in sunny Spain consisted of two weeks of rain and a case of dysentery, you may have developed a negative attitude toward Spain. Furthermore, it seems that just being familiar with something can lead to a positive attitude (Moreland and Zajonc, 1977), whereas we tend to have negative attitudes toward things that are unfamiliar. Some psychologists have proposed that this is a major cause of black-white racial hostility (Rokeach, 1968; Ashmore, 1970).

A second possible source of attitudes—in this case, negative attitudes—is the displacement of painful emotions. Displacement, as you may recall from Chapter 5, is the unconscious redirecting of painful emotions (especially hostility) away from their actual target and toward some other, "safer" target. A number of theorists, particularly of the Freudian school, have proposed that this mechanism is responsible for racial prejudice (Adorno et al., 1950). Hostility that cannot be vented against its proper object (for example, parents or employers—anyone who could strike back) is vented instead on a minority group. Vulnerable, unable to fight

These two women clearly have an attitude toward Ronald Reagan, yet chances are that they have never met him. So what is the source of their attitude? Parents? Peers? Mass media? Displacement of painful emotions? (Lawrence Frank 1980)

back, and already labeled as inferior, they constitute the ideal "safe" object.

The third source of attitudes is social influence, and it may well be the major source. After all, many of our attitudes are too tame to be based on unconscious hostility, and many of them have nothing at all to do with personal experience with the object of the attitude. Do you, for example, have an attitude toward Nancy Reagan? And have you

ACTIVITY 11.1

Because most of our attitudes are deeply ingrained in us, we rarely stop to think how they got there in the first place. Try this experiment on yourself. Take a recent newspaper, scan the major news stories, and select five that deal with social and/or political issues about which you have an opinion—for example, welfare, defense spending, a presidential policy or program. Make four columns on a sheet of paper. In the first column list the five issues. In the second column summarize how you feel about each issue. In the third column state as best you can how your attitude originated. In the fourth column write down the category in which you believe the source of your attitude falls: personal experience, displacement of emotion, or social influence.

ever had a personal encounter with Nancy Reagan? Chances are that you haven't. Indeed, the chances are excellent that your attitude toward Mrs. Reagan was picked up from parents, friends, teachers, newspapers, magazines, and the television news—in other words, through social influence. Recall Walter Lippmann's statement, already quoted in Chapter 9: "We are told about the world before we see it." Social influence often forms our attitudes long before we ever encounter the objects of these attitudes.

The Organs of Social Influence

Because social influence is such an important source of attitudes, we need to ask ourselves exactly where the influence is coming from. Who tells us about the world? We shall examine three major sources of influence: (1) parents, (2) peers, and (3) the mass media.

Parents

"The major influence upon people is people" (Bem, 1970, p. 75), and during childhood the most influential people are our parents. As children, we hear our parents express their attitudes every day: "Lying isn't nice"; "Smoking is a bad, bad habit"; "Yes, daddies go to work, but so do mommies." And because we love our parents and depend on them, we copy their attitudes. Furthermore, when we're not listening to our parents, we're listening to sources of information chosen by them. It is they who decide which schools we will attend, which books we can read, which television programs we can watch. Thus, even when they are miles away, our parents are deciding which version of reality we will see and hear.

The parent-child relationship, then, is no free forum of ideas. Even when parents consciously attempt to be open-minded and to "expose" their children to a variety of ideas

Three generations saying grace over lunch. Religious attitudes, like many other kinds of attitudes, are passed from parent to child. (Dennis Stock/Magnum)

and experiences, the exposure itself is yet another reflection of attitudes ("It is important to be open-minded"; "There's good and bad in all kinds"). In short, childhood socialization is also an intensive course in parental attitudes. The result is predictable: the attitudes of children tend to match those of their parents. A number of studies have shown this to be true. For example, elementary school children, both black and white, tend to harbor the same racial prejudices as their parents (Epstein and Komorita, 1966). They also tend to favor the same political party as their parents (Hess and Torney, 1967; Adelson, 1970), though many of them probably have only a dim notion of what a political party is.

Peers

As we have just seen, parents try to select the influences to which their children will be exposed. However, it is easier to control what a child sees on television than what

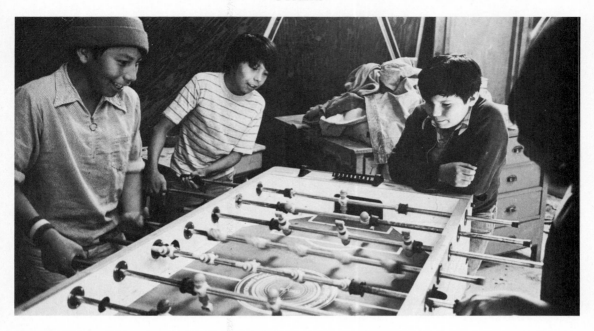

Children tend to adopt their parents' attitudes. But adolescents and young adults are more influenced by their peers—often to the great annoyance of their parents. (*top and bottom right:* Lawrence Frank 1982; *bottom left:* Joseph Daniels/Photo Researchers, Inc.)

he hears from the other kids on the block. And eventually what the kids on the block have to say becomes more important than what the parents have to say.

In the later years of adolescence, the peer group tends to replace the family as the individual's *reference group*—that is, the group whose standards we adopt and against whose standards we evaluate ourselves. This may be true particularly for adolescents who go on to college. College removes the student from home, often for the first time, and exposes her to many more, and many "weirder," ideas than were ever discussed around the family breakfast table. The result may be a dramatic unseating of parent-derived attitudes.

This process was demonstrated in an interesting study by Theodore Newcomb (1943). In the late 1930's Bennington College was already, as it is today, a center of extremely liberal political thought. Nevertheless, wealthy conservative families were used to sending their daughters there, and despite the school's liberalism, they continued to do so. To Newcomb this seemed an interesting laboratory for testing parental influence against peer influence. Would the incoming freshmen remain true to their families' conservative attitudes, or would they gradually be won over to the liberal attitudes of the faculty and upperclassmen? To answer this question Newcomb traced the political opinions of the class of 1939 through four years of college, and found that the families were the losers. As the women progressed through their four years of college, most of them—particularly the more popular and influential students—became increasingly liberal. Twenty-five years later they were still liberal, as Newcomb found out in a follow-up study (1963). Not only had peer influence replaced parental influence, but the switch was permanent—a lesson to conservative families choosing colleges for their daughters.

Mass Media

The mass media are the organs of communication—such as television, radio, newspapers, and magazines—that reach out to large masses of people. According to many social critics, those masses of people are deeply affected by what the media tell them. Television in particular is thought to have a great impact on attitudes. The "tube," we are told, can make us switch from Coke to Pepsi, from Carter to Reagan. Television is said to be a particularly powerful influence over American children, who now spend an average of six hours a day in front of it (Steinberg, 1980). To influence this enormous and dedicated audience, child-oriented commercials sing the praises of Barbie dolls and Ken dolls, while *Sesame Street* promotes interracial harmony and the ABC's.

In truth, however, we do not yet know how effective television actually is in molding or changing attitudes. Clearly, it has some influence. To take only one example, televised violence does appear to encourage violent behavior in children (Bandura et al., 1961; Liebert, 1974). But parents, it seems, can still squelch this learned aggression (Maccoby, 1964; Ross, 1981). In sum, it appears that television and other media have *some* impact on our attitudes. For children, they provide models for behavior. For adults, they are a source of information, which in turn molds attitudes. But research has not yet shown that the media have a power comparable to that of other people in forming attitudes.

THE PROCESSES OF INFLUENCE

Social influence is easy to understand on an abstract level. Yes, of course our parents have influenced us. Yes, the fact that we recently bought a pair of designer jeans must have something to do with the fact that most of our friends have a pair of designer jeans. But on another level, social influence seems quite mysterious. Why should any one subject in Sherif's experiment have felt the need to agree with the other subjects in estimating how far the light had moved? What was at stake? To move to a more disturbing example, how did Senator Joseph McCarthy manage, in the 1950s, to convince the American people that communists had infiltrated the entire federal government and the army? Indeed, how did Hitler succeed in influencing an entire nation of people to act on his anti-Semitic and imperialist attitudes? Social influence does seem, at a certain point, to defy common sense.

Social psychologists have attempted for many years to solve this mystery. They still do not have all, or even most, of the answers as to what goes on in a person's mind as he is being influenced. But they have found out that there are several distinct processes through which people can be influenced. And they have also discovered certain factors that can determine whether or not these processes will take place—whether the individual will actually be influenced.

We will examine three of the processes of social influence: modeling, conformity, and persuasion.

Modeling

Modeling, as we saw in Chapter 5, is the learning of new behaviors through imitating other people. The observer watches the other person (called the "model") perform the behavior, remembers the performance, and then reproduces the performance. We watch other people drive cars, dive off diving boards, operate computer keyboards, make omelettes, and so on. By copying them, we learn how to do the same. An immense range of behavior is learned in this way.

The reproducing of modeled behavior may take place immediately or many years later. A child who is learning hopscotch from a friend immediately copies the friend's hopping technique, but it may be twenty years before that child reproduces with her own child the baby talk that her mother used on her.

Modeling and Reinforcement

Among the mechanisms of behavioral psychology, modeling stands out as a somewhat special case. The reason for this is that modeling does not always follow the learning-through-reinforcement principle. Modeling is certainly affected by reinforcement. If the model's performance is reinforced by praise,

We don't have to see a behavior rewarded in order to imitate it. In this case, however, the act of blowing a trumpet is rewarded, as the younger child knows, by a spiffy uniform and the chance to march in a parade—all the more reason to imitate. (Constantine Manos/Magnum)

food, or some other external reward, it is more likely to be imitated. And if the act of imitation is reinforced by an external reward, it is more likely to be repeated. But as we noted in Chapter 5, modeling can also take place without any external reinforcement (Bandura, 1977). We watch our big brother swim the backstroke, and two days later we are swimming the backstroke. We hear our parents nag one another in a certain way, and ten years later we are nagging our spouses in the same way. There are no external rewards accompanying the modeled behavior, and yet we imitate it. Why?

It appears that the reinforcement lies within, in the desire to be like other people—particularly the special people with whom, in Freudian terms, we "identify." Other people, then, can influence us without even trying, and without appearing to benefit from the actions that we imitate. Simply because they are who they are, we will copy their words and deeds and absorb these words and deeds into our own personalities.*

But we do not honor everyone with imitation. As psychologists have discovered, we tend to choose as our models people with certain specific characteristics.

The Characteristics of the Model

There are three characteristics that appear to be most important in determining whether or not a person will, in our eyes, constitute a model—that is, whether we will imitate him or her. First, we tend to choose

as models people who appear to have power, people who control rewards and punishments (Bandura et al., 1963; Grusec, 1971). In a gang of neighborhood friends, for example, the leader—the child who somehow always decides who will play shortstop and who will play first base—is the one whom the others are most likely to imitate. A second determinant of modeling is rewardingness, the extent to which the model actually *has* provided rewards to the observer (Mischel and Grusec, 1966). When a person has supplied us with attention, affection, money, or any other reward, we are more likely to imitate her. The third decisive characteristic is the model's similarity to the observer (Maccoby and Wilson, 1957; Wolf, 1973). One important dimension of similarity is sex. Boys tend to imitate boys and girls tend to imitate girls—a fact that helps to perpetuate stereotyped "male" and "female" behaviors. But even similarities that seem trivial can promote modeling. In one experiment, subjects were more likely to imitate another subject's choice of nonsense syllables when they thought that this subject's musical tastes were similar to their own (Stotland et al., 1961).

These three qualities—power, rewardingness, and similarity—provide an interesting gloss on a fact that we noted earlier: that during adolescence, the influence of parents tends to take a back seat to the influence of peers. When a child is small and dependent, his parents may not seem very similar to him, but they do seem infinitely powerful, and the rewards that they provide—love, care, and approval—are the most potent, the most rewarding. Therefore it is no surprise that a young child's parents are his most powerful models and, accordingly, his greatest source of influence. But to the adolescent, striving for independence, the warm nest of parental love and approval may seem less appealing than the reward of being

---

* It should be noted that we do not copy them in every respect. Indeed, in some instances, we choose to do exactly the opposite of what we have observed in our most admired and influential models. For example, people who remember the humiliation of being spanked by their parents may choose never to spank their own children.

ACTIVITY 11.2

We often wait for others to model a behavior before acting ourselves. This is frequently the case when the behavior involves helping someone else. By taking the initiative, however, we can become models for others. Try the following experiment. Ask a friend to drop a large handful of loose papers in the middle of a busy sidewalk, pretending that it is an accident. Observe from afar how many people stop to help your friend pick up the papers. Then try the same thing a second time, using the same or a similar location at a similarly busy hour. This time, however, you should help pick up the papers, all the while pretending to be a stranger. You will probably find that when you help, others are more likely to help, too. This is a useful principle to remember when you are wishing that something would be done about bottle-recycling or cleaning up the neighborhood. If you start it, others are likely to follow.

treated as an equal by a group of equals. So he switches his loyalty to his peers. They provide him with this reward; they have the power to give it and take it away; and they constitute models similar to himself. Thus, peers become the major source of influence.

Modeling and Attitudes

Modeling, as we have seen, is the imitative learning of *behavior*. Through modeling, then, we can acquire new behaviors, but can we also acquire new attitudes? Behavior, after all, is only one component of an attitude. What about the other two components: beliefs and feelings? If we acquire a new behavior, do matching beliefs and feelings follow close behind? If we learn through modeling the behavior of petting a dog, do we then complete the process by developing warm feelings toward dogs and by embracing the belief that dog is man's best friend?

According to one theory, attitudes not only *can* be developed out of behavior, they almost always *are* developed out of behavior (Bem, 1972). First we behave in a certain way, and then we infer our feelings and be-

liefs from our behavior. To many people (including many psychologists), this theory seems to put the cart before the horse. After all, we generally assume that we act on the basis of our beliefs and feelings, not that we believe and feel on the basis of our actions. Nevertheless, experiments (including Festinger and Carlsmith, 1959) have shown that attitudes definitely can be developed out of behavior. Many examples of this process can be seen in daily life. The child, for example, certainly learns to use a knife and fork before he develops a positive attitude toward table manners, and the development of this attitude is probably based, in part, on his mastery of the knife and fork. Likewise, an adult is unlikely to switch from a negative to a positive attitude toward marijuana without first smoking marijuana. What probably happens is a very slight easing of the negative feeling and belief, then the behavior, then—if the behavior is rewarding—a serious change in feeling and belief. In other words, we often try things out before believing in them (Gerard et al., 1974). Therefore, if a model can induce us simply to develop a new behavior—pet a dog, attend

ACTIVITY 11.3

A good deal of pressure is exerted by peer groups in the matter of clothes, even in ordinary circumstances. Those who do not conform are often viewed as odd and may even be ostracized by the group. It can be a useful exercise to learn what it feels like to be on the receiving end in a situation like this. Try going to a party or to class dressed differently from the way you know others there will be dressed. Then note whether you are treated in any special way—stares, comments, or giggles—and how you feel about it. Keep this experience in mind the next time you're tempted to make amusing remarks about someone who isn't conforming to group norms in matters of clothing.

a ballet, ask a woman out on a date—a new attitude will probably grow up around this new behavior. Much behavioral therapy is based on this principle.

Conformity

A girl who went through four years of high school in matching outfits comes home from her first year of college with a wardrobe consisting entirely of blue jeans and T-shirts. "Sweater sets are corny," she tells her unhappy mother. "Jeans are—I don't know—comfortable. And to me they look just fine." Behind this change of taste is another change, a change in peer groups. The girl's old high school friends all wore matching outfits; her new college friends all wear jeans and T-shirts. She has changed her tastes to match those of her new group. This familiar phenomenon is known by the familiar name of conformity. *To conform is to change one's beliefs or behavior to make them agree with those of a group.* While modeling involves one individual's following the example of another individual, conformity involves a group member's following the example of the group.

But what is a group if not a collection of individuals? What source of influence does the group have that the individual members, taken separately, don't have? These questions, major issues in social psychology, must be addressed before we can understand conformity.

The Group and Its Norms

In the vocabulary of social psychology, a group is *not* simply a collection of individuals. Twenty strangers on a bus, for example, do not constitute a group. Rather, *a group is a collection of individuals who share a common goal, who act out roles in relation to one another, and who interact according to shared norms.*[*] For the purpose of understanding conformity, the most important part of this definition is the last item: shared norms.

We mentioned norms at the beginning of this chapter, in discussing Sherif's experiment with the autokinetic effect. *A group's norms are its "rules," its established beliefs regarding the right way to do things.* These

---

[*] Elsewhere in this book we have used the term "group" in its broader, nonsociological meaning, as any collection or category of people. This was done to avoid introducing unnecessary technical terms.

norms may be formalized and written down, as regulations or laws. More often, however, group norms exist only in the minds of the members, as an understanding of what is expected of them and what they can expect from the others. For example, a group of young girls who play together may have the understanding that it is okay to quarrel but not okay to cheat in games. Or a group of telephone company workers may have the understanding that it is not okay for any one member to work too hard and thereby make the others look bad. (Such a group was the subject of a classic sociological study [Roethlisberger and Dickson, 1939].)

Once a group's norms are established, the group places great value on them. And with good reason. Norms allow the group to function. Norms structure the interaction of the members; without this structure, they could never coordinate their efforts in order to achieve their goal. If half the members of a softball team think base-stealing is allowed and the other half think it is forbidden, the team is likely to fall apart as soon as the first player steals a base, and the game will never be finished.

Because norms are so important to the group, deviations from them are not taken lightly. If you wear a swimsuit to a formal dance, or a ball gown to a beach party, you will be met with strange looks (see Activity 11.3). If you constantly flirt with your friends' wives, you are likely to find yourself without friends. Whatever the punishment—raised eyebrows, ostracism, or worse—its purpose is to let you know that you have violated the group norm and to discourage you from doing it again.

With these facts in mind, we can now answer our earlier question: what source of influence does a group have that individuals, taken separately, don't have? The answer is: norms, backed by the power of group approval and disapproval.

A group portrait in conformity. At the same time that we adopt the outer characteristics of a group—clothing styles, mannerisms, interests—we also adopt inner habits, such as beliefs and values. (© Lawrence Frank 1981)

Conformity, the process that results from this influence, can be extremely useful to us. For example, we would learn nothing in our classes if students didn't conform to the following norm: be quiet while someone else is speaking. But what is interesting, and disturbing, about conformity is that it often goes far beyond what is useful and reasonable. This fact was demonstrated in a famous experiment by Solomon Asch.

The Asch Study

Imagine that you have volunteered to take part in a study of visual perception. You enter the room with seven other students and sit down in a row on one side of a table. You are seventh in the row. The experimenter puts two cards on the blackboard. On one card there is a single line, called the "standard" line. On the other card there are three

SOCIAL INFLUENCE: WHAT IT IS AND HOW IT OPERATES

lines, called the "comparison" lines (see Figure 11.1). Your job—and the job of the other students—is to tell the experimenter which of the comparison lines is the same length as the standard line.

On the first set of cards the answer is obvious—any idiot could figure it out. All the volunteers, including you, call out the same answer, one by one. The experimenter puts up a second set of cards. Again, the answer is quite obvious, and the volunteers all give the same answer. You settle in for what is obviously going to be a boring experiment. The experimenter produces a third set of cards, and once again the answer is perfectly clear. But now something strange happens. One by one, relaxed and confident, the six people in line ahead of you call out an answer that you *know* is wrong. You look again at the cards. The answer is obviously line number 1, but all the other students are saying that it is line number 2. Now it's your turn. What do you do? If you're like the subjects in Asch's experiment (1952), who were placed in exactly the same situation, there is only a two-out-of-three chance that you will give the answer that you know is correct.

The trick to this experiment was that it was not a study of visual perception. It was a study of conformity. And unlike you, the six other students were not subjects. They were "confederates" of the experimenter—that is, people who had been instructed by the experimenter to act out a certain role during the experiment. Their instructions were to give unanimous wrong answers on certain sets of cards. The purpose, of course, was to find out what *you* would do.

What Asch's subjects did was to conform to the group's judgment on 33 percent of the occasions when the group gave a wrong answer. In considering this percentage, it is important to note three things: (1) the subjects conformed even though they were sure

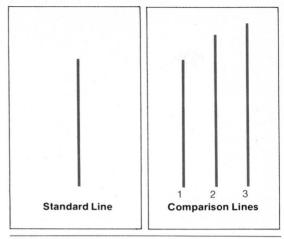

Standard Line **Comparison Lines**

Figure 11.1

that the answer was wrong; (2) the people whose judgment they conformed to were strangers, people they would probably never see again; (3) the other people put no pressure on the subject to conform. What, then, would be the rate of conformity in a more ordinary situation—that is, a situation in which (1) the person might have some doubt about his judgment, (2) the other people involved are people on whom he depends, such as friends or family, and (3) the other people put some pressure on the person? In all likelihood, the rate of conformity would be much, much higher.

This raises some very disturbing questions about the power of the group over the individual. Asch has stated these questions: "May we simply conclude that [groups] can induce persons to shift their decisions and convictions in almost any desired direction, that they can prompt us to call true what we yesterday deemed false, that they can make us invest the identical action with the aura of rightness or with the stigma of grotesqueness and malice?" (1956, p. 2) In other words, will we conform to just about anything?

Obviously, we will conform to a great deal. But why?

The Causes of Conformity

One possible explanation of conformity is the *social comparison theory*, advanced by Leon Festinger (1954). This theory states that people evaluate their opinions by comparing them with some other source of information. When there is no objective means of comparison (for example, a thermometer to tell you whether you're right in thinking you have a fever), people will resort to social comparison. That is, they will turn to other people—people similar to themselves—and ask for their opinions. ("Feel my head; do you think I have a fever?" "Look at this hat; does it look stupid?") And they will rely on those other opinions. Thus, conformity might be explained by the fact that the members of our groups (our friends, our fellow students, our family) are those similar people whose judgments we tend to adopt when we have no objective standard.

This explanation may cover some instances of conformity, but it cannot really account for what went on in the Asch experiment. After all, the subjects in that experiment had more to go on than just opinions. They *knew* the right answer, but to avoid disagreeing with the others, they gave the wrong answer. Thus, their behavior, and many other acts of conformity, may have to be explained by a more ordinary fact—our dependence on groups. As we stated in earlier chapters, and as everyone knows, other people—particularly the people in our groups (our friends, our family)—mean a very great deal to us. We depend on them for love, approval, companionship, advice, and a host of other gratifications. Therefore we think twice about risking their disapproval through nonconformity. How much is our

dissenting opinion worth, stacked against the rewards that we derive from our groups? Going along with the group is easy and safe; standing alone against the group is difficult and risky.

The Determinants of Conformity

Modeling, as we have seen, is most likely to occur if the model has certain characteristics. Likewise, there are certain factors that determine the likelihood of conformity. These factors have to do with the nature of (1) the group, (2) the question being decided, and (3) the individual.

First, the group. The larger the group is (Gerard et al., 1968), the more competent, powerful, and rewarding it seems to you (Endler, 1966; Ettinger et al., 1971), and the more unanimous it is, the more likely you are to conform (Moscovici, 1974). Unanimity in particular seems to be a powerful determinant of conformity. When Asch changed his experiment so that one of the confederates gave the right answer while the other confederates gave the wrong answer, the rate of conformity on the part of the subjects was drastically reduced.

Second, the question being decided—the issue on which the person will or will not conform. The more ambiguous the question is, and the more difficult it is to find the right answer, the more likely the person is to conform (Kiesler, 1969). When Asch varied his experiment by making the visual test harder and more confusing, the rate of conformity increased. Thus, if your coworkers told you that the boss was married when you were fairly certain he was single, you would be unlikely to accept their statement without checking, for this is something that can be checked. But if they told you that the only way to obtain fair wages was for all the employees to go out on strike—a point that

BOX 11.1
A STUDY OF OBEDIENCE

Obedience is a special form of influence in which the individual submits to the direct command of another. It is generally assumed, at least in a free society, that adults will avoid situations calling for obedience. Except in special circumstances (the army, for instance), people are resistant to taking orders. Or so we think. However, a series of famous studies conducted in the sixties by psychologist Stanley Milgram (1963, 1964, 1965), then a professor at Yale, suggests otherwise.

Milgram told his subjects that they were participating in a learning experiment. Questions would be put to another person, the so-called "victim," and if the answers were wrong, the subject was ordered by the experimenter to give the "victim" an electric shock, ranging from 15 to 450 volts. As the experiment progressed, the subject was ordered to administer ever-increasing levels of voltage, even to the point where the control panel was marked "Danger: Severe Shock." (The "victim," described to the subject as a student, was actually a confederate of the experimenter and, unbeknownst to the subject, was never shocked.) In each case of a "wrong answer," the instruction to administer the shock was made to seem like an order; in a firm tone of voice, the experimenter commanded the subject to pull the lever. However, all the subjects knew that they were simply volunteers in an experiment. They could walk out at any time. What Milgram wanted to find out was how many of them *would* walk out.

Using Yale University students as subjects, Milgram began his experiments with the victims unheard and located in another room. To his surprise, all the subjects gave all the shocks up to the maximum intensity. Milgram then had his victims appear to protest. These tape-recorded protests were set so that at 125 volts the subject heard "Hey, that really hurts"; at 180 volts, "I can't stand the pain"; at 195 volts, complaints of heart trouble; at 285 volts, an agonizing scream; and from 315 volts on, ominous silence. Still Milgram found that 65 percent of his subjects would go all the way to 450 volts. At one point, Milgram put the victim in the same room with the subject. Even then, with the screams from a visible "sufferer," twelve out of forty subjects went to 450 volts.

Milgram thought that the prestige of the university might be affecting the subjects' behavior, so he set up the same experiment in a rundown office building in Bridgeport, Connecticut, advertising in the newspaper for subjects. With invisible but protesting victims, the proportion of subjects who went all the way to 450 volts was the same as with the Yale students (65 percent). And with the victim in the same room, 48 percent of these subjects administered the full dose of shock.

Milgram's studies have been replicated by others, leaving psychologists with a number of questions about people's response to authority. We might ask ourselves how we respond to people in authority. Do we question the right of a teacher, a police officer, or anyone else to tell us what to do? How far will we go in obeying them? Under what circumstances will we disobey? Although such questions may be hard to answer in the abstract, it is helpful to be aware of our tendencies in this important area.

could be argued many different ways—you would be more likely to go along with them.

Third, the individual. Studies have found that the more intelligent and self-confident a person is, the less likely he is to conform (Stang, 1972). However, these generalizations—and those about the group and the question being decided—should not be regarded as hard and fast rules. Characteristics of the group, the question, and the individual can counteract each other. Many extremely intelligent artists and professors conformed in the face of the anticommunist witch hunts of the 1950s, probably because the groups supporting this mania were powerful enough to have such people fired from their jobs. Likewise, in a choice between your own small family and a large and unanimous group, you may choose your family, because it provides you with so many rewards.

Persuasion

As powerful and pervasive as modeling and conformity is a third process of social influence—persuasion. *Persuasion is the delib-erate exercise of influence through the transmission of information.* You should note two elements in this definition. First, "deliberate." Unlike modeling and conformity, in which the model or the group may or may not consciously attempt to influence you, persuasion is always intentional. Second, "transmission of information." In modeling and conformity, information may be transmitted, but it doesn't have to be; the power behind the influence is the psychological bond between the individual and the model or the group. Persuasion, on the other hand, depends on the transmission of information. The persuader *tells* you something—usually through words, though pictures may be used as well. That information may be true or false. In either case, the purpose is to win you over to a certain attitude.

Attempts at persuasion surround us on all sides. Indeed, our persuaders are so much there, all the time, that we simply get used to them and come to regard them as a natural part of the environment. You wake up, turn on the radio, and are told that your life will be carefree and easy if you open a checking account at Bank X. You go into the kitchen to eat breakfast, and the cereal box informs you that sweetened cereals constitute a highly nutritious breakfast. You drive to school, past numerous billboards telling you what beer to drink, what car to buy, and what airline to use. You sit down in your English class, and your professor tells you why the novel he has assigned is a work of beauty and intelligence. You join a friend under a tree, open a newspaper, and are informed by the editorial page that you should vote to reelect Congressman X. You mention this to your friend, who tries to persuade you that any newspaper using the word "congressman" instead of "congressperson" is probably sexist. You go home and are greeted by your son, who tells you all the reasons why you should increase his al-

A New York street scene, with messages from the local persuaders. (© Lawrence Frank 1982)

lowance. At dinner your husband tells you why your views on capital punishment are crazy. Then you and he go to a movie that attempts to persuade you that nuclear power plants pose an imminent danger to United States citizens.

Persuasive communications, then, are everywhere. But not all of them persuade us. What makes an attempt at persuasion successful or unsuccessful?

The Determinants of Persuasion

In persuasion, as in modeling and conformity, there are certain factors that determine whether or not you will in fact be influenced—whether the persuasion will work. These factors are characteristics of (1) the communicator, (2) the message, and (3) the audience.

The Communicator. You are in charge of a campaign to promote gun control. The local Kiwanis Club has invited you to send a speaker to their meeting next week. Whom should you send? What are the qualities that enable a person to persuade other people?

Not surprisingly, research suggests that a major asset for any would-be persuader is credibility. That is, the audience must feel that they can believe what he says. When credibility is low or damaged, the audience begins to ignore the message, as Lyndon Johnson and Richard Nixon both discovered toward the end of their terms as president. A communicator's credibility depends on two questions. First, how much expertise does he have in the subject he is discussing? If you can say to yourself, "Well, *he* should know," then you are more likely to take to heart whatever he is telling you (Aronson et al., 1963; Smith, 1973; Maddux and Rogers, 1980). The second question is: How trustworthy is he? Does that woman on the TV really believe your dog would be happier and

healthier on a diet of Chunk-O-Bits, or is she just saying that because she is paid to say it? Apparently, we are somewhat suspicious of persuaders. We trust them more if we think that they have nothing to gain, personally, from persuading us. One study, for example, found that people are more likely to be convinced by a message that they overhear than by a message aimed directly at convincing them (Walster and Festinger, 1962). Television advertisers, never far behind in such matters, have tried to capitalize on this fact by presenting, as commercials, grainy little films in which we are allowed to "spy" on some woman as she discovers and proclaims the excellence of a new laundry detergent.

The second major asset for a persuader is attractiveness, or "likeableness." We have already examined (Chapter 9) the factors that make us like people. One is similarity, a quality that is exploited daily in television commercials. When advertisers are not showing us beautiful people praising their products, they are showing us "ordinary people"—gray-haired women in housecoats, overweight men in undershirts—people they think resemble the average television viewer. Likewise, black entertainers and black athletes are hired to endorse political candidates in commercials aimed at the black television audience. The theory behind all this is that a person whom you see as similar to you has a better chance of persuading you. Several studies support this theory (among them Brock, 1965; Blanchard et al., 1974). Similarity apparently works best, however, when the specific similarity has something to do with the issue at hand (Berscheid, 1966), for example, when a "housewife" addresses housewives about floor wax.

What about all those beautiful people on billboards and in TV commercials? Physical attractiveness, as we have seen, makes people more likeable. Does it also make them more persuasive? Many studies say yes (Mills and Aronson, 1965; Horai et al., 1974; Snyder and Rothbart, 1971; Chaiken, 1979). On the other hand, another recent experiment, in which subjects were presented with arguments by either a very good-looking man or a decidedly homely man, found that the physical difference had no significant effect on whether the subjects were convinced by the argument (Maddux and Rogers, 1980). The investigators speculate that the genuine homeliness of the "non-attractive" persuader may have caused the subjects to bend over backward in an effort not to be influenced by it. (The earlier studies did not use such extremes of handsome and homely). So perhaps we are influenced by intermediate variations in physical attractiveness, but not by dramatic extremes. In any case, more research is needed on this question.

BOX 11.2
MARKETING PRESIDENTIAL POLICY

As everyone knows, television now plays a major role in presidential elections. The essence of television campaigning, whether in debates or advertisements, is the same as in any other advertising: find out what the consumers are concerned about and tailor your presentation of the product accordingly. Pollsters and media consultants tell the candidate what issues to emphasize or avoid, how to do so, and whether to stand or sit, smile or frown, while doing so. For the past two decades, every president has owed his election in large part to this clever use of techniques borrowed from media advertising.

In the past, however, the media experts were generally called in only in election years. Now they are apparently becoming part of the actual administration. President Reagan retains on his permanent staff not only pollsters and public-opinion analysts, but also his own special media consultant, a former television producer, who has his headquarters in the Executive Office Building next to the White House. These people's job, they claim, is to advise the President not on policy—he makes his own policy, they say—but on how to implement it in such a way as to make it attractive to the voters. They tell him what to play up and what to play down, in order to retain the favor of the people who voted him into office. The presidency has thus become, in the words of one analyst, a "permanent campaign" (Blumenthal, 1981).

How this works can be seen in the case of the assassination attempt. While Reagan was still in the hospital, his advisers were hurriedly polling voters on whether the shooting had affected their opinion of the President. Eleven percent of respondents claimed that it had; they now regarded him more favorably. So the advisers convened a strategy meeting to decide how best to invest this new "political capital," as one of them put it. The decision was that Reagan's first major public appearance after his release from the hospital should be a speech on the economy before a joint session of Congress. The President's economic plan was his major policy initiative. If he had gained a new edge from being shot at, that edge should be used to further the economic plan.

Such planning can also backfire, as in the case of the President's stand on the 1981 political

The Message. Leaving aside the characteristics of the communicator, there are also characteristics of the message itself that can turn the audience on or off. Research has suggested some answers to a few important questions regarding the content and style of a persuader's message.

First, is it worthwhile to marshal arguments in support of your position, or should you just state your position and not confuse the audience with supporting arguments?

You should probably state the arguments. In the study just cited, with the very handsome and very homely persuaders, the point on which the persuaders were trying to convince the subjects was that people really need only four hours sleep. Half the subjects were presented with a simple statement of opinion: "I think people should sleep only four hours a night." The other half were given the same statement of opinion plus four supporting arguments—that sleep pat-

---

upheaval in El Salvador. According to his aides, Reagan sincerely believed that the Soviet Union was wrongly interfering in El Salvador. But whether he should make a major issue of it was a question for his political strategists. They decided he should. A firm stand, they reasoned, would boost Reagan's public appeal by touching people's concerns over national security. Exactly the opposite happened. Remembering Vietnam, the public became alarmed over Reagan's aggressive stand, and his popularity dropped. The advisers then had to scurry to get El Salvador *out* of the news so that the public's fears would quiet down. According to Richard Beal, a member of the President's staff, the problem with the President's handling of the El Salvador matter was not the policy itself but "the packaging of the activity, in terms of . . . presentation to the public. It wasn't well staged or sequenced."

This type of thinking raises some serious questions. Is it in our best interests for the country to be run like an advertising campaign? Do we want the president's initiatives to be carefully "packaged"—"staged" and "sequenced"—for maximum persuasiveness? And how much *do* these marketing considerations affect presidential policy? According to James Baker, the White House Chief of Staff, social

issues are dangerous to the President's coalition: "There are some issues that are political losers. Abortion cuts both ways hard. If you come down one way or the other, you lose some people." The solution, obviously, is not to come down at all on such issues, but to stick to something that most people can agree on, such as strengthening the economy. And that is exactly what Reagan did in his first year of office, to the frustration of many people looking to him for leadership in solving pressing social issues.

The possible threat inherent in this way of running the country is not new with the Reagan administration, nor is it a Republican specialty. Previous presidents used media consultants (though not as heavily). Future presidents will probably rely more and more on such services. In the meantime, voters should ask themselves whether they want presidential policy sold to them via the same sophisticated techniques of persuasion that have been so successful in marketing radial tires and designer jeans.

Blumenthal, S. *"Marketing the President,"* The New York Times Magazine, *September 13, 1981, pp. 42-118.*

terns vary from culture to culture, that many successful people sleep less than eight hours a night, and so on. The second group came out of the experiment far more convinced of the virtues of getting only four hours sleep (Maddux and Rogers, 1980). The usefulness of arguing your case, rather than simply stating it, has been shown by other studies as well (for example, Norman, 1976).

A second question: Should you present only your own point of view, or should you state both sides of the issue? According to several studies, the answer is that it depends. One factor on which it depends is the intelligence of the audience. Intelligent audiences like to hear both sides, possibly because this technique gives the illusion of fairness (Hass and Linder, 1972). Another factor is the degree of opposition in the audience. With audiences already leaning toward your position, one-sided arguments are more effective. They strengthen what the audience already wants to believe. But with audiences that oppose your position, two-sided arguments are more effective. Apparently people want to hear their own point of view acknowledged and refuted before they will abandon it (Hass and Linder, 1972).

A third question: How useful is it to play on people's emotions, particularly the emotion of fear? "Scare tactics" are common in advertising, for good and bad causes. You see a group of people weeping at a cemetery, and the voice-over tells you how drunk drivers are keeping population growth under control. You see a woman walking down a deserted and dimly lit street, with someone lurking in the shadows behind her, and the voice-over tells you that Candidate X will preserve law and order. How effective are these fear-arousing messages? Pretty effective, according to research (Leventhal et al., 1967; Mann and Janis, 1968). But there are limits. For example, if the message is too horrible and arouses too much fear, mem-

bers of the audience may defend themselves by "tuning it out" (Bauer, 1970). This may be one of the reasons why the American Cancer Society has yet to show us a cancerous lung in their antismoking advertisements.

The Audience. The final determinant of the effectiveness of an attempt at persuasion is the nature of the audience. Certain types of people are more persuadable than others. One determinant is the need for social approval. Not surprisingly, people with a powerful need to be liked by others are more easily persuaded than those who are less concerned about what people think of them (Skolnik and Heslin, 1971). A related finding is that persuadability is affected by self-esteem (which, as you may recall, was also a factor in conformity). People with low self-esteem are apparently easier to bend to your point of view than people with high self-esteem (Zellner, 1970).

However, the determinants of persuasion, like the determinants of conformity, should not be viewed as absolutes. Every act of persuasion will involve a unique mix of these factors, and it is hard to tell which will cancel out which.

Propaganda

One special form of persuasion that deserves a brief mention is propaganda. *Propaganda may be defined as persuasion by means of deliberately deceptive information and for self-serving purposes.* In order to increase his chances of influencing you, the propagandist intentionally *distorts the truth.* And he wants to influence you not for your own sake, but in order *to benefit himself or the cause he serves.* Propaganda is often associated with large causes and large institutions, such as churches or governments. Americans, for example, may speak of communist

HELP STOP THIS

W.S.S.

BUY W.S.S.

& KEEP HIM OUT of AMERICA
NATIONAL WAR SAVINGS COMMITTEE

A World War I poster urging Americans to buy war bonds. The poster skillfully plays on fear. It also distorts the truth, making the average German soldier look like a homicidal maniac. Is this propaganda or persuasion? (Culver Pictures)

propaganda, while Russians and Chinese may speak of American imperialist propaganda.

Propaganda or Ordinary Persuasion? The above definition of propaganda raises some interesting questions. We are distinguishing between propaganda and other forms of persuasion on two counts: deliberate distortion and selfish purposes. But how honest is "ordinary" persuasion, and how unselfish is it? Television commercials, for example, are not usually called propaganda, but they are

certainly not known for their objective presentation of the facts:

A major brand of aspirin has been advertised as "100% pure aspirin." This is true, but it suggests that other brands are impure. . . . Advertisers do not shy away from claims that a product is "the biggest selling *of its kind*" or is "23% *more effective* by actual clinical tests" or "lasts *twice* as long." The specifics of comparison are usually very ambiguous or entirely absent in these cases. What is "its kind"? "More effective" than what? Lasts "twice as long" as *what*—the half-size bottle? Also note that "clinical tests" reported are usually just those which come out right! (Hollander, 1976, pp. 205–206)

As for selfish versus unselfish purposes, consider the following statistic: In 1980, business enterprises spent $10.3 billion simply to buy time for advertising on American television networks (FCC, 1981). How easy is it to imagine that this amount of money was paid out to benefit you, to save you from the embarrassment of bad breath or the "heartbreak" of psoriasis?

The same questions can be applied to more personal persuasions. When your boss tries to persuade you to come in and work overtime on Saturday, is she doing this in order to supplement your income? When your wife tries to convince you that it's time to buy a dog, does she present both sides of the argument? When she tells you that the dog will offer protection against burglars, does she also give you an estimate of how much it will cost to feed the animal and what the veterinary bill will be?

The point is that persuasion almost invariably carries a measure of propaganda. Two noted psychologists claim that propaganda, as opposed to ordinary persuasion, is *manipulative* rather than informative (Krasner and Ullmann, 1973). But if, as one dictionary states, to manipulate is "to manage or influence by artful skill" (*Random House Dictionary*, 1973, p. 872), then all persuasion is manipulative to some degree. All persuaders are using their skills, as artfully as possible, to influence our attitudes. (For a list of manipulative techniques commonly used in everyday persuasion, see Box 11.3.)

Thus, it might be said that our choice of terms often depends not on the manipulative quality of the argument but on how we feel about the cause behind it. If we favor the cause, the argument is "common sense." If we aren't sure about the cause, the argu-

BOX 11.3
TECHNIQUES OF EVERYDAY MANIPULATION

The following list summarizes some of the manipulative techniques most commonly used in persuasion or propaganda. Look for them in advertising (particularly television commercials), in speeches, and in "public statements" by politicians, businesspeople, and leaders of interest groups. You might also look for them in your own conversations with others.

1. *Transfer and Testimony.* The use of a positive symbol to endorse whatever the persuader wants you to "buy." Examples: Bill Cosby endorsing Jello; Tom Lasorda, manager of the Los Angeles Dodgers, endorsing Yoplait yogurt. The idea is that through respondent conditioning you will transfer the positive qualities of the endorser to the product.

2. *Appeal to the Expert.* "Studies in major hospitals have shown . . .," "Four out of five doctors recommend. . . ." The idea is that no matter how vaguely defined the authority is, you will take his or her word for it.

3. *Plain Folks.* A favorite of politicians. The candidate, no matter how wealthy and powerful, describes himself as a "man of the people" (Hollander, 1976, pp. 205–206). Richard Nixon used to talk about how his mother emptied bedpans and how his wife wore a "Republican cloth coat"—unlike Democratic wives who, supposedly, went nowhere without fur coats. Another politician devoted to the "plain folks" technique was Lyndon Johnson. Here is a journalist's description of Johnson appearing before a group of local politicians in Texas:

> He slouched on the podium, grinning boyishly, pulling at his ear, saying how grand it was for "me and Lady Bird to get out of the steel and stone of the cities and come back here to feel the soil of home under our feet, and draw close to all the things we hold dear while we gaze on the Texas moon." He invited all hands to "drop by and see us when you're in Washington." He reported that the coffeepot was always on, and added that "sometimes Bird bakes a buncha little cookies in the shape of the State of Texas to go with the coffee." (King, 1968, p. 40)

Ronald Reagan's habit of referring to his wife as "Mother" falls into the same category, as does his well-publicized fondness for jelly

ment is an attempt at persuasion. If we consider the cause dangerous, the argument is propaganda.

Should we then throw out the term *propaganda*? If one man's persuasion is another man's propaganda, what is the usefulness of the term? The usefulness of the term is that we can use it to describe what it is supposed to describe: not the cause, but the argument. No matter what our opinions are, we still must exercise our judgment as to how deceptive or honest an argument is, and to what degree its purpose is to benefit or exploit the audience. The term "propaganda"

---

beans. The idea (as in the television commercials featuring the man in the undershirt) is the similarity principle, discussed earlier; if you think the persuader is "like you," you will be persuaded more easily. This person *knows* the problems you face.

4. *Appeal to Self-Esteem.* "Mothers who care about their children's teeth. . .," "A man likes to feel like a man. . .," "For people of taste. . . ." The idea is that you will rush out and buy the product in order to prove to yourself that you are not a negligent parent, that you are really a man, or that you do have taste.

5. *Appeal to the Social Fears.* This is a close cousin of the appeal to the self-esteem. "Gee, how am I going to tell Dale he needs Pep-O Mouthwash?" "Ultrafem spray—for women in the know," "Water spots on the glassware! Boy, was I embarrassed," "Do you look older to him now? Lanolush Cream can erase those little wrinkles. . . ." The idea is to start you worrying about how you look, how you smell, and what others might be saying about you. Once you're worried, you'll go out and buy the product.

6. *Bandwagon.* This could be called the "all-the-kids-on-the-block" technique. Examples: "Crummy-cakes are sweeping the nation," "America's favorite dishwashing detergent." The idea is a straight appeal to conformity: if you don't want to be "out of it," you'd better jump on the bandwagon now.

7. *The Empty Slogan.* "The Democratic party is the party of war," "The Republican party is the party of depression," "Nixon's the one!" (One what?) The idea is to offer you a convenient generalization that will relieve you of the problem of having to think (Hollander, 1976).

8. *Pseudo-Statistic.* "Kills bugs three times faster than other leading products." (Which other leading products?) "Surveys of car-owners show. . . ." (Who conducted the surveys?) "During my opponent's administration, unemployment doubled." (Because a war ended?) See other examples on page 323. The idea is to inflate a half-truth into a "scientific proof" of the persuader's claim.

9. *Fuzzy Language.* Another favorite of politicians. In a now-famous example, Ronald Ziegler, Richard Nixon's press secretary, spoke of earlier statements as being "inoperative" and "misspoken" rather than as mistakes or lies. Likewise Congressman Hugh Carey of New York, when asked whether he was going to run for governor in 1974, did not say "I might"; he said "I am considering offering my capacity for state-wide leadership" (Newman, 1975, p. 89). The idea is to make the truth look better than it is through the use of vague or important-sounding words.

serves very well to describe arguments that are especially distortive and especially self-serving, even in support of a cause that we ourselves favor.

DIRECT INFLUENCE AND ADJUSTMENT

How is our adjustment affected by these powerful processes of direct social influence: modeling, conformity, and persuasion? One possible thought is that these influences constitute something of a threat to good adjustment; they intrude on our principles and eat into our integrity and independence. You may recall that in discussing conformity we raised a question that we didn't answer: Will we conform to just about anything? The same question can be raised about modeling and persuasion. If the conditions are favorable, will we imitate any behavior and yield to any persuader? Do we bend with every wind that blows? If so, we are surely in trouble.

Yet we cannot solve this problem by shutting out direct influence. To be a social creature—to have acquaintances, friends, parents, spouses, children—is to be influenced. If we had never been influenced, we would be completely unsocialized, like the isolated children described in Chapter 8. And if we wanted, now, to call a halt to influence, we would have to find a very remote cave to huddle in. In other words, we are more or less stuck with social influence. Is there any way by which it can be controlled? We have two suggestions to offer.

Reactance

You may have noticed that when someone tries to interfere with your freedom, you "get your back up" and resist the interference. For example, if you are looking for-

ward to going to a party and then someone tells you that you *must* go to this party, you may find that you no longer want to go. Staying home of your own free will seems preferable to attending a party under compulsion. In other words, when our freedom of choice is threatened or actually reduced, we try to reestablish that freedom by pulling back from whatever it is that we are being forced into. This phenomenon is called *psychological reactance* (Brehm, 1972).

Reactance can be cultivated as a defense against excessive influence. Having read this chapter, you now know some of the circumstances under which people can influence you. Hang on tightly to this knowledge. It will alert you to situations in your daily life when you are, in fact, being influenced. Influence always limits your freedom to a certain degree. Therefore, the "influence-alert" signal should result in reactance. And that reactance, that pulling back, will give you the chance you need to evaluate the influence. This brings us to our second suggestion.

An Active Approach to Influence

Not all influences are bad. (If they were, you would be an extremely bad person, since you are already a bundle of influences.) Some influences are simply neutral. For example, if you conform by wearing a jacket and tie to work, this is a fairly harmless influence. And other influences are excellent. For example, if someone is trying to persuade you to stop smoking, you might do well to bend to this influence. After all, your smoking habit is not sacred. It is not "essence of you." It is just the result of an old influence. Sometimes it is definitely worthwhile to let new influences take the place of old ones.

The point is that there are all kinds of influences—good, bad, and so-so. As we have seen, it is impossible to isolate ourselves from these influences, but it is not impossible to *choose* among them. The best defense against excessive influence is to take an active rather than a passive approach to influence.

An active approach to influence means confronting and consciously evaluating the influences that are brought to bear on you. Reactance will help in alerting you to potential influences, but you can also actively look for the things that influence you. Having read about the three processes of influence, you already know where to look.

First, models. Be aware that you model yourself after your friends and parents, and ask yourself whether the thoughts and behaviors you have picked up from them are consistent with what you want to be. Second, groups. Pay attention to the pressures applied to you in groups, and weigh those pressures against your personal beliefs. Maybe you can accommodate both the group and your principles, but if not, you owe it to yourself to make a conscious choice between them. Third, persuaders. By all means, be sensitive to persuasive communications and scrutinize them carefully. How honest is the communication? Whom does it mean to benefit? How many manipulative techniques is it using? (You might make a copy of Box 11.3, pp. 324–325, and keep it on top of your television set.) If you ask yourself these questions in the face of persuasion, you will save yourself from being the plaything of persuaders. Once again, this is not to say that you should not be persuaded. Even if the persuader is arguing entirely for his own benefit (for example, your son's argument for an increase in allowance), you may be quite willing to be influenced. But you can at least say that you *willed* the influence, rather than that you simply let it happen.

In sum, by taking an active approach, you influence yourself from within at the same time that you are being influenced from the outside. You choose your own social pressures. Consequently, despite the immense power of social influence, you retain a degree of freedom.

SUMMARY

1. *Social influence* occurs whenever we think or act in response to the prior action of another human being. In this chapter we deal with *direct influence,* in which we imitate or comply with others.

2. *Attitudes* are highly subject to social influence. An attitude is a cluster of ingrained beliefs and feelings about a certain object, and a predisposition to act toward that object in a certain way. Attitudes make social life possible by serving three important functions: organizing our experience, confirming our need for approval, and protecting our self-esteem. Attitudes arise from personal experience, the displacement of painful emotions, and social influence. Parents, peers, and the media are important sources of influence in the formation of attitudes.

3. There are three main processes through which people can be influenced. The first is modeling, which involves the learning of new behaviors through imitating other people. Modeling is a somewhat special form of learning in that it does not depend on external reinforcement. The

more powerful a person is, and the more rewarding and similar he is to the observer, the more likely he is to be chosen as a model for the observer. If, as some theorists argue, behavior can give rise to attitudes, then we may assume that, as we learn new behavior through modeling, new attitudes will follow.

4. A second process of social influence is conformity. To *conform* is to change one's beliefs or behavior to make them agree with those of a group. A *group*, in sociological usage, is a collection of individuals who share a common goal, act out roles in relation to one another, and interact according to shared norms. A study by Solomon Asch demonstrates the strength of our tendency to conform. Festinger's *social comparison theory* suggests that conformity may be the result, in part, of people's need to confirm their opinions by comparing them with the opinions of others. Conformity may also be explained as a consequence of our dependence on others. Certain characteristics of the group, the question being decided, and the individual help to determine the probability of conformity.

5. *Persuasion*, the deliberate exercise of influence through the transmission of information, is a third process of social influence. Certain characteristics of the communicator, the message, and the audience are important in determining the effectiveness of persuasion.

6. The special form of persuasion known as *propaganda* involves the use of deliberately deceptive information for self-serving purposes. The distinction between propaganda and ordinary persuasion is not clear-cut; while propaganda is manipulative, so is all persuasion, to some degree. Nevertheless, the term "propaganda" is useful in describing arguments that are especially distortive and self-serving.

7. Our adjustment is clearly affected by the powerful processes of direct influence. We cannot and should not try to avoid them altogether, yet neither should we let ourselves be helplessly controlled by them. *Psychological reactance*, our pulling back from an influence that threatens our free choice, can serve as a signal that influence is being exerted on us. We should respond to this signal by taking an active approach to influence—that is, judging and then choosing or rejecting the influence.

PROJECT

In Box 11.3 we list nine techniques commonly used in persuasion. One place where we encounter these techniques frequently is in the commercials that litter every hour of television. A great deal of time, effort, and money is spent making these brief messages as effective as possible. And with some success, apparently, for over the years the amount of money spent on television advertising has steadily increased, with some "spots" now costing advertisers hundreds of thousands of dollars.

Since it is likely that you are one of the millions of Americans influenced by these efforts at persuasion, it might be useful for you to find out just what techniques are being used and which ones do in fact have an effect on your feelings about the product being advertised. Such an exercise will help to "inoculate" you against these techniques.

Begin by reviewing the list of techniques in Box 11.3. Then spend one evening watching television during prime time—that is, 8 o'clock to 11 o'clock. (This is the period of the day when the most people are watching television; therefore, it is also the time when the most money is spent for advertising.) As you watch, keep a running record of the commercials. After each commercial, (1) note the product being advertised, (2) describe the commercial in a sentence or two, (3) list the techniques of persuasion employed by the commercial (use the numbered code provided below), and (4) on a scale of 1 to 10, rate the persuasiveness of the commercial—that is, how much the techniques employed actually made you feel positively disposed toward the product.

After you have done your ratings, review them to see which techniques consistently drew positive responses from you. Why do you think these particular techniques are persuasive in your case? Do they tell you anything about your own biases and mental habits?

Persuasive techniques:

1. Transfer and testimony
2. Appeal to the expert
3. Plain folks
4. Appeal to self-esteem
5. Appeal to social fears
6. Bandwagon
7. The empty slogan
8. Pseudo-statistic
9. Fuzzy language

SAMPLE RECORD

PRODUCT	DESCRIPTION	TECHNIQUES USED	PERSUASIVENESS RATING
Budweiser beer	Film clips of laborers toiling under hot sun, then enjoying cold beer, accompanied by song with refrain, "This Bud's for you!"	3, 7	5

<u>OUTLINE</u>

THE CHAIN OF INFLUENCE
Analyzing a Problem in a Relationship
Description
Simplicity
Objectivity
Specificity
A sample description
Functional Analysis

CHANGING YOUR SOCIAL INFLUENCE
Setting the Goal
Planning the Interaction
Avoiding cues for conflict
Creating cues for pleasant interaction
"Psyching yourself up" for new responses
Creating New Interactive Chains
Listening
Avoiding defensive responses
Giving clear messages
Revealing your interpretations
Being rewarding in general
Two-Sided Change
Contracts
A Note on Methods
Punishment
Dealing with slip-ups

12

SOCIAL INFLUENCE: HOW TO CHANGE IT

In Chapter 11 we described direct influence. But what about the subtler forms of influence? As we learned in Chapter 11, *social influence occurs whenever we think or act in response to the prior action of another human being.* We are influenced not only when someone persuades us, but also when someone says hello or goodbye, "Go to hell," or "I love you." Each of these statements calls for a particular type of response from us and thereby influences us in a particular way.

This type of influence—indirect influence—is the stuff of which our social life is made. In order to deal with this enormous topic in the space of one chapter, we will concentrate on the one area in which indirect influence most affects our adjustment—close relationships. And as usual we will concentrate on dealing with problems—in this case, the day-to-day problems of getting along with those who are close to us. As we shall see, these problems very often result from the careless use of

our social influence. And they can often be solved by learning to use social influence more wisely.

This, then, is the subject of Chapter 12: how to change social relationships by changing the way we exercise our social influence. First we will take a closer look at how reciprocal influence works. Second, we will go through the procedure for analyzing a problem in a relationship. Third, we will discuss the techniques for handling such problems by changing our method of social influence.

THE CHAIN OF INFLUENCE

In chemistry we learn that chemical elements sometimes combine in chains. Certain elements, however, can only combine with certain other elements, so that each new link in the chain determines, to some degree, what the next link will be. The same is true of social influence. Let us look at an example:

It is Sunday morning: Jay is reading the newspaper in the living room. His wife Annie, is building some shelves in the kitchen. Annie holds a long board up against the wall to see how high she wants it. But since she is the one holding it up, she can't step back to see whether the height is correct.

1. **Annie:** Can you help me with this?

2. **Jay:** In a minute.

3. **Annie:** Please—now! I'm breaking my arm here.

4. **Jay:** Oh! Why didn't you say so? Here I come. *(He comes into the kitchen and grabs the board.)*

5. **Annie:** Thanks. Whew!

If you look carefully at this rather ordinary dialogue, you will see that the responses seem to follow one another with a certain inevitability. Each statement suggests, to some extent, what the next statement will be. Each link in the chain calls for the next link. This fact of human interaction has been noted by many psychologists. One psychologist, discussing children's behavior, put it as follows: "If you want to know what child B will do, the best single predictor is what child A did to B the moment before" (Raush, 1965, p. 492). And if you want to know what Jay will say, the best predictor is what Annie said to him the moment before.

This is not to say that we can predict exactly how a human being will respond to a particular statement. People differ from one another, and therefore they have different responses to the same thing. Some people, for example, tend to come running when asked for help; others tend to run in the opposite direction. In addition to these "person variables," situational variables also affect our responses. When we're with a group,

for example, we may be less willing to help a stranger than when we are alone. Finally, we do have some choice about how we will respond to a particular statement. We are not programed to make statement *y* in response to statement *x*. Rather, we select among a number of possible responses.

Nevertheless, the fact remains that what is said to you has a powerful influence on what you will say in return. What you will say is, after all, a *response to* that prior statement. And the nature of that prior statement will make certain types of responses less likely.

To prove this to yourself, try an experiment. Take any one of the first four statements in the Jay-and-Annie dialogue and replace it with a statement of a different meaning. Now, could the *next* remark still stand as it is? Imagine, for example, that we threw out number 3 and replaced it with "Whenever you're ready." Could numbers 4 and 5 remain? No. The rest of the script would have to be rewritten. Here is one way it might go.

3. **Annie:** Whenever you're ready. *(Ten minutes later Jay finishes reading the paper and comes into the kitchen.)*

4. **Jay:** What did you want?

5. **Annie:** Forget it. Ten minutes ago you could have helped. Now you can go back to your damned paper. I do all the work in this house anyway.

This is not the only way statements 4 and 5 could be rewritten. There are a number of logical possibilities (see Activity 12.1). But given the change in statement 3, statements 4 and 5 from the first script are not among the logical possibilities.

In sum, our own remarks and actions have a profound impact on the other person's remarks and actions. Now, this fact may sound very obvious. Yes, of course, people respond to each other. We take this for granted. And that is precisely the problem. By taking it for granted, we lose sight of the fact that we help to determine other people's behavior toward us by providing the cues for their responses. We say to ourselves, "That's just the way he is," or "God knows why she acts that way." What we are forgetting is that the way she acts is a response to the way we act (Gottman et al., 1977).

The same is true of the relationship as a whole. We create half of it, and in doing so, we help create the other half. What we give, we are likely to get. Nastiness begets nastiness, and niceness begets niceness. Coldness begets coldness; intimacy begets intimacy. This is what psychologists call *reciprocity* (Patterson and Reid, 1970). It could also be called the "two to tango" principle. Whatever the term, the phenomenon can be seen in all close relationships. Marriage is perhaps the best example. As one researcher puts it, "a marital relationship comprises a never ending sequence of circular and reciprocal behaviors" (Margolin, 1981). But the same can be said of parent-child relationships, sibling relationships, and friendships.

In the principle of reciprocity, then, lies the cause of much of our interpersonal conflict. And in this principle lies our power to resolve such conflict. For if the other person's behavior toward us is a response to our behavior toward him, then we can change his behavior by changing our own. And in

Human relationships tend to follow the principle of reciprocity; whatever we give, that is what is given back to us. (© Hiroshi Hanaya/Magnum)

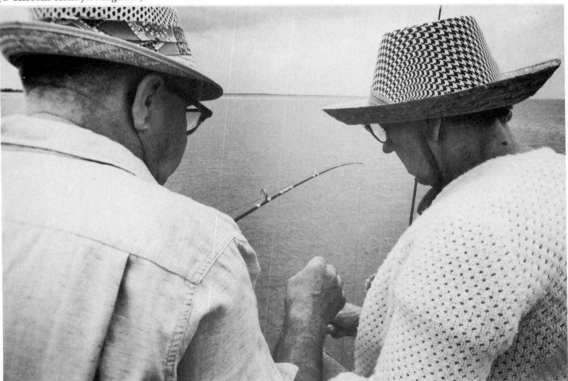

ACTIVITY 12.1

Take another look at the original Annie-and-Jay dialogue (p. 332). Using the three kinds of variables discussed above—situational variables, person variables, and individual choice—experiment with the dialogue. Here are three experiments: (1) introduce a new situational variable, such as the fact that it's a steaming hot day or that the phone rings right after Annie asks for help; (2) introduce a new "person variable," such as Jay's being an extremely irritable person—or an extremely obliging person; (3) assuming that the situation and Jay's personality are the same as in the original dialogue, substitute a different response that he could have *chosen* to make in statement 2. In each experiment, start by writing Annie's statement 1 on a fresh piece of paper. Then introduce a new variable and let the dialogue "rewrite itself" (with your help) in keeping with the change. As you will see, one change in the script changes the rest of the script.

the process we will have changed the relationship.

This doesn't mean that you can transform a relationship from nasty to nice overnight. What it does mean is that you can change specific behaviors on your part and specific conditions in the environment that help to initiate chains of negative responses. And you can create behaviors and environmental conditions that will help to initiate chains of positive responses. The result will be less pain and more pleasure in your relationship—not an unworthy goal.

First, however, you have to pinpoint the problem in your relationship and locate its specific causes. In other words, it is necessary for you to do another description and functional analysis.

ANALYZING A PROBLEM IN A RELATIONSHIP

Since we have already been through the analysis procedure several times, we will be brief this time around.

Description

In describing a problem in a relationship, you need to follow the same three rules that you applied to earlier descriptions: simplicity, objectivity, and specificity.

Simplicity

When people try to describe their interpersonal problems, they tend to speak in huge, vague generalizations: "He's just mean"; "She's a bitch." These statements may seem true enough to the person making them, but they are far too complex for analysis. The best way to ensure simplicity in your description is to pick a problematic *situation* in your relationship—a scene that you play out repeatedly. Examples: "my anger at him for flirting with other women and his defensiveness on the subject"; "the fight with my father over the yard work." (Note that both these examples include you as well as the other person. Remember the reciprocity principle. Every interpersonal problem involves at least two people.)

Objectivity

To ensure objectivity, the problem you describe should be a *behavior*—an observable, countable behavior. "If you can't count the behavior, you haven't pinpointed it properly" (Patterson, 1975, p. 50). Look back at the first example in the last paragraph: "my anger at him for flirting with other women and his defensiveness on the subject." You can't count anger or defensiveness. So you have to translate these items into concrete actions: "my nasty remarks about his flirting and his counterarguments that I am jealous and insecure." Make sure that your problem is stated just as objectively as this.

Specificity

Now you have to get specific—that is, fill in the details. (Remember: you will need these details when you begin looking for correlations during functional analysis.)

The Behavior. First, the details about the behavior itself. Not only should it be countable; it should be counted. How many times a week (on the average) does this scene take place? How long (on the average) does it last? What percentage of your time together is taken up with going through this same scene? You can gather this information in the same way that you gathered information on self-control problems—that is, through self-monitoring.*

Aside from the numbers, the precise details of your actions and the other person's actions must be described. What, exactly, do you say or do to each other? In short, you need a situational description, with dialogue. Give at least six or seven lines of the talk and back-talk. Or if actions are more important, describe them in a back-and-forth manner (for example, "He turns up the volume on the stereo. I turn it down. He turns it up. I leave the room and slam the door"). Be sure to indicate how the scene ends. Does someone leave? Does someone apologize? Does the whole thing just peter out?

The Surrounding Variables: External and Internal. You also need to fill in the details surrounding the behavior: the external and internal variables connected to the scene.

First, the external variables. Are there any environmental cues? Is there a special place (in the kitchen, in the car) where the scene usually takes place? Does it tend to occur at a particular time? Are there any special situations (trying to agree on which movie to see) or events (phone calls during dinner) that seem to trip the switch?

Second, the internal variables—thoughts and feelings that might be contributing to the problem. This is a hazier area, but you can help yourself through it by remembering the theories of social psychology described in Chapter 8. (Reminder: these are attribution theory, role theory, communication theory, and social exchange theory. You might want to turn back to pages 219–227 and review them right now.) Is there a disagreement on roles lurking behind your problem with the other person? (Do you want your mother to be your "friend," while she thinks of herself as your protective, enveloping "Mama"?) Do you attribute the other person's behavior to some special motive, a motive that annoys or angers you? (Do you suspect that your roommate makes those "helpful suggestions" because she thinks

---

* The self-monitoring of interpersonal behavior, like self-monitoring of "personal" behavior such as over-eating or smoking, is reactive (Cavior and Marabotto, 1976). So don't be surprised if you suddenly become a model of good behavior (thus cutting short the fights) once the monitoring begins. Just continue watching and recording for two or three weeks. The reactive effects will eventually diminish.

OTHERS

Certain stimuli—such as phone calls during mealtime, or even mealtime itself—can act as triggers for family arguments. (Richard Kalvar/Magnum)

she's better than you?) And are you possibly arguing over a cost-and-rewards contract? (Are you angry because he never comforts you, whereas you are always comforting him?) These thoughts and feelings—along with any other internal factors connected to the problem—should be added to your description.

A Sample Description

Here is a description of an interpersonal problem written by a woman we will call Sally. As you read it, note how the details hint at possible causes of the problem:

My problem is a running argument with my mother over the way I lead my life. What really bothers her is the fact that I'm divorced and not looking to get married again, at least not right away. But this comes out in all sorts of complaints. She disapproves of my job, my friends,

my way of raising my daughter. If I'm going out with someone and I bring him over to meet her, she tells me later what she didn't like about him. If I don't introduce her to the person I'm seeing, she thinks I'm hiding something. If I ask her to look after my daughter for the evening (she lives about ten minutes away), she says I'm going out too much and neglecting my responsibilities as a mother. If I hire a babysitter instead and she finds out, that's even worse. (I can't really afford sitters, anyway.) As for what I criticize about her, mostly it's just her attitude toward me, her constant nagging. Also her values, particularly the idea that what a woman should do is get married and stay home.

The numbers: We average about two or three arguments, or at least unpleasant conversations, per week, lasting about ten minutes apiece. I think this represents about two-thirds of the time I spend with her.

The scene: Our conversations take place either on the telephone or at her house, when I'm picking up Lauren, my daughter, or dropping her off. Here is a scene from last week that was very typical. I arrived at my parents' house around midnight to get Lauren. My mother was still up.

She: What's the hurry? Why can't you sit down for a minute?

I: My friend is waiting in the car, Mom.

She: Can't he come in?

I: I've got to get up early. If he comes in and we have a cup of coffee, we won't leave for another hour. You know that.

She: Lauren told me she takes the bus to that swimming class.

I: Mom, she's ten years old. There are no sex fiends on the bus. It's very safe.

She: How do you know? You're out fooling around. How do you know what she does?

This sort of thing goes on every time. Eventually she accuses me of being irresponsible, or hints at it. And I tell her that she makes no effort to understand me—that I'm trying to work and go to school and raise a kid, all at the same time, and that I'd be happy if she'd get off my back. If we're on the phone, we say a stilted goodbye. If I'm at her house, I tell her I have to leave and go.

The surrounding variables: As I said, this conversation takes place either on the phone or at her house. And I guess what might be triggering it is a situation where she's doing something for me or agreeing to do something for me—usually take care of Lauren. This gives her the upper hand. (But she wants *to look after Lauren. She doesn't have much else to do, and she thinks babysitters are "irresponsible kids.") As for internal variables, there definitely is a role disagreement. She sees our roles as parent and child. Even though I'm thirty-two, she still thinks she should inspect my boyfriends and tell me what to eat and how to do my hair and so forth. And I see my role as that of an independent adult. Attributions: I attribute her nagging to a desire to keep me in my place, to make me a child again, make me follow her rules. Costs and rewards: I think she figures that in return for what she does for me—babysitting for Lauren and also some financial help now and then—she should get full obedience from me. And I don't think I owe her that.*

Anyway, what I feel is anger. I need her help, but at the same time I have to defend myself constantly against her accusations. By the time I pull up in front of her house, I'm already tensed up because I know what's coming: some leading question, some critical remark. I feel as though she makes no effort at all to understand who I am or what I want out of life. Essentially, she has no respect for me as a person. She just wants to make me over into herself.

Functional Analysis

Having finished your description, you are ready for the functional analysis. In the first step, finding variables that correlate with the problem behavior, you will probably have no trouble whatsoever. In fact, you may have the problem of finding too many. It is safe to say that in interpersonal conflict there is never a single cause. Your feelings, the other person's feelings, your picture of his role, his picture of his role, your attributions, his attributions, to say nothing of external cues—all of these are very likely causes. In Sally's description, for example, you probably spotted a number of suspicious-looking variables: the role dissensus (Chapter 8), the questionable attribution,* the mother's high costs and low rewards, the fact that all the occasions for interaction involve Sally's needing a favor.

In your own functional analysis, however, we suggest that you concentrate on one particular class of variable: external cues. This category includes environmental variables—time, place, events, and situations—that seem to set the stage for the interpersonal conflict. It also includes your responses to the other person.

This latter variable, your own responses, is the crucial one. As we saw earlier in the chapter, your responses set the conditions for the other person's responses. Furthermore, it is only through your responses that you can communicate the internal variables discussed above. Role misunderstandings, mistaken attributions, cost-and-reward imbalances, wounded feelings: if you want to clear up these matters, you have to do it through speech and behavior—that is, through your responses to the other person.

Thus we repeat: in your hypothesis and in your experiments we recommend that you concentrate on external cues: events, situations, and—most of all—your responses to

---

* Sally's mother might offer an altogether different explanation for her criticisms: actual concern for her daughter's and granddaughter's welfare.

the other person. The rest of this chapter will be devoted to describing techniques for manipulating these independent variables, with the hope of changing the dependent variable: your interpersonal problem.

CHANGING YOUR SOCIAL INFLUENCE

Setting the Goal

We have spoken, in earlier chapters, about the value of setting modest goals. When you set out to improve a relationship with another person, your goals should be particularly modest. There are two reasons for this. The first is a reason we have given before: if you choose goals that are too high, you set yourself up for failure. And once you fail, you are likely to become discouraged and give up. By choosing modest goals, on the other hand, you set yourself up for success, which will encourage you to continue your efforts.

The second reason for setting modest goals in interpersonal experiments is that your achievement of your goal depends not just on you but on the other person as well. Even if you think you can change your responses to her overnight, she is unlikely to follow suit.

Thus, in the beginning, you should keep your goal at a level low enough so that *through your own efforts* you are likely to achieve it. For example, if you invariably have an argument with your boyfriend when he is late meeting you, aim at "no nasty remarks for ten minutes" the next three times he is late. (In those ten minutes you will have to deal with his lateness in more constructive ways—ways that we will describe further along in this chapter.) By the time you have achieved this goal, your pos-

itive efforts are bound to be having an effect on the other person. And then you can move your goal up a notch.

Let us look now at ways to achieve this goal.

Planning the Interaction

As we saw in Chapter 6, you can control your own behavior by planning ahead. If you don't buy snack foods when you're at the grocery store, you won't have an easy time snacking once you get home. In the very same way, you can plan your interactions with another person so as to make that painful old scene (the subject of your description) less likely to occur. There are three ways of planning: (1) avoiding cues for conflict, (2) creating cues for pleasant interaction, and (3) "psyching yourself up" for new responses.

Avoiding Cues for Conflict

If your description tells you that your problem is usually set off by some environmental cue—some event or situation—then examine this cue to see whether it could be avoided. In some cases it can't be. (Sally, for example, is not willing to spend every evening at home in order to avoid conflict with her mother.) But in many cases, the environmental cue can be avoided, and with very little sacrifice. For example, consider a woman who invariably has three or four fights with her husband every week because she wants to have a relaxed intimate talk after dinner and he wants to watch the news. Before she concludes that he prefers Dan Rather to her, she should try moving the dinner hour up so that there is a half hour for talk before the news comes on.

If you feel that you have serious problems with the other person, then cue-avoiding may seem a very simplistic suggestion. For instance, the woman in our example may have concluded that her husband has no desire to communicate with her. If she's right, then she does have a serious problem, one that will not be solved simply by avoiding setting events (cues) for quarrels. But by experimenting with the setting event, she at least gives herself the chance to find out whether that serious problem really exists. And if the problem does exist—that is, if it continues after the cue-avoiding experiment—then it can be faced squarely, rather than concealed behind a quarrel over the TV news.

Creating Cues for Pleasant Interaction

Sometimes, as we mentioned, the cue can't be avoided. Imagine that you have a part-time job at an insurance agency. Almost everything about the job is fine. It's close to home, the pay is reasonably good, and you can adjust the hours to fit your school schedule. The only problem is that the person you work directly under, the office manager, does not seem to like you. The minute you arrive, he starts griping, usually about your work, although the boss has told you that your work is fine. You've talked to the boss about your problem with this man, but he says that you'll just have to work it out somehow. What do you do? The cue for the unpleasantness is your arrival in the office. Should you quit the job?

Instead, try creating cues for pleasant interaction and using them to counteract the cue for unpleasantness. In other words, as soon as you arrive at the office, do something that almost requires a positive response from this man. For example, tell him that his daughter (her picture is on his desk) is the prettiest child you've ever seen. Or hand him a book, telling him that you heard him say he wanted to read it, so you picked it up for him at the library. He may not know what to do in response to this positive opener. In fact, he may be completely nonplused. But he will find it very hard to start in right away on what's the matter with you.

This technique, essentially the reverse of cue-avoidance, is based on the same principle: starting off the interaction with the maximum probability of positive responses. Unlike the cue-avoidance technique, the cue-creating technique probably won't solve the problem. But it will do two things that can definitely contribute to solving the problem. First, it will show that you care about the relationship—that you're willing to make an effort. Second, it will hold off negative interaction long enough to give you and the other person the chance to engage in more substantial positive communications. (These positive communications will be discussed shortly.)

"Psyching Yourself Up" for New Responses

We said earlier that we would concentrate exclusively on changing external variables. We will make one exception to this rule right now. In planning ways to improve a relationship, you must give attention to one internal variable: your feelings about changing.

Imagine, for example, that Sally is planning to use the cue-creating technique. As she comes into her mother's house, she is going to say, "Listen, Mom. They're showing *Gone With the Wind* at the Roxie on Sunday. Laurie and I are going. Do you want to come?" But as she pulls up in front of the house, her anger at her mother returns, and suddenly the plan of inviting her to the movies looks artificial and ridiculous.

Sally, then, needs to "psych herself up" for changing her responses. And you probably do, too. This can be done through self-talk.

First, ask yourself what you have to gain by following your "natural" feelings (for example, anger) and engaging in your old responses. What you have to gain is the continuation of the old problem. Is this what you want?

Second, ask yourself what you have to gain by changing your responses. An improved relationship with someone you care for. Isn't this worth more than the momentary satisfaction of giving in to your "natural" feelings? And what do you have to lose? At this point three questions may occur to you. Here are the questions, along with some reasonable answers that you can give yourself:

"Won't I feel like a fool?" Yes, in the beginning you probably will feel rather silly. When you and your mother have not exchanged a kind word in months, it's not easy to walk in, all smiles, and ask her to go to the movies with you. So expect feelings of embarrassment, swallow them, and go ahead with your plans. Once positive responses are repeated a few times, they will feel more natural, and the embarrassment will slowly disappear.

"But what if it doesn't work? What if she makes some nasty response?" Well, what of it? No one is writing this up for the local newspaper. Remember, what you are engaged in is not a contest between you and the other person. It's an experiment. If the experiment doesn't work, try a new one. Scientists do this every day.

"But doesn't it mean that I'm giving in?" No. It means exactly the opposite. It means that you're refusing to be excessively influenced by the other person's responses. It means that you're free enough and strong enough to create a new pattern of responses —a pattern that will benefit you both.

If you answer your misgivings in this way, you will be able to get through the period of doubt and embarrassment that almost always accompanies the first few experiments with positive responding. After that, positive responses will gradually become self-rewarding and automatic.

Creating New Interactive Chains

Planning the interaction helps to get you going in the right direction. But this still leaves the interaction itself. If you have an established pattern of negative responses, the easiest thing to do is to fall right back into it. What can you do, then, to prevent yourself from backsliding into negative responses and at the same time to start a chain of positive responses?

There are several positive-response techniques you can use, and the purpose of this section is to describe them. They include (1) listening, (2) avoiding defensive responses, (3) giving clear messages, (4) revealing your interpretations, and (5) being rewarding in general.

Ordinary as these techniques may seem, they are perfectly designed to serve your two purposes—preventing backsliding and starting positive responses. If you make one of these positive responses instead of a negative response, you've avoided backsliding right then and there. Furthermore, you are preventing future backsliding, since, by replacing an old negative response with a new positive response, you are weakening any conditioned cue-and-response associations that may have been leading automatically to conflict. (In this sense, these techniques represent "incompatibile behaviors," as described in Chapter 6.) Second, they initiate positive chains. Your positive response calls for a positive response from the other person, which calls for a positive response from you, and so on. Thus, you have forged the first few links of a bright new chain.

SOCIAL INFLUENCE: HOW TO CHANGE IT

Listening

Listening to another person—*really* listening—is an art that many of us never learn. Either we're too busy trying to get a word in ourselves, or we listen "with one ear," meanwhile giving the better part of our attention to the cat, the newspaper, or our fingernails. Ironically, this is particularly true in close relationships. A stranger whom you meet at a party may get your close attention, but as for your mother, your wife, your friend, your child—you've heard their routine before.

To them, however, their routine is interesting and important, and one of the best ways of improving your relationship with them is to listen to them. By doing so, you achieve three very desirable goals: (1) you show that you care about them, (2) you gather enough information so that you can make meaningful responses to what they're saying, and (3) you increase the probability that they will listen to you (Williams and Long, 1979, pp. 213–215).

Active Listening. Genuine listening involves more than just shutting up while the other person speaks. When you take the trouble to listen to someone, you should let him know, through brief remarks, that you are in fact hearing what he has to say. This is called *active listening*, and it can be achieved through two very humble techniques.

The first is simply asking questions. When your friend says to you, "I don't know

By genuinely listening to another person—looking him in the eye as he talks to you, asking him questions, and picking up on unspoken feelings—you can let him know that you care about what he thinks. And you can come to understand him better. (© Barbara Alper 1981)

what's the matter with me today," and you say "Umm" or "Yeah, I know," all you're indicating is that you're not deaf. If, on the other hand, you respond by saying, "What's the problem?" then you're indicating that you care, that you're listening, and that you want her to go on. Even when you're not confronted with a clear "opener" (as in "I don't know what's the matter with me"), questions are still very useful. When someone is describing a scene to you and you say, "And then what did he do?" you let the person know that she has your attention. She will be grateful.

The second technique of active listening is *reflecting*—that is, briefly paraphrasing back to the other person what he has just said to you. You let him speak his piece and then you give him a brief synopsis, starting with a phrase like "So what you're saying is. . ." or "So you think that. . . ." This technique, first developed by humanistic psychologist Carl Rogers (1951) and now widely used by psychotherapists, serves two purposes. First, like asking questions, it shows that you hear and value what the other person is saying. (This doesn't necessarily mean that you agree.) Second, it gives the other person a chance to correct the statement if you have misunderstood him, or if he has overstated his case. For example:

Your father: I don't see why you encourage your brother to do such stupid things.

You: So you think I'm egging him on.

Your father: Well, not exactly egging him on. But if you would just talk to him. . . .

Instead of attacking him for making an exaggerated accusation, you show him that you care about what he's saying and at the same time you get him to clarify what he means and what he wants.

Listening to Feelings. What people feel, they don't always express in plain English. Instead, they convey their feelings through "body language" (posture, facial expression, gestures), through tone of voice, and through indirect wording. Responding directly to these cues—by asking a question or by reflecting the emotional message you're picking up—is one of the most positive responses you can offer to another person. This is clearly illustrated in an experience reported by psychologist Arnold Lazarus.

ACTIVITY 12.2

By listening passively, we often forego the chance to deepen a relationship. Active listening, on the other hand, invites the person to share more of her thoughts and feelings with you. (It also creates more interesting conversations.) Pick out a person whom you would like to know better and engage her in conversation. As she talks, respond to what she says by asking questions ("But why do you think he did that?") and by reflecting ("So you think they're not going to give any raises at all this year"). You will probably find that once the person feels you are interested in what she has to say, she will say a great deal more.

A regular customer comes into the luncheonette, seeming depressed. The counterman, who has known him for years, intuitively picks up his emotional cue. And by asking "Having a bad day, George?" he gives George a chance to talk about the problem. He also lets George know that someone notices, someone cares. (Charles Harbutt/Magnum)

While being waited upon by an abrasive sales clerk, Lazarus considered three possible negative responses to the individual: (1) personally chastising him, (2) using one-upmanship (i.e., insulting him), or (3) reporting him to the manager. However, instead of verbally attacking him, Lazarus decided to respond empathically: "You seem to be having a hell of a bad day. Is something wrong?" The sales clerk proceeded to explain that his wife was in the hospital and he was very anxious about her condition. What followed was a significant conversation focusing on the man's feelings about his wife's illness. Undoubtedly, both men felt substantially better as a result of this positive, supportive interaction. (Williams and Long, 1975, pp. 196–197)

There will be times, of course, when you simply don't want to hear what the other person is communicating. You still gain more by acknowledging the message than by ignoring it. Let's look at another example. You tell your sister that you're going to the movies with a friend tonight. A hurt look passes over her face, and she says "Oh" in a muffled tone of voice. You know right away what the problem is. She has an exam tomorrow in chemistry and she needs you to drill her for the exam. But what you really want is just to go to the movie and not have to feel guilty about your sister. You may be perfectly justified in doing this, but you are not justified in ignoring her very clear communication. Even if you're not going to be swayed by it, you should acknowledge it. By saying "Look, Eileen, I know you have a chemistry exam tomorrow, but I've been waiting to see this movie for months, and tonight's the only night they're showing it," you let her know that you "hear" her feelings and care about them but that you have your own reasons for not going along with them. If you just leave without acknowledging her communication, what you're saying is that you're going to do what you want to do *and* that you don't care in the least how she feels about it. In short, refusing to listen to the other person's emotional cues is an excellent way to let him know that you don't give a damn about him.

Expressing Similarity. A final technique that will make you a better listener is to tell the person that you have had feelings similar to what he is describing to you. This technique comes quite naturally to most people. How many times have you started to tell someone about something, only to have him say, "That reminds me of the time I . . ." and then continue with his story for five minutes? The problem here is that the person is bringing up his experience not to show you that he is listening but to *stop* listening to you and get you to listen to him.

When used briefly and sparingly, however, expressions of similarity show the other person not only that you're listening and that you care, but also that you empathize—you know how he feels. This is particularly useful when the other person is explaining a subtle emotional point.

She: . . . I was just about to ring up her purchase and she said, "Just a minute there." I don't know what it was about her tone, but it made me so mad.

You: I know what you mean. I had a customer use that tone on me this morning. Snippy.

She: Yes, that's it. Snippy. So I said to her . . .

Expressing similarity is also very useful when someone is criticizing you. Here, however, it is very important to keep your comments brief:

Your roommate: When I told you that story about Nancy and me, I didn't mean for you to pass it on to Al. I ran into him today, and he gave me a long talk on how to handle women. I felt like a complete idiot.

You: I'm sorry. I didn't know you meant it to be private. I know how you feel. He gave me the same talk when Maggie and I split up.

In this way you "affirm" the other person's feeling. You may not feel that you owe the person an apology. Indeed, you may feel that the criticism is completely unfair. But you can still let him know that you have felt what he is feeling. By doing so, you show that you respect his emotional experience, even if you don't agree that you are to blame for his pain or embarrassment.

"Did she say that to you? Boy, I know how it feels . . ." By expressing similarity, you let the other person know that you understand and appreciate what she's talking about. But don't take over the conversation in order to tell *your* story. Let her go on telling hers. (© Henri Cartier-Bresson/Magnum)

Avoiding Defensive Responses

One of the major causes of negative interactions is our habit of responding defensively. We feel we've been hit, so we hit back, and then the other person hits back, and so on it goes. However, if you don't hit back, this ugly little spiral cannot take place. What, then, can you do when you feel you've been hit? There are two alternatives to consider: (1) admitting fault and (2) ignoring the "zap."

Admitting Fault. On some occasions when we feel we've been hit, we really haven't been hit at all. Rather, we have been criticized for something that really *is* our fault. Yet we still tend to respond defensively:

He: I thought you said you were going to take these books back to the library.

You: Oh, get off my back. I'll return them when I'm good and ready.

What if, instead, you admitted that you were at fault: "Oh, I forgot. I'm sorry. I'll take them back tomorrow"? In the first place, this would be a much fairer response. It concedes that the other person has a right to his complaint and even to his exasperated tone of voice. Equally important, this response is very practical. It leaves the other person no opening for an argument. (By contrast, the defensive response is an almost irresistible invitation to an argument.)

Ignoring the "Zap." Some criticisms are delivered not just in an exasperated tone of voice; they come with a "zap"—an insult or nasty crack added on.

She: Who the hell do you think you are, keeping me waiting for a half hour?

In this case you *have* been hit. What do you do?

As psychologists have pointed out (Patterson and Cobb, 1971), most remarks that are made to us are fairly mixed offerings. In responding, we choose, among several possibilities, which component of the remark we will address ourselves to. In the case of the above remark, for example, you have at least two choices as to what you will respond to:

1. The insult ("Who the hell do you think you are"). In this case you would probably choose to be insulting in return: "Oh, get off it. I spend my life waiting for you to finish preening in front of the mirror."
2. The complaint ("keeping me waiting

for a half hour"). In this case you would probably choose to explain and/or apologize: "I'm sorry. I kept trying to leave the house, but every time I put the phone down it rang again."

If you respond to the zap—which, of course, is very tempting—you allow the argument to begin. If, instead, you respond to the complaint, you short-circuit the argument before it has a chance to begin.

This does not mean that you should always respond to zappy criticisms by admitting fault. If you are at fault, by all means admit it and apologize. If, on the other hand, the criticism is unjust, say so: "What we agreed was that I would get here as soon as I could. And that's what I did." In this way, you state your case, but not aggressively. And consequently you give the other person no cue for further aggression on his part.

You should be warned that ignoring the zap is not always easy to do. After all, insults hurt; they make us angry. And the natural response is to express that anger. But if you can simply postpone this for a moment and deal with the criticism, you may find that your anger and the other person's will dissipate. Even if it doesn't, you will have given yourself a moment to frame a clear protest against the other person's unpleasant outburst.

This brings us to our next topic.

Giving Clear Messages

As communication theorists (Lederer and Jackson, 1968; Gottman, 1979) have pointed out, we often create problems in our relationships by never letting the other person know, in plain words, exactly what we want from him—never telling him, "That's what I like" or "That's what I don't like." Especially in marriage, people seem to expect one another to be mind-readers (Stuart,

BOX 12.1
PROBLEM-SOLVING TRAINING FOR UNHAPPY MARRIAGES

One approach to marriage-counselling is for the therapist to talk to the couple about their problems and help them arrive at solutions. Another approach, which many therapists are now trying, is to focus not so much on the couple's problems as on their problem-solving skills, the way they communicate with one another about sources of conflict in the relationship.

Psychologist Neil Jacobson has developed a marital treatment plan that aims at teaching couples how to deal with conflict in more positive and constructive ways. That is, he teaches couples how to do less blaming and criticizing and how to be more supportive, cooperative, and resourceful. In the early part of the treatment, the couples practice discussing their problems, whatever these may be, during the treatment hour. As they talk, the therapist coaches and corrects them, showing them how to listen carefully, make clear criticisms, avoid name-calling, generate solutions, and so forth.

Later the couple is assigned to engage in and tape two problem-solving sessions per week at home. The tapes are then analyzed by the couple and the therapist together during the treatment hour.

Jacobson (1979) recently reported results of this treatment with six severely distressed marriages. Five out of six improved substantially, and follow-up reports showed that the improvements endured after the therapy ended.

This is a hopeful new approach, very appealing in terms of practicality. Problems in a marriage change over the years. If a couple goes to a marriage counsellor who helps them work out this year's problems, there is still no telling what next year will bring. But if, instead, they learn new skills for solving a problem—any problem—then presumably they can apply these skills to whatever new conflicts arise over the years.

1969): "If she were really sensitive to me, she would know what I want," "Well, if he doesn't know how I feel, I don't see how I can tell him."

This reluctance to discuss areas of dissatisfaction not only makes it that much harder to achieve satisfaction; it also robs the couples involved of the opportunity to understand one another better on all levels—to find out who they're married to. Research indicates that when couples actually discuss their conflicts with one another, this increases each one's access to the other's interpersonal perceptions (Knudson et al., 1980). In other words, if you tell your wife (or, for that matter, your girlfriend or your mother) what she is doing that is bothering you, chances are that while the two of you are talking about the problem, even unpleasantly, you will also be gaining a clearer picture of how she sees both herself and you—information that will help strengthen the bond between you and prevent future conflict.

Clear messages, then, are all-important in a close relationship. You can help yourself in this direction by working on two basic skills: complaining constructively and giving approval.

Complaining Constructively. Many unhappy relationships consist largely of complaints. The problem, however, is not with the complaining itself. Complaining is a perfectly legitimate way of expressing dissatisfaction. The problem is with the style of complaining: vague, indirect, and nasty.

In order to improve a relationship, we have to learn how to complain more constructively. This doesn't mean you should bottle up serious grievances or sweeten them in any way. Constructive complaining simply means that you state your grievance—and nothing but your grievance—plainly and directly. You can do this by following six commonsensical rules:

1. *Make the complaint specific.* Before you open your mouth, narrow your complaint down to specific behaviors and stick to those. Don't say, "Boy, did you act like an idiot at that party!" *How* did he act like an idiot? By getting drunk and telling dirty jokes to the host's mother. So that's what you say: "You really embarrassed me last night by getting drunk and telling those jokes to Teddy's mother." Now he knows exactly what you want him to stop doing.

2. *Make the complaint plain and direct.* When you say one thing and mean another, you are usually criticizing (O'Neill and O'Neill, 1973, p. 118). The problem is that the other person picks up vaguely the fact that she is being criticized, but she never finds out exactly what she's done wrong. This usually leads to no improvement and considerable hostility. So take the responsibility for your complaint and state it clearly.

3. *Stick to the present.* Don't haul up old offenses from last month or last year. By doing this, you divert attention away from the problem at hand, and you make your criticism seem more like an attack on the other person's whole self. Furthermore, you invite him to drag up *your* old offenses.

4. *Don't add insults.* As we have already seen, many complaints come with a zap, and the zap makes it that much harder to respond constructively to the complaint. So if you want the other person to accommodate you rather than zap you back, make sure that your complaint is stated without insults. Avoid name-calling, sarcasm, ridicule, and mimicry. (These are foolproof ways of making the other person angry and thereby giving up any chance of getting her cooperation.) And avoid also the more subtle but equally insulting approach of "Let me show you how to do it, dear" (Ginott, 1965). Under this superficially pleasant phrase lies the insult of condescension. What you mean is "I think you're doing it wrong" or "I think I know a better way to do it." So say that instead.

5. *If you are very angry, just state your feelings.* Sometimes the other person makes you so angry that you have to make a very strong statement. "I wish you wouldn't act that way" or some other sober, reasonable protest simply won't do. This is when the insults usually start to roll. To ward them off, just state your feelings, as strongly as you have to (Ginott, 1965). For example: "That makes me *furious!*" This will release the emotional pressure on your side. At the same time, it still gives the other person the chance to respond constructively—something that she cannot do if you start pouring down insults on her head.

6. *Complain privately.* Don't make the other person lose face by criticizing him in front of his friends, his parents, his children, or anyone else, for that matter. Criticizing in front of a third party has the same effect

ACTIVITY 12.3

Through constructive complaining, we can communicate difficulties without destroying good relationships. Following the six rules given in the chapter, mentally rehearse the act of making a constructive complaint to a friend or a member of your family about something he or she does that annoys you. When you feel you have practiced enough, make your complaint and talk over the situation with the person. Afterward, write down what was said, what the outcome was, and whether you feel you gained or lost by making the complaint.

as insults. It shames the person being criticized and therefore gives him no opportunity to retreat with grace. The result, inevitably, is that he will not retreat; he will attack. (If not now, then tomorrow or next week.)

In sum, the whole point is to get your complaints across clearly without impinging on the other person's self-esteem. Obvious as this might seem, many of us have immense difficulties with it. Either we refrain from complaining and let other people have their way with us, or we mow them down with insults. These two problems and their solution—the middle road of proper "assertiveness"—will be discussed in greater detail in Chapter 13.

Giving Approval. Our comments about other people's behavior should not be limited to complaints. When the other person does right the thing that you think he often does wrong, give him your approval. Let's return to Sally and her mother. If they do go to the movies together and have a reasonably pleasant time together, Sally should let her mother know that she enjoyed their outing. As she is leaving, for example, she might simply say "What a nice afternoon!" (And then she might call her mother a few days later just to say hello.) As one group of

marital therapists summarized it, "reinforce the reinforcer" (Azrin et al., 1973, p. 367).

By all means, be careful to show your appreciation if the "good behavior" in question is a response to a complaint from you. Don't say to yourself, "Well, it's about time" or "That's more like it." Say—out loud, to the other person—"I really appreciate your doing that." If you've had a period of conflict with the other person, such approving comments may be very hard to produce. Produce them anyway. No matter how embarrassed your tone of voice, the other person will appreciate the fact that you recognize her efforts. And therefore she will be more likely to go on making those efforts.

Revealing Your Interpretations

As we have seen, attribution theorists claim that the key to an interaction is each person's idea of why the other person is doing what he is doing. Whether or not such attributions are really *the* key to human interaction, they are certainly *a* key. Imagine, for example, that you're having a conversation with a group of friends. Every time you open your mouth, your friend John interrupts you and finishes your thought for you. If you think that John is doing this because he always likes to dominate the conversation, you may be somewhat annoyed. But if you think that this behavior is directed specifically at you—that he is voicing your opinions for you because he considers you too inarticulate to voice them for yourself—then you may be extremely angry.

In other words, attributions do count. Therefore they should be checked for accuracy. If the cause to which you attribute someone's behavior is wounding or insulting to you, reveal it before acting on it. Calmly tell him (1) what he said or did and (2) how you interpret it. Then let him respond. It's quite possible that you're completely mistaken:

> **You:** John, every time I opened my mouth tonight, you interrupted me and finished my thought for me. To me this means that you think I'm too dumb to voice my own opinions.

> **John:** Oh, no. It's just an awful habit of mine—always trying to be the center of attention. It doesn't have anything to do with you. I'm awfully sorry. I'll reform. Just give me a dirty look if I do it again.

Here you have achieved three things: you have prevented yourself from starting a chain of negative responses on the basis of a mistake; you have reduced your anger; and you have offered a constructive complaint.

And what if the insulting attribution is correct? If it is, then it's best to get the problem out in the open and discuss it. Let's imagine, for example, that in response to your query, John had said, "Well, you really *don't* express yourself very well." Then you can ask him for more specific feedback about your speaking skills, or you can tell him to stop interrupting you no matter what he thinks of your speaking skills—or both. Whatever you decide, you now have accurate information on which to base your response.

Being Rewarding in General

As we learned in Chapter 8, social exchange theory argues that relationships are based on the exchange of costs and rewards. In keeping with this theory, a number of psychologists have proposed that the problem with unhappy marriages is simply that there are not enough rewards being exchanged (Stuart, 1969; Azrin et al., 1973). Indeed, the same could be said of any troubled relationship—between friends, lovers, parent and child, or whatever. The level of punishment (nagging, criticism, icy silences) is high, and the level of reward (praise, thoughtful acts, affection) is low.

However, this lopsided arrangement can exist only as long as *both* people maintain it. Again, remember the reciprocity principle. If you are caught in a mutual-punishment arrangement and you suddenly start sending out rewards rather than punishments, the old arrangement is destroyed. The following are some suggestions for destroying it and for creating a mutual-reward arrangement in its place.

Approval. One of the most reliable rewards is approval. We have already seen how you can use approval to reinforce those aspects of the other person's behavior that are pleasing to you. But you can also use approval simply as a gift—something you offer to the other person simply out of the desire to make her existence a little more pleasant. You can be assured that eventually the favor will be returned.

But if, at the moment, you and the other person are busy driving each other crazy, what can you find to approve of in her? Plenty, if only you look for it. Let us return to Sally and her mother, for example. From her mother, Sally receives extensive babysitting services and, as she notes, some financial help now and then. These are substantial gifts, and it wouldn't hurt her to express some forthright appreciation for them. Furthermore, there are probably many other things about Sally's mother that merit approval. Maybe, in addition to being conventional and critical, she is a good pianist, has a beautiful garden, and is unbeatable in bridge. These things, no matter how much Sally has learned to take them for granted, are worthy of praise. The same principle applies to *your* "other person." Look at her carefully and pick out the good things about her that you have taken for granted. Then start dispensing a little approval.

However, in order to make your approval truly rewarding to the other person, you should follow a few rules. First, increase your rate of approval gradually. Don't wake up one morning and start showering the other person with compliments; she will begin to wonder what you want from her. Second, praise things that the other person considers important—things that she has worked on and cares about. If she doesn't give a hang about her cooking but prides herself on being witty, praise her wit rather than her cooking. Third, be specific in your praise. Don't just say, "You were awfully witty tonight." Pick out specific details (for example, "I loved it when you said to Suzanne . . ."). This will show the person that you're not just manufacturing compliments; you really did notice. The fourth and by far the most important rule is: be sincere. Most people despise insincere praise; they rightly take it as an insult to their intelligence. Furthermore, most people can easily sniff out insincere praise. So the most crucial aspect of an approval-increasing program is the first step: finding things in the other person that you really *do* approve of.

Other Rewards. There are any number of rewards that you can use in addition to approval. Little gifts, for example. However, gifts, even more than praise, should not be overdone, lest you give the impression of

Gifts, like praise, can be easily overdone. Better reinforcers than gifts are thoughtful gestures, such as remembering to order a cake for the birthday dinner—or better yet, bringing a home-made cake. (© Leonard Speier 1982)

"coming on too strong." Better than gifts are thoughtful gestures such as doing the dishes when the other person is tired, making him a hot drink when he has a cold, volunteering to pick up the tickets for the play he wants to see, or listening sympathetically when he's had a bad day. These are the subtle little rewards of which good relationships are made. Start offering them, and you will soon find that you have created a chain of reciprocal reward.

Two-Sided Change

So far, in this chapter, we have concentrated on one person working alone rather than two people working together. We have done this for one very practical reason: It is not always easy to enlist the help of your "other person" in a program to change your relationship. However, if you *can* get the other person's cooperation, then the two of you can combine your efforts to improve the relationship.

For one thing, you can sit down together and pinpoint cues that lead to quarrels. Then you can figure out how to avoid these cues. Furthermore, each person's efforts at making positive responses can encourage efforts from the other person. When one person ignores a zap, this is a gentle reminder to the other person to make his criticism more constructive. When one person reveals an attribution that turns out to be accurate, this reminds the other person to give clearer messages. You can also *plan* interlocking rewards. For example, one person can make a point of praising the other person's efforts to be more rewarding. (He listens to you sympathetically; you tell him how grateful you are.) Or you can go one step further and establish an actual contract of planned reciprocal rewards.

Contracts

We have already discussed contracts in Chapter 6. There, you will recall, the contract provided some kind of reward for the achievement of a short-term goal in self-control. In relationship-contracts this same principle is used to create a cycle of reward. Your goal is to provide something that the other person wants, and your reward is that he provides you with something that you want. Thus, both of you are being rewarded for being more rewarding.

The beauty of contracts is that they guarantee that each party will profit from his efforts. Furthermore, contracts are helpful simply by virtue of being so specific. Rather than just deciding that they will be nicer to one another, the two parties write down exactly what rewards they will start offering one another. Box 12.2, for example, is a sample contract between (1) a husband who was

BOX 12.2
A SAMPLE CONTRACT

Below is a very simple contractual agreement between husband and wife. Note that in this type of contract, one party has to start the ball rolling by providing a reward before receiving one. The two parties can flip a coin to see who starts.

Contract: Between Sally and Richard Schneider   *October 17, 1983*

Reward to be provided	*Reward to be received*
1) Richard will arrange to go out with Sally every Saturday night (or Sunday afternoon), on the condition that: ⟶	on four out of the five evenings preceding that Saturday, Sally has sat down for twenty minutes before dinner to chat with him.
2) On four out of every five evenings (Monday–Friday), Sally will sit down for twenty minutes before dinner to chat with Richard, on the condition that: ⟶	Richard has gone out with her on the preceding Saturday night (or Sunday afternoon).

annoyed that his wife had no time to chat with him when they got home from work and (2) a wife who was annoyed that her husband was always too worn out from his home-handyman projects to go out with her on Saturday nights.

Drawing up a contract with someone who is close to you may seem rather odd and mechanical. However, such contracts have proved very helpful in propping up shaky marriages (Stuart, 1969; Weiss et al., 1974) and in improving relationships between teen-agers and their parents (Stuart, 1971). So go ahead and laugh, if you wish, as you draw up the contract. But take the contract itself seriously. If you do, you will get more of what you want—and see that the other person gets more of what he wants—out of the relationship. And thus you will have at least two new chains of positive responses.

A Note on Methods

In conclusion we offer a few practical pointers—a word about punishment and some advice on dealing with slip-ups.

Punishment

What about the use of punishment? Should penalties, for example, be built into contracts? Or if you are making a special effort to be a good listener and the other person uses this golden opportunity to lambaste you for all your faults, should you punish him by getting up and walking out? What we said about punishment in relation to self-control applies once again here. That is, avoid it.

If you have a troubled relationship, then you and the other person have already had your fill of punishment. Research has shown, not surprisingly, that unhappily married couples exchange "displeasing behaviors" at a far higher rate than happily married couples (Margolin, 1981), and the same is surely true of distressed parent-child relationships. Indeed, a troubled relationship may be defined as a reciprocal exchange of punishments, each person punishing the other in an effort to make him change (Weiss et al., 1973). As you probably know by now, such punishments do not work very well. For the most part, all they do is incite the other person to punish you back. So forget about punishing and concentrate on rewarding. If you must give negative feedback, give it in the form of a constructive complaint— that is, in the least punishing form.

One type of punishment that you should make a special effort to avoid is the one we mentioned earlier: walking out. In almost every troubled relationship there is a communication problem. The parties either yell at one another regularly or they communicate as little as possible. What they *don't* do is talk seriously about what is really bothering them. So when an argument begins, don't get up and leave. This is not only a harsh punishment to inflict on the other person; it also cuts the line of communication. Stand your ground and use everything that you have learned about listening, complaining constructively, and revealing attributions to focus the argument on the central issues.

Dealing with Slip-Ups

In any program to improve a relationship, slip-ups are bound to occur. Contracts will be broken. A listening session will end in a fight. A constructive complaint will degenerate into a nasty crack. Take these lapses philosophically. If your goals are too ambitious, modify them. If either party cannot keep to the contract, then adjust the contract accordingly. But if your goals and your contract seem reasonable, then just accept the slip-up as part of the nature of things. After all, you cannot expect yourself or the other person to change overnight. It takes time to unlearn the old scripts and learn new ones. And even when you do succeed in changing the relationship, there will still be explosions now and then. These should be taken not as a sign that you've failed, but as a sign that you're human.

SUMMARY

1. When two people interact, each one influences the other, in a chain of action and reaction. There is thus a *reciprocity* of influence, whether the influence is positive or negative.

2. The task of developing new patterns of reciprocal influence begins with the analysis of current patterns. The first step is to write a simple, objective, and specific description of the problem in the relationship. All relevant variables, both external and internal, should be included. The second step is functional analysis, which means examining the description, forming a cause-and-effect hypothesis, and manipulating the independent variable.

3. A change in interaction can be facilitated by planning ahead so that unpleasant episodes will be less likely to occur. One approach is to identify and avoid cues for conflict. You can also create cues for pleasant interaction, by starting the interaction with behaviors that elicit positive responses. And you should "psych yourself up" by preparing yourself mentally for a change in the interaction.

4. The interaction itself can be changed through the techniques of listening, avoiding defensive responses, giving clear messages, revealing your interpretations, and being rewarding in general. All these techniques substitute positive responses for negative responses and thereby help you avoid falling back into old patterns of negative influence. At the same time, they call for positive responses from the other person and thereby initiate positive chains of influence.

5. If you can enlist the other person to work with you on improving the relationship, you can aim for two-sided change. The two of you may draw up a contract specifying how you will change your behavior and what rewards you will receive from one another for doing so.

6. In working on your relationships, you should avoid using the technique of punishment; this form of influence is usually the very thing that has led to the interpersonal conflict. If and when you do slip up in your efforts, don't be discouraged. Change takes time.

PROJECT

The aim of this project, like that of earlier ones, is to get you to experiment with the techniques described in this chapter. Here we will focus on changing your way of discussing a problem in a close relationship.

1. Choose someone—a friend, your spouse, one of your parents, a brother or sister—with whom you have a generally satisfying relationship that is occasionally marred by conflict. Pinpoint a problem in that relationship,

OTHERS

some situation that repeatedly causes tension or leads to an argument.

2. Arrange to have a talk with the other person about this problem and to tape-record the conversation. Explain to the person that you will be taping the conversation so that you can go back over it and find out what changes you need to make in your communication skills. Make it clear to the person that you are not trying to "analyze" him, nor are you looking for ways to beat him in an argument.

3. Have your conversation, limiting it to ten or fifteen minutes.

4. Find some place where you can sit quietly and listen to the tape. First, listen to it from beginning to end without trying to analyze it. Then replay it, this time collecting information about your behavior by noting on a piece of paper the following items. (You probably will have to listen to the tape a couple of times to obtain all this information.)

a. The amount of time you spent talking and the amount of time the other person spent talking

b. The number of times you interrupted the other person

c. The number of times you changed the subject, bringing in something not directly related to the problem under discussion

d. The number of times you asked the person to clarify his thoughts or feelings

e. The number of times you made no response to a statement by the other person

f. The number of times you expressed your feelings

g. The number of times you reflected the feelings of the other person

h. The number of suggestions you made as to how the problem might be solved

5. If the other person is willing, have him do the same thing with his part of the conversation.

6. On the basis of the information you have gathered, decide whether or not you need to change your approach to talking out interpersonal problems. You may come to the conclusion that you did as well as could be expected. On the other hand, you may discover some areas that call for improvement. For example, did you talk approximately half the time? (A higher or lower rate of participation may indicate that you tend to dominate the conversation or fail to hold up your end.) Did you interrupt? Did you change the subject frequently? If so, these are things you might wish to work on. As for reflecting, expressing feelings, asking for clarifications, and so forth, the usefulness of these tactics has been discussed in the chapter. Are you making use of them?

7. Write down the areas in which you could improve your way of talking out a problem in a relationship.

Note: You of course cannot expect that your tape will be a perfectly representative sample of your interpersonal behavior. Like any self-monitoring exercise, it will show reactive effects (see footnote on p. 335). Both you and the other person will be on good behavior to some extent. Don't be overly concerned about this. A distorted record is better than no record at all. Furthermore, if both of you go on extremely good behavior, you may find that the taping results in a solution to your problem—which, after all, is more important than obtaining a representative tape.

HUMAN ISSUE:
CHILD-REARING

If one has never known thunderous fear when a child is lost in a crowd, or shared the sweet intensity of a small boy's secret, or felt the blissful vertigo of a little girl's first bicycle solo, then explaining mother love—or father love, for that matter (though here I must speak only for myself)—will be rather like explaining the sea to a landlocked people (Pogrebin, 1973, p. 49).

One of the most difficult tasks anyone can undertake is that of rearing a child. It involves hundreds of complex decisions that will shape another person's life; it is tremendously time-consuming; and it costs a lot of money. Not only that, but most of us have to learn how to do it without any formal training. In the words of Alvin Toffler, "Parenthood remains the greatest single preserve of the amateur" (1970, p. 243).

And yet every year some 3 million American couples bring a new child into the world. Why do they do it? And how do they deal with the great change in their lives?

CHOOSING PARENTHOOD

The very phrase "choosing parenthood" would have been unthinkable a few generations ago, and still is in many parts of the world. Children came or not, according to God's will. Now, with contraceptive devices readily available (at least in most industrialized nations), conceiving a child is, or can be, the result of a conscious decision.

Still, parenthood is not always a matter of choice. For some couples, having a child is something they do without thinking; it is a natural consequence of marriage. For other couples, it is a surprise, and not always a pleasant one. According to one survey, approximately 12 percent of births are unwanted (U.S. Department of Commerce, 1977). The lower the family income and educational level, the higher the rate of unwanted births.

For those couples who deliberately choose whether or not they will have children, the choice is not always easy. Society exerts a good deal of pressure in favor of having children. Childless people are still generally considered deprived.

In a 1978 Gallup poll, 50 percent of those questioned felt that people without children were lonely; 40 percent said that such people were unfulfilled; and 37 percent said that such people had empty lives (Blake, 1979). In the past, the pro-birth stance had a strong economic basis; the more children, the more hands on the farm. Today, pro-birth arguments tend to be psychological—that a woman is unfulfilled without children, that children improve a marriage, that parenthood is one of life's truly important experiences, not to be missed. The government even gives financial inducements to parenthood, in the form of income tax deductions. Married couples may be swayed by other reasons as well: to carry on the family name, to gain the approval of parents and friends. Some women feel that motherhood is their only way to gain an identity of their own; this is especially true among low-income, poorly educated women without marketable skills or goals.

Couples contemplating parenthood are also influenced by a number of negative considerations. More and more couples now marry for personal fulfillment and pleasure—goals that may be harder to attain with children in the way. It is estimated that from birth to high-school graduation a child generates 9,274 hours of extra housework (Espenshade, 1979) and costs, for the average middle-class family, more than $100,000 (Morrow, 1979). This is an enormous investment. People also worry about contributing to the population explosion. Said one pregnant woman with a toddler clinging to each hand: "I've come full circle right back to where my Victorian grandmother was. Granny had to hide her condition out of modesty. My belly is embarrassing . . . because it labels me a population exploder or an exploited baby machine" (quoted in Pogrebin, 1973, p. 49). Yet another factor is the expense, especially for middle-class parents who intend to send their children to college.

"It's ironic," commented one man who was considering fatherhood. "Everyone today is talking about the great freedom of choice we now have. But for those of us in the middle, the new freedom makes life complicated" (quoted in Whelan, 1977, p. 29).

Surveys of young people are interesting not only for what they reveal about present-day attitudes, but also as predictors of future population trends. One poll of 15,000 college women yielded these replies: the majority disapproved of large families (three or more children); they did not regard children as the most important reason for marriage; they favored family planning; and they thought it possible for women to pursue both a career and motherhood at the same time (Westoff and Potvin, 1967). In another survey, of both men and women, four out of five under the age of thirty agreed that it was perfectly appropriate to have no children at all (Institute of Life Insurance, 1974). And, according to census figures, 1 in 20 women today expects to have no children, as compared to 1 in 100 just ten years ago (U.S. Bureau of the Census, 1980).

One thing certain is a downward trend in births. The rate in the United States accelerated after World War II from 85.9 per 1,000 in 1945 to 118.5 per 1,000 in 1955, producing the "baby boom" that brought joy to the hearts of baby-food manufacturers. It then began a steady decline (which inevitably had to be called the "birth dearth") and reached its lowest point ever—66.7 per 1,000—in 1975. By 1980, it had risen slightly, to 68.2 per 1,000, but there is no sign that it will go much higher in the near future. Whereas the average couple twenty years ago had three children (think of the family you grew up in), today's average couple have less than two (think of the family you have created or plan to create). And they are apparently content to keep it that way.

ASSUMING NEW ROLES

The popular manual *Our Bodies, Ourselves* issues the following warning: "Often we remain upset months after the baby's birth because we expected at some point to get our lives and feelings back to 'normal.' It is important to understand that once we become mothers we will never again lead altogether the same lives" (Boston Women's Health Collective, 1973). Nor, it goes without saying, will fathers. What do the new roles of mother and father involve?

A major question is whether mothering—or "parenting," to use the new, unisex term—must be a full-time job. In the 1940s psychologists (among them Spitz, 1945) became concerned about the care infants received in institutions. As a result of their research, they argued that full-time mothering was required in order for a child to develop fully. John Bowlby (1953), a British psychoanalyst, argued that young children needed the continuous care of a mother in order not to be intellectually and emotionally damaged. If this is true, then plenty of children in this country are being damaged, for nearly half of all American mothers with children under six have jobs outside the home. However, recent research suggests that the children of working mothers suffer no ill effects (Hetherington et al., 1978). Indeed, they may benefit, becoming more self-sufficient and less prone to sex-role stereotyping (Hoffman, 1979).

What about fatherhood? Society and research alike place less emphasis on the father's role in the family. Because of the prevalence of divorce, most studies examine his role when he is *not* present. There is no clear evidence that the absence of a father is, in itself, detrimental to children. But there are at least two objective problems. One is that the average income of single-parent families headed by women (by far the majority) is far less than that of two-parent families. Indeed, 34 percent of such families live below the poverty level (U.S. Bureau of the Census, 1980). The other is that since the head of a single-parent family usually has the double burden of work and child care, children in such a household receive less attention than they do in a two-parent family.

In families where the father is present, his role is beginning to change. Rather than acting solely as breadwinners and disciplinarians, men are now spending more time with their children and taking more responsibility for their upbringing (Pleck and Lang, 1979)—an arrangement that seems to benefit the mother-child relationship as well as strengthening the father-child bond (Pederson et al., 1977). This trend may gradually change child-rearing from a full-time job for the mother to a part-time job for both parents.

However, even if parents share child-care responsibilities, children put a strain on the marriage. The year following the birth of the first child is a peak time for divorce. And in those marriages that survive, marital satisfaction tends to decline steadily from the time the first child is born, increasing once again only after the children have left home (Bell and Harper, 1977). Of course, a decline in marital satisfaction may be balanced by parental satisfaction. Since there has been little psychological research on this facet of child-rearing, we must rely on the reports of those (like Pogrebin) who have "been there."

LEARNING NEW SKILLS

Being a parent is often hard work. The romanticized television baby—cuddly, round, and cooing—bears little resemblance to the real-life baby, who is likely, at any given moment of the day, to be howling at the top of its lungs, spitting up on the rug, or rubbing applesauce into its hair. Unfortunately, many couples are totally unprepared for the realities of child-care. An attempt to fill this information gap— one that has probably done more than anything else to influence American child-rearing in the past few decades—was Benjamin Spock's *Baby and Child Care.* First published in 1945, it has since sold over 30 million copies and remains today the most popular guide for child-rearing in middle-class America.

Spock has been associated with what is called a permissive, or democratic, approach to child-rearing (although in later editions of his book he edged back from this position somewhat). According to the permissive view, children are basically innocent and good, responsive to an atmosphere of warmth and acceptance; parents are advised to be indulgent and flexible, in order to produce a spontaneous adult who will realize his or her full potential. A different attitude, more traditional and authoritarian, grows out of the view that children are basically unruly and need strong control. This approach to child-rearing—which was common in the early decades of this century—advises parents to enforce strict discipline so as to build the child's "moral character."

Research indicates that white-collar parents favor variations of the permissive approach, while blue-collar families are more apt to rely on the strict discipline favored by the traditional view (Bronfenbrenner, 1961; Newson and Newson, 1968). For parents or parents-to-be, however, it is good to remember that there are not just two ways to bring up children, but hundreds. And, in spite of all the expert advice, researchers have not been able to determine that any one approach to raising children is clearly the best.

<u>OUTLINE</u>

MAKING CONTACT
Priming Your Social Skills
Modeling   Role-playing
Priming Your Self-Confidence
Self-talk   Your clothes   Shaping
The Contact
Where to make the contact
How to open   Nonverbal behavior
The Follow-Up: More Shaping
For Women Trying to Meet Men
Handling Rejection

BECOMING ASSERTIVE
Do You Assert Your Rights?
Nonassertiveness and its consequences
Aggressiveness and its consequences
Assertiveness and its consequences
Increasing Assertiveness: A Program
Step 1: Self-monitoring   Step 2: Modeling
Step 3: Using imagery
Step 4: Systematic desensitization
Step 5: Role-playing   Step 6: The real thing
Step 7: Keep at it
Two pitfalls
The Limits to Assertiveness
When to squelch assertiveness   The white lie

FOSTERING INTIMACY
The Search for Intimacy
Making Time
Increasing Self-Disclosure
Why does self-disclosure foster intimacy?
How to begin disclosing
The limits to self-disclosure

13

THREE SOCIAL PROBLEMS: MAKING CONTACT, BECOMING ASSERTIVE, AND FOSTERING INTIMACY

In Chapter 12 we described techniques for dealing with what might be called the "general interpersonal problem"—that is, the day-to-day pains and annoyances that we cause one another in our relationships. However, many of us are plagued by certain very specific problems in the arena of social life, and these problems deserve special attention. For example, what if your major interpersonal problem is that you can't seem to meet people, particularly people of the opposite sex? Or what if you are afraid to assert your rights with the people that you do know? Or what if you have a number of pleasant relationships but no intimate relationship—no one person with whom you can truly drop the social mask and be yourself?

Aside from the "general interpersonal problem," these three difficulties—making contact, asserting oneself, and developing intimacy—are probably the most common causes of frustration in social life. Many of the techniques outlined in the last chapter

are indispensable for dealing with these problems. For example, there is no such thing as intimacy without listening, and constructive complaining is the surest route to assertiveness. But psychologists who have treated people with these problems have found that certain special combinations of techniques are particularly helpful. Those special techniques will be the subject of this chapter.

MAKING CONTACT

People need other people. This is a truth that we have already stated several times and that most people understand without the help of psychology books. Yet many people live without satisfying their need for others. Many people, indeed, are excruciatingly lonely, often as a result of the common problem called shyness.

Shyness needs to be distinguished from simple unsociability. *Unsociability* may be defined as a preference for being alone, as opposed to being with others. *Shyness,* on the other hand, is a reaction of discomfort—tension, self-consciousness, a tendency to look away, stammer, or keep quiet—in the presence of strangers or casual acquaintances (Buss, 1980). As recent research has pointed out, the two qualities are largely independent of one another (Cheek and Buss, 1981). A person may be unsociable without being shy. She has no fear of others; she would just rather be by herself. By the same token a person may be shy without being unsociable. He *wants* to make more friends, but being with new people makes him uncomfortable.

Unsociability is not what we are concerned with here. If a person truly wants to be by himself, then so be it. The problem we are addressing is shyness. What is it that makes a person shy? Some psychologists claim that the basic problem is a lack of social skills. Shy people, according to this theory, just don't know how to approach another person—how to introduce themselves, how to start up a conversation, and so on. Another theory, perhaps more widely held, is that anxiety is the main cause of shyness. This anxiety might be due to respondent conditioning (for example, the girl who laughed out loud when you asked her for a date at Teen Club), or it might be due to cognitive processes such as low self-esteem ("Why should she want to meet me?"). In either case, the shy person fears rejection. And, therefore, he would rather go on being lonely than take the risk of reaching out and having his hand slapped.

But what about the rest of us? After all, the hesitation to make contact with new people is not limited to individuals with extreme social anxiety or with minimal social skills. The fact is that a very large proportion of ordinary people are shy (Borkovec et al., 1974; Zimbardo, 1977). When we move into

a new neighborhood, we hesitate to go next door and introduce ourselves to the neighbors. When we walk into a party and can find no familiar face, our hearts sink. Why this general unwillingness to make contact? It is likely that the fear of rejection operates to some degree in all of us. It is also likely that we are feeling what our society has taught us to feel. For the norms of our culture generally discourage making contact simply for the sake of making contact. Trying to make new friends on the bus is not encouraged, nor, in our day, are we usually expected to drop in on the new neighbors. Social norms, in general, seem to militate against making oneself known to strangers, except in special situations.

Yet at the same time we have everything to gain from making as many contacts as we can. Contacts become acquaintances. And the more acquaintances we have, the larger the pool we can draw from in choosing our friends. Even when acquaintances remain simply acquaintances, they still benefit us. We can call on them for help—in getting a job, a date, a ticket to a concert. Furthermore, the larger our circle of acquaintances, the richer our social life—the more opinions we hear, the more ideas we are exposed to, the more we know of human life.

What can we do, then, to help ourselves in making contact? Let us focus specifically on the problem of meeting someone of the opposite sex. A man looking for a woman or a woman looking for a man can always go to singles bars, singles clubs, singles weekends at resorts. In these environments, the social prohibition against making contact is lifted. The problem, however, is that in its place there is heavy social pressure *to* make contact: to get or give phone numbers, or more. This pressure increases social anxieties for many people. They sit watching others make their "kills" and hate themselves for being unable to do the same thing.

w how
ely peo-

singles
p with
est for
anxiety

anxiety
simply
ural sur-
gram of
hese sug-
nose who
also use
friends. In
signed for
ger live in
man who
nan is no
aken for a
gin talking
ıny women
ce does not
re right. For
late-request-
by men (and
cultural situ-

ation). Therefore, any woman who is not ready to ask a man out can simply ignore the discussion of how to ask someone out and give her attention to the final section on how a woman can make it easier for a man to ask *her* out.

Priming Your Social Skills

Modeling

How does a boy learn how to approach a girl? By watching his older brother do it. And how did his older brother learn? By watching Burt Reynolds or Warren Beatty— or somebody else's brother. Much of this modeling is done unconsciously. But it can also be done quite consciously. As researchers have discovered, deliberate modeling is an excellent way of learning how to make contact (Twentyman and McFall, 1975; Curran, 1977).

In other words, if you don't know what to do in a male-female situation, copy somebody else who seems to be doing fine. This can be done with or without the model's cooperation. If you don't have a socially skilled friend who can help you, then just go to a party or a dance and watch carefully how other people operate. If you can get the cooperation of a friend, arrange to go with him to a place where he can demonstrate his skills for you. In either case, watch exactly what the model does: how he walks up to someone, how he introduces himself, how he starts a conversation, how much eye contact he maintains, what he does with his hands while he's talking, and how he ends the contact—or allows her to end the contact—without awkwardness. By watching carefully, you will see that the ability to meet other people is not magic; it is simply a set of skills. Even more important, you will see what skills you have to imitate.

You can begin imitating them right then and there, by going up to someone else and doing what your model did. Or you can go through the helpful intermediate step of role-playing.

Role-Playing

In *role-playing* (also called behavioral rehearsal) you rehearse a desired behavior with "actors"—people who are helping you—before you try it out in real-life situations. Therapists have found that this technique is very useful in building up "approach" and dating skills (Twentyman and McFall, 1975; Bander et al., 1975; MacDonald et al., 1973; Lipton and Nelson, 1980). It allows you to get feedback on what you're doing right and wrong. Furthermore, it gives you a chance to practice, so that you can refine your new skills and get over some of your anxieties about using them.

How, specifically, is it done? Get a friend to act the part of the "other person." (If your problems are with the opposite sex, make sure your partner is of the opposite sex.) Let's assume that you're a man trying to learn how to make contact with women. You ask your cousin to role-play with you. She stands there with a glass in her hand, pretending she's at a party, and you come up to her and engage her in at least one minute of conversation. After that minute she gives you feedback on your performance: "Don't cross your arms—it makes you look nervous"; "I loved your joke"; "Don't ask me what my major is—that's such a boring routine." Then you go through the scene again until you and she both feel comfortable with your performance.

After role-playing you should be ready to perform in real-life situations. If you feel anxious about doing this, however, you may want to put some effort into boosting your self-confidence.

Priming Your Self-Confidence

If you do feel anxious, you're not the only one. As we have seen, most people feel somewhat shy about dishing themselves up to strangers. However, if you have a history of *not* approaching people, then, by a circular effect, you may feel even more anxious and even more reluctant to approach. (Remember avoidance learning, Chapter 5.) If your anxiety is very strong, the methods that we are about to describe should help you, but in addition you would probably benefit from systematic desensitization. (The procedure is described in Chapter 7. Follow the instructions carefully.) If your anxiety is strong but not completely unsettling, you can probably use just the following methods.

Self-Talk

The most reliable technique for giving yourself the confidence to initiate contact with others is, once again, self-talk. In fact, self-talk for the purpose of reducing anxiety about making heterosexual contacts is exactly what Larry Fallon practiced at the end of Chapter 4. So before setting out to make contact, follow the self-talk procedure. We have already outlined this procedure in Chapter 4, but we will review it here:

1. *Listen to your self-talk.* When you're sitting at a party *knowing* you can't approach that person over there, verbalize your feeling. Say to yourself exactly why you can't make the contact.
2. *Talk back.* If your self-statement is questionable, then question it. ("Well, why *shouldn't* he want to meet me?") If you don't want to fall victim to a gloomy self-fulfilling prophecy, talk back to it.
3. *Act on your back-talk.* Get up and do what your positive self-statements tell

. Positive action will gen-
ulfilling prophecies—posi-

ise your self-confidence for
ou might give some atten-
thes. As social psychologists
ted again and again, clothes
ression you make on other
ld et al., 1971; Keasey and
asey, 1973). However, we're
you how to dress-to-impress.
ch advice, buy a fashion mag-
or some candid feedback from
What we are suggesting is that
impress *yourself* and thereby
your confidence. Many people,
feel particularly good about
when they're wearing some-
you're one of them, you might
treat yourself to a new shirt or
e a contact-making experiment.
can't spend the money for new
ar that outfit in which you al-
ood—the one that fits so perfectly
our eyes look bluer, or whatever.
is to make yourself feel as good
e about yourself.
ception to the dress-for-yourself
ou have a taste for bizarre and at-
tting clothing, stifle that taste for
few contact-making experiments.
rageous clothing will help you ap-
wider range of people. Then, once
e made your appeal, you can drag
Day-Glo bow tie or your green nail

g

ellent method for reducing anxieties
meeting new people is to shape the
t-making behavior—that is, allow

yourself to approach your goal in small
steps. (Each step should be preceded by self-
talk. And the successful completion of each
step should be followed by self-approval and
perhaps tangible rewards as well.)

Let's assume that you're a man who wants
to meet women, but the thought of walking
up to a live female and introducing yourself
gives you the shakes. So your first step
might be just to go to a social gathering,
look around, and leave. (Remember, the first
step in a shaping project must be very, very
easy.) Then your next step is to go to the
library and smile at a woman—then at two,
then three. The next step is to go to the
library or the student lounge, pick out an
interesting-looking woman, and make some
casual, trivial remark to her: "Do you have
the time?" "Can you tell me how to get to
the administration building?" Once you
have done this a few times, you may be
ready for the final step: actually starting up
a conversation with a strange woman. (As
you may have noticed, this procedure is similar to in vivo desensitization, Chapter 7,
but without the use of cue words.)

The Contact

You have now primed your skills and your
confidence. You're ready for the real thing:
making the contact. How do you manage it?

Where to Make the Contact

Don't try to make your first contact at a
singles bar or a "mixer" or in any other situation where contact-making is the explicit
goal. As we've mentioned, such situations
create pressure, and pressure is what you
don't need. The ideal environment is a gathering organized around some activity other
than pairing people off—for example, a political meeting (with a break for refresh-
ments), a yoga group, a photography class at

the local "Y." Such gatherings provide new people for you to meet without making too many demands. Furthermore, the activity in which the group is engaged gives you something to talk about, and it gives you a guaranteed exit line. ("Oh, excuse me, I think my slides are ready.") You will feel more comfortable about starting up a conversation if you know that you have some way of ending it.

However, if you can't find the ideal environment, just pick an environment that is pressure-free. And if possible, see to it that you have a friend in the room. This will give you social support, and it will provide you with your exit. ("Oh, excuse me. I want to say hello to my friend over there.")

How to Open

From observing your model, you probably realized one important fact of social life: to start a conversation, you don't need a brilliant opener—you just need an opener. The content of the opener can be almost anything. Its only purpose is to put the conversational ball in motion.

If you're unused to starting conversations, however, you may want some suggestions. Leonard and Natalie Zunin have written an entire book, *Contact: The First Four Minutes* (1972), about the beginning of a first encounter. In this book they give a long list of suggestions as to how you can open the conversation. The following are six suggestions based on the Zunins' list. They are the usual gambits; go ahead and take advantage of them:

1. *The Search for Identifying Data.* Here you exchange questions and answers on name, profession, major, and so on:

You: Hello. My name is Sandy. What's yours?

ΓY 13.1

ncerns to take a genuine interest in other
good way to initiate a contact, but is also
meone you see regularly in class or in your
ect of the person that *has* actually caught
mment made in class, an accent you can't
up the conversation for a few minutes. You
g than you thought. In any case, note his or
terest in others, they often suddenly take an

ient of all openers. After the exchange of names, you comment on something in the environment that the two of you share at the moment: "Wow, this punch tastes lethal," "That last speaker was excellent, wasn't he?" "I'm amazed that a folk-dance club can draw such a big crowd." This starts the conversation moving. The person's response will give you something to hook onto for your next remark.

5. *Requests for Information.* Most people like to be asked for their expert information. This makes them receptive to the "Can you tell me" opener. For example: "Can you tell me how to sign up for this club? I just came tonight for a free sample." "Can you tell me the title of the book you were talking about? I couldn't help overhearing. It sounds fascinating." "Can you tell me where you bought that suede vest? It's really the best-looking one I've ever seen." Then you can make conversation about the club, the book, or the vest for a minute and then shift gears into something more interesting.

6. *You Happened to Notice.* People also like to be told that subtle things about their behavior have caught your eye. Even if what you noticed is somewhat personal, it is still flattering that you noticed: "I noticed that

r

ect
our
to

ke you
erefore,
e excel-
he name

hear this
hair color
fire.

poetic. Ac-
you're an
everybody

au
calls y

As with giving app____ er 12), you
should make sure that you____ mpliment is
sincere, specific, and not overly effusive.

4. *Comments on the Surroundings.* This
is probably the most common and conven-

you look very confused. May I help you?" "I noticed that you sit out the fast dances. Do you mind if I sit this one out with you?" Make sure, however, that what you noticed is not *too* personal.

Nonverbal Behavior

In recent years a number of books have appeared on "body language." All of them make essentially the same point: that our bodies do much of our communicating for us, whether or not we are aware of it. And what we do with our bodies affects other people's impressions of us. In general, according to the research, people prefer people who look them in the eye (without staring), who orient their bodies toward them while they're talking, and who assume a fairly relaxed posture (Mehrabian, 1972; Harper et al., 1978; Kleinke et al., 1975).

To translate these findings into practical wisdom, try, when making a contact, to relax your body and use it to convey interest in the other person. Look him in the eye. (If you avoid eye contact, the other person will usually assume that you're bored, even though your problem may simply be nervousness.) And smile when there is something to smile at. As for body language from the neck down, try to communicate a state of moderate relaxation. Plan beforehand what you'll do with your hands (holding a drink, for example); this will eliminate nervous fidgeting. Turn your body toward the other person and ease your posture into a relaxed state, perhaps with a slight lean toward the person if you're sitting down. Avoid the pretzel look: legs crossed and arms folded across the chest. This may communicate a clamped, closed-off, "I'm-not-available" message (Mehrabian, 1972).

Above all, however, let yourself get interested in the other person and in the conver-

Her body language says that she's interested in what he is saying. Her body is relaxed. She leans forward and looks him in the eye. (Ken Heyman)

sation. If you do, then you'll become less self-conscious, and your body, accordingly, will reflect less self-consciousness. Our bodies, after all, are fairly sincere. They tend to communicate what we're really feeling. Once you feel genuine ease, pleasure, and interest, your body will automatically begin telegraphing this message.

The Follow-Up: More Shaping

What do you do after you've made contact? You have struck up a conversation with an interesting stranger. What now? If the interaction is proceeding so naturally and pleasantly that you can't stand to tear yourself away, then by all means stay. Go on talking to her, take her out for coffee, and see her home—the works. You have a new friend. Bravo!

But for most people the first contact-making experiment will not end up this way. And you shouldn't try to force it to do so.

Rather, you should shape the follow-up just as you shaped the contact.

Let's imagine that you go to a party and start a conversation with a woman. The talk proceeds smoothly enough, and she seems fairly interested. (In any case, she hasn't walked away.) You are only slightly nervous. This is what we would call a successful first contact, and we suggest that you not try to push it much further. Continue the conversation for five minutes, make some excuse as to why you have to leave, get her phone number, and *leave*. You've accomplished the first step.

Go home and pat yourself on the back. Then in a few days you proceed to the second step: calling to ask her out. Role-play the call beforehand. Once you call, make sure that the activity you propose to her is a low-pressure one. For example, your biggest worry is probably about making conversation. ("What if I can't think of anything to say?") So ask her out to a movie. In this way, you'll have to make spontaneous conversation only on the way to the movie. (And you can plan topics for this "spontaneous" conversation beforehand.) During the movie you of course won't be talking. Then when you go out for coffee afterwards, you can talk about the movie, plus other movies that it reminds you of, plus other movies in which the star of this movie appeared, and so on. (You might plan a few back-up topics as well.) If this date works out well enough, then you move on to another low-demand meeting, such as a thirty-minute coffee date. But save the leisurely romantic dinner for later, when you're ready for it.

Don't expect to be relaxed and confident on the first few dates. "Confidence comes not from thin air, but from experiences in which we succeed" (Zunin and Zunin, 1972, p. 29). And that is exactly what you are creating for yourself through shaping: a series of experiences in which you're likely to succeed. As the successes accumulate, so will your confidence.

For Women Trying to Meet Men

Today, many women feel comfortable about asking men out—and not just to accompany them to a party where they have to bring a date. Furthermore, there are many situations in which it is quite acceptable for a woman to approach a man simply for the purpose of making contact. However, if you are already somewhat shy, you may want to begin by facilitating contacts and save the contact-initiating for later, when you've gathered confidence.

How do you make it easier for a man to approach you? For one thing, don't huddle with your friends. Sit or stand alone. This makes you seem more available. And try to be responsive, no matter how nervous you are. When a man smiles at you, smile back. When he comes over to you, stop what you're doing and give him your attention. In general, do exactly the opposite of what you would do if you were trying to brush him off. Look at him rather than at the punch bowl. When he speaks to you, don't give clipped, one-word answers. Respond with interest and make new openers, so that the burden of the conversation doesn't rest entirely on his shoulders. Remember: the man is taking your responses as clues to whether or not you are interested in him. Don't give him the wrong clues.

You can pick up these and other "facilitating" responses from models, and you should definitely role-play them with a brother or a male friend. You can also make use of the shaping technique. When a man calls to ask you out, suggest low-pressure activities, such as the movie date described above. Shy women, like shy men, should progress gradually, encourage themselves with self-talk, and congratulate themselves for every small success.

Handling Rejection

What if he doesn't ask for a second date? Or, for men: What if you work up the courage to make contact and *she* suddenly excuses herself to say hello to a friend across the room? In short, how do you handle rejection?

When you set out to make contacts, you do run the risk of rejection. But if you don't try to make contacts, you almost guarantee loneliness. As the Zunins put it, "Risk not, want a lot" (1972, p. 29). Furthermore, a rejection is no catastrophe. The person isn't likely to slap you or call the police. The worst that will happen is that he will just signal lack of interest by averting his eyes or excusing himself or giving some other discreet signal.

This is not to say that rejection, if it should happen, will not hurt. Rejection is always painful. And if you're a person who is fearful of making contact, rejection may be even more painful. But if you find yourself in this situation, don't let the pain get the better of you. And don't, by any means, let it discourage you from further efforts at making contact.

To prevent yourself from becoming discouraged after rejection, use your self-talk skills. Tell yourself that the pain you're feeling is what anyone would feel under the circumstances. Then verbalize any feelings of inferiority that you may be experiencing and talk back to them. Ask yourself why this person's lack of interest in you should mean anything in particular about you. Maybe he's married. Maybe she's in love. Maybe he doesn't know a good thing when he sees it. In any case, you have no reason

whatsoever to assume that because that person wasn't for you, you should therefore give up and crawl back into your hole. You can't win every time, but the only way you can win at all is to stay in the running. Congratulate yourself on having the courage to do this. Then look around the room for someone else who seems interesting.

BECOMING ASSERTIVE

To make contact with a stranger, you must have a certain respect for your own desires. You have to believe that because you want something, it's your right to go after it. In short, you have to manifest what psychologists call assertiveness.

Assertiveness means "standing up for personal rights and expressing thoughts, feelings, and beliefs in direct, honest, and appropriate ways" (Lange and Jakubowski, 1976, p. 7). Being assertive includes any behavior in which you honestly and unselfconsciously put yourself forward: asking a stranger for directions, going to see a professor for an explanation of a grade, telling someone that you didn't get his joke. When you act on your own needs and desires—without, however, trampling on the rights of others—you're being assertive.

Assertiveness, then, is a broad category of behavior. However, psychologists have concentrated particularly on one area of assertiveness, the one that seems to give people the most difficulty. This is the area of asserting *rights*—asking people to do things you want and asking them to stop doing things that bother you. In other words, requests and complaints. Psychologists have found that many people who are otherwise well adjusted will suffer immense inconvenience rather than "impose" on others with requests or complaints. Even when smoking on buses is illegal, they will become nauseated rather than ask the person in the next seat to put out a cigarette. Even when they have paid twenty dollars for a ticket to a play, they will miss half of what is said rather than tell the people in the next row to stop talking. Needless to say, asking for cooperation in these instances is not an imposition. It is a right. Likewise, asking your friends for favors is a right. Yet many people cannot do either.

Do You Assert Your Rights?

How well do you exercise your rights? Put yourself in the following situations:

1. You are in a restaurant. You have ordered a steak, medium rare. You salivate in anticipation; all day you've been looking forward to this steak. The waitress brings your steak and you cut it. Inside, it is a perfect, uniform brown-gray. What do you do?

2. You are standing in the check-out line at the grocery store with a cart full of groceries. You wish the line would move faster because you're late for an appointment. A man with almost as many groceries as you have inserts himself into line in front of you and says, "Oh, you don't mind if I go ahead of you, do you? I'm in a rush." What do you do?

3. The friends that you invited over to dinner are due to arrive in five minutes, and you're still in your underwear, rolling out the pie crust. The phone rings. It's your sister, who always has plenty of problems and likes to talk about them at great length. She launches into a description of her current problem. What do you do?

4. You leave your car at the gas station for an oil change. When you return in the afternoon to pick it up, the mechanic hands you a bill for eighty dollars, explaining that the car needed a few other things in addition to the oil change: antifreeze, a new oil filter, a grease job, and so forth. What do you do?

5. You lent your lecture notes to your friend and now you need them back. The exam is in five days and you want to give yourself plenty of time to study. When you ask your friend for the notes, she says that she lent them to another friend, Steve. She'll get them back in a few days, she assures you. What do you do?

Nonassertiveness and Its Consequences

If your response to these situations would be a general "Er, okay," then you're engaging in nonassertive behavior. *Nonassertiveness* is the violation of your own rights by failing to express your thoughts and needs openly and thereby allowing others to disregard them. Whatever the other person thinks is okay. Whatever you think doesn't matter. Your heart may be pounding from anger, but the message you actually communicate is that your feelings don't count. Anything to avoid unpleasantness. For the goal of nonassertiveness is "to appease others and avoid conflict at any cost" (Lange and Jakubowski, 1976, p. 9).

We should point out from the beginning that you have a perfect right to behave nonassertively. You do not really harm others thereby. (However, by rewarding other people for taking advantage, you don't do them very much good either.) The only person you seriously harm is yourself. And you *do* harm yourself—emotionally, physiologically, socially, and practically.

Consider first the emotional consequences. The nonasserter, after all, doesn't feel good about herself for behaving nonassertively. Often she hates herself for it. All she knows is that she "just *can't*" make an assertive response. In the face of her powerlessness, her self-esteem withers. At the same time, unexpressed anger and anxiety

This looks like a cue for an assertive response from the man with the bald spot. By learning to respond assertively, we increase our self-respect, gain the respect of others, and stand a better chance of getting the things we need and want out of life. (Alex Webb/Magnum)

build up inside her. These emotional consequences can result in equally serious physiological consequences. It is no secret that headaches, ulcers, high blood pressure, and skin diseases often result from the stress of bottled-up emotions. The social consequences of nonassertive behavior are equally unappealing. As we have seen, people behave nonassertively in order to avoid the disapproval of others. Yet in the end, they don't gain approval. People will not love you, much less respect you, for being spineless. They may pity you, but often this pity eventually turns to annoyance and finally contempt (Alden, 1981). Nonassertiveness is a handicap in intimate relationships as well; unexpressed needs drive the wedge of dishonesty between two people.

Finally, consider the practical consequences of nonassertive behavior. Nonasserters end up with drawers full of useless items that salespeople pressured them into buying or items that turned out to be faulty when they got them home but that they couldn't bear to return. Nonasserters don't have the right change, because they can't bear to ask for it. They wait longer in checkout lines. They lend things they don't want to lend. They go to parties they don't want to attend and have long conversations with people they don't want to talk to. They tend to marry people who choose them, not people they choose. In short, nonasserters pay more.

Aggressiveness and Its Consequences

By pointing out the disadvantages of letting others walk all over you, we are not suggesting that you start walking all over others. That is aggressiveness, something altogether different from assertiveness. *Aggressiveness* is the exercise of your own rights in ways that violate other people's rights. When the aggressive person stands up for himself, he does so by insulting and humiliating others. To the line-jumper in the grocery store he does not say, "No, I can't let you go before me. I'm in a hurry too" (assertive response). He says loudly, "Who the hell do you think you are? Find some other sucker if you want to butt into line." To the problem-ridden sister on the phone he doesn't say, "Listen, I can't talk. My dinner guests are going to be here in a minute" (assertive response). He says, "Oh, bug off, Sheila. Save it for your shrink." In short, the aggressive person asserts himself by zapping the other person—hard.

The goal of aggressiveness is winning, at any cost. And the cost is great. The aggressive person may get what he wants from the other person this time, but he has bred re-

ACTIVITY 13.2

Many people confuse assertiveness with aggressiveness when they are trying to become more assertive. Distinguishing between the two is important, and you can practice it by observing others. Situation comedies on television provide numerous occasions on which people act both aggressively and assertively. After reviewing the definitions of these two terms, watch a few situation comedies. Note three examples of aggressive behavior (verbal, not physical) and three examples of assertive behavior. Write down brief descriptions of each instance, including a final sentence explaining why you classify the behavior as aggressive or assertive. This practice in distinguishing between the two types of behavior will help you to be assertive without "tipping over" into aggressiveness.

sentment in the process, and this resentment will be turned on him. Needless to say, you won't find the aggressive person surrounded by adoring friends and family.

Assertiveness and Its Consequences

We have already seen what assertiveness is. In the five situations described earlier, the assertive person would have insisted on her rights without abusing the other person. To the waitress she might have said, "This steak is well done. Could you please take it back to the kitchen? I asked for medium rare." To the mechanic she might have said, "No, I didn't ask for those things. I asked for an oil change, and that's all I'll pay for." To the note-borrowing friend she might have said, "I need those notes now, and I don't think you should have lent them to Steve without asking me. Please try to get them back to me tonight." We have already seen what she would have said to the line-jumper and the talkative sister.

What are the consequences of assertive behavior? You get things off your chest, and you may even get your way. (Not always, though. For example, you may end up compromising with the overzealous mechanic.)

Furthermore, you win the respect of others. Most important of all, you win your own respect.

To consider the psychological benefits of assertive behavior is to be reminded of the major concerns of humanistic and existential psychology. As we saw in Chapters 1 and 3, the humanists and existentialists regard adjustment not so much as an absence of problems, but as an active process of self-enhancement: the well-adjusted person is the one who chooses and acts. He feels free to make choices, acts on those choices, takes responsibility for his actions, and derives his self-respect from his freedom and his responsibility.

Such a state would be impossible to achieve without assertiveness. Indeed, assertiveness is really nothing more than the behavioral means by which we enact our freedom and responsibility. Through assertive behavior we say, in essence: "Here I am. I count. I have a right to be what I am and to want what I want. And I will answer for my decisions."

By learning to act out this message through ordinary assertive behavior, we come to believe it. And by believing it, we reap our psychological benefits. As researchers (for example, Hammen et al., 1980) have found, assertiveness results in increased self-respect and self-confidence. It enhances our sense of our own dignity and "rightness" as human beings. And it also gives us a better chance of getting our steak the way we ordered it.

Increasing Assertiveness: A Program

How do we become more assertive? Not in one jump. Assertiveness, like all the other adjustive techniques we have discussed in this book, is best learned gradually. We will present a seven-step program. (This program is based in part on the method suggested by Alberti and Emmons in their assertiveness-training manual *Stand Up, Speak Out, Talk Back!* 1975, pp. 35–38.)

Step 1: Self-Monitoring

To increase assertiveness, you must be able to pinpoint the people and situations that are most likely to bring out nonassertive-ness in you. Are there any particular people with whom you are especially afraid to speak up? (Your boss? Your girlfriend? Your father? Your professor? Your peers?) Are there any particular situations that seem to reduce you to a puddle? (Ordering in a restaurant? Dealing with salespeople?) Keep a record for at least one week of all occasions on which you were assertive and nonassertive. Be sure to include situations you avoided because they would have required assertive behavior. Record what you did and how you felt on each of these occasions.

Step 2: Modeling

Observe a person who behaves assertively. Better yet, observe her behaving assertively in one of the situations in which you behave nonassertively. Again, modeling will show you not only the skills you must learn but also the fact that assertive behavior *is* a matter of skills—not of magic. Note particularly that assertive people are not necessarily brilliant debaters. In fact, assertive people generally have no better speaking skills than nonassertive people. They just speak up,

If you want to learn to be assertive, start by watching those who are. (© Lawrence Frank 1980)

with whatever words come to them, and then stick to their point.

Step 3: Using Imagery

In a quiet moment, sit back, close your eyes, and imagine yourself behaving assertively in one of your problem situations. You don't have to copy your model. Imagine yourself being assertive in the way that seems most natural to you. Make sure that you imagine also the rewards of behaving assertively. For example, you picture yourself politely disagreeing with your English professor in class. He smiles, tells you what an interesting point of view that is, and asks you to explain it further. Your fellow students turn to hear what you have to say. What an active, probing intelligence you have!

By using this type of imagery, you ease yourself into the idea of behaving assertively and encourage yourself with the imagined rewards. Furthermore, you get a rough measure of your anxiety, which will tell you whether you need to go through Step 4.

Step 4: Systematic Desensitization

This step is optional. If imagining yourself being assertive arouses serious anxiety in you, then once again you might do well to practice systematic desensitization, according to the instructions given in Chapter 7. Make the scene you imagined, or an even more rattling act of self-assertion, the final item in your hierarchy and approach it in slow, graded steps.

Step 5: Role-Playing

Your next task is to practice assertiveness through role-playing. The scenes that you role-play will eventually be your first real-life experiments. Therefore, you must think now about what they will be. They should be scenes that you yourself can initiate. (You can't expect the assertion-requiring situation to come to you. If you go into a store expecting to find a pushy salesperson, you're sure to get a sweet grandmotherly type.) In addition, the assertions required should be only slightly difficult for you; this is shaping, not a kamikaze mission. For example, if you have mild difficulty returning items to stores, role-play the act of returning something. Then you can go to a store, buy something you don't want, and return it as your first experiment.

In your role-playing, choose an assertive person as your partner and have him give you only a slightly hard time. An example:

You: I want to return this electric knife, please.

Partner: *(pretending to be a gruff salesperson)* Well, what's the matter with it?

You: I just don't want it.

Partner: Where's the sales slip? I can't take it back without a sales slip.

You: I don't have a sales slip. It was a gift.

Partner: You're returning a *gift?*

You: Yes, I am.

Partner: Well, I can't give you a refund without a sales slip. That's store policy. You'll have to exchange it for something else.

You: I don't have time to pick out something else. I'm in a hurry. Please give me a credit slip instead.

Partner: Well, all right.

In playing your role, try to be assertive not only with your words but also with your body. Face the person, look him in the eye, and speak clearly. Then ask your partner to give you feedback. You might also tape-record the scene; this will provide excellent feedback on your words, tone of voice, speech hesitations, and so forth.

Step 6: The Real Thing

It is time to share your new skill with the world. Go out and initiate the situations that you rehearsed and be as assertive as you can. If you lose your courage, go back to role-playing. But if you handle the situation fairly well, feeling some anxiety but still getting through the task, then congratulate yourself and repeat the scene again tomorrow. However you perform, keep up the self-monitoring. Record what happened, how you felt, and what the outcome was. By showing your progress and by documenting the rewards of your self-assertions, this record will provide invaluable reinforcement.

Step 7: Keep at It

Once you have mastered in real life the few scenes that you rehearsed in Step 5, you can move up to slightly more difficult assertions. Again, you should rehearse them. If you master this second set of scenes without much difficulty, then you can drop the rehearsal step and just keep moving on to more and more demanding self-assertions. But remember the rules of shaping: make the steps gradual, reinforce yourself for every success (keep up the self-monitoring!), and don't move on to the next step until you feel perfectly comfortable—even a bit bored, perhaps—with the present step.

BOX 13.1
SAYING NO WITHOUT GUILT

In his book *When I Say No, I Feel Guilty*, Manuel J. Smith emphasizes our need to stand up for our personal rights. Here is his list of ten basic principles, which he calls

A BILL OF ASSERTIVE RIGHTS

I: You have the right to judge your own behavior, thoughts, and emotions and to take the responsibility for their initiation and consequences upon yourself.

II: You have the right to offer no reasons or excuses for . . . your behavior.

III: You have the right to judge if you are responsible for finding solutions to other people's problems.

IV: You have the right to change your mind.

V: You have the right to make mistakes—and be responsible for them.

VI: You have the right to say, "I don't know."

VII: You have the right to be independent of the goodwill of others before coping with them.

VIII: You have the right to be illogical in making decisions.

IX: You have the right to say, "I don't understand."

X: You have the right to say, "I don't care."

YOU HAVE THE RIGHT TO SAY NO, WITHOUT FEELING GUILTY.

Smith, M. J. When I Say No, I Feel Guilty. New York: Bantam Books, 1975, p. 1.

Two Pitfalls

There are two problems that you may encounter in shaping assertiveness, and you should be ready for them. The first is failure—a lapse into nonassertive behavior. You are doing very nicely with your experiments—speaking up in class, complaining about the neighbors' stereo, and so forth—when suddenly someone comes to you with an unreasonable request and before you know it, you've given in. You are now committed to taking care of your aunt's homicidal German Shepherd while she goes off on a two-week vacation.

When this happens, simply accept the fumble as natural. Nonassertive behavior, like any other automatic behavior, cannot be turned off like a faucet. It must be phased out gradually. And during the phasing-out process, slips are to be expected.

Note: When you assert yourself and don't win, this must not be counted as a failure. You can't win every time. If two people have their eye on the same parking space, someone has to lose (Alberti and Emmons, 1975, p. 82). And it may be you, no matter how assertive you've been. Just remember that the goal of assertiveness is not so much to have your way; it is to give yourself a *fair chance* of having your way. If you assert yourself and lose, or end up having to compromise, you have still done your best.

The second problem you may encounter is an unpleasant reaction from a person with whom you are being assertive. For example, when you contest the garage mechanic's bill, you may hear a few words about idiots who don't know cars or about the gall of this younger generation. In such cases, the best response is simply to ignore the zap and stick to your argument.

Even more likely, and more disturbing, are adverse reactions from people who have long-standing relationships with you and are used to having their way with you. If, after years of being nonassertive with your mother-in-law, you tell her that you can't change your plans in order to accompany her to the flower show this Sunday, she may react with anything from tears to a gall bladder attack. If you give in at this point, you are simply reinforcing the other person's dominance. So stick to your guns, kindly but firmly, and don't allow the other person to make you feel guilty. Eventually, he or she will adjust to your assertiveness and start meeting you halfway.

The Limits to Assertiveness

Should you adopt assertiveness as your main approach to dealing with other people? This, we propose, would be going a bit too far. There is something extremely unpleasant in the image of human relations as constant negotiation—constant bargaining over who has what rights and who is getting the best deal. After all, even though you have a *right* to your place in the check-out line, you may want to surrender this place to someone else if she is in a hurry and you're not. And if you do this, you should not have to feel that you've been a "sucker." In short, human interaction cannot be based entirely on the question of rights.

Some psychologists get around the how-much-assertiveness problem by claiming that assertiveness is the honest expression of *any* feeling (MacDonald, 1975), including feelings of pleasure, affection, approval, love, and so forth. Assertiveness, then, would include praising your child's artwork, kissing your mother, petting your dog, and so forth, in addition to protecting your rights. We would argue that once you broaden the term to this extent, you render it nearly useless. We would reserve the term "assertiveness" mainly for instances in which you ask the other person to attend to *your* needs. And we would add that this type of assertiveness represents only a part, albeit an essential part, of good relationships. Your needs, after all, are not the only thing that matters. There has to be giving as well as getting, listening as well as talking, agreeing as well as bargaining, love as well as justice. In addition to assertiveness, we must practice a certain acceptance.

But how do we decide when to be assertive and when to be accepting? We have already touched on this question at the end of Chapter 10. When you want something and have a right to it, or when your rights are being violated, then be assertive. But how do you know if you really have the right? Often your body will tell you; you can *feel* anger welling up inside you when your rights have been violated. From that point on, you can use your common sense to tell you whether you have the right to insist on what you want.

When to Squelch Assertiveness

There will be times when you do indeed have the right but when you may choose not to assert it. With someone who is sick or upset or extremely touchy, or with someone who is simply having a bad day, or with your grandmother, you may decide to "lay low." If your waiter clearly has too many tables to wait on, or if the fumbling phone installer is obviously new on the job, you may choose not to add to their troubles by complaining of slowness or poor service. In other words, be sensitive. This doesn't make you a pushover; it makes you a decent human being.

At the same time, you should make sure that you're not squelching your assertiveness every day of the week with the same person. If you are, then you're teaching that person that he can have his way with you by appearing unable to "take" any assertiveness on your part.

The White Lie

A final question is how candid you should be when you assert yourself. Technically, assertiveness requires the honest, direct statement of your needs or feelings. But sometimes you may choose the white lie instead.

Imagine, for example, the following situation. Your cousin calls and invites you to spend next weekend at her beach house: "I'm just dying for you to come. It would cheer me up so much." Last summer you spent several weekends at your cousin's beach house and you had a dismal time. When your cousin and her husband and their children weren't arguing, they were sitting in front of the television set. Now you are being invited to a repeat performance. What do you do?

One alternative would be to feel that you "can't" say no. After all, she needs you to cheer her up. So you end up saying yes. This is the nonassertive response, and we do not recommend it. A second alternative would be to say, "I really didn't have a good time when I visited last summer, so I think I'll stay home and read this weekend." This would be very honest. Needless to say, it would also be very effective in discouraging future invitations. But it would probably hurt your cousin's feelings very badly as well. A third alternative would be to say that you can't come because you have too much studying, a part-time job, tickets to the ballet, a hot date, or whatever. This is the white lie, and it may be the best alternative, or the least unattractive of the three unattractive alternatives.

It is impossible to state general rules about when to be blunt and when to temper assertiveness with white lies. There are arguments for both sides. On the one hand, white lies often postpone the problem rather than solve it. (If you tell your cousin that you have too much work this weekend, she may be calling back soon to invite you for the following weekend.) By contrast, honesty gets the problem out into the open and may lead to a genuine solution.

On the other hand, there are times when honesty does more harm than good. (If you tell your cousin that you didn't enjoy yourself at her house, she may stop speaking to you. Even if this doesn't bother you, it may well bother your parents, and this in turn will bother you.) You may want to save "painful honesty" for people who are close to you or people with whom you have regular contact; it is important that such people know how you feel.

We would reaffirm, however, that assertiveness is not a license to go around hurting others or making them look like fools. You don't have to scream insults at someone in order to be guilty of aggressiveness. Unnecessary excursions into "painful honesty" are often simply aggressiveness in disguise. So

by all means protect your own rights as vigorously as you have to. But don't forget that as a human being the other person has a right to decent treatment from you, just as you have a right to decent treatment from him.

FOSTERING INTIMACY

By making contact you can increase your circle of friends and acquaintances. And by asserting yourself properly, you can make your relationships with these people more honest and more satisfying. Thus, by learning these two social skills, you should be able to guard yourself against loneliness, or at least one kind of loneliness.

For centuries poets and novelists have described the feeling of being lonely in a crowd. There you are, surrounded by people you know. There's Sarah, who laughs at your jokes. There's Willie, who plays basketball

Social loneliness. (Bruce Davidson/Magnum)

BOX 13.2
LONELY, LONESOME, AND ALONE

Have you ever been lonely? Not just alone, but afraid of your aloneness, saddened by it, convinced that it means there is something wrong with you? Psychologist Steven Johnson, in his book *First Person Singular* (1977), distinguishes among three responses to being alone. One is *loneliness*, the state just described. It involves not only being alone, but "catastrophizing" over this condition, engaging in thoughts such as

> I can't stand to be alone. I am worthless without a partner. My life is devoid of purpose without someone to love. I will always be alone. Loneliness is my punishment for the wrongs that I have committed. I shouldn't have to be alone; I've been cheated. . . . (p. 121)

Loneliness, then, is a state of fear and depression, and in our society, where an increasingly large number of adults live alone, it plagues many people. According to Johnson, it doesn't have to. We can relieve our loneliness, even banish it altogether, by deciding not to run away from it. After all, most of us, when we experience loneliness, try to escape it. We turn on the television, make ourselves a drink, pick up a book we don't particularly want to read, call up a person we don't especially want to talk to. Instead, Johnson suggests, we should face our loneliness, embrace it, in order to break free of it. Facing loneliness means asking yourself what you are really feeling. As Johnson puts it, "What are the thoughts you don't want to think? What are you really afraid of? What is so bad about your own company?" (p. 119). By put-

ting these questions to yourself, you can at least end the "loneliness panic," the sense that your being alone is a catastrophe. You can also find out a good deal about yourself, including, perhaps, that you have enough inner resources to enjoy your solitude.

Even if we get over loneliness, we will still occasionally feel *lonesomeness*, the second response described by Johnson. Lonesomeness, although it is discomforting, involves no fear or self-pity. It is simply the feeling, when you are alone, that you would rather be with other people. This is a normal, healthy reaction. Like hunger, it is a signal that something is wanted. And just as we deal with hunger by eating, so we should deal with lonesomeness by seeking out people—calling up a friend or going to a place where we are likely to meet someone.

A third response that Johnson describes is *aloneness*, the enjoyment of one's own solitude. Such enjoyment may be relaxed, or it may be very intense. Indeed, Johnson claims that aloneness can be one of life's peak experiences, like love. Alone on a walk, or simply sitting in your chair at home, you savor your own company, the pleasure of being able to do what *you* want, and the delight of exploring your own thoughts and keeping them, at least for the moment, to yourself.

This chapter is devoted to helping you improve your relationships with other people. But we also have a relationship with ourselves. As Johnson suggests, this too is a relationship that can yield either pain or joy, depending on whether we are willing to work on it.

Emotional loneliness, the lack of intimacy, can attack a person even when he or she is surrounded by a noisy group of "friends." (Ken Heyman)

with you and lends you his car. There are the other people you like and give to and get from. And there you are in the midst of them, feeling isolated and alone.

It appears, then, that there are two different kinds of loneliness—social loneliness and emotional loneliness, as psychologist Robert Weiss (1973) calls them. *Social loneliness* is the lack of a social network—people to laugh at your jokes, play basketball with you, lend you their cars. When you move to a new town or enter college, what you feel is social loneliness. The cure, obviously, is to make new contacts.

Emotional loneliness, on the other hand, is the lack of an intimate relationship. It cannot be relieved simply by making con-

tacts. As we have just seen, emotional loneliness may haunt you even when you're among "friends." Outwardly you join in the action; inwardly you suffer the dull pain of aloneness. The only cure for emotional loneliness is to supply what is lacking: intimacy.

The Search for Intimacy

Intimacy may be defined as a strong attachment, characterized by trust and familiarity, between two people. It is not a necessity of life, like food or water. People can live without intimacy. But it may well be a necessity for happiness, and possibly for mental health as well. Numerous researchers have demonstrated a correlation between loneliness and serious psychological problems such as alcoholism, depression, and suicide (Jacobs, 1971; Lynch, 1976; Nerviano and Gross, 1976; Wenz, 1977; Perlman et al., 1978). Of course, such correlations, like all correlations, do not tell us which is the cause and which the result. Furthermore, the problem with many of the people studied by these researchers may have been simply social loneliness rather than emotional loneliness. Yet it is safe to assume that what lesser attachments might have prevented, intimacy would even more surely have prevented. As evidence, consider this rather poignant finding: two researchers, looking for causes of depression in old people, found that a crucial factor was the lack of a confidant. Regardless of their level of general socializing, those old people who had at least one confidant—someone to whom they could reveal private thoughts and feelings— were the ones least likely to be depressed (Lowenthal and Haven, 1968).

Intimacy, then, seems to be extremely important for good adjustment. Yet, as many social critics have pointed out, it also seems

For old people, having a confidant—a person they can talk to honestly—seems to be the best protection against the depression that plagues so many of the aged. (© Frank Siteman/Taurus)

increasingly hard to find. By now it is something of a cliché to contrast the good old days with the bad nowadays in terms of intimacy. Nevertheless, this cliché, like many clichés, may contain a solid truth. In past centuries most people lived and died in the neighborhoods where they were born. Their social contacts were fewer, more regular, and more stable. Most important of all, relationships tended to last until death intervened. In this atmosphere, intimacy developed naturally. This doesn't mean that our ancestors revealed their private lives to everyone in the village square. Actually, they probably did less "revealing" than we do. What it does mean, however, is that friends, neighbors, and spouses knew one another better, and probably trusted one another more, because of the length of their relationships and the frequency of their interaction.

By contrast, the frenetic mobility of life in modern technological societies seems to work against intimacy. As we move from one town to the next, from one job to the next, from one marriage to the next, from one social class to the next, we are constantly leaving people behind us. As a consequence, we lose whatever intimacy we have built up. And as a further consequence, we may learn, eventually, not to build up too much intimacy. In short, the pace of modern life tends to encourage superficial attachments—drive-in friendships, disposable marriages, no-risk love affairs. Easy in, easy out (Altman and Taylor, 1973). No deposit, no return.

Interestingly enough, however, our psyches have not adapted to this cultural change. Although modern life appears to discourage intimacy, we still search for it. As Carl Rogers points out, "individuals nowadays are probably more aware of their inner loneliness than . . . ever . . . before in history" (1970, p. 106). And the lonelier we feel, the more intense the intimacy we seek. No longer will we settle for the stable, predictable, humdrum attachments of our ancestors. We seek relationships that will yield total emotional gratification, white-hot communication, spiritual consummation. The honeymoon should never be over.

Paradoxically, it appears that the current popularity of divorce may be one sign of this modern hunger for intimacy. Some people have interpreted our rising divorce rate as a sign that Americans are fleeing intimacy. But according to many psychologists and sociologists, American divorce statistics reflect, on the contrary, a frantic *search* for intimacy: "High divorce rates do not indicate that marriage is no longer considered important by Americans. Rather, [they suggest] that marriage has become so important a source of emotional satisfaction that few people can endure a relationship that does not provide this" (Udry, 1974, p. 405). The fact that the vast majority of divorced Americans remarry, and quickly, strongly supports this interpretation.

Another visible sign of the current longing for intimacy is the "growth" group, which became a spectacularly popular phenomenon in the sixties and early seventies. (Under the heading of growth group we include encounter groups, sensitivity groups, and all other species of groups aimed at promoting honest and intimate communication. There used to be distinctions between these group subtypes, but such distinctions are largely blurred by now.) Growth groups vary considerably. In general, however, they share a common goal: to strip away social restraints and allow the individual to reveal to a group of fellow human beings his hidden self—his dreams and fantasies, his unspoken fears and longings. The purpose of all this self-revelation is not just "getting it off your chest." The theory is that self-revelation leads to intimacy. Once the group participant expresses his private feelings and sees them accepted by the group, perhaps even shared by other members, he will learn to accept himself. Above all, he will learn to relate to other people with more trust, more honesty, and more spontaneity.

All this sounds very helpful, and research indicates that for some people it is helpful (Campbell and Dunette, 1968; Lieberman et al., 1973). At the same time, many psychologists have raised serious questions about growth groups. For one thing, the intense emotional confrontations that often occur in such groups can be harmful as well as beneficial. One long-term study of the effects of encounter groups showed that for every two people who claimed to have benefited from the experience, one person claimed that his psychological state was *worse* as a result of his participation in the group. Furthermore, close to 40 percent of the participants reported that their lives had undergone no change as a result (Lieberman et al., 1973). This is not altogether surprising, for the sort of extremely candid self-revelation that is encouraged in growth groups is difficult to transfer to ordinary social life (Bednar and Kaul, 1978). Indeed,

given the right conditions, it is probably far easier to reveal yourself to strangers, people whom you will never see again, than it is to take the same risk with someone who is already part of your life. Carl Rogers, once a foremost advocate of growth groups, has made the same point: "You can leave the group with a real high, but there's no follow-up. It's more costly, less dramatic and more lasting to reveal something to someone you've known for years" (quoted in Keyes, 1973, p. 184).

What, then, should you do if you want to increase your intimacy? We propose that the best route is the one just suggested by Rogers. Rather than pay a psychologist or psychiatrist to help you become intimate with people you may never see in your daily life, try increasing your intimacy with the people you *do* see in your daily life—your father, your brother, your roommate, your girlfriend, your next-door neighbor. This is more difficult than joining a growth group, but it will probably yield a greater payoff. A "peak experience" that has no effect on your ordinary existence is worth less, in the end, than any experience, peak or otherwise, that will make your ordinary existence more fulfilling.

But how to go about it? There has been little research on techniques for improving intimacy, and therefore we cannot present a step-by-step program. (It is quite possible that intimacy is not something that can be created through a step-by-step program.) We can, however, put forth two suggestions: make time for others and increase self-disclosure.

Making Time

Intimacy feeds on time. Specifically, there are two time-bound factors that foster intimacy. First is the duration of the relationship. The longer you know a person, the more likely you are to become intimate with her. Second is the frequency of informal meetings. For intimacy to grow, you need to see the other person often, and these meetings should occur outside the context of formal roles (for example, employer-employee, teacher-student). Such roles, because they set rather strict rules for interactions, prevent the sort of relaxed self-revelation, mutual exploration, and general breeze-shooting that promote intimacy.

It is precisely the scarcity of these two factors—longstanding relationships and frequent informal meetings—that seems to work against intimacy in our time. As we have seen, modern mobility tends to keep our friendships brief. As for frequent and informal meetings with friends and acquaintances, these have almost gone out of style, at least for the working adult with a family. Neighbors, in general, are discouraged from simply appearing at the back door; good fences make good neighbors, as they say. Friends too are often discouraged from dropping in. We tend to see them, instead, at dinners and parties, where our roles are more strictly defined. Modern styles of architecture and city planning contribute to this lack of opportunity for informal meetings. Gone is the town square, where people used to gather and gossip. Gone is the front porch, where people used to sit and greet their neighbors. The modern American couple is to be found behind closed doors. If you want to see them, call before you come.*

And what of intimacy *within* the household? Intimacy certainly stands a better chance among family members. Yet here too modern life creates impediments. A truly astounding proportion of the time that family members spend together is spent not in interaction, but in silence—in front of the television set. (On the average weekday winter evening almost half the population of the United States is watching television [Steinberg, 1980].) When family members are not in front of the TV, they are often occupied with *instrumental behaviors*—practical pursuits aimed at survival or achievement (cooking, homework, household repairs). Not surprisingly, there is little time left over for relaxed interaction: comparing opinions on this or that, checking out how everyone's day was, speculating on what's the matter with Mr. Jones next door, and so forth.

In sum, our society doesn't offer many ready-made opportunities for informal interaction. If you want to increase your intimacy with others, you have to *create* these opportunities, literally engineer them. For example, if you would like to move beyond your superficial acquaintance with the people across the street, ring their doorbell on the spur of the moment and invite them over for something extremely informal—a cup of coffee, a drink on a hot day, a very ordinary dinner (meatloaf, not beef Wellington). If you see them puttering in the garden, go over and chat for a moment. Give and ask. If you buy a crate of tomatoes, send some over. If you need a pie plate, borrow it. The great beauty of intimacy with neighbors is the quality of relaxed, low-demand give and take. If you start this process moving, your neighbors are quite likely to reciprocate. (And if they don't, you can try the people down the block.)

To increase intimacy with people who are already your friends, try to divide the time you spend with them into smaller pieces.

---

* Among children and students, opportunities for informal interaction are much more frequent. Dropping by is accepted. (For example, "Mrs. Russo, can Vince come out and play?" "Hey, Harry, we're going down to Corby's for a beer. Do you want to come?") You don't have to call first before knocking on somebody's door in a college dormitory. Indeed, opportunities for shooting the breeze are so common in student residences that some students end up doing little else. In this way, many intimate friendships are established. But of course they often come to an end on graduation day.

THREE SOCIAL PROBLEMS

Families in living rooms with and without televisions. If you move the TV out of the room where the family tends to congregate, some family members may follow it, but others will have a nice place to fool around together. (Thomas Höpker/Woodfin Camp & Assoc.; Bill Stanton/Magnum)

That is, instead of seeing them for a five-hour dinner party every five weeks, see them for one hour every week—for a glass of wine, a cup of coffee, a walk in the park, or whatever. As more and more American women go out to work, the custom of the dinner party is becoming increasingly burdensome. It places too many demands on everyone. The brief, low-demand get-together is generally much more rewarding, both for host and guest. If you institute it, it's likely to be repeated. If you can't go to the movies with your friends, tell them to come by afterwards. Start throwing informal parties *after* dinner. If you have to work most of Saturday, invite your friends for breakfast on Sunday. And if you don't have time to make your own coffee cake, just buy one. The important thing is to see your friends, and see them without making a big production of it.

As for intimacy within the family, marriage manuals often advise that spouses go off on cozy vacations together, armed with champagne and frilly underwear, while child-rearing manuals recommend family outings. Again, however, what seems to be needed is not big "togetherness projects" but small and frequent pauses for informal interaction. So plan such pauses. Husband and wife can make a rule that the half hour before dinner is *their* half hour; the phone is taken off the hook and children are banished from the kitchen while parents have a quiet chat together. Dinnertime itself is an excellent opportunity for relaxed interaction among all family members. Indeed, it is often the one time of the day when the whole family can be induced to sit down together and talk. If your dinnertime is a social disaster—everyone reading the paper or coming and going at different times or watching television while they eat—make new rules. Get together and agree that everybody should show up for dinner on time, leave their reading material behind, steer clear of the television knob, and be ready for a chat.

(Again, you might do well to take the phone off the hook.) This simple strategy can be immensely fruitful. Through a modest half-hour interchange over dinner every night, you may find out what your son really does after school, what your wife really thinks of your moustache, and much more besides.

To sum up, we can no longer expect intimacy to flower automatically within the family. Our culture has simply created too many substitutes for intimacy-producing interaction. Therefore, if you are seeking a closer relationship with your parents, children, or spouse, you must make the time, frequently and regularly, to sit down quietly and talk with them.*

Increasing Self-Disclosure

Intimacy depends not only on whether you make time to talk, but also on what you talk about. If you confine your conversations to nonintimate material—how bad the weather has been, where you can get the best pizza in town, whether so-and-so will break up with so-and-so—intimacy has little chance to develop. If, on the other hand, you reveal something of your inner self—your hopes, conflicts, weaknesses, secret delights—then you provide the soil in which intimacy can grow.

This revealing of the inner self is called *self-disclosure*. In self-disclosure we temporarily lower our defenses and give the other person a glimpse of our more vulnerable selves. We show ourselves not as we want the world to see us, but as we know ourselves to be. We provide information that, on the one hand, could embarrass us and, on the other hand, could bring our inner self closer to the other person's inner self.

According to Sidney Jourard, the humanistic psychologist who initiated research on self-disclosure, self-disclosure is synonymous with intimacy: "This is what differentiates personal relationships of love and friendship from formal role relations—the participants seek to make their subjective worlds known to one another" (1974, p. 222). In fact, it is often an act of self-disclosure that accomplishes that crucial shift whereby a superficial acquaintance becomes an actual friend. This process is illustrated in one student's account of getting to know her roommate:

When I came on campus, I really didn't know anybody. . . . My roommate had already been here for a semester, and she helped me find my way around. She pointed out the buildings to me and showed me where my classes were.

In the first few days we talked about general stuff. Where we came from, what we were interested in. I really didn't know her very well then. One night, though, she and I were both studying in our room, and we got to talking about our personal lives. We had done the same things when we were younger, we had gotten into the same kinds of trouble. It was funny because our lives were kind of parallel to each other. We came from the same types of backgrounds.

We talked about some pretty serious things. We were talking about our boyfriends, how they were on drugs and how we didn't want to see them any more because of it. I think she knows me pretty well now. I can start to say something and she can just pick it right up and say what I was going to say. (adapted from Derlega and Chaikin, 1975, p. 57)

---

* One further suggestion: Get the television out of the room that would be the most convenient for socializing. If this means moving it out of the living room and into the bedroom or kitchen, fine. People who are trying to talk should not have to compete with the noise of the television. Furthermore, simply by reserving a comfortable, television-free place for socializing, you increase the probability of socializing instead of television-watching.

In this case, once the preliminary "feeling out" period was over, self-disclosure and intimacy came in a rush. In most cases, however, self-disclosure proceeds more gradually, along with continued testing of the other person. Both persons slowly feel their way into the relationship, gauging how much they can trust each other. Then Person A risks embarrassment by revealing some intimate fact about himself. ("I know I'm supposed to be an independent college student now, but frankly I miss my mother" or "I try to look sophisticated at parties like this, but I'm really scared to death.") Then Person B reciprocates by offering up some equally personal information about herself. Then Person A, either immediately or at some later time, responds by revealing something even more private. Again Person B reciprocates in kind. And so on it goes. In other words, bit by bit, through a spiral of reciprocal disclosures, the two people gradually drop their "cool" and reveal their inner lives.

Why Does Self-Disclosure Foster Intimacy?

As we learned earlier, intimacy is a close attachment characterized by trust and familiarity. Logically enough, the reason self-disclosure promotes intimacy is that it increases trust and familiarity (Zimbardo, 1977). By revealing to another person something that could embarrass you, you are saying, in effect, "I trust you." By responding to your disclosure without ridicule or scorn, the other person is saying, "You can trust me." And by reciprocating with a disclosure of her own, she is saying, "I will trust you in return. Now we have a pact."

At the same time, self-disclosure of course increases familiarity (Levinger, 1974). Gradually, as more and more information is re-

Self-disclosure creates attachment between human beings. (Al Kaplan/DPI)

vealed, each person can piece together the logic of the other person's thoughts and emotions. Each comes to know the other's inner self. Consequently, each can be more certain of understanding the other and of being understood. (Look, for example, at the last sentence in the student's statement cited above.)

Finally, self-disclosure deepens the attachment between two people simply by virtue of being rewarding (Davis, 1978). To the receiver, the disclosure is a gift of trust and affection. He is hearing privileged information; he is special. To the giver, self-disclosure is rewarding in several ways. First, it relieves emotional loneliness; the private self, revealed and accepted, no longer shivers in isolation. Second, self-disclosure relieves guilt and fear. As long as we conceal our mental bogeymen, they will continue to howl and cackle in the dark corridors of the mind. Once we reveal them, they look (and feel) much less threatening. Third, human beings seem to have a need to tell. This need probably accounts, in part, for the current popularity of psychotherapy. It certainly accounts for the so-called stranger-on-the-train phenomenon, whereby a person lays bare his soul to a total stranger, particularly a stranger whom he is fairly certain of never seeing again. (Growth groups, discussed above, are in a sense a special case of the stranger-on-the-train phenomenon.) Self-disclosure to a friend satisfies the same need, and it has the added advantage of creating a bond of trust with a person who, unlike the stranger or the psychotherapist, may still be part of your life ten years from now.

How to Begin Disclosing

For many people self-disclosure does not come easily. Those who grew up during the sixties, when spontaneous self-expression was widely promoted among the young, may find it easier to reveal themselves to others. But most adults have learned only too well the lesson of guarded restraint that is generally taught by our culture. Men in particular seem to have difficulty getting intimate

statements out of their mouths. If forced to "talk about feelings," they stammer, look away, grin with embarrassment, make jokes. Self-disclosure is simply too inconsistent with the stoical tough-guy image that for some reason is considered so desirable for males in our culture (Jourard and Richman, 1963; Rubin and Shenker, 1978).

Let us imagine that, male or female, you have difficulty with self-disclosure. You want to deepen the intimacy of your relationships, but you cannot imagine yourself pouring out your intimate thoughts to another person or telling him all the dark deeds and hidden sorrows of your past. Don't trouble yourself by thinking that you have to rush out and do this. As we have seen, self-disclosure usually proceeds gradually and reciprocally. Each disclosure is limited to what seems reasonably safe at the moment. And further disclosures are not usually offered until the other person has reciprocated. Self-disclosure, then, is not a suicide leap. It is a slow and natural process. All you have to do is start it moving. But how?

Several of the communication techniques we discussed in Chapter 12 are good beginner's exercises in self-disclosure. Expressing similarity, reacting nondefensively, reveal-

ACTIVITY 13.3

Because self-disclosure should come naturally in the course of a conversation, rehearsing ahead of time doesn't make sense. You might try this, however. Choose someone you know but with whom you'd like to be on closer terms. The next time the situation is appropriate—when you're having coffee together, for example, not when you're both dashing to a lecture—try disclosing something about yourself to this person. Don't force it, but if it does happen, jot down a brief summary afterward: what you said, what the response was, how you felt during the conversation, and whether you think it strengthened the bond between the two of you.

ing attributions—these responses, when they include a statement of personal thoughts and feelings, are excellent ways to open yourself up slightly to the other person. Imagine, for example, that your girlfriend accuses you of being a snob and you react nondefensively by saying, "Yes, I guess I am sort of snobbish. I don't like myself any better for it." You have revealed something of your inner, more vulnerable self. You have trusted her with the knowledge that you are not always "on top of" your feelings or actions. In return, she may feel easier about admitting her own weaknesses.

Two more excellent ways of initiating self-disclosure are expressions of approval and constructive criticisms. Just word your approval or criticism in such a way that you express some private sentiment. Don't say, "Thanks for calling." Say, "I love it when you call just to say hello." Don't say, "I wish you wouldn't do that." Say, "It hurts my feelings when you do that." And don't reserve such statements just for your spouse or boyfriend or girlfriend. The best way to deepen your intimacy with friends or members of your family is to let them know, through remarks such as these, that what they do makes a difference in your emotional life. To admit this is to express affection.

In sum, to deepen your intimacy through self-disclosure, you are not required to corner a friend and blurt out how you felt at age seven when all the kids went on the picnic without you. Self-disclosure can be achieved naturally, in the course of normal conversation, through subtly personal responses. Once it is initiated, it will increase gradually, as the other person reciprocates. Eventually, of course, you may end up telling the other person about the picnic disaster or some other wrenching experience. This will probably do you good, particularly if the other person responds by telling you about the time he wet his sleeping bag at Boy Scout camp. In any case, you will have arrived at this point naturally, through the shared satisfaction of mutual disclosure. And you will have built up enough trust between you to make such intimate disclosure possible.

The Limits to Self-Disclosure

We cannot conclude the subject of self-disclosure without a small warning: Don't overdo it. Gradual self-disclosure, encouraged by reciprocity, is not only the easiest way; it is also the most successful way. If you reveal too much too soon, you may find the other person edging away with an embarrassed smile rather than reciprocating.

The "plunger," or too-quick discloser, generally puts people off. In the first place, his behavior is simply too unconventional to inspire trust in most people. Second, other people reason, quite logically, that he is unlikely to keep their secrets if he is so indiscriminate in revealing his own (Luft, 1969). So if you want to increase your intimacy with a friend, don't overwhelm her with a hot blast of intimate revelations. Proceed slowly, slowly, one step at a time.

Even in a relationship that is already intimate, there are times when self-disclosure is excessive or out of place. You shouldn't turn your boyfriend or roommate or wife into your psychiatrist or confessor. By doing so, you force that other person always to be strong so that you can always be weak and cry on his shoulder. This is too great a burden, and eventually it will become irksome. Disclosure and vulnerability should be shared, not one-sided.

In addition, there are times when it is simply inappropriate to reveal something to another person, no matter how close your relationship. When your husband is depressed about his job, this is not the time for you to make a sincere, honest, spontaneous disclosure of the fact that you think he is less attractive since he gained weight. Likewise, if your brother's dog has just died, this is not the time to draw him into a discussion of how you feel guilty over not loving your father enough. In other words, a good deal of selfishness can slip past under the cloak of self-disclosure. If you abuse self-disclosure in this way, it will cease to be effective. Appropriate self-disclosure, like appropriate assertiveness, requires sensitivity to the other person's feelings as well as to your own.

SUMMARY

1. This chapter deals with three specific problems that plague many of us in the area of social life: making contact, asserting oneself, and developing intimacy.
2. Shyness, or discomfort in the presence of strangers and casual acquaintances, causes many people to shrink back from making contact with new people. Shyness may be due to anxiety or a lack of social skills, or both. But social skills can be primed through modeling and through *role-playing* (rehearsing social behavior with another person). And self-confidence can be increased through self-talk, through dressing to please yourself, and through shaping your approach to social situations.
3. Once you have primed your social skills and your confidence, you can begin to make contact, choosing where to do so, what conversational openers to try, and how to make use of nonverbal behavior. After the initial contact has been made, follow-ups can be facilitated through shaping. In making contact you do run the risk of rejection; self-talk is a good way to prevent a rejection from discouraging you.
4. *Assertiveness* means standing up for personal rights and expressing oneself in direct, honest, and appropriate ways. It differs from *nonassertiveness*, in which you allow others to violate your rights, and from *aggressiveness*, in which you violate the rights of others.
5. You can follow a seven-step program to increase assertiveness. Beginning with self-monitoring and modeling, you move on to use of imagery and perhaps systematic desensitization. Role-playing gives you confidence before you try out your new skills in actual situations. If you encounter failure or adverse reactions, don't give up.
6. Assertiveness has its limits. It should be used mainly when you feel your rights are being violated. There are times when a "white lie" is more suitable than strict honesty. Assertiveness must be balanced with sensitivity.
7. Our daily contacts with others stave off *social loneliness.* But we may still suffer from *emotional loneliness,* the lack of an intimate relationship with another person. *Intimacy* is a strong attachment, characterized by trust and familiarity, between two people. Some aspects of contemporary life, such as our high divorce rate and the proliferation of *"growth" groups,* reflect our need for intimacy.
8. Time is a crucial factor in the development of intimacy. The longer you know a person and the more frequently you see that person on an informal basis, the

more likely it is that intimacy will grow between you. Intimacy is also increased by *self-disclosure*, the revealing of the inner self. Reciprocal self-disclosures indicate trust, increase familiarity, and provide rewards. But self-disclosure should begin slowly and proceed gradually, with continual sensitivity to the other person's feelings.

PROJECT

To help you determine how assertive (or nonassertive or aggressive) you are, test yourself with the following questionnaire reprinted from *Your Perfect Right: A Guide to Assertive Behavior*, Robert E. Alberti and Michael L. Emmons (1974). This questionnaire has not been formally studied, with comparison groups established, so you will not be able to compare yourself with other persons of your age and sex. Its usefulness lies in drawing your attention to your own feelings and habits.

ASSERTIVENESS INVENTORY

The following questions will be helpful in assessing your assertiveness. Be honest in your responses. All you have to do is draw a circle around the number that describes you best. For some questions the assertive end of the scale is at 0, for others at 4. Key: 0 means *no* or *never*; 1 means *somewhat* or *sometimes*; 2 means *average*; 3 means *usually* or *a good deal*; and 4 means *practically always* or *entirely*.

1. When a person is highly unfair, do you call it to attention?   0 1 2 3 4
2. Do you find it difficult to make decisions?   0 1 2 3 4
3. Are you openly critical of others' ideas, opinions, behavior?   0 1 2 3 4
4. Do you speak out in protest when someone takes your place in line?   0 1 2 3 4
5. Do you often avoid people or situations for fear of embarrassment?   0 1 2 3 4
6. Do you usually have confidence in your own judgment?   0 1 2 3 4
7. Do you insist that your spouse or roommate take on a fair share of household chores?   0 1 2 3 4
8. Are you prone to "fly off the handle?"   0 1 2 3 4
9. When a salesman makes an effort, do you find it hard to say "No" even though the merchandise is not really what you want?   0 1 2 3 4
10. When a latecomer is waited on before you are, do you call attention to the situation?   0 1 2 3 4
11. Are you reluctant to speak up in a discussion or debate?   0 1 2 3 4
12. If a person has borrowed money (or a book, garment, thing of value) and is overdue in returning it, do you mention it?   0 1 2 3 4

OTHERS

13. Do you continue to pursue an argument after the other person has had enough? 0 1 2 3 4

14. Do you generally express what you feel? 0 1 2 3 4

15. Are you disturbed if someone watches you at work? 0 1 2 3 4

16. If someone keeps kicking or bumping your chair in a movie or a lecture, do you ask the person to stop? 0 1 2 3 4

17. Do you find it difficult to keep eye contact when talking to another person? 0 1 2 3 4

18. In a good restaurant, when your meal is improperly prepared or served, do you ask the waiter/waitress to correct the situation? 0 1 2 3 4

19. When you discover merchandise is faulty, do you return it for an adjustment? 0 1 2 3 4

20. Do you show your anger by name-calling or obscenities? 0 1 2 3 4

21. Do you try to be a wallflower or a piece of the furniture in social situations? 0 1 2 3 4

22. Do you insist that your manager (mechanic, repairman, etc.) make repairs, adjustments or replacements which are his/her responsibility? 0 1 2 3 4

23. Do you often step in and make decisions for others? 0 1 2 3 4

24. Are you able openly to express love and affection? 0 1 2 3 4

25. Are you able to ask your friends for small favors or help? 0 1 2 3 4

26. Do you think you always have the right answer? 0 1 2 3 4

27. When you differ with a person you respect, are you able to speak up for your own viewpoint? 0 1 2 3 4

28. Are you able to refuse unreasonable requests made by friends? 0 1 2 3 4

29. Do you have difficulty complimenting or praising others? 0 1 2 3 4

30. If you are disturbed by someone smoking near you, can you say so? 0 1 2 3 4

31. Do you shout or use bullying tactics to get others to do as you wish? 0 1 2 3 4

32. Do you finish other people's sentences for them? 0 1 2 3 4

33. Do you get into physical fights with others, especially with strangers? 0 1 2 3 4

34. At family meals, do you control the conversation? 0 1 2 3 4

35. When you meet a stranger, are you the first to introduce yourself and begin a conversation? 0 1 2 3 4

Alberti, R. E., and Emmons, M. L. Your Perfect Right: A Guide to Assertive Behavior, *4th ed. Copyright © 1982. San Luis Obispo, Calif.: Impact Publishers, Inc.*

HUMAN ISSUE:
LOVE

WARM, ATTRACTIVE, SMART, INTENSE WOMAN, *sophisticated but unfancy, domestically centered and talented, accomplished, albeit unevenly, wants substantial man, 40+, long grown up, sharp, good/active in interpersonal matters, warm, funny, reliable, who would like to fall in love and develop a life together.*

Along with the ads for apartments, Eskimo carvings, and Beethoven T-shirts appear columns of such "Personals" (some of them very personal indeed). In the true spirit of the sexual revolution, many advertisers seek a "passionate relationship" or "discreet, fantasy-fulfilling encounters." But here is a seeker who wants love. Did she meet Mr. Right? Did he fall in love? Did she? But what did she mean by falling in love anyway?

The meaning of the word *love* changes according to who or what is being loved. We speak of loving our parents, our country, pizza, Fred Astaire movies, our best friends. But it is romantic love—love between two persons of the opposite sex (to be conventional)—that we are concerned with here. It is this kind of love that we fall into, or out of.

In our culture few things are valued as highly as romantic love. Our popular songs dwell on love. Among the hottest sellers on our newsstands are "love comics" and magazines, such as *Screen Romance*, that chronicle the passions of our television and movie stars. The newest sensation in book publishing is the paperback "romance," which generally concerns the heartthrobs of a beautiful young woman and a handsome, mysterious man, often thrown together unexpectedly in a wind-swept castle. Likewise, across our movie screens pass an endless cavalcade of lovers—from *Rocky* to *Annie Hall* to *The French Lieutenant's Woman*. However cynical our times may seem, the fact is that most people in our society still take romantic love very seriously, value it highly, and feel cheated if they don't experience it.

This was not always the case. In fact, in most societies of past centuries, romantic love was looked upon as somewhere between a pleasant form of extramarital recreation (especially for the upper classes) and a dangerous psychological disturbance. People in these societies enjoyed hearing about love in plays and stories, but when it came to real life—that is, choosing a marriage partner—love

(© Joel Gordon)

(© Ellen Pines Sheffield/Woodfin Camp & Assoc.)

(© Thomas Höpker/Woodfin Camp & Assoc.)

(© Ellen Pines Sheffield/Woodfin Camp & Assoc.)

was not an issue. The same holds true in many nonindustrial societies today. Marriage partners are chosen for their financial standing, their ability to produce children, and the social position of their families. Love is beside the point.

In other words, our society's obsession with romantic love is, historically, the exception rather than the rule. This fact raises some interesting questions about love. What, as a matter of fact, *is* romantic love? And why do we experience it?

WHAT DO PSYCHOLOGISTS SAY?

Until recently, psychologists took little professional interest in the subject of love. If they thought about it at all, they were content to categorize it as an intense form of liking. During the past ten years, however, a number of researchers have bravely tackled the problem, attempting to define love, to study its causes, and even to measure it.

Zick Rubin (1973), who has done a good deal of work in this area, began his research by making a list of statements about love, taken from literature and other sources. He then asked students involved in love relationships to indicate which of the numerous statements on his list best described their feelings toward those they loved, and which were more applicable to their feelings about people they merely liked. On the basis of this survey, Rubin concluded that love was different from liking and consisted of three components: attachment, caring, and intimacy.

Attachment is the need to be with the other person, to have physical contact, and to possess him or her. It is the passionate desire that the ancient Greeks called *eros*. While attachment involves being fulfilled through another person, caring involves the desire to fulfill. It is the wish to give, to satisfy the other person. Erich Fromm, in *The Art of Loving* (1956), called it "the active concern for the life and growth of that which we love." To the Greeks, this form of love was *agape*. *Eros* and *agape* can be seen as opposing or conflicting elements in love, but Rubin suggests that they complement one another and represent the give-and-take of the love relationship.

Intimacy, according to Rubin, is a special bond between two people. It is manifest in the unspoken, mutual understanding that each has for the other. It is exclusive, involving communication that only the two lovers fully understand.

What about liking? Rubin thinks that it is at least somewhat related to loving, since we often begin by liking the person whom we come to love. But the three components of love—intense desire, the wish to fulfill, the exclusive bond—are missing. According to Rubin's surveys, the attitudes that count the most when we like someone are positive evaluations, respect and confidence, and perceived similarity.

Two other researchers who differentiate between love and liking are Ellen Berscheid and Elaine Walster (1974). In their view, friendship lacks the element of fantasy usually present in love. It also lacks the conflicting emotions, including hate, that often seem to accompany passionate love. (Lord Byron called love "a sort of hostile transaction, very necessary to keep the world going.") Friendship is also steadier than passionate love, which almost always diminishes with time.

What happens when passionate love dies out? If the relationship continues, passion may be replaced by a different sort of love, "companionate love." This emotion lacks the spine-tingling ups and downs of passionate love. Rather, it is a steady, comfortable feeling of affection for someone whose life is deeply entwined with ours and with whom we have shared experiences over a substantial period of time (Walster and Walster, 1978). Companionate love is probably the basis of most good marriages.

WHY DO PEOPLE FALL IN LOVE?

The reasons for loving, as writers and thinkers have described them, are almost as numerous as definitions of love itself. Pure pleasure, physical attraction, reciprocity, habit, frustration, proximity—all have been credited with stimulating the emotion. How does love happen? How much does it have to do with being "warm, attractive, smart, intense"—or "grown up, sharp . . . funny, reliable"?

Not much, according to Elaine Walster (1971). The crucial factors, as she sees them, are physiological arousal and the label of love itself. Walster's view of how love develops is based on a theory of emotions proposed by Stanley Schacter (1964). An emotion, he says, involves two steps. First, we experience physiological arousal. This may happen more or less spontaneously, or it may be induced by drugs or an electric shock. Second, we label the resulting feeling according to our situation. Physically, we may feel equally stirred up after watching a horror movie or being severely criticized in public. In the first case, we label our feeling as fear; in the second, we call it shame.

When it comes to love, the stimulus might vary from sexual arousal to a sudden scare or a shot of Vitamin B. The only precondition is that we feel aroused, experiencing increased heart rate, muscle tension, and so on. Once arousal has occurred, we need to label what we are feeling, and we choose a label based on social cues in the environment. Thus, if a young man is aroused, perhaps by strong anxiety, and then meets an attractive young woman at a party, he may well decide that he is in love.

The arousal theory has been partially confirmed by a recent experiment. One group of young men was asked to run in place for a few minutes. A second group listened to selections from Steve Martin's album *A Wild and Crazy Guy*. A third group listened to a gory account of a missionary being murdered and mutilated while his family watched. A fourth group listened to a tape describing the circulatory system of the frog. Then all four groups were shown a videotape of a young woman talking about a variety of subjects. When asked whether they would like to date this woman and kiss her, the three groups who had been aroused (by the exercise, the funny record, and the grisly story) responded more positively than those who had sat through the lecture on the frog (White et al., 1981).

But why, if we are aroused, do we call our feeling "love" rather than "sexual interest" or some other form of arousal? Partly because of social norms. Our society approves of love, and therefore we are likely to invoke this label. Personal standards and self-concept make a difference too. People who don't believe in sex without love will tend to "fall in love" when they are sexually aroused. Likewise, people who see themselves as romantic are more likely to label an emotion as love than those who consider themselves unromantic (Walster and Berscheid, 1971).

This theory is highly speculative. But it does help to explain the close connection between falling in love and the physical symptoms songwriters like to dwell on: hearts that go thumpety thump, chills running up and down the spine, and so on. It also may explain how love and its opposite can go hand in hand. If cues in the external situation change—the candlelight dinner gives way to a hard-fought contest for a school scholarship—the physiological arousal once labeled as love can well be relabeled as hate.

OUTLINE

HOW ENVIRONMENT INFLUENCES BEHAVIOR

ENVIRONMENTAL STRESS AND BEHAVIOR
Crowding
Calhoun's rat experiment
Population density and crowding
The human consequences of high population density
Noise
Temperature

THE BUILT ENVIRONMENT AND BEHAVIOR
Rooms
Beauty and ugliness
Furniture and seating
Buildings and Neighborhoods
The Pruitt-Igoe project
The social amenities of slums
High-rise and low-rise: Defensible space
Cities
Crime
Social indifference
The other side of the story: Freedom and variety

PERCEIVING THE ENVIRONMENT
Cognitive Maps
Selective Attention
Habituation

ADJUSTMENT AND ENVIRONMENTAL PERCEPTION
Surveying an Environment: A Step-by-Step Procedure
A Sample Environmental Survey
Changing Your Environment

14

THE ENVIRONMENT: HOW IT AFFECTS US AND HOW WE CAN AFFECT IT

A man walks along a sidewalk, stops at a newsstand, and buys a pack of cigarettes. He removes the cellophane from the top of the pack and looks around for a trash can. No trash can in sight. So he quickly drops the cellophane on the sidewalk. He lights a cigarette, blows a puff of smoke into the evening air, and then continues on his way.

On the surface, this seems a short and rather trivial segment of human action. However, human action is really only half the story. If you look again, you will see that the man is only one of the actors in the scene. There is another actor: the environment. And what is represented is not just action, but interaction—the interaction between the human being and his environment. This interaction is the subject of an entire subfield of psychology, *environmental psychology*. It is also the subject of this final chapter of our book.

At this point someone may be tempted to ask, "Where do you see interaction in that example? All I see is a man smoking a cigarette." Look again. By being what it is, containing what it contains, and not containing what it does not contain, the environment made the man's actions possible. Had the setting been the aisle of a church rather than a city sidewalk, he would not have decided to smoke. Had the sidewalk been lined with houses rather than shops, he would not have bought the cigarettes. Had there been a trash can on the corner, he would not have littered. The environment, in short, influenced his behavior. And he in turn influenced the environment. By leaving the cellophane on the sidewalk and the smoke in the air, he put a dent in his surroundings. He changed the world that would be encountered by the person walking twenty paces behind him.

In Western culture we are used to seeing ourselves as separate from the environment. It is our clay; we mold it to our will. If we want to convert a forest into a town, we chop down trees and raise buildings. If we miss the forest, we knock down the buildings, plant trees, and call the place a park. We are constantly manipulating the world around us. Yet we forget that the world is constantly manipulating us as well. In a forest we behave one way; in a building, another way; in a park, another way. Whatever our surroundings, they have a profound impact on our behavior. Indeed, some psychologists claim that we do not learn just behaviors. We learn *behaviors-in-situations*—mental sets of behavior plus time and place for enacting the behavior: "The act cannot be separated from the situation within which it occurs" (Krasner and Ullmann, 1973, p. 22).

This dynamic interaction between behavior and environment has not been ignored in earlier chapters. We have seen that study habits are affected by the desk where you study, that eating habits can be changed by changing what's in the kitchen, that intimacy can depend on where you keep your television set. These, however, are small pieces of behavior, whereas the truth is that the sum total of our lives—our thoughts, our emotions, our actions—constitutes an interaction with the environment and cannot be separated from it. Indeed, your entrance into this world may have been caused by a particularly romantic restaurant setting in which your parents had dinner twenty years ago. And the timing of your exit from this world will probably be influenced by environmental factors such as the quality of your neighborhood, the quality of your housing, and the quality of the air you breathe.

In sum, you and your environment constitute a single system—an *ecosystem*, as scientists call the interacting unit of organisms and their environment. And it is this personal ecosystem, made up of you and your world, that we will examine in the present chapter. First we will discuss in general terms how the environment molds behavior. Second, we will examine the relationship between behavior and specific environmental stressors. Third, we will see how behavior is affected by different aspects of the "built" (man-made) environment. Finally, we will take up the subject of environmental perception: How do we perceive the environment, and how can we sharpen our environmental perception for the sake of better adjustment?

HOW ENVIRONMENT INFLUENCES BEHAVIOR

We said earlier that the environment influences behavior. How? In four ways. First, the environment puts constraints on behavior; it limits what we can do. "We may not be aware of the walls of a room, yet they will determine how far we can walk in it. The height of a table will influence the way we sit at it; the number of people in a room, how comfortable we feel; the level of noise, how much we really listen" (Ittelson et al., 1974, p. 94). These constraints cut even deeper. An inner-city child who is never exposed to mountains, streams, or woods may never learn to tell an oak tree from a pine tree or a frog from a toad, and he may never learn to appreciate nature. Likewise, a child growing up in a suburb, without access to an art museum or ballet company, may grow up with a gap in her knowledge and sensitivity.

Second, the environment elicits behavior; it tells us how to act. When we walk into a church, the environment tells us to be quiet and look serious. When we enter the bleachers in a ball park, the environment tells us to laugh and cheer and call loudly for the hot-dog vendor. A living room with straight-

THE ENVIRONMENT

Certain environments elicit certain kinds of behavior. Violence comes easily in the ghetto; in its raw ugliness, the ghetto seems to call for either violence or despair. Likewise pleasureful play comes easily at the beach; that's what beaches are for. (© Harvey Stein 1980; © Geoffrey Gove)

backed chairs, all covered in clear plastic to keep the upholstery clean, tells us to sit up straight and not make a mess. A living room with big, puffy, overstuffed chairs, all covered in soft brown denim and looking lived-in, tells us to sit back and relax.

Third, the environment molds the self. The behaviors that specific environments elicit may become permanent parts of the self, determining the direction of future personality development. Consider, for example, a child whose early school years are spent in an "open classroom." In such classrooms there are no rows of desks facing the teacher. Rather, the classroom is a wide-open space filled with little islands of activity, any one of which the children may join. Given such an environment, the child may come to see learning not as the absorbing of information dispensed by authority figures, but as a process of satisfying her own individual curiosity. (Or so the progressive educators hope.) In the process, her personality will be stamped.

Fourth, environments affect the self-image. The king in his palace reads the message of his importance all around him—in the painted ceilings, the gilded and mirrored walls, the richly carpeted floors. (If he weren't important, why would everyone have gone to so much trouble?) Likewise, the child in the inner city may read in the blistering paint, littered alleys, and stinking corridors the message of his powerlessness and defeat. (If he *were* important, why would he be in a place like this?)

In sum, our surroundings tell us what we can do, what we should do, and, by extension, who we are. In the two sections that follow, we will examine specific environmental factors that have been shown to affect behavior.

ENVIRONMENTAL STRESS AND BEHAVIOR

Stress is defined by psychologists (including Lazarus, 1966) as a sense of threat accompanied by coping efforts aimed at reducing that threat. (The source of the stress is called a *stressor*.) For most people a final exam produces stress. It poses the threat of failure, a threat that we try to cope with by studying. Likewise, certain physical features of the environment appear to be clear sources of stress, resulting in coping behaviors considerably less useful than studying. We shall examine three environmental stressors: crowding, noise, and heat.

Crowding

Thirty years ago there were 2.5 billion people on this planet. Since then the population has doubled. The earth now houses almost 5 billion people. And in the next thirty years the population is expected to double once again. Yet the earth cannot double. Indeed, in thirty years the earth's resources—food, energy, drinkable water, breathable air—will almost certainly be *less* plentiful than they are now. And there will be twice as many people competing for them.

The chances are good that you will still be here in thirty years. Consider what it might be like. Twice as much pollution from human wastes. Twice as many people trying to use the buses, the roads, the parks, the water fountain. Half as much food to eat. Half the space to move around in. How will you respond to this?

Calhoun's Rat Experiment

One rather horrible answer to this question was suggested by a famous experiment with rats. The experimenter, John B. Calhoun (1962), placed 48 rats in a comfortable cage and allowed the population to increase to 80. He supplied these 80 rats with adequate food and water, and then he sat back to see what would happen. What happened was a gradual breakdown in social behavior. The rats ignored territorial boundaries. They disregarded the rituals for ending a fight and simply went ahead and killed one another. Females ceased to build proper nests and neglected their young; the infant mortality rate rose to 75 percent. Other rats became aggressive, homosexual, hypersexual, or hyperactive. Autopsies later showed that many of the rats had enlarged adrenal glands, a commonly recognized sign of stress. As we just saw, stress is a sense of threat plus an effort at coping. Clearly, the way the rats dealt with the threat of too many roommates was to cease engaging in cooperative social behavior. The rat pen had become, in Calhoun's words, a "behavioral sink."

These, however, were rats. Would human beings react in the same way to being packed in with their fellow human beings? We will try to answer this question in a moment. First we must look at how the individual sees a crowded situation.

Population Density and Crowding

Imagine yourself packed into the grandstands of a football stadium, watching the Super Bowl. What you would probably feel is excitement. Then imagine yourself trying to study in the same amount of space, surrounded by the same number of people. Very few people would feel excited by such a situation. Indeed, most people would feel extreme discomfort.

As these examples suggest, situations in which we are surrounded by a crowd of other people are not always unpleasant to us. At sports events, rock concerts, dances, rallies, and other events where stimulation is the main goal, being packed in often adds to the

High population density on Coney Island on a hot summer day. For some, this would be crowding; for others, it would be fun. (J. W. Cella/Photo Researchers, Inc.)

The Human Consequences of High Population Density

With this distinction in mind, let us now return to the question we asked a moment ago: How do human beings respond to high population density and crowding? In those temporary situations (parties, etc.) where high density produces no discomfort, we may assume that the people involved suffer no negative consequences. But when high density does produce discomfort—when density leads to crowding—then people, like rats, begin to undergo disturbing changes.

For one thing, crowding produces physiological changes. Crowded people have higher blood pressure, experience increased arousal, and are more likely to complain of illness than people who don't feel crowded (Aiello et al., 1975; D'Atri, 1975; McCain et al., 1976). As for changes in social behavior, these are harder to study, but researchers within the past decade have produced a number of relatively firm findings.

Crowding and Social Behavior. One apparent result of high population density is that it lessens interpersonal attraction. People in high-density situations tend to like one another less. One study showed that dormitory residents who had two roommates were less satisfied with their roommates than residents who had only one roommate in rooms of the same size (Baron et al., 1975).

Why should high density decrease attraction? Probably because it robs us of the ability to control our degree of interaction with others. The sense of control over social interaction appears to be a powerful human need (Altman, 1975). At times we want privacy; at times we want social stimulation. But at all times we like to know that we have the choice. Even small children seem to feel this need. According to one study, children in open classrooms, with social ac-

fun. The fact that being in a crowd may or may not be perceived as stressful has led environmental psychologists to develop a distinction between two conditions—population density and crowding. *Population density* is the number of people per unit of space. In the two situations cited above—the football game and the packed study session—the population density was equally high. Yet only one of these situations, the latter, was characterized by *crowding,* the psychological state of stress that sometimes results from high population density (Stokols, 1972, 1978). High population density, then, is an objective state: the state of being packed into a space with many other people. Crowding, on the other hand, is a subjective state: the state of wishing that you were *not* packed in with so many other people.

tivity going on constantly around them, will deliberately seek out private spots during some parts of the day. If such "privacy nooks" are not provided, the children will create their own, crawling into clothes closets, secreting themselves behind bookshelves, and so forth (Rothenberg, 1972). Thus, it seems that when people are forced on us, they become a source of stress. Small wonder that we like them less as a result.

Crowding in the Dormitory. A recent study (Baum and Davis, 1980) conducted in a college dormitory nicely demonstrates the pressures that crowding exerts on social behavior. The building in question had the standard dormitory design. Each floor consisted of a long corridor with a row of bedrooms on each side and a bathroom at each end of the hall. The number of students per floor was about 43. Before the school year began, the experimenters did a little renovating on the second floor. (See Figure 14.1.) Specifically, they took over the three bedrooms in the middle of the hall and converted them into a lounge area. By reducing the number of bedrooms, this change decreased the population of the floor. Instead of 43, it could now accommodate only 39. Thus, the population density was slightly lowered. More important, however, was the fact that the lounge area had the effect of dividing the floor into two separate units. Instead of one group of 43 women, there were now two groups of about 20 women each. What this meant was that the women in these groups could more easily predict and control whom they would meet when they stepped out into the hall and who would be brushing her teeth at the next sink in the bathroom. Compared to the women on the other floors, which remained unaltered, their social interaction on the floor was twice as manageable.

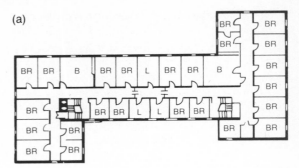

(a)

BR = Bedroom
B = Bathroom
L = Lounge

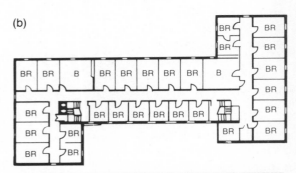

(b)

Figure 14.1 The floor plans of the altered dormitory floor (a) and the unaltered floor (b). Note that the only difference between the two is the conversion of the three middle bedrooms into a communal lounge area on the altered floor. (Source: Baum and Davis, 1980.)

The experimenters then tested and observed the social reactions of the women on the altered floor throughout the semester, comparing them to those of the women on the unaltered floor above. As they had expected, the women on the unaltered floor reported more difficulty in controlling who they were thrown together with than the women on the altered floor. They also perceived dormitory life as more hectic. As a result, they became less sociable. They made fewer friends on the floor, and when asked how often small groups were likely to form in the halls or bedrooms, they reported this as a less frequent occurrence than the women on the altered floor. Their relatively withdrawn behavior was confirmed by surreptitious observers, who reported that on the altered floor more bedroom doors were left open (an invitation for drop-ins) and there was more observable socializing going on.

Interestingly, the differences between the two floors in feelings of control and in sociability generalized beyond the residential setting. The women on the unaltered floor expressed less confidence in their ability to control experiences outside the dormitory as well as within it. As for social withdrawal outside the dormitory, this was assessed in a clever little experiment. Women from both the altered and the unaltered floor were asked, one at a time, to come to the psychology laboratory for a study of "impression formation." Each one, as she arrived, was told that the sessions were running a bit late. She was then asked to wait for five minutes in a room with another woman, who was supposedly participating in the same experiment. (Actually, the other woman was a confederate of the experimenters.) As the subject waited, the experimenters observed her behavior toward the confederate through a one-way mirror. Compared to the residents of the altered floor, the residents of the unaltered floor chose seats further away from the confederate and looked at her less than half as often during the five-minute period. Presumably as a result of what were actually minor architectural differences, the women on the unaltered floor were less sociable creatures altogether than their downstairs neighbors.

Aside from offering hints to dormitory architects, these results suggest a disturbing truth: that even slightly crowded conditions can have a widespread effect on human behavior. At the same time, the experiment forcefully underlines the difference between high population density and crowding. Remember that the population density of the altered floor was only slightly less than that of the unaltered floor. The major difference between the two living spaces was the size of the groups. Presumably because the group was smaller—and also, we may guess, because of the added lounge space—the residents of the altered floor found their social life more manageable. Therefore, they felt less crowded, more in control of their lives, and more kindly disposed toward their fellow human beings.

Crowding and Social Pathology. If crowding dampens our feelings toward others, does it also encourage aggression? It seems logical that in crowded conditions people might eventually strike out against those bumping up against them. Research in classrooms has shown that crowded children are in fact more likely to attack one another, or to choose the opposite coping method, withdrawal from interaction (Baum and Koman, 1975). However, this rule may be more applicable to males than to females. When older students were put in crowded classrooms and asked how they felt, they divided along sex lines. The women felt nervous; the men felt aggressive (Schettino and Borden, 1976).

Considering these findings, and considering the fact that slums tend to be crowded places, one might be tempted to see high population density as a cause of the various social pathologies—crime, juvenile delinquency, mental illness, alcoholism—that seem to afflict many slums. A number of researchers have tested this hypothesis. In general, they have found that high density *within* residences (as opposed to high density per acre of land) definitely correlates with social pathology, especially crime and mental illness (Galle et al., 1972; Booth and Welch, 1973, 1974; Gove et al., 1979). Children who are sleeping three to a bed have less chance of growing up to be model citizens than do children with their own rooms. Yet as we have seen in earlier chapters, a correlation is not necessarily a cause-and-result relationship. In addition to high density, there are plenty of other factors—poverty, poor housing, racial discrimination, inadequate medical care, substandard schools—that might be causing social pathology in crowded slums. Indeed, research suggests that the crucial correlates of social pathology are actually poverty and ethnic group membership (Freedman et al., 1975).

In sum, studies of large populations cannot yet give definite answers as to the effects of high population density, because it is so difficult to rule out other factors. Yet smaller-scale studies do indicate that high density can harm social relations. Although it does not reduce us to the level of Calhoun's rats, it does decrease interpersonal tolerance.*

Noise

A second important environmental stressor is unwanted sound, generally known as *noise*. Have you ever tried to study amid the sound of the neighbors' radio, the jackhammers in the street, and voices giggling in the hall? If so, then you know that noise can interfere with your work, put you in a nasty temper, and generally drive you crazy.

Several recent studies have documented the fact that noise has a negative effect on interpersonal behavior. In one experiment (Mathews and Canon, 1975), students were tested in pairs in rooms with normal, moderate, and high noise levels. However, only one of the pair was actually a volunteer. The other was a confederate. As each pair was called to begin the experiment (or so the volunteers thought), the confederate dropped a large stack of books that he or she was carrying. In the rooms with normal noise, 73 percent of the volunteers automatically stopped to help the confederate pick up the books. In the moderately noisy rooms, the percentage dropped slightly, to 68 percent. But in the very noisy rooms, only 38 percent of the students took the trouble to help. Thus, it seems that noise may decrease our concern for others.

Yet many factory workers spend seven hours a day in a terrible din without becoming alienated from their fellow human beings. How do they manage? Adaptation is of course part of the answer. But recent research indicates that another important part of the answer is the predictability of the noise.

Noise that is predictable—a subway passing underneath your house every ten minutes or a piece of machinery clanging away in a regular rhythm—is apparently easier to adapt to and produces fewer negative effects than unpredictable noise, which can damage task performance and frustration-tolerance (Glass and Singer, 1972, 1973). But why this difference? Once again, it may be a matter of control. Unpredictable noise robs the individual of his feeling that he controls his

---

* Note, however, that different people have different levels of tolerance for crowding—and also for the two other stressors that we discuss here, noise and heat. Some people, for example, are extremely sensitive to noise. Others are bothered by silence and will turn on a television set or radio just to keep them "company" while they are working around the house. In other words, what we are discussing in this section on environmental stressors are *general rules*. Individual cases, because of person variables and situational variables, may deviate considerably from the general rule.

ACTIVITY 14.1

We usually think of noise as sounds created by other people. Of course, we create noise too, though it usually doesn't bother us because we control it. However, our own noise also acts on us as a stressor, and can have undesirable effects. To get an idea of what these might be, try a simple experiment. Ask a friend to make up six arithmetic problems for you. Each problem should consist of a column of ten one-digit numbers for you to add up. Ask the same friend to time you while you add the numbers. Add the first three columns in a room with the television on at normal volume. Then turn off the television and do the remaining three. You will probably find that your calculations took more time with the television on. You should also check your answers to see if you made more mistakes while the television was on.

environment; it makes him feel helpless (Glass et al., 1969; Glass, 1977). This feeling of helplessness in turn makes him less able to tolerate difficulties, either with tasks or with human beings.

Temperature

A third environmental stressor that can dampen your love for, and tolerance of, human beings is heat. When driving through a desert on an August day, your body glued by perspiration to the automobile seat, you are much less likely to accept your five-year-old son's proposal of a game of Twenty Questions. Or if you do accept, the fact that he doesn't seem able to guess anything but "bunny" or "dog" may make you furious. In short, heat is hard on the disposition.

To test the effects of heat on interpersonal liking, a group of subjects was asked to work for 45 minutes in a room heated to 100 degrees. Then they were given a description of a stranger and were asked how much they liked him. Predictably, the strangers were much less appealing to the "hot" subjects than to another group who had been work-

ing in a room at moderate temperatures (Griffitt, 1970). Apparently, a hot day is not the ideal time to meet your boyfriend's mother.

If heat makes us like people less, does it also make us more likely to be aggressive? Possibly. Two researchers (Goranson and King, 1970), for example, looked up the daily temperatures for twelve days prior to the riots and violent incidents that occurred in various American cities during the troubled year of 1967. (This was the year of race riots in Newark and Detroit.) They found that compared with temperatures in previous years, the temperatures on the riot day and the preceding day were unusually high. The connection between heat and collective violence has since been reaffirmed in other studies (Carlsmith and Anderson, 1979). So it is possible that television newscasters were correct in suggesting that heat was partly responsible for the civil disorders of the late sixties.

A group of psychologists have recently done a series of laboratory experiments on the relationship between heat and aggression (Baron and Lawton, 1972; Baron and

Bell, 1975; Bell and Baron, 1976; Baron and Bell, 1976; Bell, 1981). Their conclusion is that a relationship definitely exists but that it is more complex than we imagine. In these experiments the subjects were put in hot rooms and then nudged toward aggression by some other stimulus—electric shocks, a movie showing an aggressive model, disagreement with another person, a negative evaluation by another person, or a combination of these. The experimenters' question was: Will heat "tip the balance," causing the person to respond aggressively to a provocation that he might have ignored in a cooler room? The answer yielded by the experiments was: yes, up to a point. As conditions became increasingly unpleasant, the volunteers, in general, became increasingly aggressive. Yet once conditions became *too* unpleasant (for example, heat combined with disagreement and negative evaluation), the level of aggression dropped off. What this suggests is that, heat or no heat, people pushed beyond a certain point will stop trying to retaliate and simply look for ways to withdraw from the scene of their misery. (This finding echoes the notion that political revolutions occur not when the oppressed masses have nothing but when they have been given a little something.) In sum, heat does increase the likelihood of aggression, but only within limits.

THE BUILT ENVIRONMENT AND BEHAVIOR

So far we have limited our discussion to environmental factors that have negative effects on social behavior. We turn now to an environmental factor that can have effects ranging from the most positive to the most negative. That factor is what is called the built environment.

The *built environment* includes all settings that have been designed and created largely by human beings (Heimstra and McFarling, 1974)—rooms, buildings, neighborhoods, towns, cities, and so forth. The built environment stands in contrast to the *natural environment*, which encompasses settings that human beings have modified only slightly or not at all. Examples would include lakes, fields, forests, the purple mountains' majesty above the fruited plain, and so forth.

Not all environments fit neatly into one type or the other. (For example, what of the lake surrounded by billboards, gas stations, and hot dog stands? How natural is this environment?) Nevertheless, if we wish to study human beings' psychological responses to settings created by human beings, there are plenty of unmistakably built environments for us to examine. Your living room, your classroom, your church, your downtown shopping area, your local pizza parlor—all these were designed, carefully or carelessly, by human beings. And as they were designed, so they will affect your behavior. Winston Churchill wrote, "We shape our buildings, and afterwards our buildings shape us" (cited in Wrightsman, 1977, p. 511). This rule could be applied to our rooms, our neighborhoods, and our cities, as well as to our buildings. Let us examine how these environments bend us to their design.

Rooms

Rooms have been a favorite subject of European novelists. This is not because these writers were terribly interested in interior design, but because they realized that rooms could provide insight into the one thing they were most interested in: human psychology. In a room described by Dickens or Balzac, for example, every object reeks of the personality of the room's inhabitants. Here is an excerpt from Balzac's famous description of the boarding-house dining room in *Père Goriot:*

> The dining room, where the walls are paneled to the ceiling, was long ago painted in some color which cannot be discerned today, and is now only a background on which layers of dirt have formed in such a fashion as to present some bizarre designs. The room is surrounded by sticky buffets holding carafes which are dirty and chipped. . . . In a corner there is a box with numbered pigeonholes for the stained and spotted napkins of the boarders. The room has those indestructible pieces of furniture, proscribed from every other place, and resting there just as the refuse of humanity come to rest in homes for the incurable. You would see there a barometer with a monk who comes forth when it points to rain, engravings so horrible as to spoil one's appetite . . . and a long table covered with oil cloth so greasy that a merry boarder can write his name on it with the end of his finger. And there are rickety chairs. . . . To explain how old this furniture is, how cracked and rotten and shaky and worn, how deformed, how lopsided, and sick and dying, we should have to embark on a description which would too long delay our start on the story and which hurried readers would not pardon. The red tiles of the floor are full of indentations caused by waxing and painting. In short, this is the kingdom of poverty without poetry: a poverty which is economical, concentrated, threadbare. If it is not yet filthy, it is spotted; if it has not holes and rags, it is about to rot away. (Balzac, 1946, pp. 7–8)

Into this room, Balzac seems to say, no joy can ever pierce. (And none ever does.) Created by pettiness and misery, it in turn creates pettiness and misery.

What novelists such as Balzac discovered a century ago, environmental psychologists are now beginning to investigate scientifically. Rooms clearly affect behavior, but how much and in what ways? Can human relationships really be influenced by the rooms in which they are carried on?

Beauty and Ugliness

One interesting line of investigation has to do with the relationship between interpersonal attraction and the beauty and ugliness of rooms. In Balzac's novel the ugliness of the boarding-house rooms carried over into human relations. Apparently the same thing happens in real life. Two investigators (Maslow and Mintz, 1956) decided to test social perception in a pretty room, an ugly room, and an ordinary room. The pretty room had beige walls, mahogany furniture, soft indirect lighting, a Navajo rug, and other pieces of art. The ugly room looked something like a janitor's storeroom. It was lit by a single bare light bulb; the walls were institutional gray; the windows were covered by discolored shades; the floor was dirty; brooms, mops, and pails were lined up against the walls. The ordinary room was the rather nondescript office of a professor. In these three different rooms subjects were shown photographs of people's faces and asked to rate them on energy versus fatigue, well-being versus displeasure, and other qualities. As Balzac would have predicted, the photographs received the highest ratings in the pretty room, the lowest ratings in the ugly room, and intermediate ratings in the ordinary room.

Furniture and Seating

A second aspect of room design, furniture arrangement, has an even clearer impact on interpersonal behavior. Consider an obvious example: the American courtroom. The first thing that strikes your eye as you walk into the courtroom is the judge's seat. Centered, elevated above the other seats, and facing the rest of the courtroom, the seat leaves no doubt as to who is in charge of this room. The witness chair is lower than the judge's, but like his, it faces the rest of the court. This seat puts the witness on the spot, forcing him to state his evidence while the whole court, including the defendant, looks him straight in the face. The seat is thus a reminder to the witness of his oath of honesty. Then consider the jury box: off to the side, placed at an angle to the rest of the seats. This placement tells the jury that they are observers, not participants; they are not to take sides. Then consider the seats of the

prosecutor and the defense attorney. They are parallel and on the same level. This arrangement tells everyone that the accusing government has no authority or advantage over the private citizen and his representative (Hazard, 1962). The defendant is innocent until proven guilty; the chairs tell us so.

In other words, furniture arrangement guides thought and action. It tells the people in the room what their roles are and how they should behave. If you placed a band of Aborigines in an American courtroom, they would probably have some idea of what to do.

Sociopetal and Sociofugal Space. One type of behavior that seating arrangements definitely control is socializing. According to one theorist (Osmond, 1957), seating can create either *sociopetal space* (literally, "companion-seeking" space) or *sociofugal space* (literally, "companion-fleeing" space). In sociopetal space, seats face one another and are close together, encouraging us to interact. In sociofugal space, seats are either placed side by side, encouraging us to ignore the person next to us and simply stare straight ahead, or they are so far apart that it is impossible to talk.

This principle was nicely illustrated by an experiment conducted in the women's geriatric ward of a Canadian hospital (Sommer and Ross, 1958). The ward had a newly redecorated dayroom, but in this seemingly cheerful room the patients were cheerless. Indeed, they seemed downright depressed, and interacted very little with one another. The investigators noticed immediately that the room, for all its new furnishings and snappy decorations, was a classic case of sociofugal space. The chairs were lined up side by side against the walls, and not surprisingly the patients sitting in these chairs spent most of their time staring off into

A bus station in a large city. Note the airport-type seats. Bolted down side by side, they make it almost impossible for people to converse with one another. And so they subtly encourage people to move on. (Alex Webb/Magnum)

ACTIVITY 14.2

Seating can affect how and what we communicate. In your home, arrange the seating so that you can speak to a person from about eight feet away, and also from about three feet away. Ask someone to discuss a problem with you, and seat yourself eight feet from him or her. After five minutes or so, move to the seat three feet away. After your conversation, jot down if and how it changed when you sat closer together. You might also try the experiment in reverse (first close, then farther away) with a different person.

space. So the investigators converted the room into a sociopetal space by arranging the chairs around tables. At first the patients didn't like this; it disrupted their old habits. But within a few weeks the frequency of their conversations had doubled, and their morale showed a striking improvement. In other words, a simple rearrangement of seating went a long way toward solving a serious adjustment problem.

What Does This Room Want From Me? By observing whether a space is sociofugal or sociopetal, you can often get some idea of what the designers of the room wanted you to do there. Airport seating, for example, is notoriously sociofugal and, according to one investigator, quite deliberately so:

> In most [airline] terminals, it is virtually impossible for two people sitting down to converse comfortably for any length of time. The chairs are either bolted together and arranged in rows theatre-style facing the ticket counter, or arranged back-to-back, and even if they face one another they are at such distances that comfortable conversation is impossible. The motive for the arrangement is the same as in hotels and other commercial places—to drive people out of the waiting areas into cafes, bars, and shops where they will spend money. (Sommer, 1969, pp. 121–122)

The seating in cafés, restaurants, and cocktail lounges, on the other hand, is sociopetal—to encourage you to stay, socialize, and spend your money. (The one exception is the long bar in a tavern or cocktail lounge. This provides a sociofugal haven for those who wish to drink alone.)

Another environment in which seating betrays the designers' intentions is the classroom. The traditional classroom arrangement, with seats arranged in rows facing the teacher, is based on the traditional image of the teacher as the authority, the source of knowledge, and the traditional image of education as the process of absorbing authoritative statements from the teacher and the book. By and large, it is a sociofugal arrangement. It discourages interaction between students, and while it allows interaction between teacher and student, it clearly indicates that such interaction is to be on a formal basis. This seating plan stands in sharp contrast to the more modern and sociopetal arrangement whereby students and teacher sit around a table, so that the teacher is deprived of a commanding position and the students face each other as much as they face the teacher. The educational theory behind this latter arrangement is that education is not something that teachers can dispense and students swallow; rather, education is a process of discovery through interaction. The teacher is there simply to aid the process of discovery, somewhat like the "facilitator" in a group therapy session.

The sociopetal arrangement, a child of the "progressive education" movement, is thought by many environmental psychologists (for example, Richardson, 1967) to be a vast improvement over the traditional scheme. Yet, as many students know, both schemes have their pitfalls. While the traditional arrangement can make the student feel uninvolved and insignificant, the sociopetal arrangement can just as easily lead to meandering and trivial discussions. (For another connection between classroom seating and behavior, see Box 14.1.)

Buildings and Neighborhoods

Buildings and neighborhoods, like rooms, control behavior. Details that might seem psychologically insignificant—the height of an apartment building, the number of apartments on a hallway, the placement of exits, the number of stairwells and elevators, the amount of communal space for informal interaction among residents—these details can go a long way to determining how the residents will lead their lives. The crime rate, the level of friendship among neighbors, and the satisfaction of residents in general often depends on just such simple matters of architectural design.

BOX 14.1
CLASSROOM ECOLOGY

How the seats are arranged in a classroom may determine what kind of education you get, but *where* you sit may determine what kind of grades you get. R. Sommer (1967), a noted environmental psychologist, sat in on a number of classes and found that students' participation in classroom discussion had a great deal to do with where they were sitting. In general, the students who participated the most were those who sat in the center seats and/or in the front row. In fact, the students who sat in the center seats of the front row participated twice as much as those in the side seats of the back row. In a more recent study (1974), Sommer found that students' grades followed almost the same pattern. The students who sat in the front and in the center of the classroom were the ones who did best.

Before you change your seat, remember that when two factors correlate, we don't necessarily know that there is a cause-and-effect relationship between them—or, if there is, which is the cause and which is the effect. It is possible that sitting squarely in front of the instructor causes a student to participate more in the class and therefore to learn more and get better grades. However, the reverse is equally possible. That is, the students who are interested in the class and who want to participate—in other words, the students who are most likely to get good grades—may deliberately choose the seats in front, all the better to participate. The students who don't care and don't want to participate—in other words, the students who are least likely to get good grades—might deliberately choose the seats in the rear, all the better to look out the window. (If you haven't done the reading, how likely are you to sit in the front row?)

So changing your seat might not help. But then again, it wouldn't hurt. . . .

Much of what environmental psychologists have learned about the psychological impact of buildings and neighborhoods has been based on the study of slums and their replacements, the so-called urban renewal projects. In the fifties and sixties it became the fashion in city planning to tear down the decrepit inner-city tenements and build in their place tall, sleek public housing units, with rents geared to low incomes. To the city planners' dismay, many of these projects soon became slummier than the slums they had replaced. Why? A few answers to this question—and a good lesson in environmental psychology—are contained in the story of the Pruitt-Igoe housing project in St. Louis.

The Pruitt-Igoe Project

Amid many high hopes, the Pruitt-Igoe housing project was opened in 1955. It was an enormous complex: 33 11-story buildings, containing almost 3,000 apartments. The apartments were simple but attractive; the hallways were vandal-proofed by wall tile and indestructible light fixtures; the design had won architectural awards. Yet within three years these buildings were complete physical wrecks. Windows were broken and boarded up. The vandal-proof hallways were thoroughly vandalized. Walls were covered with graffiti. Litter and garbage lay everywhere. The stairwells stank of urine.

Worse still, the buildings were hotbeds of crime, much of it committed by teen-agers living in the project. Assault and rape were constant threats. Those who were not committing the crimes remained behind heavily locked doors, fearful of using any of the common areas. To enter the elevators after dark was an invitation to mugging. To enter the central stairwell at any time was an invitation to rape (Yancey, 1976).

Eventually people began moving out. The vacancy rate rose to 70 percent. Finally, in 1972, the city authorities voted to tear down the project.

Post-mortems of Pruitt-Igoe pointed up a number of possible causes for this failure. The buildings were sterile and anonymous, arousing little sense of "belonging." The height of the buildings and the presence of the stairwells and other hideaways made it difficult for parents to keep an eye on their children's activities. The vandal-proof features were insulting to the residents, inviting hostility and destruction (Rainwater, 1966). But, according to those who studied the project, the major cause of its decline was the lack of facilities for promoting social ties among the residents. The buildings had very few places where neighbors could socialize informally. Hence, residents seldom became friendly with one another. One woman who lived there described the situation:

> I've got no friends here. There's none of this door-to-door coffee business of being friends here or anything like that. Down here, if you are sick you just go to the hospital. There are no friends to help you. I don't think my neighbors would help me and I wouldn't ask them anyway. . . . The rule of the game down here is *go for yourself.* (Yancey, 1976, p. 455)

This isolation of neighbor from neighbor not only made it easy for residents to ignore or harm one another. It also prevented them from developing any stake in the project, for it is often the local social network that causes people to put down roots.

The Social Amenities of Slums

The failure of Pruitt-Igoe and other urban renewal projects has caused environmental psychologists to look again at slums—or the

The Pruitt-Igoe housing project being dynamited. The Pruitt-Igoe disaster was a demonstration of the disadvantages of urban renewal housing and a lesson in certain basic principles of environmental psychology. (© The Pulitzer Publishing Co./St. Louis Dispatch)

working-class and lower-class neighborhoods that nonresidents call slums. One of the most striking aspects of these neighborhoods is the street life. As poor as they are in physical facilities (central heating, decent plumbing, and so on), most slums are rich in social facilities. Semiprivate, sociopetal spaces—the very thing that Pruitt-Igoe lacked—are everywhere. Activity is constantly spilling out of the apartments and into street corners, stoops, alleys, porches, the corner bar, or the corner grocery. Children play in the streets; women socialize on the stoops; men roll dice and shoot the breeze on sidewalks or in the alleys.

This buzzing street life—aptly called "neighboring" by one sociologist (Ottensmann, 1978)—has two important consequences (Fried and Gleicher, 1961). The first is that residents develop a strong sense of local identity. The neighborhood—not just the apartment—is "home." The second con-

sequence is that neighbors develop an intricate network of social ties. Everyone knows everyone else. If someone is sick, a neighbor looks in. If a child misbehaves, there are many adult eyes (not just his parents') watching. Both these factors, the sense of local identity and the network of social cooperation, foster a sense of belonging, discourage antisocial behavior, and, not incidentally, contribute to the residents' happiness. In short, slums generally have vast social advantages over the projects. This fact has led many writers to plead that public money be used to improve the slums rather than tear them down (Jacobs, 1961; Gans, 1962; Fried, 1963; Ottensmann, 1978).

High-Rise and Low-Rise: Defensible Space

Yet another point of difference between projects and slum housing (or between luxury apartment buildings and town houses, for that matter) is building height. And building height appears to have a definite relationship to crime rates. For example, one researcher, Oscar Newman (1972), compared crime rates in two neighboring housing projects in New York City, one with high-rise buildings and the other with three- to six-story buildings. The crime rate in the high-rise project turned out to be twice as high as that in the low-rise project.

To explain this difference, Newman introduced the concept of the *defensible space.* He defined a defensible space as a residential building small enough that the residents can control it through informal precautions. Such precautions include keeping an eye on entrances, watching children from the windows, noticing strangers who are hanging around the building, and recognizing non-residents in the hallways and challenging them, particularly if they are carrying television sets. Newman claims that once an apartment building rises beyond six or seven stories, these informal controls become difficult to impose. And unless formal controls (doormen, security guards, and so on) are instituted in their place, the space lies undefended, an open invitation to criminals.

High-rises are now an important issue in discussions of how to house the elderly. In town after town you can see "senior citizens" housing built to ten and twelve stories. It has been argued that if these high-rises are made defensible—with guards, buzzer systems, and the like—they are actually better for old people than single-story housing, because common hallways and lobbies will encourage social contacts, the very thing so many old people lack. A recent study (Devlin, 1980) measuring the benefits of high-rises vs. garden apartments for old people found that both arrangements had some advantages. The garden-apartment res-

idents liked living in a private structure and working in their gardens. The high-rise residents, as expected, praised the social benefits of sharing their building with others. However, the majority of the high-rise residents felt that a low-rise—two to five stories—was the best design, apparently because it offered a more manageable space without sacrificing the pleasures of hallway socializing. We may eventually see a trend toward "unstacking" the elderly, in those towns that can afford the space for low-rises and garden apartments.

Cities

While people may be unaware of the impact of rooms and buildings on behavior, everyone is an amateur environmental psychologist when it comes to cities. The city mouse, they know, is different from the country mouse. The city fosters certain kinds of behavior, some of it not too attractive. For one thing, the city breeds crime. For another thing, the city breeds indifference. People don't smile at you, don't give you change for a quarter, don't say they're sorry when they bump into you. The city, in short, is a social jungle. Or so we are told by our movies and magazines.

How true is this stereotype? Somewhat true, according to the research. And somewhat false as well, for it leaves out the psychological benefits of city living. Let's look at the evidence.

Crime

It is a well-documented fact that crime is a particular problem in large cities. For every 2 violent crimes reported in rural areas, and for every 3 reported in the suburbs, there are 11 reported in cities with over 250,000 population (FBI, 1978).* Why should this be so? The reasons are fairly obvious. First of all, two of the major correlates of crime, poverty and high concentrations of ethnic minorities, are to be found in abundance in the cities. Other possible causes of urban crime have already cropped up earlier in this chapter. High-rise buildings and urban renewal projects, as we have seen, are associated with crime, and they too are most common in cities. Crowding, as we have seen, can provoke aggression, and people are certainly more crowded in cities. Furthermore, high population density creates anonymity: the more people there are, the smaller the percentage of people who know you. And anonymity increases the likelihood of crime. (See Box 14.2.) In both practical and psychological terms, it is much easier to rob an unknown shopowner in front of unknown witnesses than it is to rob good old Mr. McGee, the druggist who sold you your first comic book, in front of witnesses who will see your parents in church on Sunday.

Social Indifference

The second great behavioral flaw that cities are said to foster is indifference—a general

---

* Although the common assumption that big cities have a serious crime problem is correct, the equally common assumption that the "crime capitals" of the United States are the older cities of the Northeast—New York, Buffalo, Boston, Philadelphia, Newark—is *not* correct. Actually, the major crime centers are located in the so-called "Sun Belt," the strip of cities and suburbs stretching across the southern United States from Florida to California. Of the ten cities listed by the FBI (1980) as having the highest rate of reported violent crime and property crime, only one, Atlantic City, is in the Northeast. Indeed, the majority are in Florida. They are, in order: Miami, Atlantic City, Las Vegas, Gainesville, West Palm Beach, Orlando, Sacramento, Fort Lauderdale, Phoenix, Daytona Beach, and Tallahassee. As you can see, New York, often thought of as *the* crime-ridden city, doesn't even make it into the top ten.

lack of concern for the welfare of one's fellow human beings. This urban stereotype was reinforced by a shocking incident that occurred in New York City in 1964. A woman named Kitty Genovese, returning home late at night, was beaten, stabbed, and strangled in front of her apartment building. The attack lasted for thirty-five minutes. Genovese repeatedly screamed for help, and many of her neighbors heard her. Indeed, thirty-eight different people admitted that they saw at least part of the attack from their windows. Yet incredibly, not a single person went to her aid or even bothered to call the police until Kitty Genovese was already dead.

The Genovese incident is an extreme case of what is called *bystander apathy*, the unwillingness to help others, particularly strangers, who are in trouble. It is probable that bystander apathy is more common in large cities than in small towns (Milgram, 1970; Korte and Kerr, 1975). If so, high population density may be a major cause. Several experiments have shown that the larger the number of bystanders, the less likely it is that any one of them will intervene to help a stranger in trouble (Latané and Darley, 1969, 1970).

System Overload. High population density alone, however, is not a sufficient explanation for bystander apathy. What happens psychologically to make people ignore the needs of others? Social psychologist Stanley Milgram (1970) has come up with one interesting theory. Milgram claims that bystander apathy and other forms of urban indifference (failing to give an old person your seat on the bus, failing to call the fire department when you see smoke, and so on) can be explained as the result of *system overload*. The city-dweller is bombarded by stimuli, particularly interpersonal stimuli. The sight, smell, and sound of other people

BOX 14.2
ANONYMITY AND CRIME: SOMETHING TO CONSIDER WHEN PARKING YOUR CAR

Several years ago social psychologist Philip Zimbardo (1969) set out to test the hypothesis that the anonymity of city life encourages crime. He arranged to have automobiles abandoned in two different locations: New York City and Palo Alto, California, a medium-sized suburban community. The cars' license plates were removed and their hoods were raised to signal that the autos were abandoned. Then each car was secretly watched for sixty-four hours.

The person assigned to watch the New York car did not have long to wait:

Within ten minutes the 1959 Oldsmobile received its first auto strippers—a father, mother, and eight-year-old son. The mother appeared to be a lookout, while the son aided the father's search of the trunk, glove compartment, and motor. He handed his father the tools necessary to remove the battery and radiator. Total time of destructive contact: seven minutes. (Zimbardo, 1969 p. 287)

This, however, was only the first "contact." By the end of the sixty-four hours the car had been vandalized twenty-four times, often by well-dressed, seemingly middle-class adults. What remained when the experiment was over was a useless hunk of metal. In contrast, the Palo Alto car was approached only once: when it started to rain, a passerby stopped to lower the hood so that the engine would not get wet.

According to Zimbardo, the crucial factor in the different fates of the two cars was anonymity. In a large city, where the chances of being recognized outside one's own neighborhood are extremely slim, even "upstanding citizens" can afford to take a temporary excursion into thievery. In a smaller community, on the other hand, the higher probability of being recognized and caught keeps people honest.

Zimbardo, P. G. "The Human Choice: Individuation, Reason, and Order Versus Deindividuation, Impulse, and Chaos," in W. Arnold and D. Levine, eds., Ne-braska Symposium on Motivation. Lincoln, Neb.: Univ. of Nebraska Press, 1969.

come at him from all sides. If he paid attention to all these stimuli, his mind would simply be overwhelmed. He wouldn't be able to concentrate on the things that really matter to him—his job, his family, his own private thoughts. Consequently, according to Milgram, the urbanite learns to screen out a large number of interpersonal stimuli. If a drunk is sprawled across the sidewalk, he steps over him. If there is a new clerk in the drugstore, he doesn't ask what happened to the old clerk. In sum, he automatically

protects himself from involvement with those who aren't part of his particular inner circle.

Research suggests that system overload is at least a partial explanation for bystander apathy (Sherrod and Downs, 1974; Weiner, 1976; Krupat and Epstein, 1975). But we still need to know the actual mechanics of the process. Does the high stimulus level wear people out, so that they no longer have the energy to help? Or does it cause them to adjust their standards of what they owe their fellow human beings? Or do they just notice less of what is going on around them? The last factor, decreased awareness, probably has something to do with it (Cohen and Lezak, 1977). Recently, two researchers (Korte and Grant, 1980) set out to test whether high traffic noise would affect urban pedestrians' awareness of *any* unusual stimulus, not just a person in trouble. During high traffic hours, and then again at low traffic hours, they set up a few odd sights—a woman in a funny pink party hat, another woman clutching a bright yellow teddy bear—on a sidewalk in Dundee, Scotland. After people had walked past these novelties, they were stopped and asked whether they had seen them. Even with prompting, only 35 percent of the pedestrians recalled the odd sights during the high-traffic conditions, as opposed to 56 percent during the low-traffic conditions. It was also found that during the high-traffic hours pedestrians walked faster and were more likely to keep their gaze fixed directly in front of them, which helps to explain their decreased awareness. This study gives us some insight into the stereotyped city-dweller, marching straight ahead, briefcase in hand, noticing nothing. Apparently there is a limit to how much a human being can notice, and traffic noise alone—to say nothing of the many other strong stimuli that surround the city-dweller—can push people to that limit.

The Other Side of the Story: Freedom and Variety

If the big city fosters crime and indifference, why do so many people want to live there? The answer is that crime and indifference are only the negative aspects of city life. There are positive aspects as well.

One is freedom. We have just seen that if you happen to find yourself lying drunk on a big-city sidewalk, you are unlikely to get help from passersby. If you pull the same stunt in a small town, someone will probably stop. But once he stops, he is as likely to call the police or give you a lecture on reforming your behavior as he is to go fetch you a cup of hot coffee. In other words, we shouldn't romanticize the interpersonal concern of small-town residents. Their interest in you is sometimes as meddlesome and annoying as it is helpful. In either case, it involves restrictions. Once someone knows your business, you aren't as free as you were before.

By contrast, big-city indifference confers the blessing of freedom. This is not to say that urbanites are completely free. They too have parents and lovers and spouses and children, and these intimate relationships place the same restrictions on city-dwellers as they do on small-town folk. But outside the circle of intimacy, urbanites generally leave one another alone to lead their lives as they please:

> So long as the shoe salesman performs his rather limited service for us, thereby fulfilling our rather limited expectations, we do not insist that he believe in our God, or that he be tidy at home, or share our political values, or enjoy the same kind of food or music that we do. We leave him free in all other matters—as he leaves us free to be atheist or Jew, heterosexual or homosexual, John Bircher or Communist. (Toffler, 1971, pp. 98–99)

To many urbanites this combination of freedom and privacy—the ability to go their own way without being asked what they are up to and whether it conforms to somebody else's code of proper behavior—is one of the city's most precious gifts. As a character in an old Olivia de Haviland movie once said to the unwed mother (Olivia de Haviland) who had fled the disapproval of her small-town neighbors to give birth to her baby in

New York, "The more I hear of them cozy little towns, the better I like the Bronx."

A predictable result (and possibly also a cause) of this freedom is variety of behavior. As you switch your attention from small town to big city, the increase in different *types* of behavior is much greater than could possibly be accounted for by the increase in population. Communists and the Little League, hippies and bankers, prostitutes and foreign princesses, cops and robbers—all are there, going about their different business. This variety creates an atmosphere of excitement, of endless possibilities, that for many people outweighs the psychological disadvantages of urban life.

PERCEIVING THE ENVIRONMENT

As we have noted in earlier chapters, what people see is not necessarily what is out there. This is as true of our perception of the environment as it is of self-perception and social perception. When we look at our physical surroundings, we don't see just the objective reality. Rather, we see a subjective reality. This subjective reality results from the combined impact of three factors (Baron and Byrne, 1977). The first of these is objective reality. (We do, after all, see *something* of what is out there.) The second is our personal characteristics—our needs, our tastes, our past learning experiences. For example, if you have been raised in a Kansas farmhouse, Cleveland may seem to you a loud and terrifying place. The third component of our perception of the environment is the quality of the situation. As we have noted, what seems like crowding in one situation may seem like a barrel of fun in another situation. By the same token, the quiet library that seemed to you such a wonderful place two hours ago, when you had so much

studying to do, may seem as grim as a mausoleum once you've finished your work and are ready for some action.

Cognitive Maps

An interesting illustration of the subjective quality of environmental perception is the research that has been done on cognitive maps. A *cognitive map* is an individual's mental picture, or map, of an environment. A number of researchers have asked residents of various cities to transfer their mental maps to paper. In one study (Saarinen, 1969), researchers requested maps of the Chicago Loop from a group of people who worked in the Loop and from a group of students who simply lived near the Loop. The maps produced by the students generally encompassed the whole Loop and focused on obvious external landmarks such as Lake Michigan and Lake Shore Drive. The maps produced by the workers, on the other hand, tended to focus on smaller areas and included more intricate detail. Clearly, these workers, unlike the students, *knew* the Loop, and knowing an area often means taking for granted what is big and obvious (Lake Michigan, for example) and concentrating instead on more specific and practical details (the location of Clancy's Bar, for example).

The influence of learning and personality is nicely illustrated in a study of cognitive maps of Paris (Milgram, 1976). Figure 14.2 shows Paris as drawn by a 25-year-old resident, a businessman with degrees in physical chemistry. He encompasses the entire metropolitan area of Paris in a few bold strokes of the pen. Among his landmarks, the Eiffel Tower is of course included, but it is dwarfed by a nearby skyscraper. And the entire city is dwarfed by the huge modern office complex at the upper left. This, obviously, is a young cosmopolite, with his

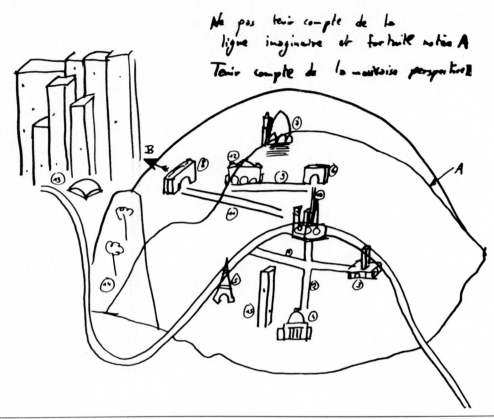

Figure 14.2 A 25-year-old businessman's cognitive map of Paris. (Source: Milgram, 1976, p. 105.)

mind on things modern and technological. In striking contrast is a map drawn by a 50-year-old woman (Figure 14.3). Rather than take on the whole city, she concentrates on a small area, the neighborhood where she had lived for fifteen years. This she maps in meticulous detail, sketching in neat little rows of trees in front of the Louvre, writing in the names of the streets, and even indicating the directions of the one-way streets. Not a single modern building is included. This, clearly, is the mental map of an older person, with a strong sense of neighborhood identity and with little concern for the skyscrapers that grew up in Paris long after she had created her own mental image of the city. Clearly, different people see the same environment in very different ways (see Activity 14.3).

We will examine briefly two processes that help to create these personal distortions of the environment: selective attention and habituation.

Selective Attention

Among the stimuli presented to us by our environment, we select what we want or need to perceive, and that is what we tend to perceive. What we don't want or need to perceive, we screen out. This process is called *selective attention* (Moore, 1979).

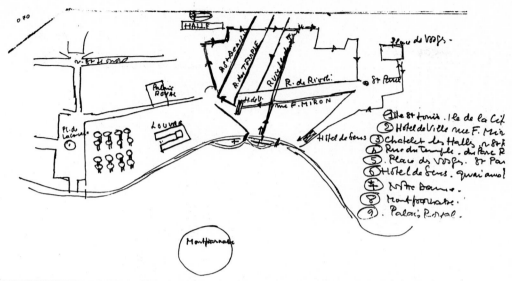

Figure 14.3 A 50-year-old woman's cognitive map of Paris. (Source: Milgram, 1976, p. 106.)

On what bases do we make our selection? One criterion is relevance. We automatically discriminate among things that are relevant and irrelevant to our needs. The former are perceived and remembered; the latter are ignored. Thus, for example, a person driving down a street will notice a stop sign that a person walking down the street won't see. Likewise, when the corner newsstand begins selling pornographic magazines, this fact will forcibly strike the attention of local adolescent boys and of local parents. It relates to their needs—positively in the case of the adolescent boys, negatively in the case of the parents. As for the local three-year-olds and sexually satisfied childless adults, they will tend to ignore the sizzling display, since it can't do much of anything for or against them.

A second criterion that determines what we will perceive in the environment is cognitive consistency. As we have pointed out in earlier chapters, the information that we are most likely to attend to about ourselves and others is the information that is consistent with our already-established impressions of ourselves and others. Environmental perception operates on the same principle. A person who loves New York City will walk down Fifth Avenue and see

ACTIVITY 14.3

Draw your own cognitive map of your school campus, and ask two other students to do the same. Then compare the three maps. What do the differences among them tell you about the interests, personalities, and past histories of the three of you?

Fifth Avenue at Christmas time, complete with numerous shoppers and a pretzel-and-chestnut seller. To some, the busy sidewalks of New York are alive with excitement and variety. To others, they are ugly, crowded, and commercialized. (Ray Ellis/Rapho/Photo Researchers, Inc.)

the handsome displays in the shopwindows, the towering spire of St. Patrick's Cathedral, the colorful flowers blooming in Rockefeller Plaza, the stylish clothes of the passersby. A person who hates New York City will walk down the same stretch of Fifth Avenue and see the bum on the corner, the dog-droppings in the gutter, the high price tags on the merchandise in the windows, and the carbon monoxide floating amid the heavy traffic. One reality. Two different expectations. And therefore two different perceptions, each consistent with the expectation.

Habituation

The second process that works to distort our perception of the environment is *habituation*—our tendency to become less aware of and less responsive to a stimulus once we have been repeatedly exposed to it (Korte and Grant, 1980). Habituation, then, means getting used to something so that you notice

it less and are less likely to do anything about it. If a person who has been raised in Florida moves to Alaska, she is likely, at first, to be painfully aware of the cold and to protect herself with layer upon layer of clothing, much to the amusement of seasoned locals. Eventually, however, she habituates: she becomes less aware of the cold and even starts going out to empty the garbage without wearing her gloves. Likewise, if you move into an apartment with a living room that is painted a horrible color of orange, the color may drive you crazy in the beginning. But gradually the room will come to seem less orange and you will stop thinking about repainting it.

Of all the aspects of environmental perception, habituation is the one that is of deepest concern to professionals involved in reforming people's attitudes toward the environment. For it is habituation that leads people to accept, without complaint, unacceptable environmental conditions. When we sit in a small room with a group of smokers, we often don't notice that the air is becoming hazy. We habituate at the same rate that the smoke level rises. Similarly, we habituate to breathing industrial pollution, to hearing jets break the sound barrier over our heads, to having to drive many miles to find a patch of grass on which to have a picnic. The more we are exposed to these things, the more natural they seem. And the more natural they seem, the less likely we are to do anything about them. If all the lakes and rivers are polluted, well, that's the way things are. If you want to swim, join the "Y."

In this way, according to environmental critics, we could witness the destruction of most of the earth's resources within our own lifetimes and not even be aware of it:

If this generation doesn't wake up, the next generation won't know any better. They'll think that swimming in filth is the normal thing to do. They'll think that the moon is supposed to be yellow. They'll think they are breathing clean air and drinking clean water because they won't know any better. (Blaushild, cited in Sommer, 1972, p. 24)

Through habituation, then, we cease to notice environmental conditions. But this doesn't mean that those environmental conditions cease to affect our behavior. People who live near airports may get accustomed to hearing sonic booms, but they may still have a difficult time getting their friends to come to dinner. People who live on streets with heavy traffic may habituate to the noise and automobile exhaust, but they still can't enjoy their front yards. Urbanites still experience more environmental stress than suburbanites, whether they notice it or not. In short, habituation does not shield us psychologically from environmental conditions. It simply stifles the will to change those conditions.

ADJUSTMENT AND ENVIRONMENTAL PERCEPTION

So far we have discussed the relationship between environment and behavior in broad, general terms: "we" feel thus and such; "people" do thus and such. Now it is time to return to the question of individual adjustment. In other words, how about you? As we have seen throughout this chapter, our physical surroundings make us behave in certain ways. How does your environment make you behave? What kind of a person is your environment making of you? And is this the person you want to be?

At this point you may reply that, given what we have just said concerning habituation, you cannot be expected to see clearly either your environment or its behavioral effects. However, if you want to see these things clearly, you *can* short-circuit the process of habituation.

Let's return to the example of the smoke-filled room. As the room gradually fills with smoke, your internal habituation machine hums along, keeping pace with the increasing pollution, and consequently you fail to notice the smoke. Let us now imagine that you leave the room for a moment. As you open the door to come back in, you finally see the foul air that you have been breathing and ask somebody to open a window. In other words, by removing yourself from an environment temporarily, you allow yourself, when you see it again, to see it more clearly, without the dulling effects of habituation.

By the same token, the best time to analyze an environment in which you spend a lot of time (for example, your bedroom, your living room, your office) is when you have been away for a while—on a trip, for example. However, if you have no trips planned, you can analyze your environment by removing yourself from it psychologically. That is, you mentally cast off the role of

BOX 14.3
SOME TIPS FOR PROTECTING
THE ENVIRONMENT

In addition to rearranging our domestic environments, all of us could use some advice on protecting the planet we live on. Many of us needlessly waste and pollute our resources without even realizing it, simply by following habits that we have developed over the years. Here is a list of suggestions for minor changes in your consumption habits. Each, by itself, seems a small thing. But practiced day after day, these alternatives could make a great difference in the environment.

1. Cut down on heat consumption by hanging on to the heat you have already produced. Insulate ceilings and walls. Buy storm windows. Put caulking and weather stripping on the joints of windows and doors.

2. When you turn up the heat 1 degree, you raise your fuel consumption 3 to 4 percent. When you turn up the heat 5 degrees, you raise fuel consumption 15 to 20 percent. So put an extra blanket on your bed and turn *down* the heat at night.

3. Don't turn on a dishwasher, clothes washer, or dryer until you have a full load. Every time you use the dishwasher, you consume 12 to 16 gallons of water. Every time you use the washing machine, you consume an average of 45 gallons of water.

4. When buying a refrigerator-freezer, remember that the new side-by-side models consume about 45 percent more electricity than the older-style models with the freezing compartment above or below the refrigerator. Self-defrosting models are also power-guzzlers.

5. Disposals, or food-waste disposers, are ecological villains. (New York City banned them years ago.) Organic food waste is one thing that *should* be dumped on the land; it fertilizes and replenishes the soil. It should not be dumped into the water system, which is where the disposal dumps it.

6. Give yourself the bath-versus-shower test. Put the plug in the bathtub drain and then take a shower. If the water gets higher than it would in a normal bath, you should be taking baths rather than showers. If, when you have finished your shower, the water is still shallower than in a normal bath, you should be taking showers rather than baths.

7. If you must use disposable paper products, don't use colored ones. The dye pollutes the waters.

8. If you must use disposable cups and plates for a picnic or party, buy the ones made of uncoated paper. These will decompose and burn much more easily than the plastic-coated ones.

9. Boycott overpackaged products, such as packages of individually wrapped cheese slices.

10. When something breaks, don't throw it out. Have it fixed. Or donate it to a charity that can have it fixed and resell it.

11. Don't buy scratch pads or writing tablets. Do your doodling, list-making, and first-draft-writing on the back of paper that has already been used.

inhabitant, take on the role of environmental psychologist, and study the environment as clinically and as objectively as possible.

Surveying an Environment: A Step-by-Step Procedure

Here are five steps you can follow in order to sharpen your perception of an environment:

1. Pick the environment to be analyzed, and make it small. Don't tackle more than one room or one limited outdoor area (that is, a back yard, not a large park) for your first analysis.

2. Draw two vertical lines down a piece of ruled paper so that you have three columns of equal size. Give those columns the headings "Physical Feature," "Psychological Message," and "Behavioral or Emotional Consequence," in that order.

3. In the first column ("Physical Feature") list the physical aspects of the environment. What is *in* this place? What do you see there?

4. In the second column ("Psychological Message") note, for each physical feature, what that feature seems to say to you. As we mentioned earlier, environments carry messages, intentional or unintentional. A classroom with traditional seating says "Listen to the teacher." A bathroom without doors on the stalls says, "We don't trust you." On your survey sheet, try to put into words the message conveyed by each of the physical features on your list. (If a physical feature says nothing to you, leave the "Message" space blank.)

5. In the third column ("Behavioral or Emotional Consequence") note, for each physical feature, what you *do* in response to that feature. How does it make you behave? If you can't think of a behavior, write down a feeling the feature elicits. Then, if you can, list behaviors that might result from that feeling.

12. Buy one-ply toilet paper and don't waste it. Remember: paper is made from trees.

13. Make sure that the detergents you are using are biodegradable and contain no phosphates. If the label doesn't say this, find one with a label that does.

14. Put a litter bag in your car and scold anyone who doesn't use it. Don't litter. Period.

15. Don't use plastic garbage bags. Put your garbage in the paper bags you bring home from the grocery store. This may mess up your garbage can a bit more, but it will mess up the planet a great deal less. So just hose out your garbage can now and then.

16. When storing food, don't cover it with plastic wrap or aluminum foil. Buy yourself a set of permanent, reusable plastic or glass containers and use them instead.

17. Buy a bicycle and use it, rather than a car, for short trips. Bikes have no vices and plenty of virtues. They are cheap; they are safe; they give you needed exercise; they are easy to park; they are quiet. But above all, they produce no pollution and use up no fuel.

18. If school or work is so far away that you can't get there by bike, use public transportation or join a carpool.

Adapted in part from Swatek, P., The User's Guide to the Pollution of the Environment. *New York: Ballantine, 1970.*

A Sample Environmental Survey

Let's look at a sample survey. The environment is one department of a large publishing company, housed on one floor of a modern office building in Manhattan. In order to give a fuller sample, the hypothetical author of the following survey (an editor in the department) will break the one-room rule and will look not only at her own office but at several features of the department as a whole:

Physical Feature	Psychological Message	Behavioral or Emotional Consequence
My Office:		
Large desk	We know you have a lot of work to do, and we want to give you the space in which to do it.	Spread papers out and work efficiently.
Bulletin board over desk	1) We thought you might like to pin up some pictures or memos. 2) Don't put pin holes in the wall.	Pin up memos. Also pin up photographs, postcards, etc., to make office seem homey.
New electric typewriter	We don't want you to have to struggle with inefficient equipment.	Type quickly. Feel important.
Extra chair next to desk	You need an extra chair for business conferences—and maybe also for socializing with a coworker.	Socialize frequently with other people in office.
Telephone hooked up to call anywhere in the world	We trust you not to call your brother in Hawaii.	High morale, sense of being regarded as a responsible, trustworthy adult. (Resulting behaviors: working late or skipping lunch hour without complaint when work requires it.)
The Whole Floor:		
Coffee station with free coffee	1) Make yourself at home. 2) We do things for you.	1) Drink 4–5 cups of coffee per day at work. 2) High morale.*

THE ENVIRONMENT

Physical Feature	Psychological Message	Behavioral or Emotional Consequence
Bulletin board next to coffee station	We try to meet some of your personal needs.	Read notices on bulletin board—dog for sale, apartment to sublet, etc.—while waiting for coffee to brew. (Feeling afterward of having had a nice little break.)
Supply cabinet, not locked	We trust you not to take home supplies for your personal use or for your friends.	High morale, sense of being regarded as a responsible, trustworthy adult.*
Long white corridors	This is a businesslike place.	Feeling of formality. (Resulting behaviors: being quiet in the halls, tendency not to horse around too much.)
A few bright red walls	This may be a businesslike place, but it's not a prison or a hospital. Cheer up.	Cheerfulness. (Resulting behaviors: smiling at people in hallways, saying hello to them.)
Dark brown wall-to-wall carpeting everywhere	1) This office should be kept as quiet as possible 2) We expect you to spill some coffee on the way back from the coffee machine to your office.	1) Speak quietly in hallways. 2) Am not too careful when carrying coffee.
Handsome wooden doors and bookshelves	This is a classy establishment.	Feeling of being important: high morale.*
Locked bathroom	Undesirable people have to be prevented from hanging around in our bathroom.	1) Carry keys when going to bathroom. 2) Cautiousness, sense of possible danger. (Resulting behaviors: locking office door and starting at strange noises when working late.)
"Make-up" room separated from bathroom proper (contains two chairs, counter, large mirror)	1) We try to make you comfortable. 2) Please comb your hair in here rather than over the sinks in the bathroom. Hair clogs the drains.	1) High morale.* 2) Sometimes chat with coworkers in make-up room. 3) Don't comb hair over sinks.

* For behaviors resulting from high morale, see behavioral consequence of desk telephone.

By adding up the psychological messages in the second column, we come up with the psychological "tone" that this environment conveys to this person: businesslike but comfortable and pleasant. And by adding up the behavioral consequences in the third column, we come up with the net behavioral impact of this environment on this person: She is relaxed, works hard, feels trusted and important, and drinks too much coffee. In other words, if the purpose of this environment is to encourage responsible hard work, it is doing its job very well.

How about your environment? If you chose your living room, does it encourage the kind of behavior you want to engage in in your living room? Does the seating allow you to converse easily with guests? Is there an easy chair with good lighting, encouraging you to read? Is there a too-available bar that keeps inviting you to get up and mix another drink? If you chose your dormitory room, is there space enough to study in? Is the room quiet enough for study? Are the walls painted hospital-green? Do you have any privacy from your roommate? If so and if not, what kind of behavior do these conditions elicit from you? Whatever space you choose to survey, train yourself to see how it molds your behavior—and how, if it were different, it would mold your behavior differently.

Changing Your Environment

In general, we are amazingly passive with regard to our environments (Sommer, 1972). Environmental psychologist Irwin Altman notes this fact:

> People . . . adapt too quickly to even the most undesirable places. For example, I have been in several conferences at which the arrangements of tables and chairs were simply not conducive to free discussion. (They represented the janitor's idea of how our meeting should be organized!) Yet people hardly ever protest such arrangements. . . . They are willing to stretch their necks to see one another, speak to people sitting behind them by twisting around, fidget in uncomfortable chairs, and so on. We are simply unwilling to *act* on our environments to make them fit what we desire. (1975, p. 213)

Part of the problem, of course, is that people simply don't notice to what degree their behavior is being molded by the environment. You, however, no longer have this problem, at least with regard to the environment you have surveyed. The psychological-messages column of your survey will tell you which aspects of this environment are threatening or depressing or insulting or even just annoying to you. Even more important, the behavioral-consequences col-

---

ACTIVITY 14.4

Look again at the sample environmental survey on pages 426–427. How would the tone of the office have been different if it had had (1) oriental rugs, (2) a pay phone, (3) a time clock, (4) murals painted by local schoolchildren in the hallways, (5) a coffee machine that required a dime, (6) Muzak, (7) metal doors, (8) a locked supply cabinet? For each of these hypothetical changes, write down the psychological message and the behavioral/emotional consequence.

umn will tell you what aspects of the environment are nudging you into undesirable behaviors. Armed with this information, you can now go to work changing your environment.

This doesn't mean that you can make your environment fit your needs entirely. If the fact that your office has no window depresses you and makes you take overlong lunch hours, you may still have to wait for a promotion in order to get a windowed office. But there are many things you *can* change. If you tend to watch television rather than read because your living room is equipped with a television set but no reading lamp, then you can move the television to the bedroom and buy a reading lamp. If you neglect to look up words you don't know because the dictionary isn't in the room where you study, you can move the dictionary. If the fact that you and your roommate eat off a minuscule card table discourages you from inviting your friends over to dinner, you might consider getting rid of some of the living room furniture and installing a big table. In other words, ask yourself what kind of behavior you want from yourself, and then rearrange the environment as best you can to make that behavior possible and probable.

By doing so, you will be exercising the one human faculty that is the main theme of this book: choice. Though we often allow our environments to push us around, we need not. By recognizing that our behavior is in part a response to environmental stimuli, we can decide for ourselves what those stimuli—and consequently, our responses—should be. In sum, we can begin to choose our lives by choosing the environments in which we live them.

SUMMARY

1. *Environmental psychology* studies the interaction between human beings and their physical environment. Our entire lives are spent influencing and being influenced by our physical surroundings. The unit of the individual and his environment is called an *ecosystem*. Within our ecosystems, the environment helps shape our behavior in three ways: by putting constraints on behavior, by eliciting certain behaviors, and by molding the self.

2. Certain aspects of the environment may cause *stress*. One form of environmental stress is *crowding*, which is caused by high *population density*. Two other environmental *stressors* are noise and heat. All three have been shown to have negative effects on interpersonal behavior.

3. The *built environment*, comprising those settings that have been designed and created largely by human beings, can have both positive and negative effects on people. The design of rooms and the location of furniture have been shown to affect interpersonal interaction—for instance, by creating *sociopetal* or *sociofugal* space. Buildings also influence behavior, as was dramatically illustrated by the Pruitt-Igoe housing project. The design of neighborhoods can encourage or discourage social interaction.

4. In cities, environmental stressors are particularly intense. Two negative types of

OTHERS

behavior associated with city life are social indifference, as illustrated by *bystander apathy*, and crime. However, cities also seem to foster freedom, variety, and excitement.

5. Three factors influence our perception of the environment: objective reality, our own personal characteristics, and the quality of the situation. An illustration of the subjectivity of environmental perception is the highly personal and individual quality of *cognitive maps*, people's mental pictures of an environment. *Selective attention*—perceiving on the basis of personal relevance and cognitive consistency—is one psychological process that distorts perception. Another is *habituation*, whereby we become less responsive to a stimulus after repeated exposure to it.

6. By studying an environment objectively, we can perceive it more clearly and see its effects on our behavior. If these effects are negative, we can change them by changing the environment.

PROJECT

In Chapter 7, when discussing study habits, we mentioned the need for environmental planning—arranging the setting in which you work. Here we suggest that, using the sample environmental survey in this chapter as a model, you conduct a formal analysis of your study environment. You may then want to rearrange that environment if, according to the results of your survey, it could be made more conducive to learning. For the purposes of this discussion, we will assume that you do most of your studying in a private environment such as a bedroom, dormitory room, living room, or den. If this is not the case—if you use the library or a lounge, for example—try to analyze it according to the same general outline.

Begin your analysis by marking off three columns on a sheet of paper and heading them with the phrases used in the sample environmental survey on pp. 426–427. In the first column, under "Physical Feature," be sure to include the following information:

1. What you can see from where you sit while studying
   a. Things outside the room (seen through windows and doorways)
   b. Inanimate objects inside the room:
      1. the desk or table at which you study
      2. articles on the desk or table
      3. articles on the wall
      4. other furniture (bed, chairs, TV, and the like)
      5. other inanimate objects (for example, food)
   c. Animate objects inside the room:
      1. plants
      2. pets (goldfish, bird, cat)
      3. other people
   d. Lighting sources and their intensity

2. What you can hear while you study
   a. Sounds from outside the room
      1. traffic sounds
      2. human activity in the adjacent rooms or outside

b. Sounds from inside the room
  1. people talking
  2. television, radio, record player
  3. other noise

3. Other sensory messages

  a. Temperature of room
  b. Air (drafts, stuffiness)
  c. Odors (cigarette smoke or cooking smells, for example)
  d. Chair you sit on (comfort/discomfort)
  e. Other sensory messages

Now turn to the second column of your sheet, focusing especially on how the physical features you have listed relate to your *studying*. For example, the psychological message of a picture, as it relates to studying, may be, "Look at me—I'll distract you." A stereo playing jazz may tell you, "Enjoy yourself, don't work so hard." Your big, soft easy chair may be saying, "Relax, make yourself comfortable, you are getting very sleepy. . . ." Other features—a blank wall, relative quiet, a straight-backed chair—may tell you, "Get busy and work, nothing else to do here."

In the third column, indicate the behavioral or emotional consequences of these environmental features as they relate to studying. If your easy chair tells you to relax, note whether you do and what effect this has on your studying. If your calendar tells you that time is important, does that help you to concentrate, or does it just make you anxious?

After you have completed your survey, go through it and make a list of the aspects of your environment that tend to interfere with studying. At this point you may see the need to change your study environment. Some interferences can be dealt with simply by removal. If your girlfriend's picture makes you daydream, move it out of sight. If the light is poor, you may have to buy a new lamp. In other words, do whatever you can to improve your surroundings. By rearranging them to the best advantage, you can create an environment that will go a long way toward helping you study more efficiently.

HUMAN ISSUE: WORK

Why work? Most people would answer that they work for a *living*—to put food on the table. But clearly money-making is not the only dimension of a job. After all, most of us spend more hours on the job than we do in any other activity of our lives, and that investment affects not only our bank balance, but our attitudes, our self-esteem and our psychological well-being. Perhaps even more than the family, work today is the central anchor of a person's identity.

CHANGING VIEWS OF WORK

It was not always so. Prior to the Renaissance, work was essentially independent of the idea of personal worth. If you worked, that meant you had the misfortune not to be rich. It certainly did not make you a better person. If anything, it was damaging to your moral worth, for it diverted your attention from spiritual matters. Then, with the rise of the merchant class in the Renaissance and, above all, with the Protestant Reformation, came the idea that work was morally improving. To work, said Martin Luther, was to serve God. And the more success you had in work (that·is, the richer you became), the more worthy you were, for your prosperity showed that you were favored by God.

This so-called "Protestant ethic" arrived in America with the Puritans and has been an important part of our culture ever since. It involves three major ideas. First, working to earn a living is a moral obligation; it is our *responsibility* to work. Second, not to work—worse yet, to remain idle while accepting support from others—is a sign of moral deficiency. (Hence, the public's attitude toward welfare recipients, of which there are now about 7 million in the United States.) Third, a person's worth depends on how much he or she contributes by working. The more important your job, the more you are valued.

After centuries of dominance, the Protestant ethic seems now to be slipping somewhat. According to Daniel Yankelovich, Americans are beginning to "look up from the grindstone" (1974, p. 47). In surveys conducted by Yankelovich (1974, 1981), people were asked what they thought of the saying "Hard work always pays off." In the mid-sixties, 72 percent of college students and 58 percent of adults agreed with the statement. In the mid-seventies, only 40 percent of college students and 43 percent of adults agreed.

The change seems to be one of expectations. People are now less likely to value work just because it allows them to pay the bills. They want their jobs to yield psychological rewards as well—fulfillment, a sense of creativity, a feeling that they are doing something truly worthwhile. This can be seen in workers' demands for interest and variety on the job. It can also be seen in the trend toward switching from high-pressure, high-paying jobs to more "menial," but satisfying work. Most of us have met the carpenter or leather-worker with the law degree. The point is that for many people money and prestige alone no longer justify long hours and high blood pressure.

This does not mean, however, that people would rather stay home than go to work. On the contrary, it appears that most people would go on working even if they didn't have to (Lesem, 1979). A study of million-dollar lottery winners found that those who had quit their jobs after striking it rich often felt aimless and dissatisfied (Kaplan, 1978).

Why? Outside of money, where is the profit in working? To begin with, work gives a pattern to people's lives, creating a day-to-day, week-to-week rhythm. Second, it provides a network of informal social relationships. If you were at home and wanted to have lunch with a friend, you would have to arrange a date, get dressed, drive to the restaurant, and so on—a "big production." At work, all you have to do to lunch with a co-worker is sit down and open your brown bags together. Third, work gives us an identity; it tells us who we are and what our status is. Fourth, work provides a basis for self-esteem. This is partly because it makes us feel that we are doing our duty. (The Protestant ethic, though slipping, is by no means dead.) Also, a job allows us to demonstrate our competence and test our skills. "A job tells the worker, day in and day out, that he or she has something to offer" (Special Task Force to the Secretary of HEW, 1972, p. 14).

WORK AND THE INDIVIDUAL

Though many people do not begin drawing a paycheck until they are in their twenties, the process of career choice begins in early childhood (Roe, 1973; Lambert et al., 1976). As children, we begin forming the attitudes and interests that will affect our choice of a job, and we develop (or don't develop) the achievement-motivation that will determine how ambitiously we pursue our careers. It is also in childhood that we learn which jobs are really open to us. After all, the choice of a career is not an utterly free decision. It is affected not just by individual interests and ambition, but also by such factors as social class, race, and sex (Pavalko, 1971). Upper-middle-class children are steered toward white-collar work; working-class children, toward blue-collar work. These expectations are made clear relatively early. If the bank president's son announces at age five that he wants to be a fireman when he grows up, that's okay. If he is still saying the same thing at age fifteen, his parents are likely to have a serious talk with him. But chances are that he will have gotten the message long before fifteen, since his school and his peer group, both determined by his social class, will have already oriented him toward the white-collar professions. By fifteen, as a matter of fact, job limitations have already been imposed, in the form of educational decisions. Teenagers who have entered their high school's "vocational training" program are probably not headed for white-collar jobs. Significantly, many of the schools that upper-middle-class children attend have no vocational training programs whatsoever. It is simply assumed that all the students are headed for college, and many for graduate school, so as to enter white-collar professions.

WOMEN AND WORK

How about the bank president's daughter? If she wants to be a sales clerk at Woolworth's, will this occasion a parental outcry? Twenty-five years ago, such a question would probably not even have been asked. The bank president's daughter, it was assumed, would grow up to marry a bank president, or something just as good, and stay home with the children. As a general rule, the only women who worked were those who had to. This situation has rapidly changed. Within the past ten years the number of women with full-time jobs has more than doubled, and women now constitute almost half of the country's labor force (U.S. Bureau of Labor Statistics, 1980).

But they do not have the same jobs as the men. The increase in the number of women workers has not been accompanied by a corresponding increase in their access to desirable jobs. Eighty percent of all women workers still hold the three most typical low-status female jobs: secretary, sales clerk, and waitress. Only 6 percent of women workers are managers, and only 17 percent belong to unions. Not surprisingly, women are also paid less than men. A woman with four years of college earns less, on the average, than a man with an eighth-grade education. For every dollar that a man earns, a woman earns approximately 59 cents—the same income gap that existed forty years ago. While the 1964 Civil Rights Act guaranteed women equal opportunity for work and equal pay for equal work, this ideal is still a long way from realization.

Things are changing, however. One reason so many women are confined to low-status jobs is that many of these women were educated during the years when it was generally assumed that women neither needed nor could handle high-status jobs. Hence, they received shorter and poorer educations; they also had lesser expectations and ambitions. Small wonder, then, that few of them entered high-status jobs. Women's job opportunities will improve as women's education improves. And it is improving. Over half of all college students are now women, and every year more and more women enter law school, medical school, and business school. As these women go out and become lawyers, doctors, and business executives, they will serve as role models for the next generation of girls, who will thus feel more free in their choice of profession. At the same time, the success of these women will lessen the prejudice of our society (women included) against women in responsible positions, so that when the next generation comes through, there will be less job discrimination. All this is happening, but it takes time.

CAREER CHANGE

When asked in high school or college to make career decisions, most of us assume that whatever the decision, it will be final. We will become a French teacher or an insurance adjustor or an airplane mechanic, and that will be that, until we retire. But the fact is that most people, in the course of their careers, make six or seven major changes in their work pattern. Some people switch from one career to a wholly unrelated one, like the lawyer-become-carpenter mentioned earlier. More commonly, people will move over into a related profession—for example, the English teacher becoming a magazine editor. Even more commonly, people will shift from one type of job to another within the broad boundaries of a single profession, as in the case of the teacher who becomes the school principal or the assembly-line worker who is promoted to foreman.

The reasons for job change are many. In some cases, one is simply forced to change. Most dancers and athletes, by the time they reach forty, must find a new job whether they like it or not. Likewise, if a company switches over from typewriters to word processors, its typists will either have to learn word-processing or move to another company. In other cases, people find that the job they are doing no longer serves their personal needs and goals. For the young man of thirty, the pressures and long hours of being an obstetrician in private practice may seem quite manageable. But if, at forty, he has a heart attack, or finds that he has no time to spend with his family, or simply wants more fun out of life, he may want to move over into a lower-pay, lower-pressure job in the local clinic.

On the other hand, many people who would love to change their work pattern don't, because somehow they feel "locked in" in their present jobs. The major reason is money. In a survey of people who saw themselves as "locked in," 42 percent felt they could not find another job with the same salary and fringe benefits (Quinn and Staines, 1979). Another reason for toiling on at an unloved job is reluctance to change residence. In the survey just cited, 62 percent of the people said they would not move 100 miles to take a new job. Presumably, the comforts associated with having roots in a community—knowing the neighbors, having friends and relatives nearby, knowing where to get the best pizza—make up for the boredom of the job.

For almost all workers, the major change in work pattern is retirement. For some, retirement offers new freedoms—time to rest, time for interests that were previously squeezed out by work. But for very many people, retirement simply spells loss: loss of income, loss of social contacts, and above all loss of a sense of usefulness and purpose. (Old people are major subscribers to the Protestant ethic.) In 1978, because of such problems, the mandatory retirement age for government workers was pushed up to 70, and many private companies have followed suit.

THE FUTURE OF WORK

Income, hours, and working conditions in the 1970s were the best ever, but worker attitudes apparently were not. As the Protestant ethic loses hold—and with it, the idea that work is valuable *in itself*—people have begun to look critically at their jobs and have found much to dislike: dullness, repetitiousness, bureaucratization, overspecialization. When asked whether they would choose the same kind of work if they could live their lives over again, only 43 percent of white-collar workers and 24 percent of blue-collar workers said yes (Quinn and Staines, 1979). People are now looking for fulfillment, and apparently there are simply not enough jobs that offer this elusive reward. Many jobs are just jobs.

Industry is making some attempts to remedy this discontent, by "rehumanizing" the work place. Assembly lines have been rearranged to make tasks less repetitious. Workers have been given new opportunities for training, so that they can be promoted into more responsible positions. Efforts have also been made to draw workers into the company's decision-making processes. Finally, some companies have experimented with new work schedules, offering options such as part-time work and also "flex-time," where employees map out their own 7-hour schedule within an 8-AM-to-6-PM span. The objective, in general, is to relieve the workers' sense that they are simply "cogs in the machine." At the same time, automation is progressing at a very rapid pace, and it is hard to say whether this will improve work conditions, by freeing workers from dull, humdrum tasks, or increase dissatisfaction by making people feel even more acutely that they are simply serving a dehumanized mechanism.

APPENDIX

GETTING HELP

—

Throughout this book we have assumed that people are capable of solving for themselves most of the problems they encounter in everyday living. There are occasions, though, when help from some outside source seems necessary. Here we want to give you an idea of what some of those occasions might be, and indicate the kinds of resources available to you if and when you do seek help.

WHEN HELP MAY BE NEEDED

In dealing with problems in your day-to-day life, there are at least three types of situations in which you may need some outside help. One is when you can't identify what is troubling you. You may be suffering from a symptom that bothers you a great deal—anxiety, insomnia, or depression, for example—but find yourself unable to figure out what is causing it. A second situation is when you have an idea of what your problem is, but don't know how to solve it. For instance, you know that you're having trouble with your parents because you fight with them almost every time you see them, but you can't find a way to stop this misery. In the third type of situation, you may have identified your problem and you may even have an idea of how to solve it, but you find yourself unable to do so. Let's say that you're working and going to school at the same time, and many nights you're so tired that you can't sleep. You take a sleeping pill, but then have trouble getting started in the morning, so you resort to more pills, different pills. These enable you to get through the day, but you're still "hyped up" at night—and so on. Here you know that you should break this cycle, but you can't seem to do it.

What all this boils down to is that you look for help when you feel helpless. Whatever your problems and however you have tried to analyze them, the important point is that you can't seem to cope with them yourself.

NONPROFESSIONAL HELP

Help is available wherever you can find advice, information, encouragement, or feedback. In this book we have tried to provide you with ways to deal with problems. Other books and magazines that deal with psychology can also offer you guidance in problem solving. But written sources (and this includes our book) are limited because the advice they offer must be general enough to apply to a large number of people. Furthermore, many of the popular psychological self-help manuals are based not on psychological research but on opinion and guesswork. (This does not include our book.) So use caution when you turn to written sources for help. If you are in any doubt, ask your instructor for advice.

Another source of help—one on which many of us depend daily—is friends and family. They may not be experts, but don't underestimate their value. Other people can help you in all three of the situations we described above. When you're trying to identify a problem, talking to someone about it may in itself clarify the issue. Other people can also help you in dealing with a problem that you've identified. It may be that they have had a similar difficulty, though they never discussed it with you until now. If so, their way of handling it may give you useful clues. (And the mere fact that someone close to you has had, and survived, a problem like yours can be immensely reassuring.) If you know what you should do but can't seem to do it, friends or relatives can give you encouragement. Whether you act on the strength of their arguments, or simply out of a desire not to disappoint them, you'll be doing what you know you should do.

In some cases, however, friends and relatives can be a source of confusion and misdirection rather than help. Even the most well-meaning people may not understand your problem or may offer inappropriate advice. So use care in selecting those in whom you confide.

Another source of nonprofessional support is the self-help group. Members of such groups pool their resources and share their experiences with a similar problem. Most of these groups focus on a specific area; Weight Watchers and Alcoholics Anonymous are two examples. If you want to find out whether there is a self-help group in your area that addresses itself to your problem, consult the telephone directory, ask a professional (a psychologist, doctor, or guidance counselor, for example), or check with a community agency such as the United Fund or a mental health clinic.

PROFESSIONAL HELP

If you feel that books, friends and relatives, or self-help groups are not the answer for you, it may be appropriate to seek professional help—psychotherapy. Consulting a professional does not mean that you are a failure or a "crazy." It simply means that you have decided to go to an expert, much as you would go to an accountant for help with taxes or to a lawyer for help in a legal matter.

Psychotherapy may be defined as a series of interactions between a therapist—a trained professional—and a client who is troubled and/or is troubling others. Its aim is to help clients change their feelings or behavior so that they can function more constructively. There are three major psychological approaches to therapy: the psychodynamic, the humanistic-existential, and the behaviorist. We shall summarize each of these, and also deal briefly with group therapy.

The Psychodynamic Approach

This approach is based on the theories of Freud, which we outlined briefly in Chapter 1. The classic method of treatment is the technique developed by Freud himself—psychoanalysis. Here the client and the analyst normally have three or more sessions a week, with the client lying on a couch and the analyst sitting somewhere out of his field of vision. The goal is to have the client overcome the harmful effects of early traumatic events that have weakened his ego, forcing him into self-defeating behavior. The client gains insight by dredging up repressed memories and emotions from his unconscious. The classic method for doing this is free association, in which the client expresses verbally whatever goes through his mind, without suppressing anything. Another way of getting at the unconscious is through the analyst's interpretations of the client's dreams. The traditional analyst takes a nondirective approach; that is, she does not speak often, and when she does, it is usually to help the client interpret his own remarks.

Psychoanalysis is time-consuming (typically, it takes several years) and expensive. There have also been modifications of Freud's theories by later theorists such as Karen Horney and Erik Erikson. For these reasons, among others, today's typical psychodynamic therapy is rather different from rigorous psychoanalysis. In the usual case, therapist and client will sit face to face and meet only once or twice a week. Therapy may last only a year or only a few months. The therapist may also take a more directive approach, asking questions, making judgments, and giving the client advice on his everyday problems.

Psychodynamic therapy is the subject of much debate. It rests on assumptions that cannot be scientifically proved—for example, the existence of the unconscious. However modified, it still consumes a great deal of time and money. Furthermore, it tends to be of most benefit only to certain types of patients, particularly those who are good at talking about their personal problems—a skill that not all of us share. Finally, no one really knows how well psychodynamic therapy works, or even whether it *does* work. Yet many of those who have been through it feel that the insights they have gained are well worth the effort.

The Humanistic-Existential Approach

This approach to therapy is based on the idea that people are not at the mercy of repressed traumas, but can control their own lives. Its goal is to help clients realize who they are and what they want, so they can begin to exploit their full potential. The relationship between therapist and client is flexible, but usually they sit face to face and aim for an intimate, warm atmosphere.

The best-known humanistic therapy is client-centered therapy, developed by Carl Rogers. As the name indicates, the client is the focus of the treatment. She talks about whatever she wants to, and the therapist listens sympathetically. In his nondirective role, he does not interpret. Instead, he tries to mirror and clarify his client's feelings. Because the therapist is accepting, the client learns to accept herself; by gaining insight, she can abandon self-destructive behaviors and reach self-actualization.

Existential therapy was pioneered in the United States by Rollo May. It too relies on people's capacity to control their own lives, but, less optimistic than the humanistic approach, it sees existence as a struggle to establish a value system. Because of the existentialist emphasis on the uniqueness of the individual, therapeutic techniques vary widely, depending on the needs of the individual client (and on the style of the individual therapist). In general, however, therapist-client conversations focus on the client's deciding what her values really are and then improving her life by making new choices based on those values.

Objections to humanistic-existential therapies are similar to the criticisms leveled at the psychodynamic approach. For these therapies, like psychodynamic therapy, are aimed at articulate clients who have time and money to spend. The results of humanistic-existential therapies have not been subject to much objective evaluation, although Rogers has used and encouraged evaluation techniques such as the Q-sort (see the Chapter 3 project, pp. 85–87). Nevertheless, both practitioners and clients claim that these methods enable people to gain the confidence and clarity they need to lead truly meaningful lives.

The Behaviorist Approach

Unlike the insight therapies just discussed, behavioral therapy does not focus on the total personality of the patient, but on specific, measurable behaviors. This approach is based on the theory that maladaptive behavior, like other behavior, is learned and therefore can be unlearned.

Behavior therapists take a forthrightly directive approach, advising, instructing, and encouraging their clients. They use many of the techniques discussed in this book. For example, a therapist may help a client develop a functional analysis and specify a target behavior; then she may instruct him in the procedures necessary to attain the target. The client learns to change his behavior according to the principles of respondent and operant conditioning, using techniques such as shaping, modeling, desensitization, and the like.

Behavior therapy has been criticized as manipulative and superficial because it concentrates on eliminating specific symptoms rather than addressing itself to the patient's life as a whole. But it has the advantage of being less costly in time and, therefore, in money. Furthermore, because it focuses on measurable behaviors, the results of this therapy can be measured with a high degree of precision, and some of those results are extremely encouraging.

Group Therapy

As the name indicates, the distinguishing characteristic of this technique is that rather than seeing the individual client privately, the therapist meets with a number of clients in a group. And it is assumed that the clients will benefit as much (if not more) from their interactions with each other than from their interactions with the therapist leading the group.

A group may consist of a random assortment of members, or it may be limited to certain types—for example, married couples, a family, homosexuals, or alcoholics. Group therapy may be oriented toward a psychodynamic, humanistic, or behaviorist approach. Assertiveness training is one type of behavioral therapy that is often conducted in groups. A humanistic variant of group therapy is the growth group (see Chapter 13), which may take many different forms: some are characterized by no-holds-barred emotional outpourings; others use sensory awareness exercises (staring, touching, and so on) to loosen inhibitions.

Group therapies are generally less expensive than individual therapy. They also have the advantage of treating clients in an interpersonal setting, where they have the benefit of immediate feedback from others. (Clients may also feel an enhanced self-esteem because they can help fellow group members.) However, controlled testing has not yet proved the effectiveness of most group therapy. And there seems to be some danger that the intensity of a group situation—particularly an encounter group—may actually have destructive effects on particularly vulnerable members.

A Cautionary Note

During the sixties and early seventies there was a rapid proliferation of both individual and group approaches to therapy: sensitivity training, est, psychic healing, biorhythm, the Reichian approach, the Rolfian approach, and so on. Some of these methods have now receded from view; others, such as est, have remained popular. As a general rule, you should exercise caution before becoming involved in any of these newer movements. Few of their methods have been adequately tested. While they have their enthusiastic adherents, they also have their (less publicized) failures, even disasters. If you are interested in any of these approaches, check with several professional persons and ask for their advice. Make sure that there is a professional in charge of the treatment and that he or she is licensed, certified, and trained in psychology. Finally, beware of promises of instant results and life-changing consequences. Seldom are such promises fulfilled.

DECIDING ON A PROFESSIONAL

If you do want professional advice or assistance, to whom do you go? The title on the door says merely "Ph. D." or "M.D." Should you expect to lie on a couch for the next five years, or will you just be given a prescription for tranquilizers and sent on your way with a hearty handclasp?

To begin with, there is a wide variety of professionals. A psychiatrist is a medical doctor with residency training in psychiatry (the treatment of mental disorders). Psychiatrists generally use some sort of psychodynamic approach. A psychoanalyst—a psychiatrist with additional training in analysis—will engage in more or less classic psychoanalysis; so will a lay analyst, a person without a medical degree who has studied analytic techniques. (Both the psychoanalyst and the lay analyst have been analyzed themselves.)

In addition, there are psychologists (people with a Ph.D. in psychology); clinical psychologists (psychology Ph.D.'s who have specialized in counseling patients); and psychiatric social workers (people with a master's degree in social work and special training in psychiatry). All of these professionals—and psychiatrists as well—may use any of the counseling approaches described above or combinations of them. In fact, it has been estimated that at least half of all practicing psychotherapists in the United States do not fall neatly into any single category.

When deciding to go to a professional, there are several steps you can take. Begin by asking for recommendations. Talk with your instructor, and perhaps also with someone in your school's counseling service. Other good sources for recommendations are physicians and members of the clergy. Once you have one or two names, try to check out reputations through the professional sources available to you. (For instance, if your priest gives you a name, you might check it out with your instructor.) Next, call the professionals and ask about their training, degree, and experience; a good therapist will not hesitate to give you this information. You might also want to find out what approach they follow and what goals they aim for in treating people. Finally, make your first visit to the professional an exploratory one: learn as much as you can about how he or she does therapy, and how your own problems might be dealt with. Don't make a second appointment unless the arrangement seems right for you.

Most people seeking psychotherapy are too unhappy or too shy or in too much of a hurry to engage in comparison shopping. This is too bad, since therapists, like any other kind of professional, have different methods—and different personalities. If, on the first visit, something tells you that this person's method is not for you or that you simply don't like him, then go elsewhere. This approach to selecting a therapist, while it may take a little time, will save you from wasting a great deal more time (and money) in a therapy that is wrong for you.

GLOSSARY

active listening Carefully listening to what another person is saying, and asking questions or "reflecting" to indicate that you are listening.

adjustment Each person's continuous interaction with his self, with other people, and with his environment.

adjustment model The view that "normal" and "abnormal" behavior are defined by the quality of the individual's adjustment.

affective disorder A form of psychological disorder characterized mainly by extreme and inappropriate emotions—either extreme despair (depression), extreme elation (mania), or an alternation between the two (bipolar affective disorder).

agape The Greek term for the caring type of love; the active concern for the life and growth of that which we love.

aggressiveness Asserting your own rights in ways that violate other people's rights.

alienation In existential theory, a feeling of meaninglessness in life.

analysis The act of studying something by examining its essential features and their relationship to one another.

androgyny A term combining the Greek words for "man" and "woman" and meaning our recognition and expression of both masculine and feminine traits in ourselves.

antecedents Stimuli that precede a response.

anxiety A feeling of fear (realistic or unrealistic) accompanied by a state of increased physiological arousal.

anxiety attack A temporary state of almost unbearable anxiety, accompanied by physiological reactions such as shivers, gasping, and pounding heart.

armchair desensitization Desensitization in which anxiety-provoking stimuli are imagined rather than actually confronted.

assertiveness Standing up for personal rights without violating the rights of others.

association A learned mental connection between two different things.

assumed content In a social perception, the material that is added by the perceiver to enhance and support her fundamental impression.

attitude A cluster of ingrained beliefs and feelings about a certain object and a predisposition to act toward that object in a certain way.

attraction Liking another person.

attribution theory In social psychology, the theory that social interactions are governed by people's interpretations of other people's behavior.

autonomic nervous system That part of the nervous system that controls the muscles and glands that produce the body's involuntary responses, particularly to emotion.

avoidance learning The process whereby a person, after having encountered an unpleasant stimulus, will arrange his responses so as to avoid any further encounter with that stimulus.

baseline The description of a behavior before any efforts are made to change that behavior.

behavioral theory A psychological theory that emphasizes the role of learning—through such mechanisms as modeling, respondent conditioning, and operant conditioning—in the development of human behavior.

behavior therapy A form of therapy that aims at helping the client increase or decrease specific behaviors through such techniques as shaping, modeling, and desensitization.

built environment Settings that have been designed and created largely by human beings.

bystander apathy The unwillingness to help others, especially strangers, who are in trouble.

central trait A personality characteristic that we place at the center of our perception of another person, organizing the rest of the perception around this trait.

circular relationship A relationship between two or more variables in which each variable is both the cause and the effect of the other(s).

client-centered therapy A form of therapy, developed by Rogers, in which the therapist mirrors and clarifies the client's feelings in order to help her accept herself and begin actualizing her potential.

clinical psychology The area of psychology that deals with the treatment of emotional and behavior problems.

cognition Mental processing, including learning, perceiving, thinking, and "knowing."

cognitive behaviorism A branch of behavioral psychology that views behavior as a response primarily to mental events.

cognitive consistency The experience of having our beliefs fit comfortably with one another and with reality.

cognitive dissonance The state of discomfort experienced when two cognitions (beliefs or perceptions) conflict with one another.

cognitive map A mental picture of an environment.

cognitive restructuring Changing one's thoughts by means of self-talk.

communication theory In social psychology, the theory that people's statements to one another are the key to social interaction, since these statements serve to define the relationship for the participants.

companionate love Comfortable feelings of affection for someone whose life is deeply entwined with ours and with whom we have shared experiences over a substantial period of time.

complementarity The degree to which two people's personality needs mesh.

conceptual anchor The child's earliest experience of himself, positive or negative. This is the basis on which the self-concept is developed.

conditioned reinforcer A stimulus to which we have attached positive or negative value through association with a primary reinforcer or a previously established conditioned reinforcer.

conformity The individual's changing of her beliefs or behavior to make them agree with those of a group.

consequence A stimulus that follows a response.

correlation A relationship between two variables whereby they change, by increasing or decreasing, at the same time. (The two variables are called *correlates.*)

coverant A mental sentence or image that a person rehearses in order to help himself engage in or avoid a specific behavior.

covert reinforcement The process whereby a person rewards herself mentally for a desired behavior, by praising herself silently or by imagining future rewards for this behavior.

crowding Stress resulting from high population density.

cue A discriminative stimulus that triggers a certain behavior. (Cues are also called *setting events.*)

defensible space According to Newman, a residential building small enough so that the residents can control it through informal precautions.

delusion A false belief, as when a person who is not the Virgin Mary firmly believes that she is the Virgin Mary. Delusions are often involved in psychosis.

denial A defense mechanism whereby the individual simply denies the existence of an event or feeling that is threatening to his self-concept.

dependent variable In a hypothesis, the variable that you guess is changing as a result of changes in another variable (the independent variable).

description The first step of functional analysis, consisting of a simple, objective, and specific account of the target behavior.

desensitization A method of controlling anxiety by having the person encounter or imagine the anxiety-provoking stimulus while in a state incompatible with anxiety (for example, deep muscle relaxation).

determinism The idea that people's behavior is largely caused by forces over which they have no control.

developmental psychology The study of how human beings change as they grow and develop.

devil effect A negative primacy effect.

direct influence Social influence in which we imitate others or comply with their wishes.

discrimination The process of learning to distinguish among similar stimuli and to respond to each one differently.

discriminative stimulus A stimulus for which, through discrimination, we learn a specific response and that eventually comes to "trigger" that response.

displacement A defense mechanism whereby the individual transfers an emotion from an unacceptable object to a safer one.

distributed practice A method of learning whereby the material is learned a little bit at a time over an extended period.

ecosystem The interacting unit of organisms and their environment.

ego In Freudian theory, the thinking, perceiving, remembering, and decision-making part of the mind. The ego mediates between the demands of the id, the superego, and reality.

emotional loneliness According to Weiss, the lack of an intimate relationship.

environmental planning Arranging external cues so that they will trigger desired behaviors.

environmental psychology The study of the interaction between human behavior and the environment.

eros The Greek term for passionate love.

existential theory A psychological theory that stresses individual freedom and responsibility. According to existential theory, good adjustment means developing and acting on one's own unique set of values.

experimental psychology The laboratory study of general psychological principles via experimentation.

experimentation Making changes in an independent variable (such as study habits) to see whether this causes changes in a dependent variable (such as grades on examinations).

extinction The process whereby a behavior is followed by the removal of the stimulus that is reinforcing it, with the result that the behavior is weakened.

fear hierarchy A graded series of anxiety-provoking cues used in desensitization.

functional analysis The examination of a behavior and the events and situations surrounding it in order to discover cause-and-effect relationships.

generalization The process whereby an organism, conditioned to respond in a certain way to a particular stimulus, will also respond to similar stimuli in the same way.

generalized anxiety disorder A behavior pattern characterized by constant and extreme anxiety, sometimes escalating into panic attacks.

group In sociological terms, a collection of individuals who share a common goal, who act out roles in relation to one another, and who interact according to shared norms.

group norms Group standards as to what is acceptable and unacceptable behavior.

group therapy A form of psychotherapy in which the therapist meets with a number of clients as a group.

habituation Becoming less aware of and less responsive to a stimulus once you have been repeatedly exposed to it.

hallucination A false sensory perception, as when a person hears devils talking to her. Hallucinations are often involved in psychosis.

halo effect A positive primacy effect.

humanistic theory A psychological theory that stresses human potential and the importance of self-actualization—that is, the individual's realization of her potential.

hypothesis A theory stating that one specific factor (the independent variable) is causing another specific factor (the dependent variable).

id In Freudian theory, that part of the mind that consists of inborn sexual and aggressive drives.

identification In Freudian theory, the process whereby the child, emerging from the Oedipus complex, adopts the mannerisms, values, and moral standards of the parent of the same sex.

implicit theory of personality A set of beliefs about which traits go with which in the human personality.

impression management Our habit of adjusting our words and behavior in such a way as to produce a desired impression on the people observing us.

incompatible behavior A behavior that makes another behavior—one that a person is trying to control—difficult or impossible to perform.

independent variable In a hypothesis, the presumed cause of changes in another variable (the dependent variable).

indirect influence Social influence in which we respond to the behavior of another person without direct imitation or compliance.

inferred qualities Qualities that we add to our perception of another person on the basis of wishful thinking and implicit theories of personality.

intellectualization A defense mechanism in which the individual hides unacceptable feelings behind a smokescreen of intellectual analysis and thereby avoids the pain of confronting these feelings directly.

intermittent reinforcement The reinforcement of a behavior only after a number of responses or only at intervals in time.

intimacy A strong attachment, characterized by trust and familiarity, between two people.

in vivo desensitization Desensitization in which the person actually confronts the anxiety-provoking stimuli rather than simply imagining them.

law of effect A law, formulated by Thorndike, stating that responses that lead to satisfying consequences will be strengthened and are therefore likely to be repeated, whereas responses that lead to unsatisfactory consequences will be weakened and are therefore unlikely to be repeated.

learning A relatively permanent psychological change that occurs as a result of experience.

massed practice A method of learning whereby the material is learned in large chunks in one or a few sessions.

medical model A view of psychological disturbance as analogous to physiological disease.

modeling The learning of a new behavior by imitating another person performing that behavior.

motivation The state of arousal that a person experiences when working toward a goal.

natural environment Settings that human beings have modified only slightly or not at all.

negative correlation A correlation between two variables whereby one increases as the other decreases.

negative reinforcement The process whereby a behavior is followed by the removal of an unpleasant stimulus, with the result that the behavior is strengthened.

negative self-punishment The process whereby a person subjects himself to some freely avoidable unpleasant stimulus in order to punish himself for a lapse in self-control.

nonassertiveness Violating your own rights by failing to express your thoughts and needs openly and thereby allowing others to disregard them.

norms (see *group norms*)

observational learning Learning by watching others.

obsessive-compulsive disorder A behavior pattern in which the individual, against her will, either repeatedly thinks a disturbing thought (an obsession) or repeatedly engages in some unnecessary act (a compulsion) or both.

Oedipus complex According to Freud, the stage

that all children go through, between the ages of three and six, when they long to get rid of the parent of the same sex and take sexual possession of the parent of the opposite sex.

operant conditioning The learning process in which actions are strengthened or weakened by their consequences, according to the law of effect.

passionate love Love characterized by intense desire, the wish to fulfill, and an exclusive bond.

perceived locus of control A person's idea of who or what controls his life.

performance measure A means of description whereby the individual's behavior is observed and objectively recorded.

person variables According to interaction theory, internal variables such as abilities, habits of mind, expectations, values, and plans.

personality psychology The study of how human beings differ in their behavior.

persuasion The deliberate exercise of influence through the transmission of information.

phobia (see *phobic disorder*)

phobic disorder A behavior pattern characterized by an intense and overwhelming fear of something that (as the person realizes) poses no major threat.

physical self The body and all the biological activity going on inside the body.

population density The number of people per unit of space in a given area.

positive correlation A correlation between two variables whereby both variables either increase or decrease at the same time.

positive reinforcement The process whereby a behavior is followed by a pleasant consequence, with the result that the behavior is strengthened.

positive self-punishment The process whereby a person deprives herself of a freely available reinforcer in order to punish herself for a lapse in self-control.

Premack principle The principle, formulated by Premack, that a behavior that a person voluntarily performs with high frequency can be used to reinforce a behavior that the person performs with low frequency.

primacy effect The power of a first impression to affect our later perceptions of a person.

primary reinforcer A pleasant or unpleasant stimulus to which we respond instinctively, without learning.

productive personality Erich Fromm's ideal of good adjustment; a personality capable of love and bent on fulfilling its potential.

projection A defense mechanism whereby the individual, experiencing an impulse that is threatening to his self-concept, unknowingly transfers the unwanted impulse to another person and then poses as the innocent victim.

propaganda Persuasion by means of deliberately deceptive information and for self-serving purposes.

Protestant ethic The belief, arising out of the Protestant Reformation, that to work is to serve God and that success in work indicates one's favor in the eyes of God.

proximity In social psychology, one person's geographical closeness to another person and therefore her availability for interaction.

psychoanalysis A form of psychotherapy, developed by Freud, that aims at uncovering unconscious conflicts that are interfering with the individual's adjustment.

psychodynamic theory A psychological theory, derived from Freud, that emphasizes instinctive drives and the power of the unconscious.

psychological reactance Pulling back from something you feel you are being forced into.

psychology The study of the human mind and of human behavior.

psychosocial stages According to Erik Erikson, developmental periods characterized by crises in the individual's relationships with others.

psychotic disorders Psychological disturbances in which the person sees a severely distorted picture of reality. Psychosis often involves false sensory perceptions (hallucinations) and/or false beliefs (delusions).

punishment The process whereby a behavior is followed by an unpleasant consequence, with the result that the behavior is weakened.

reactance (see *psychological reactance*)

reaction formation A defense mechanism in which the individual represses a feeling that is threatening to his self-concept and then claims to have exactly the opposite feeling.

reactive A process that affects a behavior without being intended to do so is said to be reactive. Self-monitoring, for example, often results in improvement in the behavior being monitored.

reciprocity   The process whereby people respond to us as we respond to them.

reference group   A group whose standards a person adopts and against whose standards she evaluates herself.

reinforcer   A pleasant or unpleasant stimulus that strengthens a behavior.

repression   A defense mechanism whereby the individual unknowingly forces out of his conscious mind an unacceptable impulse or memory.

respondent conditioning   The process whereby a neutral stimulus is paired with a pleasant or painful stimulus with the result that the organism learns to respond to the neutral stimulus as it would to the painful or pleasant stimulus.

role   (see *social role*)

role conflict   The situation in which a person's roles impose conflicting demands on her.

role demands   Cues that people give to elicit role-appropriate behaviors from others.

role dissensus   Disagreement between role partners as to what is expected of one or both of them.

role failure   Failure to fulfill role expectations.

role partners   Two or more people enacting social roles in an interaction.

role-playing   Rehearsing a desired behavior with "actors"—people who are helping you—before you try it out in real-life situations. (Role-playing is also called *behavioral rehearsal.*)

role theory   In social psychology, the theory that social interactions are governed by the appropriateness of people's behaviors to their roles.

schizophrenia   A form of psychosis characterized mainly by severely disturbed thought processes.

selective attention   Perceiving, in an environment, what we want or need to perceive and screening out what we don't want or need to perceive.

self   A hypothetical construct referring to the complex set of physical, behavioral, and psychological processes characteristic of the individual.

self-actualization   In humanistic theory, the process of realizing one's own unique potential.

self-as-process   The constant flow of our thoughts, emotions, and behaviors.

self-concept   The individual's own personal view of himself.

self-contract   A self-control technique whereby a person writes out her behavioral goal, her behavioral requirements for achieving it, and the rewards that she will give herself for meeting these requirements within a certain time period.

self-control   The process whereby a person, for the sake of a long-term goal, deliberately avoids engaging in some habitual or immediately gratifying behavior that is freely available to him and instead substitutes a behavior that is less habitual or offers less immediate gratification.

self-disclosure   Revealing private information about yourself to another person.

self-esteem   The degree to which a person likes and respects herself.

self-fulfilling prophecy   A statement or belief that, by means of changing a person's expectations of himself or others, comes true.

self-ideal   A person's image of what she would like to be.

self-monitoring   A means of self-description whereby the individual keeps regular, precise, and objective records of his behavior—for example, how many cigarettes he smokes every day and when and where he smokes them.

self-report   A form of description in which a person says what she feels and thinks.

separation anxiety   The fear and distress shown by a child around the age of one to two years when separated from his parent or caretaker.

setting event   (see *cue*)

shaping   The learning of a specific desired behavior through reinforcement of responses that more and more closely approximate that behavior.

shyness   A reaction of discomfort (tension, self-consciousness, a tendency to look away, stammer, or keep quiet) in the presence of strangers or casual acquaintances.

situational description   The description of a habitual behavior as it occurs in one specific situation.

situational variables   According to interaction theory, external variables that can affect a person's behavior.

social comparison theory The theory, advanced by Festinger, that people often have doubts about whether their opinions are correct and that they try to resolve these doubts by comparing their opinions to some other source of information.

social exchange theory In social psychology, the theory that relationships are determined primarily by their costs and rewards to each of the participants.

social influence The process whereby we think or act in response to the prior action of another human being.

socialization The process by which children learn the beliefs, values, and behaviors that are acceptable to their society and necessary for social interaction.

social loneliness According to Weiss, the lack of a social network.

social perception The individual's view of another person.

social psychology The study of interpersonal behavior.

social role The sum total of the expectations for behavior in a given position in a social structure.

social self The thoughts and behaviors we adopt in response to other people and to the society in general.

sociofugal space Space in which seating arrangements discourage people from interacting.

sociopetal space Space in which seating arrangements encourage people to interact.

SQ3R method A study method involving five steps: survey, questioning, reading, reciting, reviewing.

statistical model The conceptualization of abnormal behavior as any behavior that deviates substantially from the statistical norm.

stereotyping Classifying people on the basis of their membership in a group and automatically assuming that they possess a cluster of traits that we associate with that group.

stimulus-narrowing A self-control technique in which a person, in order to increase or decrease a certain behavior, allows herself to engage in that behavior only in one specific situation.

stranger anxiety The fear and distress shown by a child around the age of eight to twelve months when approached or held by a stranger.

stress A sense of threat accompanied by coping efforts aimed at reducing that threat.

stressor A source of stress.

sublimation A defense mechanism whereby the individual rechannels impulses away from forbidden outlets and toward more creative outlets that are acceptable to the self-concept.

superego In Freudian theory, that part of the mind that consists of the internalized moral standards of the society (the conscience).

system overload According to Milgram, the city-dweller's overexposure to stimuli, especially interpersonal stimuli.

third-variable problem A situation in which two correlates may be mistaken for cause and effect when in fact they are both being caused by another factor.

unconscious In Freudian theory, the level of the mind that contains repressed memories and desires.

unsociability A preference for being alone as opposed to being with others.

variable A thing that can change.

Permissions Acknowledgments continued from page *iv*

BIBLIOGRAPHY

Chapter 1

Bandura, A. *Social Learning Theory.* Morristown, N. J.: General Learning Press, 1971.

Bootzin, R. R., and Acocella, J. R. *Abnormal Psychology: Current Perspectives,* 3rd ed. New York: Random House, 1980.

Carpenter, T. "I'm Writing as Fast as I Can: Two Cheers for Valium," *Village Voice* (January 7, 1980), pp. 1–19.

Colligan, D. "That Helpless Feeling: The Dangers of Stress," *New York Magazine* (July 14, 1975), pp. 28–32.

Conway, F., and Siegelman, J. *Snapping.* Philadelphia: Lippincott, 1978.

Erikson, E. H. *Childhood and Society,* rev. ed. New York: Norton, 1963.

Frankl, V. E. *Man's Search for Meaning.* Boston: Beacon Press, 1962.

Freud, S. *Beyond the Pleasure Principle* (1920), in J. Strachey (ed.), *The Standard Edition of the Complete Psychological Works of Sigmund Freud,* Vol. 20. London: Hogarth Press, 1953.

Fromm, E. *The Art of Loving.* New York: Harper & Row, 1956.

————. *Escape from Freedom.* New York: Holt, Rinehart and Winston, 1941.

————. *Man for Himself.* New York: Rinehart, 1947.

Hartmann, H. *Ego Psychology and the Problem of Adaptation.* New York: International Universities Press, 1958.

Holmes, T. H., and Rahe, R. H. "The Social Readjustment Rating Scale," *Journal of Psychosomatic Research,* 11 (1967), 213–218.

Holmes, T. S., and Holmes, T. H. "Short-Term Intrusions into the Life Style Routine," *Journal of Psychosomatic Research,* 14 (1970), 121–132.

Laing, R. D. *The Politics of Experience.* New York: Pantheon, 1967.

Mahoney, M. J. *Cognition and Behavior Modification.* Cambridge, Mass.: Ballinger, 1974.

Maslow, A. H. *Motivation and Personality.* New York: Harper & Row, 1954.

————. *Motivation and Personality,* 2nd ed. New York: Harper & Row, 1970.

Mead, M. *Culture and Commitment.* New York: Natural History Press, 1970.

Meichenbaum, D. H. (ed.). *Cognitive Behavior*

Modification: An Integrative Approach. New York: Plenum Press, 1977.

Mischel, W. "Toward a Cognitive Social Learning Reconceptualization of Personality," *Psychological Review*, 80 (1973), 252–283.

Rice, B. "Messiah from Korea: Honor Thy Father Moon," *Psychology Today* (January 1976), pp. 36–47.

Rogers, C. R. *Client-Centered Therapy: Its Current Practice, Implications, and Theory.* Boston: Houghton Mifflin, 1951.

Sarason, I., Johnson, J. H., and Siegel, J. M. "Assessing the Impact of Life Changes: Development of the Life Experiences Survey," *Journal of Consulting and Clinical Psychology*, 46 (1978), 932–946.

Singer, M. T. "Coming Out of the Cults," *Psychology Today* (January 1979), pp. 72–82.

Szasz, T. S. "The Psychiatrist as Double Agent," *Transaction*, 4 (1967), 16.

Toffler, A. *Future Shock.* New York: Random House, 1970.

Watson, J. B. "Psychology as the Behaviorist Views It," *Psychological Review*, 20 (1913), 158–177.

Human Issue: Abnormal Psychology

American Psychiatric Association. *Diagnostic and Statistical Manual of Mental Disorders* (DSM-III). Washington, D. C.: American Psychiatric Association, 1980.

Chapter 2

Bandura, A., Grusec, J. E., and Menlove, F. L. "Vicarious Extinction of Avoidance Behavior," *Journal of Personality and Social Psychology*, 5 (1967), 16–23.

Brim, O., Jr. "Personality Development as Role Learning," in I. Iscoe and H. Stevenson (eds.), *Personality Development in Children.* Austin: University of Texas Press, 1960.

Fenigstein, A., Scheier, M. F., and Buss, A. H. "Public and Private Self-Consciousness: Assessment and Theory," *Journal of Consulting and Clinical Psychology*, 43 (1975), 522–527.

Frankel, J. J., and Merbaum, M. "Effects of Therapist Contact and a Self-Control Manual on Nailbiting Reduction," *Behavior Therapy*, 13 (1982), 125–129.

Franklin, B. *The Autobiography of Benjamin Franklin.* New York: Pocket Library, 1954.

Gergen, K. "Multiple Identity," *Psychology Today* (December 1972), pp. 31–66.

————, and Taylor, M. "Social Expectancy and Self-Presentation in a Status Hierarchy," *Journal of Experimental Social Psychology*, 5 (1969), 79–92.

Goffman, E. *The Presentation of Self in Everyday Life.* Garden City, N. Y.: Doubleday Anchor, 1959.

Kuhn, M. H., and McPartland, T. S. "An Empirical Investigation of Self-Attitudes," *American Sociological Review*, 19 (1954), 68–76.

Mischel, W. *Introduction to Personality*, 2nd ed. New York: Holt, Rinehart and Winston, 1976.

Newtson, D., and Czerlinsky, T. "Adjustment of Attitude Communications for Contrasts by Extreme Audiences," *Journal of Personality and Social Psychology*, 30 (1974), 829–837.

Skinner, B. F. *Science and Human Behavior.* New York: Free Press, 1953.

Snyder, M. "The Many Me's of the Self-Monitor," *Psychology Today* (March 1980), pp. 33–92.

————. "The Self-Monitoring of Expressive Behavior," *Journal of Personality and Social Psychology*, 30 (1974), 526–537.

————, and Monson, T. "Persons, Situations and the Control of Social Behavior," *Journal of Personality and Social Psychology*, 32 (1975), 637–644.

Underwood, B. J. "Ten Years of Massed Practice on Distributed Practice," *Psychological Review*, 68 (1961), 229–247.

Chapter 3

Anderson, N. H. "Primacy Effects in Personality Impression Formation Using a Generalized Order Effect Paradigm," *Journal of Personality and Social Psychology*, 2 (1965), 1–9.

Aronson, E., and Mettee, D. R. "Dishonest Behavior as a Function of Differential Levels of

Induced Self-Esteem," *Journal of Personality and Social Psychology,* 9 (1968), 121–127.

Asch, S. E. "Forming Impressions in Personality," *Journal of Abnormal and Social Psychology,* 41 (1946), 258–290.

Butler, J. M., and Haigh, G. V. "Changes in the Relation between Self-Concepts and Ideal Concepts Consequent upon Client-Centered Counseling," in C. R. Rogers and R. F. Dymond (eds.), *Psychotherapy and Personality Change.* Chicago: University of Chicago Press, 1954.

Caplan, F. (ed.). *The First Twelve Months of Life.* New York: Grosset & Dunlap, 1973.

Chodorkoff, B. "Self-Perception, Perceptual Defense, and Adjustment," *Journal of Abnormal and Social Psychology,* 49 (1954), 508–512.

Coleman, J. *The Adolescent Society.* New York: Free Press, 1961.

Cooley, C. H. *Human Nature and the Social Order.* New York: Scribner, 1922.

Coopersmith, S. *The Antecedents of Self-Esteem.* San Francisco: Freeman, 1967.

Deaux, K., White, L., and Farris, E. "Skill versus Luck: Field and Laboratory Studies of Male and Female Preferences," *Journal of Personality and Social Psychology,* 32 (1975), 629–636.

Ephron, N. *Crazy Salad: Some Things About Women.* New York: Bantam Books, 1976.

Epstein, S. "The Self-Concept Revisited," *American Psychologist,* 28 (1973), 405–416.

Erikson, E. H. *Identity: Youth and Crisis.* New York: Norton, 1968.

Festinger, L. *A Theory of Cognitive Dissonance.* Stanford, Calif.: Stanford University Press, 1957.

————, and Carlsmith, J. M. "Cognitive Consequences of Forced Compliance," *Journal of Abnormal and Social Psychology,* 58 (1959), 203–210.

Fitch, G. "Effects of Self-Esteem, Perceived Performance, and Choice on Causal Attribution," *Journal of Personality and Social Psychology,* 16 (1970), 311–315.

Freud, S. *Civilization and Its Discontents.* London: Hogarth Press, 1949 (original edition, 1930).

————. *The Problem of Anxiety.* New York: Norton, 1936.

Fromm, E. *Man for Himself.* New York: Holt, Rinehart and Winston, 1947.

Hilgard, E. R., and Bower, G. H. *Theories of Learning,* 3rd ed. New York: Appleton-Century-Crofts, 1966.

Horowitz, F. D. "The Relationship of Anxiety, Self-Concept and Sociometric Status among 4th, 5th and 6th Grade Children," *Journal of Abnormal and Social Psychology,* 65 (1962), 212–214.

Hraba, J., and Grant, G. "Black Is Beautiful: A Reexamination of Racial Preference and Identification," *Journal of Personality and Social Psychology,* 16 (1970), 398–402.

Jacobs, L., Berscheid, E., and Walster, E. "Self-Esteem and Attraction," *Journal of Personality and Social Psychology,* 17 (1971), 84–91.

Jahoda, G. "A Note on Ashanti Names and Their Relation to Personality," *British Journal of Psychology,* 45 (1954), 192–195.

James, W. *Psychology: The Briefer Course.* New York: Holt, 1910.

Jourard, S. *Healthy Personality.* New York: Macmillan, 1974.

————, and Remy, R. M. "Perceived Parental Attitudes, the Self and Security," *Journal of Consulting Psychology,* 19 (1955), 364–366.

Kardiner, A., and Ovesey, L. *The Mark of Oppression: Explorations in the Personality of the American Negro.* Cleveland: World Publishing, 1951.

Maliver, R. "Anti-Negro Bias among Negro College Students," *Journal of Personality and Social Psychology,* 2 (1965), 770–775.

Maracek, J., and Mettee, D. "Self-Esteem, Level of Certainty and Responsibility for Success," *Journal of Personality and Social Psychology,* 22 (1972), 98–107.

Mead, G. H. *Mind, Self and Society.* Chicago: University of Chicago Press, 1934.

Mettee, D. R. "Rejection of Unexpected Success as a Function of the Negative Consequences of Accepting Success," *Journal of Personality and Social Psychology,* 7 (1971), 332–341.

Moss, H. A., and Kagan, J. "The Stability of Achievement and Recognition-Seeking Behavior from Childhood to Adulthood," *Journal of Abnormal and Social Psychology*, 62 (1961), 543–552.

Moustakas, C. E. *Finding Yourself, Finding Others*. Englewood Cliffs, N. J.: Prentice-Hall, 1974.

Nicholson, J. *Portrait of a Marriage*. New York: Bantam Books, 1974.

Rogers, C. R. *Client-Centered Therapy*. Boston: Houghton Mifflin, 1951.

—————. "A Theory of Therapy, Personality and Interpersonal Relationships, as Developed in the Client-Centered Framework," in S. Koch (ed.), *Psychology: A Study of Science*, Vol. 3. New York: McGraw-Hill, 1959.

Rohrbaugh, J. B. *Women: Psychology's Puzzle*. New York: Basic Books, 1979.

Rosenberg, M., and Simmons, R. *Black and White Self-Esteem: The Urban School Child*. Washington, D. C.: American Sociological Association, 1971.

Rotter, J. B. *Social Learning and Clinical Psychology*. Englewood Cliffs, N. J.: Prentice-Hall, 1954.

Serbin, L. A., and O'Leary, K. D. "How Nursery Schools Teach Girls to Shut Up," *Psychology Today* (December 1975), pp. 57–58, 102–103.

Stephenson, W. *The Study of Behavior*. Chicago: University of Chicago Press, 1953.

Sullivan, H. S. *The Interpersonal Theory of Psychiatry*. New York: Norton, 1953.

Weir, R. H. *Language in the Crib*. The Hague: Morton, 1962.

Human Issue: Sex-Role Development

Bem, S. "The Measurement of Psychological Androgyny," *Journal of Consulting and Clinical Psychology*, 45 (1974), 155–162.

Friedan, B. *The Feminine Mystique*. New York: Dell, 1964.

Gagnon, J. H. *Human Sexualities*. Glenview, Ill.: Scott, Foresman, 1977.

Heilbrun, C. "Reorganizing the Androgynous Human," in Robert T. Francoeur and Anna K. Francoeur (eds.), *The Future of Sexual Relations*. Englewood Cliffs, N. J.: Prentice-Hall, 1974.

Mead, M. *Growing Up in New Guinea*. New York: New American Library, 1930.

Millett, K. *Sexual Politics*. Garden City, N. Y.: Doubleday, 1970.

Money, J., and Ehrhardt, A. *Man and Woman, Boy and Girl*. Baltimore: Johns Hopkins University Press, 1972.

Reinisch, J. M. "Prenatal Exposure of Human Fetuses to Synthetic Progestin and Estrogen: Effects on Personality," *Nature*, 266 (1977), 561–562.

Tunnell, G. "Sex Role and Cognitive Schemata: Person Perception in Feminine and Androgynous Women," *Journal of Personality and Social Psychology*, 40 (1981), 1126–1136.

Wiggins, J. S., and Holzmuller, A. "Psychological Androgyny and Interpersonal Behavior," *Journal of Consulting and Clinical Psychology*, 46 (1978), 40–52.

Chapter 4

Bandura, A. *Social Learning Theory*. Englewood Cliffs, N. J.: Prentice-Hall, 1977.

Beck, A. T. *Cognitive Therapy and the Emotional Disorders*. New York: International Universities Press, 1976.

Beck, P., and Burns, D. "Anxiety and Depression in Law Students," *Journal of Legal Education*, 30 (1979), 270–290.

Burns, D. D. *Feeling Good: The New Mood Therapy*. New York: Morrow, 1980a.

—————. "The Perfectionist's Script for Self-Defeat," *Psychology Today* (November 1980b), pp. 34–52.

Cobb, N., Kahn, A., and Cath, S. H. "How Your Self-Image Controls Your Tennis Game," *Psychology Today* (June 1977), pp. 40–53.

Cooley, E. J., and Spiegler, M. D. "Cognitive versus Emotional Coping Responses as Alternatives to Test Anxiety," *Cognitive Therapy and Research*, 4 (1980), 159–166.

Ellis, A. "Rational Psychotherapy," *Journal of General Psychology*, 59 (1958), 35–49.

——————. "Rational-Emotive Therapy," in R. Corsini (ed.), *Current Psychotherapies*. Itasca, Ill.: Peacock, 1973.

——————, and Harper, R. A. *A New Guide to Rational Living*. North Hollywood, Calif.: Wilshire, 1978.

Goldfried, M. R., and Davison, G. C. *Clinical Behavior Therapy*. New York: Holt, Rinehart and Winston, 1976.

Greenburg, D. *How to Make Yourself Miserable*. New York: Random House, 1966.

Haney, C., and Zimbardo, P. G. "The Socialization into Criminality: On Becoming a Prisoner and a Guard," in J. L. Tapp and F. L. Levine (eds.), *Law, Justice, and the Individual in Society: Psychological and Legal Issues*. New York: Holt, Rinehart and Winston, 1977.

Horney, K. *Neurosis and Human Growth*. New York: Norton, 1950.

Kanter, N. J., and Goldfried, M. R. "Relative Effectiveness of Rational Restructuring and Self-Control Desensitization in the Reduction of Interpersonal Anxiety," *Behavior Therapy*, 10 (1979), 472–490.

Lazarus, A. A. *Behavior Therapy and Beyond*. New York: McGraw-Hill, 1971.

Linehan, M. M., Goldfried, M. R., and Goldfried, A. P. "Assertion Therapy: Skill Training or Cognitive Restructuring?" *Behavior Therapy*, 10 (1979), 372–388.

Mahoney, M. J. *Cognition and Behavior Modification*. Cambridge, Mass.: Ballinger, 1974.

——————, and Avener, M. "Psychology of the Elite Athlete: An Exploratory Study," *Cognitive Therapy and Research*, 1 (1977), 135–141.

Meichenbaum, D. H. *Cognitive-Behavior Modification: An Integrative Approach*. New York: Plenum Press, 1977.

——————. "Self-Instructional Methods," in F. H. Kanfer and A. P. Goldstein (eds.), *Helping People Change*. New York: Pergamon Press, 1975.

——————, and Cameron, R. "The Clinical Potential of Modifying What Patients Say to Themselves," *Psychotherapy: Theory, Research, and Practice*, 11 (1974), 103–117.

——————, Gilmore, J. B., and Fedoravicius, A. "Group Insight Versus Group Desensitization in Treating Speech Anxiety," *Journal of Consulting and Clinical Psychology*, 36 (1971), 410–421.

Meyers, A. W., Cooke, C. J., Cullen, J., and Liles, L. "Psychological Aspects of Athletic Competitors: A Replication across Sports," *Cognitive Therapy and Research*, 3 (1979), 361–366.

Mischel, W. "Toward a Cognitive Social Learning Reconceptualization of Personality," *Psychological Review*, 80 (1973), 252–283.

Moustakas, C. E. *Finding Yourself, Finding Others*. Englewood Cliffs, N. J.: Prentice-Hall, 1974.

O'Leary, K. D., and Wilson, G. T. *Behavior Therapy: Application and Outcome*. Englewood Cliffs, N. J.: Prentice-Hall, 1975.

Perls, F. S. *In and Out of the Garbage Pail*. New York: Bantam Books, 1972.

Reisman, D., with Glazer, N., and Denny, R. *The Lonely Crowd*. New Haven, Conn.: Yale University Press, 1950.

Shrauger, J. S., and Terbovic, M. L. "Self-Evaluation and Assessments of Performance by Self and Others," *Journal of Consulting and Clinical Psychology*, 44 (1976), 564–572.

Thoresen, C. E., and Mahoney, M. J. *Behavioral Self-Control*. New York: Holt, Rinehart and Winston, 1974.

Watson, J. B. *Behaviorism*. Chicago: University of Chicago Press, 1924.

Zimbardo, P., Haney, C., Banks, W., and Jaffe, D. "The Psychology of Imprisonment: Privation, Power and Pathology." Unpublished paper, Stanford University, 1972.

Chapter 5

Aronfreed, J. *Conduct and Conscience*. New York: Academic Press, 1968.

Bandura, A. *Social Learning Theory*. Morristown, N. J.: General Learning Press, 1971.

——————, and Kupers, C. J. "Transmission of Patterns of Self-Reinforcement through Modeling," *Journal of Abnormal and Social Psychology*, 69 (1964), 1–9.

——————, and Mischel, W. "Modification of Self-Improved Delay of Reward through Exposure to Live and Symbolic Models," *Journal of Personality and Social Psychology*, 2 (1965), 698–705.

——————, and Whalen, C. K. "Transmission of Patterns of Self-Reinforcement through Modeling," *Journal of Abnormal and Social Psychology*, 69 (1964), 1–9.

Bettelheim, B. "Individual and Mass Behavior in Extreme Situations," *Journal of Abnormal and Social Psychology*, 38 (1943), 417–452.

Bolles, R. C. *Theory of Motivation*. New York: Harper & Row, 1975.

Bryan, J. H., and Walbek, N. H. "Preaching and Practicing Generosity: Children's Actions and Reactions," *Child Development*, 41 (1970), 329–353.

Dennis, W., and Najarian, P. "Infant Development under Environmental Handicap," *Psychological Monographs*, Vol. 71, No. 7 (1957).

Ferster, C. B., and Skinner, B. F. *Schedules of Reinforcement*. New York: Appleton-Century-Crofts, 1957.

Freud, S. *New Introductory Lectures on Psychoanalysis*. New York: Norton, 1933.

Jenkins, W. O., McFann, H., and Clayton, F. L. "A Methodological Study of Extinction Following a Period of Continuous Reinforcement," *Journal of Comparative Physiological Psychology*, 43 (1950), 155–167.

Kanfer, F. H., and Karoly, P. "Self-control: A Behavioristic Excursion into the Lion's Den," *Behavior Therapy*, 3 (1972), 398–416.

Kaplan, A. *The Conduct of Inquiry: Methodology for Behavioral Science*. Scranton, Pa.: Chandler, 1964.

Langer, E. J., and Rodin, J. "The Effects of Choice and Enhanced Personal Responsibility for the Aged: A Field Experiment in an Institutional Setting," *Journal of Personality and Social Psychology*, 34 (1976), 191–198.

Lefcourt, H. M. "The Function of the Illusion of Control and Freedom," *American Psychologist*, 28 (1973), 417–425.

——————. "Internal versus External Control of Reinforcement: A Review," *Psychological Bulletin*, 65 (1966), 206–220.

MacKay, J. R. "Clinical Observations on Adolescent Problem Drinkers," *Quarterly Journal of Studies in Alcoholism*, 22 (1961), 124–134.

McMahon, A., and Rhudick, P. "Reminiscing, Adaptational Significance in the Aged," *Archives of General Psychiatry*, 10 (1964), 292–298.

Mischel, W. *Personality and Assessment*. New York: Wiley, 1968.

——————. "Processes in the Delay of Gratification," in L. Berkowitz (ed.), *Advances in Experimental Social Psychology*, Vol. 7. New York: Academic Press, 1974.

——————. "Theory and Research on the Antecedents of Self-Imposed Delay of Reward," in B. A. Walker (ed.), *Progress in Experimental Personality Research*, Vol. 3. New York: Academic Press, 1966.

——————, and Liebert, R. M. "Effects of Discrepancies between Observed and Imposed Reward Criteria on Their Acquisition and Transmission," *Journal of Personality and Social Psychology*, 3 (1966), 45–53.

——————, and Mischel, H. N. "A Cognitive Social Learning Approach to Morality and Self-regulation," in T. Lickona (ed.), *Morality: A Handbook of Moral Behavior*. New York: Holt, Rinehart and Winston, 1976.

Mowrer, O. H. "Learning Theory and the Neurotic Paradox," *American Journal of Orthopsychiatry*, 18 (1948), 571–610.

Provence, S., and Lipton, R. *Infants in Institutions*. New York: International Universities Press, 1962.

Robbins, D. "Partial Reinforcement: A Selective Review of the Alleyway Literature since 1960," *Psychological Bulletin*, 76 (1971), 415–431.

Rodin, J., and Langer, E. J. "Long-Term Effects of a Control-Relevant Intervention with the Institutionalized Aged," *Journal of Personality and Social Psychology*, 35 (1977), 897–902.

Rotter, J. B. "Generalized Expectancies for Internal Versus External Control of Reinforcement," *Psychological Monographs*. Vol. 80, No. 609 (1966).

——————, Chance, J. E., and Phares, E. J. (eds.). *Applications of a Social Learning Theory of Personality*. New York: Holt, Rinehart and Winston, 1972.

Sears, R. R., Maccoby, E. E., and Levin, H. *Pat-*

terns of Child Rearing. New York: Harper & Row, 1957.

Seligman, M. E. P. Helplessness—On Depression, Development and Death. San Francisco: Freeman, 1975.

Skinner, B. F. Science and Human Behavior. New York: Macmillan, 1953.

Strickland, B. R. "Locus Control and Health-Related Behavior." Paper presented at 15th Intra-American Congress, Bogotá, Colombia, 1974.

Thoresen, C. P., and Mahoney, M. J. Behavioral Self-Control. New York: Holt, Rinehart and Winston, 1974.

Verplanck, W. S. "The Control of the Content of Conversation: Reinforcement of Statements of Opinion," Journal of Abnormal and Social Psychology, 51 (1955), 668–676.

Watson, J. B., and Rayner, R. "Conditioned Emotional Reactions," Journal of Experimental Psychology, 3 (1920), 1–14.

Weber, M. The Protestant Ethic and the Spirit of Capitalism. New York: Scribner, 1958.

Williams, J. L. Operant Learning: Procedures for Changing Behavior. Monterey, Calif.: Brooks/Cole, 1973.

Wilson, C. "Existential Psychology: A Novelist's Approach," in J. F. T. Bugental (ed.), Challenges of Humanistic Psychology. New York: McGraw-Hill, 1967.

Wood, H., and Duffy, E. "Psychological Factors in Alcoholic Women," American Journal of Psychiatry, 123 (1966), 341–345.

Chapter 6

Abrams, D. B., and Wilson, G. T. "Self-Monitoring and Reactivity in the Modification of Cigarette Smoking," Journal of Consulting and Clinical Psychology, 43, (1979), 577–583.

Bandura, A. Principles of Behavior Modification. New York: Holt, Rinehart and Winston, 1969.

————. "Punishment Revisited," Journal of Consulting Psychology, 26 (1962), 298–301.

————. Social Learning Theory. Morristown, N. J.: General Learning Press, 1971.

Bornstein, P. H., Mungas, D. M., Quevillon, R. P., Kniivila, C. M., Miller, R. K., and Holombo, L. K. "Self-Monitoring Training: Effects on Reactivity and Accuracy of Self-Observation," Behavior Therapy, 9 (1978), 545–552.

Broden, M., Hall, P. V., and Mitts, B. "The Effect of Self-Recording on the Classroom Behavior of Two Eighth-Grade Students," Journal of Applied Behavior Analysis, 4 (1971), 191–199.

Coates, T. J., and Thoresen, C. E. How to Sleep Better. Englewood Cliffs, N. J.: Prentice-Hall, 1977.

D'Zurilla, T. J., and Goldfried, M. R. "Cognitive Processes, Problem-Solving and Effective Behavior," in M. R. Goldfried and M. Merbuam (eds.), Behavior Change through Self-Control. New York: Holt, Rinehart and Winston, 1973.

Ferster, C. B., Nurnberger, J. I., and Levitt, E. B. "The Control of Eating," Journal of Mathematics, 1 (1962), 87–109.

Frederiksen, L. W., and Simon, S. J. "Modifying How People Smoke: Instructional Control and Generalization," Journal of Applied Behavior Analysis, 11 (1978), 431–432.

Goldfried, M. R. "The Use of Relation and Cognitive Relabeling as Coping Skills," in R. B. Stuart (ed.), Behavioral Self-Management. New York: Brunner/Mazel, 1977.

Goldiamond, I. "Self-Control Procedures in Personal Behavior Problems," Psychological Reports, 17 (1965), 851–868.

————. "Self-Reinforcement," Journal of Applied Behavior Analysis, 9 (1976), 509–514.

Homme, L., Csanyi, A. P., Gonzales, M. A., and Rechs, J. R. How to Use Contingency Contracting in the Classroom. Champaign, Ill.: Research Press, 1969.

Johnson, S. M., and White, G. "Self-Observation as an Agent of Behavioral Change," Behavior Therapy, 2 (1971), 488–497.

Kanfer, F. H. "The Many Faces of Self-Control, or Behavior Modification Changes Its Focus," in R. B. Stuart (ed.), Behavioral Self-Management. New York: Brunner/Mazel, 1977.

————. "Self-Management Methods," in F. H. Kanfer and A. P. Goldstein (eds.), Helping People Change: A Textbook of Methods. New York: Pergamon Press, 1975.

Komaki, J., and Dore-Boyce, K. "Self-Recording: Its Effects on Individuals High and Low in Motivation," Behavior Therapy, 9 (1978), 65–72.

Lando, H. A. "Successful Treatment of Smokers with a Broad-Spectrum Behavioral Approach," *Journal of Consulting and Clinical Psychology*, 45 (1977), 361–366.

Mahoney, M. J. "Self-Reward and Self-Monitoring Techniques for Weight Control," *Behavior Therapy*, 6 (1974), 416–418.

—————, and Mahoney, K. "Fight Fat with Behavior Control," *Psychology Today* (May 1976), pp. 39–43, 92–94.

—————, and Thoresen, C. E. *Self-Control: Power to the Person*. Monterey, Calif.: Brooks/Cole, 1974.

McFall, R. M. "The Effects of Self-Monitoring on Normal Smoking Behavior," *Journal of Consulting and Clinical Psychology*, 35 (1970), 135–142.

—————. "Parameters of Self-Monitoring," in R. B. Stuart (ed.), *Behavioral Self-Management*. New York: Brunner/Mazel, 1977.

McKenzie, T. L., and Rushall, B. S. "Effects of Self-Recording on Attendance and Performance in a Competitive Swimming Training Environment," *Journal of Applied Behavior Analysis*, 7 (1974), 199–206.

McReynolds, W. T., and Paulsen, B. K. "Stimulus Control as the Behavioral Basis of Weight Loss Procedures," in G. J. Williams, S. Martin, and J. Foreyt (eds.), *Obesity: Behavioral Approaches to Dietary Management*. New York: Brunner/Mazel, 1976.

Menges, R. J., and Dobroski, B. J. "Behavioral Self-Modification in Instructional Settings: A Review," *Teaching of Psychology*, 4 (1977), 168–173.

Nelson, R. O. "Methodological Issues in Assessment via Self-Monitoring," in J. D. Cone and R. P. Hawkins (eds.), *Behavioral Assessment: New Directions in Clinical Psychology*. New York: Brunner/Mazel, 1977.

Nisbett, R. E. "Hunger, Obesity, and the Ventromedial Hypothalamus," *Psychological Review*, 79 (1972), 433–470.

Premack, D. "Catching Up with Commonsense, or Two Sides of a Generalization: Reinforcement and Punishment," in R. Glaser (ed.), *The Nature of Reinforcement*. New York: Academic Press, 1971.

—————. "Reinforcement Theory," in D. Levin (ed.), *Nebraska Symposium on Motivation*. Lincoln: University of Nebraska Press, 1965.

Romanczyk, R. G. "Self-Monitoring in the Treatment of Obesity: Parameters of Reactivity," *Behavior Therapy*, 5 (1974), 531–540.

Rosenbaum, M. "A Schedule for Assessing Self-Control Behaviors: Preliminary Findings," *Behavior Therapy*, 11 (1980), 109–121.

Schmidt, J. A. *Help Yourself: A Guide to Self-Change*. Champaign, Ill.: Research Press, 1976.

Skinner, B. F. *Walden Two*. New York: Macmillan, 1948.

—————. *Science and Human Behavior*. New York: Macmillan, 1953.

Stuart, R. B., and Davis, B. *Slim Chance in a Fat World*. Champaign, Ill.: Research Press, 1972.

Thoresen, C. E., and Mahoney, M. J. *Behavioral Self-Control*. New York: Holt, Rinehart and Winston, 1974.

Turkewitz, H., O'Leary, K. D., and Ironsmith, M. "Generalization and Maintenance of Appropriate Behavior through Self-Control," *Journal of Consulting and Clinical Psychology*, 43 (1975), 577–583.

Viorst, J. *How Did I Get to Be Forty . . . and Other Atrocities*. New York: Simon and Schuster, 1976.

Winnett, R. A., Neale, M. S., and Grier, H. C. "Effects of Self-Monitoring and Feedback on Residential Electricity Consumption," *Journal of Applied Behavior Analysis*, 12 (1979), 173–184.

Chapter 7

Abrams, J. L., and Allen, G. J. "Comparative Effectiveness of Situational Programming, Financial Payoffs, and Group Pressure in Weight Reduction," *Behavior Therapy*, 5 (1974), 391–400.

Beneke, W. M., and Harris, M. B. "Teaching Self-Control of Study Behavior," *Behavior Research and Therapy*, 10 (1972), 35–41.

Breen, L. J., Endler, N. S., Prociuk, T. J., and Okada, M. "Person × Situation Interaction in

BIBLIOGRAPHY

Personality Prediction: Some Specifics of the Person Factor," *Journal of Consulting and Clinical Psychology*, 46 (1978), 567–568.

Castro, L., and Rachlin, H. "Self-Reward, Self-Monitoring and Self-Punishment as Feedback in Weight Control," *Behavior Therapy*, 11 (1980), 38–48.

Chapman, C. B., and Mitchell, J. H. "The Physiology of Exercise," *Scientific American*, 212 (1965), 88–96.

Clark, F. "Self-Administered Desensitization," *Behavior Research and Therapy*, 11 (1973), 335–338.

Cohen, E. A., Gelfand, D. M., Dodd, D. K., Jensen, J., and Turner, C. "Self-Control Practices Associated with Weight Loss Maintenance in Children and Adolescents," *Behavior Therapy*, 11 (1980), 26–37.

Counts, D. K., Hollandsworth, J. G., and Alcorn, J. D. "Use of Electromyographic Feedback and Cue-Controlled Relaxation in the Treatment of Test Anxiety," *Journal of Consulting and Clinical Psychology*, 46 (1978), 990–996.

deVries, H. A. "Immediate and Long-Term Effects of Exercise upon Resting Muscle Action Potential Level," *Journal of Sports Medicine and Physical Fitness*, 8 (1968), 1–11.

Ellis, A., and Harper, R. A. *A New Guide to Rational Living*. North Hollywood, Calif.: Wilshire, 1976.

Ellis, H. C. "Motor Skills in Learning," in H. C. Ellis (ed.), *Fundamentals of Human Learning and Cognition*. Dubuque, Iowa: Wm. C. Brown, 1972.

Endler, N. S., and Hunt, J. M. V. "Generalizability of Contributions from Sources of Variance in the S-R Inventories of Anxiousness," *Journal of Personality*, 37 (1969), 1–24.

Ferster, C. B., Nurnberger, J. I., and Levitt, E. B. "The Control of Eating," *Journal of Mathematics*, 1 (1962), 87–109.

Folkins, C. H., and Amsterdam, E. A. "Control and Modification of Stress Emotions through Chronic Exercise," in E. A. Amsterdam, J. H. Wilmore, and A. N. DeMaria (eds.), *Exercise and Cardiovascular Health and Disease*. New York: Yorke, 1977.

—————, and Sime, W. E. "Physical Fitness Training and Mental Health," *American Psychologist*, 36 (1981), 373–389.

Fox, L. "Effecting the Use of Efficient Study Habits," *Journal of Mathematics*, 1 (1962), 76–86.

Gaul, D. J., Craighead, W. E., and Mahoney, M. J. "Relationship Between Eating Rates and Obesity," *Journal of Consulting and Clinical Psychology*, 43 (1975), 123–125.

Goldfried, M. R. "The Use of Relaxation and Cognitive Relabeling as Coping Skills," in R. B Stuart (ed.), *Behavioral Self-Management*. New York: Brunner/Mazel, 1977.

—————, Decenteceo, E., and Weinberg, L. "Systematic Rational Restructuring as a Self-Control Technique," *Behavior Therapy*, 5 (1974), 247–254.

—————, and Goldfried, A. P. "Cognitive Change Methods," in F. H. Kanfer and A. P. Goldstein (eds.), *Helping People Change: A Textbook of Methods*. New York: Pergamon Press, 1975.

—————. "Importance of Hierarchy Content in the Self-Control of Anxiety," *Journal of Consulting and Clinical Psychology*, 45 (1977), 124–134.

Goldiamond, I. "Self-Control Procedures in Personal Behavior Problems," *Psychological Reports*, 7 (1965), 851–868.

Gravel, R., Lemieux, G., and Ladouseur, R. "Effectiveness of a Cognitive Behavioral Treatment Package for Cross-Country Ski Racers," *Cognitive Therapy and Research*, 4 (1980), 83–89.

Green, L. "Temporal and Stimulus Factors in Self-Monitoring by Obese Persons," *Behavior Therapy*, 9 (1978), 328–341.

Greiner, J. M., and Karoly, P. "Effects of Self-Control Training on Study Activity and Academic Performance: An Analysis of Self-Monitoring, Self-Reward, and Systematic Planning Components," *Journal of Counseling Psychology*, 23 (1976), 495–502.

Harris, G., and Johnson, S. B. "Comparison of Individualized Covert Modeling, Self-Control Desensitization and Study Skills Training for Alleviation of Test Anxiety," *Journal of Consulting and Clinical Psychology*, 48 (1980), 186–194.

Harris, M. B. "Self-Directed Program for Weight Control: A Pilot Study," *Journal of Abnormal Psychology*, 74 (1969), 263–270.

Hilyer, J., and Mitchell, W. "Effect of Systematic Physical Fitness Training Combined with Counseling on the Self-Concept of College Students," *Journal of Counseling Psychology*, 26 (1979), 427–436.

Homme, L. E. "Control of Coverants, the Operants of the Mind," Perspectives in Psychology, XXIV, *Psychological Record*, 15 (1965), 501–511.

House, J. S. "The Effects of Occupational Stress on Physical Health," in J. O'Toole (ed.), *Work and the Quality of Life*. Cambridge, Mass.: MIT Press, 1974.

Israel, A. C., and Saccone, A. J. "Follow-Up of Effects of Choice of Mediator and Target of Reinforcement on Weight Loss," *Behavior Therapy*, 10 (1979), 260–265.

Jacobson, E. *Anxiety and Tension Control: A Physiological Approach*. Philadelphia: Lippincott, 1964.

Kanter, N. J., and Goldfried, M. R. "Relative Effectiveness of Rational Restructuring and Self-Control Desensitization in the Reduction of Interpersonal Anxiety," *Behavior Therapy*, 10 (1979), 472–490.

Katell, A., Callahan, E. J., Fremouw, W. J., and Zitter, R. E. "The Effects of Behavioral Treatment and Fasting on Eating Behaviors and Weight Loss: A Case Study," *Behavior Therapy*, 10 (1979), 579–587.

Kazdin, A. E., and Wilcozon, L. A. "Systematic Desensitization and Nonspecific Treatment Effects: A Methodological Evaluation," *Psychological Bulletin*, 83 (1976), 729–758.

Kendall, P. C. "Anxiety: States, Traits—Situations?" *Journal of Consulting and Clinical Psychology*, 46 (1978), 280–287.

Kientzle, M. J. "Properties of Learning Curves under Varied Distributions of Practice," *Journal of Experimental Psychology*, 39 (1946), 187–211.

Kingsley, R. G., and Wilson, G. T. "Behavior Therapy for Obesity: A Comparative Investigation of Long-Term Efficacy," *Journal of Consulting and Clinical Psychology*, 45 (1977), 288–298.

Kirkland, K., and Hollandsworth, J. G. "Effective Test Taking: Skills-Acquisition versus Anxiety-Reduction Techniques," *Journal of Consulting and Clinical Psychology*, 48 (1980), 431–439.

Lang, P. J. "The Mechanics of Densensitization and the Laboratory Study of Human Fear," in C. M. Franks (ed.), *Behavior Therapy: Appraisal and Status*. New York: McGraw-Hill, 1969.

Locke, S. "Stress May Damage Cell Immunity," *Science News*, 113 (1978), p. 151.

Loro, A. D., Fisher, E. B., and Levenkron, J. C. "Comparison of Established and Innovative Weight-Reduction Treatment Procedures," *Journal of Applied Behavior Analysis*, 9 (1979), 141–155.

Maher, B. A. *Principles of Psychotherapy: An Experimental Approach*. New York: McGraw-Hill, 1966.

Mahoney, M. J., and Avener, M. "Psychology of the Elite Athlete: An Exploratory Study," *Cognitive Therapy and Research*, 1 (1977), 135–141.

————, and Mahoney, K. "Fight Fat with Behavior Control," *Psychology Today* (May 1976), pp. 39–43, 92–94.

Manno, B., and Marston, A. R. "Weight Reduction as a Function of Negative Covert Reinforcement (Sensitization) Versus Positive Covert Reinforcement," *Behaviour Research and Therapy*, 10 (1972), 201–207.

Martic, M. "Results of Psychological Testing of Coronary Paths in a Longitudinal Study of the Follow-Up Effects of Training," in U. Stocksmeier (ed.), *Psychological Approach to the Rehabilitation of Coronary Patients*. New York: Springer, 1976.

Martinek, T. J., Cheffers, J. T., and Zaichkowsky, L. D. "Physical Activity, Motor Development and Self-Concept: Race and Age Differences," *Perceptual and Motor Skills*, 46 (1978), 147–154.

McGowan, R. W., Jarman, B. O., and Pedersen, D. M. "Effects of a Competitive Endurance Training Program on Self-Concept and Peer Approval," *Journal of Psychology*, 86 (1974), 57–60.

Mead, M. "One Vote for This Age of Anxiety,"

BIBLIOGRAPHY

New York Times Magazine (May 20, 1956), pp. 13, 56, 58.

Meyers, A. W., Stunkard, A. J., Coll, M., and Cooke, C. J. "Stairs, Escalators and Obesity," *Behavior Modification*, 4 (1980), 355–359.

Morgan, W. P. "The Mind of the Marathoner," *Psychology Today* (November 1978), pp. 38–49.

Morris, A. F., and Husman, B. F. "Life Quality Changes Following an Endurance Conditioning Program," *American Corrective Therapy Journal*, 32 (1978), 3–6.

Newman, A., and Brand, E. "Coping Response Training versus In Vivo Desensitization in Fear Reduction," *Cognitive Therapy and Research*, 4 (1980), 397–408.

Paul, G. L. *Insight versus Desensitization in Psychotherapy*. Stanford, Calif.: Stanford University Press, 1966.

Phillips, R. E., Johnson, G. D., and Geyer, A. "Self-Administered Systematic Desensitization," *Behaviour Research and Therapy*, 10 (1972), 93–96.

Richards, C. S., McReynolds, W. T., Holt, S., and Sexton, T. "Effects of Information Feedback and Self-Administered Consequences on Self-Monitoring Study-Behavior," *Journal of Counseling Psychology*, 23 (1976), 316–321.

Robinson, F. P. *Effective Study*, 4th ed. New York: Harper & Row, 1970.

Rosen, G. M., Glasgow, R. E., and Barrera, M. "A Controlled Study to Assess the Clinical Efficacy of Totally Self-Administered Systematic Desensitization," *Journal of Consulting and Clinical Psychology*, 44 (1976), 208–217.

Saccone, A. J., and Israel, A. C. "Effects of Experimenter versus Significant Other-Controlled Reinforcement and Choice of Target Behavior on Weight Loss," *Behavior Therapy*, 9 (1978), 271–278.

Shelton, T. O., and Mahoney, M. J. "The Content and Effect of 'Psyching-Up' Strategies in Weight-Lifters," *Cognitive Therapy and Research*, 2 (1977), 275–284.

Solomon, E. G., and Bumpus, A. K. "The Running Meditation Response: An Adjunct to Psychotherapy," *American Journal of Psychotherapy*, 32 (1978), 583–892.

Spence, K., and Norris, E. "Eyelid Conditioning as a Function of the Intertrial Interval," *Journal of Experimental Psychology*, 40 (1950), 716–720.

Spiegler, M. D., Cooley, E. J., Marshall, G. J., Prince II, H. T., Puckett, S. P., and Skenazy, J. A. "A Self-Control versus a Counterconditioning Paradigm for Systematic Desensitization: An Experimental Comparison," *Journal of Counseling Psychology*, 23 (1976), 83–86.

Stuart R. B., and Davis, B. *Slim Chance in a Fat World*. Champaign, Ill.: Research Press, 1972.

Stunkard, A., and Kaplan, D. "Eating in Public Places: A Review of Reports of the Direct Observation of Eating Behaviors," *International Journal of Obesity*, 1 (1977), 89–101.

Suinn, R. "Behavioral Methods at the Winter Olympic Games," *Behavior Therapy*, 8 (1977), 283–284.

Taylor, J. A. "A Personality Scale of Manifest Anxiety," *Journal of Abnormal and Social Psychology*, 48 (1953), 285–290.

Underwood, B. J., and Schulz, R. W. "Sources of Interferences Associated with Differences in Learning and Retention," *Studies of Distributed Practice*, XX, *Journal of Experimental Psychology*, 61 (1961), 228–235.

Vinokur, A., and Selzer, M. L. "Desirable versus Undesirable Life Events: Their Relation to Stress and Mental Distress," *Journal of Personality and Social Psychology*, 32 (1975), 329–337.

Walker, J. M., Floyd, T. C., Fein, G., Cavness, C., Lualhati, R., and Feinberg, I. "Effects of Exercise on Sleep," *Journal of Applied Physiology*, 44 (1978), 945–951.

Weingarten, G. "Mental Performance during Physical Exertion: The Benefit of Being Physically Fit," *International Journal of Sport Psychology*, 4 (1973), 16–26.

Williams, R. L., and Long, J. D. *Toward a Self-Managed Life Style*, 2nd ed. Boston: Houghton Mifflin, 1979.

Wooley, S. C., Wooley, O. W., and Dryenforth, S. R. "Theoretical, Practical, and Social Issues in Behavioral Treatments of Obesity," *Journal of Applied Behavior Analysis*, 12 (1979), 3–26.

Wolpe, J. *The Practice of Behavior Therapy*, 2nd ed. New York: Pergamon Press, 1973.

Zitter, R. E., and Fremouw, W. J. "Individual versus Partner Consequation for Weight Loss," *Behavior Therapy*, 9 (1978), 808–813.

Chapter 8

Allport, G. "The Historical Background of Modern Psychology," in G. Lindzey and E. Aronson (eds.), *Handbook of Social Psychology*, 2nd ed., Vol. 1. Reading, Mass.: Addison-Wesley, 1968.

Aronson, E. "Some Antecedents of Interpersonal Attraction," in W. J. Arnold and D. Levine (eds.), *Nebraska Symposium on Motivation, 1969*. Lincoln: University of Nebraska Press, 1970.

Bateson, G., Jackson, D., Haley, J., and Weakland, J. "Toward a Theory of Schizophrenia," *Behavioral Science*, 1 (1956), 251–264.

Berne, E. *Transactional Analysis in Psychotherapy*. New York: Grove Press, 1961.

————. *Games People Play: The Psychology of Human Relationships*. New York: Grove Press, 1964.

Bettelheim, B. *Children of the Dream*. New York: Macmillan, 1969.

Biddle, B. J., and Thomas, E. J. *Role Theory: Concepts and Research*. New York: Wiley, 1966.

Bowlby, J. *Attachment and Loss. Vol. 1: Attachment*. New York: Basic Books, 1969.

————. "The Nature of the Child's Tie to His Mother," *International Journal of Psycho-Analysis*, 39 (1958), 350–373.

Casler, L. "Maternal Deprivation: A Critical Review of the Literature," *Monographs for the Society for Research in Child Development*, 26 (1961), 1–64.

Clausen, J. (ed.). *Socialization and Society*. Boston: Little, Brown, 1968.

Davis, K. *Human Society*. New York: Macmillan, 1948.

Firestone, L. J., Kaplan, K. J., and Russell, J. C. "Anxiety, Fear and Affiliation with Similar-State versus Dissimilar-State Others: Misery Sometimes Loves Miserable Company," *Journal of Personality and Social Psychology*, 26 (1973), 409–414.

Frank, E., Anderson, C., and Rubinstein, D. "Marital Role Strain and Sexual Satisfaction," *Journal of Consulting and Clinical Psychology*, 47 (1979), 1096–1103.

Fromm, E. *The Art of Loving*. New York: Harper & Row, 1956.

Gewirtz, J. L. "A Distinction between Attachment and Dependency in Terms of Stimulus Control," in J. L. Gewirtz (ed.), *Attachment and Dependency*. New York: Halsted Press, 1972.

Goffman, E. *Relations in Public: Micro Studies of the Public Order*. New York: Basic Books, 1971.

Goldenson, R. M. "Prenatal Development," in L. R. Best and M. K. Jaffe (eds.), *The Encyclopedia of Human Development*. New York: Doubleday, 1970.

Goldfarb, W. "Effects of Psychological Deprivation in Infancy and Subsequent Stimulation," *American Journal of Psychiatry*, 102 (1947), 18–33.

Harlow, H. F. "The Nature of Love," *American Psychologist*, 13 (1958), 673–685.

————. "Love in Infant Monkeys," *Scientific American*, 200 (1959), 67–74.

———— and Harlow, M. H. "The Effect of Rearing Conditions on Behavior," *Bulletin of the Menninger Clinic*, 26 (1962), 213–224.

————, and Harlow, M. H. "Learning to Love," *American Scientist*, 54 (1966), 244–272.

————, Harlow, M. H., and Suomi, S. J. "From Thought to Therapy," *American Scientist*, 59 (1971), 538–549.

Harlow, H. F., and Zimmerman, R. R. "Affectual Response in the Infant Monkey," *Science*, 130 (1959), 421–432.

Heider, F. *The Psychology of Interpersonal Relations*. New York: Wiley, 1958.

Heron, W. "The Pathology of Boredom," *Scientific American*, 196 (1957), 52–56.

Homans, G. C. *Social Behavior: Its Elementary Form*. New York: Harcourt Brace, 1961.

Jackson, D. "Family Interactions, Family Homeostasis, and Some Implications for Conjoint Family Psychotherapy," in J. H. Masserman (ed.), *Individual and Family Dynamics*. New York: Grune & Stratton, 1959.

Jones, E. E., and Harris, V. A. "The Attribution of

Attitudes," *Journal of Experimental Social Psychology,* 3 (1967), 1–24.

Jones, E. E., and Nisbett, R. E. "The Actor and the Observer: Divergent Perceptions of the Causes of Behavior," in E. E. Jones, D. E. Kanouse, H. H. Kelley, R. E. Nisbett, S. Valins, and B. Weiner (eds.), *Attribution: Perceiving the Causes of Behavior.* Morristown, N.J.: General Learning Press, 1972.

——————, Rock, L., Shaver, K. G., Goethals, G. R., and Ward, L. M. "Pattern Performance and Ability Attribution: An Unexpected Primacy Effect," *Journal of Personality and Social Psychology,* 10 (1968), 317–341.

Kelley, H. H. "Attribution Theory in Social Psychology," in D. Levine (ed.), *Nebraska Symposium on Motivation, 1967,* Vol. 15. Lincoln: University of Nebraska Press, 1967.

——————. *Attribution in Social Interaction.* Morristown, N.J.: General Learning Press, 1971.

——————. "The Process of Causal Attribution," *American Psychologist,* 28 (1973), 107–128.

Lederer, W., and Jackson, D. *The Mirages of Marriage.* New York: Norton, 1968.

Mead, G. H. *Mind, Self and Society.* Chicago: University of Chicago Press, 1934.

Miller, A. *Death of a Salesman,* in B. Atkinson (ed.), *New Voices in American Theater.* New York: Modern Library, 1955.

Minuchin, S. *Families and Family Therapy.* Cambridge, Mass.: Harvard University Press, 1974.

Nisbett, R., Legant, P., and Marecek, J. "The Causes of Behavior as Seen by Actor and Observer." Unpublished manuscript, Yale University, 1971. Cited by E. Jones and R. Nisbett in *The Actor and the Observer: Divergent Perceptions of the Causes of Behavior.* Morristown, N.J.: General Learning Press, 1971.

Patterson, G. R., and Cobb, J. A. "Stimulus Control for Classes of Noxious Behaviors," in J. F. Knutson (ed.), *The Control of Aggression: Implications from Basic Research.* Chicago: Aldine, 1971.

Provence, S., and Lipton, R. *Infants in Institutions.* New York: International Universities Press, 1962.

Rabin, A. I. *Growing Up in the Kibbutz.* New York: Springer, 1965.

Rheingold, H. L., and Eckerman, C. O. "Fear of the Stranger: A Critical Examination," in H. W. Reese (ed.), *Advances in Child Development and Behavior.* Vol. 8. New York: Academic Press, 1973.

Rutter, M. "Maternal Deprivation Reconsidered," *Journal of Psychosomatic Research,* 16 (1972), 214–250.

Sarbin, T. R., and Allen, V. L. "Role Theory," in G. Lindzey and E. Aronson (eds.), *The Handbook of Social Psychology,* 2nd ed., Vol. 1. Reading, Mass.: Addison-Wesley, 1968.

Satir, V. *Conjoint Family Therapy,* rev. ed. Palo Alto, Calif.: Science and Behavior Books, 1967.

Scanzoni, L., and Scanzoni, J. *Men, Women and Change.* New York: McGraw-Hill, 1976.

Schachter, S. *The Psychology of Affiliation.* Stanford, Calif.: Stanford University Press, 1959.

Shaw, M. E., and Costanzo, P. R. *Theories in Social Psychology.* New York: McGraw-Hill, 1970.

Spitz, R. A. "Hospitalism: An Inquiry into the Genesis of Psychiatric Conditions in Early Childhood," *Psychoanalytic Study of the Child,* 1 (1945), 53–74.

Sullivan, H. S. *Schizophrenia as a Human Process.* New York: Norton, 1962.

Swensen, C. H. *Introduction to Interpersonal Relations.* Glenview, Ill.: Scott, Foresman, 1973.

Thibaut, J. W., and Kelley, H. H. *The Social Psychology of Groups.* New York: Wiley, 1959.

Zimbardo, P., and Formica, R. "Emotional Comparison and Self-Esteem as Determinants of Affiliation," *Journal of Personality,* 31 (1963), 141–162.

Zubek, J. (ed.). *Sensory Deprivation: Fifteen Years of Research.* New York: Appleton-Century-Crofts, 1969.

Human Issue: Sex

Comfort, A. *The Joy of Sex.* New York: Simon and Schuster, 1972.

Ellis, A. "Healthy and Disturbed Reasons for Having Extramarital Relations," in G. Neubeck (ed.), *Extramarital Relations.* Englewood Cliffs, N. J.: Prentice-Hall, 1969.

Gilmartin, B. "Swinging: Who Gets Involved and How?" in R. W. Libby and R. N. Whitehurst (eds.), *Marriage and Alternatives: Exploring Intimate Relationships.* Glenview, Ill.: Scott, Foresman, 1977.

Hunt, M. *Sexual Behavior in the 1970's.* New York: Dell, 1974.

Kinsey, A. C., Pomeroy, W. B., and Martin, C. E. *Sexual Behavior in the Human Male.* Philadelphia: Saunders, 1948.

Kinsey, A. C., Pomeroy, W. B., Martin, C. E., and Gebhard, P. H. *Sexual Behavior in the Human Female.* Philadelphia: Saunders, 1953.

Knapp, J., and Whitehurst, R. N. "Sexually Open Marriage and Relationships: Issues and Prospects," in R. W. Libby and R. N. Whitehurst (eds.), *Marriage and Alternatives: Exploring Intimate Relationships.* Glenview, Ill.: Scott, Foresman, 1977.

Luckey, E. B., and Nass, G. D. "A Comparison of Sexual Attitudes and Behavior in an International Sample," *Journal of Marriage and the Family,* 31 (1969), 364–379.

Reiss, I. *The Social Context of Premarital Sexual Permissiveness.* New York: Holt, Rinehart and Winston, 1967.

————. *The Family System in America.* New York: Holt, Rinehart and Winston, 1971.

Tanner, J. M. "The Secular Trend Towards Earlier Physical Maturation," *Tydshrift voor geneeskunde,* XLIV (1966), 527–535.

Tavris, C. "The New *Redbook* Report on Sexual Behavior in Females," *Redbook* (October 1974), pp. 109–199.

————. "The New *Redbook* Report on Sexual Behavior in Males," *Redbook* (February–March 1978), pp. 111–181.

U. S. Department of Health, Education and Welfare. *Age of Menarche, United States.* Series 11, No. 133. Washington, D. C.: Government Printing Office, 1979.

Wolfe. L. "The Sexual Profile of That Cosmopolitan Girl," *Cosmopolitan* (September 1980), pp. 254–265.

Chapter 9

Aronson, E. "Some Antecedents of Interpersonal Attraction," in W. J. Arnold and D. Levine (eds.), *Nebraska Symposium on Motivation, 1969.* Lincoln: University of Nebraska Press, 1970.

————, and Linder, D. "Gain and Loss of Esteem as Determinants of Interpersonal Attractiveness," *Journal of Experimental Social Psychology,* 1 (1965), 156–171.

————, Willerman, B., and Floyd, J. "The Effect of Pratfall on Increasing Interpersonal Attractiveness," *Psychonomic Science,* 4 (1966), 227–228.

Asch, S. "Forming Impressions of Personality," *Journal of Abnormal and Social Psychology,* 41 (1946), 258–290.

————. *Social Psychology.* Englewood Cliffs, N. J.: Prentice-Hall, 1952.

Bell, A. P., and Weinberg, M. S. *Homosexualities: A Study of Diversity Among Men and Women.* New York: Simon and Schuster, 1978.

Bennett, R., and Eckman, J. "Attitudes toward Aging: A Critical Examination of Recent Literature and Implications for Future Research," in C. Eisendorfer and M. P. Lawton (eds.), *The Psychology of Adult Development and Aging.* Washington, D. C.: American Psychological Association, 1973.

Berscheid, E., and Walster, E. *Interpersonal Attraction.* Reading, Mass.: Addison-Wesley, 1969.

Bickman, L. "The Effect of Social Status on the Honesty of Others," *Journal of Social Psychology,* 85 (1971), 87–92.

Brigham, J. C. "Ethnic Stereotypes," *Psychological Bulletin,* 76 (1971), 15–38.

Broverman, I. K., Broverman, F. E., Clarkson, P. S., Rosenkrantz, P. S., and Vogel, S. R. "Sex-Role Stereotypes and Clinical Judgments of Mental Health," *Journal of Consulting and Clinical Psychology,* 34 (1970), 1–7.

Bruner, J. S., Shapiro, D., and Tagiuri, R. "The Meaning of Traits in Isolation and in Combination," in R. Tagiuri and L. Petrulla (eds.), *Person, Perception and Interpersonal Behavior.* Stanford, Calif.: Stanford University Press, 1958.

Buchanan, B. A., and Bruning, J. L. "Connotative Meaning of First Names and Nicknames on Three Dimensions," *Journal of Social Psychology,* 85 (1971), 143–144.

BIBLIOGRAPHY

Byrne, D. *The Attraction Paradigm.* New York: Academic Press, 1971.

——————, and Wong, T. S. "Racial Prejudice, Interpersonal Attraction, and Assumed Dissimilarity of Attitudes," *Journal of Abnormal and Social Psychology,* 65 (1962), 246–253.

Catton, W. R., Jr., and Smirich, R. J. "A Comparison of Mathematical Models for the Effect of Residential Propinquity on Mate Selection," *American Sociological Review,* 29 (1964), 522–529.

Chomsky, N. *Language and Mind,* enl. ed. New York: Harcourt Brace Jovanovich, 1972.

Clark, K. B., and Clark, M. P. "Racial Identification and Preference in Negro Children," in T. M. Newcomb and E. L. Hartley (eds.), *Readings in Social Psychology.* New York: Holt, 1947.

Dion, K. "Physical Attractiveness and Evaluations of Children's Transgressions," *Journal of Personality and Social Psychology,* 44 (1972), 207–213.

——————. "Physical Attractiveness, Sex Roles and Heterosexual Attractiveness," in M. Cook (ed.), *The Basis of Human Sexual Attraction.* London: Academic Press, 1981.

——————, and Berscheid, E. "Physical Attractiveness and Social Perception of Peers in Preschool Children." Mimeographed research report, University of Minnesota, 1972.

——————, Berscheid, E., and Walster, E. "What Is Beautiful Is Good," *Journal of Personality and Social Psychology,* 24 (1972), 285–290.

Eagelson, O. W. "Students' Reaction to Given Names," *Journal of Social Psychology,* 23 (1946), 187–195.

Epstein, R., and Komorita, S. "Childhood Prejudice as a Function of Parental Ethnocentrism, Punitiveness, and Outgroup Characteristics," *Journal of Personality and Social Psychology,* 3 (1966), 259–264.

Erikson, E. H. *Childhood and Society,* 2nd rev. ed. New York: Norton, 1963.

Feldman, J. M. "Stimulus Characteristics and Subject Prejudice as Determinants of Stereotype Attribution," *Journal of Personality and Social Psychology,* 21 (1972), 333–340.

Feldman-Summers, S., and Kiesler, S. B. "Those Who Are Number Two Try Harder: The Effect of Sex on Attributions of Causality," *Journal of Personality and Social Psychology,* 30 (1974), 846–855.

Festinger, L., Schachter, S., and Back, K. *Social Pressures in Informal Groups: A Study of Human Factors in Housing.* New York: Harper & Row, 1950.

Gagnon, J. H. *Human Sexualities.* Glenview, Ill.: Scott, Foresman, 1977.

——————, and Simon, W. E. *Sexual Conduct: The Social Sources of Human Sexuality.* Chicago: Aldine, 1973.

Garwood, S. G. "First Name Stereotypes as a Factor in Self-Concept and School Achievement," *Journal of Educational Psychology,* 68 (1976), 482–487.

Goldberg, P. A. "Are Women Prejudiced Against Women?" *Transaction* (April 1968), pp. 28–30.

Gollin, E. "Forming Impressions of Personality," *Journal of Personality,* 23 (1954), 65–76.

Harari, H., and McDavid, J. W. "Name Stereotypes and Teacher Expectations," *Journal of Educational Psychology,* 65 (1973), 222–225.

Hendrick, C. "Attitude Change and Behavior Change." Unpublished manuscript, Kent State University, 1972.

Hoffman, M. L. "Development of Moral Thought, Feeling, and Behavior," *American Psychologist,* 5 (1979), 45–57.

——————. "Personality and Social Development," in M. R. Rosenzweig and L. W. Porter (eds.), *Annual Review of Psychology,* Vol. 28. Palo Alto, Calif.: Annual Reviews, 1977.

Jennings, M., and Niemi, R. "The Transmission of Political Values from Parent to Child," *American Political Science Review,* 62 (1968), 169–184.

Kelley, H. H. "The Processes of Causal Attribution," *American Psychologist,* 28 (1973), 107–128.

Kephart, W. M. *The Family, Society, and the Individual,* 3rd ed. Boston: Houghton Mifflin, 1972.

Lawson, E. D. "Semantic Differential Analysis of Men's First Names," *Journal of Psychology,* 78 (1971), 229–240.

Lippmann, W. *Public Opinion.* New York: Macmillan, 1922.

Lott, A., Aponte, J., Lott, B., and McGinley, W. "The Effect of Delayed Reward on the Development of Positive Attitudes toward Persons," *Journal of Experimental Social Psychology*, 5 (1969), 101–113.

McArthur, L. Z., and Friedman, S. A. "Illusory Correlation in Impression Formation: Variations in the Shared Distinctiveness Effect as a Function of the Distinctive Person's Age, Race, and Sex," *Journal of Personality and Social Psychology*, 39 (1980), 615–624.

McDavid, J. W., and Harari, H. "Stereotyping of Names in Popularity of Grade School Children," *Child Development*, 37 (1966), 453–459.

McNeill, D. *The Acquisition of Language*. New York: Harper & Row, 1970.

Mead, G. H. *Mind, Self and Society*. Chicago: University of Chicago Press, 1934.

Meyer, J. P., and Pepper, S. "Need Compatibility and Marital Adjustment in Young Married Couples," *Journal of Personality and Social Psychology*, 35 (1977), 331–342.

Moss, M. K., and Andrasik, F. "Belief Similarity and Interracial Attraction," *Journal of Personality*, 41 (1973), 192–205.

Muhr, M., and Bogard, K. "Sex, Self-Perception and the Perception of Others." Paper presented to the Eastern Psychological Association, Boston, 1972.

Murstein, B. "Physical Attractiveness and Marital Choice," *Journal of Personality and Social Psychology*, 22 (1972), 8–12.

Newcomb, T. M. *The Acquaintance Process*. New York: Holt, Rinehart and Winston, 1961.

Piaget, J. *Play, Dreams and Imitation in Childhood*. New York: Norton, 1951.

————. *The Origins of Intelligence in Children*. New York: International Universities Press, 1952.

————. *Six Psychological Studies*. New York: Random House, 1967.

Rokeach, M. *Beliefs, Attitudes and Values*. San Francisco: Jossey-Bass, 1968.

Rosch, E. "Principles of Categorization," in E. Rosch and B. B. Lloyd (eds.), *Cognition and Categorization*. Potomac, Md.: Erlbaum, 1978.

Rubin, K. H., and Schneider, F. W. "The Relationship between Moral Judgment, Egocentrism, and Altruistic Behavior," *Child Development*, 44 (1973), 661–665.

Saghir, M. T., and Robins, E. "Homosexuality: I. Sexual Behavior of the Female Homosexual," *Archives of General Psychiatry*, 20 (1969), 192–201.

Schneider, D. J. "Implicit Personality Theory: A Review," *Psychological Bulletin*, 79 (1973), 294–309.

Seyfried, B. A., and Hendrick, C. "When Do Opposites Attract? When They Are Opposite in Sex and Sex-Role Attitudes," *Journal of Personality and Social Psychology*, 25 (1973), 15–20.

Sheposh, J. P., Deming, M., and Young, L. E. "The Radiating Effects of Status and Attractiveness of a Male upon Evaluating His Female Partner." Paper read at the annual meeting of the Western Psychological Association, Seattle, 1977.

Sigall, H., and Landy, D. "Radiating Beauty: The Effects of Having a Physically Attractive Partner on Person Perception," *Journal of Personality and Social Psychology*, 28 (1973), 218–224.

Thompson, S. K. "Gender Labels and Early Sex-Role Development," *Child Development*, 46 (1975), 339–347.

Trotter, R. J. "Language evolving," *Science News*, 109 (1975), 378–383.

White, G. L. "Physical Attractiveness and Courtship Progress," *Journal of Personality and Social Psychology*, 39 (1980), 660–668.

Human Issue: Midlife and Aging

Barnett, R. C., and Baruch, G. K. *The Road Taken*. New York: McGraw-Hill, 1981.

Braceland, F. J. "Senescence—The Inside Story," *Psychiatric Annals*, 2 (1972), 10.

Erikson, E. *Childhood and Society*, rev. ed. New York: Norton, 1964.

Fried, B. *The Middle-Age Crisis*. New York: Harper & Row, 1967.

Levinson, D. J., Darrow, C. N., Klein, E. B., Levinson, M. H., and McKee, B. *The Seasons of a Man's Life*. New York: Knopf, 1978.

Masters, W. H., and Johnson, V. E. *Human Sexual Inadequacy*. Boston: Little, Brown, 1970.

Neugarten, B. C. *Middle Age and Aging*. Chicago: University of Chicago Press, 1968.

Sheehy, G. *Passages.* New York: Bantam Books, 1977.

Tavris, C. "The New *Redbook* Report on Sexual Behavior in Females," *Redbook* (October 1974), pp. 109–199.

————. "The New *Redbook* Report on Sexual Behavior in Males," *Redbook* (February-March 1978), pp. 111–181.

————, and Sadd, S. *The Redbook Report on Female Sexuality,* 2nd ed. New York: Dell, 1977.

Terkel, S. *Division Street: America.* New York: Pantheon, 1967.

Trippett, F. "Looking Askance at Ageism," *Time* (March 24, 1980), p. 88.

U. S. Bureau of the Census. *Statistical Abstract of the United States, 1979.* Washington, D. C.: Government Printing Office, 1979.

Chapter 10

Bach, G. R., and Wyden, P. *The Intimate Enemy: How to Fight Fair in Love and Marriage.* New York: Avon Books, 1969.

Bower, G. "On Injecting Life into Deadly Prose: Studies in Explanation-Seeking." Paper presented at Western Psychological Association Convention, Seattle, 1977.

Cohen, C. E. "Person Categories and Social Perception: Testing Some Boundaries of the Processing Effects of Prior Knowledge," *Journal of Personality and Social Psychology,* 40 (1981), 441–452.

Frank, E., and Kupfer, D. J. "In Every Marriage There Are Two Marriages," *Journal of Sex and Marital Therapy,* 2 (1976), 137–143.

Hastie, R. (ed.). *Person Memory: Cognitive Basis of Social Perception.* Hillsdale, N. J.: Erlbaum, 1980.

Heller, J. *Something Happened.* New York: Knopf, 1974.

Jones, E. E., and Davis, K. E. "From Acts to Dispositions: The Attribution Process in Person Perception," in L. Berkowitz (ed.), *Advances in Experimental Social Psychology,* Vol. 2. New York: Academic Press, 1965.

Knudson, R. M., Sommers, A. A., and Golding, S. L. "Interpersonal Perception and Mode of Resolution in Marital Conflict," *Journal of*

Personality and Social Psychology, 38 (1980), 751–763.

Luckey, E. G. "Implications for Marital Counseling of Self-Perceptions and Spouse Perceptions," *Journal of Counseling Psychology,* 7 (1960), 3–9.

Nisbett, R. E., and Ross, L. *Human Inference: Strategies and Shortcomings in Social Judgment.* Englewood Cliffs, N.J.: Prentice-Hall, 1980.

Rausch, H. L., Barry, W. A., Hertel, R. K., and Swain, M. A. *Communication, Conflict, and Marriage.* San Francisco: Jossey-Bass, 1974.

Rosenhan, D. L. "On Being Sane in Insane Places," *Science,* 179 (1973), 250–258.

Ross, L. "The Intuitive Psychologist and His Shortcomings: Distortions in the Attribution Process," in L. Berkowitz (ed.), *Advances in Experimental Social Psychology,* Vol. 10. New York: Academic Press, 1977.

Schneider, D. J., Hastorf, A. G., and Ellsworth, P. C. *Person Perception,* 2nd ed. Reading, Mass.: Addison-Wesley, 1979.

Swensen, C. H. *Introduction to Interpersonal Relations.* Glenview, Ill.: Scott, Foresman, 1973.

Tunnell, G. "Sex Role and Cognitive Schemata: Person Perception in Feminine and Androgynous Women," *Journal of Personality and Social Psychology,* 40 (1981), 1126–1136.

Wicklund, R. A., and Brehm, J. W. *Perspectives on Cognitive Dissonance.* Hillsdale, N.J.: Erlbaum, 1976.

Williams, A. M. "The Quantity and Quality of Marital Interaction Related to Marital Satisfaction: A Behavioral Analysis," *Journal of Applied Behavior Analysis,* 12 (1979), 665–678.

Human Issue: Marriage

Belkin, G. S., and Goodman, N. *Marriage, Family and Intimate Relationships.* Chicago: Rand McNally, 1980.

Bernard, J. *The Future of Marriage.* New York: Bantam Books, 1973.

Bradburn, N. M. *Psychotherapy and the Objectivist Ethics.* New York: Nathaniel Branden Institute, 1969.

BIBLIOGRAPHY

Cadwallader, M. "Marriage as a Wretched Institution," *The Atlantic* (November 1966), pp. 62–66.

Chiriboga, D., and Cutler, L. "Stress Responses among Divorced Men and Women," *Journal of Divorce*, 3 (1979), 121–135.

Glick, P. C., and Norton, A. J. *Marrying, Divorcing, and Living Together in the U. S. Today.* Washington, D. C.: Population Reference Bureau, 1977.

——. *Update: Marrying, Divorcing, and Living Together in the U. S. Today.* Washington, D. C.: Population Reference Bureau, 1979.

Hacker, A. Cited in "The American Family: Future Uncertain," *Time* (December 28, 1970), pp. 34–40.

Kephart, W. M. *Family, Society, and the Individual*, 3rd ed. Boston: Houghton Mifflin, 1972.

Knupfer, G., Clark, W., and Room, R. "The Mental Health of the Unmarried," *American Journal of Psychiatry*, 122 (1966), 844.

Mead, M. "Marriage in Two Steps," *Redbook* (July 1966), pp. 48–49.

O'Neill, W. *The American Sexual Dilemma.* New York: Holt, Rinehart and Winston, 1972.

Pietropinto, A., and Simenauer, J. *Husbands and Wives: A Nationwide Survey of Marriage.* New York: Times Books, 1979.

U. S. Bureau of the Census. *Statistical Abstract of the United States, 1980.* Washington, D. C.: Government Printing Office, 1980.

Yllo, K. "Nonmarital Cohabitation: Beyond the College Campus," *Alternative Lifestyles*, 1 (1978), 37–55.

Chapter 11

Adelson, J. "What Generation Gap?" *New York Times Magazine* (January 18, 1970), pp. 1–98.

Adorno, T. W., Frankel-Brunswik, E., Levinson, D. J., and Sanford, R. H. *The Authoritarian Personality.* New York: Harper & Row, 1950.

Aronson, E. *The Social Animal.* San Francisco: Freeman, 1972.

——, Turner, J., and Carlsmith, M. "Communicator Credibility and Communicator Discrepancy as Determinants of Opinion Change," *Journal of Abnormal and Social Psychology*, 67 (1963), 31–36.

Asch, S. E. *Social Psychology.* New York: Prentice-Hall, 1952.

——. "Studies of Independence and Conformity: I. A Minority of One Against a Unanimous Majority," *Psychological Monographs*, Vol. 70, No. 9, Whole #416 (1956).

Ashmore, R. D. "Prejudice: Causes and Cures," in B. E. Collins (ed.), *Social Psychology.* Reading, Mass.: Addison-Wesley, 1970.

Bandura, A. *Social Learning Theory.* Englewood Cliffs, N.J.: Prentice-Hall, 1977.

——, Ross, D., and Ross, S. A. "A Comparative Test of the Status Envy, Social Power, & Secondary Reinforcement Theories of Identificatory Learning," *Journal of Abnormal and Social Psychology*, 67 (1963), 527–534.

——, Ross, D., and Ross, S. A. "Transmission of Aggression through Imitation of Aggressive Models," *Journal of Abnormal and Social Psychology*, 63 (1961), 575–582.

Bauer, R. A. "Self-Confidence and Persuasibility: One More Time," *Journal of Marketing Research*, 7 (1970), 256–258.

Bem, D. J. *Beliefs, Attitudes and Human Affairs.* Monterey, Calif.: Brooks/Cole, 1970.

——. "Self-Perception Theory," in L. Berkowitz (ed.), *Advances in Experimental Social Psychology*, Vol. 6. New York: Academic Press, 1972.

Berscheid, E. "Opinion Change and Communicator-Communicatee Similarity and Dissimilarity," *Journal of Personality and Social Psychology*, 4 (1966), 670–680.

Blanchard, F. A., Weigel, R. H., and Cook, S. W. *The Effect of Relative Competence of Group Members upon Interpersonal Attraction in Cooperating Interracial Groups.* Unpublished manuscript, Institute of Behavioral Science, University of Colorado, 1974.

Blumenthal, S. "Marketing the President," *New York Times Magazine* (September 13, 1981), pp. 42–118.

Brehm, J. W. *Responses to Loss of Freedom: A Theory of Psychological Reactance.* Morristown, N. J.: General Learning Press, 1972.

Brock, T. "Communicator-Recipient Similarity and Decision Change," *Journal of Personality and Social Psychology*, 1 (1965), 650–654.

BIBLIOGRAPHY

Chaiken, S. "Communicator Physical Attractiveness and Persuasion," *Journal of Personality and Social Psychology*, 37 (1979), 1387–1397.

Endler, N. S. "Conformity as a Function of Different Reinforcement Schedules," *Journal of Personality and Social Psychology*, 4 (1966), 175–180.

Epstein, R., and Komorita, S. "Childhood Prejudice as a Function of Parental Ethnocentrism, Punitiveness, and Outgroup Characteristics," *Journal of Personality and Social Psychology*, 3 (1966), 259–264.

Ettinger, R., Marino, C., Endler, N., Geller, S., and Natziuk, T. "Effects of Agreement and Correctness on Relative Competence and Conformity," *Journal of Personality and Social Psychology*, 19 (1971), 204–212.

Federal Communications Commission. "Television Broadcast Financial Data." Public notice, Washington, D. C., 1981.

Festinger, L. "A Theory of Social Comparison Processes," *Human Relations*, 7 (1954), 117–140.

——————, and Carlsmith, J. "Cognitive Consequences of Forced Compliance," *Journal of Abnormal and Social Psychology*, 58 (1959), 203–210.

Gerard, H. B., Connolley, E. S., and Wilhelmy, R. A. "Compliance, Justification, and Cognitive Change," in L. Berkowitz (ed.), *Advances in Experimental Social Psychology*, Vol. 7. New York: Academic Press, 1974.

——————, Wilhelmy, R., and Connolley, E. "Conformity and Group Size," *Journal of Personality and Social Psychology*, 8 (1968), 79–82.

Grusec, J. E. "Power and the Internalization of Self-Denial," *Child Development*, 42 (1971), 93–105.

Hass, R. G., and Linder, D. E. "Counterargument Availability and Effects of Message Structure and Persuasion," *Journal of Personality and Social Psychology*, 23 (1972), 219–233.

Hess, R., and Torney, J. *The Development of Political Attitudes in Children*. Chicago: Aldine, 1967.

Hollander, E. P. *Principles and Methods of Social Psychology*. New York: Oxford University Press, 1976.

Horai, J., Naccari, N., and Fatoullah, E. "The Effects of Expertise and Physical Attractiveness upon Opinion Agreement and Liking," *Sociometry*, 37 (1974), 601–606.

Katz, D. "The Functional Approach to the Study of Attitudes," *Public Opinion Quarterly*, 24 (1960), 163–204.

Kiesler, C. A. "Group Pressure and Conformity," in J. Mills (ed.), *Experimental Social Psychology*. New York: Macmillan, 1969.

King, L. L. . . . *And Other Dirty Stories*. New York: New American Library, 1968.

Krasner, L., and Ullmann, L. P. *Behavior Influence and Personality*. New York: Holt, Rinehart and Winston, 1973.

Leventhal, H., Watts, J. C., and Pagano, F. "Effects of Fear and Instructions on How to Cope with Danger," *Journal of Personality and Social Psychology*, 6 (1967), 313–321.

Liebert, R. M. "Television Violence and Children's Aggression: The Weight of the Evidence," in J. deWitt and W. W. Hartup (eds.), *Determinants and Origins of Aggressive Behavior*. The Hague: Mouton, 1974.

Maccoby, E. "Effects of the Mass Media," in M. Hoffman and L. Hoffman (eds.), *Review of Child Development Research VI*. New York: Russel Sage Foundation, 1964.

——————, and Wilson, W. C. "Identification and Learning from Films," *Journal of Abnormal and Social Psychology*, 55 (1957), 76–87.

Maddux, J. E., and Rogers, R. W. "Effects of Source Expertness, Physical Attractiveness, and Supporting Arguments on Persuasion: A Case of Brains over Beauty," *Journal of Personality and Social Psychology*, 39 (1980), 235–244.

Mann, L., and Janis, I. "A Follow-Up Study on the Long-Term Effects of Emotional Role-Playing," *Journal of Personality and Social Psychology*, 8 (1968), 339–342.

Milgram, S. "Behavioral Study of Obedience," *Journal of Abnormal and Social Psychology*, 67 (1963), 371–378.

——————. "Issues in the Study of Obedience: A Reply to Baumrind," *American Psychologist*, 19 (1964), 848–852.

——————. "Some Conditions of Obedience and Disobedience to Authority," *Human Relations*, 18 (1965), 57–76.

Mills, J., and Aronson, E. "Opinion Change as a

Function of Communicator's Attractiveness and Desire to Influence," *Journal of Personality and Social Psychology*, 1 (1965), 173–177.

Mischel, W., and Grusec, J. E. "Determinants of the Rehearsal and Transmission of Natural and Aversive Behaviors," *Journal of Personality and Social Psychology*, 3 (1966), 197–203.

Moreland, R. L., and Zajonc, R. B. "Is Stimulus Recognition a Necessary Condition for the Occurrence of Exposure Effects?" *Journal of Personality and Social Psychology*, 35 (1977), 191–199.

Moscovici, S. "Social Influence I: Conformity and Social Control," in C. Nemeth (ed.), *Social Psychology: Classic and Contemporary Integrations*. Chicago: Rand McNally, 1974.

Newcomb, T. *Personality and Social Change*. New York: Dryden Press, 1943.

————. "Persistence and Regression of Changed Attitudes: Long-Range Studies," *Journal of Social Issues*, 19 (1963), 3–14.

Newman, E. *Strictly Speaking: Will America Be the Death of English?* New York: Warner Books, 1975.

Norman, R. "When What Is Said Is Important: A Comparison of Expert and Attractive Sources," *Journal of Experimental Social Psychology*, 12 (1976), 294–300.

Roethlisberger, F., and Dickson, W. *Management and the Worker*. Cambridge, Mass.: Harvard University Press, 1939.

Rokeach, M. *Beliefs, Attitudes and Values*. San Francisco: Jossey-Bass, 1968.

Ross, A. O. *Child Behavior Therapy*. New York: Wiley, 1981.

Sherif, M. "A Study of Some Factors in Social Perception," *Archives of Psychology*, No. 187 (1935).

Skolnik, P., and Heslin, R. "Approval Dependence and Reactions to Bad Arguments and Low Credibility Sources," *Journal of Experimental Research in Personality*, 5 (1971), 199–207.

Smith, R. G. "Source Credibility Context Effects," *Speech Monographs*, 40 (1973), 303–309.

Snyder, M., and Rothbart, M. "Communicator Attractiveness and Opinion Change," *Canadian Journal of Behavioural Science*, 3 (1971), 377–387.

Stang, D. J. "Conformity, Ability and Self-Esteem," *Representative Research in Social Psychology*, 3 (1972), 97–103.

Steinberg, C. *TV Facts*. New York: Facts on File, 1980.

Stotland, E., Zander, A., and Natsoulas, T. "The Generalization of Interpersonal Similarity," *Journal of Abnormal and Social Psychology*, 62 (1961), 250–256.

Walster, E., and Festinger, L. "The Effectiveness of Overheard Persuasive Communications," *Journal of Abnormal and Social Psychology*, 65 (1962), 395–402.

Wolf, T. M. "Effects of Live Modeled Sex-Appropriate Play Behavior in a Naturalistic Setting," *Developmental Psychology*, 9 (1973), 120–124.

Zellner, M. "Self-Esteem, Reception and Influenceability," *Journal of Personality and Social Psychology*, 15 (1970), 87–93.

Chapter 12

Azrin, N. H., Naster, B. J., and Jones, R. "Reciprocity Counseling: A Rapid-Learning-Based Procedure for Marital Counseling," *Behaviour Research and Therapy*, 11 (1973), 365–382.

Cavior, N., and Marabotto, C. M. "Monitoring Verbal Behaviors in a Dyadic Interaction," *Journal of Consulting and Clinical Psychology*, 44 (1976), 68–76.

Ginott, H. G. *Between Parent and Child*. New York: Avon Books, 1965.

Gottman, J. *Marital Interaction: Experimental Investigations*. New York: Academic Press, 1979.

————, Markman, H., and Notarius, C. "The Topography of Marital Conflict: A Sequential Analysis of Verbal and Nonverbal Behavior," *Journal of Marriage and the Family*, 39 (1977), 461–477.

Jacobson, N. "Increasing Positive Behavior in Severely Distressed Marital Relationships: The Effects of Problem-Solving Training," *Behavior Therapy*, 10 (1979), 311–326.

BIBLIOGRAPHY

Knudson, R. M., Sommers, A. A., and Golding, S. L. "Interpersonal Perception and Mode of Resolution in Marital Conflict," *Journal of Personality and Social Psychology,* 38 (1980), 751–763.

Lederer, W., and Jackson, D. D. *The Mirages of Marriage.* New York: Norton, 1968.

Margolin, G. "Behavioral Exchange in Happy and Unhappy Marriages: A Family Cycle Perspective," *Behavior Therapy,* 12 (1981), 329–343.

O'Neill, N., and O'Neill, G. *Open Marriage: A New Life Style for Couples.* New York: Avon Books, 1973.

Patterson, G. R. *Families.* Champaign, Ill.: Research Press, 1975.

—————, and Cobb, J. A. "A Dyadic Analysis of 'Aggressive' Behaviors," in J. P. Hill (ed.), *Minnesota Symposia on Child Psychology,* Vol. 5. Minneapolis: University of Minnesota Press, 1971.

—————, and Reid, J. B. "Reciprocity and Coercion: Two Facets of Social Systems," in C. Neuringer and J. L. Michael (eds.), *Behavior Modification in Clinical Psychology.* New York: Appleton-Century-Crofts, 1970.

Raush, H. L. "Interaction Sequences," *Journal of Personality and Social Psychology,* 2 (1965), 487–499.

Rogers, C. *Client-Centered Therapy.* Boston: Houghton Mifflin, 1951.

Stuart, R. B. "Operant-Interpersonal Treatment for Marital Discord," *Journal of Consulting and Clinical Psychology,* 33 (1969), 675–682.

—————. "Behavioral Contracting within the Families of Delinquents," *Journal of Behavior Therapy and Experimental Psychiatry,* 2 (1971), 1–11.

Weiss, R. L., Birchler, G. R. and Vincent, J. P. "Contractual Models for Negotiation Training in Marital Dyads," *Journal of Marriage and the Family,* 36 (1974), 321–330.

—————, Hops, H., and Patterson, G. R. "A Framework for Conceptualizing Marital Conflict, a Technology for Altering It, Some Data for Evaluating It," in L. A. Hamerlynck, L. C. Handy, and E. J. Marsh (eds.), *Behavior Change: Methodology, Concepts and Practice.* Champaign, Ill.: Research Press, 1973.

Williams, R. L., and Long, J. D. *Toward a Self-Managed Life Style,* 2nd ed. Boston: Houghton Mifflin, 1979.

Human Issue: Child-Rearing

Bell, R. Q., and Harper, L. V. *The Effect of Children on Parents.* Hillsdale, N.J.: Erlbaum, 1977.

Blake, J. "Is Zero Preferred? American Attitudes toward Childlessness in the Late 1970s," *Journal of Marriage and the Family,* 41 (1979), 245–257.

Boston Women's Health Collective. *Our Bodies, Ourselves.* New York: Simon and Schuster, 1973.

Bowlby, J. *Child Care and the Growth of Love.* Baltimore: Penguin Books, 1953.

Bronfenbrenner, U. "The Changing American Child—A Speculative Analysis," *Journal of Social Issues,* 17 (1961), 6–18.

Espensade, T. J. "The Cost of Children," in J. G. Wells (ed.), *Current Issues in Marriage and the Family,* 2nd ed. New York: Macmillan, 1979.

Hetherington, E. M., Cox, M., and Cox, R. "The Development of Children in Mother-Headed Families," in H. Hoffman and D. Reiss (eds.), *The American Family: Dying or Developing.* New York: Plenum Press, 1978.

Hoffman, L. W. "Maternal Employment: 1979," *American Psychologist,* 34 (1979), 859–865.

Institute of Life Insurance. *Youth—1974.* New York: Institute of Life Insurance, 1974.

Morrow, L. "Wondering if Children are Necessary," *Time* (March 5, 1979), p. 42.

Newson, J., and Newson, E. *Four Years Old in an Urban Community.* Chicago: Aldine, 1968.

Pederson, F. A., Anderson, B. T., and Cain, R. L. "An Approach to Understanding Linkages between the Parent-Infant and Spouse Relationships." Paper presented at the Society for Research in Child Development, New Orleans, 1977.

Pleck, J. H., and Lang, L. "Men's Family Work: Three Perspectives and Some New Data," *Family Coordinator,* 28 (1979), 481–488.

Pogrebin, L. C. "Motherhood!" *Ms.,* 1 (May 1973), 47–50, 96–97.

Spitz, R. "Hospitalism: An Inquiry into the Genesis of Psychiatric Conditions in Early Childhood," Part I, *Psychoanalytic Studies of the Child*, 1 (1945), 53–74.

Spock, B. *Baby and Child Care* (originally published under the title *The Common Sense Book of Baby and Child Care*). New York: Duell, Sloan and Pearce, 1945.

Toffler, A. *Future Shock*. New York: Random House, 1970.

U. S. Bureau of the Census. *Statistical Abstract of the United States, 1980*. Washington, D. C.: Government Printing Office, 1980.

U. S. Department of Commerce. *Current Population Reports*. Special Studies No. 63, Series P-23. Washington, D. C.: Government Printing Office, 1977.

Westoff, C. F., and Potvin, R. H. *College Women and Fertility Values*. Princeton, N. J.: Princeton University Press, 1967.

Whelan, E. "A Baby? . . . Maybe," *Ms.*, 5 (April 1977), 26, 28–29.

Chapter 13

Alberti, R. E., and Emmons, M. L. *Your Perfect Right: A Guide to Assertive Behavior*, 2nd ed. San Luis Obispo, Calif.: Impact Publications, 1974.

——————. *Stand Up, Speak Out, Talk Back!* New York: Pocket Books, 1975.

Alden, L., and Cappe, R. "Nonassertiveness: Skill Deficit or Selective Self-Evaluation?" *Behavior Therapy*, 12 (1981), 107–114.

Altman, I., and Taylor, D. *Social Penetration: The Development of Interpersonal Relationships*. New York: Holt, Rinehart and Winston, 1973.

Bander, K. W., Steinke, G. V., Allen, G. J., and Mosher, D. L. "Evaluation of Three Dating-Specific Treatment Approaches for Heterosexual Anxiety," *Journal of Consulting and Clinical Psychology*, 43 (1975), 259–265.

Bednar, R. L., and Kaul, T. J. "Experimental Group Research: Current Perspectives," in S. L. Garfield and A. E. Bergin (eds.), *Handbook of Psychotherapy and Behavior Change: An Empirical Analysis*. New York: Wiley, 1978.

Borkovec, T. D., Stone, N. M., O'Brien, G. T., and

Kaloupec, D. G. "Evaluation of a Clinically Relevant Target Behavior for Analog Outcome Research," *Behavior Therapy*, 5 (1974), 503–513.

Buss, A. H. *Self-Consciousness and Social Anxiety*. San Francisco: Freeman, 1980.

Campbell, J. P., and Dunette, M. D. "Effectiveness of T-Group Experiences in Managerial Training and Development," *Psychological Bulletin*, 70 (1968), 73–104.

Cheek, J. M., and Buss, A. H. "Shyness and Sociability," *Journal of Personality and Social Psychology*, 41 (1981), 330–339.

Curran, J. P. "Skills Training as an Approach to the Treatment of Heterosexual-Social Anxiety: A Review," *Psychological Bulletin*, 84 (1977), 140–157.

Davis, J. D. "When Boy Meets Girl: Sex Roles and the Negotiation of Intimacy in an Acquaintance Exercise," *Journal of Personality and Social Psychology*, 36 (1978), 684–692.

Derlega, V. J., and Chaikin, A. L. *Sharing Intimacy*. Englewood Cliffs, N. J.: Prentice-Hall, 1975.

Hammen, C. L., Jacobs, M., Mayol, A., and Cochran, S. D. "Dysfunctional Cognitions and the Effectiveness of Skills and Cognitive-Behavioral Assertion Training," *Journal of Consulting and Clinical Psychology*, 48 (1980), 685–695.

Harper, R. G., Wiens, A. N., and Matarazzo, J. D. *Nonverbal Communication: The State of the Art*. New York: Wiley, 1978.

Jacobs, J. *Adolescent Suicide*. New York: Wiley, 1971.

Johnson, S. *First Person Singular*. Philadelphia: Lippincott, 1977.

Jourard, S. M. *Healthy Personality*. New York: Macmillan, 1974.

——————, and Richman, P. "Disclosure Output and Input in College Students," *Merrill-Palmer Quarterly*, 9 (1963), 141–148.

Keasey, C., and Tomlinson-Keasey, C. "Petition-Signing in a Naturalistic Setting," *Journal of Social Psychology*, 89 (1973), 313–314.

Keyes, R. *We the Lonely People: Searching for Community*. New York: Harper & Row, 1973.

Kleinke, C. L., Staneski, R. A., and Berger, D. E. "Evaluation of an Interviewer as a Function of Interviewer Gaze, Reinforcement of Subject

BIBLIOGRAPHY

Gaze, and Interviewer Attractiveness," *Journal of Personality and Social Psychology*, 31 (1975), 115–122.

Lange, A. J., and Jakubowski, P. *Responsible Assertive Behavior*. Champaign, Ill.: Research Press, 1976.

Levinger, G. "A Three-Level Approach to Attraction: Toward an Understanding of Pair Relatedness," in T. L. Huston (ed.), *Foundations of Interpersonal Attraction*. New York: Academic Press, 1974.

Lieberman, M. A., Yalom, I. D., and Miks, M. B. *Encounter Groups: First Facts*. New York: Basic Books, 1973.

Lipton, D. N., and Nelson, R. O. "The Contribution of Initiation Behaviors to Dating Frequency," *Behavior Therapy*, 11 (1980), 59–67.

Lowenthal, M. F., and Haven, C. "Interaction and Adaptation: Intimacy as a Critical Variable," *American Sociological Review*, 33 (1968), 20–30.

Luft, J. *Of Human Interaction*. Palo Alto, Calif.: National Press Books, 1969.

Lynch, J. J. *The Broken Heart: The Medical Consequences of Loneliness in America*. New York: Basic Books, 1976.

MacDonald, M. L. "Teaching Assertion: A Paradigm for Therapeutic Intervention," *Psychotherapy: Theory, Research and Practice*, 12 (1975), 60–67.

————, Lindquist, C. U., Kramer, J. A., McGrath, R. A., and Rhyne, L. L. "Social Skills Training: The Effects of Behavior Rehearsal in Groups on Dating Skills." Unpublished manuscript. 1973.

Mehrabian, A. *Nonverbal Communication*. Chicago: Aldine-Atherton, 1972.

Nerviano, V. J., and Gross, W. F. "Loneliness and Locus of Control for Alcoholic Males: Validity against Murray Need and Cattell Trait Dimensions," *Journal of Clinical Psychology*, 32 (1976), 479–484.

Perlman, D., Gerson, A. C., and Spinner, B. "Loneliness among Senior Citizens: An Empirical Report," *Essence*, 2 (1978), 239–248.

Rogers, C. *Carl Rogers on Encounter Groups*. New York: Harper & Row, 1970.

Rubin, Z., and Shenker, S. "Friendship, Proximity and Self-Disclosure," *Journal of Personality*, 46 (1978), 1–22.

Smith, M. J. *When I Say No, I Feel Guilty*. New York: Bantam Books, 1975.

Steinberg, C. *TV Facts*. New York: Facts on File, 1980.

Suedfeld, P., Bochner, S., and Matas, C. "Petitioner's Attire and Petition Signing by Peace Demonstrators: A Field Experiment," *Journal of Applied Social Psychology*, 1 (1971), 278–283.

Twentyman, C. T., and McFall, R. M. "Behavioral Training of Social Skills in Shy Males," *Journal of Consulting and Clinical Psychology*, 43 (1975), 384–395.

Udry, J. R. *The Social Context of Marriage*. Philadelphia: Lippincott, 1974.

Weiss, R. S. *Loneliness: The Experience of Emotional and Social Isolation*. Cambridge, Mass.: MIT Press, 1973.

Wenz, F. V. "Seasonal Suicide Attempts and Forms of Loneliness," *Psychological Reports*, 40 (1977), 807–810.

Zimbardo, P. G. *Shyness*. Reading, Mass.: Addison-Wesley, 1977.

Zunin, L., and Zunin, N. *Contact: The First Four Minutes*. New York: Ballantine, 1972.

Human Issue: Love

Berscheid, E., and Walster, E. "A Little Bit about Love," in T. L. Huston (ed.), *Foundations of Interpersonal Attraction*. New York: Academic Press, 1974.

Fromm, E. *The Art of Loving*. New York: Harper & Row, 1956.

Rubin, Z. *Liking and Loving: An Invitation to Social Psychology*. New York: Holt, Rinehart and Winston, 1973.

Schachter, S. "The Interaction of Cognitive and Physiological Determinants of Emotional State," in L. Berkowitz (ed.), *Advances in Experimental Social Psychology*. New York: Academic Press, 1964.

Walster, E. "Passionate Love," in B. I. Murstein (ed.), *Theories of Attraction and Love*. New York: Springer, 1971.

————, and Berscheid, E. "Adrenaline Makes the Heart Grow Fonder," *Psychology Today* (October 1971), pp. 46–50.

————, and Walster, G. W. *A New Look at*

Love. Reading, Mass.: Addison-Wesley, 1978.

White, G. L., Fishbein, S., and Rutstein, J. "Passionate Love and the Misattribution of Arousal," *Journal of Personality and Social Psychology*, 41 (1981), 56–62.

Chapter 14

Aiello, J., Epstein, Y., and Karlin, R. "Effects of Crowding on Electrodermal Activity," *Sociological Symposium*, 14 (1975), 43–57.

Altman, I. *The Environment and Social Behavior*. Monterey, Calif.: Brooks/Cole, 1975.

Balzac, H. de. *Père Goriot* and *Eugénie Grandet*. New York: Modern Library, 1946.

Baron, R. A., and Bell, P. A. "Aggression and Heat: Mediating Effects of Prior Provocation and Exposure to an Aggressive Model," *Journal of Personality and Social Psychology*, 31 (1975), 825–832.

————, and Bell, P. A. "Aggression and Heat: The Influence of Ambient Temperature, Negative Affect, and a Cooling Drink on Physical Aggression," *Journal of Personality and Social Psychology*, 33 (1976), 245–255.

————, and Byrne, D. *Social Psychology: Understanding Human Interaction*, 2nd ed. Boston: Allyn & Bacon, 1977.

————, and Lawton, S. F. "Environmental Influences on Aggression: The Facilitation of Modeling Effects by High Ambient Temperatures," *Psychonomic Science*, 26 (1972), 80–83.

Baron, R. M., Mandel, D. R., Adams, C. A., and Griffen, L. M. "Effects of Social Density in University Residential Environments." Unpublished manuscript, University of Connecticut, 1975.

Baum, A., and Davis, G. E. "Reducing the Stress of High-Density Living: An Architectural Intervention," *Journal of Personality and Social Psychology*, 38 (1980), 471–481.

————, and Koman, S. "Differential Response to Anticipated Crowding: Psychological Effects of Social and Spatial Density." Unpublished manuscript, Trinity College, 1975.

Bell, P. A. "Physiological, Comfort, Performance,

and Social Effects of Heat Stress," *Journal of Social Issues*, 37 (1981), 71–94.

————, and Baron, R. A. "Aggression and Heat: The Mediating Role of Negative Affect," *Journal of Applied Social Psychology*, 6 (1976), 18–30.

Booth, A., and Welch, S. "The Effects of Crowding: A Cross-National Study." Unpublished manuscript, Ministry of State for Urban Affairs, Ottawa, Canada, 1973.

————. "Crowding and Urban Crime Rates," Paper presented at the Midwest Sociological Association, Omaha, 1974.

Calhoun, J. B. "Population Density and Social Pathology," *Scientific American*, 206 (1962), 139–148.

Carlsmith, J. M., and Anderson, C. A. "Ambient Temperature and the Occurrence of Collective Violence: A New Analysis," *Journal of Personality and Social Psychology*, 37 (1979), 337–344.

Cohen, S., and Lezak, A. "Noise and Inattentiveness to Social Cues," *Environment and Behavior*, 9 (1977), 559–572.

D'Atri, D. "Psychophysiological Responses to Crowding," *Environment and Behavior*, 7 (1975), 237–252.

Devlin, A. S. "Housing for the Elderly: Cognitive Considerations," *Environment and Behavior*, 12 (1980), 451–466.

Freedman, J. L., Heshka, S., and Levy, A. "Population Density and Pathology: Is There a Relationship?" *Journal of Experimental Social Psychology*, 11 (1975), 539–552.

Fried, M. "Grieving for a Lost Home," in L. J. Duhl (ed.), *The Urban Condition*. New York: Basic Books, 1963.

————, and Gleicher, P. "Some Sources of Residential Satisfaction in an Urban Slum," *Journal of the American Institute of Planners*, 27 (1961), 305–315.

Galle, O. R., Gove, W. R., and McPherson, J. M. "Population Density and Pathology: What Are the Relations for Man?" *Science*, 176 (1972), 23–30.

Gans, H. *The Urban Villagers*. New York: Free Press, 1962.

Glass, D. C. *Behavior Patterns, Stress and Coronary Disease*. Hillsdale, N.J.: Erlbaum, 1977.

————, and Singer, J. E. "Experimental Studies of Uncontrollable and Unpredictable Noise," *Representative Research in Social Psychology*, 4 (1973), 165–183.

————, and Singer, J. E. *Urban Stress.* New York: Academic Press, 1972.

————, Singer, J. E., and Friedman, L. N. "Psychic Cost of Adaptation to an Environmental Stressor," *Journal of Personality and Social Psychology*, 12 (1969), 200–210.

Goranson, R., and King, D. "Rioting and Daily Temperature: Analysis of the U. S. Riots in 1967." Unpublished manuscript, York University, 1970.

Gove, W. R., Hughes, M., and Galle, O. R. "Overcrowding in the Home," *American Sociological Review*, 44 (1979), 59–80.

Griffitt, W. "Environmental Effects on Interpersonal Affective Behavior: Ambient Effective Temperature and Attraction," *Journal of Personality and Social Psychology*, 15 (1970), 240–244.

Hazard, J. N. "Furniture Arrangement as a Symbol of Judicial Roles," *ETC: Review of General Semantics*, 19 (1962), 181–189.

Heimstra, N. W., and McFarling, L. H. *Environmental Psychology.* Monterey, Calif.: Brooks/Cole, 1974.

Ittelson, E., Proshansky, H., Rivlin, L., and Winkel, G. *An Introduction to Environmental Psychology.* New York: Holt, Rinehart and Winston, 1974.

Jacobs, J. *The Death and Life of Great American Cities.* New York: Random House, 1961.

Korte, C., and Grant, R. "Traffic Noise, Environmental Awareness and Pedestrian Behavior," *Environment and Behavior*, 12 (1980), 408–420.

————, and Kerr, N. "Responses to Altruistic Opportunities under Urban and Rural Conditions," *Journal of Social Psychology*, 95 (1975), 183–184.

Krasner, L., and Ullman, L. P. *Behavior Influence and Personality.* New York: Holt, Rinehart and Winston, 1973.

Krupat, E., and Epstein, Y. "I'm Too Busy: The Effects of Overload and Diffusion of Responsibility on Working and Helping." Unpublished paper, Boston College, 1975.

Latané, B., and Darley, J. M. "Bystander Apathy," *American Scientist*, 57 (1969), 244–268.

————. *The Unresponsive Bystander: Why Doesn't He Help?* New York: Appleton-Century-Crofts, 1970.

Lazarus, R. S. *Psychological Stress and the Coping Process.* New York: McGraw-Hill, 1966.

McCain, G., Cox, V., and Paulus, P. "The Relationship between Illness Complaints and Degree of Crowding in a Prison Environment," *Environment and Behavior*, 8 (1976), 283–290.

Maslow, A. H., and Mintz, N. L. "Effects of Esthetic Surroundings: I. Initial Effects of Three Esthetic Conditions upon Perceiving 'Energy' and 'Well Being' in Faces," *Journal of Psychology*, 41 (1956), 247–254.

Mathews, K. E., and Cannon, L. K. "Environmental Noise Level as a Determinant of Helping Behavior," *Journal of Personality and Social Psychology*, 32 (1975), 571–577.

Milgram, S. "The Experience of Living in Cities," *Science*, 167 (1970), 1461–1468.

————. "Psychological Maps of Paris," in H. M. Proshansky, et al. (eds.), *Environmental Psychology*, 2nd ed. New York: Holt, Rinehart and Winston, 1976.

Moore, G. T. "Knowing about Environmental Knowing: The Current State of Theory and Research on Environmental Cognition," *Environment and Behavior*, 11 (1979), 33–70.

Newman, O. *Defensible Space.* New York: Macmillan, 1972.

Osmond, H. "Function as the Basis of Psychiatric Ward Design," *Mental Hospitals*, 8 (1957), 23–30.

Ottensmann, J. R. "Social Behavior in Urban Space: A Preliminary Investigation Using Ethnographic Data," *Urban Life*, 7 (1978), 3–22.

Rainwater, L. "Fear and the House-as-Haven in the Lower Class," *Journal of the American Institute of Planners*, 32 (1966), 23–31.

Richardson, J. E. "The Physical Setting and Its Influence on Learning," in J. E. Richardson (ed.), *The Environment of Learning.* New York: Weybright and Talley, 1967.

Rothenberg, M., and the children of P. S. 3. "Planning at P. S. 3." Unpublished manuscript, City University of New York, 1972.

Saarinen, T. F. "Perception of the Environment." Resource paper No. 5, Association of American Geographers, 1969.

Schettino, A. P., and Borden, R. J. "Sex Differences in Response to Naturalistic Crowding: Affective Reactions in Group Size and Group Density," *Personality and Social Psychology Bulletin*, 2 (1976), 67–70.

Sherrod, D., and Downs, R. "Environmental Determinants of Altruism: The Effects of Stimulus Overload and Perceived Control on Helping," *Journal of Experimental Social Psychology*, 10 (1974), 468–479.

Sommer, R. *Personal Space: The Behavioral Basis of Design*. Englewood Cliffs, N.J.: Prentice-Hall, 1969.

————. *Design Awareness*. New York: Holt, Rinehart and Winston, 1972.

————. "Classroom Ecology," *Journal of Applied Behavioral Science*, 3 (1967), 489–503.

————. *Tight Spaces*. Englewood Cliffs, N.J.: Prentice-Hall, 1974.

————, and Ross, H. "Social Interaction on a Geriatrics Ward," *International Journal of Social Psychiatry*, 4 (1958), 128–133.

Stokols, D. "In Defense of the Crowding Construct," in A. Baum, J. Singer, and S. Valins (eds.), *Advances in Environmental Psychology*, Vol. 1. Hillsdale, N.J.: Erlbaum, 1978.

————. "On the Distinction between Density and Crowding: Some Implications for Future Research," *Psychological Review*, 79 (1972), 275–277.

Swatek, P. *The User's Guide to the Pollution of the Environment*. New York: Ballantine, 1970.

Toffler, A. *Future Shock*. New York: Random House, 1970.

U. S. Federal Bureau of Investigation. *Uniform Crime Reports*. Washington, D. C.: Government Printing Office, 1978.

————. *Uniform Crime Reports*. Washington, D.C.: Government Printing Office, 1980.

Weiner, F. "Altruism, Ambience and Action: The Effects of Rural and Urban Rearing on Helping Behavior," *Journal of Personality and Social Psychology*, 34 (1976), 112–124.

Wrightsman, L. S. *Social Psychology*, 2nd ed. Monterey, Calif.: Brooks/Cole, 1977.

Yancey, W. L. "Architecture, Interaction and Social Control: The Case of a Large-Scale Public Housing Project," in H. M. Proshansky, et al. (eds.), *Environmental Psychology*, 2nd ed. New York: Holt, Rinehart and Winston, 1976.

Zimbardo, P. G. "The Human Choice: Individuation, Reason, and Order Versus Deindividuation, Impulse, and Chaos," in W. Arnold and D. Levine (eds.), *Nebraska Symposium on Motivation*. Lincoln: University of Nebraska Press, 1969.

Human Issue: Work

Kaplan, H. R. *Lottery Winners*. New York: Harper & Row, 1978.

Lambert, N. M., Hartsough, C. S., and Zimmerman, I. L. "The Comparative Predictive Efficiency of Intellectual and Nonintellectual Components of High School Functioning," *American Journal of Orthopsychiatry*, 46 (1976), 109–122.

Lesem, C. "The Motivation to Work," in C. Kerr and J. Rosow (eds.), *Work in America: The Decade Ahead*. New York: Van Nostrand Reinhold, 1979.

Pavalko, R. *Sociology of Occupations and Professions*. New York: Peacock, 1971.

Quinn, R. P., and Staines, G. L. *The 1977 Quality of Employment Survey*. Ann Arbor, Mich.: Institute for Social Research, 1979.

Roe, A. "Perspectives on Vocational Development," in J. M. Whiteley and A. Resnekoff (eds.), *Perspectives on Vocational Development*. Washington, D.C.: American Personnel and Guidance Association, 1973.

Special Task Force to the Secretary of Health, Education and Welfare. *Work in America*. Cambridge, Mass.: MIT Press, 1972.

U. S. Bureau of Labor Statistics. *U.S. Working Women: A Data Book*. Washington, D. C.: Government Printing Office, 1980.

Yankelovich, D. "The Meaning of Work," in J. M. Rosow (ed.), *The Worker and the Job*. Englewood Cliffs, N.J.: Prentice-Hall, 1974.

————. "New Rules in American Life: Searching for Self-Fulfillment in a World Turned Upside Down," *Psychology Today* (April 1981), pp. 35–91.

NAME INDEX

NAME INDEX

NAME INDEX

NAME INDEX

SUBJECT INDEX

SUBJECT INDEX

SUBJECT INDEX

SUBJECT INDEX

SUBJECT INDEX

ABOUT THE
AUTHORS

James F. Calhoun is Associate Professor of Psychology at the University of Georgia and Director of the Psychology Clinic there. He received his B.A. degree from the University of Florida and earned both his M.A. and Ph.D. from the University of Illinois. He has taught at the State University of New York at Stony Brook, where he was Director of the Psychology Clinic. His primary area of interest is clinical psychology, particularly social perception change, community psychology, spouse abuse, depression, marital adjustment, and human relations. He has been a Fellow of the American Council of Education. He is coauthor of *Understanding Abnormal Psychology* (1983), and his articles have appeared in the *Journal of Abnormal Psychology* and the *Journal of Consulting and Clinical Psychology.*

Joan Ross Acocella is a professional writer. She has researched and written numerous articles in various areas of the social sciences, and she is coauthor of *Abnormal Psychology: Current Perspectives.*